Sidney and Spenser

The Poet as Maker

To Craig,
with Thanks for all
the challenges.

1-3-90

Sidney and Spenser
The Poet as Maker

S. K. Heninger, Jr.

The Pennsylvania State University Press
University Park and London

Library of Congress Cataloging-in-Publication Data

Heninger, S. K., Jr.
  Sidney and Spenser: the poet as maker / S. K. Heninger, Jr.
    p. cm.
  Bibliography: p.
  Includes index.
  ISBN 0-271-00666-8
  1. English poetry—Early modern, 1500–1700—History and criticism.
2. Sidney, Philip, Sir, 1554–1586—Criticism and interpretation.
3. Spenser, Edmund, 1552?–1599—Criticism and interpretation.
4. Authors and readers—England—History—16th century.
5. Imitation (in literature) I. Title.
PR531.H44   1988
821'.3—dc19   88–39036
                                                             CIP

To Dr. and Mrs. James Thorpe

Contents

Preface

In 1598 when Francis Meres assembled the "similitudes" that comprise his *Palladis tamia: Wits treasury,* he included a section on "Reading of bookes" (fols. 266ᵛ–267). Under this topic, quite appropriately, he quoted a sentence from one of Plutarch's best-known essays, "How the Young Man Should Study Poetry," repeating a commonplace that underlay the humanist curriculum of *litterae humaniores:*

> As we see our selves in other mens eies, so in other mens writinges we may see, what becometh us, and what becommeth us not.

This aphorism indicates an interest in the act of reading that was common in the Renaissance. Poetry was an art of discourse based upon a model of social exchange. Authors viewed their writings as instruments of societal policy—as a means of fashioning gentlemen, to use Spenser's words, or of moving men to well-doing, to paraphrase Sidney. And readers, to complete the aim of such writing, interacted with the text in meaningful ways in order to know themselves. At the end of the sixteenth century in England, as Meres shows, a great deal of attention was paid to expository methods and to the reading habits those methods induced. As Plato had argued memorably in the *Republic,* literature is an agent of much power in the commonwealth, and its deployment requires careful supervision.

Sidney and Spenser, who reached their artistic maturity as the 1580s began, recognized this potential of poetry, and each launched an ambitious program of writing to exploit it. These two authors signaled a new era in English letters, and while they responded in individualistic ways to the literary tradition that then prevailed, they set the course of literature in England for centuries to come. Milton as their heir and successor adapted their expository methods to his own genius and purposes, and he educated an audience in how to read poetry that we ourselves still participate in. With these poets, allegory in England transmutes to fiction.

This study is concerned centrally with this transformation in narrative strategies and with the historical circumstances that encouraged and sustained it. For English writers this change was largely effected by the reintroduction of Aristotelian imitation as the quiddity of the poetical art. In his *Defence of poesie* Sidney proclaims unequivocally, almost contentiously, that poetry is first and foremost an art of imitation as Aristotle had defined it in the word *mimesis*. As its distinctive feature, poetry no longer reflects heavenly beauty or echoes cosmic harmony—it isn't rhyming and versing that make a poet, Sidney insists. Instead, poetry becomes a depictive art, an activity that produces images, a narrative with semantic content.

Other arts, of course, were also mimetic. Music, for example, reproduced the ratios of the cosmic scheme in its tuning system and its rhythms. Painting reproduced in homologous fashion what the eye sees when we look about. But in its metrics, poetry could repeat the measures of music; and by means of the colors of rhetoric and descriptive narrative, it could achieve the effects of painting. Therefore poetry was the *prima inter pares* in the family of the arts.

This superiority of poetry as both a formal art conveying the numerical basis for music and a descriptive art conveying the pictorial basis for painting was made possible by the suppleness of its medium. Music was an aural art, while painting depended upon visual effects; but the medium of language allowed poetry to produce "speaking pictures," as Plutarch had noted and Horace confirmed. The new poetry consisted of images encoded in a verbal system addressed simultaneously to both ear and eye. It was this capaciousness of language that had allowed poetry to assume preeminence among the arts by the sixteenth century, so in this study we shall be continually concerned with Renaissance notions of how language accomplishes its communicative function of engaging a reader.

Our challenge will be to explain, as I earlier formulated it, the transmutation of allegory to fiction. Now, to be more explicit, we shall investigate why the Elizabethans abandoned the Platonist assumption that the verbal system of a literary work is a veil through which the reader peers in order to discern its inner form, some antecedent and autonomous idea. Also, how they fundamentally revised the rhetorical model of poetical discourse, the model of *res* and *verba,* where the verbal system serves as clothing to cover a serious matter, the apparel over some prefabricated invention that is disposed into an argument before it ever reaches the stage of elocution.

It will be my contention that Sidney, by assimilating the principles of Aristotelian mimesis, devised a poetics that assigns meaning to the verbal system itself, independent of anterior systems of thought. In Sidney's poetics of making, language is the means of creation, and the poet reenacts the divine imperative preserved in the opening of John's Gospel: "In the beginning was the Word . . ." No longer is a poem seen as the versified codification of something else. Writing is making, so the verbal artifact is self-sufficient, containing its own raison d'être, its own meaning. Such a poetics requires new narrative strategies on the part of the poet, as well as new reading strategies among the audience. Out of this novelty the novel is born. Furthermore, poetry has now become a process, not a substance. It has become a performative act on the part of both poet and reader.

As my last sentences suggest, this study will go some distance, I hope, toward explaining the renewed interest in Sidney, and especially in the *Arcadia,* that has occurred in the last decade. Sidney was aware of the problems inherent in any theory of meaning or of signifying or of reading, and in his *Defence of poesie* he makes rudimentary efforts to deal with these problems and formulate his own solutions. Being thoroughly trained in the rhetoricism of the humanists, he not surprisingly thinks of these problems in terms appropriate to the language arts. He would have appreciated Derrida's fascination with *différance,*[1] for example, and would have understood what Barthes meant when he said that *Sarrazine* (and, indeed, any fictive text worth reading) is "a galaxy of signifiers, not a structure of signifieds."[2] He would have applauded the subtle methods by which de Man extends a text beyond referentiality and raises it to an intellectual activity that

ceaselessly constitutes, undoes, and reconstitutes itself, so that ultimately it reflects upon the unreadability of narrative.[3] Most remarkably, perhaps, Sidney preempted the deconstructionists by
making both philosophy and history subspecies of an archi-
literature which he calls "poetry," and he promoted the principle
of self-reflexivity in poetry, that "literature is a mode of writing
distinguished by its quest for its own identity"[4]—for example, by
characterizing Xenophon's *Cyropaedia* and More's *Utopia* as "absolute" poems.

But Sidney was not a postmodern man. Plato, not Saussure, was
his point of reference in theorizing about language. With Cratylus,
and the majority of writers in his day, Sidney believed that words
do have inherent meanings fixed in the nature of things, and probably fixed by the deity as part of the providential scheme. The
opportunity for adjustment and movement in this orthodox view
of language came with the arrival of Aristotle's *Poetics* as a dominant influence on literary theory. As a neo-Aristotelian, Sidney
raised questions about the nature of representation and implemented experiments that we might say ran their course through
the intervening centuries and now have reached their culmination
in the present-day vogue for deconstructing a text. But we must
remember that while Sidney would have understood the positions
taken by Derrida and Barthes, and while in a very real way he
prepared for the anti-authoritive arguments of these theorists, he
himself would not have gone so far.

Not only would Sidney have been inhibited by his faith in the
holy scriptures, but he would have seen a threat to his plan of
using literature in the cause of societal reform (if language is impugned, it loses its suasive force). Sidney was too strongly conditioned by the literate culture of his time—grounded in Cicero, and
behind him, in Plato. Sidney shared more than simply a nostalgic
fondness for a theory of language that joined signifier and signified by a sacred bond innate in the universe from its creation and
revealed by Adam in his naming of the creatures. This was a bond
stronger than the social conventions of our structuralists, and im-
pervious to the postern attacks of our deconstructionists. After all,
God had sent his only son to mediate between heaven and earth,
and this holy Word ensured the viability of language. Logocen-
trism was not yet a dirty word. I therefore shall cite recent theo-

rists not to bring their assumptions and methodologies to bear upon the texts of Sidney and Spenser, but rather to suggest how these poets shaped the conditions that made the new poetry possible and shifted it toward the modern direction.

My debts to scholarly friends and friendly scholars are too numerous to list separately, but many will recognize a personal contribution to this study. My thanks to each of them for both particular help and general encouragement. The obligation acknowledged in the dedication, however, stands above the rest. My wife shares my pleasure in publicly proclaiming it.

1
Leicester House, 1579–80

When *Spencer* saw the fame was spredd so large,
Through Faery land of their renowned Queene:
Loth that his Muse should take so great a charge,
As in such haughty matter to be seene,
To seeme a shepeheard then he made his choice,
But *Sydney* heard him sing, and knew his voice.[1]

When the first three books of *The Faerie Queene* were published
in 1590, they were ornamented by several commendatory poems.
Walter Raleigh led off with two sonnets hyperbolic in their praise,
rating Spenser's ability to bestow fame above that of Petrarch and
Homer. Gabriel Harvey followed, writing officiously in the six-line
stanza of the January and December eclogues of *The Shepheardes Calender* and signing himself "Hobynoll," and he emphasized Spenser's successful transition from pastoral verse to heroic. Next are two short ten-line poems, one signed "R.S." and the
other "H.B.," neither of whom can be identified with any degree
of certainty; and the last is a four-stanza poem, again in the metrics of "January" and "December," signed "Ignoto"—and unknown the author has remained. Taken as a whole, these commendatory verses offer a great deal of current opinion about
Spenser's progress as a poet since *The Shepheardes Calender;* and
although this opinion is aimed at enhancing Spenser's reputation,
it nonetheless tells us something about his intentions and achievements.

The epigraph at the beginning of this chapter appears in the

commendatory poem not yet mentioned, the next to last in the
series. It bears the initials "W.L.," who for lack of a likelier candidate is usually identified as William Lisle, translator of at least
portions of Du Bartas and of Heliodorus and of Vergil.[2] Like the
last of the commendatory poems, it comprises four stanzas in the
metrics of "January" and "December," the verse form by now regularly associated with Colin Clout. It continues the extravagant
praise of Spenser and once more takes note of his successful exchange of the pastoral guise for the more grandiose trappings of
epic.

What is most noteworthy in Lisle's poem, however, is the suggestion that Sidney took an immediate hand in Spenser's career
and redirected it. In the first stanza, by means of an elaborate
conceit, Lisle recalls how Achilles was disguised as a woman to
escape service in the Trojan War until discovered by Ulysses. Just
so, Lisle says in the second stanza (quoted above), Spenser would
have remained in the retiring role of modest shepherd if Sidney
had not advised him to speak more openly and forcefully. According to Lisle, it was Sidney who recognized Spenser as the appropriate voice to proclaim the queen's largesse as Gloriana. It was
Sidney who convinced Spenser to launch upon a project so ambitious and so politically hazardous as *The Faerie Queene*. The
third stanza of Lisle's poem begins:

> And as *Ulysses* brought faire *Thetis* sonne
> From his retyred life to menage armes:
> So *Spencer* was by *Sidneys* speaches wonne,
> To blaze her fame not fearing future harmes.

In the final stanza of his poem, Lisle acknowledges Spenser's success in *The Faerie Queene;* just as Achilles triumphed over all
who contended with him, "so *Spencer* now to his immortall
prayse, / Hath wonne the Laurell quite from all his feres." But,
Lisle concludes, Spenser would never have attempted so daunting
an enterprise without Sidney's encouragement: "What though his
taske exceed a humaine witt, / He is excus'd, sith *Sidney* thought
it fitt." With only three books of *The Faerie Queene* in print, out
of twelve books promised (with a hint that twelve more might be
contemplated), Lisle understandably expresses doubt that such a

mammoth undertaking lay within the reach of "a humaine witt." But all is made right, and Spenser is exonerated from presumption, "sith *Sidney* thought it fitt."

Although the commendatory verse by Lisle (or whomever) does express a contemporary view, perhaps it overstates the influence Sidney had on Spenser. After all, the two men had not been in geographical proximity since July 1580, when Spenser departed for Ireland, and even then the opportunity for personal exchange lasted little more than a year. So Lisle is referring to events of at least a decade earlier than 1590, events to which he was not a party. Moreover, he is perhaps consciously contributing to the legend of Astrophil, the talented poet and generous patron. He seizes the occasion of Raleigh's patronage of Spenser to reflect additional glory upon Sidney, now dead. Even more likely, Lisle is invoking the magical name of Sidney to add luster to the achievement of Spenser, aspiring to be England's laureate. Nonetheless, overstatement or not, Lisle's poem posits a direct relationship between Sidney's opinions and Spenser's poetry, and there's additional evidence that the two young poets may have exchanged views during a period which proved crucial in each of their careers. Therefore it behooves us to accumulate this evidence and evaluate it for the bearing it has upon the literary accomplishments of both Sidney and Spenser. The first exhibit is *The Shepheardes Calender,* published in December 1579 and dedicated to Sidney.

By early July 1579 Spenser was employed by Robert Dudley, earl of Leicester and Sidney's uncle.[3] Spenser had left London ten years before, a precocious schoolboy of seventeen on his way to Cambridge. His formative years at the university, filled with serious study and religious controversy, came to an end in 1576 with an M.A. Then he took a while to find a suitable position. Two years later, though, Spenser resided in Bromley, Kent, serving in the household of John Young, the newly elected bishop of Rochester, who had been master of Spenser's college at Cambridge. From there, it became an easy step to Leicester House in London. Spenser was now a lively and engaging gallant in his mid-twenties, somewhat bookish perhaps, but nonetheless attracting the attention of influential men of affairs. He hoped to make a place for himself in the turbulent politics of the Elizabethan court.

Leicester, of course, was one of the busiest men in the realm.[4]

By reason of high birth, good looks, boldness, and a becoming flamboyance, he attracted enormous power. He had been Elizabeth's friend since adolescence and, except for brief periods when he resisted her peremptoriness, continued to be her most intimate courtier. He was also leader of a dominant faction of powerful nobles dedicated to English nationalism and the Protestant reformation—two causes not easily distinguishable to them. This group, which included Sir Henry Sidney and Sir Francis Walsingham, Sidney's father and his future father-in-law, looked to Leicester to maintain easy access to the queen.

Throughout 1579 Leicester's faction was especially agitated because Elizabeth appeared determined to marry the duc d'Anjou, younger brother of the king of France and next in line for the French crown.[5] This matrimonial alliance had the advantage of binding together England and France in a common front against Spain, but in England objection to the marriage was widespread among nobles and commoners alike. Disapproval was based not so much on the difference in ages—Anjou was twenty-three, and Elizabeth twice his age—as on the difference between their professed religions. Whatever other arguments were advanced against this marriage, the objection rested mainly upon the simple fact that Anjou was a Catholic. More specifically, he was the son of Catherine de' Medici, who in popular opinion was responsible for the St. Bartholomew's Day massacre that had decimated the Protestant community in Paris. The intervening seven years had, if anything, intensified religious animosity. Therefore, when Elizabeth received Anjou's agent in January 1579 and flattered him with favors, the political group around Leicester foresaw a serious challenge. Later, in August of the same year when Anjou himself arrived in London and the queen appeared to be infatuated with the young Frenchman despite his ugliness, Leicester's faction became increasingly fearful. Concerted action was necessary to block this threat to their position at court. There were machinations within the Privy Council to prevent the marriage, and considerable private advice, largely unwelcome, directed to the queen herself.[6]

It is impossible to say exactly when Spenser had joined Leicester's retinue—perhaps several months earlier than July. And it is equally difficult to say what he was intended to do. If he served as

Leicester's secretary, the usual assumption, there is no evidence that he was entrusted with letter writing or with any other confidential duties.[7] According to a letter sent in October to his Cambridge crony, Gabriel Harvey, Spenser expected to leave soon on short notice for a trip abroad,[8] a common assignment for a confidential agent. But this mission never came about, and the reasons for its cancellation, as well as its purpose, remain unknown. Even if we accept the authenticity of the Spenser-Harvey correspondence (a very risky thing to do), there is room for suspicion that Spenser's expectation of foreign service had no basis in fact— mere puffery or joking on his part. In any case, other than this claim in a letter published by Harvey, there is little indication of how Spenser filled his days in Leicester's service. For the most part, it seems, he was left to read his books and write his poetry.[9] In the best humanist tradition, he sought to get ahead by skill in the language arts.

Certainly Spenser leapt eagerly into a literary career. By December 5 he had ready for the press *The Shepheardes Calender,* which was probably printed before the end of the month. He may have composed many of these eclogues during the previous year while employed by the bishop of Rochester,[10] but under Leicester's roof he revised his text to reflect the political events of 1579 and completed it for publication.[11] He also composed a more pointed, less coy political satire against the French marriage of Elizabeth, entitled "Mother Hubberds Tale," which was not published until 1591, when Spenser's miscellanea were collected in a volume entitled *Complaints.* This lengthy beast fable, mordant with Chaucerian irony, may or may not have been solicited by Leicester. In any case, it is likely to have proved an embarrassment to him, and it is often blamed for Spenser's being shipped off to Ireland the following summer.[12]

If we believe the Spenser-Harvey correspondence published in June 1580, Spenser at the time had a number of additional works on hand. Most of these have been lost, although a few may be identified as more or less determinate passages in *The Faerie Queene* and elsewhere.[13] In October 1579 he wrote to Harvey about "*My Slomber,* and the other Pamphlets," which he had meant to address to Edward Dyer; but now he was cautiously considering Leicester as the dedicatee.[14] By the next April, Spenser had ready for the press two major poems, *Dreams* and *The Dying Pelican,* which Harvey saw and approved, and two other works, *Nine Comedies* in English and *Stemmata Dudleiana* in Latin, which Harvey liked but thought could use a bit of cutting and polishing.[15] None of these seems to have been actually printed, at least in their original form. Another long work nearing completion that April was entitled *Epithalamion Thamesis,*[16] which is generally conceded to have found its eventual way into Book 4 of *The Faerie Queene,* where the marriage of the Thames and the Medway occurs. By this date Spenser was also working on *The Faerie Queene.*[17]

In his commentary on *The Shepheardes Calender,* the elusive E.K. (whom I identify as Harvey[18]) cites another work by Spenser ready for publication by the end of 1579, a treatise presumably in prose entitled *The English poete.* This is the most tantalizing of the "lost works" because it would indicate that Colin Clout was giving serious thought to the theory of his art. In the argument to the October eclogue, E.K. praises this "booke," which had "lately come to my hands," and announces his intention of publishing it. According to E.K., it propounded the same view of poetry as that in "October"—that is, a poetics dependent upon "enthusiasm" in its literal meaning of divine inspiration. William Webbe in 1586 mentions this work again, though without having seen it (he undoubtedly picked up the title from E.K.'s notice).[19] But nothing more is known about it, and I confess to a strong suspicion that it existed only as a figment of Harvey's officiousness, hardly substantiated by Webbe's wan echo. Spenser was not much given to theorizing about poetry. If there ever was such a treatise as *The English poete,* though, this is the most regrettable loss among all of Spenser's works that have not come down to us.[20]

Another poetizing member of Leicester's household was Edward Dyer, already appreciated at court as a lyricist of considerable talent. Dyer was an honorable and urbane (if somewhat impecunious) gentleman, who had long been a faithful friend and retainer of the Dudleys. He had joined Leicester's retinue in 1565, and he continued to fill a busy post, responsible for a variety of serious as well as delicate matters. Nonetheless, he found time to read the many new texts available for humanists and to compose graceful lyrics, which he sang to his friends. Some few of these may still be identified among the pages of anonymous verse that fill manuscript anthologies and printed miscellanies of the late sixteenth century. Dyer was almost a decade older, and several social ranks higher, than Spenser, but he may well have noticed the eager Cambridge scholar who had recently joined the staff. It appears that both Spenser and Harvey at one time or another considered dedicating works to him, although neither actually did.

Among those of Spenser's own age, the most illustrious visitor at Leicester House was Philip Sidney, a frequent caller and sometime resident. Philip's mother was a Dudley, sister of Leicester as well as sister of Ambrose Dudley, earl of Warwick. Both these men, two of the most powerful in the realm, were then childless; so Philip, as their eldest nephew, was heir to each. Philip's father, Sir Henry Sidney, was an equally important man, if not so celebrated. At various dates he served Elizabeth with unusual distinction as Lord Deputy of Ireland and as Lord President of Wales. Philip, at this time a dazzling young gentleman of twenty-five, seemed destined to surpass them all in brilliance.

Philip had studied for three years at Oxford under the most able of England's scholars, and perhaps had also spent some time at Cambridge while Spenser was there. For three more years, from May 1572 to May 1575, he had visited the cultural centers of Europe with such success that he established the Continental tour as a sine qua non of the cultivated English gentleman. He had made extended stops in Paris, Frankfurt, Vienna, Venice, Strasbourg—captivating his hosts and leaving behind a train of friends and admirers wherever he went.[21] He exemplified all the comely virtues, the living epitome of wit and noblesse. His combination of intellect, dependability, tact, courage, and personal charm was unmatched in the realm. A biographer must work at finding faults.[22] As Spenser claims in "Astrophel" with unmitigated admiration, "Ne spight it selfe that all good things doth spill, / Found ought in him, that she could say was ill" (lines 23–24).

Since his return to England in 1575, Sidney had applied his considerable ability in pursuit of the obvious career. His family had always assumed that he would become an active courtier, and he burst upon the London scene with boundless vitality. For reasons not fully clear, however, the queen was reluctant to employ him for any service of consequence.[23] Although Sidney faithfully attended court and handled his family's affairs with aplomb, Elizabeth gave him no preferment beyond the ceremonial office of royal cupbearer. Perhaps his persistent advocacy of a protective league with the other non-Catholic nations of Europe antagonized her powerful advisers such as Lord Burghley and the earl of Oxford, and therefore rendered the queen cautious in her recognition of Sidney. In the spring of 1577 she had sent him on a diplomatic nicety to Emperor Rudolph II in Prague and to Count Ludwig of the Palatinate in Heidelberg, and he had returned with concrete proposals for a Protestant league.[24] He also had entertained a proposition to marry the eldest daughter of William of Orange, and thereby to become lord of Holland and Zeeland.[25]

So Elizabeth was wary in her dealings with this engaging and capable young courtier who had a following, as well as a mind, of his own.[26] Despite his willingness to serve, Sidney was offered no state employment. As a result, he felt neglected and longed for something to exercise his political and martial talents. He thought of accepting various invitations to fight against Spain in the Netherlands, but the queen refused her permission for military service under a foreign command. We must not think of Sidney as languishing indolently; he was busily engaged in myriad matters— but not in matters of his choice, not in matters that he deemed consequential. In this state of frustration, he had turned to writing a narrative in which to weigh some opinions about government, especially about the problems of divine law and human justice. Denied the use of the sword, he resorted to the pen.[27] The result, after a few years, was the *Arcadia.*

By 1579 Sidney had also begun to express himself in verse. Many of the poems in the *Arcadia* were probably written by this time, as well as poems from the collection known as *Certain Sonnets.*[28] In May either of 1578 or 1579 Sidney had composed songs for *The Lady of May,* a brief entertainment presented before the queen when she visited Leicester at Wanstead. Moreover, for many years he had been on familiar terms with Edward Dyer, and with this kindred spirit Sidney had begun experiments in classical meters. They were attempting to fit English words to long and short syllables, with an eye to writing quantitative verse.

When Spenser joined Leicester's service, according to the Spenser-Harvey correspondence, it was these metrical experiments that seemed of most importance to him. In early October 1579 he reported with considerable excitement and a touch of pride that these two gentlemen had made him privy to their poetical discussions: "As for the twoo worthy Gentlemen, Master *Sidney,* and Master *Dyer,* they have me, I thanke them, in some use of familiarity."[29] After assuring Harvey that they had also spoken well of him, Spenser continued by giving more precise information about the substance of these discussions. By Spenser's account, interest centered in what the title page of the printed correspondence calls "artificiall versifying":

> And nowe they have proclaimed in their ἀρείῳ πάγῳ, a generall surceasing and silence of balde Rymers, and also of the verie beste to: in steade whereof, they have by authoritie of their whole Senate, prescribed certaine Lawes and rules of Quantities of English sillables, for English Verse: having had thereof already greate practise, and drawn mee to their faction.

It seems that Harvey also had been experimenting with quantitative verse in English, and Spenser agreeably declares: "I am, of late, more in love wyth my Englishe Versifying, than with Ryming: whyche I should have done long since, if I would then have followed your councell." A major portion of the remaining letters in this published correspondence then demonstrates this artificial versifying, both by theoretical considerations and in practical exercises. It must be remembered that Harvey edited and published this correspondence for his own ends,[30] and much of what appears even in a letter attributed to Spenser may be in substantial part a reflection of Harvey's ambitions. Nonetheless, we know from the several examples of quantitative verse in the *Arcadia* that Sidney did try his hand at this anomaly, and in *The defence of poesie* he speaks favorably of the "ancient versifying" (119.29–120.5). No experiments of this sort by Dyer have survived, if they ever existed.

The question of whether the Areopagus was a formally convened coterie has already spilled much scholarly ink, and more is hardly called for. The evidence has been thoroughly sifted and rather firm conclusions drawn on both sides of the debate. For my part, I agree with what seems to be consensus now and doubt that

the Areopagus existed as an exclusive club with its own membership and manifesto.[31] I take Spenser's and Harvey's references to
an ἀρείῳ πάγῳ to be playful or, less charitably, presumptuous.
When Harvey replied to Spenser's report of a poetical Senate at
Leicester House, he amplified the hyperbolic allusion to the Athenian law court and overtopped Spenser's erudite exuberance:

> Your new-founded ἄρειον πάγον I honoure more, than you will
> or can suppose: and make greater accompte of the twoo worthy
> Gentlemenne, than of two hundreth *Dionisii Areopagitae,* or the
> verye notablest Senatours, that ever *Athens* dydde affourde of
> that number.[32]

I conclude that the Areopagus was a product of Spenser's and
Harvey's high-spirited joking, most likely a pipedream of the over-
confident Harvey, and those who have viewed it in the image of
Ronsard's Pléiade have seen an elephant on the face of the moon.
There was no poetical academy dubbed the Areopagus with fixed
rules and regular meetings.

In sum, although the opportunity for acquaintance existed, it
can be only a surmise that Sidney and Spenser actually met. The
historical evidence is sketchy at best. We can conclude with reasonable certainty that Spenser was in service with Leicester for at
least a year before leaving for Ireland in July 1580, but his residence in Leicester House is attested only by the address of one of
the questionable letters to Harvey. Furthermore, how he occupied
himself other than by writing is uncertain. Biographical data for
Sidney during this year are somewhat more plentiful, though we
cannot allot how much time he spent in London or at Wilton or
perhaps at other places. Evidence from the Spenser-Harvey correspondence is unreliable because Harvey edited the text to suit
his own ambitious motives, so that alteration of facts and doubtful
interpretation of events are rife. Even if we take the letters to be
relatively pristine, there's still the problem of knowing what is serious and what is raillery. Spenser's poetry pretends to familiarity
with Sidney, but that may be discounted as a hopeful expression
of what he wished might be, rather than a dependable statement
of what actually took place. The evidence from Sidney's works is
discouragingly slight, as we might expect—a single reference to

The Shepheardes Calender in the latter part of *The defence of poesie,* and even there he does not mention the name of its author.

Of one thing we might be sure: Spenser was more awed by Sidney than the reverse. Sidney was the cynosure of his generation, and despite his youth, or perhaps partly because of it, he was already a bright light in Elizabeth's star-studded court. In contrast, Spenser could at best claim distant kinship to a northern family of some social standing. Sidney had traveled widely, meeting the powerful and the learned of Europe on equal terms. Because of straitened means, Spenser had never left the shores of England. Sidney was assured of a glorious future. Spenser was struggling for recognition, even a livelihood. The social disparity between them is difficult for the modern mind to comprehend.

After Sidney's death in the autumn 1586, however, his ghost haunted the poetry of Spenser. "Astrophel," published in 1595, is a supreme example of hero worship, although little of genuine emotion or of personal reminiscence is discernible behind the pastoral mask.[33] In a similar burst of adulation, when Spenser directs to the Countess of Pembroke one of the dedicatory sonnets for his *Faerie Queene,* he devotes the octet to remembrance of her brother, "that most Heroicke spirit, / The hevens pride, the glory of our daies."[34] Again Sidney is the summation of all that is most admirable. But even in this thicket of epithets, Spenser recalls him primarily as a partner in poetry; he now rests in heaven, "crownd with lasting baies," and the paean culminates in recognition that it was Sidney "who first my Muse did lift out of the flore, / To sing his sweet delights in lowlie laies." Once more in *Colin Clouts Come Home Againe,* Sidney as Astrophel is placed reverentially at the end of all those worthy shepherds who worship Cynthia and immortalize her fame in verse (lines 448–51).

Most touching to those aware of the close ties that centered on Sidney and shattered at his death is "The Ruines of Time," Spenser's belated tribute to the Dudley family. Addressed to the Countess of Pembroke, Leicester's niece and Sidney's sister, it was composed shortly before 1591, when it appeared as the opening item in the volume of *Complaints.* Like "Astrophel," this is a flawed piece, but movingly eloquent in some passages. In the lengthy headpiece that dedicates "The Ruines of Time," Spenser recalls his debt to Sidney, and he conceives the work as a lasting expression of gratitude to those who helped him at the beginning of his poetic career. It has an envoy at the end, addressed to the "immortall spirite of *Philisides*," the surrogate of Sidney in the *Arcadia;* "and with last duties of this broken verse," Spenser says, he intends "to decke thy sable Herse" (lines 673–79). Especially cogent is the strong feeling of obligation flowing toward Sidney throughout this work, "this moniment of his last praise" (line 682).[35] For Spenser, Sidney once more was "the Patron of my young *Muses*," as he reiterates in the dedication, remembered with "most entire love and humble affection." And that, I think, encapsulates what Spenser felt for Sidney. De Selincourt is no doubt correct that "Spenser's love for Sidney was probably the deepest formative influence upon his life and character."[36]

So Spenser admired Sidney without stint. How much—how often or how highly—Sidney thought of Spenser is another matter. Legend, however, posits a personal relationship from an early date, as William Lisle's commendatory poem indicates. According to the anonymous author of the brief "Life of Mr. Edmond Spenser" that prefaces the 1679 folio of his collected works, Sidney immediately perceived the genius of Spenser and took considerable pains to ensure his recognition. When Spenser first came to London, according to this account, he applied to those "who, in likelyhood, might give him Encouragement, and Patronage." Sidney was an obvious choice:

> Mr. *Sidney* (afterward Sir *Philip*) then in full glory at *Court,* was the Person, to whom he design'd the first Discovery of himself; and to that purpose took an occasion to go one morning to *Leicester-House,* furnish't only with a modest confidence, and the Ninth *Canto* of the First Book of his *Faery Queen:* He waited not long, e're he found the lucky season for an address of the Paper to his hand; who having read the Twenty-eighth *Stanza of Despair,* (with some signs in his Countenance of being much affected, and surpris'd with what he had read) turns suddenly to his Servant, and commands him to give the Party that presented the Verses to him Fifty Pounds; the Steward stood speechless, and unready, till his Master having past over another *Stanza,* bad him give him an Hundred Pound; the Servant something stagger'd at the humour his Master was in, mutter'd to this purpose, That by the semblance of the Man that brought the Paper, Five Pounds

would be a proper Reward; but Mr. *Sidney* having read the following *Stanza,* commands him to give Two Hundred Pounds, and
that very speedily, least advancing his Reward, proportionably to
the heigth of his Pleasure in reading, he should hold himself ob-
lig'd to give him more than he had: Withal he sent an invitation
to the Poet, to see him at those hours, in which he would be most
at leasure. After this Mr. *Spenser,* by degrees, so far gain'd upon
him, that he became not only his Patron, but his Friend too;
entred him at *Court,* and obtain'd of the *Queen* the Grant of a
Pention to him as *Poet Laureat.*[37]

Though written within living memory, this anecdote, despite the
realistic detail, is undoubtedly apocryphal. Nonetheless, it testi-
fies to a seventeenth-century tradition for Spenser's indebtedness
to Sidney.[38]

Another more nearly contemporary opinion comes from Philip
Massinger, who some time between 1615 and 1623 sent to the
earl of Pembroke a letter which contained the following verses:

> Unimitable Spencer ne're had been
> So famous for his matchlesse Fairie Queene
> Had he not found a Sydney to preferr
> His plaine way in his Shepheards Calendar.[39]

According to Massinger, Sidney knew *The Shepheardes Calender*
at an early date and encouraged Spenser to turn from pastoral to
an epic treatment of Elizabeth. But Massinger had no firsthand
knowledge of either Spenser or Sidney, and he may be doing nothing more than echoing Lisle in his commendatory verses for *The
Faerie Queene.*

Certainly Sidney was linked to *The Shepheardes Calender*
after its publication, and could have been involved with it by the
autumn 1579. In *The defence of poesie,* written about this time,
Sidney praises *The Shepheardes Calender,* although with reservations about its use of archaic language.[40] Beyond that, however,
there is no mention of Spenser in Sidney's writings.[41] Some readers have seen a Spenserian imitation in Philisides' pastoral fable
in the old *Arcadia,* beginning "As I my little flocke on *Ister*
banke,"[42] but Sidney had no need of Spenser as a model, in mat-

ters either pastoral or amorous. Astrophil was a different sort of wooer than Colin Clout, and the *Arcadia* a different sort of narrative than anything Spenser wrote. Since Sidney's work reveals no awareness of Spenser, we can safely conclude that, even if Sidney met Spenser at Leicester House, after his departure from London in July 1580 Spenser was of negligible consequence in Sidney's busy life.

What strikes me when looking at the writings of Sidney and of Spenser, though, is how extraordinarily productive the year 1579–80 proved to be for both. When Spenser entered Leicester's service, he may have had in hand some of the eclogues for *The Shepheardes Calender* in varying degrees of completion, but during the next few months he revised and polished them extensively in readiness for publication. He may have had under way several of the dozen or so lost works that are cited in the Spenser-Harvey correspondence and in Ponsonby's headpiece to the *Complaints* volume, and he continued to work on these projects. If we can believe E.K., which I doubt, he also brought to completion his theoretical treatise, *The English poete*. Most important, in the course of this annus mirabilis before his expatriation in Ireland, Spenser began the consuming literary work of his lifetime, *The Faerie Queene*. He had sent portions of it to Harvey before April 1580, when he wrote to ask for the return of his manuscript and for Harvey's judgment. William Lisle implies that Sidney also looked over the early drafts, and Spenser's anonymous biographer of 1679 states this to be a certainty.

On Sidney's side, he had begun the *Arcadia* by this time, although it is impossible to say how far he had gotten. Scholarly opinion is fairly well agreed, however, that he virtually completed the old *Arcadia* by the end of 1580, with most of the writing done in the preceding year.[43] Many poems in the collection known as *Certain Sonnets* also belong to this period, although no one can say which ones.[44] *Astrophil and Stella* belongs to a later date, for the most part after Penelope Devereux's marriage in November 1581.[45] But according to the best-informed opinion, *The defence of poesie* was written during the winter of 1579–80.[46]

So was there ever a personal exchange between Sidney and Spenser? The question remains moot, but I seriously doubt it.[47] As James J. Higginson shrewdly observed long ago, the biographers of Spenser, not Sidney, have argued for a relation that went beyond the cool one of casual benefactor and grateful underling.[48]

Whether they actually met, however, or actually discussed this or that, is incidental to my concerns. With T. S. Eliot, I could draw the widest possible perimeter and say, "Between the true artists of any time there is, I believe, an unconscious community."[49] Or I might apply to Elizabethan London what Walter Pater said of the Medicis' Florence: "Here, artists and philosophers and those whom the action of the world has elevated and made keen, do not live in isolation, but breathe a common air, and catch light and heat from each other's thoughts."[50] Sidney and Spenser lived at the same time, although at vastly different social levels; and they adapted to the same cultural formation. As a structuralist would say, they responded to the same codes, though each according to his individual genius. They were both poets in the humanistic tradition, with its respect for the past, its privileging of the language arts, and its faith in God-given reason. In consequence, the important relationship between them is best revealed not by fitful glimpses into their daily lives but by examining their works in a common light.

Although no *English poete* by Spenser is available, Sidney's theoretical tract fortunately is very much with us. Therefore in order to compare these two poets my plan is to analyze Sidney's *Defence of poesie* with an eye to deriving a poetics from it. In its function as *apologia,* it is a retrospective and summary work, and it provides—for Spenser as well as for us—what Eliot has called "the historical sense," that necessary awareness of all that has gone before in the literary tradition.[51] The individual talent must place itself in relationship to the cumulative practice of our predecessors, capitalizing upon that intertextuality. Sidney's *Defence* is in that spirit, progressing as it does from general theory through the delineation of genres to the evaluation of contemporary poets.

The meaning of many passages in Sidney's *Defence* is elusive, as anyone who sets out to determine a precise reading soon realizes. But though the treatise is intricate and convoluted, and though at first glance it seems to contain inconsistencies and even contradictions, it remains faithful to certain postulates. Therefore any particular passage should be interpreted as part of a total argument. There's a main thrust or general thesis that controls the discourse and conditions the import of any segment of it. Quite early in the *Defence* Sidney states with unwonted directness that poetry is an "art of imitation" (79.35); and this, it seems to me, is the basic assumption that underlies his argument and gives it cohesion. In consequence, reading Sidney's tract is largely an exercise in determining his view of what poetry imitates and how it accomplishes this imitation.

As preparation for an analysis of the *Defence* each of the three succeeding chapters looks at the "art of imitation," but each from a different perspective. Chapter 2 considers imitation as a generic feature common to all of what we today call the fine arts, and it delineates a model which lays out the components of the mimetic process, as well as their variations and their interactions. Chapter 3 examines imitation in each of the fine arts in turn, identifies the grounds for interrelationships between the various arts, and narrows the focus to imitation in the verbal medium, the distinctive vehicle for poetry. Chapter 4 surveys in chronological order the earlier critics mentioned by Sidney to see what they have to say about imitation in art, especially verbal art. Eventually, with the many possibilities for an imitative art set firmly forth and clearly in view, we come in Chapter 5 to an exposition of Sidney's poetic theory. In Chapters 6 and 7, finally, we arrive at a poetical praxis first for Spenser and then for Sidney by examining their works in the light of *The defence of poesie*. While these two poets share much, it is their differences that justify the length and minuteness of this study.

2

A Model for the Art of Imitation

All the arts which make up our culture have a common bond and as it were by a certain relationship comprise a family.[1]

In contrast to the preceding chapter, which revives the historical moment when Sidney and Spenser might have shared Leicester House, this chapter leads in another direction and deals only with theory. It is not concerned with facts, but with hypothetical schemes. Specifically, it constructs a model for the artistic event based upon the premise that art is imitation.[2] From Aristotle until the present century, this premise has been an a priori assumption, explicit or implicit, in most Western theories of art. It has been variously interpreted, however, and put to a wide assortment of uses.

Sidney flaunts his commitment to poetic imitation as defined by Aristotle. In a prominent passage from *The defence of poesie*, he declares: "Poesy therefore is an art of imitation, for so Aristotle termeth it in the word μίμησις" (79.35–36). This is a central statement in Sidney's poetics,[3] what is designated as the *propositio* in the rhetorical division of his treatise. But what might Sidney have meant by it? Before turning to his *Defence* for our complicated answer, we should set out the possibilities in any "art of imitation" so that we may see more clearly what choices Sidney made. In this chapter, then, I shall identify the several elements essential to such a system and determine the range of their interrelationships.

Although *mimesis* as representation of some version of nature was the prevailing doctrine for many centuries, from the Renaissance until our own, we are well aware that art as imitation in this commonest sense is an outmoded aesthetic and that other systems based upon other principles are also feasible. Art as imitation culminated in the realistic novels of the last century,[4] in impressionism in the graphic and plastic arts, and in tone poems in music.[5] But after literary realism came naturalism and the radical innovations of Eliot and Joyce, after impressionism came cubism and abstract (even nonobjective) painting, and after tone poems came new tuning systems and an abandonment of harmony. As E. H. Gombrich observes, "Toward the end of the nineteenth century, the whole comfortable idea of the imitation of nature disintegrated, leaving artists and critics perplexed."[6] There was, in fact, no common agreement about what constitutes "nature," much less about how to imitate it. The resultant perplexity accounts for the frenetic nothing-sacred experimenting of our own time. Driven by frustration, and later energized by release from convention, artists in every medium have been remarkably inventive in devising alternative modes of expression that defy the traditionalist assumption that art is imitation.

But in this study we need concern ourselves with contemporary theory only in a comparative way—that is, the assumptions that underlie a modern movement may clarify by comparison the assumptions that underlie art as imitation. Conversely, our anatomy of imitative theory may define more sharply the distinctive characteristics of certain modern movements by showing where they diverge from the tradition. As a system, art as imitation solves many problems that plague contemporary theory before they become problematical. For example, since the work of art is imitating *something,* we can posit certainly that the something being imitated is an ultimate determinant of the artifact, so we prevent a number of questions about its mode of existence and final meaning. The ontological *situs* of the artifact resides in the object being imitated. Again, since *someone* has executed the imitation, there's a clear assumption that an active human intellect has been at work. Consequently, the imputing of authorial intention is no fallacy.[7] So the theory of imitation that we construct will sail breezily past many of the rockiest shoals of recent controversy. Perhaps we won't even notice them.

To see poetry in its largest network of relations,[8] we need only recall the dictum of Cicero that serves as an epigraph to this chapter. We should remember that poetry belongs to a large and various class known as "the arts," a loose confederation which includes a considerable number of distinct members. Today it is usual to designate six pure arts: painting, sculpture, music, architecture, and dance, as well as poetry.[9] There are also several mixed arts, such as emblem-books, madrigals, concrete poems, ballet, and opera; and the multimedia artifact has become the cliché of recent exhibitions. But our discussion of the pure arts can be easily extended to the mixed arts, so I shall pay them little attention. I shall begin by talking about "the arts" in general, although whatever I say about the genus in this chapter will be applicable to poetry in particular. Having looked at the arts as a family, we can proceed to distinguish poetry from its siblings, thereby obtaining a clearer view of its unique constitution. Sidney, incidentally, adopted a similar strategy in *The defence of poesie* (cf. 78.1–30).

In discussing any theory, the definition of terms is of fundamental importance, and particularly so in this study because language evolves. What a word meant in Sidney's day can vary considerably from what it means in ours. Especially the technical terms of the critical lexicon, reflecting as they do the ontology and epistemology which prevail at any given time, change in their implications from period to period. Sidney tended to use words precisely, and therefore when interpreting a statement by him we must be sure to understand his vocabulary. The term "poetry" itself provides an example of the difficulty, as footnote 8 demonstrates. Other terms which have radically changed in meaning include "poetical," "artificial," "fiction," "story," and "image"—the terminology of a poetics that is now four centuries out of date. But we must be careful about our vocabulary as well, because words convey hidden assumptions that affect meaning in basic ways.[10] Many critical terms in our lexicon incorporate the unexamined premises of the twentieth century, and they are as inappropriate when talking about Elizabethan poetry as "measures" and "fore-conceit" when applied to Pound and Fowles. In consequence, we shall take every precaution to use precise terms and to be aware of any implications or connotations or biases that a term, whether Elizabethan or modern, may conceal.

Even the word "art" carries an invisible freight of assumptions and secondary meanings. As commonly used today, the term is a compression of "the fine arts." In turn, the phrase *les beaux arts* designates a rather large class of loosely identified human activities which were not grouped together as a class until the eighteenth century.[11] For us in the post-Romantic era, "art" most likely implies originality, imaginativeness, a heightened response to the world—something out of the ordinary. It doesn't at all mean what its etymology suggests. *Ars* for the Romans meant first of all a skill that could be mastered after proper instruction and sufficient practice, so there were an *ars medica,* an *ars militaris,* and an *ars grammatica,* as well as an *ars poetica*—and Ovid prepared even an *ars amatoria.* For Sidney, as for the Romans, the word "art" indicated a skilled discipline, such as logic or astronomy; and when he thought of the "arts," it was definitely not as "fine arts."[12] So unless we take precautions, the word "art" may casually imply an entire aesthetic, Roman or Romantic. In this discussion, we shall use it in as antiseptic a way as possible, merely as a generic term, with no preconceptions about the origin of art, its philosophy, or its purpose. For the sake of convenience, we must resort to the abstract term "art," although admittedly it is inappropriate for the sixteenth century. And we must remember that this term, like most conventions, conceals a cultural bias.[13]

Now on to the project in hand: constructing a model for the theory of art based upon imitation. This is a surprisingly simple task. Such a system contains a determinate number of components, and these components enter into a fixed number of easily discernible relationships. To make a beginning, any theory of art as imitation presupposes four isolable elements: an artifact, the artificer who made the artifact, an object which the artificer imitated in making the artifact, and a percipient who observes the artifact. This list is exhaustive and exclusive. Nothing else enters into the system.

Although we can identify and discuss each of these elements as a separate component, the dynamics (and consequently the results) of the system derives from their interaction. Each element affects and is affected by every other element. Again to be exhaustive in a mathematical way, any theory of art as imitation presupposes six relationships between these four components: the relation between artificer and artifact, the relation between artificer and object of imitation, the relation between object of imitation and artifact, the relation between artifact and percipient, the relation between percipient and artificer, and the relation between percipient and object of imitation. What we have delineated may be codified in a rudimentary diagram.[14]

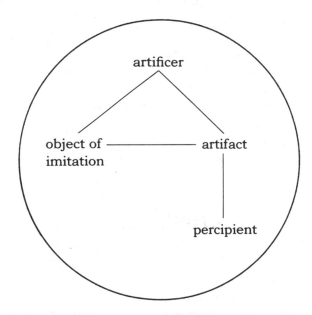

The diagram is encircled to suggest that each of the four components derives its character by virtue of its relationships with the other elements to form a system. As in a Saussurian model, none is an absolute. The elements inhere in the whole, and for their identity—perhaps even for their existence—are dependent upon it. Furthermore, the summation of these relationships is an entity in its own right, a whole which in some sense is greater than the sum of its parts. The circle embodies the result of both the creative act by the artificer and the perceptual act by the percipient. It incorporates a both-and synthesis rather than an either/or dialysis. The totality of the interaction among the four basic components constitutes, then, what we may call the "art event." This term implies a human artificer and a human percipient, and an inanimate artifact, as well as an object of imitation that may be anything; and each of these components participates actively in a process taking place in both time and space.

The art event begins with the artificer's choice of an object of imitation, and it culminates in the percipient's comprehension of the artifact. That terminus completes the artistic process. Then, however, the percipient is likely to turn critic. He stands outside the self-sufficient system, indicated here by the circle, wishing to probe and dissect it, and ultimately to evaluate it, either as art or as life, and perhaps as both. To use the vocabulary of Wittgenstein, he interprets the work according to the rules of a "game" dictated by his particular culture, by his particular geographical location and period in history.[15]

Consequently, this complex of relationships inside the circle must be placed within a larger context of reality. Outside our diagram lies a realm of experience known to the percipient, and this larger reality provides a basis for comparison that permits assessment of the art event. While experiencing the work of art, the percipient resides within its sphere, an inhabitant of what has come to be called the "world" of the artifact,[16] and he is governed by its laws. He must slough off his preconceptions and prejudices in order to achieve a radical innocence; otherwise, he violates the integrity of the work and prevents a successful engagement with it. But eventually the percipient withdraws from this "world" in order to gain perspective upon it.[17] He removes to his own world. The percipient's reality then becomes a context, comprising both cultural and personal facts, within which the artifact must fit.[18] This encompassing reality therefore engages in a reciprocal exchange with all elements of the art event, both individually and in toto. While the art event and its constituent elements will modify to some extent the percipient's consciousness, his awareness will determine the circumference of meaning for the art event. Indeed, the act of criticism may be described as the analysis of this interpenetration between art and reality.[19] The knowledge of the percipient, personally acquired or culturally induced, is what allows the artifact to have meaning.

We may grow uneasy if someone objects that reality is not readily determined. First, are we talking about the personal reality of the percipient, which would vary from one individual to another; or the reality of the artificer, which for purposes of comprehension the percipient should temporarily adopt; or an absolute reality, such as that which the physical sciences purport to describe or that which resides with the deity (however that concept may be defined); or a spontaneous and highly subjective circumstance which happens to be your or my reality at the moment. To follow the ramifications to the point where they vanish over the horizon, there is no common agreement among natural philosophers about the make-up of ultimate reality. At various times it has been authoritatively defined, and is still defined today, in a number of mutually exclusive ways: for example, the realm of Platonic ideas, the Judeo-Christian God, the world of sense-perceptible nature, human percepts of that nature, concepts in the individual human psyche (innate, or arrived at logically or irrationally), quanta of matter, or of energy, etc. There is a welter of possibilities for the "reality" within which the percipient evaluates the artifact.

Each of these possibilities, however, is no more than a variant which can be fitted into our hypothetical model. Each will result in a particular application, but will not jeopardize our general theory. If we take Platonic ideas to represent ultimate existence, for example, art will be the palpable projection of those ideas, the means whereby the immaterial realm of essences is deduced into the world of our mortal senses. If we believe in a Judeo-Christian God and in the doctrine that all inheres within His being, art will be the manifestation of His attributes and will. If we hold that ultimate reality resides in the items of physical nature, art will be a representation of some time-space continuum. If we place ultimate reality in the individual's sense perception of the environment, art will be an empirical description of those surroundings as an individual views them. If we place ultimate meaning in an individual's more subtle mental responses to his surroundings, art will be a subjective and psychological expression of the artificer's inner life. If we propose that the ultimate constituents of reality are quanta of matter or of energy, discrete units of being arranged in space, we must expect pointillism and action painting and the narrative atomism of Eliot and Faulkner.

But all of this is simply to say that whatever is taken to be the ultimate constituents of our universe will directly affect the art event. In a fundamental way, the reality of the artificer has been a determinant of the artifact. With varying degrees of self-conscious intent, he has composed his work of art in accordance with what he assumes to be real, or true. And we as percipients have the choice of several different realities within which we may fit the art event. We may choose one exclusively—for example, we may examine the artifact from what we reconstruct to be the artificer's point of view and talk about "artistic intention"; or we may disregard the artificer's reality, on the grounds that it is irrelevant to us or impossible to reconstruct accurately, so we examine the artifact from our personal point of view and talk about "audience response"; or we may examine the artifact as though looking at it through the eyes of a Platonist, or a Puritan, or a Freudian, or a Jungian, or a Marxist, or a Feminist—or a Thomist or a Buddhist or a Taoist of the thirteenth century in Tsientsin. As Wittgenstein observes, "An entirely different game is played in different ages."[20] We may fit the artifact into any one of numerous cultural formations.

Furthermore, we may opt for pluralism, in which case we fit the artifact successively into any number of "realities." We may, for example, begin by relating the artifact to what we reconstruct to have been the artificer's reality and arrive at a determination of the art event within those circumscribed limits of time and place and personality. We may then in turn, however, place the resultant version of the artifact within the circumstances of the contemporary world, so that we make it relevant to our own times. Moreover, going one step farther, each of us may view it from his personal point of view as a Freudian or Marxist or Feminist—or even as the unique combination of these and other points of view that is *mei generis*. When we relate the art event to reality, the important thing is to be conscious of the choice we are making among the limitless variety of "realities" that we can readily distinguish.[21]

If the percipient is satisfied with his spontaneous and unexamined response to the artifact and does not wish to proceed further in his experience of it, he may bring to bear upon it no more than the ephemeral reality constituted by his current state of mind. The percipient does not turn critic, except perhaps to the casual extent of expressing an unsupported liking for or disapproval of the artifact—what we call, in the physiological terms it deserves, a "gut response." In contrast, if the percipient wishes to find incontrovertible truth in the artifact, he may bring to bear upon it some absolute system of values, such as religious doctrine or scientific fact, and he approves or disapproves to the extent that the art event confirms his preconception of wherein lies truth.

Usually, however, criticism proceeds somewhere between these two extremes of spontaneity and absolutism. If we wish to reconstruct what the artificer might have meant, we must take the trouble to resurrect (as fully and accurately as possible) the world he inhabited, because the artifact is a reflection of the artificer's worldview. The ultimate constituents of his universe have conditioned the artifact. But when the percipient as critic assesses the significance of the art event, he measures it against what *he* assumes to be true. The percipient's reality is brought to bear upon the artifact. In consequence, criticism of art as imitation proceeds by at least two steps. It proceeds by the determination of at least two realities, which may or may not be congruent: the reality accepted by the artificer and that accepted by the critic. In addition to identifying the postulates which underlie the reality of the artificer, the percipient as critic must take the trouble to identify the postulates of his own reality, his own a priori assumptions and so-called self-evident truths, because they to a large extent determine what he looks for (and therefore finds) in a work of art. What we have said, then, suggests the large number of ways in which reality may be formulated and points to the need to identify the reality of both the artificer and the percipient. But our thesis that the art event inheres in a larger reality (and probably in more than one) is still valid.

To return to the firmer ground of basics, it is appropriate now to consider each of the four components in our model as an individual element per se, for the moment without respect to anything else. In our mutually responsive system with its network of relationships, we could begin with any of the four components, since each is essential to the whole and each is integrally related to every other.

Let's begin, however, with the artifact—although in doing so, we should recognize that this choice may not be entirely neutral. We're heeding the dictates of the phenomenologists and their followers, who elevate what is observed to the position of greatest prominence. An earlier generation would probably have started with the artificer, the artist himself; while a generation earlier still may well have begun with the object of imitation, the original of the artifact; and the coming generation seems bent on raising the percipient to preeminence. The critical cliché of the moment, with its revealing Marxist vocabulary, is Roland Barthes's pronouncement that "the goal of literary work (of literature as work) is to make the reader no longer a consumer, but a producer of the text."[22] Or perhaps by starting with the artifact we are acting in accord with an even more prevalent bias in our culture, the bias engendered by empirical science, which takes as primary what we perceive with our senses. In any given instance, the artifact is immediately before us, while the artificer and the object of imitation, and probably the percipient (as an objective rather than hypothetical entity), are not. Or perhaps the artifact as the residue of the artistic process *is* primary. René Wellek and Austin Warren echo the Russian Formalists and in their seasoned study, *Theory of Literature,* assert without more ado: "The natural and sensible starting-point for work in literary scholarship is the interpretation and analysis of the works of literature themselves."[23] Practicing critics in the other arts would no doubt say something comparable. To be a music critic, I suppose, one must attend concerts, or perhaps listen to recordings. At least we must concede, though, that our reason for awarding pride of place to the artifact admits several explanations and warns us to suspect biases even in our mode of proceeding.

To proceed nonetheless, the *artifact,* as the etymology of the term indicates, is the thing made by the exercise of art. It exists as an autonomous item—that is, externalized by its maker, separate from the object which it imitates, and present before the person who perceives it. The term "artifact" is not wholly satisfactory because it suggests that the work of art is an item produced by a skilled craftsman, like a ceramic pot or a wooden table. The alternative "artifice," however, is even less satisfactory because it would currently imply an intent to deceive. Therefore let's use the term "artifact," although we must remember that the work of art is not merely the end-product of a teachable craft. The artifact carries the personal imprint of an original practitioner, what sometimes is called his "style." Two portraits of the same person by two different painters, for example, will bear an unmistakable resemblance to the sitter, while at the same time each will be distinguishable from the other by virtue of technique, and thereby can be attributed to the appropriate painter.

The artifact may appear in a wide, almost endless, variety of media: for example, stone or wood or metal, colors on a two-dimensional surface, words to be heard or read, nonverbal but audible vibrations in the air (e.g., musical notes), movements of the human body, enclosures of space for the purpose of human habitation. The "medium," as the etymology of this term indicates, determines the means by which the artifact is made known and is knowable (its epistemology). The medium also differentiates the artifact from other artifacts that imitate the same object of imitation though in different media. A poem and a painting, for example, may depict the same motif from mythology—the judgment of Paris or the rape of Europa—but the medium of each artifact distinguishes it from the other and prevents confusion of the two. When the Laocoön statue was discovered in Rome in 1506, several scholars immediately compared it to Vergil's account of the episode in the Aeneid (2.199–227), but with the expressed intention of demonstrating the superiority of description over depiction, or vice versa. So the medium in which the artifact appears is of prime importance.

The artificer is he who produces the artifact. He plays an initial and necessary role in our model, exercising what Alois Riegl and Wilhelm Worringer call the "artistic volition."[24] Some aestheticians, such as George Santayana,[25] include in their definition of art the requirement that it be the product of an intellect conscious of its artistic aim; and like Worringer, they use the factor of artistic volition to set apart works of art from works of nature, such as birdcalls and sunsets. Later theorists, however, have proposed removing the artificer as a fit subject of inquiry, arguing that investigation of his mind leads beyond aesthetics into the psychology of artistic creation.[26] And Barthes argues ingeniously that an author is self-slain, self-obliterated in the very act of submitting his thoughts to the neutral medium of language.[27] The artificer, however, is not so easily excluded from our consideration. If art is imitation, it is the artificer who does the imitating. A birdcall or a sunset cannot be studied profitably as a product of *mimesis;* a madrigal or a landscape painting, though, usually can be. If art is art rather than nature, it is the artificer who makes it so.

The term "artificer" is simply the anglicized form of the Latin *artifex,* which like "artifact" derives from *ars + facere.* Two other terms, "artist" and "artisan," also come to mind. We should avoid "artist," however, because in twentieth-century English the term suggests ethereality. As *Webster's Third New International Dictionary* defines it, the term means "one who professes and practices an art in which conception and execution are governed by imagination and taste"—that is, "a person skilled in one of the fine arts." Conversely, "artisan" today suggests a lack of originality, a constrained following of a prescribed method, perhaps even a repetition of someone else's design. Again to quote *Webster's Dictionary,* an artisan is "one trained to manual dexterity or skill in a trade." As we shall see, these two alternatives to "artificer" were called into being by different possibilities in the relationship between artificer and object of imitation. So both "artist" and "artisan" stray from neutrality. While "artificer" may seem archaic or affected, it is the preferable term because it has the least subversive connotations. It is, moreover, the term used by Sidney.[28]

In the preponderance of cases, the artificer is a single person, although two or more persons may collaborate on a single artifact. In such an instance the artifact is likely to be a compound item, like a lyric set to music, and each collaborator has responsibility for one element in the complex. In folk art, such as the ballad or quilting, it may be argued that an entire nation is the artificer; though more likely, I suggest, a single person is the progenitor of a prototypical artifact that successive artisans have reproduced with or without modification. For the purposes of our discussion, however, we may assume that the artificer is a single person who has produced the artifact.

The *percipient* is he who perceives the artifact. He may be reader, auditor, spectator, viewer, visitor—depending upon the medium of the artifact. But "percipient," despite its cumbrousness, is the best umbrella-term under which to gather all the possibilities, whatever the medium. The percipient is the end term in the art event.

Immediately there arises the question of whether a percipient is essential in a theory of art as imitation. Wouldn't the artifact exist whether or not anyone observed it? This question raises the extremely difficult problem of determining the mode of existence of an art work, thrust into recent prominence by the phenomenologists. But in the immediate context here, we need deal with only the objective-subjective conundrum. Does the actuality of an event reside in the causal object or the perceiving subject? The problem is well-known in its juvenile formulation: Would a tree falling in the forest make any noise if no one were there to hear it? An answer of either yes or no is defensible. But I shall answer practically, while recognizing objections, that if no one observes the falling tree, neither aurally nor visually nor tactually, concurrently or *post facto,* then for all intents and purposes the event has not taken place. It would remain unknown, if not unknowable. If someone claims to have witnessed the tree falling in an apocalyptic vision, I admit to some difficulty. But an apocalyptic vision is no more than the future construed as the here-and-now, so we can deal with it as a present fact. Otherwise, we can say that the falling tree unobserved by a percipient is a possibility put forward for our consideration *in potentia,* but it is not an actual deed. We must consider it as merely a proposition, rather than a fait accompli. And works of art cannot be dealt with at the inchoate stage of proposition only. They must be actualized because their physical state and the sense perception of that datum are essential factors in the art event. To use Sidney's vocabulary, the "*idea* or foreconceit" is not "the work itself" (*Defence* 79.7–8).

So I conclude that a percipient is a necessary constituent in the theory of art as imitation. To exclude him is to make the art event a closed, static system, sterile and remote. Someone must perceive the artifact to make it real—"real" in the literal sense of being a *res,* a palpable object.[29] Furthermore, what the artifact is attempting to achieve (its teleology) is directed at the percipient. Without him, the artistic process would have no aim, no end result.

The importance of the percipient becomes even more evident when we consider alternatives. What happens if we exclude the percipient from the art event—if we paraphrase John Stuart Mill and hold that "all art is of the nature of soliloquy"?[30] If we deem the purpose of the artistic process merely to be self-announcement by the artificer, a desire to make manifest one's own inner life, we have departed from a theory of art as imitation and generated a system known as expressionism. In such a system the artificer is governed by a desire to express his emotional being via the artifact, so the artifact becomes an extension of the artificer. Artifact and artificer are essentially one. Moreover, there's no room for an extraneous object of imitation. A painting of a pair of shoes, for an example by Van Gogh, is simply a statement of how the painter feels about those shoes, regardless of what the shoes are actually like. The shoes as objective entities vanish. Attention is riveted on the artificer/artifact, and all else is obliterated. But even in expressionism, the artificer usually posits a percipient to be known to. Soliloquy predicates an auditor. The artificer contrives the artifact with some audience in mind, and reaches certain conscious choices (such as that of medium) accordingly.[31] If the percipient is inserted into the system, however, expressionism may be seen as a special sort of mimetic art, where the artificer himself has become the object of imitation in a process of communication.

In a more extreme case, we may deem the artistic process to be a kind of innate impulse to create, the result of the mind's ineluctable need for imaginative activity. Then the artifact is totally reflexive, referable to the artificer only. And art is reduced to mental therapy for a self-absorbed patient. We may pity and fear and even admire such an artifact, but it exists inviolate, if not unreachable, within its own unalterable uniqueness. We cannot participate as a partner in the art event that it generates, but can only submit to it. And no matter how completely we think we empathize or how engrossing our emotional reaction, our role is indeterminate. We cannot judge the appropriateness or accuracy of our response. We are reacting spontaneously, without adequate guidance—as though to a Rorschach blot, which indicates no more than a subjective predilection for one option among an infinite range of possibilities. Such an artifact does not allow a meaningful engagement between percipient and artificer. The art event does not come off. In the theory of art as imitation, a significant role must be permitted to a sentient and animated percipient.

But after the aestheticism of Walter Pater there is little need to argue for the importance of the percipient. The focus of the art event has now shifted to that component in our model. Much art of this century, especially that which is nonobjective, aims not at imitating what was preexistent or at expressing an emotional state which has already been felt. Rather, the art event is something current and aims at a new experience for the percipient in a continuous present. It contains its own raison d'être, without reference to imitation or expression. The artificer merely supplies raw materials for an occasion, and the percipient is invited to make of them what he can, or even what he will. In such a system, the art event is aborted if a percipient does not appear to perform this function.

As a consequence, in our time great emphasis is placed upon how much the percipient must do to bring off the art event. Recent theorists have paid increasing attention to audience response, both individual and collective, and perhaps the greatest contribution to criticism that our century has made lies in a new awareness of how the percipient interacts with an artifact. Some theorists have escalated the percipient to a position of such importance that he seems to have subsumed the other elements in our system. The percipient is not only the observer, but also the subject and even the author of the artifact—not only the end-all, but the be-all of the artistic process.[32]

While we might not wish to indulge the affective fallacy to that extent, at the very least we must concede that when a percipient observes the artifact, his faculties of perception revise it to some degree because of his individual proclivities and limitations. For this reason, we have distinguished between the artifact as a fixed object of unchanging identity and the percipient's comprehension of it, the product of what we have called the "art event."[33] Of course, the art event is a derivation from the artifact—indeed, the result of the percipient's processing of it. So the artifact is the exclusive stimulus for the art event, and therefore its major determinant. The art event is simply the artifact modified by the percipient in the act of perception (what the artificer and the object of imitation contribute to the art event is crystallized in the artifact). So the percipient has no right to obtrude into the art event anything which is not implicit in the artifact. To deem otherwise would be to allow an artifact to mean anything, and thereby effectively to deny the possibility of meaning.

But while the artifact does not change, the art event derived from it will vary from percipient to percipient, so that an artifact will generate as many different art events as there are percipients. Furthermore, the effect of an artifact upon the same percipient at different times will generate different art events. Nonetheless, all these art events derive from the same artifact, and therefore constitute a set. Each member of this set (each of the several art events deriving from the same artifact) will share some characteristics with other members of the set, though not necessarily all the characteristics that appear commonly among members. This series of responses constitutes a "family," as Wittgenstein defined such a group,[34] and may be used to identify the work of art. The artifact is not destroyed or even disintegrated by a succession of percipients, but only revised in each particular instance.[35]

But this is to get away from basics and into the relationships between the components of our model. And we have one element, *the object of imitation,* yet to consider. An object of imitation is the unique feature of imitative art. Other systems have an artificer, an artifact, and a percipient, but no other system presumes such a fixture as an object of imitation. It locates the terminus a quo from which the artistic process originates. It is the ontological *situs* of the art event, providing that "structure of determination," to use a phrase from Wellek and Warren (152), that endows the artifact with a permanent and irreducible identity, despite any subjective interpretation to which the artifact might be submitted.

Given its radical importance, we should not be surprised that the object of imitation is the most difficult of the four components to deal with. And, in fact, theorists have not paid much attention to it. In actual practice, of course, the object of imitation is the least accessible, most recessive element in the art event. It is often not easily descried. But apart from practical considerations, the object of imitation is difficult to deal with for two additional reasons: first, the range of possibilities is greater than for any other element in our system, equal to the infinite variety in the worlds we can either perceive with our senses or imagine in our minds;[36] and second, conditioned as we are by the assumptions of modern technology, we are accustomed to think that only physical objects actually exist, and therefore that only physical objects can be objects suitable for imitation.

It is indeed a measure of our cultural bias how easily we assume that only concrete things are objects. But nothing is farther from the fact. An object—in the philosophical sense, something the mind has set apart for the purpose of study—need not be physical. Conceptual ideas may also be objects, and until the last few centuries have always been taken to be so. Examples are justice or friendship, eternity or infinity, chaos or cosmos, heaven or hell. Each of these is an object if we describe it in terms which make it external to our mind. The point may become less arguable if we recall that the most advanced of the physical sciences, particle physics, is dedicated to defining at least one of these examples—to determining what happens as a particle approaches a velocity equal to the speed of light, when theoretically its mass becomes infinite.

In actual fact, then, conceptual ideas as well as physical phenomena can be objects, and consequently objects suitable for imitation in art.[37] As E.K. observes in his gloss on Spenser's October eclogue (line 93), "Beauty . . . is an excellent object of Poeticall spirites." Indeed, the availability of concepts which submit to imitation provides the basis for the literary mode known as allegory. As an example from that genre, a typical figure named Everyman encounters a figure manifesting death and thereby renders concrete a doctrine that would otherwise remain abstruse. The fiction, however, is a mere appearance that illustrates an immaterial truth. There is no doubt that the essence of the artifact is the doctrine, not the narrative. The ontological bias that conditioned earlier poets such as Dante and Spenser was diametrically opposed to the phenomenalism that has influenced current modes of thought, so they were prone to take concepts as their objects of imitation much more readily than items or events in our physical surroundings.

In any case, the range of possibilities for the object of imitation is extremely wide. At one end—the end where we feel most at home—the object of imitation is something that the artificer has experienced in the course of contact with the physical world. He attempts to reproduce in facsimile a sight or sound or touch—sometimes even a taste or a smell, at least by suggestion. Often in such instances the object of imitation is not simple—perhaps some highly articulated phenomenon with many parts that fills a large quantity of space or a long period of time, or both—and the artificer must reproduce many sights or sounds or touches, and prob-

ably even a combination of these sense experiences. But the physical thing being imitated is reproduced, with considerable
attention to accuracy and completeness, as a coordinate sense experience for the percipient. The artificer takes pride in the success
of this illusion.

At the opposite end of our scale—the end where we no doubt
feel most uncertain and uneasy—the object of imitation is something that the artificer has experienced in his intellectual or spiritual activity divorced from the concrete world of physical things.
It is an idea in the Platonic sense or a belief in the Judeo-Christian
sense. The artificer has observed this object of imitation in the
course of his inner life, as a result of divine revelation or of meditation, or he might know it as an innate idea by virtue of instinct.
A seminal example of imitation of this sort stands at the wellhead
of Western art: Phidias's statue of Zeus at Olympia and his Athena
Parthenos, as Cicero reminded his own generation and instructed
all those that followed, were not sculpted in imitation of any human features, but rather exemplified the idea of divine majesty
which Phidias conceived in his mind. As Cicero describes their
creation, "That great sculptor, while making the image of Jupiter
or Minerva, did not look at any person whom he was using as a
model, but in his own mind there dwelt a surpassing vision of
beauty; at this he gazed and all intent on this he guided his artist's
hand to produce the likeness of the god" (*Orator* 2). Rather surprisingly, the pragmatic Cicero goes on to associate this "surpassing vision of beauty" with "the patterns of things" (hae rerum for-
mae), which Plato calls ἰδέαι.[38]

Until the revolutionary philosophy of Locke, who discredited
innate ideas, mankind ranged rather easily along the scale of
being, participating in physicality with the lower ranks of nature
and participating in divine reason with the angels and God. Our
sensibilities were not dissociated, and we moved unhindered between the world of thought and the world of sense experience. But
later developments introduced a disjunction between these two
adjacent realms. Empiricism subordinates the world of thought to
the world of sense experience, making ideas dependent upon
data; while positivism goes even farther and casts doubt upon the
very possibility of concepts. The problem faced by the latter-day
artificer who chooses an idea as an object of imitation then be-

comes how to bridge these two worlds, how to represent and make knowable that which is actually immaterial.

To the preempiricist, though, like Dante or Spenser, this problem was readily solved because an obvious example pointed to an answer. The deity has faced the same difficulty in manifesting His ideas—hence the holy scriptures and the book of nature. The Bible is a *direct* statement of the divine intention, while *indirectly* we discern the divine intention by reading the book of nature, whose recognized purpose is to reveal the immaterial attributes of its author. As Psalm 19 proclaims, "The heavens declare the glory of God, and the firmament sheweth His handiwork." Quite readily the mortal artificer assumes a similar stance toward his audience, and he may likewise converse in two modes. The artificer may adopt the guise of inspired prophet and like a *vates* address his audience directly. Or he too may create a universe to exemplify his thought—what we call narrative fiction, complete with characters who act and suffer, who transgress and fall, in a recognizable setting. It is this sort of artificer whom Sidney designates a "maker" and a "right" (i.e., authentic) poet (*Defence* 77.35, 80.28). As Shelley observed, "Few poets of the highest class have chosen to exhibit the beauty of their conceptions in its naked truth and splendour; and it is doubtful whether the alloy of costume, habit, &c., be not necessary to temper this planetary music for mortal ears."[39] But for such a poet, ideas rather than things are still the gist of his discourse—actually, his discourse is ancillary to his ideas.

A phenomenon (an item or event) in physical nature, then, and a conceptual idea define the extremes on a scale for possible objects of imitation. Few artificers, of course, work at either extreme, although some attempt it. Realism and naturalism are movements that strive toward the painstaking representation of physical things. The trompe-l'oeil painting reproduces the exact image of familiar objects grouped in space, even the illusion of open windows and distant prospects. The dance of the mime such as Marcel Marceau similarly seduces our senses. The tranche-de-vie story is also, at least by profession, an effort at representational art, and so is much (though not all) of the drama. In contrast, there is some art which is solely intellectual,[40] projecting that which is not physical. Most instrumental music without lyrics, certainly the most advanced forms such as the fugue,[41] and dance other than the pantomimic operate at this end of the scale. Abstract or non-objective painting suggests an attitude, maybe no more than a vague feeling or the possibility of relationships, but it represents nothing. Pure allegory renders discernible a doctrine that might otherwise go unheeded, and it is clear that the episodes that make up the fictive narrative are not in themselves to be taken as real in terms of our workaday world.

Between the extremes of a physical phenomenon and a conceptual idea, however, lie an unlimited number of possibilities for the imitated object. The degree of physicality can range from almost all to almost nothing, in an inverse proportion to the degree of metaphysicality. Herrick's poem "To Daffodils," for example, imitates in approximately equal parts the flowers as they bloom in the garden and as they express the concept of mutability. His daffodils are indissolubly both sense datum and concept. But along this continuous range from phenomenon to idea, it is cogent to locate at least two distinct nodes. For the object of imitation, an artificer may use an *abstraction* or a *type*. We must define these terms carefully, because they are often confused.

Working away from the physical end of the scale toward the middle, we can identify a node where the object of imitation is an abstraction drawn from several particular items. For example, a sculptor may mold a female face in the likeness of some notion of beauty which he has abstracted from his experience of looking at a number of beautiful women. The artifact then represents beauty in the abstract rather than a particular beautiful woman; but the "abstraction," as the etymology of that word indicates, has been literally "drawn from" concrete examples.[42] The artificer who implements this method usually intends to surpass nature by idealizing it; or, less commonly, he may wish to denigrate nature, in which case he produces the grotesque.[43]

An exemplary instance of art by abstraction is reported by Cicero. Wishing to paint Helen of Troy "so that the portrait though silent and lifeless might embody the surpassing beauty of womanhood," Zeuxis assembled the five most beautiful virgins of Croton and drew his image of ideal beauty from their features.[44] This anecdote was well-known in the Renaissance. Petrarch festoons Juno's temple in Croton with paintings by Zeuxis, although he appropriates the portrait of Helen and reassigns it to Juno herself:

> Here stood
> the austere image of the goddess-queen
> for which five lovely maidens, in the nude,
> had served as models for his brush to yield
> a distillation of the beautiful,
> as if the painter, having failed to find
> in one sole body all the graces sought,
> had drawn from many the one perfect form.[45]

The Petrarchan mistress of the popular sonnet sequence—with her starry eyes, cherry lips, pearly teeth, and ivory neck—is a similar distillation, where the particular beauties are dissolved in an idea of feminine perfection. In the eighteenth century this process of abstracting and idealizing the actual led to a theory that all the arts could be reduced to the single principle of imitating "beautiful nature," *la belle nature*,[46] and ultimately to the classification of the *beaux arts* as we know them.[47] In turn, this search for the universally beautiful in nature generated esthetics as a distinct academic discipline.

Counter to the process of abstraction, we may begin at the conceptual end of the scale, but again work toward the middle, and identify a node where the object of imitation embodies a concept in a particular example. Thereby the general is rendered knowable through the uniqueness of a specimen, the type. Kenelm Digby, for example, repeats the commonplace that "Man is a little world, an exact *type* of the great world, and of God himself."[48] In practice, a poet often takes the type a step farther and indicates an actual person, living or dead, as the exemplar of a virtue or of a vice. Shelley recognized this strategy as a distinctly poetical ploy: "A poet considers the vices of his contemporaries as the temporary dress in which his creations must be arrayed, and which cover without concealing the eternal proportions of their beauty" (12).

Dante used any number of contemporaries for this purpose. The artifact then depicts a particular person, but not to reveal that person's individuality. Rather, the individual is seen as typical of a concept that can best be, perhaps can only be, expressed in this manner.[49] In the proem to Book 1 of *The Faerie Queene* Spenser exemplifies this use of the term and its implications when he invokes the patronage of Elizabeth, whom he identifies as the local embodiment of Gloriana, who in turn is the "type" of glory which serves as his object of imitation:

> Shed thy faire beames into my feeble eyne,
> And raise my thoughts too humble and too vile,
> To thinke of that true glorious *type* of thine,
> The argument of mine afflicted stile.
>
> (1.proem.4.5–8; italics mine)

Here an individual personage, Elizabeth, proves to be a particular example of a type, Gloriana, who represents the quality or value of glory, an idea.[50] So an object of imitation may be either idea or sense datum, or something in between—abstraction or type.

Having defined the individual elements in the theory of art as imitation, we may now proceed to examine the several relationships between these elements. In addition to inhering in the whole art event, each element is related to every other on a one-to-one basis. Looking again at the diagram on page 21, we see the following interchanges: (1) artificer and artifact; (2) artificer and object of imitation; (3) object of imitation and artifact; (4) artifact and percipient; (5) percipient and artificer (through the artifact); and (6) percipient and object of imitation (through the artifact). Each of these relationships involves a mutual response between the two components—that is, it comprises a dynamic two-way interaction, rather than the complete control of an agent over a wholly passive receptor. The two components affect one another; and while an equilibrium may be reached with one or the other dominant, the relationship is still fluid, that of *agere* and *pati*. Therefore again, as in the case of delineating the range of possibilities for the object of imitation, we can define two extremes for each relationship while recognizing that either extreme is difficult to execute and that an infinite number of possibilities lie along the scale between them.

    1. The relation between artificer and artifact appears to be straightforward, although there are interesting possibilities. The artificer has the initial creative impulse, and chooses the object of imitation and the medium for the artifact. It is here also that questions about genre, about form, and about style are decided, al-

though these decisions may be tentative and may be adjusted during the course of completing the artifact. As the artifact emerges, in fact, as it assumes an identity and becomes an object in its own right, it inevitably begins to affect the artificer and modifies his choices. At one extreme, the artificer conceives the artifact in its entirety at once, and then proceeds through a largely mechanical operation of setting it down—on paper, on canvas, in stone, whatever.[51] At the other extreme, the artificer thinks of the creative process as a dynamic, even spontaneous, occurrence which is itself the proper subject matter of art, and the artifact is the record of that happening. The artifact takes over, leads a life of its own, while the artificer becomes as docile, even obedient, as possible.

Some artificers claim to withdraw from the artistic process once it is started, so that the artifact develops according to some automatic directive quite independent of the artificer. James Joyce, for example, suggested that the artist should turn away from his work like some indifferent deity and pare his fingernails.[52] But such a claim, if taken literally, is impossible, if only for logistical reasons. Falstaff or Scarlet O'Hara may assume human dimensions in the writer's mind, but they cannot pick up a pen and record their own stories. Such a claim of independence for the artifact is an affectation, of course, or it suggests a direction in which the artificer would like to move (Joyce's case), or it is a literary device to generate verisimilitude (*David Copperfield*), or it is itself the subject matter of the artifact (the myth of Pygmalion's Galatea, especially as Shaw reworked it). We must conclude that the artifact does undoubtedly develop under supervision of the artificer, although the degree of control varies, and conscious control may come close to nil. There may be attempts at completely unconscious literary composition—Coleridge and Yeats offer notorious examples—and attempts, such as those of Arp and Duchamps, to introduce the element of chance into the plastic arts. But these attempts have not been conspicuously successful. The artificer must participate to some considerable extent in the artistic process.

In our century the creed of formalism has endowed the artifact with authority over its own organization and meaning, and has relegated the artificer to an obscure position not only as unmoved but as nonmoving.[53] Especially literary criticism, starting with T. S. Eliot and John Crowe Ransom, has tended to hypostatize the artifact, claiming that it embodies its own reality, giving it an autonomous status, detached from the author. Relating the artifact to the artificer, and explaining it or interpreting it in that context, has called forth the scornful charge of "intentional fallacy." Some theorists argue that it is impossible to determine the intention of an artificer since he is not an immediate presence available for interview; and even if he were, he might not be willing to divulge his secrets, or he might not himself be consciously aware of his intention, or he might not be in control of what the artifact eventually means.

The classic and most judicious statement of this position is an essay by William K. Wimsatt, Jr., and Monroe C. Beardsley, entitled "The Intentional Fallacy."[54] Many have followed them in arguing that "the design or intention of the author is neither available nor desirable as a standard for judging the success of a work of literary art" (3). The point of this argument is to shift critical attention from the author to his work, so that a new aesthetic to deal with the phenomena of the artifact is required.[55] Such an aesthetic is duly laid out by these theorists, and their principles have had wide effect:

(a) The intention of the poet is not "a *standard* by which the critic is to judge the worth of the poet's performance" (4). What the poet intended and what he actually produced might be widely differing entities, and must be recognized as such. Later in the essay the authors draw a meaningful distinction between "criticism of poetry" and "author psychology" (10).

(b) Poetry is immediate and concrete experience for the reader, to be distinguished from practical messages, which are successful only if we correctly infer the intention. In consequence, practical messages "are more abstract than poetry" (5). To use Ransom's phrase, poetry is "the world's body."

(c) The poem presents a dramatic event, "the response of a speaker (no matter how abstractly conceived) to a situation (no matter how universalized)" (5). But since the poet is banished from the poem, the critic hypothesizes a "dramatic speaker," so the obvious need for an origin lies within the poem's own bounds. Then, "we ought to impute the thoughts and attitudes of the poem immediately to the dramatic *speaker*" (5), rather than to the poet.[56]

(d) "The poem is not the critic's own and not the author's (it is detached from the author at birth and goes about the world beyond his power to intend about it or control it). The poem belongs to the public. It is embodied in language, the peculiar possession of the public" (5).[57] Hence a poem is a "verbal icon"; its meaning resides in its words. They are the only data, the only phenomena, which are available to the reader in the task of interpretation.

This fruitful line of inquiry has application in the criticism of other than literary works of art. But an aesthetic that deals with artifacts as "icons" divorced from any antecedents lies outside our domain of inquiry. Such an aesthetic pointedly ignores both imitator and imitated object. It denies that art might be imitation, and it is uninterested that art might be personal expression. In fact, it lies perilously close to the magic land where a chunk of driftwood is a piece of sculpture and a birdcall is a madrigal. The artifact is an item which suddenly heaves into our consciousness, and it should be dealt with like any other object in physical nature.[58]

Refutation of the position propounded by Wimsatt and Beardsley has been undertaken by E.D. Hirsch, Jr., who argues that the intention of the author is the only valid basis for literary interpretation.[59] At least tacitly, Hirsch is working within a framework of art as imitation. Hirsch does not conclusively refute Wimsatt and Beardsley, however, because their arguments are based upon different systems of poetic theory. They are arguing from different premises and do not engage the same issues. Wimsatt and Beardsley consider poetry to be a special sort of discourse, while Hirsch insists that a poem should submit to the same kind of hermeneutical exegesis as any other verbal composition. Moreover, Wimsatt and Beardsley are talking about "the success of a work of literary art"; and there is still a question of whether that depends upon "validity in interpretation" or upon the impact the artifact has upon an impressionable percipient. Should the success of an art work be measured in terms of how well it can be validated as the artificer's intention, or in terms of how much a percipient may make of it? We may even wonder if *what* a poem means is more pertinent to critical evaluation than *how* the poem means—or, perhaps, if *what* a poem means is pertinent to critical evaluation at all. Should the verity of Milton's theological doctrine be a factor in evaluating the success of *Paradise Lost?* Hirsch makes some neat distinctions—for example, between "meaning" and "significance," and between "interpretation" and "criticism"[60]—but he doesn't completely close the gap or remove the difficulty that the intentional fallacy implies. We are likely to line up behind Hirsch or behind Wimsatt and Beardsley depending upon whether in our own poetic theory we assume that meaning is implied by the author in a public text or imputed by the reader from a self-contained text.

A corollary question that arises from the same discussion is whether an artifact is forever inextricably linked with the artificer, or whether upon publication it achieves an identity independent of its origins. The latter alternative is consistent with the proposition that art is timeless or universal. Though art begins in the mundane, in the everyday experience of the artificer, he transmutes his private particulars into an item which is public and unconditional in its truthfulness. It has value at all times and in all places. The realm of art is "ethereal" in the literal sense that Aristotle would have meant: the items in it have undergone a transmutation, and therefore are no longer vulnerable to the decay that besets the mutable things of our terrestrial world, although they are still visible to our mortal sight.[61] In modern terms, the artistic object is enduring and impersonal, enjoying in perpetuity an existence of its own detached from the author.[62] The diametric opposite is to root the artifact in its origins and to see it as an occasional piece—to treat it as a datum of historical evidence to document a period, or a datum of anthropological evidence to document a culture, or a datum of biographical or psychological evidence to document an individual person.

But here we have returned to the range of possibilities with which we began our discussion of the relationship between artificer and artifact. At one extreme, the equilibrium of this relationship resides near the artifact, so that it is dominant in our consideration, almost independent of its maker. At the other extreme, the equilibrium resides near the artificer, so that the artifact is little more than pertinent evidence about him and his milieu. The artificer—and the critic—may choose to work near either end of this scale, or anywhere in between.

2. In the relation between artificer and object of imitation, the equilibrium may similarly be placed anywhere along a range between two extremes. The object of imitation, whether physical or conceptual, has attracted the notice of the artificer, and he has chosen to imitate it in the artifact. If he scrupulously respects the identity of the object of imitation and reproduces it faithfully, so that the artifact is a replication of the object of imitation, we have one extreme. The object of imitation dominates and determines the nature of the artifact, which becomes a mere facsimile of the original. But of course the artificer in viewing the object of imitation will revise it to some degree in the very act of cognition, so he acts upon it as well as being acted upon by it. The artificer may, in fact, intentionally distort the object of imitation for his own purposes. It is here that the concept of "style" acquires meaning, because style is the technique by which the artificer adapts the object of imitation and makes it his own.[63] At the extreme in this direction, the artificer domineers, and the artifact is a gross revision of the imitated object. For some ulterior motive he exploits the object of imitation, perverting it as much as necessary to serve his end. The original object of imitation may be barely discernible in the resultant artifact, barely identifiable.

The two extremes in this relationship between artificer and object of imitation define the terms "artisan" and "artist" that we have glanced at earlier (page 28). The "artisan" is he who faithfully reproduces the object of imitation as it has become standardized, following the rules of that craft and exercising traditional skills. The "artist" is he who assumes a license to disregard rules and snatch a grace beyond the reach of art. The term "artist" in this refined sense is a relatively recent innovation in our language,[64] and reflects a changing philosophy of art in our culture. It became prevalent as a result of the Romantic movement with its reverence for the individual genius. So the artisan imitates to manufacture a reproduction, while the artist creates anew.

One theory of art, ultimately traceable to Plotinus,[65] obviates the need for an object of imitation. We may call it "the theory of inherent form," because it is based upon the thesis that residual forms inhere within portions of matter. The role of the artificer is then reduced to realizing this potential within the medium itself. He reveals what is already present by removing the excess material that obscures it. For example, within the block of stone, there is a form struggling to be free, and the task of the sculptor is simply to release it. No less an artist than Michelangelo professed such a theory,[66] and more recently it has shaped the most innovative work of two sculptors so dissimilar as Rodin and Brancusi.[67] Gertrude Stein and others have suggested a similar potential in the verbal medium when they argue that a reader struggles to find meaning in a sequence of words, no matter how unrelated, until he arrives at some resolution which seems satisfying. But if practised conscientiously, in either stone or language, in no sense is this an art of imitation.

A much more sophisticated theory of art, traceable to Kant and Cassirer, recognizes the initial determinacy of the object of imitation, but during the artistic event the object of imitation is transformed into something more complex. Following Susanne Langer, its most popular exponent, we may call it "the theory of symbolic transformation" because it is based upon the thesis that a phenomenon may undergo a process of "symbolization." From the immediate significance of an item or event in his experience, the artificer extrapolates a symbolic meaning that raises the particular instance to a generality. In this theory, the artifact serves as a receptacle for what the object of imitation means at a higher level of abstraction. In consequence, the artifact includes both a particular and a general reference. It includes both a denotation (with the object of imitation as its referent) and a connotation (with the conception in the mind of the artificer as its referent).[68] But already we have encroached upon our next topic.

3. The artifact and the object of imitation are related in the way that a derivative is related to its original. To continue with the terminology of Langer, the artifact is a "symbol" of the object of imitation. As Langer defines the term, "Symbols are not proxy for their objects, but are *vehicles for the conception of objects*" (60– 61)—that is, the symbol conveys thought about its object without the object being physically present or even without representing the object in any verisimilar way.[69] The "symbolization" of the imitated object does give it a new identity, and the artifact acquires a measure of independence from both the object of imitation and the artificer.

The closeness of the relationship between object of imitation and artifact depends largely upon the degree of distortion introduced by the artificer, either consciously or unconsciously. The medium of the artifact may also introduce a degree of distortion, because the medium imposes certain technical limitations. It is difficult, for example, for a painter to construct a narrative within a single frame; and because of quite different limitations, a musician is similarly unable to tell a story without the complement of a script. Conversely, the verbal description of a scene—assessed strictly as a visual image—is patently less effective than a picture ("A picture is worth a thousand words"); and the verbal description of a mood—assessed strictly as an emotional occasion—is patently less effective than an appropriate piece of music ("Say it in music").

The medium may also impose certain limitations because of tradition and convention, the codes of the cultural formation. A number of distinct "genres" have developed, and both artificer and percipient recognize their potency so that much can be conveyed simply by the invocation of a genre.[70] A poem is a "mock-epic," or a painting is a "still life," or a musical composition is a "sonata." By applying such a label, the artificer designates that his artifact is a member of a class, and thereby, as if in shorthand, he indicates a great deal about it. The drawback, though, is that working within the dictates of a genre is restrictive as well as convenient. Abuse of the traditional and conventional characteristics of the class constitutes a violation of "decorum." The artifact must accord with the object of imitation within certain bounds acknowledged by the artificer and acceptable to the percipient. Of course, if the artificer wishes to be insouciant or revolutionary, he may flagrantly violate the expected codes and produce an artifact that recklessly subverts the object of imitation.

It is evident how the object of imitation acts upon the artifact: it is the original of the artifact and a continuing referent for its meaning. Using the familiar linguistic model of Saussure, we might say that the imitated object is the *signifié,* while the artifact is the *signifiant,* both together comprising the sign. How the artifact acts upon the object of imitation, however, is not so readily discerned. The object of imitation would seem to be a fixed datum, unchangeable. Yet, the artifact as a new version of something familiar may give both artificer and percipient a deeper understanding of the original, and consequently a richer experience of it. After dealing with something in a work of art, we may be more appreciative of its correspondent in physical nature or more receptive to an idea which presents itself for our consideration. For example, after perusing Dürer's engraving of a hare, we may see more in the next rabbit that hops across our path; or after reading Dr. Johnson's *Rasselas,* we may more readily comprehend the vanity of human wishes. By sharpening the sensibility of the percipient, the artifact endows the object of imitation with increased significance. It is even possible in an extreme case, as in symbolist art, that the object of imitation exists only by virtue of its incarnation in the artifact.

When the object of imitation is itself an artifact of a similar kind which inheres in an established tradition, we have a special case of a most interesting sort: for example, when Milton writes a Homeric epic, or when Matisse paints an odalisque after Ingres and Delacroix, or when Gilbert Scott builds a Gothic monument to memorialize Queen Victoria's husband. The artificer blatantly reinterprets a convention, adapting it to his own purposes, and thereby demands that the percipient reexamine that convention and revise its import. As a new member of a previously defined class, the recent artifact alters, however slightly, the total makeup of that class. Consequently, any component in the imitated object which derives from a genre, or even from tradition and convention, must be adjusted to take into account the recent artifact, the new addition to that set. Eliot makes this point in his well-known essay, "Tradition and the Individual Talent": "The existing monuments form an ideal order among themselves, which is modified by the introduction of the new (the really new) work of art among them" (5).[71] The poet must write with an awareness of this immense body of precedents, this residual and cumulative component in any art work which itself becomes an object of imitation.

So the relationship between object of imitation and artifact is likely to be dynamic at least to some small extent in every instance, and the degree of replication may range from exact to tenuous. The artifact may be an attempt at exact representation of the imitated object, or the similarity may be vague, sufficient only for the barest outlines of the imitated object to emerge. The relationship is further complicated by the fact that the object of imitation may be a physical phenomenon or it may be a conceptual idea (pages 33–38). John Crowe Ransom acknowledged this dichotomy and built a poetics upon it:

> A poetry may be distinguished from a poetry by virtue of subject-matter, and subject-matter may be differentiated with respect to its ontology, or the reality of its being. . . . The recent critics remark in effect that some poetry deals with things, while some other poetry deals with ideas. The two poetries will differ from each other as radically as a thing differs from an idea.[72]

But all that we have said holds for either case, whether a poetry of "things" or a poetry of "ideas." The artifact embodies the essence of the imitated object. Finally, in the theory of art as imitation this relationship, as Ransom recognized, is fundamental to an exegesis of the artifact's meaning because the being of the artifact originates with the object of imitation. To be simplistic, the artifact exhibits the object of imitation as it has been modified by the artificer and as it is offered to the percipient for comprehension.

4. The most spectacular achievements of twentieth-century criticism have resulted from investigating the relationship between artifact and percipient. Using the techniques of several new disciplines such as symbolic logic, semiotics, and stylistics, we have been able to suggest more analytically than before how a work of art expresses meaning, or conversely how a percipient knows an artifact. Here we see the essential interaction between these two elements: the artifact works upon the percipient, while of course the percipient also works upon the artifact. At one extreme, the artifact is complete and precise, and the percipient must struggle to realize its potential, to know it in its nearly inviolable selfhood. At the other extreme, the artifact is a largely undefined stimulus, the merest hint, to which the percipient is invited to respond in a personal freewheeling fashion.[73] At either extreme, however, and all along the intervening range of possibilities, the percipient distorts the artifact to a lesser or greater degree in the perception of it; and therefore the term "art event," as we have suggested, is useful to distinguish the percipient's comprehension of the artifact from the artifact itself.[74]

The relationship between artifact and percipient is largely a matter of epistemology, and our extremes may be defined in terms of phenomenalism and the theory of innate ideas. Since Plato, some aestheticians have postulated that the mind is naturally stocked with all possible ideas, and perceiving an artifact is merely responding to a stimulus by bringing forward the correspondent idea innate in the mind (cf. *Phaedrus* 249E–250A). This aesthetic gives epistemological control of the relationship to the percipient. Once he is stimulated, his mind is the determining agent for meaning. Other aestheticians, however, are strict phenomenalists and postulate that the mind knows only what it perceives with the senses. In fact, there is no other reality but phenomena, so for knowledge the mind is dependent upon its percepts of sense data. Assuming that the mind is an innocent instrument, this aesthetic gives epistemological control of the relationship to the artifact. The art event subsists in the phenomena which reveal the artifact, so it is the determining agent for meaning. Empiricists take a stand somewhere in the middle: although, as Aristotle said and Locke confirmed and Freud professed, there is nothing in the intellect which was not first in the senses, the mind does maintain a log of past experience, and this memory consciously or unconsciously conditions the percipient's response to any particular artifact. The debate about the activity or the passivity of the human intellect during the perceptual act continues to rage, with the tide of battle tending now to one side and then to the other.

There is another consideration in this highly volatile relationship between artifact and percipient. Should we think of the perceptual act as conclusive, the perception of a finished and determinate artifact? Or should we think of the perceptual act as a continuing process that determines the artifact in the very act of knowing it? I am, of course, talking about questions of "closure." [75] Just as the artificer may conceive of the artifact as an entirety before engaging in the actual production of it (a sort of *natura naturata*), so also the percipient may approach the artifact in a comparable spirit and treat it like a permanent object, a finished product sufficient unto itself and forever fixed. The percipient comprehends the artifact, and that's that. Or, just as the artificer may see the artifact as the dynamic record of a creative experience that he is undergoing (a sort of *natura naturans*), so also the percipient may approach the artifact in this spirit, so that the artifact is the dynamic process of experiencing it. And this process may not definitely terminate. In this latter case, the artifact and the art event will be congruent. Examples here may be instructive: a lyric poet may tell us post facto about his loneliness on a particular occasion in the past, or he might wish to have us share concurrently his experience of what it is to feel lonely; comparably, we may read to find out about someone else's loneliness, or to indulge a sentimental impulse to feel lonely ourselves. Crucial decisions about the appropriate methodology for interpretation depend upon these choices.

A closely related consideration in our analysis of the perceptual act has to do with the extent of its duration. The act of cognition may be instantaneous, completed almost at once, approaching an epiphany; or it may be discursive, stretching over a long period of time—perhaps never reaching a final end. Some media adapt more readily to one condition than the other, a distinction that Lessing parlayed into a clear separation of spatial arts from temporal arts.[76] Painting and sculpture tend to be perceived instantaneously, although further examination may reveal nuances not noticed at first. The immediacy of the spatial arts, being visual, approaches an actual encounter with the object of imitation. Poetry, in contrast, tends to be perceived discursively and is therefore a temporal art. The syntax required by verbal meaning demands that words be strung out in a cumbrous system, even though a poem may eventually achieve an effect of totality and organic oneness. In general, counter to what occurs in the spatial arts, the dispersiveness of poetry induces a psychic distance between the percipient and the object of imitation. Again, our selection between possibilities—whether we treat the artifact as an extemporal or a durational object—will play a large part in devising a methodology for interpretation. Our choice, in fact, will predetermine to a large extent what we find in any given artifact.

There is yet another contingent consideration in the relationship between percipient and artifact, one bearing upon what happens in successive encounters with the same artifact. What takes place, for example, when we read a poem for the second, or the third or fourth or fifth, time?[77] Or even more crucially, because there are additional variant factors in the presentation (performers and sets as well as a text), what takes place when we see a play

on successive occasions? To compound the question to its uttermost, what is the relation of the most recent film of *Macbeth* I've
seen to an earlier film of *Macbeth* I previously saw, and to the
several different stage productions of the play I've sat through
over the years, and to what went on in my mind when I first read
the play? And as a side issue, what is the relation of all this to
Verdi's *Macbeth,* or even to a painting of Macbeth and the
Witches that hangs on the walls of the Folger? Frye states the
problem succinctly: "Direct experience, even if it is concerned
with something already read hundreds of times, still tries to be a
new and fresh experience each time, which is clearly impossible if
the poem itself has been replaced by a critical view of the
poem"[78]—but he leaves the matter at that impasse.

So far we have dealt with the epistemology of this relationship:
how is the artifact known by the percipient? But there are correlative questions that concern its teleology: for what purposes is the
artifact directed at the percipient? Ever since Plato, critics have
assumed that art has an immediate and profound effect upon our
behavior, for either good or ill. Horace proposed that poetry
should teach as well as please, and others have repeated this dictum with an admonition that it should please only in order to
teach. For these reasons, the Church has often preempted authority over the graphic and plastic arts and drama, while from the
time of the Sophists until the last few hundred years the art of
poetry was usually subsumed in the schools under rhetoric, the
"art of persuasion." Political parties have frequently suppressed
all art but their own propagandistic efforts to disseminate the
party ideology. Today certain guarantees for freedom of expression have lessened the imperative of art's teleology, although there
is still ample evidence that art is used as an agent to induce cultural conformity. So in examining the relationship between an artifact and its percipient, there's good reason to look for an ulterior
motive behind the artistic effort. We must take into account the
ethical or didactic or propagandistic element in its teleology. This
element, of course, is intended by the artificer and aimed at the
percipient.

5. The relationship between artificer and percipient is necessarily at one remove—that is, the artificer must approach the percipient through the artifact, and conversely the percipient must

work in the opposite direction and use the artifact as a means of approaching the artificer. What the artificer contributes to the art event is incorporated into the artifact, which becomes the vehicle of his intent. Conversely, the percipient if he engages in critical analysis of the artifact will look behind it to its originator. Those who squeamishly desist from committing the "intentional fallacy" would deny this reasonable right of the percipient to explore every avenue that might lead to meaning; but as we have seen (page 41), they do not in any case concur in a theory of art as imitation.

Among the six relationships that we have identified, only this one between artificer and percipient involves an interaction between two human beings. In this relationship, communication occurs, and critics displaying a wide variety of stripes deal with art as though it were some sort of communication.[79] In the succinct words of George Heard Hamilton, "Because each work of art originates in the mind and feelings of a human being, it reaches its destination in the mind and feelings of another."[80] In the even more succinct words of Wordsworth, a poet "is a man speaking to men."[81] But other theorists make a distinction between poetry and ordinary conversation. Frye, for example, perhaps echoing Matthew Arnold, insists, "Poetry is a *disinterested* use of words: it does not address a reader directly."[82] Nonetheless, if we think of art as communication between artificer and percipient, here also we may construct a scale of possibilities and identify an extreme at each end. The artificer may express himself so assertively and unmistakably that he brooks little initiative on the part of the percipient. The percipient is necessarily passive.[83] Or the percipient may act so aggressively as he responds that he takes over the conversation, once begun, and hardly listens further to the artificer. The percipient is very active indeed. In this relationship between artificer and percipient there is the tentativeness, even unresolvable ambiguity and chance for error, that always inheres in social intercourse.

As an extraordinary ploy, the artificer may address the percipient directly in a blatantly extracurricular gesture—for example, the annotation that Eliot appended to *The Waste Land*. In the same vein, the title of a work provides an opportunity for explanations or for announcing contexts, and the artificer may exploit it for these purposes. He may use the title to locate his work geo-graphically (*The Grand Canyon Suite*), or to indicate its genre (*The Tragedy of Romeo and Juliet*). Printed stage directions and program notes at concerts and inscriptions on buildings perform the same function by approaching the percipient outside the con-fines of the artifact. Sometimes an artificer dextrously inserts the extraneous into the artifact by means of a headpiece or an epi-logue, and sometimes he even integrates himself into the work of art so that he appears nominally as its purveyer. In a lengthy headpiece Milton self-consciously calls attention to his neoclassi-cism before allowing a reader to proceed to the verse of *Paradise Lost,* and a Renaissance painter kneels prominently among the worshippers in an altarpiece. Or Dante and Chaucer at least seem to speak directly to their audience, so that it is difficult to distin-guish poet from narrative voice. But by and large this is now con-sidered poor technique because it thrusts the artificer too far for-ward into the limelight, upstaging the artifact.

A modern tendency in criticism, following the New Critics, has been to separate the poet himself from a persona through whom he speaks. And sometimes, especially in fictive narrative, the ar-tificer explicitly pretends that someone else is communicating through the artifact. In these cases the persona is a disguise with an ulterior motive: perhaps to permit the expression of dangerous opinions without reprisal against the author (Spenser's "Mother Hubberds Tale"), or to give a semblance of verisimilitude to the story (Conrad's *Heart of Darkness*), or to give the narrative an additional dimension by seeing it from the perspective of a third person with a significantly different point of view (James's *Portrait of a Lady*).

In most media the artificer cannot address the percipient di-rectly within the artifact, but must instead remain a grey emin-ence. In contrast to the narrative purportedly related by its au-thor, we have the drama, the most objective of the literary modes. The dramatist must speak only through his characters; he cannot step out from the wings and explain to the audience what he means—although prologues and epilogues (and sometimes solilo-quies and choruses) are a way of getting around this restriction, and our century has witnessed astonishing cleverness in circum-venting the objectivity of the drama. The other arts militate against the unabashed intrusion of the artificer even more rigorously. Only rarely does a painter presume to include himself in a canvas (self-portraits are a genre apart), and a musician—or a sculptor, a choreographer, or an architect—can't interrupt his composition for a personal appearance. These media do not permit such license. In all the arts other than literature, it is difficult for the artificer to manipulate the percipient except via the artifact.

When the percipient turns to act upon the artificer, he also is severely limited—again, largely to the artifact alone.[84] The artifact should rightly be the focus of his attention, since the artificer is physically out of reach. Of course, the percipient may go beyond the artifact and search out additional information about the artificer in other sources, and this will become part of the paraphernalia by which he interprets the artifact. The percipient, in fact, may go to great lengths to reconstruct the biography and milieu of the artificer. Such research is scholarship, however, and though it may be a legitimate component of critical analysis, it is not integral to the viewing process itself. It is an act of criticism rather than an act of perception.

Problems attendant upon the relationship between artificer and percipient usually center upon the reliability of the artificer. Wordsworth insisted upon his "sincerity"; and commenting upon Wordsworth, Pater made stipulations about the poet's self-awareness.[85] Is he sensitive to his surroundings, conscious of his own impressions, gifted in expressing them? More recent critics have raised questions about the rhetorical stance of the artificer. Does he mean what he says, or does he, deliberately or inadvertently, adopt poses which must be seen through? So far, the "sincerity" of the percipient has not been called into question, although he too must be a responsible party for communication to take place. It is assumed that the percipient is capable of comprehension and, equally important, not perverse—what Dryden calls "the reasonable reader,"[86] perhaps even what Fish calls "the informed reader."[87] The danger, of course, is that even an informed and sympathetic viewer finds in the artifact what he is predisposed to look for. So the relationship between artificer and percipient is strained at best, and depends upon the good will and honest effort of both parties.

6. In any theory of art as mimesis, the relationship between percipient and object of imitation is the most tenuous and delicate of all, yet this is the interaction that gives purpose to everything else. If the percipient fails to comprehend the object of imitation, which is the touchstone for the entire imitative process, the artistic effort is flawed at best, and perhaps wildly misdirected. The ontological basis of the art event, the primary meaning of the artifact, resides with the object of imitation, and the motive for the imitative act is to reveal it. To this end, the artifact is a projection of the object of imitation. Unless the artificer addresses the percipient directly by means of a device such as prologue or footnote, the imitated object is made apparent to the percipient only by means of the artifact. Conversely, the percipient has access to the object of imitation only through this distorted derivative.

If the object of imitation is faithfully reproduced by the artifact, it will be fully evident and will likely prevail with the percipient. He can contribute little of his own to the clearly revealed physical phenomenon or conceptual idea, and will likely subside into passivity. The artifact does it all. If, however, the object of imitation is heavily veiled or but obscurely suggested, the percipient must exercise considerable ingenuity in discerning it. He becomes actively involved in the artistic process. The percipient is called upon to fantasize in his attempt to reconstitute the object of imitation. At the extreme, his contribution to the art event may be so large that the reconstituted object of imitation becomes little more than a projection of his own self-image. The subjective fallacy marks this extreme.[88] When the subjective fallacy is operative, the object of imitation is reduced to a figment of the percipient's imagination, and critical anarchy ensues.

But always the object of imitation is distorted to some degree in the artifact, and always the percipient exercises his faculties (and thereby introduces further distortion) when viewing the artifact. Here in this transmission lies the crux of the problem. In the theory of imitation, on what can interpretation be based? How can the percipient reconstruct the object of imitation using only its imperfect replica, the artifact? In Sidney's terms, how does the reader use the narration in fiction to discover the author's profitable invention (*Defence* 103.14–16)? Moreover, how does the percipient credit the possibility that distortions of the imitated object are intended by the artificer with significative consequences? The obvious procedure would be to investigate to what extent and in what ways the artificer revised the object of imitation in production of the artifact, and for what purposes he made these modifications.

Langer suggests that as a basic procedure we seek to detect the "significant form" of the artifact (262–65),[89] which it shares with the object of imitation—indeed, which is supplied by the object of imitation. Just as the artifact is a "symbol" of the object of imitation, in Langer's sense of the term (page 44), so understanding the artifact consists in abstracting a meaning, in making a "diagram" of the relationships between its parts. This structure is the irreducible essence of the artifact, which it shares with the object of imitation: "It is a *form* that appears in all versions of thought or imagery that can connote the object in question, a form clothed in different integuments of sensation for every different mind" (71). Perception of an artifact varies from observer to observer, as we have noted; but since each interpretation incorporates the same network of relationships among its parts, all interpretations share this "fundamental *pattern* . . . [so] that we can talk about the 'same' house despite our private differences of sense-experience, feeling, and purely personal associations." An interpretation that doesn't fully realize this "fundamental *pattern*" is inadequate. An interpretation that in an idiosyncratic way proposes a different pattern is wrong. Such an aesthetic is satisfied by discovery of this "significant form," which in a Platonic way is taken to be the essence of the imitated object.

If the percipient can so much as identify the object of imitation, he may do independent research and reconstruct it from resources outside the artifact. For example, to evaluate Constable's "View of Salisbury Cathedral," a spectator might compare it to a photograph of the cathedral or might even visit the site (not just to determine the verisimilar accuracy of the painting, but to assess Constable's modification of what he had seen). Such an investigative project, like research on the artificer, is scholarship. But how do we identify and take into account the distortion purposely introduced by the artificer—what the artificer has added, deleted, or emended in order to convey the quiddity of the imitated object as he views it? This is the overarching problem in the interpretation of imitative art: how to comprehend the artifact in terms of what the artificer is imitating and of how he has willfully modified that object.

But even if we accurately discern the artifact, clearly detect the object of imitation, and sympathetically understand the artificer, our duties *as a critic* are not at an end. Criticism goes beyond perception. The critic must evaluate as well as perceive. Having reconstructed the object of imitation, he must ask the pragmatic question, "How worthwhile is the artifact?" Sometimes this question takes a philosophical turn, "How *true* is it?" Or a moral turn, "How *good* is it?" Or an aesthetic turn, "How *beautiful* is it?" But each of these variant questions requires the critic to measure the artifact against some standard outside itself. The history of civilization shows that only rarely have we been satisfied by an aesthetic of art for art's sake; and only recently, in the wake of formalism, have we pontificated that the artifact is sufficient unto itself, a self-reflexive icon. So in articulating our theory, we must realize that a larger reality looms beyond the art event, and ultimately conditions its significance. As Pope asserted so memorably, the universal norms which he with his age conflated in the term "Nature" are "at once the *Source*, and *End*, and *Test* of *Art*."[90]

By the act of criticism the percipient ascertains if the artifact is valid or fraudulent, valuable or worthless. Of course, if the artificer denies seriousness to his work, the percipient acts without license if he lades it with import. If the intent of the artificer is merely to entertain rather than to convey values, we may cherish the artifact for its fun, but not for its Truth. But even to enjoy the fun, the percipient must determine whether he can fit the artifact into his own scheme of things, whether there is sufficient common ground to allow even a frivolous response, or whether the artifact must remain a distant anomaly of no significance to him. Today we are not amused, for example, by pastoral romances, despite their popularity in the seventeenth century, or edified by the academic paintings submitted for the Prix de Rome in the early nineteenth century. And who knows what future generations will make of our pop music?

To implement a doctrinaire aesthetic program, an artificer may pointedly deny any relationship between his artifact and a larger reality—for example, in a movement such as art for art's sake, or even more outrageously in an outburst such as dada. To deal with this insouciance, the percipient must be consciously aware of the implications of such a denial, and he must accept the prohibition against measuring the artifact against the actuality of experience. The artifact becomes "play" in the most effete and least demanding sense. But even here the artifact generates meaning by affirming the doctrinaire aesthetic which it exemplifies. Life, like art (it says), is ridiculous—perhaps sadly so, but nonetheless ridiculous. Or as the surrealists were commenting at the mid-point in our century, life is unpredictable, mysterious, unsettling, inexplicable. Our theater has, by serious intent, become absurd. By and large, however, art is a rational and earnest business, as attested by the centuries of devoted efforts on the part of artificers and percipients alike, and we expect something positive from it. Hence the considerable labor expended upon criticism, in both theory and practice.

From this model for the art of imitation there emerges no inexorable methodology for criticism, because there are no inexorable rules for mimetic art. Anatomizing the several relationships that make up the system does not yield a surefire way of evaluating the artifact, or even of reconstituting the object of imitation. In any case, my intention has been hypothetical rather than prescriptive, suggesting boundaries rather than plotting routes. And I have refrained from making definite proposals because I don't wish to preempt Sidney, whose well-articulated poetics in *The defence of poesie* is the tale that calls forth this lengthy prologue. Chapter 5, however, will set forth Sidney's poetical theory in detail and will indicate the appropriate way to analyze a poem in accord with that poetics.

Any theorist, however, who does propound a critical methodology should bear in mind the full range of possibilities within each of the relationships delineated in this chapter, especially if he concurs in the commonplace that art is imitation. If he doesn't accept this premise, he must overtly dissociate himself and his theory from what has, rightly or wrongly, acquired the prevalence of a self-evident maxim. For all art is *not* imitation—divine inspiration, expressionism, symbolist art, dada, what I shall call "iconism" from the phrase "verbal icon,"[91] affective stylistics, and self-

reflexivity prove the point. Each of these modes obviates or ignores an object of imitation. And all artifacts should not be treated
as though all art *were* imitative. Different artistic premises require
different techniques of analysis, and these decisions should be explicitly stated. Fortunately, our theorists and practicing critics
have become increasingly circumspect in doing so, and several
new journals are devoted primarily to that purpose.

3
Imitation in the Arts

> The last of the fine arts is literature. . . . It appeals to the sense of hearing far less immediately than music does. It makes no appeal to the eyesight, and takes no help from the beauty of colour. It produces no palpable, tangible object. But language being the storehouse of all human experience . . . it follows that, of all the arts, poetry soars highest, flies widest, and is most at home in the region of the spirit.[1]

In the last chapter we considered all the arts indiscriminately as a class. What we said about "art" applies to poetry, however, since poetry is a member of that class. To make the argument at any point applicable specifically to poetry, simply change the term "artificer" to "poet," "artifact" to "poem," and "percipient" to "audience" (to "hearer" or, more usually in our day, "reader").[2] There is no need to change the term "object of imitation," the distinctive feature of any mimetic theory of art. Our model of imitation, then, is adaptable in every detail to those artifacts made public through the medium of words.

But poetry is a special category of artifact. Because of its verbal medium, the literary art has certain distinctive properties which set it apart. Of course, in some respects a poem may be like a painting or like a musical composition—or even a statue, a dance, or a building.[3] Poetry can be contrived to simulate certain characteristics of this or that fine art. Most easily, if we judge from the frequency of attempts, poetry is likened to painting on the one hand and to music on the other. But since the medium of poetry differs from the media of painting and of music, the assimilation of poetry to either of its sister arts can be carried only so far. There are limitations to how far a verbal system can be transmuted into or intermeddled with something nonliterary.

These attempts at assimilating poetry to painting or to music are highly instructive, though, as we shall see, and indicate a great deal about poetic imitation. And the reasons why poetry refuses to be completely transformed into any of the other arts are equally instructive. They stem from the linguistic identity of poetry. Ultimately, imitation in poetry—as distinct from imitation in music or in the visual arts—depends upon the nature of its medium, language. So we shall spend some time exploring those topics about language that bear upon its mimetic capacity, especially those topics that proved of special interest in the Renaissance. But again, because our notion of the arts has changed radically since Sidney's day, we must pause to clarify our terminology.

Like Sidney, I will use the word "poetry" for all artful literature, whether in verse or prose,[4] and I'll allow it to subsume the equally common Elizabethan term, "poesy."[5] Furthermore, I will follow Elizabethan usage and designate the word "poem" as a generic term for all artifacts expressed through a verbal medium. "Poem" comes from the same etymological root as the word "poet"—that is, as Sidney points out, the Greek verb ποιεῖν, "to make" (*Defence*, 77.34).[6] A "poet," then, is a maker, and a "poem" is that which has been made. "Poem" is a cognate, in fact, with the word "fiction," which comes from the past participle *fictus* of the Latin verb *fingere*, similarly "to make."[7] A "fiction," like a "poem," is that which has been made. The two words are synonyms from roots that mean the same thing in two different languages, Latin and Greek. John Marston, for example, in 1598 could publish this couplet:

> For tell me *Crittick,* is not *Fiction*
> The soule of Poesies invention?[8]

The act of making, Marston implies, ποιεῖν or *fingere*, is basic to the art of poetizing. "Fiction" is integral to the "poem" like soul to body.[9]

The association of prose with "fiction" and of verse with "poetry" is a post-Renaissance development. Late in the seventeenth century, during the same period that saw the separation of the physical sciences from the arts, prose in England acquired a reputation for directness and honesty through its recommendation by the Royal Society. In contrast, as Dryden claimed, poets enjoy a "poetic license" to go beyond actual fact, and he explained: "Poetic License I take to be the liberty which poets have assumed to themselves, in all ages, of speaking things in verse, which are beyond the severity of prose."[10] The separation of prose from poetry, completed by the mid-eighteenth century,[11] reflects certain aesthetic postulates, certain assumptions about literature. As Hegel later took to be self-evident, prose deals with "the world of Nature," while verse conveys "the life of Spirit."[12] Prose is one thing, and verse another, clearly distinguishable like what is real and what is ethereal. Consequently, the novel, claiming realism, hit upon prose as its proper vehicle. But this distinction has served its purpose in our cultural evolution, has grown impractical, and now is being sloughed off.[13] The demarcation between poetry and prose fiction has been blurred, often intentionally. We are returning to a holistic view of literature more in line with Sidney and his contemporaries, although the intervening history of the words "fiction" and "poem" may not allow us to employ these terms with the same meaning as they did.

In any case, for Elizabethans "fiction" was not "fictitious" (a modern sense of the word, paralleling the evolution of "artificial" to mean "sham").[14] Even though fiction was imagined by the poet, it was not invalid. One of Sidney's major aims in the *Defence* was to prove that the poet does not lie. "Fiction" was a synonym for "poem," which likewise was made up, but true.[15] Moreover, fiction was not limited to prose. Nor was a poem necessarily cast in verse (certainly rhyme was no requirement, as Sidney and Milton both contended). After noting the derivation of "poet" from ποιεῖν, Jonson summarizes his definition of the term: "A *Poet* . . . is not hee which writeth in measure only; but that fayneth and formeth a fable, and writes things like the Truth."[16] *Caveat lector.* In this discussion we shall use "poem" as a generic term, meaning any literary artifact, verse or prose, that involves "fiction." And we shall use "fiction" in the sense of "making," as though it were "the soule of Poesies invention."

These definitions and warnings make it clear that our investigation has a historical dimension and our findings have historical boundaries. We are dealing with a particular body of art whose contours are determined by time and place—the Renaissance in Western Europe. We may not slip off the mortal coil of historicity. As we noted in the last chapter, the artifact and the real world of the artificer interpenetrate. As Wittgenstein would have it, we must know the rules of the cultural "game" that is being played.

The period that contains our discussion runs roughly from the opening of the fifteenth century to the end of the last, a half millenium that witnessed a radical shift in the prevailing ontology of our culture. These centuries are identified as a coherent epoch in human history by what I shall call the relocation of reality. In 1400 the ultimate constituents of reality were located in a Platonist-Christian heaven among the attributes and intentions of a transcendent deity. Gradually during the course of this period, however, the cosmological postulates of Christianity gave way to new scientific laws arrived at empirically, so the ultimate constituents of reality were relocated among the observed data of physical nature.[17] Consequently, our study begins with the incipient interest in validating our sense-perceptible universe during the early Renaissance in Italy and continues until the beginning of our own century when empiricism could no longer withstand the challenges of atomism and relativism and subjectivism. This is the period when it could be argued with reasonable conviction that art is replicative imitation of some sort. In the time of Alberti, such a doctrine was enunciated as an innovation, replacing medieval attitudes toward art; by the time of Picasso, despite the ingenious efforts of the Impressionists, the theory of art as a representation of objective nature, no matter how defined or how interpreted, was no longer viable.

At the opening of this period, however, carrying over as a generality from the Middle Ages, ultimate meaning resided with God, and all things inhered in His inclusive substance. God was a prior order of being which preexisted and outlived any physical or conceptual object and any cognizant subject. He was the premise which underlay (as substance) any act of knowing or of stating or of comprehending. In consequence, art and its constituent elements inhered in this larger system grounded in the deity. Art was placed in the service of praising God, and the products of art were seen as a means of acquaintance with the imperative of God's will. Art was subservient to religious worship and teaching.

Reinforcing this attitude, though redefining it in new terms, the Florentine Platonists saw art as the embodiment in palpable form of the essences that comprise the ideal world of being. As Ficino interpreted Plato and his followers, "God is the supreme source and light within whom shine the models of all things, which they call ideas,"[18] and therefore activity of the human psyche should be directed toward comprehension of those divine ideas. But being mortal, debilitated by the limitations that time and space impose upon mankind, we cannot directly comprehend those *exemplaria* which locate the absolute being of all things. For our understanding, we require material projections of them. And this is the function that art serves. As Ficino comments by way of continuing his digest of Platonic doctrine, "Men never remember the divine unless they are stirred by its shadows or images, as they may be described, which are perceived by the bodily senses." So a work of art is a shadow (umbra) or an image (imago) of some immortal idea, which is thereby rendered sense-perceptible, and consequently knowable to us. An artifact is a metaphor in the literal sense of that term,[19] translating an immaterial concept into an actuality for cognition by the human community. To meet these conditions, an art work must be an imitation of an idea, conceived in the mind of the artificer, adumbrating the mind of the deity. In 1568 when Vasari wrote about design (disegno), which he called "the parent of our three arts, Architecture, Sculpture, and Painting," he described it as the mediating factor between the artificer's inner and outer worlds: "Design," he said, "is not other than a visible expression and declaration of our inner conception."[20]

But implicit in Ficinian aesthetics is an allowance for the validity of physical nature. Because the godhead had created our universe, it reflects the perfection of cosmic order. In the words of Thomas Campion, "Lovely formes do flowe / From concent devinely framed."[21] These lovely forms which emerge into our consciousness are palpable manifestations of "heavenly beauty" and "heavenly love," to use Spenser's terms. In consequence, our visible universe, being a metaphor for God's idea of cosmos, is perhaps the fittest object for imitation. To cite an Augustinian cliché, nature is God's art. In its multitudinous variety and down to its minutest particle, nature bears the imprint of divinity. Hence the artist's awed attention to the details of nature that the eye perceives. The mathematics of linear perspective, a reworking in visual terms of the nonvisual notion of harmony, was formulated to demonstrate that despite the welter of apparently haphazard events there is a mathematical underpinning which preserves the merciful scheme of providential order.[22] So already by the mid-fifteenth century in Ficino's Italy there had begun to emerge an ambiguous interpretation of mimesis: while art must be truthful to the ideal order prescribed by the deity, it may shamelessly imitate the world that lies open to our senses.

Gradually, this concession evolved into an imperative: art *must* imitate physical nature. As the location of ultimate reality shifted from the Christianized version of Plato's realm of essences to the empiricist's world of observable nature, a work of art became a representation of what exists in fact, rather than a presentation of what is *supposed* to be in ideal principle. By the mid-sixteenth century, Aristotle's *Poetics* had been resurrected and freshly interpreted to support this doctrine: ποιητική, the act of making, consists in representing the actions of men in naturalistic surroundings. And the new scientific method of empirical observation instructed the artificer in the ways to observe and present the objects he wished to imitate. A work of art became a congeries of data exactly described rather than an embodiment of concepts. Eventually, in its origin an artifact derived from the items of observed nature rather than from the ideal world of being. Genre painting and topographical poetry were two of the inevitable results, although the relocation of reality affected the postulates of all mimetic art.

By the time of Sidney and Spenser, the relocation of reality was well under way; they lived, in fact, when the conflict was at crisis. According to orthodoxy, absolute truth resided with a Platonizing deity in a Christian heaven; but increasingly in practice, thinking men reached their conclusions on the basis of data obtained from sense experience. In a Platonic system, an item of physical nature is conjoined to its originating essence in the same way that an image depends upon its original object. The world of physical nature is a replication of the idea of cosmos in the divine mind. But in the brave new world of the empiricists, matter exists in its own right, divorced from anterior concepts and independent of all but material causes.

In consequence, by the late sixteenth century a disjunction had developed between the sense-perceived particular and the Platonic essence, and this disjunction led to a difficult choice for the artificer that in fact proved to be a dilemma: which of the two—transitory but actual *particular* or permanent but speculative *essence*—is the proper object of imitation in art? Various rapprochements were attempted, such as the use of "types" on the one hand, and of "abstractions" on the other (pages 36–38). As we might have predicted, however, imitation of things replaced the imitation of ideas as empiricism took over from idealism on all fronts, philosophical and theological as well as artistic. As a final concession, uneasy theorists devised some notion of *la belle nature,* a refinement of reality that could serve as object of imitation.[23] But it was nature still, though nature idealized. And the pretense of idealizing nature soon gave way to unbridled realism. In historical capsule, this is the evolution of art as imitation during the period that is relevant to Sidney and Spenser.

The central problem of the Renaissance aesthete, therefore, was how to abide by the strictures warning against the seductiveness of art without foregoing the new attention to sensuous detail that made it so exciting. Resourcefully, he argued that art could be allowed to imitate physical nature if it was conceived as harmonious, divinely ordered according to mathematical principles. Such a view quantified nature and rendered it submissive to descriptive analysis. Furthermore, recalling Plato's advocacy of music and the related mathematical arts in the *Republic,* theorists managed to condone the delights deriving from art by assigning it an educative function. The harmony and proportion evident in art teach us about celestial beauty and love, even about God's attributes. The end (instruction) justifies the means (sensuousness). The sensuous means, in fact, are necessary to art, because of humanity's—especially fallen humanity's—limitations. How else is a mere mortal, confined to sense perception for information (said the empiricists), to understand the otherwise ineffable truths that art purports to teach? Art is the best teacher, in fact, because—

and here Horace comes in handy—it both pleases and instructs. But at least in the earlier stages of the Renaissance, the aim of explaining the beauties and mysteries of the providential design was more important than the sensually gratifying expression of it, so art could be patronized by those in power, whether Christian or humanist, or (more usually) both.

We have already noted the semantic difficulties that inhere in the word "art" and the cultural bias that it inevitably conceals (page 20). In Sidney's day, practicing an "art" demanded an acquired skill to a greater extent than imagination or creativity. Moreover, "the fine arts" were not defined as a class or in our terms until late in the eighteenth century—until after the triumph of empiricism. It is therefore anachronistic to talk of "the fine arts" in the Renaissance. No such class had been identified, and there was no possibility of hypothesizing such a category until the ontological *situs* of an artifact was placed in the sense impressions by which it is perceived—that is, until the triumph of empiricism. Only then could the beauty of works of art be located wholly in their observed phenomena. Until then the beauty, and therefore the ultimate meaning of the work of art, was located in the Platonic essence of Beauty or in the Christian absolute of Deity, of which the artifact was a shadow or a reflection, or perhaps an image. Despite the forward strides made by Alberti,[24] during the Renaissance the time was not yet ripe for a concept such as "aesthetics," the study of beauty in art per se, embracing all of what we call the arts. Before the eighteenth century each of them had undergone independent development and served disparate purposes. As a consequence, each had its private history. When we talk about the relation of poetry to the other arts in the 1580s, therefore, it is necessary to consider the status of each art at that time.[25]

Without question, the most reputable of the arts was music.[26] For Sidney, it was "the most divine striker of the senses" (*Defence*, 100.34–35). The reasons for this preeminence of music, however, may be difficult for us to appreciate. At the end of the Middle Ages it held a secure place in the quadrivium—an honor that none of our other "fine" arts could claim; and its prominence in the curriculum could be traced back through Boethius and Augustine and Quintilian to the Greeks themselves.[27] This authoritativeness continued into the sixteenth century. Castiglione's Count recalled "that Plato and Aristotle will have a man that is well brought up, to be also a musitien" (89; cf. 118–20); and a hundred years later Henry Peacham was still giving the same advice.[28] In Elizabethan England every gentleman was expected to have some knowledge of music and even to play an instrument, the lute or at least a recorder (young ladies, of course, performed on the virginal). Among the arts, proficiency in music was the mark of gentility. While composing lyrics was permitted a gentleman, no courtier or lady made a habit of publicly painting pictures. The pictorial arts, including drama, required apology in the Renaissance, but music carried its own approval. It was music, in fact, that lent its terminology to the most cherished beliefs of the time: the angels appeared as a heavenly choir, and nature aspired to universal harmony.[29]

The basis for this high esteem lay in a musical tradition that not only stretched back to antiquity, but also offered a clear exposition of its tenets.[30] Through the quadrivium, the Renaissance had inherited a fully articulated theory of music. Arithmetic was the quadrivial science of numbers as aggregates of units; geometry was the science of numbers as indivisible quantities; astronomy was the science of these quantities in motion. Music, however, was distinguished as the science of the relationship between numbers, what is called "proportion." Indeed, the notes of the musical scale are determined by strict ratios worked out between the first four integers: 1, 2, 3, 4.[31] Moreover, since the fourteenth century, mathematical proportion had been displayed not only in the harmonies, but also in the rhythms of music, in the relation of whole notes to half notes, quarter notes, and so forth.[32] According to the formulation of Boethius, who had institutionalized this subject matter in the quadrivium, instrumental music (including song) must be an echo of the *musica mundana,* the universal harmony that allowed the creation of the universe and maintains its orderliness. Furthermore, the *musica mundana* is echoed in the *musica humana,* the harmony that pervades the well-ordered human microcosm.[33]

In the long-standing tradition of Boethius, then, a musical artifact repeats the *musica mundana,* no matter how faintly; and its ultimate object of imitation, no matter how recessive, is the idea of cosmos. The purpose of the musician is to make his listener aware of the music of the spheres, which except through art is otherwise inaudible to mortal ears. Because the soul of the listener is informed by the same harmonies as the heavens, instrumental music activates the latent music of the soul, so the human microcosm intuitively reverberates in sympathy with the celestial song.[34] In the words of Ficino, "By the ears . . . the soul receives the echoes of that incomparable music, by which it is led back to the deep and silent memory of the harmony which it previously enjoyed."[35] Ficino extends this mimetic theory to the other arts as well: "It is this music that orators, poets, painters, sculptors and architects seek to imitate in their work."[36] In such an aesthetic, there is no question about the mode of existence of the artifact or about its theme; these are determined a priori by the concept of cosmos. The musical composition is a reiteration of—the audible equivalent for a shadow or reflection of—the cosmic scheme, and it leads the auditor to contemplation of that immaterial absolute. This is the tradition of *musica speculativa,* of course, and may have little to do with *musica practica,* and even less with popular music. Nevertheless, to the educated and uneducated alike, this doctrine would have been acknowledged as the reason for music's privileged position among both the arts and the sciences.

The ancient reverence for music was still strongly felt in Elizabethan London. In 1570 Henry Billingsley published his translation of Euclid in a monumental volume, for which John Dee wrote a celebrated preface. At the time, Dee was the most respected mathematical practitioner in England, an authority consulted by the most powerful and knowledgeable in the realm, and in his preface he surveys the thirty-odd mathematical sciences, which he meticulously individualizes. Writing about music in the orthodox tradition, he reminds us, "*Astronomie* and *Musike* are Sisters, saith *Plato*" (b2ᵛ).[37] Most important, though, he indicates the benefits of listening to music:

> From audible sound, we ought to ascende to the examination: which numbers are *Harmonious,* and which not. And why, either, the one are: or the other not. I could at large, in the heavenly motions and distances, describe a mervailous Harmonie, of *Pythagoras* Harpe with eight stringes.

Dee here alludes to a time-honored practice of assigning a musical note to each of the planets as well as placing each planet under the tutelage of a Muse. Discovery of this heavenly concert was ascribed to Pythagoras, and the resultant octave of musical notes was emblematized as his eight-stringed lyre. It had long been a seminal topos in both music and astronomy, since it described the music of the spheres in the most precise detail.[38] Like the symphony of the Muses, it served as a synecdoche for universal harmony, for that all-embracing network of mathematical relationships that informs the cosmos. Listening to music puts us in touch with those formal patterns and imbues us with love for that divinity which shapes our ends.

Such sentiment was often directed to a specifically Christian purpose. Pierre de la Primaudaye, for example, informs us "that this science is given of God to men . . . to the end that by the sounds & songs which they heare, they might be stirred up to praise God the giver of them."[39] Well into the next century, music was exalted as the mathematical science that echoes the infinite variety of God's creation and produces a sympathetic response in the listener's soul. In the words of Henry Peacham, "Infinite is the sweete varietie that the theorique of Musicke exerciseth the mind withall, as the contemplation of proportions, of Concords and Discords, diversitie of Moodes and Tones, infinitenesse of Invention, &c."[40]

Today, in the backwash of Romanticism, we are likely to see music in a different way and cannot easily assess its purpose or importance in the Renaissance. The contemporary musical theorist cannot be so precise about the object of music's imitation—if he thinks of music as imitation at all. Of course, music can reproduce audible phenomena in the physical world, such as a birdcall or cannon shot or the clippety-clop of donkey hooves in the Grand Canyon; and already by the fourteenth century Guillaume de Machaut was introducing such effects into his songs. A later Frenchman, Clement Jannequin (fl. 1529–60), made a career of composing concerts of birds and street vendors and battling armies. This is the musical equivalent of onomatôpoeia, however, never successfully used alone in music any more than in poetry. So what does modern music refer to? It is, in fact, difficult to say. If we reply that music is the projection of an emotion or a mood, drawing upon our Romantic sensibility, we are verging toward an expressionistic theory and excluding music from membership among the mimetic arts. By this description, music becomes a means of expressing what is otherwise subliminal and for evoking what cannot otherwise be easily reached.[41] Music is not an imitation of anything that can be readily identified.[42]

To turn far back in time, music in the culture of classical Greece was analyzed in terms of eight modes (or scales), and each of these was thought to represent a particular ethos as a natural attribute.[43] For example, the Phrygian mode was warlike; the Lydian mode, voluptuous; the Dorian mode, dignified. This theory is expressive in a certain sense because each mode was held to generate its correspondent emotion in the listener. During the Renaissance, some of the more thoughtful humanists made explicit efforts to reform contemporary music by striving to produce these so-called "effects" of music.[44] But these "effects" are cosmic moods, not idiosyncratic feelings; and the auditor's response is not uniquely personal, but microcosmic. Each of these modes evoked its particular ethos in the auditor's psyche because the musical artifact was thought to embody the absolute essence of martialness or amorousness or temperateness. Instrumental music reproduced in sensible form the otherwise futile potency of these mere concepts, so that they were rendered efficacious. To indicate how Malacasta induces the pervasive sensuality of Castle Joyous, for example, Spenser notes that "all the while sweet Musicke did divide / Her looser notes with *Lydian* harmony" (3.1.40.1–2).

In similar manner, so went an oft-repeated tale, the musician Timotheus had aroused Alexander the Great from indolent feasting to preparations for battle; and then, seeing the warrior inflamed with valor, Timotheus changed to a different mode and mollified him into placidity—all to show the power of music.[45] In a corresponding tale from biblical literature, David restored harmony to the jangled mind of Saul.[46] The doctor hired by Cordelia likewise ministers to the mad Lear with the same sort of musical therapy. The gist of these stories is that by means of music some inchoate and bodiless value is rendered operative in human affairs. But that value is not undefined. It is harmony, that universal harmony, which closes full in man. The *musica humana* is occasioned by the palpable rendition of *musica mundana*.

Architecture, unlike music, was not a theoretical discipline with its own place in the approved curriculum. Rather, it was an applied science, a mechanical rather than speculative art[47]—an "art" in the original sense of the word. It was highly regarded, however, because of its long service to the Church and because of its usefulness to those who hankered after earthly grandeur and fame. Moreover, like music, architecture can realize in sense-perceptible form the potencies of numerical proportion; indeed, since the twelfth century, architecture and music had been sister arts because of their shared ability of making palpable the formality of God's creation.[48] Therefore, in the phrasing of John Dee, architecture belongs "among those *Artes Mathematicall,* which . . . may deale with Naturall thinges, and sensible matter" (d3).

Early in the Renaissance, as Dee goes on to indicate, the manual of Vitruvius with its emphasis upon proportion had been installed as the unquestioned authority for architecture, instituting a neoclassicism that prevailed for centuries. According to Vitruvius, beauty depends upon symmetry, the harmonious arrangement of parts within a total design. Furthermore, the proportions that insure beauty have their prototype in the human body, the microcosm—as the neoplatonists saw it, God's masterwork.[49] The parts of a building, then, both in its floor plan and on its facade, should cohere in a beauteous whole just as the members of our body fit together in that image of God that Genesis proclaims man to be.[50] It took the authority of Vitruvius, however, with his praise for mathematical proportion, to elevate the architect above the rank of craftsman, and to endow secular architecture with seriousness and high purpose.

The architect, even if we may not often think of him in this way, proceeds by realizing a design that in origin is immaterial, though not nonexistent. From a plan in his mind he produces an extended construct.[51] Like the musician, as Alberti carefully explains, the architect puts into the material form of an artifact the beauty which is latent in mathematical proportion. The architect, in fact, with his plan or *ratio* was seen to be the archetypal creator. In the words of Ficino, "As the design of a whole building and of its parts exists in the mind of an architect, so the design of this whole world and of its parts exists in the divine intelligence."[52] The mortal architect, working in palpable materials, follows the creative habits of the heavenly *opifex*. And what this typus of the architect employs as the object of his imitation can be readily designated: the scheme of cosmos. Into the spatial and temporal coordinates of our world he projects the potencies of the cosmic design which resides eternally in the mind of deity,[53] although it may not be eternally realized in fact.

For that reason, both practicing architect and musician alike fashioned their artifacts according to the mathematical ratios which most easily express the perfect proportions and harmonies inherent in that concept of cosmos. About 1450, Alberti wrote: "The same Numbers, by means of which the Agreement of Sounds affects our Ears with Delight, are the very same which please our Eyes and our Mind. We shall therefore borrow all our Rules for the finishing our Porportions, from the Musicians, who are the greatest Masters of this Sort of Numbers."[54] In 1624 Sir Henry Wotton was still looking back to Alberti and recalling his instruction about "reducing *Symmetrie* to *Symphonie,* and the *harmonie* of *Sounde,* to a kinde of *harmonie* in *Sight.*"[55] As strange as it might seem to us, architects painstakingly constructed their buildings to echo the ratios implied in the musical scale.[56] As Alberti carefully explains, a room that is twice as long as it is wide, for example, embodies the proportion 2/1, the octave; while a room that is half again as wide as it is high embodies the proportion 3/2, the diapente or fifth. So at least for the beginning of our era, historically speaking, we can say that the object of imitation in both music and architecture was the concept of cosmos in the mind of God. Immaterial though it is, this idea can be rendered palpable by the application of proportion and harmony to physical matter—that is, by the actualization of mathematical ratios in something which is sense perceptible, like a musical composition or a building.

In contrast to music and architecture, the depictive arts were shown little respect by the conservative theorist.[57] They had very limited status in the educational program—indeed, Plato had warned against them, and the Church was openly suspicious of their appeal to the senses. In the *De remediis utriusque Fortunae* when Petrarch's Joy confesses, "I am delighted with pictures, and painted tables," his Reason warns, "The pleasure and admiration thereof, is able privily to remoove and withdrawe the minde from contemplation of higher matters."[58] At best, painting and sculpture were decorative arts (in the pejorative sense), firmly subordinated to architecture in its service to religion.[59] When the visual arts were able to serve an educative mission—retelling a biblical tale or recalling a saint—they were condescendingly permitted. But not until the late Renaissance were painting and sculpture freed from the church wall and altarpiece, and allowed to develop independently. Easel-painting had begun only in the fifteenth century; until then, pictures did not have frames. The frame, in fact, represents the window through which we look at the natural scene outside purportedly depicted by the painting. This development necessarily awaited the formulation of fixed-point perspective by Brunelleschi and Alberti.[60]

What training in the depictive arts a scholar might receive was strictly conditioned by their usefulness. In the traditional curriculum the art of drawing, γραφική, was assigned a minor role as a sort of mnemonic aid. A sketch may serve as the reminder of a particular place or event. Aristotle had listed drawing (along with writing, gymnastics, and music) among the four customary disciplines in education (*Politics,* 1337b22–27), and on his authority Castiglione approves of painting for the courtier, even though, as Castiglione snidely observes, "Now a dayes perhappes [it] is counted an handycraft and ful litle to become a gentleman" (91). Nonetheless, γραφική has its uses, "and especiallye in warre to drawe oute countreys, plattefourmes, ryvers, brydges, castelles, houldes, fortresses, and suche other matters, the which thoughe a manne were hable to kepe in mynde (and that is a harde matter to doe) yet can he not shewe them to others" (92). The practical advantage of an ability to draw had been apparent to those who trained young men in the chivalric arts, and Chaucer's Squire possesses the skill to "portraye," as well as joust and dance and compose poetry, no doubt as part of his preparation for military service.[61] Sir Thomas Elyot, with limited enthusiasm, acknowledges the usefulness of the graphic and plastic arts, and in *The Governour* includes a chapter which concedes "that it is commendable in a gentilman to paint and kerve exactly, if nature therto doth induce hym."[62] Elyot cites several examples of notable persons who did indeed paint or sculpt—all of whom, incidentally, were Roman emperors of a less-than-exemplary reputation. For Richard Mulcaster, Spenser's headmaster at the Merchant Taylors' school, γραφική is admitted into the curriculum on Aristotle's authority, although Mulcaster himself puts little stock in "the setting of colours."[63]

Spenser had little opportunity to see avant-garde painting, and Sidney, for all his enlightenment and his interest in Renaissance painters, didn't think of painting as the vivid, sensuous art that we associate with the Italy of his time. He seems, in fact, rather conservative in his views, and in one passage of *The defence of poesie* narrowly circumscribes what painting can be reasonably set to achieve. "The painter," Sidney asserts, "should give to the eye either some excellent perspective, or some fine picture, fit for building or fortification, or containing in it some notable example (as Abraham sacrificing his son Isaac, Judith killing Holofernes, David fighting with Goliath)" (104.18–22). Like most men of his day, Sidney thought of painting as the utilitarian art of γραφική or as the visualization of a moral lesson drawn from the Bible.[64]

But once the possibility that art might imitate physical nature was allowed, the depictive arts came into their own.[65] Early apologists such as Alberti had argued for the respectability of painting, and soon many masters of the brush were eagerly acclaimed for their achievements—usually, for their success at verisimilitude. Vasari epitomizes the accomplishment of Masaccio, for example, in a summary statement of praise: "It was he who, eager for the acquirement of fame, first attained the clear perception that painting is no other than the close imitation, by drawing and colouring simply, of all the forms presented by nature, exhibiting them as they are produced by her."[66] Paintings and statues are visibilia, like the things they portray; so Giovanni Paolo Lomazzo, author of the most extensive sixteenth-century manual on painting, sculpture, and architecture, calls attention to "that admirable workemanshippe, whereby the immoveable and senselesse picture seemeth as it were to moove, daunce, runne, call, strike with the hande, and moove his whole body forwards, backwards, on the right hand, and on the left."[67] Lomazzo also marvels that though limited to a two-dimensional surface, the painter creates perfectly the illusion of space: "The Painter by helpe of his colours representeth uppon a plaine the thicknesse and *eminencies* of any bodie, the flesh, hayre, apparrell, and the light it selfe, whereby all these things are seene: And that which is more strange, how on a flatte surface hee can expresse three or fowre men one behinde another, yea a whole army." Lomazzo epitomizes the Renaissance painter's pride in verisimilar representation.

The plastic media of painting and of sculpture—and of bas-relief, that intermediate art so popular in the Renaissance—give these arts an advantage in the depiction of physical nature, and this advantage accounts for their rapid rise as imitation came to mean the reproduction of what the eye sees. Although some of the most admired painters, such as Leonardo and Raphael, carefully borrowed the principles of harmony and symmetry for their com-positions,[68] and although Lomazzo later in the century still used the musical intervals to prescribe the proper proportions of the human figure,[69] painting and sculpture in this period evolved from an impetus other than the mathematical. Their roots did not lie in Boethius's quadrivium. There was no *pictura speculativa,* only *graphice practica.*

Success in practice, however, bestowed an unwonted approval upon the pictorial arts, and before long they openly challenged the others for dominance. The *paragone,* a comparison between the several arts, became a common topos in the writing about art. In his famous example of this genre, Leonardo argues strongly that painting is superior to poetry, largely because of its advantage in verisimilar depiction.[70] As Leonardo says, "Though poetry is able to describe forms, actions, and places in words, the painter employs the exact images of the forms and represents them as they are" (55). A painter reproduces his object of imitation in a homologous fashion. Painting takes the prize even from sculpture because the use of color allows it to reproduce most exactly what the eye perceives (78, 104–5).

In the Renaissance it would have been meaningless even to speak of the dance as an art, except perhaps as it actualized the rhythms of music. Dancing boasted no theory of its own divorced from music, and consequently could claim no artistic status.[71] Plato had identified dancing with γυμναστική, the exercise of the body which on a lower level corresponds to music, the exercise of the psyche; and through the use of rhythm in gymnastics, the af-finity between dance and music was emphasized, to the enhance-ment of the former.[72] Aristotle also had approved gymnastics as one of the four customary studies, along with the language arts, music, and drawing (*Politics* 1337b22–28). Mulcaster, wary apologist for his curriculum at the Merchant Taylors' school, defended dancing and claimed for it an educative purpose:

> Howsoever *daunsing* be or be thought to be, seing it is held for an exercise, we must thinke there is some great good in it, though we protecte not the ill, if any come by it. Which good we must seeke to get, and praie those maisters, which fashion it with *order* in time, with *reason* in gesture, with *proportion* in number, with *harmonie* in *Musick,* to appoint it so, as it may be thought both seemely and sober.[73]

But by and large this healthful effect of dancing was forgotten. In the sixteenth century, dancing was little more than recreation for the poor on holidays and at most a social grace for the aristocracy, and inevitably it caught the baleful eye of the prude.[74] When Petrarch's Joy announces, "I delyght in dauncing," his more sober Reason chides, "By singyng there is some sweetenesse conceyved, which many tymes is profitable, and holy: by dauncing never any thyng but lasciviousnesse".[75]

From the same instincts that produced the maypole and morris dancing, however, there arose some notion of nature as a series of rhythmic movements. The planets turn in their predictable courses, the seasons follow one another in a well-modulated cycle, and even the four elements, despite their continual transformation one into another, maintain an equipoise as they change places in perpetual round. These regulated motions of *natura naturans* were seen as dance on a cosmic scale.[76] During the sixteenth century in France a sophisticated coterie devised the ballet as a means of figuring forth the universal order,[77] and at the end of *A Midsummer Night's Dream* the fairies dance in a ring to suggest the social concord which resolves that play. Because of its alliance with music, dance had this metaphoric capacity as an image of the cosmic design. With the opening of Ovid's *Metamorphoses* also in mind, Sir John Davies exploited this potential in his playful/profound philosophical poem *Orchestra,*[78] where Antinous woos the reluctant Penelope by enticing her to dance and thereby to participate in that ordered creation presided over by Love:

> *Dauncing* (bright lady) then began to be,
> When the first seedes whereof the world did spring,
> The Fire, Ayre, Earth and Water did agree,
> By Loves perswasion, Natures mighty King,
> To leave their first disordred combating;
>> And in a daunce such measure to observe,
>> As all the world their motion should preserve.
>>> (17.1–7)

But even for Davies, "Sweet *Musick*. . . [is] Dauncings only life" (46.1). Therein, and nowhere else, lay the aesthetic value of dance. It was sometimes pantomimic, at least in part, and less often expressive; but except as γυμναστική, it was rarely a serious pursuit.

The status of poetry near the end of the sixteenth century is much more difficult to assess. The factors influencing its reputation were more numerous and diverse than is true for any of the other arts. While particular poems and particular poets were greatly admired, and although certain genres such as epic and tragedy were beyond reproach, there was ardent disagreement over what sort of activity poetry might be.[79] George Puttenham, for instance, offers four quite distinct possibilities:

> It is therefore of Poets thus to be conceived, that if they be able to devise and make all these things of them selves, without any subject of veritie, that they be (by maner of speech) as creating gods. If they do it by instinct divine or naturall, then surely much favoured from above. If by their experience, then no doubt very wise men. If by an president or paterne layd before them, then truly the most excellent imitators & counterfaitors of all others.[80]

According to Puttenham, a poet may invent ex nihilo like a creating deity, or may compose under the influence of divine inspiration, or may write out of personal experience, or may follow classical models. Each of these possibilities presumes a different poetics.

Sidney in his tersest definition of poetry opts for yet a fifth possibility, a new poetics in England. "Poesy," he says, "is an art of imitation, for so Aristotle termeth it in the word μίμησις" (*Defence*, 79.35–36). But even if it were agreed that poetry results from mimesis, what might be the proper object of that imitation and how might poetry go about its business of imitating? Furthermore, there were pointed questions verging into ethics about its teleology: what is the purpose of poetry and what is its effect upon the young? Plato, the most revered of philosophers, had actually denied most poets a place in his commonwealth, and Italian critics were locked in debate over whether the moralistic Dante shouldn't give way to the more pleasurable Petrarch. Finally, incipient in these practical questions were the aesthetic questions: what constitutes beauty in poetry and how can one evaluate it? The wide range of responses to these problems accurately reflects the proliferation of worldviews that marks the Renaissance as an age of transition in our cultural history. The idealists differed from the materialists; those who still believed in a finite cosmos from those who claimed heretically that the universe is unbounded. Not even the powerful force of philosophical syncretism could identify a central tradition, despite its aspiration to synthesize; and by the time of Donne, as we know, all coherence was gone. Especially poetry, it seems, suffered from this divisiveness of opinion. As George Gascoigne commented in 1575, "*Quot homines, tot Sententiae,* especially in Poetrie."[81]

A great deal of the confusion about poetry arose from the fact that it had not held a clearly defined place in the medieval curriculum. To our surprise and disappointment, poetry (like painting and sculpture) was not one of the seven liberal arts. To be sure, some poetry was taught in the schools. Since the prime of Athens, the epic at least was used as a textbook, especially for moral instruction; and Ovid and several later poets were also regularly read, even if metamorphosed by heavy-handed allegorization. But poetry was not recognized as a fully legitimate discipline. In the trivium, the grammarians drew a distinction between prose and verse, and therefore usually offered information about the length of syllables and the rudimentary rules of poetic meter;[82] and the rhetoricians dealt with language as *oratio,* or discourse, which tacitly included poetry,[83] and also they offered a description of the numerous figures of speech. So certain aspects of poetry might be briefly accommodated under grammar or rhetoric, and even on occasion under logic.[84] But poetry was a waif without a home. It was graciously tolerated only while providing illustrative examples to substantiate those established disciplines which had been authoritatively codified. In the most respected encyclopedias of the time—such as Oronce Finé's edition of Gregor Reisch's *Margarita philosophica* (1535), Pierre de la Primaudaye's *L'Académie françoise* (1577), or Stephen Batman's revision of Bartholomaeus' *De proprietatibus rerum* (1582)—poetry per se received no mention at all. The reason for this neglect is unmistakable: unlike the members of the trivium and quadrivium, poetry could boast no rigorous theory.

So the position of poetry in the scheme of learning was uncertain. Eminent grammarians, logicians, and rhetoricians lingered from earlier ages, but no undisputed authorities for poetry. By banishing poets from his *Republic,* Plato had disqualified himself as an acceptable spokesman on poetical matters, and Aristotle's *Poetics* was virtually unknown until the Renaissance had fairly well run its course. Eventually, when Aristotle *was* introduced as an aggressive contender in the second half of the sixteenth century, he was interpreted in a biased way as a refutation of Plato and a moralizer of poetry.[85] Because Aristotle was best known in the schools for his *Ethics, Organon,* and *Rhetoric,* the recovery of his *Poetics* tended to identify poetry with the other arts of discourse taught to schoolboys. Horace was also a school text; his *Ars poetica* had been known and respected throughout the Middle Ages and was praised with renewed ardor by the humanists. But the decorous precepts of Horace are so bland that his poetical advice had been easily assimilated into the rhetorical tradition and meddled with that of Aristotle. And if none of the classical authorities carried full weight, needless to say no theorist of the Middle Ages was acceptable to Renaissance poets. So in 1580 there was no poetic theory that represented received opinion, among either poets themselves or theorists, and there was not much likelihood of reaching consensus. As a result, critics were busily engaged in polemics and in proselytizing, and a surprisingly large number of literary treatises were published. Sidney's *Defence of poesie* is a member, albeit one of the more thoughtful and noteworthy members, of this milling throng.

Nonetheless, the charms of poetry, as well as its usefulness as a socializing agent, were acknowledged by most. The humanists, if anything, exaggerated its value. Coluccio Salutati, for example, one of the most influential social engineers of the early Renaissance, had proclaimed: "Poetry preempts the entire trivium and quadrivium, all of philosophy and knowledge, both human and divine, and all of the learned disciplines."[86] A century later the Venetian humanist, Giorgio Valla, innovatively for his time, accorded *poetica* equal status with grammar, rhetoric, and logic (S5), and he devoted a separate book of his esoteric encyclopedia to this subject (EE6ᵛ–HH3).[87] What we are witnessing here, of course, is a breakdown of the medieval organization of knowledge in the trivium and quadrivium, and the humanists' preference for the *litterae humaniores*. So, although poetry could claim no fixed place in the curriculum, it came to enjoy a considerable degree of respectability.

The respect accorded poetry derived in large part from its affinities to music.[88] As Puttenham observed, "Poesie is a skill to speake & write harmonically: and verses or rime be a kind of Musicall utterance, by reason of a certaine congruitie in sounds pleasing the eare" (64). Dicus in the old *Arcadia* agreed: "Since verses had their chief ornament, if not end, in music, those which were just appropriated to music did best obtain their end" (89.12–13). Put simply, the meters of poetry echoed the measures of music, and the lyric or song, the conflation of these sister arts, was firmly ensconced as the delight of the cultivated.

In the most revered classical tradition, as humanists knew, music and poetry were closer than mere sisters. They were more like Siamese twins. Their proximity, in fact, is epitomized in the word "music" itself. Etymologically, "music" comes from the Greek μουσική, which Liddell and Scott define as "any art over which the Muses presided, esp. poetry sung to music." Μουσική, then, was a composite art, embracing whatever the Muses taught in their ninefold diversity as handmaidens to Apollo. It had a verbal component as well as a melodic line, and more nearly approached the modern notion of "poetry," perhaps, than that of "music." Indeed, Plato with unusual curtness had pronounced: "When there are no words, it is very difficult to recognize the meaning of harmony or rhythm, or to see that any worthy object is imitated by them" (*Laws* 669E). Plato regularly used μουσική in this sense of a verbal art with harmony and rhythm,[89] and Plutarch followed his example.[90] Spenser adheres to this tradition: "Musicke," he says, "is wise words with time concented."[91] It was Homer, preceded only by the legendary Orpheus and Amphion, and perhaps contemporary with the psalmist David, who served as the prototypical poet/musician.

This conception of μουσική as a conflation of music and poetry with emphasis on its formal properties—that is, "speculative" as opposed to "practical" music—persisted throughout the Middle Ages. It explains why poetry was not itself one of the seven disciplines specified as the "liberal arts"; poetry, at least in this guise, was subsumed under music and required no separate treatment. The nearly total identification of the two, as well as the medieval obsession with formality, is forcefully exemplified by Augustine's tract, *De musica*. In this treatise, the first five of the existing six books are quite appropriately given over to a discussion of poetic meter, and the last is introduced by an epigraph which stresses the importance that number as form holds for the psyche: "The mind is raised from the consideration of changeable numbers in inferior things to unchangeable numbers in unchangeable truth itself."[92]

In the centuries that intervened between Augustine and Sidney, especially after the thirteenth century, music and poetry pulled apart and tended to go their separate ways. The descriptive and narrative powers of poetry were developed at the expense of its capacity to express conceptual patterns. By the end of the Middle Ages, the romance vied with the lyric as the dominant literary genre. Nonetheless, throughout this period the concept of μουσική remained a viable aesthetic principle and enjoyed renewed vitality in trecento Italy. Dante's *Divina commedia* with its semantics of numerical structure is a product of it. Even purer products of the formal requirements that μουσική imposed upon poets are the sonnet and the sestina, poetic forms which were invented in the earliest Renaissance and which we are only now beginning to read correctly as semiotic systems with their own nonverbal codes.[93]

With the turn of the sixteenth century, under the stimulus of humanism and its renewed interest in classical art, there were overt efforts to reinstate the ancient notion of μουσική.[94] As Thomas Elyot observed, reflecting the continuing influence of the rhetorical tradition and citing the authority of Quintilian (1.4.4), "Without musike gramer may nat be perfecte; for as moche as therin muste be spoken of metres and harmonies, called *rythmi* in greke" (1: 165). Under the tutelage of the grammarians, poetry had always displayed an affinity for music. They seconded the principle that the meters of poetry are equivalent to the measures of music. By 1507 in Germany, to exploit this affinity, Peter Treibenreif, protegé of the noted humanist Konrad Celtes, had published several settings of odes by Horace as an aid to students learning the meters of classical Latin.[95] In addition, as the century wore on, there was a growing concern among musicians that music reflect the expressive meanings of the text it set. This sentiment was epitomized by Gioseffo Zarlino in his *Istitutioni harmoniche* (Venice, 1558).[96] It culminated in the unique achievement of the late Italian madrigal, that perfect wedding of words and melody,[97] rightly seen as a typical genre of the Renaissance. And the movement went beyond the madrigal to eventuate in the opera.[98]

The most pointed attention to theory in this movement, however, came in France. Pierre de Ronsard was the earliest and most successful poet to publish musical accompaniment with his poems: his *Amours* (Paris, 1552) contains a supplement of ten settings, one of which will do for any of the 150 or so sonnets printed in the volume.[99] Other members of the Pléiade showed a similar concern for making poetry consonant with music, and Jean-Antoine de Baïf became the most ardent and disciplined advocate of the movement. Shortly before 1570 Baïf formally incorporated an Académie de Poésie et de Musique which by announced intention implemented the classical concept of μουσική. In addition to concerts restricted to members of the Académie (and therefore poorly documented), Baïf and his associates wrote vernacular poetry in quantitative rather than accentual meters,[100] what they called *vers mesurés*.

Soon thereafter across the Channel, the group that Spenser jocularly dubbed the Areopagus engaged in similar experiments.[101] It is clear that Sidney began by thinking of the poet as a metrician who weighs his syllables and composes with musical measure in mind. In one of his more memorable vignettes, he depicts the poet as coming forward "with words set in delightful proportion, either accompanied with, or prepared for, the well enchanting skill of music" (*Defence* 92.7–9). In Spenser's December eclogue, Colin Clout recalls that in his youth he was "somedele ybent to song and musicks mirth" (line 40), and E.K. supplies a gloss equating the two arts: "Music that is Poetry as Terence sayth Qui artem tractant musicam, speking of Poetes" (i.e., *Phormio,* prol. 17). Milton, the heir of Sidney and Spenser, wrapped himself in singing robes, and in a deeply personal poem apostrophized the "harmonious Sisters, Voice and Verse," imploring them, "Wed your divine sounds" ("At a Solemn Music," 2–3). As late as 1763, John Brown, a protégé of Warburton with a penchant for anthropological speculation, was still arguing for the union of poetry and music on the grounds of a natural consanguinity. By that time, of course, opera was a well-established genre with a tradition of its own.

Most of this speculation about the union of voice and verse took its cue from Platonic doctrine. When Plato planned for μουσική to be the staple of education in his ideal commonwealth, he was thinking of the discipline as this inextricable combination of what we call music and poetry.[102] But as Renaissance theorists were well aware, he was thinking of it more in terms of its formal properties than in terms of its subject matter or of its physiological or emotional effects upon the listener. Unlike the other arts, μουσική is defined by its origin with the Muses rather than by its medium, so its ontological *situs* lies in the realm of ideal essences.

The Muses themselves played in symphony under the direction of Apollo—evidently, a mythological version of universal harmony. According to Macrobius, "The Muses are the song of the universe,"[103] and this image was specified in such detail that each Muse was assigned a planetary sphere to regulate its note in the celestial concert. As Ficino reminds us, "The ancient theologians maintained that the nine Muses were the musical songs of the eight spheres, and in addition the one great harmony arising from all the others."[104] When the Muses inspired a poet, what they conveyed was knowledge of this divine music, this cosmic perfection—in the words of Milton, "that undisturbed Song of pure concent" ("At a Solemn Music," 6). They made available to the poet an awareness of this esoteric beauty beyond sense perception, beauty which is formal and conceptual rather than material, the beauty which Plato postulates in the *Phaedrus* as the terminus for the soul's struggle to soar aloft (246E–247E).

When the demiurge created our universe, this heavenly beauty served as the pattern, and its formal properties organized time and space into an extended system. In the succinct words of Thomas Campion, "The world is made by Simmetry and proportion, and is in that respect compared to Musick, and Musick to Poetry."[105] This is an application of the topos that nature is God's art.

Moreover, the mathematical forms of the heavenly beauty were imprinted as well upon the human soul. Cristoforo Landino states confidently: "While they were in the celestial realm, our souls were participators in that harmony which resides in the eternal mind of God and which brings about the heavens' motions."[106] Gregor Reisch identifies the authority for such a statement: "Plato affirmed that man's soul is composed of musical proportions."[107] In consequence, our souls can apprehend directly the harmonies and rhythms of μουσική. In the syncretic tradition conflating Plato, Aristotle, Plutarch and their numerous scholiasts, E.K. glossed line 27 of the October eclogue: "What the secrete working of Musick is in the myndes of men, aswell appeareth hereby, that some of the auncient Philosophers, and those the moste wise, as Plato and Pythagoras held for opinion, that the mynd was made of a certaine harmonie and musicall nombers, for the great compassion and likenes of affection in thone and in the other."[108]

Because μουσική exemplifies the harmonies and proportions that inform our world, Plato saw it as the best means of teaching about the universe and the place of mankind in it. Music manifests the intention of the godhead. Plato was furthermore interested in music because it embodies conceptual patterns which he thought essential to a healthy state of mind. Perhaps most concisely in the *Timaeus,* he had stated the importance of music for the human psyche:

> Music . . . was bestowed upon us for the sake of harmony. And harmony, which has motions akin to the revolutions of the soul within us, was given by the Muses to him who makes intelligent use of the Muses, not as an aid to irrational pleasure (as is now supposed), but as an auxiliary to the inner revolution of the soul. (47C)

The Muses, Plato insists, make music available to us not for the irrational pleasure of sensual gratification, which has nothing to do with reason, but rather for the rational purpose of ordering our psyches. Recalling Plato, Castiglione exactly summarizes the reasons for a humanist's attention to music:

> It hath bene the opinion of most wise Philosophers that the world is made of musick, and the heavens in their moving make a melody, and our soule framed after the very same sort, and therfore lifteth up it self and (as it were) reviveth the vertues and force of it with musick. (89)

By means of music, the soul is appropriately ordered so that microcosm and macrocosm are attuned. In the terminology of Boethius, *musica humana* accords with *musica mundana*. This doctrine has been cheerfully elaborated by a long line of Christian exegetes, from Macrobius and Augustine through the medieval encyclopedists down to Du Bartas and Spenser.[109]

Since the human psyche bears the imprint of these numerical patterns, it joyously recognizes and conforms to them whenever our senses perceive them in a work of art. Although the soul when incorporated into mortal flesh is hindered in its perception of the heavenly forms—and, the Calvinist would add, further hindered by Adam's lapse into sinfulness—we can still respond to the *musica mundana* rendered palpable in manmade music. According to Landino, "Even if these human harmonies are a far cry from the celestial harmony, nevertheless (because they are, as it were, likenesses and images of it), they lead us to a certain ineffable recollection of heavenly things and inflame us with the most ardent desire of flying back to our former fatherland so that we might truly know that very music of which this is an adumbration."[110]

The same effect is achieved by harmonious proportion in any work of art, including the metrics of a poem when rightly ordered. As Richard Willes, a contemporary of Sidney and Spenser, explains:

> Since poetry is speech drawn together, as it were, by a fixed law of measure—in which there is not only a bond of feet, but also a rhythm and harmony—it comes about that there is wonderful pleasure in the art. The ears of the audience are spellbound by this and their spirits softened, because of the affinity which music has with the human soul.[111]

Willes recognized that music and poetry exhibit formal properties not only in the proportions that determine the notes of the musical scale, but also in the metrical units comprised of long and short intervals of sound. The soul responds immediately to such neatly calculated symmetry, recapturing its perfection as an image of the divine idea.

This tradition that bolstered the psyche by recollection of the consonances that prevail in the macrocosm led to the love lyric of Elizabethan England, a refinement of the madrigal (actual musical notes are omitted, although μουσική is implied still in the metrics).[112] In Plato's *Symposium* (187C), Eryximachus offers a famous definition of music, which Thomas Morley translated as "a science of love matters occupied in harmonie and rythmos."[113] The interchangeability of love and music had been again proclaimed by Erasmus in one of his best known adages, *Musicam docet amor.*[114] Like his Petrarchist cousins, Shakespeare's Orsino knew that music is the food of love[115] because it (like love) leads to the presence of beauty, to that ecstasy where the soul literally stands outside the body and views the pure form of cosmic perfection. So play on! And the madrigalists did, to the delight of all those courtiers who sentimentally pursued the ideal of neoplatonic rapture. Colin Clout reported that it did exist—though only atop Mount Acidale; and even there a mortal, albeit a poet, can hope for no more than an evanescent glimpse. But like the nightingale, who sings most sweetly when pained most sharply by the thorn of her despair—"most musical, most melancholy!"[116]—the madrigalists played on and on, lacerating themselves with thoughts of lovelessness and mutability and mortality. With them, lyrics to be heard reached a high mark.

But a separation between poetry and music had already long before begun. The widespread use of printing transformed poetry into something other than a primarily aural event.[117] As poetry came to be more commonly read than heard, the verbal text assumed a definite appearance on the page. Lessons learned from the *Greek Anthology* suggested that lines of type could be arranged to produce shapes, and individual poems could be interconnected to produce extended figures such as coronas and architectural structures such as temples. A poem became a visible object, even tangible. In our own century, poets such as e. e. cummings and the concrete poets have energetically explored this capacity of poetry to provide visual experience.

A more subtle shift away from music resulted from a change in what poetry's proper object of imitation should be. Μουσική imitated the cosmos, with its mathematical relationships that inhere in conceptual forms; and the metrics of poetry, like the measures of music, express the proportions that order the macrocosm. As the sixteenth century wore on, however, the force of this neoplatonist imperative diminished. Despite the brief revival of quantitative verse by humanists in France and England, the Reformation abetted the search for a new, less ornate aesthetic. Thomas Wilson voices a not-infrequent bias against versification as a papist practice:

> I thynke the Popes heretofore (seeyng the peoples folie to be suche) made all our Hymnes & anthemes in rime, that with the singyng of men, plaiyng of organnes, ringyng of belles, & rimyng of Hymnes, & Sequencies the poore ignoraunt might thinke the Harmonie to be heavenly, & verely beleve that the Angels of God made not a better noise in heaven.[118]

For Sidney the separation between poetry and music had proceeded to the point where a poem no longer required meter—witness his *Arcadia*. According to Aristotle's *Poetics,* recently resurrected, poetry depended upon imitating the actions of men; and "fiction," as we have defined it in Elizabethan terms, became the essential ingredient of poetry. Aristotle specifically disallows verse as a necessary component for a poem; and Scaliger aside,[119] in the new poetics the poet at basis is a maker of fictions rather than a metrist. Mimesis of the visibilia of cosmos rather than mimesis of its form became the motivating concern of poetic theory, so poetry's ties with music through a shared emphasis on formal properties were loosened. Poetry became more descriptive and less ratiocinative. Concomitantly, freed from the requirement of imitating the numbers and measures of the cosmic scheme, poetry accepted a system of accentual versification rather than the antique metrics of quantitative verse.[120]

Music also diverged from the concept of μουσική. As early as the fourth century B.C., Aristoxenus had proposed a theory of music based not upon strict mathematical ratios like the Pythagorean tuning system, but rather accommodated to what pleases the ear. In this tradition, fully recognized in musical manuals, the art of music is dealt with as a wholly aural experience, a sense response in defiance of its intellectual implications.[121] Sidney was familiar with this long-standing division among musical theorists and carried it over to his consideration of poetic prosody. In his discussion of quantitative meter in the *Defence,* he finds something to commend in both the "ancient" and "modern" rules for versification. "The ancient," he says, is "more fit for music, both words and time observing quantity"; but the modern, he continues, "with his rhyme, striketh a certain music to the ear" (*Defence,* 119.35– 120.2).[122] In the age of empiricism that followed, it was the music with appeal "to the ear"—music as unmixed aural experience— that superseded the platonist notion of music as μουσική.

Actually, the separation of music from μουσική was completed in the seventeenth century. Music acquired a theory which directed interest to its medium of expression and the means of its being perceived. With Descartes, there came a diverting of attention from the cosmological to the subjectively psychological, so that the immediate effects of music on the auditor took precedence over its metaphysical import. Descartes opened his *Compendium musicae* with a chapter entitled, "The *Object* of this Art is a *Sound.*"[123] From the start, the empirical basis for the musical event is paramount. "The *End*" of music, Descartes continued, is "to delight and move various Affections in us." Once again, interest in music is concentrated upon its ability to move the passions, as in the Greek theory of musical modes (page 70). When the essence of the musical artifact shifted from its cosmic patterning to its emotive effect, however, the formal properties that previously had joined poetry and music were degraded, and each art began to develop artistically independent of the other. For the first time, in fact, music flourished as an autonomous event, freed from a verbal text or from some other activity (such as dancing or praying or marching) to give it the substance of meaning. Instrumental music finally came into its own, carried its own justification.[124]

In the eighteenth century, despite the sincere efforts of some retrospective theorists such as John Brown, poetry and music remained fairly well separated. Pope recognized that the aural arts

shared certain propensities to produce that beauty which gave rise
to the discipline of aesthetics in his time:

> *Musick* resembles *Poetry,* in each
> Are *nameless Graces* which no Methods teach,
> And which a *Master-Hand* alone can reach.
> (*Essay on Criticism* 143–45)

But music sang to the emotions, while poetry spoke to the intellect. So Pope was scathing towards the critics "who haunt *Parnas-
sus* but to please their Ear, / Not mend their Minds"; and he likened them to those who go to church "not for the *Doctrine,* but
the *Musick* there" (337–43). Pope chose to expatiate upon the
cosmic design (upon φύσις, Nature) in explicit argument rather
than in metrical patterns. Nonetheless, he supplemented his direct description of order by reflecting it more subtly in the forms
of his poems.[125]

Late in the century, a group of poets began ostentatiously to
present themselves as singers, and Rousseau found music and language to share a common primitive origin.[126] Under such stimulus,
poetry in the nineteenth century again moved toward amalgamation with music, as did also the other arts. As a tenet of Romanticism, it was argued that art should express feeling; and music, the
argument continued, freed from the material constraints imposed
by the media of the depictive arts, is the purest and most spontaneous expression of that sort.[127] Schopenhauer elevated this sentiment to a philosophical principle; music, he said, expresses the
universal Will itself, while the other arts imitate only the physical
manifestations of that Will.[128] So poetry should approach music in
order to effect its expressive aims. As a consequence, Verlaine and
his followers paid close attention to the "music" of their verse; and
from the other side, Liszt and his followers wrote "tone poems."
When reverie became the *summum bonum* of art, music was the
yardstick by which to measure artistic achievement. Even painting under the brush of Whistler became a series of "symphonies"
and "nocturnes." The elevation of music reached its high point in
the Aesthetic Movement: in the terse statement of Pater, "All art
constantly aspires towards the condition of music."[129] For Pater
and his disciples, therefore, the lyric was "the highest and most

complete form of poetry" because of its rapprochement with music; "the very perfection of such poetry often appears to depend, in part, on a certain suppression or vagueness of mere subject, so that the meaning reaches us through ways not distinctly traceable by the understanding."[130]

Crystallizing out of this aestheticism at the beginning of our century was some realization that music and poetry do indeed have affinities. Browning had fashioned several poems with music in mind,[131] while Mallarmé had publicized an ambition to compose symphonies with words.[132] These poets and others, however, emphasized the aural similarities between music and poetry rather than their shared formal properties. Sidney Lanier had announced the principle with utmost succinctness: music and verse, he said, are "the two species of the art of sound."[133]

The poet who explored this possibility most arduously was Gertrude Stein, who experimented with words as sounds at the expense of their denotation, and to the amused horror of her contemporaries wrote poems and operas that made little sense as literary art had been usually perceived. Just as the cubist painter disintegrates his subject matter and by ambiguity and indeterminacy dissolves it in his medium, so Stein dismembered her discourse and produced a continuous present composed more of sound than of semantics. Even her repetitions determine intervals and define sequences in the manner of musical phrases. But her brilliant innovations were too far advanced for her time, and perhaps too extreme in any case, because there is a limit to how far words can be dealt with as sound alone—a limit beyond which they cease to be words at all and become nonsense syllables. Nonetheless, Stein's depreciation of the semantics of language and her concentration upon its aural effect open up for poetry new ways of meaning.

At the same time, somewhat in the classical spirit, other poets became sensitive to music as a formal art and attempted to organize their words according to musical structures. Eliot, for example, wrote "preludes" and "quartets"; and Wallace Stevens placed Peter Quince at a clavier. It is Conrad Aiken, though, who most conscientiously pursued the symphonic form and in his cadence and imagery sought an approximation to musical expression.[134] These poets are thinking of the poem as an entity in its own right, dependent for continuing existence upon neither poet nor reader. The poem is hypostatized, with its own formal arrangement; and it is this potential for formality that drove these poets to shape their works in imitation of the nonsemantic syntax of music. Passages become movements in a larger whole, drawing their meaning from the larger context as well as from the denotation of their words. Much of the meaning of these poems is conveyed through their arrangement of parts, with shifts in tone and repetition of motifs—hence the entente cordiale with music. In this respect, these modern poets are like the poets of the *Divina commedia* and *The Faerie Queene*, similar practitioners of μου- σική in their attention to the formal properties of poetry and their exploitation of the potential that musical form has for metatextual statement.

Poetry and music, in sum, can be paired as sister arts on the basis of several distinct similarities. Considered in terms of what they express, both can echo the idea of cosmos as it is realized in the symphony of the planetary spheres. At the microcosmic level, both can convey the emotions and moods of the artificer, so poetry and music share a capacity for expressiveness. Considered in terms of how they are perceived, both provide aural experience for the listener, so words and musical notes are fused as sound. When poetry is assimilated to music as aural experience, however, it separates from the other arts, all of which must be seen to be perceived. If poetry is to be heard rather than read, we have returned to an earlier notion of the poetic event as a recitation or performance. We are very near the Homeric practice of μουσική. And it is in these terms that poetry receives its most sophisticated comparison with music. As Jonson said, a poet practices the art of "expressing the life of man in fit measure, numbers, and harmony."[135] Poetry, then, is most fruitfully allied with music in its formal properties, and especially in those formal properties which reflect that cosmic beauty entrusted to the care of the Muses.

In the dying wake of New Criticism and its obsession with "imagery," we might assume that painting is the art to which poetry is most easily assimilated.[136] Prompted by a residual Romanticism, we might think of poetry as the description of emotion and as the attempt to elicit a corresponding emotion from the reader, so that poetry becomes immediate experience for its audience, like sense data perceived. Especially if we hypostatize the poem in the modern manner, viewing it as an autonomous object in its own right divorced from the author, it will be descriptive, depictive—recreating a little episode, a vignette, *une tranche de vie*. Eliot's *Waste Land* is a collage of poems of this sort. It is in this depictiveness—this ability to present an actuality within a frame—that poetry is most evidently like painting. We can see in our mind's eye—as well as hear with our mind's ear and feel along our pulse—what the poem has to show. Usually poems of this sort are short, so the beginning and end are definite and fully visible from any point, like the margins of a picture. Such poems tend to be narrowly focused rather than panoramic, about plums in the icebox rather than the Trojan War. A poem of this kind is a word picture composed of a few telling and compelling details, painted in a few bold strokes. Under these circumstances, the poem is a quasi-visual, rather than primarily aural, experience.[137]

Of course, a poem may be contrived as a fully and genuinely visible object, making its appeal to the actual eye and not the mind's eye. A poet may actually shape his poem, quantifying the individual lines and placing them in such a way as to suggest a simple figure when the poem is viewed as a unit.[138] In this instance, the poem is thoroughly reified, made into a palpable thing with definite contours, with significant shape. Then we have *carmina figurata,* an extreme of poetry as visual experience which at various times has attracted poets. Such poems appear in the *Greek Anthology,* and George Herbert's "Easter Wings" and "The Altar" are well known.[139] But such efforts are obviously forced, and their net effect is primitivistic simplicity at best, and more likely crudeness. No great poet has pursued shaped poems systematically. Moreover, even in the *carmen figuratum* the burden of the poetic statement remains with the denotation of the words. The shape is complementary to, but also subsidiary to, the verbal system. The shape seems but an echo to the sense.

Recently some poets have used words to produce shaped poems in a more radically innovative way. Led by Claudel and Apollinaire,[140] they deal with words as objects themselves, capable of being divided into portions and distributed and reassembled, capable of being grouped together by wholes or parts in a wide and clever variety of physical structures that generate meaning by their arrangement. The total effect as a shape depends upon visual perception, and the relationship between parts is, at least initially, spatial. The result is a poetry so dense in its actuality that its practitioners have dubbed themselves "concrete poets."

The concrete poets are fascinating because of their ingenuity and laudable because of their honesty (naiveté?). But of course the movement is limited by how far a verbal system can be turned into a physical object before it loses the semantic value of its own syntax. For their meaning, words are more dependent upon grammatical relationships than upon spatial arrangement. Just as poetry as aural experience is limited by how far words can be edged toward pure sound before they become nonsense syllables, so poetry as visual experience is limited by how far words can be transformed into pure visual percepts and still remain semantically viable. When concrete poetry comes off best, some denotation of the verbal system inheres in and gives support to the physical arrangement; but great care must be taken lest extraneous connotations intrude and disrupt, so that the entire construct comes tumbling down like a house of cards.[141] Without being patronizing, we can say, I think, that concrete poems are symptomatic of our times, and, while admirable, are likely to be a passing fad. Like Gertrude Stein, who exaggerated the aural potential of language at the expense of its other qualities, the concrete poets in their exaggeration of the visual potential of language are doomed to something short of complete success. Nevertheless, they have a great deal to teach us about language and how it works. They have carried to a logical and literal conclusion the modern injunction to objectify the verbal system of a poem.

Most germane to our interests, the concrete poets staunchly push toward an absolute reality, a thingness, for a poem, a goal that many other contemporary poets also strive to reach, although in a different way. The poet with a penchant for formality may draw word pictures in the manner of the modern painter, such as Kandinsky or Klee, who provides seemingly unrelated elements which the percipient is invited to put together in a personally meaningful fashion. William Carlos Williams, for example, in his famous poem about two white chickens in the rain beside a red wheelbarrow, is a poet of this persuasion. While the concrete poets make shapes out of words and generate meaning out of structural relationships, Williams in that poem uses words to describe things that exist in a relationship which is similarly configural. And everything depends upon a status quo which the reader must abstract for himself. Williams's poem, like a generic still life in painting, speaks only to the point of what conditions permit these objects to exist together.[142] The objects themselves, the subject matter—though sharply delineated—is incidental.

In a poem entitled "Still Lifes," one of the last he wrote, Williams argues for the interchangeability of poetry and painting, indicating how both poem and picture reduce reality to an abstract pattern:

> All poems can be represented by
> still lifes not to say
> water-colors, the violence of
> the Iliad lends itself to an arrangement
> of narcissi in a jar,
> The slaughter of Hector by Achilles
> can well be shown by them
> casually assembled yellow upon white
> radiantly making a circle
> sword strokes violently given
> in more or less haphazard disarray[143]

The poet, says Williams, like the painter, abstracts reality to produce a formal arrangement of circles and lines, heightened by colors such as yellow and white. The "haphazard disarray" of slanting strokes, derived perhaps from the stems of narcissi in a jar, can be used to represent the violence and casualness of human death—in this instance, the slaughter of Hector by Achilles. But again, for Williams it is the conditions of existence that focus the attention of poet and painter.

Both Williams and the concrete poets approach the goal of reducing language to picture, although Williams is still using words as signifiers for other objects, while the concrete poets take words to be objects themselves. In consequence, Williams must make his pitch to the mind's eye, while the others may appeal directly to the actual eye. But not even the concrete poets can collapse completely the barrier between the verbal and the merely spatial.

Words are not just objects in space like any other thing we perceive with our senses, and a poem can never be simply an extended construction, no matter which eye, mind's or body's, views it. Necessarily a poem retains some properties of a linguistic system that transcend physical embodiment.

A concrete poem, then, pushes language as far as it can go toward total objectification, toward *realization*, and consequently toward being a purely sensual experience. Its historical antecedent, the shaped poem, is also notable as a similar experiment in visualizing poetry, even if not so single-mindedly, since it merely weds sense *to* shape rather than dissolving sense *in* shape. The shaped poem is partly visual, not wholly so. Both shaped poem and concrete poem, though, make their appeal to the actual eye, to the sense faculty that observes the other objects that surround us in physical nature.

There is another kind of poetry which may be called depictive, however, and even a word picture, but which derives from a totally different poetics. In poetry of this sort, words are deployed syntactically like colored forms laid contiguously on a canvas. A poet may paint a picture with language by piling up descriptive details, adding descriptive line after line to his literary work just as a painter adds stroke after stroke to his canvas until he fills it and compiles a reproduction of what he wishes to portray.

By the Renaissance, the prototype for such poetry had long been available in the Εἰκόνες or *Imagines* of Philostratus the Elder, and a lengthy line of imitators had followed his example. Perhaps holding in mind Aristotle's injunction that art should imitate human actions, Philostratus in the opening sentence of his work reveals the impetus for his verbal portraits: "Whosoever scorns painting is unjust to truth; and he is also unjust to all the wisdom that has been bestowed upon poets—for poets and painters make equal contribution to our knowledge of the deeds and the looks of heroes."[144] Philostratus proceeds to give sixty-five brief portraits (ranging from 25 to 75 prose lines) of such legendary figures as Phaëton and Pasiphaë, placed in a stereoscopic setting and caught in their most telling act. His purpose and his technique are unmistakable: he is using language as a pictorial agent to convey information. Each verbal picture is truly an icon or image—a faithful representation of a memorable topos.

Such a word picture is likely to be a fuller and more carefully accurate description than the literary vignette of the twentieth-century poet, and may well be static, without movement or action. It is a richly detailed snapshot rather than a reel from an early movie. More significant for its differentiation from shaped and concrete poems, it makes its appeal not to our actual sense faculties, but rather to our so-called "mind's eye," as Philostratus is careful to instruct his audience in the first item (296K.5–10).

So what is this "mind's eye," and what assumptions does it impose upon the poet and his reader? In this concise verbal formulation, the concept of the mind's eye is primarily a rhetorical doctrine that goes back to the earliest origins of the *ars bene dicendi* in Aristotle, Cicero, and Quintilian.[145] Since the art of speaking well sought to sway an audience, most figures of rhetoric were aimed at producing certain effects, certain experiences for those in attendance at the oration. Many rhetorical figures were designed specifically to create a quasi-visual image so compelling in lifelike detail that it seems to materialize before the eyes of the listeners—indeed, the audience is transformed into a group of spectators. The audience sees what the speaker is painting in words. Rhetorical figures purporting to achieve this effect were legion: examples are *hypotyposis, demonstratio, descriptio, effictio, imago, similitudo, tractatio.*[146] In discussions of style, all these depictive figures sought to produce an effect known by the Greek term ἐνάργεια or the Latin *evidentia.*[147] This strategy of creating a visual impression came so naturally to the rhetorician that rhetoric was regularly compared to painting as an image-producing art, and its figures of speech came to be known as "colors."[148]

Because of his popularity in the Renaissance, Quintilian is an appropriate authority to explain the theory and practice of those rhetorical figures which by artful illusion activate the mind's eye. In his rules for oratorical effectiveness, he gives a prominent place to ἐνάργεια, which he glosses as *evidentia.* Quintilian explains:

> Ἐνάργεια . . . or, as some prefer to call it, representation, is something more than mere clearness, since the latter merely lets itself be seen, whereas the former thrusts itself upon our notice. It is a great gift to be able to set forth the facts on which we are speaking clearly and vividly. For the oratory fails of its full effect,

and does not assert itself as it should if its appeal is merely to the hearing, and if the judge merely feels that the facts on which he has to give his decision are being narrated to him, and not displayed in their living truth to the eyes of the mind. (8.3.61–62)[149]

To accommodate the word picture drawn by the orator, to explain how the purely verbal is translated into the convincingly visual, Quintilian predicates the existence of some auxiliary sense faculty which allows the mind to see. And he goes on to encourage its exploitation:

> Though the attainment of such effects is, in my opinion, the highest of all oratorical gifts, it is far from difficult of attainment. Fix your eyes on nature and follow her. All eloquence is concerned with the activities of life, while every man applies to himself what he hears from others, and the mind is always readiest to accept what it recognizes to be true to nature (8.3.71).

The rhetorician labors under an empiricist injunction to follow nature. He uses his imagination to fashion images by recollection of his sense experience. Moreover, the audience will not be swayed by what taxes their credulity or what fails to stir their imagination. But the rewards of appealing to the mind's eye, Quintilian assures his students, are accessible and bountiful.

From here the existence of the *mentis oculi* became a commonplace, a basic assumption that conditioned all discourse. In a passage of extreme importance for making poetry respectable, Erasmus drew heavily upon Quintilian and adapted the theory to the written rather than the spoken word:

> The fifth method of enrichment primarily involves ἐνάργεια,[150] which is translated as *evidentia* "vividness." We employ this whenever, for the sake of amplifying or decorating our passage, or giving pleasure to our readers, instead of setting out the subject in bare simplicity, we fill in the colours and set it up like a picture to look at, so that we seem to have painted the scene rather than described it, and the reader seems to have seen rather than read. We shall be able to do this satisfactorily if we first mentally review the whole nature of the subject and everything connected with it, its very appearance in fact. Then we should give it substance with

appropriate words and figures of speech, to make it as vivid and clear to the reader as possible. All the poets excel in this skill, but Homer above all.[151]

Erasmus is here recalling the topos, based upon Cicero, that Homer is more a painter than a poet. In a discussion of blindness and in a series of stories recounting how men have overcome blindness, Cicero reports:

There is the tradition also that Homer was blind: but it is his painting not his poetry that we see; what district, what shore, what spot in Greece, what aspect or form of combat, what marshalling of battle, what tugging at war, what movements of men, of animals has he not depicted so vividly that he has made us see, as we read, the things which he himself did not see?[152]

For Cicero, and for Erasmus in his wake, Homer writes with such enargeiac power that, as we read, we visualize what he describes. In this respect also, he is the father of poets.

About the same time that Erasmus was exercising the mind's eye in the service of poetry, Leonardo in his comparison of poetry and painting used the phrase *occhio tenebroso* to designate a faculty that looks inward into the imagination in distinction from the bodily eye which perceives the things of nature.[153] Later in the century the literary critic Castelvetro similarly differentiated between the *occhi della mente* and the *occhi della fronte* in his subtle discussion of Aristotelian mimesis.[154] So in Sidney's day the notion of a mind's eye was a viable concept very much in evidence in criticism of the arts as well as in rhetoric. The inward eye of the mind saw with a clarity and validity equal to that of our sense faculties. It was, in fact, the mental counterpart to our outer-directed faculties for perceiving physical nature.

In this poetics dependent upon the mind's eye, the poem itself is not viewed as a visible object. Its configuration on the page is inconsequential. Rather, the poem is seen as an agent of description, construed as a product of language. The poem is not immediate experience for the reader, but rather its verbal system produces secondary effects that are admittedly vicarious and insubstantial. This gap between what is immediate and what is vicariously induced results in a discontinuity that is difficult for an empiricist to breach. What we know from such description is secondhand, not verified by our senses. It is in this context that "artificiality" becomes a term of deprecation. The "art" is "made" in the sense of being deceptively contrived. Art is illusion.

So we must look more searchingly at the hypothesis of a mind's eye. The very formulation of the phrase admits a self-contradiction; it purports to identify the eye, a sense faculty, with the mind, the intellective faculty. But the point of having both an eye and a mind is to recognize the distinction between these two faculties—quite apart from physiology and psychology, to differentiate between experience that occurs in our material environment with its *objective* phenomena and experience that occurs in the mental realm divorced from time and space where *subjective* phenomena prevail. To merge the mind and the eye is a willful prevarication, a monstrous hedge in order to blur this differentiation.

The confusion that might result from an assumption of the mind's eye is glaringly evident in Peacham's chapter on poetry in his *Compleat gentleman*. In a passage that springs directly from the rhetorical tradition, Peacham defines the term *enargeia*,[155] the ability to present compellingly lifelike images, which Peacham translates as "efficacy":

> *Efficacie* is a power of speech, which representeth a thing after an excellent manner, neither by bare words onely, but by presenting to our minds the lively *Idaeas* or formes of things so truly, as if wee saw them with our eyes; as the *places in Hell*, the fierie Arrow of *Acesta*, the description of *Fame*, the flame about the Temples of *Ascanius*.(84)[156]

In this statement Peacham assumes a mind's eye to which the language of the poet presents images of places and people. The variety of subject matter is notably broad, suggesting inexhaustibility: there are the several regions of Hell; a god, Apollo Acestor, with the fiery dart by which he inflicts illness; the personification of an abstract concept, Fame; and a legendary hero, Ascanius, the son of Aeneas who was predestined to greatness. The poet, Peacham implies, can describe any of these items with utter convincingness. The description is accurate (it "representeth a thing after

an excellent manner") and effective ("so truly, as if wee saw them
with our eyes"). The words of the poet, though, present not the
outward appearance of things, but rather their "*Idaeas* or formes,"
which our mind can respond to because, as Plato explains, it is
itself comprised of similar ideas and forms. But why "lively" (i.e.,
lifelike)? And why "as if wee saw them with our eyes"? Peacham
is groping for a theory of how language creates images and what
sort of images it produces.

The theoretical problems that Peacham is grappling with are
not easily resolved, and perhaps can be dealt with only by avert-
ing them. The link between language and its effects is as tenuous
as that between language and its origins, and any hypothesis
about it is little more than a reflection of the theorist's cosmology,
his ontology and epistemology. In our century, however, theorists
have become compulsive about the relationship between literary
artifact and percipient, and have predicated the existence not only
of the artifact, but of the percipient himself, upon a satisfactory
answer. Not only does a poem cease to be a poem if it fails to
produce palpable effects, but we cease to be alive if we are not
physiologically responding to poetic stimuli. We must continuously burn with a gemlike flame. Rather than the question, does
a tree fall in the forest if no one hears it, the question as put by
Pater has become, do we exist if a tree doesn't fall in the forest?
Our reality, being subjective, depends upon what we perceive.
Phenomenologists, by conflating subject and object, have largely
negated both and have led us into a theoretical morass. At the
least, as empiricists we are prone to subordinate the mind to the
eye, so that we think we *extoll* our mental life by assigning it
the function of "seeing." "Imagery" is real; thought is not.

In neoplatonist doctrine, however—and in the thinking of most
Elizabethans—the mind is far superior to the eye because it links
mankind by virtue of intelligence to the angels and God. What
the mind seeks to see is Truth, not the phenomena of nature, except as they are an aid toward perceiving the truth that lies behind
them. Plato as a basic tenet had separated the world of being from
the world of becoming, and his legion of followers throughout the
centuries would have been extremely sensitive to his dieresis, sensitive to a far greater extent than we are likely to be. In this cosmology, the things that comprise the world of becoming are hier-

oglyphs, as Thomas Browne said, palpable manifestations of their counterparts among the ideal essences: "This visible world is but a picture of the invisible."[157] Painting as accurate representation of nature without this ulterior dimension of hieroglyph—and poetry that similarly sets forth only visibilia—was highly suspect. Plato had been wary of painting as mere appearance, and this suspicion had persisted through the Middle Ages. According to Isidore of Seville, "*Pictura* is an image presenting the appearance of something, which when it is seen leads the mind to a recollection of the original"[158]—as a mnemonic aid, γραφική had a limited usefulness. It should not be forgotten, though, that the painting is a likeness, not an equivalent; Isidore continues, "*Pictura*, however, sounds almost like *fictura*, for it is a feigned image, not the truth."

So painting was illusionary, deceptive. As Agrippa noted in his well-known treatise *De incertitudine et vanitate scientiarum et artium* (1531), "It deceiveth the sighte . . . and with counterfaited measures, maketh the thinges seene whiche are not."[159] Even linear perspective could be turned to the proof of painting's fraudulence, since the *illusion* of depth was created on a patently two-dimensional surface—and the more accurate and successful the perspective, the more shockingly cunning the deception. If a neoplatonist wished to disprove the truthfulness of painting, he could not devise a more effective scheme for doing so than linear perspective. As Lomazzo confesses, "Such is the vertue of Perspective, that whiles it imitateth the *life*, it causeth a man to oversee and bee deceaved";[160] and again, "The skill of the workeman consisteth in shewing False and deceitfull sightes insteede of the true" (188). Painting merely "seems," to use Spenser's canny verb. And purely descriptive poetry aroused the same suspicions. Plato's ghost raised an admonitory finger whenever an artifact appealed too openly to the senses.

The alternative was to see a painting as a symbol or emblem— some sort of semantic sign rather than merely a representation of natural data—and thereby to give it a purpose and a significance that guaranteed respectability. In a preface certainly known to Sidney, Henri Estienne argues that the Greek verb γράφειν means both to write and to draw; and he notes that good painters always take their subjects from the best poets, so that Homer's

verses describing Zeus provided the source for the famous painting of Zeus by Euphranor as well as the famous statue by Phidias.[161] A similar tack is taken by Lomazzo. In his preface, Lomazzo justifies painting by assimilating it to "writing," which was
"first invented to preserve the memory of the Sciences" (2).[162]
Painting and poetry may then fuse in a joint function as the storehouse of esoteric knowledge, a cultural memory. "Writing is nothing else, but a picture of *white* and *black,*" Lomazzo contends; and
he continues: "Whence the Egyptians, under the pictures of
beasts and other living thinges, used to deliver all their sciences,
and other secrets, both sacred and prophane: so that unto them
Painting served as a treasury, where they reserved the hidden
riches of their mysticall knowledges to all succeeding ages." When
making this statement, it is likely that Lomazzo had in mind the
collection of ideograms and explicatory comments attributed to
Horapollo, a classical text that the Renaissance rediscovered in
1419 and greatly revered;[163] perhaps he had an eye also on its
extensive derivative, the *Hieroglyphica* of Giovanni Pierio Valeriano, first published at Basle in 1556. This sort of book, which
reveals arcane lore by means of both picture and verbal text in
tandem, is characteristic of the humanists' penchant for syncretism. Painting and language are parallel avenues leading to the
same *domus aurea,* an inner sanctum where truth and beauty are
revealed as one. In this tradition, to meet the expectation that it
preserve the hard-earned wisdom of a culture, painting acquires
meaning. A picture becomes semantic, and iconography ($<$ ἐικών,
picture $+$ γράφειν, to write) is born.

It was in this capacity for semantics that painting most nearly
approached poetry, as Leonardo in the prime of the Renaissance
ably argued. In his *Paragone,* Leonardo recalls Plutarch (pages
105–7) and makes a telling statement about how closely these two
arts are related:

> Painting is poetry which is seen and not heard, and poetry is a
> painting which is heard but not seen. These two arts, you may
> call them both either poetry or painting, have here interchanged
> the senses by which they penetrate to the intellect. (58)[164]

In Leonardo's thinking, painting and poetry are interfused in their
common purpose of addressing the intellect. They are both ra-

tional enterprises, and may exchange their media in pursuit of this common goal, so that painting appeals to the ear and poetry to the eye. They are paired most fruitfully not in their shared powers of description, not in their production of imagery, but rather in their ability to express meaning.

The emblem book, which arrived on the scene fully developed in the early 1530s with the publication of Alciato's *Emblemata,* is the predictable product of this compatibility. An emblem is neither poetry nor painting, but a compound larger than the sum of both. The visual and the verbal are used together in a complementary fashion to produce a whole with a meaning greater than either of its components could generate alone.[165] By 1552 Barthélemy Aneau was proudly acknowledging the dual nature of the emblem by entitling his handsome collection *Picta poesis.* The emblem book, of course, is the perfect marriage of painting and poetry, just as the madrigal is the happy wedding of poetry to music. No time in our cultural history has been more propitious than the Renaissance for such cohabitation among the arts.[166] Notice, though, that in the emblem book the art to make the greater accommodation is painting. It is painting which assimilates to poetry, while poetry foregoes little of its essential character. In the emblem, painting denies those properties that defined it as γρα-φική and becomes largely symbolic, a visibilium whose raison d'être resides in its implied meaning.

There is one poetic genre, the epigram, which retains the fossilized imprint of a union between poetry and the depictive arts. In its origin, as its etymology records, the epigram was a brief statement inscribed on an object to indicate its significance.[167] On an altar, for example, there was a comment about the god to whom the altar was dedicated, or over a portal a statement announced: "Abandon hope all ye who enter here." As a first degree of sophistication in the development of the epigram, the object began to speak in its own right, attracting the attention of every passerby and delivering its message. The art object that speaks—the tomb that admonishes the approaching wayfarer, for example, or the classical urn that edifies with aphorisms about beauty and truth— is close to a concrete poem, both being objects with a meaning. Rather than language being reduced to a shape, however, a shape is given the ability to speak. Eventually the epigram gained independence from what it should appear upon, but it still bears the marks of its genesis as a speaking object. This origin dictates its conciseness, its concreteness—only a few highly suggestive details.[168] It is a word picture rather like Williams's white chickens beside the red wheelbarrow—both terse, both depicting actual things, both loaded with a meaning to be inferred from sparse information that at first glance gives the semblance of being casual.

In its most sophisticated and fully articulated development, the epigram becomes a poem describing an object with symbolic meaning—what Hagstrum calls "iconic poetry" (17ff.).[169] The prototype for this genre in the Western tradition is the passage describing the shield that Hephaestus made for Achilles in Homer's *Iliad,* a passage extracted by George Chapman in 1598 for separate translation and publication, which he interprets as a depiction of cosmos. For the Renaissance, an even more important example of this genre was Cebes's *Tabula.*[170] Its influence was perhaps as wide as, and more subtle than, Homer's. In this masterpiece (whose origin is uncertain, though generally ascribed to a follower of Plato in late classical times), a pilgrim traveling along his way of life arrives at a temple where a large but cryptic picture hangs. As the wayfarer stands in puzzlement, an ancient priest steps forward and explains its meaning. It is, not surprisingly, an allegory of the human condition, proceeding episodically from birth to a consummation in religious understanding. The table of Cebes is complete unto itself, autonomous; but often a passage of "iconic poetry" is embedded in a longer work. Especially in epic poetry the minute depiction of an artifact—such as a painting, tapestry, bas-relief, shield, or bowl—became so much a stock in trade as to warrant its own technical term, *ekphrasis.*[171]

So poetry can be depictive in several quite distinct ways. Just as it assimilates to music on the basis of various shared qualities, so poetry has a variety of affinities to painting. The potential of poetry for visual experience, depending upon which affinity is developed, may dictate several different poetics. The indefiniteness of the term "imagery" for the New Critics—they used it to cover almost any effect of a poetic passage—indicates that a poem can approach a quasi-visual existence from many different directions. It may be a shaped poem, a concrete poem, various sorts of word picture, an emblem or epigram or ekphrastic icon. The quasi-visual result, by the same token, can serve widely divergent ends, from highly informative to merely sensual.

After the mid-sixteenth century, two classical dicta crop up almost invariably in any discussion comparing poetry to painting and frequently occur in the most offhand conversation about the arts. It is clear that both were données, hardly to be challenged in their gist, although subject to a vast range of interpretation and application. One comes from Horace: "Poetry is like painting"—readily familiar in its Latin original, *ut pictura poesis.* The other is taken from Plutarch: "Poetry is a speaking picture, and painting is a mute poem"—almost equally well-known to the Renaissance in its Latin formulation, *Poëma loquens pictura, pictura tacitum poëma debet esse.*[172] The prevalence of these easy assertions requires that we look closely at each. Let's take Plutarch first—not that he came first in time, but because he more fully displays the grounds for comparing poetry and painting.

In his essay, "Whether the Athenians were more renowmed for martiall armes or good letters," as Philemon Holland translated it in 1603, Plutarch reverentially cites a predecessor, Simonides of Ceos, the great lyric poet,[173] who reportedly had said (again, in the words of Holland): "Picture was a dumbe poesie, and poesie a speaking picture."[174] Although this statement was appropriated by later theorists for a variety of purposes, in context it provided a fixed reference for assessing the complementarity of poetry and history, a relationship of considerable concern to Aristotle and thence to Sidney and his contemporaries. In this essay, Plutarch is at pains to show that although the Athenians are famous for their achievements in philosophy, art, and literature, they are even more remarkable for their military feats—a thesis so foreign to Plutarch's usual way of thinking that some have called it a tongue-in-cheek exercise in devil's advocacy.

The essay begins by noting that men of letters are dependent upon great men of action for their subject matter, a sentiment endorsed by Spenser in the October eclogue. According to the direct logic of Plutarch, "If you take away men of action, you shall be sure to have no writers of them" (981). Plutarch has in mind the historians (ἱστορικοῦ), such as Thucydides and Xenophon, whom he mentions. It is their function to record as accurately as possible the brave deeds of soldiers, and thereby the historians achieve a certain nobility themselves: "For surely there is a certaine image of glorie, which by a kinde of reflexion, as in a mirrour, doth rebound from those who have atchieved noble acts, even unto them that commit the same to writing" (982). The similitude between writing history and reflecting events as in a mirror is significant; the emphasis is upon accuracy and completeness in the written report. Obviously, Plutarch is thinking of literature of a certain kind, as an exact image of actuality.

From here, Plutarch glides smoothly into a consideration of painting, another depictive art which records faithfully the activity of battle. As an example, he describes in detail the famous painting by Euphranor which depicted the Athenian victory over Epaminondas at Mantineia (incidentally, the locale for Sidney's *Arcadia*). But this meticulous description is merely preparation for the conclusion that the painting, regardless of its vividness and vitality, is unmistakably derivative, subordinate to the reality it portrays: "But I suppose you will not compare the wit or judgement of a painter, with the courage and policy of a captaine, nor endure those, who preferre a painted table before a glorious trophae; or the vaine shadow before the reall substance and thing indeed" (983). And it is in this context that painting and poetry are compared. The next sentence cites Simonides to the effect that painting is dumb poesy and poesy is a speaking picture. Although Plutarch uses the word "poesy" (ποίησις), he is thinking of it as a record of events, in the sense of our word "history." The successful poet will be the one who like the painter captures the vivacity of commotion:

> For looke what things or actions painters doe shew as present and in manner as they were in doing, writings doe report and record as done and past; and if the one represent them in colours and figures, and the other exhibit the same in words and sentences, they differ both in matter and also in manner of imitation, howbeit both the one and the other shoote at one end, and have the same intent and purpose. And hee is counted the best historian who hath the skill to set out a narration, as in a painted table with divers affections, and sundry conditions of persons, as with many images and pourtraictures. (983)

Plutarch conceives of poetry as a narrative of events, as ἱστορία. Equally without doubt, his intention is to denigrate poetry. Like painting, poetry is derivative. Just as we are not to prefer "the wit or judgement of a painter" over "the courage and policy of a captaine," so we are not to prize a victory ode over the glorious trophies of war. A painting or a poem is but a "vaine shadow," says Plutarch, that palls in the presence of "the reall substance and thing indeed."

Plutarch ascribes reality to the phenomena of physical nature, which the arts image as best they can. In consequence, despite his disparagement of poetry in this instance, he proved quite congenial to the neo-Aristotelians who looked forward to an empiricist aesthetic based upon sense perception of the phenomenal world. In their hands, *historia* evolved to *istoria* and thence to "story," a fictive narrative with the illusion of reality, an attempted replication of the actions of men which acquires its authority from the convincingness with which it simulates human activity. Plutarch nudged poetry toward a rapprochement with history, toward realism.

In the 1580s, however, Plutarch's "speaking picture" was still more closely aligned with the emblem book than with history, and its value lay more in its semantic possibilities as a combination of verbal and visual elements than in its accuracy and verifiability as a record of historical event. When Sidney defines poetry as "a speaking picture" (*Defence* 80.1–2; pages 267–69), he does not have in mind the restrictive concept of poetry as verbal depiction of actuality, a word picture. Rather, he is thinking of poetry as a "picture," a visual experience, a depiction which is static when considered synchronically, but which also incorporates a diachronic dimension through its use of language, a verbal experience which necessarily is discursive, as indicated by the participle "speaking." Actually, the phrase "a speaking picture" is a neat encapsulation of both verbal *and* visual, of both verb (process) *and* noun (entity), of both dynamic *and* static, of both timeliness *and* timelessness. This phrase joins together exactly those elements that Lessing would rend asunder.

It is within this syncretic tradition of speaking pictures that Sidney wrote the *Arcadia* and *Astrophil and Stella*. As this tradition developed, a poem became an account of human affairs, a sequence of enjambed episodes, a continuous narrative with a plot. In accord with Aristotle, it need not be based upon actual event; but like a picture, it must give the illusion of a lively reality. In fact, the justification for poetry becomes this capacity for lifelike fiction. Although poetry is inferior to painting in its ability to represent a busy scene, and both fall short of complete truth, "even poetry," as Plutarch conceded, "hath a grace, and is esteemed, for that it describeth and relateth things as if they had beene done, and which carie a resemblance of truth" (984).

The other cliché of Renaissance art theory, *ut pictura poesis*,[175] is not so well defined by its original context and not so clearly directed in its thrust. It was lifted from Horace without due notice of its origins and put to a shameless variety of promiscuous uses. It can, in fact, mean almost anything about poetry or painting. Being brief, it could be tossed off as a bon mot, an offhand flourish of learning. Being unspecific, it covered an underlying confusion of thought and allowed the sort of unprincipled adaptation that made poetry a purely descriptive art like representational painting.

In its initial appearance, however, *ut pictura poesis* is not a phrase to occasion much notice. It comes from the *Ars poetica,* a document of considerable importance in the history of criticism, and one that was widely known and highly respected throughout the Renaissance. But this phrase is carelessly used by Horace, inconspicuously imbedded in the text quite far along toward the end. Those who have ripped it from its place and assigned it compelling significance have appropriated Horace's authority in a cause of their own making. In Horace's lines *ut pictura poesis* means merely that poetry is like painting in certain incidental and trivial ways: some pictures delight more when seen up close, others when viewed from a distance; some when seen in strong light, others when viewed in semidarkness; some only when seen the first time, others when viewed repeatedly. Thomas Drant's translation of Horace in 1567, known to both Sidney and Spenser, catches the disposition of the phrase exactly:

> A Poesie is picture lyke,
>   the which if thou stande nere,
> Delytes the muche: sum picture more

if further of thou were.
This hathe a better grace in darke,
   and this in open day,
The scanning skill of viewinge iudge
   can it no whit afraye.
This Poesie hath had his tyme
   it was well liked once,
An other hath bene lykd ten tymes,
   An, *A per se* for nonce.[176]

In Drant's words, "A Poesie is picture lyke"—but that a poem be like a picture in exact likeness to life is a limitation on both poetry and painting that the well-mannered and equivocating Horace is not likely to have tolerated.

Nevertheless, by the mid-sixteenth century Horace's innocuous phrase was frequently read as a directive: a poem, like a painting, should provide a quasi-visual image true to nature. Boccaccio some centuries earlier had defended poetry on these grounds: "The poet tries with all his powers to set forth in noble verse the effects, either of Nature herself, or of her eternal and unalterable operation. . . . so vividly set forth that the very objects will seem actually present in the tiny letters of the written poem."[177] As painting in the Renaissance became increasingly lifelike and illusionary—obsessed with a determination to re-present a scene by the use of perspective, by modelling to suggest plasticity, by the deployment of light (indeed, by any means at all)—it drew poetry along in the direction of pictorialism. Jonson epitomized the prevailing sentiment at the end of the sixteenth century:

> *Poetry,* and *Picture,* are Arts of a like nature; and both are busie about imitation. It was excellently said of *Plutarch, Poetry* was a speaking *Picture,* and *Picture* a mute *Poesie.* For they both invent, faine, and devise many things, and accommodate all they invent to the use, and service of nature. (*Timber* 8:609–10)

For Jonson, the poet devises images, like the painter, and subordinates his work to nature—not to "human" nature or the "universal" nature that the Augustans followed, but the physical nature which the empiricist saw with recently opened eyes.

When we come to look at poetry in relation to the other arts, then, we quickly discern that poetry is like each of the others in certain respects. With painting, for example, poetry shares a capacity for projecting visual images; with music, it shares a capacity for generating aural experience and, even more important, formal patterns. So poetry can be easily compared to, and often almost assimilated to, either of these other arts. Word pictures face toward painting, while lyric poems tend toward music. We can point also to poems that resemble a statue, a building, or even a dance[178]—at least in some features. This condition is necessary for all the arts to inhere in the same class.

What remains in this chapter is to separate poetry from the other arts, and this last observation provides a good place to start. Poetry is like painting in some ways, like music in other ways, and like sculpture, architecture, and dance in yet different ways. But what "ways" are we talking about? An answer involves consideration of several factors: the mode of existence of art works, the means of their presentation, and, though perhaps not essentially, the end to which they are directed—that is, the ontology, epistemology, and teleology of the arts.[179]

Clearly—and this is the important point here—poetry is not like painting or like music or like any of the other arts in *all* respects. Poetry is not exactly like any other art. Furthermore, poetry is not like painting and music—or like sculpture and architecture and dance—in the same respects. Those qualities which it holds in common with painting, for instance, it does not share with music. So what is the operative *differentia* for distinguishing the arts one from another?

The only dependable *differentia* among the arts that persists across the board resides in the means of their publication, in how the artifacts are presented to their prospective audience. Each of the arts can deal with the same subject matter, projecting the same object of imitation, so their ontology may be the same. We saw this to be the case for all those arts subsumed under the classical concept of μουσική, and in the Renaissance even painting, sculpture, and architecture took on the harmony of celestial music in the symmetry of their compositions. Only in the twentieth century, after the elevation of the percipient at the expense of both artifact and artificer, have we needed an Ingarden to explain the mode of existence of a literary work in terms of multiple readings. Moreover, each of the arts can be directed to the same end, ranging from amusement through edification to outright indoctrination. Their teleology may be the same: to please, to move, to instruct. But the arts do not share a common strategy of appeal to the public, so the way in which they are known, their epistemology, varies. Although artifacts exemplifying the various arts may make similar statements and may have comparable effects, the means by which they operate do differ. Since Aristotle's *Poetics*,[180] the artistic medium has been a legitimate instrument to differentiate between the arts.

Each of the arts, in fact, has its characteristic medium, a physical presence so distinctive as to be its evident hallmark. Who is likely to express this principle more elegantly than Pater? As a basic tenet of his aestheticism, he declares: "The sensuous material of each art brings with it a special phase or quality of beauty, untranslatable into the forms of any other, an order of impressions distinct in kind."[181] As Pater observes, though with less detail, poetry uses words; painting uses colored forms or lines on a flat surface; music uses vibrations in the air whose frequency is determined by mathematical ratios; sculpture uses stone or wood or metal—some durable substance that can be modelled in three dimensions; dance uses movements of the human body; architecture uses volumes of space enclosed for habitation. In our cultural past for the most part the distinction between media has been respected as a matter of artistic decorum, sometimes to the seemingly absurd point of precluding a mixture of genres, such as comic and tragic scenes in a single drama.

On occasion, however, an artificer contrives to blur the distinction that these media impose, and this tendency today is quite strong. The concrete poem, for example, is offered as a physical object, despite the presence of language, and it impinges upon painting for its interest in the configuration of extended forms— in what the painter calls "composition."[182] Conversely, the cartoon, with or without caption, impinges upon literature for its verbal statement. Several theorists and even more artificers have worked hard to obliterate the demarcation between media. The result can be terribly exciting (literally), a lively development of the Romantic penchant for synesthesia. The new sculpture and the new drama and the new music claim to provide a "total environment" for the art event, and the other arts are attempting to follow suit so far as technical limitations permit. They approach the percipient through several, if not all, of his senses. Aldous Huxley's "feelies" have verily come to pass at our neighborhood picture show.

The present-day compulsion to conflate the arts is easily explained and bears inversely upon our theme. If we accept the necessity of a percipient in the art event (pages 28–29), all the arts are equally related by at least one quality: each depends upon our sense faculties for its mode of being perceived. Perceiving an artifact in whatever medium requires attention to its sensory data. Moreover, since our culture is dominated by positivism and phenomenalism, we assume that something exists only by virtue of its sense-perceptible phenomena and that we can know about it only by observing those facts. Therefore in this empiricist aesthetic only sense experience is real. Only sense experience can substantiate the observed object and activate the observing subject. In consequence, to be real, art must be an immediate, sensuous experience. In another culture, art may be aimed at psychic orderliness, for example, as in the case of Plato's republic, or at *contemptus mundi,* as in the case of the medieval Church. But in ours, art is expected to produce palpable effects of a sensuous sort. In such an aesthetic, priority is assigned to the common quality shared by all the arts—namely, that their artifacts are perceived by our sense faculties. Since all the arts are transmitted to an audience by sensory data, our hunger for sense experience makes each of them equally effective; and the greater the number of arts involved in the "total environment," the greater the involvement of the percipient in the art event. Hence the conflation of the arts in our century.

But whether we admire or deplore the stimulation provided by multi-media artifacts, the current tendency to intermeddle the arts should not blind us to other possibilities. From classical times, in fact, there has been a sharp awareness of the individuality of the arts—Aristotle's impulse, if anything, was analytical—and that awareness has persisted through the centuries.[183] Even today, the distinctness of genres continues as a norm which enriches the multi-media artifact and conditions its meaning—perhaps, even, provides the circumstance that makes its meaning possible. So to distinguish between the arts is not a perversity, despite the fact that at the moment it might not be fashionable. Rather, it is a traditional exercise condoned by long practice and demanded by the historicity of our investigation.

Focusing upon their means of publication, we might classify the arts in several ways, and of course various criteria produce different classifications. The arts may be described according to the sense faculty by which they are primarily perceived, so we have the visual arts and the aural arts. Huxley toyed with the notion of tactile art, and the olfactory and gustatory arts remain seductive (although largely unexplored) possibilities. In a culture committed to empiricism, time and space are ever-present values, and at least since Lessing there have been attempts to separate the spatial arts (painting and sculpture) from the temporal arts (poetry and music), with dance and architecture enjoying the privileges of both parties. Sometimes a group may be identified by the willful dominance of the artificer in the artistic process, so we have the creative arts; or by the requirement that an agent mediate between the artifact and the percipient, so we have the performing arts;[184] or by the fact that perception of the constituents which comprise the artifact is sequentially fixed, so we now have the "serial" arts.[185] Most usefully, however, following the analytical lead of Aristotle (*Poetics* 1447a18–b10), the arts are characterized by their media, so we have the plastic arts, the graphic arts, the rhythmic arts, the verbal arts, and so forth.

Poetry, evidently, is one of the verbal arts. There are, of course, several others—most important, perhaps, oratory and history and philosophy, though theology and law also depend upon the use of language. A goodly portion of Sidney's *Defence* is given over to the separation of poetry from both history and philosophy in order to show how poetry is superior to both. In any case, in English letters since Sidney poetry has been an autonomous art of verbal discourse. And to continue the Aristotelian analysis from class to genus to species, as Sidney does, poetry in turn may be anatomized into several sorts, such as "heroic, lyric, tragic, comic, satiric, iambic, elegiac, pastoral, and certain others" (*Defence* 81.18–19). But at least in what immediately follows, we shall deal with poetry holistically rather than according to its kinds.

Since what distinguishes poetry from the other fine arts is its medium, we must now consider the nature of language as it was taken to be in the Renaissance. After Ficino, and at least indirectly even before him, the basic document in any philosophical discussion of language was Plato's *Cratylus*.[186] This dialogue, noteworthy in the Platonic canon for its singleness of purpose and relentless method, was the most comprehensive treatise on the theory of language inherited from classical times. It underlay Cicero's *De oratore* and Augustine's *De doctrina Christiana,* and from Pico della Mirandola to Thomas Hobbes it received renewed attention during the Renaissance.

In the *Cratylus* Plato is concerned to determine how words mean, so it is an exercise in semantics. In the course of the dialogue, he entertains three possibilities: 1) language is an *arbitrary* set of conventions agreed upon by its users, so that words are contrivances devised by humans and have no intrinsic meaning; 2) words do have *intrinsic* meanings, so that language is a system of signs predetermined in nature which reveal the otherwise hidden characteristics of things; and 3) the meanings of words have been prescribed by divine decree, so that language is fixed and sacrosanct. In the course of the *Cratylus,* each of these positions is enunciated and defended, though eventually demolished. As a result, this dialogue stops even farther than most from reaching a conclusion. But it formulates many important problems with language, and ultimately expands to problems of ontology and of epistemology.

The question under debate, framed at the outset by Hermogenes in opposition to Cratylus, is whether names bear some natural and spontaneous relationship to the things they designate, or whether they are a set of conventions agreed upon by common consent (383A–B). At issue is the dependency of a verbal signifier upon what it signifies. Hermogenes argues that nothing has been assigned its name by nature; rather, the correctness of a name is simply a matter of agreement among those who use it (384C–D).[187] But Socrates counterargues:

> Things have some fixed reality of their own, not in relation to us nor caused by us; they do not vary, swaying one way and another in accordance with our fancy, but exist of themselves in relation to their own reality imposed by nature. (386D–E)

In the Timaean cosmology, things have an objective existence independent of any perceiving mind—that is, in the world of being. Therefore, since this essence precedes the name, it must be the determinant of that name. The relationship between name and essence, in fact, is the same as the relationship between physical object and idea in the theory of mimesis that Plato expounds in the *Republic* (pages 137–38): the word is an imitation of the essence it nominates just as a chair, let's say, is a representation of chairness. A verbal system intended to communicate an idea, then, is an imitation of that idea, a verbal artifact, a metaphor in the literal sense of transferring meaning from one level of existence to another.[188] So naturally there is an inherent relationship between the words and the idea they represent by imitation. In its simplest statement, Socrates's argument is that "the name is an imitation of the thing named" (430B).

But this mimetic theory of language runs into difficulty as well, because language, unlike painting, does not permit the homologous representation of the objects it imitates. A painter reproduces the shapes and colors of his object of imitation by means of shapes and colors, but the letters and syllables of language do not reproduce the objects they signify in the same direct manner. Application of the mimetic theory of language by analogy to painting reduces language to onomatopoeic effects, a patently unsatisfactory inference. And so it goes. Cratylus attempts to recoup some of the authority for language: "He who knows the names knows also the things named" (435D), an assumption relied upon by magi in their incantations. But the dialogue ends inconclusively, or perhaps even negatively, with Socrates admitting:

> How realities are to be learned or discovered is perhaps too great a question for you or me to determine; but it is worth while to have reached even this conclusion, that they are to be learned and sought for, not from names but much better through themselves than through names. (439B)

The validity of language, perhaps also its utility, is denied.[189] There is even incipient agnosticism: knowledge is beyond us.

The residue of this dialogue, what we are left with at its end, consists in two antithetical propositions: on the one hand, words are intrinsically related to the things they designate (that is what the Middle Ages and magicians remembered about the dialogue); but on the other hand, the knowledge of things may not be derived from names. The net result is an uneasy recognition that while absolutes such as beauty and other ideas do exist (439D–E), language is inadequate as a means of expressing such truths.

The last point has been elaborated in recent literary theory. Cratylus argued that language is a semantic system of verbal signs which have precise meanings derived from the essence of what they designate. Following Saussure, however, most theorists agree with Plato's Hermogenes that language is a set of social conventions, and therefore they see language as a semantic system of verbal signs *without* predetermined, and consequently precise, meanings. Indeed, a word in the Saussurian scheme derives its imputed meaning by negative definition, in contradistinction to all those possibilities in a system of paradigmatic options which it is *not*. Furthermore, some recent theorists see language as a system of signs which act merely as undefined stimuli upon the percipient with quite uncontrollable (and therefore unpredictable) results. Much of the present confusion and frenetic activity in literary theory is a response to this linguistic assumption, because it invalidates our data in literary analysis.[190] Echoing the *Cratylus,* no doubt unwittingly, theorists of the last two decades have regularly called into question the semantic capability of language. In consequence, we have the hermeneutist shoring up the validity of language, while the deconstructionist tears it down. The semiotician has the advantage, at least for the moment, because he doesn't deal with words per se, but only (he says) with how words (and other signs) might generate meaning. Actually, though, despite our elaboration of the problems, and despite the widespread homage to Saussure, we are not much nearer a solution than were Socrates, Cratylus, and Hermogenes. Different people use language in different ways—with different assumptions and for different purposes.

A much more definite and positive theory of language held sway in the Hebraic-Christian tradition, where in fact it occupied a place of considerable prominence. In the book of Genesis, following the hexaemera, the first act of Adam was to name his fellow creatures (2:19–20), thereby distinguishing them one from another and endowing each with its appropriate identity.[191] As William Hunnis paraphrases the biblical text in standard fourteeners:

And God did bringe all beastes and foules,
   to view of Adams Eye,
Which was to see, what kynde of name,
   he then would call them by.
And Adam called every Beast,
   and every Fowle by name,
As wee do use at this same day,
   to nominate the same.[192]

This episode comes immediately after the passage which describes the tree of knowledge with its forbidden fruit and just before the creation of Eve—indeed, the creation of Eve is integral to this process of naming things, because she proves necessary for the identification of Adam, separating him as "man" from the other creatures. She is his essential counterpart, his supplement, defining his distinctive qualities. It is Adam who calls her "woman" since, as the text explains, "she was taken out of Man" (2:33).[193]

This act of naming extended eventually to all items in the universe, from the highest to the lowest, and paralleled at the human level, within the finite coordinates of time and space, the divine act of creation which had produced our world in the first place. Adam created a verbal universe which renders knowable (and discussable) the fullness of the cosmos which before Creation had resided in the mind of God. Until Adam named things, there was verbal chaos; although the items of nature existed, they had no communicable meaning, and consequently no recognizable identity. As Louis LeRoy comments, "Man could not of him selfe, without the helpe of God discerne innumerable thinges contained in the world by their proper names, which otherwaies had remained unknowen" (fol. 18^v). Such an analogy between Adam *nominans* and the divine Creator makes the use of language a creative activity, almost godlike in its potential, almost calling things into existence. For this reason, the poet, the artificer who employs language as his medium, was considered impious or divine by turns, a devilish magus or a godlike creator.

When Adam assigned names to the things he perceived with his mortal senses, he did not act capriciously or arbitrarily; according to La Primaudaye, "If hee had not named them as he should, hee had brought in great confusion in nature."[194] Adam was bound to

accord with the innate qualities of each item as God had created
it. Agrippa explains:

> *Adam* therefore that gave the first names to things, knowing the
> influencies of the Heavens, and properties of all things, gave them
> all names according to their natures, as it is written in *Genesis,*
> where God brought all things that he had created before *Adam,*
> that he should name them, and as he named any thing, so the
> name of it was, which names indeed contain in them wonderfull
> powers of the things signified.[195]

In this tradition, as Cratylus had argued, there is an inviolable
relationship between words and what they designate.[196] Language
is at basis a system of hieroglyphs, to borrow a term from the
Egyptians; words make knowable the otherwise ineffable nature
of the things they signify. When Juliet petulantly asks, "What's in
a name?" she has in mind this tradition (*Rom.* 2.2.43). And her
rejection of it—"That which we call a rose / By any other word
would smell as sweet"—indicates the degree to which her girlish
passion has overthrown her reason and blocked out her schooling.[197] Gloucester's evil son, Edmund, with greater malice follows
the same specious argument when he refuses to allow that the
epithet "bastard" predisposes him to baseness (*Lr.* 1.2.6–10).

So the system of language was perfectly analogous to the system of creation: each word was predetermined by something God
had created, and Adam's task was merely to render explicit for
mortal comprehension what God had intended. Our universe
could be conceived as a vast system of words, translating into language what God had in mind when He created it. Furthermore,
since each thing by omnipotent design was specified by its own
word (indeed, had been called into being by God conceiving its
name), there was in the beginning only one language. And that
language, of course, without much question was Hebrew. At the
dawn of human history everyone by necessity had used the same
set of letters and the same vocabulary instituted by the deity.
Everyone spoke Hebrew.

That is, everyone spoke Hebrew until the Tower of Babel. This
affront against deity was rightly seen not only as an aspiration to
godhead in the physical dimension of the Tower's height, but also

as a transgression through the abuse of language. The tyrant Nimrod who proposed the Tower had used persuasive rhetoric to convince his fellows to participate in the scheme, and he was successful because all spoke the same tongue. The punishment then fits the crime. After God destroyed the Tower, mankind was divided into several nations, each speaking its own distinct language, unintelligible to the rest.[198]

Quite appropriately, this incident from the Old Testament was explained as an analogue to the Fall, the prototypical instance of humanity's disobedience in seeking forbidden knowledge. Eve's seduction by the serpent's discourse, then her seduction of Adam and his reasoned acquiescence—their transgressions against God's express word and the resultant alteration in God's perfect plan— all this abuse of language was a diametric counterpart to Adam's naming things. It was commonly agreed that the serpent exercised his guile through language, and his success depended in large part upon his usurpation of this human capacity for verbal expression: "The serpent did not use a worde or two when he spake to the woman, but did use a sensible and distinct communication." William Alley, the learned bishop of Exeter, goes on to assign blame for this perversion to Satan himself: "It can no otherwise be concluded, but that the Serpent did speake, by the instinct and instigation of the ill aungell" (fol. 68ᵛ-69). So in the realm of words as elsewhere in the realm of nature, Eve undid what Adam had accomplished. Just as universal order at the human level had been achieved through language in the beginning, so universal disarray resulted from the corruption of speech and thence of reason.

As the compensatory phase in the providential design, however, Christ appeared as λόγος, God's word made flesh.[199] Through His gospel, there is hope for the restitution of that initial state of innocence when names did directly mean what they signify. The New Testament, read literally, is proof that God's word shall prevail. Typologically, *Fiat lux* transmutes to "Christ is risen." The whole scheme of creation, death, and resurrection—the pattern of the fortunate fall—was clearly reflected in this dynamics of language.[200] Speech, the expression of reason, is the clearest evidence that humanity is an image of deity; and, though fallen, if he cultivates his linguistic competence, a mortal may regain a large measure of the paradise lost.[201] "We shall be saved by the word" is more than a shallow liturgical pun. As Philippe Duplessis-Mornay said with reference to Christ: "We cal him *Logos,* which some translate *Word* or *Speech,* and othersome *Reason.*"[202]

Another potent concept of language arose from the Hermetic tradition. In this discipline, the inventor of language was Hermes Trismegistus, or Thoth, to use his Egyptian name, who was secretary to the gods and tutelary deity for the arts.[203] This legend was interpreted in the Renaissance to mean that language mediated between sacred knowledge and the devotee who sought to understand such hidden mysteries. A word was a palpable counter for an impalpable referent, making it sense-perceptible and therefore knowable to the reader. Under these circumstances, words are little more than hieroglyphs,[204] and language is simply one of many semiotic systems which disclose a preexistent and self-sufficient, though immaterial, state of being.

In such a view, a verbal statement, like the impresa and the emblem or any other system of signs, is an enigmatic publication which may be opaque to the ignorant, but which the adept can penetrate to its hidden significance. Indeed, the items of physical nature are themselves palpable symbols of a non-material truth, so there are "tongues in trees, books in running brooks, / Sermons in stones, and good in every thing" (Shakespeare, *AYL* 2.1.16–17). The items of creation comprise, in a common phrase, "God his great booke of nature," which La Primaudaye goes on to gloss: "I meane the admirable frame of this Univers, or whole world. Wherein the infinite varieties and sorts of creatures, like so many visible wordes, doe proclaime and publish unto man the eternitie, infinitie, omnipotency, wisedome, justice, bountie, and other essentiall attributes of his dread and soveraigne creatour."[205] Walter Raleigh concurs in his most sanctimonious manner: "This visible world," he writes, "is also the understood language of the Almightie, vouchsafed to all his creatures, whose Hieroglyphical Characters, are the unnumbred Starres, the Sunne, and Moone, written on these large volumes of the firmament: written also on the earth and the seas, by the letters of all those living creatures, and plants, which inhabit and reside therein."[206] Thomas Browne, that indefatigable seventeenth-century man of science, could still confidently proclaim belief in nature as a book of hieroglyphs: "In this masse of nature there is a set of things that carry in their front, though not in capitall letters, yet in stenography, and short Characters, something of Divinitie, which to wiser reasons serve as Luminaries in the abysse of knowledge."[207] The Hermetic theory of language, promulgated by such handbooks as Horapollo's *De sacris Ægyptiorum notis* and Valeriano's *Hieroglyphica,* permeated Renaissance culture and greatly enhanced the richness and range of its art.

Closely allied with the Hermetic view of language, and in most ways confirming it, was the theory of language that stemmed from the Cabala. The Cabalistic use of words carried particular authority, since the original language before Babel was generally conceded to have been Hebrew; and especially in religious and magical contexts the Cabala's reliance upon vocables was widely copied. In the Cabalistic tradition, ultimate being, usually conceived as light, is transcendent, beyond the limits of human knowledge, as well as undiminishable. There proceeds from it, however, a series of emanations that degenerate gradually toward materiality. Words are then seen as verbal equivalents of the concepts, values, and potentialities that originate from this sacrosanct source. The series of emanations from the divine light which eventuates in our palpable world is paralleled by the unfolding of a divine vocabulary. The tetragrammaton, the unutterable name of God vulgarly transliterated "Jehovah," holds a special place of importance as the *fons et origo* of these coordinate processes.[208] The continuum of creation, an ongoing activity which fills both conceptual and perceptible worlds, is then regarded as a proliferation of this sacred word, a verbal incarnation of this otherwise indescribable divinity. Particular terms for the Cabalist, as for the Hermetist, represent what is knowable of a divine wisdom, and etymologizing is a revered methodology for learned inquiry. Johann Reuchlin's *De verbo mirifico,* first published at Basle in 1494, was an ingenious and persuasive example of this technique, demonstrating how "the miracle-working word" is the name "Jesus" derived by permutation from the tetragrammaton.[209]

As a more pedestrian theory of language, the Cabalist saw words as equivalents to the things they identified in accordance with the Hebraic-Christian belief that Adam named his fellow creatures. It was assumed that letters of the alphabet, being the basic constituents of the verbal system, correspond to the basic

constituents of created nature. In consequence, as Agrippa concludes, the system of Hebrew letters comprises the basis for the
order of nature:

> There are therefore two and twenty letters, which are the foun-
> dation of the world, and of creatures that are, and are named in
> it, and every saying, and every creature are of them, and by their
> revolutions receive their Name, Being, and Vertue.[210]

According to Agrippa, and the multitude who followed his doctrine, verbal order is a precondition for order in the world of actualities. The word is endowed with this ability to effect and control. Language is an instrument for converting will into action.

In the Renaissance, then, there were several distinguishable
theories of language, though in the hands of the humanists they
tended to coalesce in syncretistic fashion. What they all have in
common is an allegiance to a dualistic cosmology, comprising a
realm of conceptual entities and a corresponding region of experiential actualities, and words mediate between these two mutually exclusive orders of existence, binding them together. As
Dante had early explained according to his orthodoxy, "Human
beings, for the communicating of their thoughts among each other,
required some sign which was both rational and sensible."[211] All
these theories of language assume an anterior system of knowledge which may be expressed by means of words because there is
a predetermined and inviolable relationship between names and
what they signify. Words enjoy a privileged status in the universal
scheme. They lead an amphibious life, equally at home in the
world of thought and in the world of things.[212]

In this survey of Renaissance theories of language we have not
so far taken into account the attitudes and practices stemming
from Aristotle and Cicero, what may broadly be called the rhetorical tradition. We have concentrated upon the philosophical and
theological aspects of language rather than its practical application. For the moment, linguistic *praxis,* especially rhetoric, lies
beside our point, since Aristotle and Cicero and their followers
were concerned primarily with the effect of words upon an audience, the end product of language, rather than with the basis of
meaning in language, its theoretical origin. Cicero, for example, is

content merely to note that the orator employs words of various sorts: "The words we employ then are either the proper and definite designations of things, which were almost born at the same time as the things themselves; or terms used metaphorically and placed in a connexion not really belonging to them; or new coinages invented by ourselves" (De oratore 3.37). Blithely ignoring the Cratylus, Cicero accepts each of these three sorts of words as equally valid. The question of how language means, though, had been a serious issue in philosophical inquiry since the time of Plato. It came to renewed prominence in the theology of Augustine[213] and in the writings of Isidore, who dealt with natura rerum as a system of etymologies, and it was revived with vigor by the Renaissance humanists.

The result was a lively interest in language and a deep respect for its powers of instruction.[214] Neoplatonist, Protestant, Hermetist, Cabalist—all bent words to their purpose and used them in much the same way. What Cicero did contribute was a general agreement that speech is an adjunct of reason, confirming the biblical view that speech, the ability to make reason known, is God's greatest gift to humankind. In Cicero's formulation, taking advantage of the verbal play that Latin allows, oratio is next to ratio.[215] Words render efficacious the activity of the intellect; as Sidney says, "The end of speech . . . [is] for the uttering sweetly and properly the conceits of the mind" (Defence 119.23–24). A word bridges the discontinuity between the world perceived with the senses and the world knowable to the intellect alone, permitting easy intercourse between the two.

Mornay, a Protestant apologist of particular attractiveness to the Sidney circle, explains the mechanism whereby language connects human utterance to the immaterial concepts of the mind. Like the devoutly religious man he was, Mornay begins by recognizing the sacred tradition of calling Christ the λόγος, and he continues by placing this practice in the philosophical tradition:

> When we call him Speech or Word, it is according to the doctrine of the Philosophers, who have marked that there is in man a dubble Speech; the one in the mynd, which they call the inward Speech, which wee conceyve afore we utter it; and the other the sounding image thereof, which is uttered by our mouth and is

> termed the Speech of the Voyce; eyther of both the which we
> perceyve at every word that wee intend to pronounce. (3: 267)

Here the amphibious nature of language is clearly delineated.
The uttered word is designated a "sounding image" of the fore-
conceit in the mind of the speaker; it renders palpable the immaterial idea. Rather as Socrates had described language in the *Cratylus,* the word is a metaphor which by a process of imitation
translates meaning from one level of existence to another.

Relying upon a psychology which is basically empiricist, Mornay then suggests how the mind arrives at its ideas: "The witte or
understanding doth by and by conceyve an inwarde Speech uppon the thing which is offered unto it, and begetteth or breedeth
that conceyt in our mynde as it were by a suddein flash of Light-
ning." The mind receives aural data which it processes for use in
thought by formulating its impression in words, "and afterward
our mynd uttereth it more at leysure by the voyce." Mornay admits the inadequacy of language to image forth the mind completely or accurately—"the which voyce (notwithstanding) is unable to represent or expresse the inward Speech perfectly."
Nonetheless, the value of language in human affairs is not to be
disparaged, since it offers man a God-given means of bringing his
inner thoughts to life. Echoing Cicero, Mornay proclaims:

> Now, the speech of the mynd is very Reason it self: and looke
> what the speech of the mynd reasoneth and debateth, that doth
> the voyce utter, and eyther of them is the image of the next that
> went afore. For looke what proportion is betweene the voyce or
> Speech of the mouth, and the Speech of the mynd; the like pro-
> portion is betweene the Speech of the mynd, and the Speech of
> the understanding.

Mornay sees language as a series of images, a series of metaphors
linking various levels upon which the human mind operates. It
leads from the physical level of uttered speech (the "Speech of the
mouth"), to the internal realm of immaterial thought ("the speech
of the mynd [which] is very Reason"), and eventually into the innermost reaches of the psyche ("the Speech of the understanding").

According to Mornay, then, the act of reasoning is largely a process of verbalization. As Agrippa says about a word, "It self being sensible, doth make it self and all things sensible, as light maketh it self and all things visible."[216] Language is illumination, the condition of human knowledge. It allows humanity to rise above the brutish beasts.[217] In the great chain of being, mankind inhabits the nexus between the region filled by the lower orders of physical nature and that presided over by the lord of hosts, between the material and the spiritual. Language gives us the means of relating one to the other, of annealing the breach in our own constitution. Language provides a vehicle of communication not only between one human and another, but also between body and soul.

So for humanists language endows poetry with a distinctive quality: the capacity to operate equally in both the concrete and the conceptual realms. It possesses fruitful ambiguity. Mimetic discourse originates with an object of imitation which has itself both physical and metaphysical status, and produces an artifact which similarly acts on both levels coordinately and at the expense of neither. The poem is at once material and conceptual.

In the Renaissance even the apologists for painting conceded this advantage to poetry. Lodovico Dolce, for example, that man of polite letters at the center of sixteenth-century Venice, published in 1557 a dialogue on painting which he entitled *Aretino*, in honor of an outspoken contemporary. When asked to define "what exactly painting is," Aretino impatiently rejoins that "the answer is easy and understood by everyone," implying a consensus. But he proceeds to a fuller response with characteristic forthrightness:

> To put it briefly, then, I say that painting is nothing other than the imitation of nature; and the closer to nature a man comes in his works, the more perfect a master he is. This definition is, however, somewhat narrow and defective, in that it fails to distinguish the painter from the poet—the point being that the poet too goes to trouble over imitation. I add, then, that the painter is concerned to imitate, by dint of lines and colors (whether it be on a flat surface of panel, wall or canvas), everything that presents itself to the eye; while the poet, through the medium of words, characteristically imitates not only what presents itself to the eye, but also what presents itself to the intellect. (97)

Echoing Alberti and Leonardo, Aretino declares that painting is simply the *imitatio naturae*. But he goes further and distinguishes painting from poetry, which also imitates nature. Painting, Aretino says, reproduces only what the eye perceives; but poetry, in contrast, has available as well the conceptions of the intellect. By extension, Aretino implies that painting employs a medium which presents itself to the eye alone; but poetry, through the medium of language, can in addition make an appeal to the mind. For this reason, the art event in poetry has the potential to be the most nearly complete of all the arts, and the most satisfying for the percipient.[218]

In consequence, those with a literary bias, harking back to Cicero and Augustine, dubbed literature the *prima inter pares* among the arts. Because of the capaciousness of language and its ability to express our perceptions from the most sensuous to the near-divine, poetry encompasses all activity and develops to the fullest the possibilities for human knowledge. Poetry is a culmination, a summation. As Sidney concludes, poetry is "void of no gift that ought to be in the noble name of learning" (120.31–32). It assimilates that overarching knowledge which Aristotle called ἀρχιτεκτονική; it achieves that irresistible suasiveness that Cicero ascribed to *eloquentia*. As Symonds characterized the Renaissance in the epigraph that introduces this chapter, the humanists displayed a new fascination with language because it is "the storehouse of all human experience." In consequence, "Poetry soars highest, flies widest, and is most at home in the region of the spirit."

4
Critics on Imitation

> Howe greatly are we beholden unto the great and famous writers,
> who being conversant many hundred yeeres before us here upon
> the earth, in their divine wittes, and most godly ordinances, doo
> yet lyve, dwel, and talke with us.[1]

Although Sidney wrote *The defence of poesie* when he was
scarcely past his mid-twenties, his display of learning is remarkable. He had, of course, the best of educations: private tutors,
school at Shrewsbury, university at Oxford, and a Continental tour
of long duration that placed him in touch with many eminent
scholars.[2] Under such propitious circumstances, Sidney indulged
a natural inclination toward learning; and while he rarely sounds
pedantic, it is clear that he read a great deal. He was familiar with
the classics, philosophers and poets alike, and was au fait with
literature and the other arts on the Continent. At a court populated by men and women of extraordinary intellect, he stood out
as a young man who had begun to realize his early promise. His
writings show him to be conversant with the best authors, and he
was now prepared to contribute to that conversation.

In this chapter we shall look at those several authorities mentioned by Sidney who had themselves dealt with the question of
imitation in the arts. It will be instructive to note the various
choices that major critics known to Sidney had made among the
possible relationships between artificer, object of imitation, artifact, and percipient. By going through these earlier theorists in

methodical sequence, we can discern a cumulative history—the sort of sweeping perspective surveyed by Sidney himself. It leads inexorably to the next chapter, since Sidney had in mind these authors when he wrote the *Defence*. They constitute the intertextual matrix for his own discourse. Equally important, we shall see how a theory of art as imitation can be—and has been—adapted to suit a number of quite different programs. Even mutually exclusive poetics have been put forward, all in the name of *mimesis*.

Or rather, most usually, in the name of Aristotle. When Sidney says that "Poesy . . . is an art of imitation," he cites Aristotle, the most eminent of authorities. In the annals of literary theory, Aristotle reigns supreme, and his name is inextricably linked with *mimesis*. But even before Aristotle, Plato had used this term to define the artistic process. Since in an immediate way Aristotle was responding to Plato, we shall do well to begin with him.

Plato presents something of a problem to the historian of philosophy because several of the dialogues bear upon art theory and not all of them are readily compatible.[3] Plato seems to be of two minds, and perhaps to speak with two tongues. In the *Republic* Plato castigates the arts, especially poetry, and in the end expels most poets from the commonwealth, much to the embarrassment of apologists for poetry. But in the *Ion* and the *Phaedrus* Plato allies poetry with inspired utterance and raises the poet to a special status approaching divinity, a topos endlessly repeated by supporters of the poetic art. Sidney was aware of these contrary opinions to be gleaned from the Platonic corpus, and he felt the need to refute Plato's charges against poetry. As Sidney insists, poetry was "not banished, but honored by Plato" (*Defence* 109.3). Plato's blame or praise of the arts, however, is not our focal concern, although that does demonstrate how the critic measures the artifact against a greater reality. More relevant to our inquiry is the relationship he posits between artificer and object of imitation, resulting in an artifact and eventual effect upon the percipient.

To analyze the Platonic dialogues in terms of our model in chapter 2, we should begin with the *Timaeus*. This late dialogue claims particular authority in any discussion of Plato's theory of art because it offers a cosmogony in which a divine artificer frames our universe by an artistic process. The relationship therein posited between artificer, object of imitation, and artifact is, in fact, fundamental to any systematic study of Plato's thought, and especially to the concept of mimesis delineated in Book 10 of the *Republic* and to the concept of poetic inspiration proposed in the *Phaedrus* and the *Ion*. The *Timaeus* provides the necessary coordinates for a reconstruction of Plato's larger concerns with ontology and epistemology. Therefore we turn to the *Timaeus,* a dialogue that until our own scientific era has always been preeminent in the canon, and the only Platonic dialogue that was even known during the long centuries of the medieval period.

The *Timaeus* was one of Plato's last writings, but in point of narrative time it is a continuation of the lengthy discussion about the just commonwealth contained in the *Republic*. Socrates and some few of his friends—most important of whom is Timaeus of Locris, an astronomer of Pythagoras's school—direct their attention to the creation and constitution of our universe, to φύσις, the traditional topos since Empedocles of *de natura rerum*. After a few preliminary pleasantries and Solon's account of the myth of Atlantis, which Sidney mentions early in the *Defence* (75.8–11), the dialogue is given over completely to Timaeus, who offers a carefully detailed and precise cosmogony.[4]

Timaeus begins by reiterating the doctrine known commonly as Plato's theory of ideas (27D). He notes that things in the physical realm undergo continual alteration. They are always changing into something else, and never arrive at a fixed identity. They are always *becoming*. Our immediate environment is a world of becoming, of perpetual change, without visible permanence. The fixed identity of the items in this world, therefore, must reside at some level beyond our sense perception of them. To provide a continuing identity for a changing object—for example, for a deciduous tree proceeding through its seasonal cycle (budding, leafing, bearing fruit, shedding its leaves)—there must be a permanent *being* (or "essence" <L. *esse*) at some level beyond the realm where its alterations occur. To continue the example, at some place in the scheme of things there must be an unalterable idea of treeness to provide an ontological *situs* for every individual tree we perceive, and that idea is any tree's essence, its true being. Each essence is conceived as an immaterial form ("form" = Gr. ἰδέα[5]) divorced from matter, though of course these "ideas" may be imposed upon

matter to produce the material shapes that appear in our physical environment, such as a tree. To emphasize the difference between a physical object and the idea that literally informs it, Timaeus recalls Plato's dichotomy between a world of *becoming* and a world of *being*, between the mutable world that we inhabit and the immutable world of the essences.

The world of being is the ontological *situs* also of such nonphysical concepts as justice, wisdom, and beauty. They too constitute ideas, and they too may be imposed upon matter so that they are reflected in the phenomena of the physical world of becoming. An object or event is beautiful, for example, when it embodies the idea of beauty.[6] It is more or less beautiful to the extent that it approximates the ideal form of absolute beauty. But more of this in a moment.

In the dialogue, Timaeus next glances at the epistemology implied by his scheme and acknowledges that the world of becoming is perceived by exercise of our senses, while the world of being may be known only by exercise of the mind. The former is "sensible"; the latter, "intelligible." Furthermore, study of the world of being alone permits absolute knowledge, because only its constituents have permanent, and therefore identifiable, existence. Consequently, study of the world of being can lead to valid *belief,* while study of the world of becoming can lead at best to uncertain *opinion.* All of this from the *Timaeus* is fundamental in Plato's thought and can be confirmed by many other passages of his writings.

Timaeus's cosmogony proceeds by noting that everything which comes into existence must of necessity result from some cause (28A). Our universe has not always existed; but rather it must have come into existence, since it has sense-perceptible qualities and nothing which is material is permanent. Therefore our universe must have had a beginning; and it must have had a cause, as well as a beginning. This cause is nominated by a highly significant epithet: "the Maker and Father of this All" (ὁ ποιητὴς καὶ πάτεϱ . . . τοῦ παντός, 28C). The creating deity, then, is a "poet"; and as later centuries extended the trope, the poem which he produces is the book of nature. Timaeus acknowledges the difficulty, even impossibility, of revealing this ultimate *causa sine qua non* to mortals, and consequently turns his attention to the paradigm (what we would call the object of imitation) that the divine "architect" followed in his creation.

The creating deity used as his object of imitation the ideas in the world of being, because he wanted our universe to approximate perfection. In effect, he combined the ideal forms with preexistent matter, thereby insuring a relationship between the world of becoming and the world of being. The physical objects in the world of becoming are material replicas of the ideal forms, metaphors which reify ideas. But since matter has inherent limitations (its becomingness), they are necessarily imperfect replicas. The Timaean deity is beneficent—"the Cosmos is the fairest of all that has come into existence, and He the best of all the Causes" (29A)—but he is not omnipotent (29E–30B). He cannot fully mend the imperfections of matter. Flaws in the system result from the deficiencies of its material components, whence the origin of evil.

In the course of this discussion, Timaeus makes a point of primary importance for art theory. He ascribes the perfection of the cosmos to the fact that the creating deity used ideal forms as a paradigm, and he generalizes so that the point is applicable to any creative act:

> When the artificer [ὁ δημιουργός] of any object, in forming its shape and quality, keeps his gaze fixed on that which is uniform [i.e., an essence], using a model of this kind, that object, executed in this way, must of necessity be beautiful; but whenever he gazes at that which has come into existence and uses a created model [i.e., a physical item], the object thus executed is not beautiful. (28A–B)

In this theory, an essence from the realm of ideas emerges into palpability through the material of the artifact. Conversely, the beauty of the artifact derives from its embodiment of the correspondent ideal form. As Socrates concludes in the *Philebus,* "The qualities of measure and proportion invariably constitute beauty and excellence" (64E). So the artifact literally incorporates these ethereal qualities, and its beauty results from the glimpse it allows into the world of being, the source of measure and proportion. Comprehension of such an artifact will lead to absolute knowledge because it leads to recognition of the original ideas. In contrast, however, comprehension of an artifact that copies an item from the world of becoming cannot lead to knowledge, because what it reproduces (and therefore its ontological *situs*) has no orderly arrangement or even fixed identity.

When the deity fashioned our universe, the principal form he utilized was the tetrad arrangement of the basic qualities (hot, cold, moist, dry) derived from the Pythagorean tetraktys. Proceeding in a mathematical manner and implementing proportion, from these basic qualities the demiurge produced the four elements: fire, air, water, earth (31B–32C).[7] By proliferating this tetrad of two pairs of reconciled opposites, he continued to produce the other systems of physical creation, such as the bodily humours, the seasons, and the cardinal winds. In consequence, the tetrad inheres in every constituent system of creation; it is a persistent pattern projected through innumerable physical manifestations. It is what a structuralist would call a "model": a diagram of the relationships between the parts of a system divorced from the particular subject matter in which the system manifests itself.

Two other propositions in the *Timaeus* are particularly germane to art theory. In order to correlate the world of becoming with the world of being, and thereby to imbue it with beauty and truth and goodness, the creating deity took two momentous steps: he instituted a world soul, and he established the orderly movement of the heavenly bodies known as "time." Because of these beneficent acts, our universe is rendered predictable, and perhaps to a large degree understandable.

Before creating the world's body, the demiurge created for the world a soul (ψυχή), an immaterial form to act as liaison between the ideal and the physical. Like the tetrad, the world soul is primarily a mathematical concept which, when extended, insures a prevalent mathematical order. In its creation, the demiurge proceeded in one direction to expand 2, the basic even number, and in another direction to expand 3, the basic odd number. By geometric progression he expanded each of these numbers to its cube, the limit of physical extension (2, 4, 8; and 3, 9, 27), producing a form similar to the Greek letter Λ (34C–36A).[8] This lambda is the form of the world soul which animates the world's body, although it is not visible as a structure or shape would be.

After the world's body was informed by the world soul, as a final act the deity instituted "time" to insure that our universe resembles as nearly as possible what it copies, the idea of cosmos. This paradigm, of course, is perfect and eternal, and the created world could not be endowed with these qualities because of its materiality. However, the demiurge aimed to make our world "a movable image of Eternity" (37D); and to this end, he placed the heavenly bodies in orderly motion to mark the passage of time. The sun and moon and planets go in perfect cycles and measure the units of time, such as days and months and years (39C). Since these units are endlessly repeated as the heavenly bodies roll in their courses, they extrapolate to eternity. Time as this sort of movement and duration, however, did not begin until that instant when the demiurge gave physical extension to what was previously only an idea in his mind, so the timely and the timeless are firmly distinguished.

Recognition of the dualistic cosmology set forth in the *Timaeus* is requisite to an understanding of what Plato says about art in the other dialogues, especially his discussion of mimesis. The most intensive analysis of art as imitation occurs in the *Republic,* so we shall profitably turn our attention to it. The arts are treated with great respect in this description of the ideal commonwealth, and two long passages in particular suggest the relevance that Plato assigns poetry in human affairs.

A considerable portion of Books 2 and 3 of the *Republic* is concerned with how those who are to rule in the city formulate their values. Late in Book 2 Socrates and Glaucon reach agreement on the most desirable traits in a ruler: "The love of wisdom, then, and high spirit and quickness and strength will be combined for us in the nature of him who is to be a good and true guardian of the state" (376C). The ensuing discussion becomes an overview of the principles that should prevail in the education of those who will be wardens of the commonwealth, the philosopher kings.

The discussion opens with the recognition that education was currently aimed at training both body and mind, with "gymnastics for the body, and for the soul, music" (376E). Furthermore, training in music begins earlier for the child than training in gymnastics, and the telling of tales comes under the category of music (as usual in Plato, what we call "poetry" is a sort of μουσική). One of the earliest influences upon the child, therefore, is fiction. To prevent the child from forming adverse opinions contrary to those we wish him to hold as an adult, Socrates urges that we institute "a censorship over our story-makers, and what they do well we must pass and what not, reject" (377B–C).

Socrates's censure of the poets, however, is not based on moral grounds alone (i.e., that they mislead the youth of the city), but on aesthetic grounds as well: "When anyone images badly in his speech the true nature of gods and heroes, [he is] like a painter whose portraits bear no resemblance to his models" (377E). Just as we decry the painter who distorts his material, so should we reprove the poet who is not faithful to his object of imitation. Socrates is concerned that the deity be represented in poetry only in accordance with his true nature—that is, as perfect. In consequence, Socrates lays down two principles which poets must honor: (1) to remove the possibility that what is evil in the world may be imputed to the deity, he is made less than omnipotent, although responsible for what is good ("God is not the cause of all things, but only of the good," 380C); and (2) since the perfect cannot alter itself except for the worse, and since the deity would not conceivably demean himself by such alteration, then he neither changes shape as poets relate nor stoops to other sorts of deception ("God is altogether simple and true in deed and word, and neither changes himself nor deceives others by visions or words or the sending of signs in waking or in dreams," 382E). If a poet breaks either of these rules, he will be denied performance in the theater and blacklisted for use in the classroom.

Book 3 opens with confidence that the preceding discussion has shown how poetry must be censored if the youth "are to honour the gods and their fathers and mothers, and not to hold their friendship with one another in light esteem" (386A)—that is, for socialization of the younger generation to be possible. The next question is how to insure the inculcation of bravery. Since bravery is undercut by a fear of death, the act of dying must be depicted as glorious and existence in the underworld as pleasurable. Not only must heroes be shown to be above sorrow, but also above uncontrolled laughter (388E); and the gods too must not be depicted as overpowered by mirth. Since the future rulers need "the virtue of self-control," poetry should induce the young "to be obedient to their rulers and themselves to be rulers over the bodily appetites and pleasures of food, drink, and the rest" (389D–E). Poetry, in short, should recite the admirable deeds of gods and heroes as models of conduct for the young. The gods must be shown better than men, rather than made in man's wavering image. Finally, when depicting the circumstances of ordinary men, poets must not show an unjust man who is happy or a just man who is wretched, because such a practice militates against a prevalent sense of justice (392A–C).[9]

To this point, Plato has been concerned mainly with the teleology of poetry—with the effect it has upon its audience, which is considerable. Plato always sees poetry and the other arts in a sociopolitical context. But now he leaves the subject matter of poetry and considers its technique.

Socrates makes an important distinction between two modes of narration: poets "proceed either by pure narration or by a narrative that is effected through imitation [μίμησις], or by both" (392D). In practice, this means that (1) the poet relates the narrative in his own voice, or (2) he employs the theatrical technique of having characters speak their own lines, or (3) he uses both modes alternately. As an example of each of these possibilities, Socrates cites (1) the dithyramb (i.e., lyric poetry), where the poet speaks in his own voice; (2) tragedy and comedy, where characters speak on stage to the exclusion of the poet; and (3) the epic, where the poet's narration often gives way to direct discourse among the characters. According to this definition of mimesis, only when a poet speaks through his characters does he effect his narration through imitation (393C). Plato proposes a theory of poetry as imitation, but restricts it to the theater or to direct discourse in a story. Narration without direct discourse, as in lyric poetry and in the descriptive passages of epic, is not mimetic. For Plato here, mimetic means representational, and human beings in action are the only acknowledged objects of imitation.

In the subsequent passage, Socrates sets out to disparage the poet who imitates in this fashion, or at least to circumscribe his license. First, he notes that someone who does one thing only is better at it than someone who does many different things; therefore the poet, who imitates many different actions, does nothing very well. Next, he notes that by imitating an action, the imitator gains a familiarity with the action that leaves him conditioned by it. Consequently, he concludes, the poet should imitate only good actions lest he (and his audience) be adversely affected by the imitation. The consensus among Socrates and his two interlocutors is unanimous that the theater (as well as those portions of epic transmitted as direct discourse) is pernicious unless it presents only admirable deeds. Similarly for songs and melodies, the other sorts of μουσική in addition to tales, only good actions may be presented, as well as musical modes and rhythms that are conducive to goodness (398C–400E). So also the other arts—such as painting, weaving, architecture, furniture-making—all must be censored (401B–D). When practiced in this fashion, the arts will lead to the most desirable of ends: restoration of the psyche so that it participates in that cosmic harmony which is right love (403A).

The other long passage in the *Republic* dealing with the relevance of poetry in human affairs occupies most of the last book. In the preceding book, Plato concludes the description of the just commonwealth, "The city whose home is in the ideal" (592A–B), and Book 10 begins by returning to the practical consideration of art in such a society. Socrates says again that "imitative" poetry should not be allowed because "that kind of art seems to be a corruption of the mind of all listeners who do not possess as an antidote a knowledge of its real nature" (595B). When Glaucon asks for an explanation, Socrates replies by posing a question: "Could you tell me in general what imitation [μίμησις] is?" (595C). A lengthy discussion ensues which attempts to answer this question.

Socrates begins by reaffirming the dichotomy between the world of being, consisting in ideas, and the world of becoming, consisting in the physical objects of the phenomenal world. If a craftsman wishes to produce an artifact—for example, a chair or a table—he fashions the item after the form of its essence, which he bears in his mind. The essence is antecedent to the item as the object of imitation is antecedent to the artifact. Anyone who makes a palpable image of something else is an artisan of this sort, and each of us is capable of reproducing in one way or another the full range of physical items in nature. Glaucon himself, for example, most readily by using a mirror, could reproduce images of everything that is visible: the heavenly bodies, earthly creatures, and so forth.

Glaucon interrupts, saying that he could reproduce the *appearance* of these items, but not their actuality, not their essence and truth (596E). Socrates seizes the point, and notes that the painter too makes an image comparable to that seen in the mirror, in the sense that the painting is an appearance only and not the imitated object itself. Following this aperçu, the crux of the ensuing discussion becomes the ambiguity of the image and its validity. Is an image a responsible representation of the object it projects, or is it a deceptive apparition?

In the *Sophist* Plato elaborates the possibility that an image might be illusory. There he intends to discredit the sophists, who misled the youth of Athens by professing to teach things which do not submit to easy instruction. They achieve their chicanery by producing images which deceive the percipient—paintings, which may be seen only at a distance and therefore not very clearly, and poetry, "by virtue of which it is possible to bewitch the young through their ears with words while they are still standing at a distance from the realities of truth" (234C). The sophistical faculty which generates the phantasms that deceive is designated the φανταστική in contradistinction to the faculty which produces images of true likeness, designated the εἰκαστική (235Bff.).[10]

To return to the *Republic,* Socrates now relentlessly pursues an answer to the question about the validity of an image. He specifies three levels at which anything may be said to exist: first, there is the idea of the thing, immaterial though absolute, residing in the world of being; second, there is the perceptible object, incorporating the ideal form but residing in the transient world of becoming; and third, there is the work of art copied from the physical object, itself a physical item though of an order different from the object that it copies. Taking a chair as his example, Socrates demonstrates the three levels at which a chair may be said to have existence: first, as the idea of chair, coexistent with the deity and unchanging, but to the mind of man intelligible only, not sensible; second, as a physical chair in imitation of the ideal chair, produced by a carpenter and existing in the phenomenal world, and therefore apparent to human sense; and third, as a depiction of a chair in imitation of the carpenter's chair, produced by a painter and existing in some way in the phenomenal world, but participating in a different sort of existence than that enjoyed by the carpenter's chair. In addition to the world of being and the world of becoming, Socrates recognizes a world of art. And there is a hierarchical relationship between essence, physical object, and artifact.

In this hierarchy, level two is a metaphor for level one, produced mimetically; and similarly, level three is an imitation of level two. The painter's chair is an imitation of an imitation. Therefore, Socrates concludes with crushing finality, "The mimetic art is far removed from truth" (598B). For this reason, painting "can reproduce everything, because it touches or lays hold of only a small part of the object and that a phantom." So we must remember that an artificer's imitation is several removes from true existence, and we must not be deceived by it. When viewing art, recognition of how it transforms truth is the antidote we must apply lest we be misled. Socrates expresses an admiration for Homer, going back to boyhood; but even Homer, the greatest of poets, is no more than a creator of phantoms with no record of practical public service. The poet, Socrates insists, "knowing nothing but how to imitate, lays on with words and phrases the colours of the several arts in such fashion that others equally ignorant, who see things only through words, will deem his words most excellent, whether he speak in rhythm, metre and harmony about cobbling or generalship or anything whatever" (601A). But the poet is a deceiver, so beware.

Furthermore, poetry and painting stimulate the inferior elements of the soul because they imitate things in the phenomenal world, which have no fixed identity and therefore no absolute truth. The additional metamorphosis of a physical object wrought by art removes it completely from the realm of rational knowledge and leaves it open to comprehension only by means of the emotions. In the world of art, reason gives over to passion. This is the basis of the old quarrel between philosophy and poetry (607B).[11] The arts, in fine, tend to destroy the rational faculty, while they stimulate those very emotions that ought to be decried and discouraged. Therefore, Socrates and Glaucon agree, "We can admit no poetry into our city save only hymns to the gods and the praises of good men" (607A). At the end of this condemnation of poetry, Socrates acknowledges its power, expresses regret that poetry has been excluded from their ideal community, and leaves open the possibility that poets may yet be admitted if they or their advocates can show that poetry "is not only delightful but beneficial to orderly government and all the life of man" (607D). The assessment of poetry, however, remains negative.

We are disappointed by Socrates's disparagement of poetry and alarmed by the recommendation for censorship. But to ban art which demeans the gods and heroes is not mere prudery or excessive zeal to exercise authority. Socrates is a philosophical optimist, believing that the creating deity is benevolent and that the universe is beautiful, at least in its form. Perfection resides at the first level of existence with the ideas, and extends into the second level of existence, where these ideas are interfused with matter. Therefore art, which holds the mirror up to nature, must reflect this perfection, even though at two removes from it. An art which does not discover this perfection contravenes the principle of mimesis and consequently is bad on artistic grounds. In a wholesome world presided over by a benign deity, art to represent its paradigms must be likewise ideal. To do otherwise is not so much to be immoral as to be inadequate as imitation (377E).

At first glance, poetry seems to fare better in the *Ion* than in the *Republic*. Following the consensus of Renaissance commentary,[12] Sidney observes that Plato "in his dialogue called *Ion,* giveth high and rightly divine commendation unto poetry" (*Defence* 108.31–32). A careful analysis, however, shows this not to be the case.

The *Ion* explores at a practical level certain issues that Book 10 of the *Republic* deals with more explicitly; and in his exchange with the rhapsode named Ion, Socrates leads us to a shattering conclusion. Since the poet is an imitator describing things of the phenomenal world, and since things of the phenomenal world are but projections of ideas in the essential world of being, the artificer who writes a poem about a chair, for example, operates even farther from the truth than does the artisan who has manufactured the chair. Furthermore, someone who performs a work of art, such as a rhapsode reciting a poem, is yet one step farther from the world of essences, and therefore knows even less of truth than does the artificer.

Ion is such a rhapsode, one of the most successful, whom Socrates meets and engages in conversation. Though Ion specializes in reciting Homer, Socrates quickly shows that he should have equal competence in reciting other poets who deal with the same subject matter. And since Homer dealt with most subject matters, Ion should be competent to recite the other poets too, even though they are inferior to Homer—just as the same critic is able to judge both the good and the bad in any art. But, Ion asks, why is he more interested in Homer than the other poets, who actually bore him? To this Socrates replies that Ion's ability to perform Homer comes neither from art nor from knowledge (532C). Rather, Ion's talent is "a divine power, which moves you like that in the stone which Euripides named a magnet" (533D). Then comes Socrates's famous image of poetry likened to a chain of iron rings suspended from a magnet. Just as the magnet "attracts iron rings, . . . [and] imparts to them a power whereby they in turn are able to do the very same thing as the stone, and attract other rings" (533D–E), so poetry is a chain of influences. A Muse is the source of power, and she inspires the poet, who passes on the influence to the rhapsode, who in turn transmits it to his audience. The poet, then, is dependent upon a Muse for his power, and composes only when under her ministration; and the rhapsode sequentially operates under the power of his poet.

Soon after comes the oft-repeated image of the poet as a bee, flitting hither and yon to gather material for his poem: "The songs they bring us are the sweets they cull from honey-dropping founts in certain gardens and glades of the Muses—like the bees" (534A–B). But immediately there is reassurance that although the poet is raving and like a flitting bee, what he says is valid:

> What they [poets] tell is true. For a poet is a light and winged and sacred thing, and is unable ever to indite until he has been inspired and put out of his senses, and his mind is no longer in him. (534B)

As in the *Apology* (22B–C) and in the *Phaedrus* (244A–245A), the poet and the prophet are seen as madmen rapt by divine inspiration, and therefore as fortunate beneficiaries of a special dispensation.

This is the portion of the *Ion* most frequently remembered, and taken out of context it extolls the poet. It makes him a privileged, even holy, creature, with direct access to truth. In context, however, the passage denigrates the poet. As a price for having access to truth, the poet must forego consciousness, because "every man, whilst he retains possession of that [his reason], is powerless to indite a verse or chant an oracle" (534B). The poet who submits to being rapt beyond his senses loses control of his personal identity and consequently of his poetic faculty.

Socrates's ulterior purpose, in fact, is to demonstrate that poetry is not an art: "not by art do they [poets] utter these things, but by divine influence; since, if they had fully learnt by art to speak on one kind of theme, they would know how to speak on all" (534C). The poet, actually, is little more than a mindless vassal of the deity, an amanuensis recording and transmitting the divine will. Socrates classifies poets with "soothsayers and godly seers." Their distinction lies not in any native talent or learned skill or practical knowledge of our world, but only in having been chosen by the deity as an instrument of expression.

Socrates then suggests, and Ion concurs, that a rhapsode during his performance is similarly out of his senses, inspired by the poet. In turn, the audience are rapt out of their senses, inspired by the rhapsode. So the image of the magnet and iron rings is demonstrated in practice (535C–536D). There are, of course, many chains of influence, which result in different sorts of poetry:

> One poet is suspended from one Muse, another from another. . . . And from these first rings—the poets—are suspended various others [the rhapsodes], which are thus inspired, some by Orpheus and others by Musaeus; but the majority are possessed and held by Homer. (536B)

Ion is one of these; and that is why he falls asleep when other poets are performed, but responds vigorously to Homer. Because, Socrates repeats, "Your skill in praising Homer comes not by art, but by divine dispensation" (536C).

Socrates continues to reveal the hollowness of Ion's performing skills by mounting the predictable argument that a rhapsode is but an interpreter of a poet, who in turn is but an interpreter of the phenomenal world, and therefore a rhapsode is but an interpreter of an interpreter, considerably removed from the source of truth. Furthermore, the rhapsode is not able to practice the arts (such as the *ars medica* or the *ars militaris*) about which he sings; so his learning is book learning, useless and suspect, as opposed to practical experience. Ion, though knowing the *Iliad* by heart, is not adept in the art of warfare; to the contrary, there is an unbreachable difference between reciting the exploits of a general and leading an army on the battlefield. So Socrates gives Ion a choice: to be a performer who deceives his audience by pretending to possess knowledge that he does not have, or to be one of the passive rings in the chain of poetic influence, sharing through Homer the power of a Muse but knowing nothing himself. In concise terms, Ion is faced with a choice of appearing "dishonest or divine" (542A). Being foolishly willing to forego any claim to creativity, Ion says, "It is far nobler to be called divine." So Socrates, disparagingly, bestows this epithet upon him (and, by implication, upon the other rhapsodes and the poets): "Then you may count on this nobler title in our minds, Ion, of being a divine and not an artistic praiser of Homer" (542B).

Poetry as Socrates degrades it in the *Ion* can hardly be said to fit the definition of mimetic art. Either the poet is rapt by divine inspiration so that he is a patient rather than an agent, or at best, as in the image of the magnet and iron rings, an innocent transmitter. Or the poet is a fraud who pretends to know what he doesn't know, and his poem is questionably related to the phenomenal world and even less closely related to the world of being. The *Ion,* on balance, severely constrains the poetic art. Neither is poetry the repository of dependable knowledge nor does it result from human skill.

In the *Symposium,* however, poetry has a broader meaning. In fact, Plato uses ποίησις as a generic term for any creative act that calls something into existence. The passage is incidental and its implication for the theory of mimesis is not developed; but still, it may have bearing upon Landino's and/or Sidney's conception of poesy and the poet. It is Diotima speaking to Socrates who makes the comment: "Of anything whatever that passes from not being into being the whole cause is composing or poetry [ποίησις]; so that the productions of all arts are kinds of poetry, and their craftsmen are all poets [ποιηταί]" (205B–C). Even though all creative activity may rightly be called poetry in its literal sense derived from ποιεῖν, reminiscent of the *Timaeus* and predictive of Aristotle, Diotima goes on to limit the term to its more accustomed meaning:

> A single section disparted from the whole of poetry—merely the business of music [μουσική] and metres [μέτρα]—is entitled with the name of the whole. This and no more is called poetry; those only who possess this branch of the art are poets.

So once again poets are designated as those who transpose from one level of existence to another, from not being into being, and they work presumably by mimesis. Finally, they are distinguished by the measured medium in which they work, by music and meter—not, significantly, by language as a semantic system.

One of Plato's most laudatory statements about poetry occurs casually in the *Phaedrus*. In this pleasant dialogue, Plato's excursion into pastoralism, Socrates explains why we should admire and perhaps envy the lover, even when he appears to act foolishly, as though he had lost his senses. Madness is not ugly, Socrates argues, but rather a "divine gift." The prophet, the poet, the sinner undergoing expiation through suffering, as well as the lover, are all mad by divine dispensation, and in this state are allowed to glimpse the heaven of celestial forms, absolute beauty and truth and goodness.[13] Socrates has this in particular to say about the *furor poeticus*:

> A third kind of possession and madness comes from the Muses. This takes hold upon a gentle and pure soul, arouses it and inspires it to songs and other poetry, and thus by adorning countless deeds of the ancients educates later generations. But he who without the divine madness comes to the doors of the Muses, confident that he will be a good poet by art, meets with no success, and the poetry of the sane man vanishes into nothingness before that of the inspired madman. (245A)

The *Phaedrus* associates the poet with the lover, the seer, and the anguished sinner, and not only excuses their irrational behavior but actually assigns it a benevolent cause and a beneficent effect.

In this theory, neither skill nor reason is adequate for poetry; the divinely induced fit is a necessary condition for poetic creation.

Plato's most incisive analysis of mimesis, the topic of greatest interest to Aristotle and Sidney, occurs in the last book of the *Republic,* so now we must pursue some of its ramifications. To begin with what this theory of imitation is not, in the words of R. G. Collingwood, Plato does not commit "the blunder of regarding the work of art as a reduplication of perceptible objects, whose value, so far as it has a value, is therefore the same in kind as the value of the objects which it reduplicates."[14] The artifact is not an exact replica of some physical object of imitation at the same level of existence in the phenomenal world, nor is it an imitation in the neoclassical sense of being a creditable reproduction of some acceptable artistic model. Rather, the act of imitation involves a transposition from one level of existence to another. When a carpenter makes a chair incorporating the idea of chair, he is imitating in this sense. He translates an idea across the line that marks off the world of becoming from the world of being, and embodies that formal essence in a physical object. This translation across the discontinuity between two levels of existence is a "metaphor" in the literal sense, although the carpenter is but an "artisan."

Similarly, in this system when an "artist" imitates a physical object in a work of art, he likewise effects a metaphor. He transposes from one level of existence to another, crossing the discontinuity between the world of becoming and the world of art. Art is permanent because it transcends the phenomenal world that we inhabit. It escapes the ravages of ravenous time. This was the strong point of Shelley's defence of poetry: it "makes immortal all that is best and most beautiful in the world; it arrests the vanishing apparitions which haunt the interlunations of life" (32). Although this theory bestows a certain status upon art because of that release from mutability, at the same time it weakens art's claim to value because it removes art an additional step from the site of essential truth. Mimesis results in an appearance only.

But while this theory has the negative implication that art is twice removed from truth and therefore less valid than the phenomenal world, there is also a saving grace that rescues art from total depravity. We have differentiated three levels of existence: (1) the world of being, (2) the world of becoming, (3) the world of art. When turned around and considered from level three through level two to level one, mimesis does imply an arguable epistemology. Each of these three levels of existence for the artifact, though distinct, is nonetheless related to the others. During its descent in this hierarchy, the essence has undergone a change in its mode of existence when it translates to a physical object, but nonetheless the essence has been a major determinant of that physical object by literally informing it. Analogously, the physical object has been a determinant in the work of art which imitates it; it has served as an original for the representation. We can safely say, therefore, that each level is an approximation, however inexact, of the level above it—what Socrates calls a "phantom" of its original. To use the terminology of Langer, the work of art is a symbolic transformation of something that is itself a symbol of an idea (page 44). Consequently, in level three there is at least a glimmer of level one—so that, if we wish to think positively about art, the artifact does provide a glimmer of a glimpse of truth. An imitation, although it is only an appearance in the sense of false seeming, is also an image with some degree of authenticity. As Socrates observes in Book 2 of the *Republic*, "We begin by telling children fables (μῦθοι), and the fable is, taken as a whole, false, but there is truth in it" (377A). So an artifact, even if an imitation of an imitation, is not devoid of value, although we may have difficulty reversing the process of its creation and reconstituting the essence that was its origin.

Nonetheless, it is this difficulty, this uncertainty, which leads Socrates to conclude that poetry is trivial. An idea is twice metaphorized during its translation into art, and thereby removed from the laws that govern sense perception (i.e., the world of becoming) as well as the laws that govern rational thought (i.e., the world of being). Since it is neither percept of a real object nor concept of an idea, the artifact is reduced to being emotion. This conclusion explains the strong appeal of poetry, while it points to the danger poetry holds for the inexperienced and unapprised. Art leads to an acquaintance with something neither actual nor rational. To refute this position was the primary aim of Aristotle in the *Poetics*, and after him of Sidney.

In several scattered passages Plato compares poetry and painting as though they were related arts,[15] without taking any notice that they operate through different media. Moreover—and this is a principle overlooked by many historians of art theory—Plato consistently classifies poetry as a sort of music. Any number of passages operate on this assumption,[16] and none to my knowledge presumes to the contrary. Plato thought of poetry as μουσική, primarily a vocal tradition performed by rhapsodes, whereas we are more likely to think of it as printed texts. As a result, for Plato poetry is first of all a metrical system composed of rhythms (audible proportions), rather than a semantic system of verbal signs.

To conclude with Plato's theories that bear upon art, we should note that he persists in a cosmology which recognizes the transient world of becoming as an embodiment of ideas that reside in an immutable world of being. Along with this cosmology, without exception, is an ontology which lodges truth and value with the ideas, intelligible rather than sensible. Within the framework of this strict ontology, however, Plato in diverse dialogues proposes several different theories of poetry. In the poetics derived from the *Timaeus* the poet is a busy agent who uses the ideal forms as objects of imitation and bodies them forth in his artifact, so he repeats at a lower level the divine act of creation. His making is analogous to the demiurge's creative activity, and his poem is analogous to our extended universe, the book of nature. In strong contrast, the artist in the *Republic,* though still a self-prompted imitator, must select objects of imitation only from the phenomenal world. He imitates in the sense of re-presenting something physical as accurately as his medium (and his skill) will permit. In yet other dialogues, in the *Ion* and the *Phaedrus,* the poet loses the ability to initiate and direct the creative act; he becomes passive, dependent upon inspiration from above. But the poet does regain access to the essential ideas, so his poems, like those of the Timaean maker, express eternal verities—usually, far beyond his own awareness.

So Plato wanders in his thinking on art. Where he remains most nearly constant is in his view of the audience. Throughout the dialogues, Plato's concern with the percipient is wholly teleological—that is, he considers only the effect an artifact will have upon the percipient. Though deeply and directly affected by the artifact, the percipient is most likely unable to assess its validity or worth. Certainly, he doesn't contribute to its meaning, or even interpretation. The art event is directed at him; but his role, as explicitly defined in the *Republic* and the *Ion,* is the naive recipient.

In the *Poetics* Aristotle responds to Plato's views on art, particularly those expressed in the *Republic*. Aristotle was a member of the Academy as student and teacher for nearly twenty years, and many scholars date the *Poetics* early in Aristotle's career, in large part before the death of Plato.[17] It is no surprise, then, that Aristotle's arguments should be formulated in terms which Plato had introduced. Aristotle dealt with the problems of art theory that Plato had shown to be problematical, especially those attendant upon *mimesis,* and in pretty much the same vocabulary. Of course, Aristotle adapted Plato's propositions, often in such radical ways as to take them out of Plato's mouth.[18] But much of the confusion that surrounds the *Poetics* results from a failure (or a refusal) to recollect its Academic context.

The confusion is compounded by the indeterminacy of what it is that poetry is supposed to imitate. At the opening of his second chapter, Aristotle casually mentions that poets should imitate "men in action" (1448a1), an object of imitation that seems to be left intentionally broad, even vague, in order to encompass all human experience. By the time the discussion has narrowed to drama, however, even this has been transformed to a much more tenuous statement: "Tragedy is an imitation not of men as such but of an action, a career, a man's happiness" (1450a16–17). Not only the how of mimesis is left enigmatic, but also its what. In consequence, despite the great deal that Aristotle eventually says about the concept, exactly what it implies has been a perennial bone of scholarly contention. The term has been variously interpreted to accord with almost any poetics. Confirmed by a passage in the *Physics*, where Aristotle posits that "art imitates Nature" (194a22), mimesis has been called upon as license for a theory that art is the verisimilar depiction of physical detail, holding a distortionless mirror up to visible nature.[19] Contrariwise, however, Aristotle has been summoned to support a theory that art is the ideal representation of a beauty that exists nowhere except in art, *la belle nature.*[20]

Aristotle begins the *Poetics* in a businesslike way by announcing his subject matter and the direction his investigation will take.

His subject is "the poetic art," a term that appears in the opening phrase of the treatise and has become its title, περὶ ποιητικῆς. This term infolds several assumptions. First, poetry is a kind of "making" in general, since ποιητική comes from the verb ποιεῖν. It applies to more than literary artifacts—indeed, it covers such diverse arts as choreography and composing for musical instruments, as well as mundane skills such as manufacturing chairs. Second, the term is used as a verbal with an active force, so that ποιητική is a process comprising phases. Sometimes Plato's term ποίησις is used (e.g., as early as 1447a10), and even more strongly it suggests the act of producing rather than the finished product, which is the ποίημα. Third, the discussion will be speculative, treating the art of poetry in a holistic way as theory, rather than prescribing actual methods for composing a poem or criticizing individual works. Specific poets and poetic works may be cited, but largely for purposes of illustrating a theoretical argument rather than demonstrating an artistic technique or interpreting a particular poem.

Of prime significance, the art of making is characterized at once by its dependence upon imitation (1447a13–16),[21] and there can be little doubt that Aristotle plans to continue Plato's discussion of mimesis, while extending and altering it. Following Plato, Aristotle classifies composition for the flute and lyre in a category with the epic, tragedy and comedy, and the lyric as sorts of poetic imitation. Μίμησις, like ποίησις, has a strong verblike component, and is more literally translated as "imitating" rather than "imitation." Mimesis is what the poet does when composing a poem. So more accurately we should speak of poems as "imitatings" in the crescive sense, instead of "imitations," which is retrospective of what has already taken place. A poem, at the very least, has both a past and present tense—past with respect to the artificer and its composition, but present with respect to the percipient and its current comprehension.

With Aristotle mimesis becomes the quiddity of poetry. Precisely how imitation is accomplished, however, receives no immediate clarification, and emerges only gradually as the discussion develops. Scattered comments about imitation occur throughout the treatise, usually incidental to other topics; but actually the concept is never pointedly defined. The thrust of the treatise moves rapidly from a pronouncement extolling mimesis, which makes the artifact dependent upon some external object of imitation, to a consideration of the elements of tragedy and their internal relationships within the individual poem—that is, from a mimetic theory to a formalistic one. At an early stage Aristotle pronounces the formalist's creed: "In everything that is beautiful, whether it be a living creature or any organism composed of parts, these parts must not only be orderly arranged but must also have a certain magnitude of their own; for beauty consists in magnitude and ordered arrangement" (1450b8–9).

Nonetheless, brushing past these obscurities, Aristotle quickly establishes his subject matter by characterizing it as a sort of mimesis, and then with equal briskness indicates his method. He will deal with "the poetic art as a whole," he says, but he will proceed by defining the several species of ποιητική and by identifying the several components that enter into the poetic process. The method will be orderly and analytical. To discriminate between the various species of poetry, Aristotle lists three criteria by which distinctions may be made. The various sorts of imitation, he explains, employ different media, different objects of imitation, and different modes of imitation.

Beginning with the first of these *differentiae,* Aristotle scrupulously classifies the several sorts of imitation that he has mentioned. They achieve mimesis, he notes, through three media: rhythm (ῥυθμός), speech (λόγος), and melody (ἁρμονία). All use rhythm; but some use speech without melody, some use melody without speech, while some use both melody and speech. The art of the flute and the lyre, for example, uses only rhythm and melody, without speech. In contrast, there is a sort of art in either prose or verse, such as the epic, which uses only rhythm and speech, without melody. Aristotle here identifies a literary art which is independent of melody, and thereby clarifies the difference, indistinct in Plato, between poetry and music, which heretofore as μουσική had included poetry.[22] In passing, Aristotle also laments that there is no common term to cover all the imitative arts that depend upon language without melody (what we have just called "poetry"). More importantly, he comments that *poets* deserve that name because they have the ability to produce an imitation, not because they compose in verse. Therefore someone, such as Empedocles, who casts a scientific work in verse is not ipso facto a poet, since he can lay claim to the title by virtue of metrics alone. Poethood is achieved not by choice of subject matter or by use of verse, but only by exercise of mimesis (cf. esp. 1451a36–b5). This is a crucial point, because it identifies the poet specifically as a *maker* in the special sense of imitating. Sidney will concur.

The second *differentia* between the species of making, a distinction based upon the objects which serve as the ground for imitation, proves to be a blunt instrument. All the mimetic arts, we are told, "imitate men in action." The differentiation that results is a rather crude dialysis, deriving solely from the fact that some poets imitate men of high character, while others imitate men of low character. Indeed, the only effective discrimination between species that Aristotle accomplishes with this criterion is the separation of tragedy from comedy: "The latter tends naturally to imitate men worse, the former to imitate men better, than the average" (1448a18–19). All the mimetic arts, however, take men in action as the proper objects of imitation—though, perhaps, we should more rightly say "the actions of men," since what men do rather than who men are provides the substance of imitation. Plot takes precedence over character; perhaps, even, character is revealed only through action (1450a15–24), especially through moral choice (1450b7–10, 1454a16–20). For this reason, devising the plot becomes the most important phase of the poetic act as Aristotle delineates it.

Finally, the third *differentia* for discriminating between the species of making is based upon the method employed in representing the objects of imitation. Aristotle returns here to the passage in Book 3 of the *Republic* (392D–395B) where Plato distinguishes between imitation through authorial narrative and imitation through theatrical presentation of characters speaking as though independent of an immediate author. Even if their media remain the same as well as their objects of imitation, one poetic work may differ from another by employing the narrative mode, the dramatic mode, or a combination of the two. The Homeric epic is cited as an example of the combined form, but we must recall Plato to supply the lyric as an example of the authorial narrative, while comedy/tragedy is the obvious example of the dramatic mode. What is new here is Aristotle's implication that drama is superior to narrative because it more completely realizes the potential of mimesis. Since the quiddity of poetry is imitation, and since drama to a greater degree than narrative achieves an objective state of imitation, drama is more essentially poetic than narrative (cf. 1448b34–49a6). This judgment will weigh heavily in Aristotle's preference for tragedy over epic.

Rather disconcertingly, at this point Aristotle does not continue by identifying the several parts of the poetic art, as the opening sentence of the *Poetics* has led us to expect. Instead, he turns to a new topic: the origin of the art of poetry. This tactic, however, strengthens his insistence that a poet be known above all else by the ability to produce an imitation. Toward that end, he opens this discussion by noting that ποιητική derives from two "natural" causes—perhaps what we would call its psychological explanation. Aristotle observes that "imitation is a part of men's nature from childhood, and he differs from the other animals in the fact that he is especially mimetic and learns his first lessons through imitation" (1448b6–9). That is, the child learns to perform practical acts by watching how adults perform them. Moreover, since melody and rhythm, like the imitative impulse, are innate, "at the beginning those who were endowed in these respects . . . gave birth to poetry out of the improvisational performances" (1448b20–24). In short, the origins of poetry lie in the instinctive impulse to imitate, which is common to all humans, and in an extraordinary facility with melody and rhythm, which is granted to a talented few.

Incidental to this passage, Aristotle touches upon a matter frequently noted in the Renaissance and potentially of considerable importance. He explores the reason why an imitation calls forth a pleasurable response even though the object of imitation in its actuality may be abhorrent or fearsome. As examples of what he has in mind he mentions wild beasts and cadavers.[23] Aristotle concludes that percipients derive pleasure from such an imitation "because in their viewing they find they are learning, inferring what class each object belongs to" (1448b16–17).[24] Implicit in this argument is an assumption, however sublimated, that art is imitation in terms of two of the three levels of existence that Socrates outlines in Book 10 of the *Republic* (pages 137–38). By the mimetic act, that which is abhorrent or fearsome is removed from the phenomenal world, where its unpleasantness is inescapable, and transported to the realm of art, where it is perceived within a different order of existence. As a result of the mimetic process, the object of imitation is refined, purified of what makes it repugnant in its natural state. Nevertheless (and here Aristotle parts company with Socrates), there is sufficient relationship between the artifact and its object of imitation to allow the percipient to infer knowledge about the object in its original, natural environment. Aristotle sees the artifact as an imitation that transforms the physical object, but as a relatively accurate image rather than a deceptive appearance. Therefore art is a valid vehicle of knowledge.

In addition, Aristotle hints at an aesthetic dimension to the artifact that calls forth a pleasurable response independent of the practical knowledge about the phenomenal world which the imitation may convey. "Because if the viewer happens not to have seen the object before," Aristotle suggests, he will still derive pleasure from its imitation: "The copy will not produce the pleasure *qua* copy, but by virtue of its workmanship or its finish or some other cause of that kind" (1448b17–19). Unfortunately, Aristotle does not pursue the point beyond this simple assertion. But the passage allows for the possibility that the art event be a largely aesthetic experience, simply pleasurable; while for Plato in the *Republic* the teleology of art, in contrast, must be the inducement of morals in the citizenry.

Having differentiated several species of the poetic art and having glanced at its origins in human nature, Aristotle turns to examine smaller and smaller divisions of the general subject. He confines his attention to the sort of ποιητική expressed through the verbal medium, and further restricts his scope to one sort of this poetry, that which imitates by the mode of theatrical presentation. Preparatory to separating tragedy from comedy, Aristotle again notes that the dramatic poet when selecting an object of imitation has a choice between the actions of noble men and the actions of worthless men. In passing, he observes that Homer was a dramatic (as well as narrative) poet of incomparable skill who excelled in depicting both sorts of actions, thereby providing the prototypes for both comedy and tragedy.

Soon, however, Aristotle has narrowed his focus to the genre of tragedy alone (1449b21–22). Because, for him, this is the most fully developed of the poetic genres, he chooses it as the example to be dealt with in detail. Aristotle assumes, though, that the other poetic genres—epic, comedy, lyric—share the same qualities with tragedy except in those specific ways that he indicates. The differentiation between epic and tragedy seems to be intact within the existing text of the *Poetics* (1449b9–20, 1455b16–23, 1459a17–62b15). The differentiation between comedy and tragedy can be inferred, at least in its broad outline (1448b34–49a6, 1449a32–b9, 1451b12–15). At best, though, we can only speculate upon Aristotle's differentiation between lyric and tragedy.

The detailed analysis of tragedy is beside our central point, and therefore we need not linger over what Aristotle says about this circumscribed portion of ποιητική. Because today the *Poetics* is probably best known for its influence upon the concept of tragedy, its pronouncements specific to that topic are the most familiar section of the treatise. In consequence, to recall the terrain, it will suffice merely to indicate a few notorious peaks: the basic definition of tragedy ("an imitation of an action which is serious, complete, and has bulk, in speech . . . ," 1449b24–28), the enumeration of six "parts" in tragedy ("plot and characters, speech-composition and thought, visual appearance and song-composition," 1450a10–11), the analysis of plot with a list of its qualities and parts (1450a15–b3, 1450b21–54a15, 1455b24–56b10), the characterization of the tragic hero (1453a7–22), the proposition of catharsis (1449b27–28, 1452a38–b3, 1453b1–14), and the argument that tragedy is superior to epic and the other literary genres (1461b26–62b15). This theoretical study of tragedy is intensive, yet complete.

More germane to our purpose will be a digest of those comments about mimesis which Aristotle tosses off incidental to his discussion of tragedy. There are a considerable number of such comments; and although they glance but obliquely at the mimetic process, when taken in toto they provide a remarkably coherent view of it. First let's consider imitation as the poet must deal with it in the act of composition, and then we shall look at it from the point of view of the audience.

Underlying the entire discussion are two principles established early in the *Poetics:* imitation is the sine qua non of poetry, and the actions of men comprise the appropriate object of imitation. What draws special attention, though, is construction of the plot (μῦϑος). "Since it is the plot which is the imitation of the action" (1450a4–5), as Aristotle observes, the plot assumes primary importance. It is the essence of the poetic process, the integrated summation of the media, object, and mode of the imitating. Aristotle defines the term simply and concisely: plot is "the arrangement of the events" (1450a5); and shortly thereafter, "the structure of the events" (1450a15).

But the events to be described in poetry are not actual occurrences observed by the poet, not eyewitness accounts faithfully recorded. As Aristotle says deliberately, "The poet's job is not to tell what has happened but the kind of things that *can* happen, i.e., the kind of events that are possible according to probability or necessity" (1451a36–38). As Sidney closely echoes Aristotle, the "right poets . . . to imitate borrow nothing of what is, hath been, or shall be; but range, only reined with learned discretion, into the divine consideration of what may be and should be" (*Defence* 81.3–6). So the imitation should not reproduce deeds which have been performed as a matter of fact in our experiential world; instead, the poem should present what is likely to occur according to what Aristotle calls "probability or necessity."

Here Aristotle is bringing into play his theory of the universal, an entity somewhere between the absolute being of a Platonic idea and the transient existence of a physical phenomenon.[25] For Aristotle, a "universal" is a concept arrived at by a mental process, by abstracting the common qualities from a wide range of examples—by what the logician calls inductive reasoning, and what the empiricist of a later century would call the scientific method. As applied to poetry, the poet surveys the possibilities that might obtain in a given circumstance and decides what is most likely to occur. Although the resultant imitation does not present what has been—that is, the imitation is not a verisimilar replication of one particular action which has already taken place—it nonetheless grows out of human experience. It is the distillation of what has been observed to happen most naturally, a mental construct comprising the universal aspects of an action. It has the veracity of hypothesis based upon observed data. Through this theory of the universal, Aristotle relates the fictive world of the poem to the actual world of physical occurrence.

By the same token, however, since by definition the universal holds for general application, any particular instance that does not comply with it can be discounted and ruled out as anomalous. Such an instance is exceptional, and therefore irrelevant. On its way to becoming probable or necessary, the universal rules out the partial and accidental, so an imitation achieves an unimpeachable generality and acquires an authority, a truthfulness, that is greater than actuality itself. A poem describes a superreality—what should be, rather than what has occurred in any particular case; and consequently poetry is more philosophical and serious than history (1451b6–8). Sidney carefully repeats this argument in the *Defence* (87.34–88.9).

It is especially pertinent to note that Aristotle recurrently insists upon the primacy of plot in poetry.[26] In the opening sentence of the *Poetics,* when he first announces his subject matter, he states that his treatise will deal with ποιητική and with "how the plots should be constructed if the poetic process is to be artistically satisfactory." Plot provides "the foundation or as it were the soul of the tragic art" (1450a38), and presumably the μῦθος[27] plays a similar part in the production of other species of poetry. Epic, too, for example, imitates a unified action, although its plot is episodic rather than tightly integrated (1455b16–23, 1459a17–21, 1459b17–29, 1462b10–12). Plot is anterior to poem, then, just as soul is anterior to (and semi-independent of) body, an analogy that Renaissance theorists never tired of drawing (page 515 [n. 8]).

Aristotle returns to this point and gives quite practical advice to the poet about the proper phases of composition: "The argument of the play, whether one is taking it 'ready-made' [i.e., already in the culture] or is composing it himself, should be first drafted in general terms, then expanded with episodes" (1455a34–b2). Aristotle draws a clear distinction between the plot and the episodes which express it. As quoted earlier, plot is the "arrangement" or the "structure" of events, not the events themselves. It is a plan which is later realized in full dimension, a diagram which interrelates the sequence of palpable scenes. For this reason, the plot must be artfully crafted, strictly unified. The poet cannot represent all the events from a period of time or all the deeds of the hero; rather, the poet must select and arrange carefully in order to achieve a unity of action. Each episode in the drama must contribute to a single whole, must submit to positioning on the frame of cause-and-effect (1451a16–35, 1455b13–14), which is the plot itself.

Being the "soul" of the poem, plot eludes concreteness. It is an immaterial form, a universal condition, which receives a local habitation in the images projected by the poet. Plot is the mediator between "spectacle" and "thought," the dominant that holds in union these two as well as the other three elements of tragedy. To use Sidney's terms, it is the "*idea* or fore-conceit" of a work (*Defence* 79.7–8).

Further support for the conceptual dimension assigned here to plot can be marshalled from Aristotle's comments about characterization. While plot is first in the list of elements comprising a tragedy, character is second—but, surprisingly to us, a decidedly poor second. In a bit of overstatement to make his point, Aristotle declares: "A tragedy cannot exist without an action; it can without expressions of character" (1450a24–25). Characters serve only as agents of the plot, the counters that make it palpable. They are not unique individuals with a personality and inner life of their own, verifiable in history or by observation. Rather, their very existence depends upon the requirements of plot, and their nature is revealed solely by their participation in it.

Furthermore, "what poetic composition aims at," Aristotle says, is the presentation of a typical character, "what kinds of thing a certain kind of person will say or do in accordance with probability or necessity" (1551b9–10).[28] In consequence, he continues, although the poet necessarily resorts to characters for the purpose of materializing a theme, the poet does not think of them independent of plot; indeed, the poet gives his characters particular names only after the plot is completed (1551b11–12).[29] As Sidney observes, "The poet nameth Cyrus or Aeneas no other way than to show what men of their fames, fortunes, and estates should do" (*Defence* 103.26–28). Historical personages appear in such a fiction not as facts, but as types. Since a character receives the individuation of a name only after the plot is completed, the name of a character is likely to reveal his or her type: for example, Basilius and Gynecia, or Una and Duessa. The name of the character indicates that character's contribution to the schema that we have called "plot."

In the actual composition of a poem, as Aristotle intimates

(1453b25–26, 1455a34–b1), there are two possibilities that should be resolved: (1) the poet begins with a concept (such as "patience"), which he imagines forth in episodes that by their sequence unfold his theme; or (2) from the matter of an existing story (such as the tale of Griselda), the poet induces a universal, abstracts a significance, selecting and arranging the episodes to provide a meaningful plot.[30] Each possibility is viable and can be documented by examples from literary history. Book 1 of Spenser's *Faerie Queene,* for instance, exemplifies the first, while Shakespeare's *King Lear* exemplifies the second. The first possibility is primarily Platonic, locating the ultimate being of the poem in an anterior idea. The second is more characteristically Aristotelian, recognizing the existence of data, the need to identify and classify, and the semiotics of system. But the two are not mutually exclusive by some implacable contrariety, and the thrust of Aristotle's argument, drawing upon the practice of poets, allows for the second to subsume the first. The poet chooses a tale (either ready-made or of his own devising) which implies his meaning *in potentia,* and then he relates the tale by means of a plot deployed in episodes in such a way as to enhance the visibility of that meaning. Just as the Timaean godhead in the act of creation combines rational form with inchoate matter to achieve perceptible cosmos, so the poet arranges his narrative material to disclose its inherent significance. Idea and universal coalesce, like form and content.

Whatever else, it is clear that when Aristotle designates plot as the most important element in a poem, he is not thinking of mimesis as verisimilar re-presentation of a past action. Just the opposite. This is most evident when he draws a sharp distinction between the poet and the historian. History, Aristotle pointedly repeats, "tells what has happened," in contradistinction to poetry, which tells "the kind of things that can happen" (1451b5–6). The historian and the poet may describe the same events, the historian may even write in verse; but the sites of their respective truths are miles apart. In history, reality resides among the data of physical occurrence; in poetry, reality lies with the mental construct which a sensitive observer abstracts from his experience. This observation leads to a momentous conclusion, a triumphant affirmation of the poetic imagination that has formed the basis of most apologies for poetry ever since: "That is why the writing of poetry is a more philosophical activity, and one to be taken more seriously, than the writing of history; for poetry tells us rather the universals, history the particulars" (1451b6–9). At least in part, this is Aristotle's rebuttal of Plato, who had concluded that poetry is trivial or even deceptive. Aristotle restores value to the literary art.

Even the epic poet differs radically from the historian. The epic poet selects and organizes certain facts from a given period of time in order to produce a unified action (1462b10–13), while the historian is duty-bound to recount "all the events that happened during that time involving a single man or a number of men" (1459a23–24). Although writing about past events and ordering his materials in episodic sequence, the epic poet has no inviolable commitment to time and space. The events he describes defy the laws of physics as he generates the universal aspects of his hero, and he begins *in medias res* to indicate at the outset that chronology is not a constraint. Universals, of course, are timeless.

To summarize, the prescription that poetry must imitate universals deriving from the actions of men rules out any notion that poetry is restricted to imitation of a direct or narrow sort. The poet has a license (which should be interpreted as an imperative) to fashion after his own proclivities. He is not simply to reenact certain events, but rather to order events in a sequence that generates meaning. That sequence, that form, determined in large part by the poet, is the plot.

And yet, once the plot has been devised, the poet must then work it out by visualizing the actual episodes that comprise it. He chooses dramatic characters in a setting, a fictive time and place; and as Aristotle notes, "They carry on the imitation by their own action" (1449b31–32). The characters produce a continuous pageant, the "spectacle," to embody the plot of the poet and to provide conspicuous data for instruction of the audience.

Early in the *Poetics* Aristotle notes the similarity in this respect between poetry and the plastic arts: "In the same way that certain people also imitate many things by making images of them with colors and shapes . . . so in the case of the above-mentioned arts [i.e., the species of ποιητική] they all perform the imitation in rhythm, speech, and melody" (1447a18–23). Imitation, then, implies the production of images[31]—"imitation" and "image," in fact, share the same etymological root.[32] And the "imagination" is that mental faculty by which the poet produces images and by which the audience perceives them. Imitation, image, and imagination are all integral aspects of the same process, which is the essence of ποιητική. The first is the activity itself, the second is the product, and the third the human means by which the process is accomplished. If poetry is an art of *imitation,* its palpable expression is an *image* of the plot bodied forth by the *imagination* of the poet and in turn comprehended by the *imagination* of the audience.

So after constructing the plot, the poet must then reify it by turning his conceptual schema into material "things"—that is, the poet must produce images. He first conceives of the episodes in his own consciousness, employing what later came to be known as the mind's eye,[33] as an aid to expressing the plot in language. According to Aristotle's precise instruction, "One should construct one's plot and work it out with the dialogue while keeping it before one's eyes as much as possible—for in this way, seeing it most vividly, as if one were present at the actual events, one can invent suitable business and is least likely to overlook possible discrepancies" (1455a22–26). The poet uses language to record the cavalcade of fictive events which he occasions in his consciousness.

Although the imitating derives from a mental construct of the poet, the "universal" aspects of the action rather than an actual occurrence, it must nonetheless be lifelike. The image must accord with our experience of daily life. As Aristotle reasonably observes, "It is the character who rages or expresses dejection in the most natural way who stirs us to anger or dejection" (1455a32–33). Indeed, the poet must be careful to exclude anything that undermines the naturalism of the presentation, such as exits or entrances that contradict the imagined geography of the play. It is easy for the poet to nod, so Aristotle warns about "offenses against the sense-perceptions that necessarily attend on the poetic art" (1454b15–16). Since poetry deals in imagined rather than actual events, it is readily susceptible to violations of what is plausible. As noted in the last paragraph, the poet is "likely to overlook possible discrepancies," so he must be on guard lest a slip of his pen destroy the illusion of actuality.

At a performance, then, what exactly does an audience "hear" and the spectators "see"? Although the plot embodies universals presenting what might be rather than what is or has been, what the audience actually experiences are sense impressions of various sorts, mainly auditory and visual—that is, palpable images. The audience is asked to respond to a continuous series of speaking pictures. This response is immediate and to a clearly defined stimulus, so the art event begins with sense perception. Nonetheless, to discern the plot, to construe the imitation, to turn these sensory data into meaning must be the appropriate conclusion to such a presentation. The art event does not stop with the sentient, or even the emotional. Although Aristotle says little about the audience's reception of drama's images, presumably the human psyche possesses faculties that permit the percipient to comprehend the episodes as presented and in turn to reach an understanding of the poem. As we shall see, according to Aristotelian psychology the pivotal faculty in this mental operation is the imagination, which receives sense data from the common sense and processes it for use by the reason (pages 262–66). The transmission and interpretation of the artifact is a complex process, involving an uninterrupted movement from sensuous to rational.

Aristotle notes that spectacle and music render the drama sensuous and "make the pleasure all the more vivid." Nevertheless, the effectiveness of poetry is not entirely dependent upon a verisimilar performance: "This vividness can be felt whether it is read or acted" (1462a18–21). While reading a poem at home as opposed to attending the theater, we participate in a comparable process of transcribing images into meaning by use of the imagination. Although in one case the data are visible and audible from a stage, while in the other the data are linguistic from a page, the end result of both art events is similar: comprehension of the plot, understanding of the argument. Unquestionably, however, one mental experience is different in some way from the other. So with respect to the process of mimesis, how does reading a poem differ from watching a play?

Aristotle himself provides the appropriate terms of reference for dealing with this question. Seeing a play and reading a poem are two activities which may be differentiated by one of the criteria that he proposed as a means of analyzing ποιητική into its various species: for its *mode* of imitation, a play depends upon dramatic presentation, while the written poem depends upon authorial narrative. As its hallmark, the drama is the imitation of an action which is acted out in performance by the characters. Certainly, for the percipient there is a qualitative difference between what the bodily eye and ear witness upon a stage and what the mind's eye sees while reading a text. Although Aristotle for convenience tends to overlook this difference (cf. 1450b18–19, 1462a11–17), at least on one occasion he inadvertently acknowledges this complication. When stressing the desirability of astonishing an audience, he notes that "the epic has more room [than tragedy] for the irrational (which is the chief source of astonishment), by reason of the fact that we cannot actually see the person who is performing the action" (1460a12–14).[34] The assumption is that the epic poet can get away with more than the dramatist because a play takes place in full view of the audience, while the action of an epic transpires more obscurely in the mind's eye of the reader.

But for Aristotle tragedy has the edge over epic precisely because drama provides immediate sensory experience for the spectators and therefore more fully realizes the potential of mimesis to produce objective artifacts. As a species of imitation, in fact, drama verges toward painting. Its medium, of course, is language; but in performance the visible episodes of a play assimilate many of the properties of painting: its clarity, its forcefulness, its propensity for lifelike detail. Drama lies somewhere between the largely sensuous experience of looking at a painting and the largely mentalistic experience of reading a poem, while embracing both. Like the emblem, it is a composite work of art—both verbal and visual—although kinetic rather than static, a movable image of mortality rather than a still life.

When the verbal image of poetry is conjoined with the visual image of painting, as in drama, the resulting combination has a double potency. The visual and the verbal impinge upon the senses at one and the same time, acting coordinately, mutually enhancing one another. This is why drama has the edge over its siblings in the poetic family, although Aristotle never states it quite so baldly for fear of fueling the charges leveled against drama for being vulgar (see 1461b26–62a4). Aristotle devotes the closing pages of the *Poetics* to a *paragone* among the poetic arts, however, and when he argues for the superiority of tragedy over epic, his reasons come down essentially to this affinity of drama for painting. Tragedy wins the competition on two scores: it is the most vivid and the least discursive, both of which are painterly qualities.

For Aristotle, then, the imitation that identifies a poem as ποιη- τική has all the qualities of rational discourse, but also mimesis leans it toward verisimilar description. Imitation implies that pro- duction of an image will be its ultimate fruition.[35] If Ascham understood anything of the *Poetics,* it was this point:

> *Imitation,* is a facultie to expresse livelie and perfitelie that ex- ample: which ye go about to folow. And of it selfe, it is large and wide: for all the workes of nature, in a maner be examples for arte to folow. (*Scholemaster* 264)

On occasion (1460a5–11), mimesis is almost synonymous with dramatic performance. But even in poems intended to be read rather than seen on stage, imitation readily lends itself to the rhe- torical practice of *enargeia,* producing a sense impression for an audience as though the object were physically present. Poetry be- comes a speaking picture, an image with semantic content.

The voluminous writings of Cicero, the heir of Greek culture and the embodiment of what was taken to be most noble in Roman civilization, provided a well-stocked storehouse for the Renais- sance humanist seeking knowledge of a glorious past. From the time of Petrarch, Cicero held a prominent place among the most honored of ancient authors, and his writings were read and re- vered for the urbanity of their style as well as the weightiness of their subject matter. He was the scholar's mentor and the aristo- crat's man of letters. His *humanitas* gave humanism both its name and character. The Renaissance was a rebirth, before all else, of the Ciceronian ideal.

By profession Cicero was an orator, at first in the courts of law and then in politics, and he became the consummate rhetorician. He saw language primarily as an instrument for wreaking his will upon an audience. But on occasion Cicero rises above the imme- diate and the practical, and ponders the larger consequences of language. Like Plato in the *Republic,* he considers the lasting ef- fect of literature, and hence the relationship between literature and society. He is concerned at basis with "oratory," public address, and with "rhetoric," the art of persuasion; but he often seems to be talking about poetry when he uses the terms *ars dicendi* and *eloquentia*. Again like Plato, Cicero believes that the art of letters is a major factor in communal life, as well as in the life of the individual, and consequently is worthy of careful study—although unlike Plato, he does not recommend censorship by the authorities.

With Cicero's rhetoric, the percipient of the literary work is raised to a new eminence. He becomes the explicit *terminus ad quem* for the art event. Cicero announced that the aim of oratory is threefold: to prove, to please, and to sway (probare, delectare, flectere); and he delineated three corresponding styles: plain, middle, and high (*Orator* 21).[36] Quintilian, perhaps the favored rhetorician of the Renaissance, slightly reformed his predecessor. The orator, he claimed, must instruct, move, and please his listeners (doceat, moveat, delectet; 3.5.2, 8.proem.7). Nonetheless, Quintilian reinforced Cicero's pedagogic thrust, and Renaissance critics transferred this doctrine wholesale from oratory to poetry, often confusing it with Horace's dictum that poetry should teach and delight. Minturno, for example, completes the transfer without a bobble: "In his verses the poet should speak in such a way as to teach, delight, and move."[37] With equal confidence, Scaliger applies it to tragedy: "The play is presented not so much to amaze and terrify the spectators . . . as to teach, move, and delight them."[38] The art event in this rhetorical tradition is aimed at altering the mental state of the percipient.

In his earliest work, the *De inventione*, Cicero proclaims the thesis that the *ars dicendi* has brought humans from a wild state in nature to a comfortable community, and the theme of *humanitas* is introduced in a memorable passage that became a commonplace in Renaissance thought:[39]

> There was a time when men wandered at large in the fields like animals and lived on wild fare; they did nothing by the guidance of reason, but relied chiefly on physical strength; there was as yet no ordered system of religious worship nor of social duties; no one had seen legitimate marriage nor had anyone looked upon children whom he knew to be his own; nor had they learned the ad-

vantages of an equitable code of law. And so through their ignorance and error blind and unreasoning passion satisfied itself by
misuse of bodily strength. (1.2)

It was the proper use of language that permitted humanity to
emerge from this savage condition and establish those institutions—religion, marriage, parenthood—which allowed for development of the human potential. In the *De oratore,* a later and
mature work (indeed, his major textbook for rhetoric), Cicero returns to the praise of the language arts in much the same terms:

> What other power could have been strong enough either to gather
> scattered humanity into one place, or to lead it out of its brutish
> existence in the wilderness up to our present condition of civili-
> zation as men and as citizens, or, after the establishment of social
> communities, to give shape to laws, tribunals, and civic rights?
> (1.8)

Cicero saw the art of letters as the force allowing humanity to rise
above depravity, build cities, and satisfy aspirations for a rich
though ordered life. Culture is a product of language. As Sidney
says in a Ciceronian vein, "Poetry . . . hath been the first light-
giver to ignorance, and first nurse, whose milk by little and little
enabled them to feed afterwards of tougher knowledges" (*Defence*
74.8–12).

For Cicero, however, as for Plato, the auditor is not entitled to
an individual, unique response. His interpretation may not be
idiosyncratic. Rather, the purpose of the artful work is to induce
a common response in all the auditors, what is now known fash-
ionably as intersubjectivity, so the literary effort is an acculturating agent, binding the community together, establishing a norm
which demands compliance. This norm, nowhere more passion-
ately proclaimed than in his defence of Archias the poet,[40] was
called *humanitas* by Cicero. And its salient feature is language,
our ability to use words as a means of communicating thoughts.
For Cicero the highest development of this ability is *eloquentia*
itself.[41] Therefore literature, the produce of eloquence, becomes
the identifying feature of humanity, our central activity, our
preoccupation; and literary works, later to be called the *litterae
humaniores,* become the staples of education.

Sidney and his generation in England were on the forward edge of realizing the benefits of neoclassicism, and they still subscribed to the tenets of a Ciceronian poetic. Literature performs a social function, fashioning gentlemen and noble persons, as Spenser put it. Elizabethans took at face value the imperative of *humanitas,* and confirmed it by the special status which language bestows upon humanity in the scheme of things. Speech is next to reason, the distinctive human faculty; or, in the punning formulation which Latin allowed to Cicero, *oratio* is next to *ratio.*[42] It is the ability to speak, the capacity for rational conversation, that sets humankind apart from the other animals:

> What in hours of ease can be a pleasanter thing or one more characteristic of culture [humanitas], than discourse that is graceful and nowhere uninstructed? For the one point in which we have our very greatest advantage over the brute creation is that we hold converse one with another, and can reproduce our thought in word. (*De oratore* 1.8)[43]

Culture and reason and speech and literature coalesce into a single activity, and mastery of the *litterae humaniores* becomes our chief aim as members of society.

In a later paragraph of the *De oratore,* Cicero associates the poet directly with the orator:

> The truth is that the poet is a very near kinsman of the orator, rather more heavily fettered as regards rhythm, but with ampler freedom in his choice of words, while in the use of many sorts of ornament he is his ally and almost his counterpart. (1.16)[44]

To satisfy the grammarians, the poet may be constricted by the need to versify his utterance, but he has a mandate freer than that of the orator in matters of vocabulary; and both are alike in their dependence upon figures of speech. The greatest similarity between poet and orator, however, lies in the wide range of their interests and responsibilities: "In one respect at all events something like identity exists, since he sets no boundaries or limits to his claims, such as would prevent him from ranging whither he will with the same freedom and license as the other." With the world lying before him, the poet, like the orator, must be learned in all disciplines.[45] Here Cicero returns to the problem raised by Plato in the *Ion:* Must the poet have practical knowledge of what he writes about? Is there a separation between literature and life? Cicero, because of his commitment to rhetoric and his belief that the teleology of art is to induce certain behavior in its percipients, cannot permit such a separation.

In yet another excerpt from the *De oratore,* Cicero turns to what makes for the successful use of language. The master of the *ars dicendi* requires a certain native talent, of course, but mostly it is a matter of education. He must study appropriate models and practice the rules by performing exercises:

> Let this then be my first counsel, that we show the student whom to copy, and to copy in such a way as to strive with all possible care to attain the most excellent qualities of his model. Next let practice be added. (2.22)[46]

We can detect here, at least incipiently, a theory of imitation as the following of acceptable models, a theory that Horace also will propose, as we shall see. But this theory of imitation is quite different from any notion of *mimesis* that Plato or Aristotle discussed. It presupposes a neoclassical reverence for past masters and an aping of their style.

Before leaving Cicero, we should note his most practical instruction. Although his organization of the rhetorical exercise is not original, the Renaissance credited him with its division into five parts: *inventio, dispositio, elocutio, memoria,* and *pronuntiatio.* In his derivative treatise, *De inventione,* Cicero carefully defines each term as tradition had specified it:

> Invention is the discovery of valid or seemingly valid arguments to render one's cause plausible. Arrangement is the distribution of arguments thus discovered in the proper order. Expression is the fitting of the proper language to the invented matter. Memory is the firm mental grasp of matter and words. Delivery is the control of voice and body in a manner suitable to the dignity of the subject matter and the style. (1.7)[47]

This system, with some slight adjustment, can be accommodated to Timaean poetics, as Cicero invites: "Whatever ability I possess as an orator," he says, "comes not from the workshops of the rhetoricians, but from the spacious grounds of the Academy" (*Orator* 3).[48] In such a platonist reading of the rhetorical doctrine, *inventio* provides the idea which is then bodied forth by *dispositio* and *elocutio,* thereby making the idea palpable to others. At the very least, note that the concepts are anterior to, and therefore independent of, language, so the first two steps, *inventio* and *dispositio,* the discovery of and arrangement of the argument, necessarily come before *elocutio,* the framing of the argument in actual words. This processive composition, carefully laid out in steps, induces the separation between *res* and *verba* that comes to characterize the arid rhetoric taught in Elizabethan schools.

Little of what Cicero has to say derives directly from any theory of mimesis. Although he shows familiarity with Aristotle's *Rhetoric,* he was unmindful of the *Poetics.* Cicero simply did not think of art as imitation. For him, the primary, if not the only, art was that of rhetoric—the verbal expression of preconceived argument with the intention of swaying an audience. Cicero identifies literature, poetry along with oratory, as the willful act of an author who is not only conscious of using language, but craftily manipulating it to achieve some quite specific end. The orator/poet, if successful, remains in firm control of the art event. His objects of imitation are perhaps thoughts rather than Platonic ideas, mental constructs devised pragmatically by the distillation of topoi drawn from other authors or by the operation of logic upon observed phenomena. His artifact is a series of reasoned statements presented in well-chosen language—a torrent of words, now gushing, now murmuring, to be judged largely by its effects upon a patient audience, but saved from the speciousness of sophism by the wide-ranging education and social consciousness of the author. The *ars dicendi* is deployed as propaganda, but for a laudable purpose, for the implementation of those civilized and civilizing values summed up in *humanitas.*

During the Renaissance it was widely assumed that Horace had open before him Aristotle's *Poetics* when he composed his verse epistle known since Quintilian as the *Ars poetica.*[49] While this is unlikely, since there is no evidence that the *Poetics* was known directly during the Augustan age, Horace does seem to follow Aristotle's lead in many ways. He focuses upon drama, for instance, emphasizing the importance of the plot. But the temperaments of these two critics could hardly be at greater variance, and their treatises reflect the dissimilarity. While Aristotle is ruminative and theoretical, Horace is genial and practical. Moreover, not only is the *Ars poetica* noticeably more casual than the *Poetics,* but it also differs in orientation. As Weinberg succinctly notes: "The one is essentially concerned with the internal structure of poems as these become beautiful objects of contemplation, the other with the making of poems which will have a specific effect upon a given audience at a particular time" (1:56). By Sidney's day, nonetheless, Horace and much of Aristotle had melded to produce a single tradition with a strong rhetorical bias.[50] Cicero, standing in the background, provided an equally powerful third member of a triumvirate who presided over eloquence.

Horace wrote the *Ars poetica* at the end of his career, after many years as a practicing poet, and it bears the mark of long experience and common sense. Like Cicero, he keeps constantly in mind the question, How does the poet achieve his desired effect upon the audience? Although his main concern centers upon the relation between artificer and percipient, Horace does pay some fleeting attention to questions relating to imitation. He counsels the would-be poet, for example, "Either follow tradition or invent what is self-consistent" (119), suggesting the two possibilities in constructing a plot that Aristotle had identified (page 155). Again, he stresses the care with which the poet should select and arrange the materials for his plot and the need to achieve unity of action (146–52).

Horace is most strikingly reminiscent of Aristotle, however, when discussing the manner of presentation in poetry. He takes over the two modes of imitation posited by Aristotle (and, before him, by Plato): that is, narration and dramatization. "Either an event is acted on the stage," Horace says, "or the action is narrated" (179). Furthermore, in line with Aristotle, Horace gives preference to drama over narrative because it is more effective in moving an audience: "Less vividly is the mind stirred by what finds entrance through the ears than by what is brought before the trusty eyes, and what the spectator can see for himself" (179–82). As in the *Poetics,* vividness is a valuable quality, because Horace recognizes the distinction between images directed to the sense of sight and those presented to the mind's eye.

Nevertheless, nothing may jeopardize the propriety of the presentation. Decorum is constantly required. Therefore "what should be performed behind the scenes"—that is, whatever is shocking or inexplicable—must not be shown on stage; rather, "an actor's ready tongue will narrate [it] anon in our presence." The convention of the *nuntius,* carried over from Greek tragedy, preserves the credibility of the performance. By utilizing the mind's eye for matters such as Medea's murder of her children or Cadmus's transformation into a snake, decorum will be maintained. There is a qualitative difference between what the mind's eye perceives and what would be seen if the offensive action were rendered visible by dramatic reenactment. Otherwise, however, drama is superior to narrative because of its pictoriality, as with Aristotle.

But his confirmation of Aristotle aside, Horace is better known for practical pronouncements than theorizing, and when we talk about poetry, several commonplaces are most frequently referred to him. His style lends itself to the pithy phrase or memorable line—actually, during the Renaissance the *Ars poetica* was commonly reduced to a set of precepts or rules.[51] For example, the very title is a critical aphorism: the *ars poetica,* with the inescapable implication that poetic composition is a skill to be learned by practice (cf. 289–308, 379–90, 408–18). Native talent is essential, but not sufficient by itself. Horace, in fact, points to a dichotomy between innate genius and acquired proficiency, between *natura* and *ars:* "Often it is asked whether a praiseworthy poem be due to Nature or to art" (408–09). In poetic composition, of course, both are necessary. Excellence must be sought by cultivating nature's gifts as well as by learning the craft of poetry. The *ars poetica* is a demanding discipline, a serious career.

Even more familiar is the Horatian dictum that poets should both teach and delight, mixing the useful with the sweet. Because of his satires, Horace was seen during the Renaissance as a rather strict moralist;[52] and Sidney, like most critics of the time, echoes Horace's tags: *aut prodesse . . . aut delectare* (333–35), or *utile dulci* (343). This authority bolstered the claim that poetry is an edifying experience.

Equally ubiquitous after the mid-sixteenth century was the phrase *ut pictura poesis* (361). Invariably it was taken out of context and twisted to the particular bias of the critic using it. Eventually, supplemented by Plutarch's dictum that "poetry is a speaking picture," it became the slogan of those who wanted to ally poetry with painting, making them "sister arts" (pages 108–9). Because Horace was a critic of such long-recognized authority, his opinion in this matter carried especial weight.

Horace is often cited as authority for a sort of non-Aristotelian imitation—that is, the imitation of other writers whom the critics approve, the so-called "classics."[53] Horace assumed that the poet is well-read and sensitive to predecessors, so he did not belabor the point that the poetic art is a cumulative venture, a product of intertextuality. But a terse suggestion—such as, "Handle Greek models by night, handle them by day" (268–69)—readily rigidified into a commandment.

Following literary models is a salient feature of the neoclassical spirit, and this is what most English humanists before Sidney meant by "imitation."[54] The breach between art and nature was often obviated by urging this kind of imitation: the poet should follow nature; but since the early poets, especially Homer and Vergil, lived in a pristine age, nature is best discerned in their works, so following nature means following the classical authors. This argument was first fully formulated by Vida in his *Poeticarum libri III* (Rome, 1527),[55] and it still commanded a respectful hearing in the days of Alexander Pope. But imitation as the copying of literary models, of course, has little to do with Aristotle's *mimesis*. It may, in fact, relate poetry more closely to libraries than to the actions of men. More rightly it is seen as application of the rhetorician's advice to read and emulate the best of what has gone before.[56] Imitation of this sort provides the basis primarily for what the rhetoricians call "style," a concern that to Sidney seemed to divert poetry from its proper mimetic function. He was openly scornful of those who "keep Nizolian paper-books of their figures and phrases" (*Defence* 117.26–27).

Horace nowhere deals explicitly with *mimesis* in the Aristotelian sense of the term, although he does seem to expect some limited sort of mimetic activity. He says, for instance, "Fictions [ficta] meant to please should be close to the real, so that your play must not ask for belief in anything it chooses" (338–39). This statement implies that the artificer must consciously select his subject matter and his medium, and that the object of imitation inheres in the phenomenal world. Furthermore, the poem must be in some way lifelike.[57] At his most magisterial, Horace resorts to direct counsel: "I would advise one who has learned the imitative art to look to life and manners for a model, and draw from thence living words" (317–18). The proper study of mankind is man. But the precept offers no instruction about *how* life is to be imitated, and of course it is easier said than done. The *Ars poetica* begins with the famous description of the unacceptable painter who joins disparate elements to produce a composite creature that defies actuality—a human head on a horse's neck joined to the body of a bird with a fish's tail—and the poet who does the same is equally unacceptable. This opening passage, prominently placed, similarly supports a theory of imitation as some kind of accurate representation of visibilia. The poets generate images of a wide and fascinating variety, but they may not contravene what is natural.

Although Horace recognizes the Muse,[58] there is an unstated rejection of any theory that poetry is the product of divine inspiration, as the tradition stemming from Plato's *Ion* and *Phaedrus* would have it. Indeed, the sketch of the insane poet that ends the *Ars poetica* may well be a satire of such raving and fantasizing; certainly, the unshaved and unbathed Democritus who "shuts out from Helicon poets in their sober senses" (295–98) is a parody of the inspired versifier. For Horace, poetry results from a controlled and rational process. His program for success consists in careful assimilation of the best models, ceaseless effort to perfect the style of a poem, and heedful attention to criticism from friends with knowledge and sensibility. The Horatian poet is more a talented tinkerer than an ambitious maker of fictive worlds. Sidney's greatest debt to Horace derives from the moral force ascribed to his incidental comment that poetry should instruct as well as please.

As the golden noon of Rome shaded toward a barbarous twilight, a number of lively writers brightened the deepening gloom. One of the more luminous was Plutarch, an amiable polymath, garru-

lous yet thoughtful. He was very much a man of his world, having
studied in Athens and lectured in Rome, quite comfortable on the
academic side of natural philosophy and ethics. Eventually, he
returned to Chaeronea, his birthplace in Boeotia, where he busied
himself in public affairs and wrote most of the large corpus we
have from his hand.[59] He has never lost his appeal.

Plutarch was read widely in the Renaissance, holding a place in
the popularity poll approximately between Ovid and Seneca, and
somehow combining the raciness of one with the sententiousness
of the other. He was best known for his parallel lives of Greeks
and Romans, the favorite haunt of Elizabethan poets in search of
narrative detail; but also his extensive collection of essays, entitled
the *Moralia,* was greatly admired and frequently quoted. For the
humanists, especially, Plutarch served as a singular authority on a
variety of topics, from Plato's notion of the soul to the origin of
thunderstones, the historiography of Herodotus, and the Egyptian
mysteries of Isis and Osiris.

The most literate of authors, Plutarch is continuously aware of
his craft. As Sidney observes, "Who reads Plutarch's either history
or philosophy, shall find he trimmeth both their garments with
guards of poesy" (*Defence* 109.19–20). So reading his works provides constant insight into his views about literature, both from
his incidental comments and from his actual practice. One essay,
however, concentrates upon the literary questions that have concerned us, and therefore we shall focus our attention upon it. In
the *Moralia,* the essay bears the title Πῶς δεῖ τὸν νέον ποιη-
μάτων ἀκούειν, which Philemon Holland expansively translates,
"How a yoong man ought to heare poets, and how he may take
profit by reading poemes."[60] As the title suggests, this is a didactic
essay, obviously in reaction to Plato's strictures against poetry, especially the charge that poetry misleads the inexperienced. The
question to be faced is how the young should read poetry since it
describes scurrilous events, such as the sexual indiscretions of the
gods.

Plutarch begins by readily admitting that literature is a sensual
delight. And like eating and drinking it must be used with mod-
eration, for the good it can cause rather than the hedonism of
overindulgence. But even so, literature contains bad things, descriptions of people and events that cannot be approved, and consequently the young must be supervised in their reading.

As a safeguard against being misled, the youthful reader at the outset must accept as a maxim that poets tell lies.[61] A poem, intentionally or unintentionally, is fictitious. At the least, a poet colors the truth, diverting it from possible painfulness to what is pleasant. Furthermore, it is this artifice of fictioneering, more than any other poetical practice, which identifies the poet: "Not metre nor figure of speech nor loftiness of diction nor aptness of metaphor nor unity of composition has so much allurement and charm, as a clever interweaving of fabulous narrative" (16B). For Plutarch poetry is primarily *historia,* the telling of a story. Like Aristotle, Plutarch argues that the verses of Empedocles and other versified works in the didactic mode are not genuine poems even though they display meter and a lofty style. They are not poetry for the simple reason that they are not a story, a fiction: "We do not know of any poetic composition ($\pi o \acute{\iota} \eta \sigma \iota \varsigma$) without fable or falsehood" (16C). Poetry may indirectly convey a truth, but the poem ipso facto is false.

Actually, it is the very falseness of poetry, Plutarch maintains, that makes it effective:

> Just as in pictures, colour is more stimulating than line-drawing because it is life-like, and creates an illusion, so in poetry falsehood combined with plausibility is more striking, and gives more satisfaction, than the work which is elaborate in metre and diction, but devoid of myth and fiction. (16C)

It is their fictionality that makes poems satisfying and memorable; and the ability to deceive, to create illusion, allies the poet with the painter.

This observation sets up an extended comparison of painting and poetry as sister arts:

> We shall steady the young man still more if, at his first entrance into poetry, we give a general description of the poetic art ($\pi o \iota \eta$-$\tau \iota \varkappa \acute{\eta}$) as an imitative art ($\mu \iota \mu \eta \tau \iota \varkappa \grave{\eta} \ \tau \acute{\epsilon} \chi \nu \eta$) and faculty analogous to painting. And let him not merely be acquainted with the oft-repeated saying that "poetry is articulate painting, and painting is inarticulate poetry,"[62] but let us teach him in addition that when we see a lizard or an ape or the face of Thersites in a picture, we are pleased with it and admire it, not as a beautiful thing, but as a likeness. For by its essential nature the ugly cannot be-

come beautiful; but the imitation (μίμησις), be it concerned with what is base or with what is good, if only it attain to the likeness, is commended. (17F–18A)

Both painting and poetry depend upon mimesis and may deal with the same subject matter, submitting to the same critical analysis. Plutarch has in mind here the re-presentation of objectified nature for poetry as well as painting.[63] Both the painter and the poet draw from what is observable in nature—a lizard or an ape or the face of Thersites—and both are bound to reproduce the object of imitation in reasonable facsimile. A poem becomes a speaking picture.

Furthermore, the aesthetic evaluation of the artifact is based upon the accuracy of the reproduction instead of the appreciation of beauty it may induce in the percipient: "We are pleased with it and admire it, not as a beautiful thing, but as a likeness." Aesthetic pleasure derives not from the inherent goodness or evil of the subject matter, but rather from the professional competence of the artificer. In evaluating the imitation, then, Plutarch draws a sharp and crucial distinction between *what* is imitated and *how* it is imitated. We may disapprove of *what* is imitated, keeping peace with Plato, while at the same time we might very much admire *how* the artificer has gone about his mimetic project. Plutarch establishes a certain aestheticism, the grounds for admiring the artistry of a painting or a poem quite apart from its content (18B). Shortly, Plutarch repeats the point: "It is not the same thing at all to imitate something beautiful and something beautifully" (18D). Plutarch gets around Plato's charge that poetry debauches the young through its depiction of vice by saying that we may appreciate the artistry of the technique rather than accept the truth of the subject matter. "He who always remembers and keeps clearly in mind the sorcery of the poetic art," Plutarch assures us, "will not suffer any dire effects or even acquire any base beliefs" (16D–E).

In fact, the subject matter of the poem, even though salacious in and of itself, may be turned to a didactic purpose. It may be ironically perverted and used to inculcate morality by negative example, since what the poet recounts is not true in terms of the actual, phenomenal world. Poetry is not what *has* happened, but rather the poet makes up a fiction: "Philosophers, at any rate, for admonition and instruction, use examples taken from known facts; but the poets accomplish the same result by inventing actions of their own imagination, and by recounting mythical tales" (20B–C). The poet's fiction is what *might* happen—as Aristotle said, according to probability or necessity; and it is intended for instruction. As Sidney concurs, "A feigned example hath as much force to teach as a true example" (*Defence* 89.9–10).

According to the teleology of this poetics, reading poetry develops a judgmental faculty, an ability to distinguish between vice and virtue. In a passage which Sidney echoes, Plutarch next declares: "The imitation (μίμησις) that does not show an utter disregard of the truth brings out, along with the actions, indications of both vice and virtue commingled" (25C). And in his most Aristotelian moment, Plutarch continues: "Poetry (ποίησις) is an imitation (μίμησις) of character and lives, and of men who are not perfect or spotless or unassailable in all respects, but pervaded by emotions, false opinions, and sundry forms of ignorance, who yet through inborn goodness frequently change their ways for the better" (26A). In Plutarch's mimetic *historia,* the characters are a mixture of good and bad, like Aristotle's tragic hero with his flaw. Although with a sort of Platonic optimism Plutarch thinks that characters tend to improve their ways because of some inborn goodness, nevertheless in kinetic fashion, through their actions, they display wrong as well as right.

Plutarch gives several examples of how the reader may benefit from dissecting the motivation of a character, but the case of the virginal Nausicaa's attraction to Odysseus will suffice here. "If, on the one hand," Plutarch begins," Nausicaa, after merely looking at a strange man, Odysseus, and experiencing Calypso's emotions toward him, being, as she was, a wanton child and at the age for marriage, utters such foolish words as these to her maidservants"—and Plutarch quotes the line from Homer in which the Phaeacian princess expresses her desire for the naked man washed upon the shore—"then are her boldness and lack of restraint to be blamed" (27A–B). "But if, on the other hand," Plutarch adds, "she sees into the character of the man from his words, and marvels at his conversation, so full of good sense, and then prays that she may be the consort of such a person rather than of some sailor man or dancing man of her own townsmen, then it is quite right to admire her." The reader is placed in the position of judging Nausicaa. By such analysis of human motive in a fictive circumstance the young reader is instructed in the business of making moral judgments, and thereby taught to respond rationally when faced with moral choices in his own life. But note that these are *moral* judgments that the reader is making, not aesthetic evaluations of the poet's technique. Plutarch has shifted the ground of his argument.

Actually, as Plutarch warms to the task of justifying poetry, he forgets its speciousness and thinks only of its delightful benefits:

> The bee, in accordance with nature's laws, discovers amid the most pungent flowers and the roughest thorns the smoothest and most palatable honey; so children, if they be rightly nurtured amid poetry, will in some way or other learn to draw some wholesome and profitable doctrine even from passages that are suspect of what is base and improper. (32E–F)

So the falsehood and ugliness of poetry are transmuted to sweetness and light. The metamorphosis from barefaced lie to manifest truth is completed (36D). Poetry is given a responsible place in educating the young and in holding together the social fabric: "The young man has need of good pilotage in the matter of reading," Plutarch concludes, "to the end that, forestalled with schooling rather than prejudice, in a spirit of friendship and goodwill and familiarity, he may be convoyed by poetry into the realm of philosophy" (37B). Since literature requires the judicious assessment of good and bad, it serves as an exercise in reasoning, so the old quarrel between poetry and philosophy is settled.[64]

Plutarch, in fact, goes farther than that. He tacitly follows Aristotle in the basic premise that "poetry is an imitation of character and lives" (26A). Despite his frequent platonist orientation, he moves poetry out of the realm of heavenly beauty and into the world of palpable percept. He directs poetry away from μουσική and toward *historia,* fictive narrative. As a pedagogue, he places the reader in active engagement with the text in order to allow moral judgments about the fictive characters. Literature merges with ethics, which thence leads to a life of private and public virtue. In Plutarch, Sidney found an authority to corroborate his own views about the techniques and purposes of poetry, and the several references to Plutarch in Sidney's *Defence* are far from casual.

Cristoforo Landino (1424–98) shone brightly in that firmament of humanists set in place by the Medicis.[65] He was the lesser light of the Florentine Academy for the many decades of the fifteenth century when Ficino proved to be its sun.[66] Although as a seminal intellect Ficino is far better known, Landino in his own day was greatly admired. And for good reason. He led a busy life, embodying in perfect balance those qualities necessary for both the *vita activa* and the *vita contemplativa* expounded so gracefully in the first book of his oft-reprinted *Disputationes Camaldulenses* (c.1480). Throughout his long life, Landino performed a series of municipal duties in addition to his cloistered scholarship and private tutoring, in the most honorable tradition of civic humanism.

Landino was a humanist in the sense that he placed mankind in the central position as nexus between the physical world and the angelic orders, as Augustine had prescribed[67] and the Florentine Platonists had confirmed. But he was a humanist also in the more restricted sense that literary texts fascinated him, and he handled them with a new pedantic devotion to the circumstances of their origin. Landino transmitted to the sixteenth century an important store of classical works, which he edited with the humanist's rigor on the one hand and with an infectious enthusiasm on the other. We are not likely to overestimate the influence of Landino on the later understanding of Vergil or Horace or Pliny.

Although Landino was fairly well eclipsed by the end of the sixteenth century, his reputation lingered because of his editorial work. Probably most important was his edition of Dante's *Divina commedia,* first published at Florence in 1481 with illustrations designed by Botticelli. This massive text, with generous prefatory matter and extensive annotation, was kept in print for well over a century. It is likely that Sidney knew Dante through this volume as it was published at Venice in 1578, a near-exact reprint of the edition published earlier at Venice in 1564.[68]

Sidney mentions Landino in the final sentences of *The defence of poesie,* in the peroration, and his reference to "a divine fury" which produces poetry suggests that Sidney had in mind a brief essay entitled "Furore divino" which prefaces the edition of the *Divina commedia*. The tone of this entire passage of the *Defence* is somewhat frivolous, so it is difficult to ascertain what Sidney's attitude toward Landino might have been. It's unlikely, though, that Sidney recalled Landino merely to excoriate him. I suggest that he looked to Landino as a respected authority, but one from whom he was separated by time and place. Sidney acknowledges Landino's platonist premise: poets "are so beloved of the gods that whatsoever they write proceeds of a divine fury" (121.16–17); but in the face of recent developments in literary theory, he cannot accept its consequences. Nonetheless, Landino was a shaping influence on much of Sidney's thought, especially those notions having to do with the reverend antiquity of poetry, the definition of the poet as maker, his golden world, the role of the Muses in poetic composition, and the requirement of versification in a poem. The magnitude of his effect upon Sidney has not been fully assessed.

In any case, Landino provides a prototype for the learned humanist, well-read in the vast libraries that wealthy patrons had amassed and adept in the new methodologies of scholarly inquiry. He represents the fullest development of a neoplatonist aesthetic, assimilating the literary theory of the Middle Ages while corroborating and modifying it by recourse to the recently recovered Platonic corpus. He was fundamentally influenced by Cicero, politely deferential to Horace, and knowledgeable about Aristotle in general, although ignorant of the *Poetics* itself. Landino epitomizes the orthodox aesthetic at the opening of the sixteenth century, before the boom in criticism occasioned by the impassioned advocacy of Aristotle's mimetic theory.

Landino sets forth a theory of poetry most forthrightly and completely in the collection of theses which introduce his annotated text of Dante's *Divina commedia;* and since Sidney's reference to Landino points precisely to this material, it is appropriate that we concentrate our attention here. After a brief proem and an extended defence of Dante against calumniators, Landino proceeds in a series of *topica* to praise the Florentines for a variety of activities—for their learning, their eloquence, their music, their painting and sculpture, their civil law, and their business acumen. Then comes an account of Dante's life, followed by the three interrelated essays of greatest interest to us: "What Is Poetry and the Poet, and About Its Divine and Very Ancient Origin," "The Divine Frenzy," and "That the Origin of Poets Is Ancient."[69] These three essays in Sansovino's editions are printed as an autonomous unit in the textual apparatus.[70]

In the first essay, Landino begins by usurping the authority of "all the most serious philosophers" to magnify the poet: "No sort of writer may be found who either by the loftiness of his eloquence or by the divine quality of his wisdom has at any time been equal to the poet" (140.28–31). In this passage poetry is associated with Ciceronian *eloquentia* and with the Platonic notion that poets have access to celestial wisdom. Landino goes on to mention Aristotle—"a man of great genius and for learning the most notable since Plato"—who, according to Landino, continued in this praise-giving vein and believed that "in the earliest times priests and poets were the very same" (140.31–34).[71] Not only is the poet the most admirable of writers, but also poetry is the most esteemed of all the arts, and for several reasons: (1) poetry is a comprehensive art, embracing all the others; (2) it has metrical structure and submits to the ornamentation of rhetorical figures; (3) it records all human experience; (4) it makes even ordinary subject matter seem heavenly; (5) in the tradition of Horace, it both teaches and delights. Poetry achieves this distinction because it derives from a divine frenzy—and by reference to the *Ion* and the *Phaedrus,* Landino indicates that his argument is a redaction of Plato.

Landino's interpretation of the *Phaedrus* is especially revealing because it shows how readily Plato was turned into a devout Christian who believed in God's providence: "The noted philosopher [Plato] adds that the Muses at times infuse this divine spirit into the least likely people, because divine providence wishes to show that the most famous poems are not the inventions of wise men, but instead are gifts of God" (141.36–142.3). Caedmon comes to mind, Langland's *Piers Plowman,* and perhaps the ploughboy poets of the late eighteenth century.

Of even greater relevance is Landino's introduction of the Muses at this point and his description of their role. It is the Muses who choose the poet, no matter how unlikely a candidate he may appear to be, and they pour into him the divine spirit, inducing the poetic fit. Furthermore, they act on behalf of God himself, so a poem is the result of His beneficence. Poetry, like mercy, drops unstrained from heaven. Landino concludes by again citing Plato, who "affirms in the *Phaedrus* that no one, not even the most diligent or the most erudite, becomes a poet unless he is stirred by the divine frenzy" (142.3–5); and he shores up the authority of Plato by quoting Ovid (*Fasti* 6.5–6) and by offering a string of rapid references to Democritus,[72] Origen, and Cicero.

This elaboration of divine frenzy as a prerequisite for poetry leads to a discussion of poets as prophets. They are seers, the mouthpieces of deity: "God willed *ab initio* that his mysteries be announced to the people by the poets" (142.13–14). This was the view held by the Romans, Landino reports, and he gives a supportive etymology for *vates:* "a word meaning *a vi mentis*—that is, 'with vehemence,' 'with agitation of mind'" (142.18–19).[73]

The Greeks, however, held a different view. They traced the meaning of the word "poet" to the verb ποιεῖν, "to make," as Sidney also notes to distinguish *poeta* from *vates* (*Defence* 77.32–34). And in a passage of prime importance for understanding Sidney's theory of poetry, Landino develops a poetics based upon this etymology: "The Greeks derived the word 'poet' from the verb *poiein,* which is halfway between 'creating' [creare], which is what God does when out of nothing He brings something into existence, and 'making' [fare], which is what men do when in any art they compose out of matter and form" (142.20–24). As an initial but undeclared premise, Landino assumes an analogy between the poet as maker and the divine artificer who produced our universe. In line with a long-standing theological debate, however, Landino distinguishes between the Hebraic-Christian God, who performed the miracle of *creatio ex nihilo,* and the Timaean godhead, who is less than omnipotent and performs the appreciably less wondrous feat of simply imposing form upon preexistent matter. Jove creates; Plato's demiurge merely makes.[74] As a mortal creator/maker, the poet operates somewhere between these two fictive acts: "Although the fiction of the poet is not produced entirely out of nothing, yet it is far from 'making' and comes close to 'creating'" (142.24–26). It would be impious to claim that the poet creates with the same freedom from constraint as God, and Landino declines to go that far; yet, the poet achieves a level of creativity closer to *creatio ex nihilo* than to the simple reworking of what already exists.

This scholastic splitting of terms ends abruptly, however, subsumed in an *O! altitudo* as Landino proclaims the loftiest praise for poetry. The discussion leads triumphantly to one of the great topoi in medieval literary theory, which Landino announces with all the certitude and admiration that had accrued to it over the ages: "Indeed, God is the highest poet, and the world is His poem" (142.26–27). Jove *poeta* inscribes each creature in the book of nature, laying before our view the vast and informative account of Creation. The biblical hexaemeron, a tidy summary, is realized in extended fact. Landino draws upon the Book of Wisdom (11.20) for the traditional gloss on this time-honored lore, and now makes explicit the previously implied analogy between the poet and his deity:

> Just as God arranges His creation—that is, the visible and invisible worlds which is His work—according to number, measure, and weight (as the prophet proclaims: *Deus omnia facit numero, mensura, et pondere*), so the poet constructs his poem with the number of metrical feet, with the measure of short and long syllables, and with the weight of sentiment sayings and of passions. (142.27–32)

In His creation of the universe, God is a metrician—a geometer, an architect, a musician. "The visible world," as a result, submits to measurement. It is an extended construct submitting to quantification. It exists in space and time; it is dimensional and durational. So much for the visible world. But "the invisible world," though immaterial, is similarly arranged by metrics. In the Pythagorean-Platonic tradition, numbers are forms—insubstantial, unless imposed upon matter, but nonetheless existent.[75] They are essential—that is, of absolute essence, existing forever unchanged and unchangeable in some aspatial and atemporal condition that is distinct from the visible world, but yet its counterpart. An other; and yet, the same. When we remember that ἰδέα in Greek means "form," we can see in this vocabulary a progression from unadulterated ideality to complete physicality as we proceed from idea to form to number to quantity to palpable thing. We can see how, by virtue of metrification, "the visible and invisible worlds which is His work" are held together in the same continuum, comprising the full range of possible human experience, from wholly "sensible," to use Plato's terms, to wholly "intelligible." By the same token, we see how the visible world of things and the invisible world of ideas are inextricably interlinked by numbers, those forms which underlie each, although at different levels of existence. Forms are the mediating agents between *idea* and *res objecta sensibus,* between ideal and actual. The two worlds are correlated by those formal properties that inhere as numbers coordinately in both.

This notion of the creating deity as mathematician is easily applied to the poet, who similarly metrifies, although necessarily at a level somewhat below the divine. But "just as God arranges His creation" according to the formal patterns that derive from ideas eternally resident in His mind, so the poet disposes his material according to number, weight, and measure. He follows the biblical injunction to observe mathematical proportion—an injunction attributed to Solomon, who exemplified it in the building of his temple,[76] and who in turn followed the architectural model of Moses, who had set the example in his building of the tabernacle.[77] Numerical patterning is demonstrated in the metrical order of the poem, in its every feature. To image the forms in the divine mind, in fact, is poetry's basic function, its most important significance. These forms provide its primary meaning. In this poetics, the formal properties of an artifact are its essential quality— literally, its raison d'être.

When Landino enunciates this poetics, he is not, needless to say, being original. Far from it. He is thoroughly orthodox, and can speak with such brevity for this reason. He assumes that his readers are familiar with this doctrine and assent to its validity without coercion. It comes straight out of the Middle Ages, requiring only the slightest adjustment to accord with Landino's neoplatonism, and it can be traced ultimately to Augustine. In all probability, Landino knew it directly from that source.[78]

In order to understand this poetics as Augustine formulated it, we must place it in the larger context of his teaching. Augustine is the Church Father who most successfully amalgamated Platonic doctrine with his Christianity. He wrote a chapter on Platonism, for example, entitled, "On the philosophy that has come nearest to the true Christian faith."[79] Unlike some Church Fathers, Augustine did not reject pagan literature as despicable competition to the holy scriptures; rather, like Clement of Alexandria, a syncretist of the broadest scope, he saw value in the writings of pre-Christian Greece and Rome, especially in those authors who extolled virtue. For Augustine, Plato and Pythagoras and their followers had advocated a virtuous life thoroughly compatible with the dictates of the Christian deity. In turn, the Florentine Platonists found Augustine thoroughly compatible with their syncretistic impulses.

In the early Church, and through most of its history, there was suspicion of the arts. It was feared that a response to beauty, especially in the graphic and plastic arts, would lead to earthy, sensuous experience, away from God. To counter that hostile sentiment, Augustine sought to legitimize the aesthetic response. How can that which is beautiful and therefore pleasurable be good for us rather than destroyingly seductive? His answer, compelling in its simplicity, is that even the physical has been created by God. An artifact is ultimately a creature of God, reflecting His will through the handiwork of a mortal artisan.[80] In consequence, the artifact, like a natural creature, participates in God's charity and in His attributes, including the platonist virtues of goodness, truth, and beauty.

Augustine could argue for the value of literature with particular success because it appears in the medium of words, and words have a large conceptual component. They are perceived not merely as sense experience by the ear, but their more significant element, their semantics, is comprehended by the mind. Augustine adopted the theory of Cratylus that words have an inherent meaning assigned by nature, or perhaps even by God. And because literature is conveyed in language with its natural signification (words too are God's creatures), literature carries something of the divine imperative. Remember, Christ himself, the son whom God had sent to create the world and to mediate between God and humanity, appeared as the Word, the λόγος—in Anglo-Saxon, the Gospel.[81] So for Augustine, language and literature had a special status in the scale of value.[82]

In his "De musica," Augustine explores and reveals those formal properties of poetry, quite divorced from its verbal component, which ally poetry with music: the quantification of syllables, the rhythms, the length of lines. The meters of poetry are equated to the measures of music—both arts are arranged according to *numero, mensura, pondere*.[83] The "De musica" is a highly specialized treatise dealing with that affinity, detailing the formal features of poetry. For a full-scale poetics, however, including the semantic potential of poetry's verbal component, we must go to Augustine's other writings. The *De civitate Dei*, his best known and most admired work during the Renaissance, provides the evidence for constructing a comprehensive theory of poetry—indeed, a theory of art in its broadest ramifications.[84]

The *De civitate Dei* is meant to be didactic, teaching us to prefer the heavenly city of God over the earthly city of fallen man, but it is not a systematic exposition of a subject matter or discipline. Instead, it offers a large, rather loosely organized collection of short essays, each of which is a response—a well-informed, intelligent, sensitive response—to a topic of interest to Augustine. Usually the topic relates to religious doctrine as it pertains to or derives from cosmology or the communal life of humans, often in historical perspective. In one place or another, Augustine touches upon a sufficient number of aesthetic issues to allow us quite readily to infer his theory of art.

In accord with the *Timaeus* as well as the book of Genesis, Augustine asserts that God created the cosmos:

> The universe itself, such is the perfect order of its ever-shifting and constant motions and so fair the spectacle it affords of all things visible—the universe cries aloud . . . that it was created and that it could only have been created by a God who is ineffably and invisibly great and ineffably and invisibly beautiful. (11.4)

According to Augustine's theology, God created the universe *ex nihilo* rather than out of what had previously existed; as Augustine states flatly elsewhere, "God made the world from nothing."[85] For Timaeus, the poetizing deity did not create the forms or the matter or the abyss; rather, he "imitates" in his creation by translating the ideal forms to a sense-perceptible level—that is, by projecting the ideal forms into preexistent matter. The eternal forms are his objects of imitation, and matter is his medium. For Augustine, however, God needs no extraneous patterns for creation. The ideal forms reside in His mind, are part of His being, so He can create *ex nihilo*. He supplies both object of imitation and medium. As Raleigh tersely explains, "Before that beginning, there was neither primary matter to bee informed, nor forme to informe, nor any being, but the eternall" (3). In consequence, creation is more the product of an individual mind, the *mens dei*.

Furthermore, God created the universe because He is good and it is good—it is, in fact, an objectification of His goodness. Therefore evil occurs only as an absence of this natural goodness, this divine beneficence.[86] Evil is an abeyance rather than a presence. To say that it exists in its own right would be to commit the Manichean heresy.[87] In any case, creation for Augustine is more the product of a personal will, free of extraneous determinants such as imperfect matter or flawed patterns. At the level of divine activity, creation is what Augustine calls "providence," as he explains full of awe in a chapter entitled, "Of the universal providence of God, by whose laws all things are ruled":

> The supreme and true God with his Word and Holy Spirit, which three are one, is the one almighty God, the creator and maker of every soul and every body. It is by participation in him that happiness is found by all who are happy in verity and not in vanity. He made man a rational animal, combining soul and body. When man sinned, God did not permit him to go unpunished, nor yet did he abandon him without mercy. To the good and to the evil he gave being, possessed also by stones; germinative life, possessed also by trees; conscious life, possessed also by animals; and intellectual life, possessed also by angels alone. From him comes all limit, all form, all order; from him comes measure, number and weight; from him comes whatever exists in nature, whatever its kind and whatever its worth; from him come seeds of forms and forms of seeds and movements in seeds and forms. He gave also to flesh a source, beauty, health, fruitfulness in propagation, arrangement of limbs and the saving grace of harmony. To the irrational soul also he gave memory, sensation and appetite; to the rational soul he gave in addition mind, intelligence and will. Neither heaven nor earth, neither angel nor man, not even the inner organs of a tiny and despised animal, not the pin-feather of

a bird nor the tiny flower in the meadow nor the leaf on the tree did God leave unprovided with a suitable harmony of parts, a peace, so to speak, between its members. It is impossible to suppose that he would have excluded from the laws of his providence the kingdoms of men and their dominations and servitudes. (5.11)

Augustine praises God from whom all creatures flow. God has made man a rational being, comprised of disparate halves, soul and body, capable of moral choice. He has placed man midway in the chain of being, sharing physicality with the lower orders of nature but participating also in the intelligible realm inhabited by angels. He has arranged His handiwork according to number, weight, and measure so that He might manifest His benign attributes through the resultant beauty and order. He has imbued each of His multitude of creatures with correspondent formal features, so that each enjoys its own "suitable harmony of parts"; yet each resonates within the universal harmony of a mathematical cosmos. This totally rational scheme is unmistakable evidence of His eternal providence—precisely that attribute of deity Milton sought to assert in *Paradise Lost*.

The last quotation indicates how humanity fits into this grand design. Mankind is, of course, one of God's products, the final and most favored of His creatures. And man, like the universe, is an objectification of God himself. Man is made in God's image (12.24)—of all God's creatures, he most nearly approaches likeness to God, and this superiority makes him lord of creation.[88] But in a sense mankind and creation are also cognates, both projections of God's will, both beneficiaries of His providence. Both are ordered and maintained by the same cosmic forces; they share the same formal properties. To use a technical term, man is a "microcosm," composed of the same mathematical proportions and harmonies as the universe.

We can now discern a teleology for art and an epistemology by which to achieve this end. In Augustine's world, the purpose of art, as indeed of everything, was to acquaint man with God, the ultimate and inclusive being. Therefore art must make man aware of his own microcosmic nature, so that he understands his position in the universe and his relationship to deity. This purpose is achieved by displaying the proportions and harmonies latent in the cosmos in order to awaken the proportions and harmonies latent in the microcosmic percipient.[89] When the city of God has been established on earth and celestial happiness is ubiquitous, the human soul will take its place in the heavenly choir of eternal praise to God. Just so, the work of art, embodying cosmic beauty, touches a sympathetic chord in the soul of the percipient and reminds him of this future beatitude:

> All those numbers belonging to corporeal harmony, of which I have already spoken,[90] which now are hidden, will appear, arranged through all parts of the body, within and without. A delight in the rational beauty of these, and all other things whose wondrous greatness will there be seen, will inflame the hearts of all rational beings to praise their great Creator. (22.30)

The "rational beauty" of the artifact—that is, its beauty displayed in numbers ("rational" <L. *ratio*)—will then be explicit as well as implicit, and it will affect the percipient both outwardly and inwardly. These palpable proportions, expressed in musical terms as harmony, will favorably coordinate the physical members of the body and simultaneously activate the nascent forms of the psyche. Thus awakened, the soul will clap its hands and sing, joyfully praising God, the architect of universal order. In this aesthetic, proportion and harmony become the criteria for excellence, and mathematics becomes the appropriate means for analyzing an artifact. Symmetry (<Gr. "with measure") becomes the basis for art.[91]

But notice that symmetry informs the artifact from the inside rather than being imposed upon it as a prefabricated configuration from without. These are *ratios,* a relationship abstracted from quantity, not quantification itself;[92] these are mathematical schemata, inherent rather than external, ideas rather than tangible or extended structures. Augustine makes a clear distinction between implicit and explicit form:

> Now there are two kinds of form. First, there is the form that is applied externally to each and every physical substance, as is done by potters, smiths and other artisans of this sort, who even paint and fashion shapes that resemble the bodies of animals. And second, there is also the form that has inherent efficient

causes deriving from the secret and hidden discretion of a living and intelligent nature, which, without being made itself, makes not only natural physical forms but also the very souls of living beings. The first-mentioned kind of form we may attribute to the several craftsmen, but the latter only to one craftsman, creator and founder, God, who made the world itself and the angels when no world and no angels existed. (12.26)

In fashioning an artifact, the artisan—whether potter, blacksmith, or even painter—begins with a concept in his mind, and projects this "form" onto material to produce a sense-perceptible work of art. This form is thereby rendered palpable by the artifact, becoming explicit. In contradistinction to this explicit form, however, there is another which is recessive, latent in "the secret and hidden discretion of a living and intelligent nature." This second form resides in the mind of God. This invisible and uncreated "nature" is the origin not only of all "natural physical forms," but even of "the very souls of living beings"—that is, of the souls that comprise the forms. This primordial "nature" is the original and infinitely capacious *mens dei,* from which all creatures flow:

God himself, by the work which he still carries on, causes seeds[93] to develop from their numbers, and from certain hidden and invisible folds to evolve into the visible forms of this beauty that we see. God himself in wondrous wise unites the incorporeal and corporeal nature, the first to rule, the second to be ruled, and by mating and joining them makes a living creature. (22.24)[94]

The form for the artifact, then, emerges from this reservoir of divine thought, enters the mind of the artisan, and eventuates in the artifact, where it is perceived in the only way our mortal senses allow, as a mathematically proportioned arrangement of physical matter.

The task of the artisan now becomes evident: he must insure the congruence of these outer and inner forms. The didactic purpose of art is achieved only when the forms in the mind of the artisan are an accurate reflection of the divine nature, when *mens dei* and *mens poetae* coincide. Or perhaps this is the role of the Muses, to insure this coincidence. Then art reveals the ultimate being of the deity by discovering those forms that render knowable to us those of His attributes within the bounds of human knowledge. Otherwise, without art, even this much knowledge of the deity might be beyond us.

We are now in a position to draw several aesthetic conclusions. First, beauty is objective, absolute, outside ourselves. It resides with the deity, although we are allowed glimpses of it through its reflections in art and nature. In addition, we contemplate beauty; we do not create it. At most, an artisan might disclose it. Finally, a thing pleases because it is beautiful, not the other way round. Sensual pleasure is not the aim of art; rather, it aims at an enhanced consciousness of those aspects of our being that identify us as blessed creatures of God.

We can also now delineate more precisely the epistemology of the art event. The percipient begins with sense perception of the artifact, observation of its phenomena; but from that initial experience of it, he turns away from the sensible world, and proceeds into the intelligible world of numbers, forms, ideas, essences, ultimate being. Since mortals are limited creatures, sense perception is a necessary prelude to analysis in order to comprehend the numbers, but only an ancillary to full understanding. Art, in fact, leads us away from sensory excitement toward the realm of intellectuality, toward our orientation with the angels, toward an awareness of the "harmony of [our] parts" and of our consonance with universal harmony. Art is subservient to religious experience, if not religious experience itself. Works of art, and creatures of nature as well—whatever belongs to the palpable universe—are beautiful to the extent that they reveal the divine goodness and enable us to appreciate it; but having attracted our sensuous interest, the physical object must not detain us at the sensual level.[95]

So symmetry is not merely an external feature of a work of art, but its very essence—the form which not only determines its being, but bestows being upon it. In a larger context, symmetry reveals the benevolent will of God through His creation; His love is demonstrated by the congruence and harmony everywhere evident in the universe (19.13). Symmetry comprises these interrelationships between parts, which *may* be quantified as mathematical proportions (as in music or in architecture or in poetry), but which like *caritas* is not an extended structure. Symmetry expresses a conceptualized relationship of part to part, removed from the dimensional and durational world of space and time.

Another sort of symmetry, closely related, depends upon the

abstracted relationship between a part and the whole in which it inheres. For example, if the whole comprises fifteen units and a part comprises six, we have a mathematical proportion $\%_{15}$, which may be abstracted to a non-quantified ratio $\frac{2}{5}$. Again, this ratio is an immaterial form rather than an extended structure. This kind of symmetry, relating part to whole rather than part to part (synecdoche rather than metonymy), is close to what Plotinus defined as beauty,[96] a definition adopted by Alberti and promulgated by him until it became a norm in the Renaissance.[97] Giovanni della Casa, for example, expounds it in the cause of good manners: "Where jointly & severally, every parte & the whole hath his due proportion and measure, there is Bewtie." Goodness walks hand in hand with beauty, so it is incumbent upon gentlemen to act with "due proportion and measure"—for "that thing may justly be called fayer, in which the saide proportion and measure is found" (102).

This symmetry arising from the relation of part to whole may be demonstrated in a simple way by the system of the four seasons comprising the year.[98] Each season is defined in terms of the position it occupies in the entire cycle, with emphasis upon the otherness which distinguishes it from its three counterparts. For example, spring is the only period when growth begins. Summer is the period of mature growth, autumn the period of harvest, and winter the period of quiescence; but spring is defined in a Saussurian way as what the other seasons are not. It is true the seasons follow one another in a predetermined series; they are related to one another by sequence in a diachronic system. But each is most clearly defined by its unique function in the total cycle, rather than as the successor of one season and the precursor of another. Spring is differentiated by what occurs then and at no other time. And the year, viewed synchronically, is said to be symmetrical, "with measure," comprising four equal parts. A season (any season) may be represented by the ratio $\frac{1}{4}$.

When beauty is defined as symmetry based upon the relationship between parts and the whole, the basic form of art becomes the paradox of multeity in unity. The extension of the artifact in time and space represents a proliferation, a multeity; beneath its variety, however, lies a unifying form, a wholeness—just as, for example, there are four autonomous seasons, but taken together they make up a year. This underlying wholeness refers ultimately, of course, to the Oneness that is God. It is logocentric. Numbers provide the necessary extension and variety in the artifact, as in the cosmos, in order to make it palpable. But just as in the infinite variety of the cosmos we perceive the unifying hand of God behind natural order, so in the variety of the artifact we perceive the unifying hand of the artificer—or better yet, we perceive his unifying concept, the unifying mind, the *mens poetae*.

In practical application, the aesthetic of multeity in unity was frequently intensified into the reconciliation of opposites, *concordia discors*. Augustine provides a far-reaching example in his chapter, "The beauty of the universe which, as God has arranged it, becomes even more brilliant by the contrast of opposites." Here Augustine implements his usual philosophical optimism and turns evil into good:

> Now God would never create any man, much less any angel, if he already knew that he was destined to be evil, were he not equally aware how he was to turn them to account in the interest of the good and thereby add lustre to the succession of the ages as if it were an exquisite poem enhanced by what might be called antitheses. . . . So, just as beauty of language is achieved by a contrast of opposites in this way, the beauty of the course of this world is built up by a kind of rhetoric, not of words but of things, which employs this contrast of opposites. (11.18)[99]

"The course of this world"—its mutable yet orderly operation—like "an exquisite poem," is rendered beautiful by the rhetorical figure of *antithesis*—by pairs of opposites, such as life and death, wealth and poverty, day and night. In fact, the beauty of this various world, Augustine generalizes, "is built up by a kind of rhetoric . . . which employs this contrast of opposites."

But in one of those mysterious ways by which God works, the result of this opposition is cohesion rather than divisiveness. The figure *antithesis* depends upon the identification of two contraries which oppose one another, and yet inhere within the same continuum—indeed, define one another by opposition, exist as exact counterparts. Again, an other, and yet the same, as in the continuum embracing the visible and invisible worlds. The rhetoric of such a scheme, its dynamics, demands the oscillation from one extreme to the other, proceeding systematically through all the intervening mediate stages.[100] In the universe at large, such alternation is necessary for the fulfillment of God's plan, for the full realization of what He implied in the vast design. The perpetual round of night and day, for example, is our assurance that providence is at work. To be exhaustive, complete, creation must encompass the extremes on all sides, and the opposites must be reconciled in a stable, albeit constantly mobile, unity.[101] And a poem, to be "exquisite," must embody and demonstrate the same inclusive form. It too must encompass and reconcile extremes, imaging forth the paradox of multeity in unity. Herein lies beauty, as well as truth and goodness, an icon of *caritas*.

These virtues are to be discerned even in the opposition of evil to good—indeed, especially in this pair of opposites. Evil is not an essence in its own right; it achieves definition only in terms of good, as something contrary to good, the counterpart of good. Therefore Augustine has no difficulty in explaining evil out of existence. Through the paradox of reconciling opposites, evil is turned into good. The archetypal form here is the idea of the fortunate fall. The multeity implied in the opposition of evil and good is shown to consist within the unity of divine providence.

The multifariousness of this world, including opposites, subsists within the Oneness of God. "The succession of the ages as if it were an exquisite poem" reveals this religious truth. The endless repetition of a finite cycle, like day and night or the four seasons or "the succession of the ages," discloses a schema, a ratio, an underlying wholeness of the world, God's poem. As Landino says with a similar religious impetus, "God is the highest poet," simply because He can master the greatest variety in His design. He has encompassed the farthest extremes. And as Thomas Browne was to say in the dying moments of this paradoxical tradition, *Certum est quia impossibile est.*[102]

In the reconciliation of opposites, the paradox of multeity in unity is expressed as a spatial concept (although as Augustine reminds us, it is a form, not a structure—that is, it is spatial like a schema, not concretely or quantifiably so). We may also, however, express the paradox of multeity in unity as a temporal concept (again, temporal in a nonquantified sense). Then we have a favored methodology of biblical exegesis known as typology. In this context, a "type" is a character or event in the Bible which prefigures another character or event. The *typus* represents its later equivalent, although predating it in chronological time. Usually something in the Old Testament is a type of something in the New Testament—as Augustine says of the Old Testament, "There the promised gifts are earthly blessings, but even then spiritual men understood . . . the eternity which was signified by those temporal things" (4.33). In consequence, the effect (and therefore the signification) of something in the Old Testament, though bound by time, was the same as some celestial promise in the New Testament.[103] For example, Moses smiting the rock with his rod and bringing forth water, which saves the Israelites in the desert, is a type for the piercing of Christ's side on the cross, whence flows the blood that brings salvation to mankind (13.21). A "type" is in time what a "metaphor" is in space: just as a metaphor in a Platonic context is a translation from one *level* of being to another (page 63), so a type is a translation from one *period* of being to another.

In Book 15 of the *De civitate Dei,* Augustine interprets the Bible, an exercise in hermeneutics as he saw it. He is particularly interested in the book of Genesis: the slaying of Abel by Cain, the long life of Methuselah, the Giants who then lived on the earth, the flood and Noah. His wish is to relate these incidents to the city of God, to give them doctrinal significance. He does this by typology. As an example, he uses Noah's ark as a type of the celestial city, which Augustine elaborates in a chapter entitled, "That the ark which Noah was ordered to make symbolizes Christ and the church in every detail":

> We doubtless have here a symbolic representation of the City of God sojourning as an alien in this world, that is, of the church which wins salvation by virtue of the wood on which the mediator between God and men, the man Christ Jesus, was suspended. The very measurements of the ark's length, height and breadth symbolize the human body, in the reality of which it was prophesied that Christ would come to mankind, as, in fact, he did come. . . . And as for the door that it received on its side, that surely is the wound that was made when the side of the crucified

one was pierced by the spear. This is the way by which those who
come to him enter, because from this opening flowed the sacra-
ments with which believers are initiated. Moreover, the order that
it should be made of squared beams contains an allusion to the
foursquare stability of saints' lives, for in whatever direction you
turn a squared object, it will stand firm. In similar fashion, everything else mentioned in the construction of this ark symbolizes
some aspect of the church. (15.26)

So the forms evident in the construction of Noah's ark prefigured
the church of Christ, the eternal city of God. The beneficence
shown to Noah and his family foretold the salvation to come
through Christ. A multeity of types—items bound by time and
space, such as the rock smitten by Moses and the door of Noah's
ark—are unified in the sacred truth of redemption through
Christ's suffering.

The significance of typology for the exegesis of fictive narrative
is suggested in Augustine's next chapter, entitled clumsily though
lucidly, "That we should agree neither with those who accept only
the historical account of the ark and the flood without any allegorical connotations nor with those who reject their historical reality
and defend their symbolic significance alone." Here Augustine
makes the point that a type is true both as fact and as fiction—or,
as he puts it, both as history and as allegory.[104] He begins:

No one should suppose, however, that this account of the flood
was written to no purpose, or that we are to look here only for the
historical reality of events without any allegorical connotations,
or, conversely, that these events did not take place at all but represent only symbolic discourse, or that, whatever it is, it has absolutely nothing to do with prophecy about the church. (15.27)

Augustine wants it both ways: this fictive narrative has value both
in the ethereal realm of the spirit and in the rough-and-tumble of
everyday affairs. This poem, like "the course of this world," includes all possibilities and encompasses both extremes. After disposing of every conceivable argument against the historicity of the
biblical story of the flood, Augustine concludes Book 15 with this
sweeping statement: "We must believe that the transmission of
this account in a written history was a wise action, that the events

did take place, that they do have a symbolic significance and that this significance points figuratively to the church."

A typological exegesis of God's poem, then, whether holy scripture or profane creation, shows the world to be put together rather like an epic, with validity as both history and allegory. There are two coordinates of time, chronological and eternal. Necessarily we as mortals begin *in medias res*—but no matter, since before and after, here and there, then and now, are in the end the same. An underlying veracity assured by God's benevolence dissolves all occasions into a seamless whole. Events pass by . . . but each occurrence is a prophecy, asserting eternal providence. Each episode, when viewed aright, is an epic forecast foretelling what is yet to come. We can read creation temporally like a narrative poem, since creation proceeded in time and space, though eventually we arrive at a static timelessness.

The hexaemeron, in fact, provides our paradigm for reading. It concludes in a sabbath, an all-embracing system when change, by virtue of complete fulfillment, shall be no more. Multiples shall be unified; and opposites, reconciled. The possibilities will have been exhausted, and the possible permutations will have been fully realized in an infinitely inclusive, congenerous oneness presided over by God. The mortal poet devises his poem in imitation of God's poem in order to proclaim this promised end. Spenser reaches this "Sabaoths sight" as the culmination of both *Fowre Hymnes* and the Mutabilitie Cantos (7.8.2.9).

This long digression on Augustine may seem to have taken us away from Landino. But it was necessary because Landino and the humanists following him—Erasmus, Vives, Cheke, Ascham, Sidney—took for granted a knowledge of Augustine's aesthetics, whether or not they accepted as valid his theory of art. Landino fairly well adopts it wholesale, melding it with Plato's texts to produce a Muse-inspired poetics. Du Bartas a century later follows a similar course, although elevating the Christian at the expense of the Platonic. His Urania is a "heavenly Muse," of the same sisterhood as Milton's, and she speaks of the "sacred *Phrenzie*" that raises the poet "above the Heav'ns bright-flaming Arches":

> Thence, thence it is, that Devine *Poets* bring
> So sweet, so learned, and so lasting *Numbers,*

> Where Heav'ns and Natures secret Works they sing,
> Free from the power of *Fates* eternall slumbers.[105]

Others, of course, rejected Augustine's theory of art, especially the neo-Aristotelians. No one simply ignored it, however, until long after Sidney. But now to return to Landino.

After directing attention to the Augustinian aesthetics by signaling with the familiar dictum, "God is the highest poet, and the world is His poem," Landino indicates an end to this phase of his argument. "I shall not carry this comparison further," he says (142.32–33), presumably because elaboration of a topos so well-known would be tiresome. Instead, in the best humanist fashion, he reinforces the Augustinian platitude with a fancy bit of classical learning. The divine providence that initiated poetry in Augustine's Christian scheme and supervised its production is identified with the Muses of the platonist tradition. "But I will add," Landino continues, "that Apollo and the nine Muses looked after the poets" (142.33–34). And with an ostentatious display of syncretism, etymologizing elegantly and citing an all-but-sacred authority, he demonstrates conclusively that Apollo and Jove are one and the same deity, and that the Muses represent the nine angelic orders:

> By Apollo they meant none other than Almighty God, who is One and without division, just as the name "Apollo" signifies in Greek [i.e., ἀ + πολλοί, "not many"].[106] Macrobius in his *Saturnalia*, wishing to demonstrate the oneness of the deity and to refute any notion of His divisibility, refers to Apollo all the names of the various gods as well as their powers.[107] The poets are therefore under the protection of Apollo and the nine Muses—that is, of the nine angelic choirs. (142.34–143.6)

Probatum est. Learning is a wondrous thing, even if the etymology is spurious. Poetic inspiration has always flowed from a divine source: Apollo, the Muses, Jove, Christ, the angels—what's the difference? Landino then terminates this first essay by coming to the inevitable conclusion: "Poets therefore are akin to God, and also to the primum mobile—that is, Jove—and to all the nine celestial spheres, which are the Muses, because from the latter they receive the divine influence" (143.12–14).[108] Poetry is μου-σική.

The second essay, entitled "The Divine Frenzy,"[109] returns to this topic and treats it specifically, although Landino is not concerned with the inspiration that moves the poet to compose in the first place so much as with the effect of the poetry, which raises the reader to ecstasy. The "divine frenzy" here is that of the percipient rather than the artificer. After lining up an impressive roster of authorities—"Pythagoras, Empedocles, Heraclitus, and finally the divine Plato," to whom he soon adds Hermes Trismegistus—Landino recalls "that our souls, before descending into our bodies, contemplate in God, as in a mirror, the wisdom, justice, harmony, and beauty of the divine nature" (143.16–22). These attributes of the deity are seen as reflections of the forms immanent in His innermost being. They are ideas, conceived directly by the human soul in its pristine state. When the soul descends into the body, though, the immediate experience of witnessing those divine forms is eradicated from the memory by draughts from Lethe. Nonetheless, the soul retains a lingering recollection of its former existence and longs to return to that vaguely remembered state of bliss. Plato's *Phaedrus* is cited as the text that explains how "philosophers recover their wings, because through meditation they free themselves from the body; and, filled with the godhead, they ascend to God" (143.31–32). Such an "introspective experience" (astrazione), Landino says, is called a "frenzy."

The purpose of art, then, as we have seen in the aesthetics of Augustine, is to recall the ideal forms and provide the introspective experience that leads to this divine frenzy. In a passage strongly reminiscent of Augustine, Landino explains the correlation between the visible world and the invisible, and confirms that a physical object may reflect the beauty of divine forms:

> We cannot recall divine things except by certain images in earthly things, which are almost like shadows of the divine, even though they can be comprehended by the bodily senses. St. Paul, the teacher of the people, confirmed this, as well as Dionysius the Areopagite, who said, "The invisible things of God are seen by us through what is here made visible." Therefore human knowledge

is an image of divine knowledge, and the music of our earthly
instruments is an image of divine harmony. (144.1–8)

The human knowledge conveyed by art is validated as an image
of divine knowledge, since "the music of our earthly instruments
is an image of divine harmony." Thereby the mortal poet/musician
achieves his aim of edifying an audience: "Through our ears, then,
our mind perceives the pure numbers and the musical harmonies,
and by these images it is moved to contemplate the celestial harmony with a greater seriousness" (144.11–14). Again Plato is
called as witness, though this time the text is the *Timaeus,* to certify that "this harmony is of two sorts": one is immaterial, implicit,
recessive, "in the eternal mind of God"; while the other is palpable, explicit, obtrusive, "in universal order and in the planetary
movements." Both, of course, are coordinated, "whence arises the
marvelous concert of nature" (144.14–17). The artificer attempts
to reproduce this harmony in order to awaken the correspondent
forms latent in the psyche of his percipient—"and this is what
Plato called 'poesy'" (144.31–32). Turning finally to the poet
rather than his audience, Landino concludes this essay by echoing
the *Phaedrus*: "This divine frenzy, as we said when dealing with
the poetic art, is supposed to proceed from the Muses; therefore
whoever attempts to become a poet without this divine frenzy
strives in vain" (144.35–145.1).

In the last of these three essays, as Landino himself says, he
"turns to praise the poetic faculty." His strategy is to emphasize
the antiquity of poetry and the notable achievements of poets,
especially in their efforts to raise mankind from savagery and depravity. In a Ciceronian vein, though with a Christian twist, Landino extols the earliest poets, whom he sees as prototypical clergy:

> It is likely that the first men in whom any religious feelings were
> stirred and awakened soon employed their wits in praise of God
> and in prayers, and they worked industriously to devise a more
> elegant way of speaking and to order their words and to compose
> them in definite numbers and feet. (145.5–9)

The first poets are identified as poet/priests who use language for
the acculturating purpose of religion.[110] Two examples are given,

both found in Horace (*Ars poetica* 391–96) and both familiar figures in the Renaissance roll of legendary singers: Orpheus, who
"with his lyre . . . was able to lead to a rational and civil life all
those who used physical force to oppress and trample others, as
well as all those who were barbarous or stupid or almost bestial";
and Amphion, who "with the sweet sound of his lyre . . . gathered
all the wandering men scattered in forest and cave to live in an
orderly community" (145.9–16). In an echo of Cicero, Landino
continues at some length to expound the allegorical significance of
Amphion and his music: "With the sweetness of his verses he
brought together those men who, without laws and customs, lived
as solitary vagabonds in the neighboring mountains" (145.23–24).

Citing Plutarch's *De musica* as his touchstone, Landino next
launches into a brief history of μουσική, starting with the
Greeks—and going behind them to the Syrians, Egyptians, and
Hebrews. Inevitably, "King" David is singled out for special mention because of his psalms, although David's status is somewhat
clouded by the uncertainty of his dates (the new learning here gets
in the way of the old sentiments). Solomon, Isaiah, and Moses are
also cited among the Hebrews, although again the new learning
complicates the standing of Moses by conflating him with Mercu-
rius Trismegistus since both had been credited with the invention
of language. Job is mentioned for his "elegiac verses" (145.26–
146.16). To terminate this historical sketch, Landino jumps from
the most ancient authors to his native Italy and quickly reviews
the poets of Rome. Livius Andronicus is thought to be the earliest
to write tales, though Cato shows that adulatory odes had long
been sung at banquets, and Livy reports that Numa Pompilius,
the second king of Rome, had established the practice of singing
verses at public sacrifices (146.16–23).

Landino now pauses to survey the ground he has covered:

> We have seen what poetry is and how it originates not from mor-
> tal wit, but from a divine frenzy which is infused into human
> breasts; and we have pointed out where the name *poet* comes
> from. Moreover, we have said that no other group of writers in
> antiquity were more estimable. (146.24–28)

What remains to be done, Landino says (looking toward Horace),
"is to indicate how useful and how pleasing the poet is to us, both

in public and in private" (146.28–29). The public usefulness of
poetry lies mainly in its alliance with oratory. Again following Cicero, Landino sees the *ars dicendi* as the distinctive faculty of
humanity; and poetry, at least the schemes and figures of speech,
is the chief ornament of speaking well. "Who does not know," Landino asks, "how much spirit, how much splendor, how much dignity the poet brings to the orator?" (146.32–34). For our private
hours, in contrast, poetry provides matter to be deliberated and
pleasant recreation. "Who does not know how splendidly the
poets have dealt with philosophical thought," Landino asks, "especially Homer, Vergil, and Dante" (147.7–10). Furthermore, he
points to "an ineffable delight and an indescribable pleasure in
poetry, upon which the ear and the mind feast as though it were
the sweetest ambrosia" (147.16–18). For these reasons, Landino
decides, all nations have always honored their poets; and Mae-
cenas, the patron of poets, is deserving of the highest approbation.
By way of conclusion, Landino recapitulates the several attain-
ments of poets:

> If, therefore, the poets are not human but divine, if they alone
> among writers include in their works all there is to know, if they
> are the most ancient of all the other writers, if we always find in
> them usefulness and delight together, if we find in them unlimited
> rules and examples of fine speech and upright living, we must
> with the most diligent study and greatest industry devote our-
> selves to understanding them. (148.11–17)

Poetry is defended from attack and recommended, rather in the
manner of Plutarch, for study. The poet, contrary to Plato's argument, takes an honored place in the community. He personifies
humanitas.

Sidney mentions Julius Caesar Scaliger no less than four times in
The defence of poesie,[111] and an awareness of Scaliger's *Poetices
libri septem* (Lyons, 1561) pervades Sidney's treatise. Many passages of the *Defence* echo the language of the *Poetice*, and Sidney
takes over from Scaliger some classificatory schemes and some
arguments about *energeia* and about Vergil.[112] It would be strange,
in fact, if Sidney did not show evidence of knowing the *Poetice;*

at the time of his writing the *Defence,* Scaliger's work was the most highly praised of the numerous poetical treatises that had leapt into print since the mid-sixteenth century. Scaliger was clearly the authority to contend with, and Sidney treated him with utmost respect.

Scaliger (1484–1558) had been a prominent figure on the European stage of public affairs during the first half of the sixteenth century.[113] He began his distinguished career as a military man in service with the Emperor Maximilian. From that violent life he withdrew at the age of 29 and sought to become a Franciscan, though he soon returned to the dangerous world of combat. But again at the age of 40 he retired from active service, took up medicine as a profession, and devoted himself to the study of natural science and of languages, especially Greek and Latin. He settled in Agen near Périgord, married happily, and produced a large family, including a son equally famous for learning, Joseph Justus Scaliger. Scaliger père published several volumes of Latin poems, which justly enhanced his reputation as a man of letters; and he published separate volumes dealing with Aristotle, Theophrastus, Hippocrates, and Cicero, as well as an outstanding Latin grammar. He also flamboyantly engaged in well-publicized controversies with eminent figures such as Erasmus, Nostradamus, Dolet, Rabelais, and Cardan. He was a profoundly learned man, even if also proud and opinionated. As a scientist, he paved the way for empiricism; as a polemicist, he seemed at least incipiently a Protestant. He was one of those Renaissance geniuses who took all knowledge for his province and used the world as his laboratory.

By the time Scaliger's *Poetice* was published (posthumously), the *Poetics* of Aristotle had been a staple of literary criticism for over half a century.[114] A Greek text was available to Angelo Poliziano by 1483,[115] and Giorgio Valla published a Latin translation in 1498.[116] By 1501 Valla was promulgating its principles in his own writings; he understood the significance of mimesis and acknowledged the importance of plot.[117] The great surge of interest in the *Poetics* came, however, with the superlative edition of Francesco Robortello, *In librum Aristotelis de arte poetica explicationes* (Florence, 1548), containing a revised Greek text and a new Latin translation, interspersed with a lengthy, energetic, and provocative commentary. This was followed rapidly by other translations, commentaries, paraphrases, and digests. By 1561 the *Poetics* had come to dominate literary studies. Scaliger rode the crest of this Aristotelian wave, the title of his own treatise archly reproducing Aristotle's. His literary theory floats buoyantly on the rising tide of sentiment in favor of the *Poetics* as it broke over and submerged the orthodox poetics of divine inspiration.

It would be worse than oversimplification, however, to see Scaliger simply as an Aristotelian. The texts of Aristotle were merely the starting point for his own investigations. Scaliger had studied the scientific works of Aristotle carefully, and wrote important commentaries on Aristotle's treatment of plants and animals.[118] Scaliger admired his predecessor as a natural philosopher, and it was in this vein that he read the *Poetics*. He modified Aristotle to make him current, bringing to bear upon the original material the vast store of writings that had accumulated in the interim as well as the keen judgment of a forceful intellect. In the process of this revaluation, though, Scaliger rejects or refutes much of what Aristotle had proposed. For example, the three criteria by which Aristotle analyzes poetry—media, objects, and modes of imitation (*Poetics* 1447a16–18)—are barely noticed in the *Poetice* (12). Scaliger's harsh critique of Aristotelian *mimesis* occurs in the final book (347).

Most fundamentally and significantly, in fact, Scaliger lays aside mimesis as the requisite feature of literary composition, the basic tenet of an Aristotelian poetics. Although he professes to accept the traditional etymology of "poet" from ποιεῖν—expounded, for example, by Landino—he lightly passes by it (3). Instead, he states contentiously: "The word poet is not, as popularly supposed, derived from the fact that the poet employs the fictitious, but from the fact that he makes verse."[119] The name of "poet" comes *non à fingendo,* not from fictioneering, but *à faciendo versu,* from making verse.[120] For Scaliger, the poet is still primarily a metrician rather than an imitator.

In a prefatory epistle, Scaliger dedicated the *Poetice* to Sylvius, the eldest of his four sons. It was probably begun in the late 1540s when Sylvius was a student in Paris, in the same spirit as Scaliger's study of the Latin language, *De causis linguae latinae libri tredecim* (Lyons, 1540)—as an aid to his sons' education, but also as a larger gesture of contributing to the republic of letters.[121] In any case, the *Poetice* took up a great deal of Scaliger's final decade, and he completed it but two months before his death. It is, like all his work, painstaking, unyielding, full of detail, totally free of self-scrutiny. As the dedicatory epistle makes clear, Scaliger was willing to promote poetry because, still rather in the spirit of Cicero, he sees it as an acculturating factor in human society and as a moralizing factor in each individual life.

When we open the covers of Scaliger's *Poetice,* we are immediately apprised of its studious arrangement. The title page announces seven precisely labelled sections: (1) "Historicus," which takes an historical view of several poetical topics, most notably the origin of language, of poetry, and of the various literary genres; (2) "Hyle," a transliterated Greek word associated with Aristotle meaning "matter," which in this instance is confined largely to poetic meters; (3) "Idea," another transliterated Greek word suggesting Plato although not exclusively indicating him, which in this instance is applied to questions of characterization and style; (4) "Parasceve," yet another transliterated Greek word meaning "preparation," which here has to do with the composition of poetry; (5) "Criticus," devoted to practical criticism, mainly comparisons between Greek and Latin poets who have dealt with the same subject matter; (6) "Hypercriticus," a loose continuation of the preceding section, though now centering on Latin poetry as a corpus, which Scaliger reviews by periods and generally prefers to Greek poetry; and (7) "Epinomis," a catchall label from Greek which serves as title of a Platonic dialogue associated during the Renaissance with Plato's *Laws,* but which here may well be translated "appendix." In this vast tome Scaliger touches upon almost every conceivable topic having to do with poetry. We, however, shall extract only those passages which seem of direct consequence for Sidney's *Defence,* most particularly Scaliger's discussion of imitation. This will be but a fraction of the whole, a disjointed sampling drawn from scattered pages.

Like a good Ciceronian, Scaliger opens his treatise by noting the importance of language in the development of our human community:

> Since man's development depended upon learning, he could not do without that agency which was destined to make him the par-

taker of wisdom. Our speech is, as it were, the postman of the mind, through the services of whom civil gatherings are announced, the arts are cultivated, and the claims of wisdom intercede with men for man. (1)

Oratio is here placed next to *ratio,* fulfilling the basic need for communication in an organized society.

Scaliger soon separates several sorts of writing and proposes a classification that Sidney also follows. There are, Scaliger observes, the discourse of philosophers, which is the most rational and logical use of language; the oratory of statesmen, which calls for more vigorous and less exact expression; and a third class which employs narrative and submits to embellishment. This third sort in turn comprises two distinct kinds of writing, history and poetry. So history and poetry are separated from philosophy and oratory, though they themselves are linked together by their dependence upon event and by their figurative richness. But Scaliger takes care also to distinguish between these two narrative genres:

They differ, however, in that one professes to record the fixed truth, and employs a simple style of composition, while the other either adds a fictitious element to the truth, or imitates the truth by fiction, of course with more elaboration. (2)

The former, clearly, is History, concerned with "setting forth actual events"; while "the latter was called Poetry, or Making, because it narrated not only actual events, but also fictitious events as if they were actual, and represented them as they might be or ought to be." The language, as well as the thought, is Aristotelian: in contrast to history, which records the actual fact, poetry presents the actions of men according to probability or necessity. It is no surprise, then, when Scaliger concludes this paragraph with what seems to be a forthrightly Aristotelian summary statement: "Wherefore the basis of all poetry is imitation."

Immediately, however, Scaliger begins to modify this endorsement of mimesis. "Imitation," he admonishes, "is not the end of poetry, but is intermediate to the end." In line with the contemporary tendency to conflate Aristotle with Horace, Scaliger explains that "the end is the giving of instruction in pleasurable form"; and he adds, in a foretaste of the Protestant's excuse for the language arts, "For poetry teaches, and does not simply amuse, as some used to think." But Scaliger is evidently dissatisfied with this bare apologia, so he goes on to distinguish the utilitarian function of rational discourse from the pleasure-giving effects of μουσική:

> Whenever language is used, the purpose, of course, is to acquaint the hearer with a fact or with the thought of the speaker, but because the primitive poetry was sung, its design seemed merely to please; yet underlying the music was that for the sake of which music was provided only as a sauce.

The pragmatic Scaliger approves the language arts as communication. The scholarly Scaliger, however, recalls the conflation of poetry with music through their shared formal properties. A worldly humanist would have exonerated the sensuous pleasure of poetry on the grounds of its Augustinian aesthetic. The edifying effect upon the reader justifies the incidental beauty. But Scaliger, with a kind of Malvolian abstinence, dissociates the rational meaning from the pleasant sound. He belittles the loveliness of "primitive poetry" so that its music becomes a mere sauce which frivolously disguises the meat of serious thought beneath. Beauty, as the Christian humanist feared, has become a distraction, a seduction from truth. At best, Scaliger is uneasy with his Aristotelian pronouncements about imitation. He longs for the old aesthetic, when poetry and music were sister arts devoted to displaying the divine beauty, yet he cannot overcome his commitment to reason and his suspicion of passion. His rigid intellect does not permit the religious rapture that μουσική induces.

Instead, he returns to the practical ends of poetry and reiterates, "It imitates that it may teach." Whatever the poet describes—councils of war, tempests, battles, various strategems—all is for the purpose of instruction. Scaliger cites Euripides as he appears in Aristophanes's *Frogs,* and quotes a scene where the tragedian assigns poetry a moralizing role in society. He cites also Plato's *Ion,* though to disagree by perversely misunderstanding it. In Scaliger's system, the poet must dependably know what he writes about in order to be a competent instructor in those disciplines, whether warfare or navigation or what else. "The poet is the imitator of things, the rhapsodist is he who acts out the imitation," and by attending the performance the audience learns useful information for the successful pursuit of whatever is being sung about. This is a curious notion of imitation—more contra-Platonic than pro-Aristotelian. The poet imitates by re-presenting our workaday world, and the poem becomes an exposition of actual fact.

Scaliger then takes another tack, although still insisting upon the utilitarian nature of the language arts. He asks leadingly, "Is there not one end, and one only, in philosophical exposition, in oratory, and in the drama?" He conclusively answers his own question in the affirmative: "All have one and the same end—persuasion" (3). The philosopher, the statesman, and the poet are again lined up, and now are all made rhetoricians. The language arts are bent toward influencing an audience. This is why all the modes of discourse, poetry as well as philosophy and oratory, must be true, not fictitious. "Persuasion," Scaliger sensibly points out, "means that the hearer accepts the words of the speaker"; and he concludes, "The soul of persuasion is truth." Imitation here at most can be the accurate reporting of facts with no more bias than can be hidden by a convincing speaker. Lest we resort to *eloquentia* and introduce an aesthetic dimension to the presentation, Scaliger sternly reminds us, "By no means are we to accept the popular idea that eloquent speaking, rather than persuasion, is the end of oratory." So the arts of language are assimilated to the *ars dicendi* of Cicero and Quintilian, and in turn the suasive ability of oratory is directed to the moral betterment of both the individual and his community (5).

Yet at the end of this first chapter, Scaliger again identifies several different sorts of discourse. There is oratory, but also philosophy and poetry. The philosopher may use characters in his exposition, as when "Socrates introduces Diotima or Aspasia, and Plato brings forward Socrates" (7); and the orator in his eulogies "in like manner interjects personifications." Furthermore, since the eulogist must needs rely upon biographical anecdote, "This allies him with the historian," who similarly in his turn has frequent recourse to characterization in his reporting. This round-robin of an argument leads circuitously to an unstated conclusion that all these verbal arts are likely to represent men in action, and therefore call into play the narrative mode. That observation allows Scaliger to return to his topic, poetics, and to render it guarded praise:

> But it is only poetry which includes everything of this kind, excelling those other arts in this, that while they, as we have said above, represent things just as they are, in some sense like a speaking picture,[122] the poet depicts quite another sort of nature, and a variety of fortunes; in fact, by so doing, he transforms himself almost into a second deity. (7–8)

Scaliger here seems to release the poet from the stricture, which is placed upon the other verbal arts, to "represent things just as they are." The poet does not merely record fact. Rather, to some unspecified but limited degree he has license to imagine: "The poet depicts quite another sort of nature, and a variety of fortunes." By this exercise of the imagination, the poet becomes a creator in the footsteps of the heavenly Creator, as the Augustinian aesthetic had prescribed: "He transforms himself almost into a second deity."

Scaliger in this new-found enthusiasm for poetry throws caution to the winds and contradicts his earlier argument that poetry, like the other arts of language, has persuasion as its aim and therefore must be factual. The *other* language arts are confined to verifiable subject matter: "Of those things which the Maker of all framed, the other sciences are, as it were, overseers (actores)" (8).[123] Poetry, however, creates a second nature:

> But since poetry fashions images of those things which are not, as well as images more beautiful than life of those things which are, it seems unlike other literary forms, such as history, which confine themselves to actual events, and rather to be another god, and to create.[124]

It is this argument—praising poetry as an inclusive and imaginative art, and elevating the poet to a near-divine status—that Sidney takes over from Scaliger (*Defence* 78.22–26). Sidney, however, unlike Scaliger, takes pains to accommodate the Augustinian maker to the Aristotelian imitator. In contrast, this passage in Scaliger's *Poetice* is isolated, incongruous with its context, and inconsistent with the main argument in this chapter demanding persuasiveness (and therefore truthfulness) of poetry.

The fact that the first chapter closes with such claims for poetry might explain why the second chapter opens with the bold assertion that the poet is a versifier above all else. It may well have been the Augustinian notion that the poet is "another god," creating according to number, weight, and measure, that led Scaliger to insist upon metrics in poetry. In the second chapter of Book 1 Scaliger defines the poet as he who makes verses rather than fictions (9). And just as Aristotle had postulated that the impulse to imitate is born in us, so Scaliger finds an innate impulse to versify: "The propensity for rhythm (vis numerosa), the medium of poetry, is an instinct with man." [125] Continuing to trace the development of poetry from this natural rhythmic impulse in human speech, Scaliger notes that poets soon sought the patronage of the Muses: "They arrogated to themselves, as guardians, the protection of the Muses, the Muses by the inspiration of whom they had discovered what was concealed from others." These poets seem very much like the divinely inspired singers of Landino who in their poetic frenzy are privileged to see what others cannot. These are the true poets, Scaliger assures us; and he continues, "Those, on the other hand, who lacked this inspiration, and simply composed metrical narratives, were called versifiers." Already Scaliger's definition of the poet à *faciendo versu* is found wanting; a versifier belongs to a lower order of artificers. Versification may be necessary to poetry, but it is not sufficient.

Scaliger does not address this inconsistency in his argument, however, but rather directs our attention, as though for diversion, to some fanciful etymologies of the word "Muse." His investigation into the nature of poetry trails off into learned but obfuscatory chitchat about invention and judgment and other only vaguely related matters, with breezy references to Cicero, Vitruvius, Mimnermus, Plutarch, Vergil, Plato, Pindar, Theocritus, and Aristotle. Scaliger dwells upon the rich tradition that surrounded the Muses (lore of equal interest to Landino), offering a numerological explanation of why there are *nine* Muses, recalling the musical analogy between notes and heavenly bodies and Muses, and wondering about the relation of the Muses to Mnemosyne and to Jove and to Osiris. This obsession with the Muses, pretty much a show of learning for its own sake, aligns Scaliger with the syncretic humanists of the previous century rather than the empirical scientists of the next. The flimsiness of the discussion is indicated by this sentence which introduces an anecdote: "That the Graces and pleasure and the Muses and good health are related, may be gathered from the oracle which Plutarch records as delivered to the Argive Telesilla" (14). This is hardly the logical discourse we had been led to expect.

It is therefore with some relief that we find Scaliger returning to the methodical analysis which aligns him with Aristotle. "We may make a threefold classification of poets," he suddenly says in a new breath; and he lists, in Aristotelian fashion, the criteria for his categories: "according to poetical inspiration, age [i.e., epoch], and subjects." He then examines each of these categories in turn.

The first distinguishes between three modes of inspiration: (1) "some men are born inspired"; (2) "others, born ignorant and rude, and even averse to the art, are seized on by the divine madness, and wrested from their lowliness"; and (3) yet others are "aroused by the fumes of unmixed wine, which draws out the instruments of the mind, the spirits themselves, from the material parts of the body" (15). Plato, seconded by Aristotle, is cited as authority for the assumption that "there are diversities of inspiration." What is most interesting, however, is the importance assigned to the Muses: "The poets invoke the Muses," Scaliger avers, "that the divine madness may imbue them to do their work" (15). As poetic theory, this is no advance over Landino.

The second category classifies poets "according to the age in which they wrote," and again there are three divisions. Because this thumbnail history of poetry may have provided Sidney with information, we should have it in its entirety:

> First, there was that pristine, crude, and uncultivated age, of which only a vague impression remains. No name survives, unless it be that of Apollo, as the originator of poetry. Then there is the second and venerable period, when religion and the mysteries are first sung. Among the poets of this period are numbered Orpheus, Musaeus, and Linus; Plato includes Olympus also. Of the third

period Homer is the founder and parent, and it includes Hesiod and other such writers. (15)[126]

From here the account degenerates into inconclusive speculation about chronology—for instance, whether Musaeus or Homer was earlier.

The third category, and the most pertinent because it most nearly parallels a passage from Sidney,[127] classifies poets "according to subject-matter." There is great variety in this category—"as many kinds as there are styles of subjects treated." But to render the topic manageable, Scaliger reduces the possibilities to three main heads:

> The first is that of the religious poets. Such are Orpheus and Amphion, whose art was so divine that they are believed to have given a soul to inanimate things. The second is that of the philosophical poets, and these again are of two sorts—natural, as Empedocles, Nicander, Aratus, and Lucretius; and moral, including the political, as Solon and Tyrtaeus; the economical, as Hesiod; and the general, as Phocylides, Theognis, and Pythagoras. (16)

Scaliger further comments gallantly that women authors also merit praise, and he names several, though Sappho is the only one likely to be known today. He raises the question of whether prophecies, such as the Sibylline oracles, should be judged as poetry; but he declines to do so on the grounds that "they do not narrate past events, but predict future ones," so he regards the oracles as the "actual utterance of the things disclosed by the gods." With regard to Roman poetry—"our poetry," according to Scaliger, and almost always superior to the Greek—it is generally agreed to have begun during the Second Punic War. Next comes a miscellaneous query: "Why does Horace question whether or not comedy is poetry?" (17). Scaliger most assuredly thinks it worthy of such a title.

Then Scaliger raises another question that bears more closely upon the basis of his poetic theory. Ever since Aristotle it had been continuously and hotly debated whether a natural philosopher such as Empedocles or a historian such as Herodotus was a poet simply if he wrote in verse. Aristotle had raised the issue in order to declare in the negative; for him, the act of mimesis identifies the poet, and composing in verse or not is incidental. Later, the argument had been broadened to include Roman historians, such as Lucan.[128] So this is the precise question that Scaliger now asks: "Was Lucan a poet?" His answer, without hesitation, is affirmative, and his reasoning is typically pragmatic: "Lucan must differ from Livy, and the difference is verse." Scaliger extends this observation to a generality: "Verse is the property of the poet." Again, it is the *faciendum versu* that designates the poet, not his subject matter—nor the inspiration of the Muses, and certainly not the ability to "imitate" as Aristotle had defined the term. The argument in this chapter has come full circle.

Book 2 of the *Poetice* is entitled "Hyle" and deals with the "matter" of poetry, which Scaliger interprets as language, and especially as language that can be metrified by rhythm. It begins with the statement that "poetry consists of two basic parts, substance and form,"[129] and both are due for discussion—the one in this book, and the other in the following book, entitled "Idea." Scaliger then begins the analysis of what the *materia* of poetry might be.

For this discussion Scaliger adopts the vocabulary of the rhetorician and uses the terms *res* and *verba*.[130] The *res* of poetry is its conceptual component, "the very thing which is written of." The *verba* are the actual words, the medium of the poem. Scaliger's strategy is to prove that the substance of poetry is *verba*, not *res;* and this conclusion allows him to proceed with showing how words can be deployed in metrical patterns in order to satisfy his requirement that poetry be in verse. His argument, however, is circuitous, not to say disjunctive; and though he accomplishes his immediate aim of introducing a book which lays out the multifarious poetic meters, in the process he condones a theory of imitation that seriously undermines the main thrust of his larger argument that poetry must be truthful in order to persuade.

Scaliger begins this portion of his argument by testing the hypothesis that "the very thing which is written of is the substance of the poem." He notes that often the distinction between *res* and *materia* is collapsed, so that the contents of a poem are taken to be its substance: "They call the subjects and the materials of poetry two sides of the same coin, and not without cause, since the Greeks have said they lie close together." He rejects the hypothe-

sis that *res* is the *materia* of poetry, however, and bases this negative conclusion on a cogent comparison between a poem and a
statue:

> In the same way that a statue of Caesar is Caesar's image, so also
> the poem that describes him is his physical representation. But
> bronze or marble is the substance of the statue, not Caesar. Cae-
> sar is the object, as the philosophers say, and the ultimate refer-
> ent.

Scaliger argues that the bronze or marble of a statue belongs to
the statue *qua* artifact and has nothing to do with who is being
represented. He distinguishes, rightly, between the medium of the
artifact and the nature of the imitated object. Analogously, the
words of a poem, being its medium, are equivalent to the bronze
or marble of the statue, and therefore the *verba* and not the *res*
are the substance of a poem. The *res* may be the object of imitation, but it is not the material of the artifact.

So far, so good. We seem to be heading toward a phenomenalist
aesthetic. An artifact is comprised of its phenomena—brass,
marble, words, whatever. But curiously, Scaliger pauses at this
point and brings Plato into the discussion. "If we follow Plato," he
observes, "we shall make the opposite judgment." And he proceeds to outline a Platonic aesthetic whereby an artifact is informed by an essential idea to which it gives a palpable existence.
"Plato distributed the order of things in this way," Scaliger says,
and he repeats in brief the theory of mimesis that Plato expounds
in the final book of the *Republic:*

> First, there is an absolute and incorruptible form. In the second
> place, from that form a corruptible thing may be produced, which
> is the image of that form. In the third position, Plato puts the
> picture or literary work—they are produced in the same way.
> Since they are derived from the projected images of the original
> forms, they are merely the images of appearances.

As Scaliger paraphrases Plato, the artifact (picture or literary
work) is "in the third position," twice removed from the originating
idea. Far from impugning the validity of the artifact, however,
which was the point of Plato's argument, Scaliger assumes that the

artifact embodies a corresponding essence from the realm of ideas and accurately conveys its significance. Apparently, he is not aware of, or not bothered by, the inconsistency of taking the *verba* to be the substance of a poem while its ultimate being lies in its *res,* its idea or form. Scaliger has opened a breach between the world of physicality and the realm of ideas, dissociating *verba* from *res.* This detour through a Platonic landscape has brought him to an impasse.

Scaliger tries to get back on track by signaling to his avowed mentor, Aristotle, who had related form and content through the famous analogue of a mold imprinting itself in wax. By an agile mental leap, Scaliger assumes a similar relation between Platonic idea and its replication as palpable object in the physical world.[131] This mimetic theory of Plato, he says, "accords with the Aristotelian demonstration by which we understand the design of a bath to be in an architect's mind before he constructs the bath, where the same would be both form and ultimate referent." By such a maneuver, Scaliger pretends to have annealed the breach he had introduced between idea and artifact, between *res* and *verba.*

Therefore Scaliger confidently asks, "What is the substance of poetic language [oratio] other than letters, syllables, and words?"; and just as confidently, he adds, "It is air, or parchment, or the mind in which they exist as it were in subjection"—all leading to his triumphant conclusion: "Consequently, bronze will be the substance in the statue of Caesar, and words in poetry."[132] Not realizing the inappropriateness of his argument, not to mention its inner contradictions, Scaliger continues with the comparison between a statue and a poem:

> In the statue the position expresses activity, motion, a standing still, a sitting down, or something of this sort; in poetry all this is in the alignment and arrangement of the words. In the statue the toga and armor serve as ornaments and accoutrements; in poetry that part is played by rhythm or meter, rhetorical figures, and colorful language.

Just as toga and armor are the outer dress of a statue, so the "rhythm or meter, rhetorical figures, and colorful language" are the visibilia of a poem. Scaliger seems unconcerned that he has minimized its conceptual component to the point of negligibility; he has argued out of existence its *res.* In his pragmatic fashion, however, he has set up his next three books: "In this second book the substance of poetry will be discussed [i.e., poetic meter]; in the third, its form; and in the fourth, its ornamentation."

Book 3 of the *Poetice,* entitled "Idea," is devoted to the subject matter of poetry. Scaliger opens with what he by this point, unwarrantedly, takes to be a proven premise: "The poem, as has been said, is a kind of imitation." This statement raises in his mind four questions which require investigation: "(1) what we are imitating, (2) why we are doing the imitation, (3) to what end we imitate, and (4) by what means we imitate." [133] By answering these questions, Scaliger claims, "We shall be more searching than Aristotle." Actually, the second and third questions have already been answered: "In the first book of this treatise on poetry, we demonstrated its use, as well as its origin and ultimate nature; and our reason for imitating is so that man's life might become better ordered." The fourth question has been partially answered in Book 2 on poetic meter and will be further addressed in Book 4: "In the next book we shall say how we do this imitation, though in an earlier part of this work the various sorts of meter were treated as well as the numerical laws [rationes] by which we imitate." What remains, then, is the first question: "Now let's see what is worth imitating."

Again dividing his topic into *res* and *verba,* Scaliger proceeds to postulate some relationship between words and what they signify. According to Scaliger, the *res* exists before and independent of the *verba,* and determines their meaning, rather as Cratylus long ago had argued: "The things themselves [res] constitute the ultimate referent [finis] of language [oratio], while words [verba] are their notations [notae]; and because of this, words take their form [forma] from the things themselves, the form by which they are what they are." [134] Scaliger feels uncomfortable, however, in this proximity to Cratylus and his medieval followers, so he takes pains to dissociate himself from that theory of language. He explains testily:

> We have named this book "Idea," though not because we have made the same error as the Platonists and consider that words are by their nature created by the things they describe. Words are not

such and so because the things they represent are of a certain sort
or a certain size. Rather, it is we who determine the language
[oratio].

By a great wrench of tradition, Scaliger wrests from nature the
power of bestowing meaning upon words and invests it in the
speaking individual. Far in advance of his time Scaliger prepares
for a theory that sees language as the subjective expression of a
human mind. Momentary thoughts determine language in such a
system, not eternal absolutes or natural laws or even social conventions. Unfortunately, however, Scaliger does not explore the
possibilities of such a theory beyond the rhetorician's use of language to sway an audience.

Book 4 of the *Poetice,* although as announced it deals with the
practical business of composition, has very little to say about poetry as an art of imitation. Its most important pronouncement for
our purposes comes in chapter 7, "Numerositas." There we are
told again that "meter is the soul of poetry"; and, by way of rein-
forcement, that "no kind of poetic expression is without meter." [135]
In this least theoretical of the seven books, mimesis is forgotten.

Book 5 of the *Poetice* is almost equally disappointing. This
book, entitled "Criticus," demonstrates the role of the critic in literary studies, and the first chapter bears the heading "De imitatione et judicio." The sort of imitation that Scaliger has in mind,
however, is the imitation of classical models, the kind associated
most frequently with Horace; and the sort of judgment to be exercised also follows Horatian precepts. Although all poets do not
depend upon the imitation of predecessors, Scaliger observes—
the first poets had no models to follow—he nonetheless thinks
that most poets should resort to this kind of copying. After an
approving glance at Cicero and a longer look at Horace's imitative
practices, Scaliger concludes: "A two-fold judgment should therefore be applied—first, we should select only the best for imitation;
second, we should peruse carefully all we produce, as if it were
not our own work, and we should criticize it severely." [136] So much
for the theoretical principles of "imitation and judgment." The rest
of Book 5 is given over to the comparison of Greek and Roman
poets, and Book 6 continues the work of the practical critic in a
methodical survey of Roman poetry.

Book 7, though, returns to questions occasioned by Aristotelian imitation. In this book, entitled "Epinomis" or "revised opinions," Scaliger goes back over several passages that he has now reconsidered, because he wishes to make additional comments. It would be reassuring if this overview reconciled inconsistencies and smoothed over discontinuities, but unfortunately this is not the case. In any event, Scaliger does touch upon many of the topics that we have already scrutinized; and although his review of them here is far from systematic, we are obliged to follow his string of second thoughts.

Scaliger begins by positing a theory of imitation, in both nature and art, that goes back ultimately to the last book of Plato's *Republic,* where forms from the realm of ideas are projected into matter, producing physical objects which in turn serve as objects of imitation for the artificer. Scaliger had summarized this Platonic aesthetic in Book 2 of the *Poetice,* and had taken a firm stand as its advocate. Now, though, he wishes to replace the Platonic cosmology with an Aristotelian worldview, so that reality resides among the quantifiable things of physical nature rather than with the ideal essences in Plato's world of absolute being. In consequence, he redefines the word *res:* it is no longer the rhetorician's "thing which is written of," but rather the empiricist's "thing" which is observed by the senses. "Everything that exists," Scaliger exclaims in his opening sentence, "is designated by the term 'thing.' "[137] Moreover, mimesis no longer involves imitating an object which in turn is an imitation of an idea, as in Plato's system; rather, in a way supposedly approved by Aristotle, mimesis involves no more than re-presenting something—"an ox, a man, an oak tree"—that already exists in its own right. "Materials are borrowed from nature," Scaliger explains, and "a shape is imposed upon them." In other words, mimetic art is nothing other than the replication of a portion of nature selected by the artisan. He repeats what he sees in the world about him: a house is a refined imitation of a cave, the shoemaker takes his cue from the hoofs of animals, and the weaver follows the practice of spiders.

Scaliger proposes no very elegant theory of art; indeed, his notion of artistry is wholly practical, as his examples indicate, devoid of any interest in beauty for itself. He propounds a view exactly opposite to aestheticism. As his first thesis, he announces "the fact that every imitation is done for a purpose";[138] and he ponderously documents this point: statues are erected to commemorate venerable men, and swords are fabricated for the defence of their owners. "No imitation is done for its own sake alone," Scaliger concludes; "art always looks outside itself at what might be conducive to something else." This is no art for art's sake.

Having established the utilitarian purpose of art, and having defined imitation as the re-presentation of natural things, Scaliger narrows his view to the distinguishing feature of poetry, its medium, and again turns his attention to language. He has rejected the Cratylian position that a word is the communicable portion of an entity that antecedes the word, although Scaliger's theory of language can be best understood in a Cratylian context. Cratylus postulates that a word signifies an object, physical or conceptual, to which it is naturally and inextricably related. Cratylus, however, places ultimate reality among the immaterial essences in Plato's realm of ideas; while Scaliger, as we have noted, relocates reality among the objects of physical nature. Therefore Scaliger gives priority of existence to those physical objects; they are his original "things." And a word is a sign for, an abstraction from, such a "thing." "It is clear," he says with his customary self-confidence, "that all our speech is nothing other than an image, for names themselves are conceptions of things."[139] The name is an insubstantial derivation from the material thing, a conception of it.

But how does this linguistic theory accord with the theory of language developed so painstakingly in Book 2, when Scaliger argued for the palpability of language in order that it might submit to metrification? There, we recall (pages 211–12), Scaliger proved that words are the *materia* of a poem just as bronze or marble is the substance of a statue. Here, words are abstractions. The inconsistency is glaringly evident.

Again, though, Scaliger is unaware of or indifferent to self-contradiction, and without hesitation he continues to pontificate about the use of language for the purposes of imitation in poetry. A word is an insubstantial image of a thing in a one-to-one relationship, but Scaliger suggests also how words conjoin in discourse. He has at least a rudimentary notion of syntax: "Bare words taken by themselves signify what various things are, as 'man,' or 'whiteness'; but put together they mean this—'a white man.' "[140] Then quite graphically he demonstrates how poetic images are constructed from verbal materials:

> All of those arts which employ language [oratio] as their medium are constituted by imitation. But imitation is not of one sort alone, any more than there is only one sort of thing [res]. One kind of imitation is the simple designation, as in the statement, "Aeneas fights." Another kind of imitation adds ways and circumstances. Some verbal examples: "with the sword," "armed," "on a horse," "furiously." This produces the actual appearance [facies] of a man who is fighting, not only his action. In this way circumstances of place, of emotion, and of occasion are added, so that they flesh out the imitation and endow it with a real sense of time and actual speech and relevance. Thereby arises, besides uniformity of style and fineness of delineation, a sense of shadow, light, background, the emphasis of certain parts, vigor, effectiveness. Poets shape [effingere] all these things when they shape their works.

Scaliger readily certifies language as a valid medium for imitation. Furthermore, he identifies two sorts of imitation which language allows: the straightforward account and the account embellished by descriptive detail. "In this way," he says, "circumstances of place, of emotion, and of occasion are added"; and he notes that details of time and location "flesh out the imitation." Scaliger sees this descriptive capacity of poetry as its chief ornament.

How innovative! What Scaliger recommends is something new in literary theory; at least, no one earlier had made the point so baldly. Poetry is primarily a descriptive exercise. By demonstrating the depictive potential of language, Scaliger impels poetry toward painting as its sister art. Words are no longer quantifiable entities to be metrified into the formal patterns of verse. Rather, the poet uses language to paint word pictures—albeit, in Scaliger's example, pictures of men in action, like the epic hero, Aeneas.

It is significant, I think, that in his example Scaliger specifies the depiction of the human figure rather than movements or gestures. He says about the verbal description of Aeneas in battle, "This produces the actual appearance of a man who is fighting, not only his action." Implicit here is a criticism of Aristotle. Early in the *Poetics,* Aristotle had declared that poetry is an imitation of the actions of men, rather than of men in action; and in his discussion of tragedy he repeatedly insisted upon the prominence of plot at the expense of characterization. But Scaliger, like most critics of his day, reversed Aristotle's ranking of the genres and preferred epic to tragedy—largely because the epic hero provides a moral exemplum for the sort of instruction that Renaissance theorists thought poetry should effect. Poetry depicts individual men in full-bodied clarity, easily discerned and emulated, not hazy universals of what might be or should be. Poetry, to serve Scaliger's purpose, must offer a concrete example.

Not surprisingly, Scaliger turns to an outright chastisement of Aristotle:

> Aristotle made imitation the whole purpose of the poet, and to man alone of all living creatures he attributed this ability as a distinctive characteristic. Once Aristotle had set down this theory, he often repeated it and continually supported it. But he drew us into two absurdities. His first error was that he did not put poetry [poesis] alone in this class, but put epic verse [epopoeia], the mimes of Sophron, the dialogues of Alexamenes of Teos about philosophy, written in a loose style, all in the same class together. His other error occurred when he said that the history of Herodotus, had it been confined by the laws of meter, would nonetheless have been a history. His first error was so silly, that he made the epos a kind of relaxed speech. As for the second error, this is hardly the case with history. It will not be a history, but a historical poem.[141]

Scaliger protests that Aristotle's definition of ποιητική is so lax that almost any verbal construct falls into it; while, at the same time, Aristotle excludes history from the poetic category, even versified history. Absurd! But, of course, Scaliger has grossly perverted Aristotle's theory of imitation, and it is his own misconceptions that make Aristotle appear at fault.

While snidely pointing out the errors of others, Scaliger remains oblivious to his own. This harangue is a prelude to Scaliger's oft-stated thesis: "The end of poetry is not imitation, but pleasurable teaching, by which the soul is led to right reason; and thereby man arrives at that perfect condition which is called blessedness."[142] He goes on to offer the observation—which he finds objectionable, but which both Aristotle and Sidney were quite willing to

accept—that if imitation is made the distinguishing feature of poetry, anyone who imitates, in prose as well as verse, will be a
poet.[143] Even Plato, Scaliger deduces, "will become a poet in his
Laws, even though he excludes the poet from his laws"—a point
that horrified Scaliger, though it delighted Sidney (*Defence*
75.11–21).

The full implications of Aristotelian mimesis are never understood by Scaliger, much less accepted by him. For several lines he
continues to scratch his head in puzzlement:

> Even the agent in the marketplace will become a poet, when he
> explains his master's orders in his own words. And the epic poet,
> when he introduces a speaking character, will be a poet; although
> when he speaks in his own person, he will not be. By the same
> token, the part of the *Iliad* which is from the mouths of made-up
> personages will be a poem, but that part which is from Homer
> will not be a poem.[144]

Scaliger is troubled by Aristotle's distinction between imitation by
direct discourse and by authorial narrative (1448a19–24). Aristotle had preferred the former because it allows fuller opportunity
to develop the potential of mimesis. Scaliger does not understand
mimesis and has already declared in favor of narration. Hence the
contretemps.

Scaliger wonders also about the poetic genres that are not narrative in character, such as "lyric poems, drinking-songs, paeans,
elegies, epigrams, satires, silvae, epithalamions, hymns" ([7.2]
347). How can they be said to depend upon imitation? Of course
they are not mimetic poetry, at least as Scaliger has defined imitation. He is dogged in his persistence that versifying is the distinctive activity of the poet, and he mutters one last grievance
against Aristotle: "He does not do rightly in cheating Empedocles
of the name of poet."[145]

Scaliger by this point has exhausted himself, as well as us, so he
moves to close this review of Aristotelian mimesis. His opening
gambit is safe, a reprise of Horace: "The purpose of the poet is to
instruct with delight."[146] He adds a humanistic note, pointing to
the civic function of poetry: "Poetry is a part of the state."[147] To
achieve these noble aims, he confirms that poetry must be truth-

ful: "It is therefore the property of speech to express facts."[148] And so he arrives at his thundering conclusion, ticking off each point as though it were proved:

> A poem does not arise from imitation, for not every poem is an imitation. Nor is everyone who imitates a poet. Poetry does not arise from fiction or falsehood, for poetry does not lie—or if it does, it does so consistently. So poetry and non-poetry would amount to the same thing. Finally, in all speech there is imitation, for words are the images of things. The purpose of the poet is to instruct with an accompanying pleasure.[149]

Except for the last sentence echoing Horace, Sidney would have disagreed with every point.

In actuality, Sidney is much more of an Aristotelian than Scaliger. Like Aristotle, Sidney is willing to forego versification in order to implement fully a theory of imitation based upon universals, upon representing what might be or should be. Scaliger willfully misunderstands Aristotle's concept of mimesis, interpreting imitation at some times as the following of classical models à la Horace, and at others as the accurate description of physical phenomena. Although Scaliger was eager to write under the aegis of Aristotle, he either did not properly construe his acknowledged master or intentionally subverted him. For, counter to Aristotle, Scaliger insists upon versification, he does not allow that truth may arise from fiction, and he assigns poetry a forthrightly moralizing function.

Scaliger, in fact, never resolved his divided loyalties. He never fully relinquished the orthodox poetics based upon divine inspiration and expressed through metrification. He was too much a product of Italian humanism, too well-read in the ancient literature, too appreciative of μουσική. His own poems attest to his conservatism. But since Scaliger was not interested in the orthodox poetics as a philosophical system—Renaissance man that he was, he deplored medieval attitudes—versification survived for him as a vestige, a fossilization of the old beliefs. Eventually, versification became incongruous with the new poetics of a genuinely Aristotelian *mimesis,* so by the mid-sixteenth century numbers and measures had sloughed off as a requirement. Already in certain passages of Scaliger we can see poetry nudged in the direction of painting, with description—not metrification—as its dominant feature. But Scaliger did not attempt to settle this conflict.

As a result, his treatise is more a compilation of forcefully argued points than a self-consistent theory of poetry. Unlike Weinberg, I do not find Scaliger "basically an orderly thinker, capable of seeing the necessary consequences of his distinctions and of creating a subordination of his ideas to guiding principles" (2:744).[150] Weinberg classified Scaliger as an Aristotelian and therefore liked him. Rather, I see Scaliger in muddled dilemma, neither Augustinian nor Aristotelian, an indecisive theorist whose agility as author and critic never overcame the inertia of the pedant's love of things antique. He refused to think through the necessary consequences of his apparent Aristotelianism, which called for a rejection of the orthodox poetics based upon the formal properties of metrification.

As we shall see in the next chapter, Sidney was sensitive to the literary issues raised by earlier theorists, but he remained very much of his own mind. He was attentive to his predecessors, but no one of them seemed conclusive or complete. Several questions about imitation were still pending. Sidney faced those questions squarely, formulated the problems in manageable terms, and with good will and good sense set about providing solutions. He came as close to smoothing over the difficulties as anyone has ever come. His defence of poetry not only protected it from attackers, of which there were increasing numbers, but also set it in a new place of honor among our most cherished institutions.

5

The Defence of Poesie:
Language and Imitation

The conceits of the mind are Pictures of things, and the tongue is the Interpreter of those Pictures.[1]

What really comes before our mind when we *understand* a word?—Isn't it something like a picture? Can't it *be* a picture?[2]

In *The defence of poesie* Sidney puts forward a radical poetics that marks an advance over the neoplatonist aesthetic of proportion and harmony. In Italy already for centuries the civic humanists had cultivated the language arts to serve the ends of the godly city on earth. Sidney respected that tradition, but he felt the need to adjust to a worldview which increasingly questioned the primacy of Platonic essences and relocated reality among the phenomena of observed nature. Consequently, he depreciated the formal properties of poetry which lead to intellection in pursuit of goodness, truth, and beauty. Poetry should result not only in well-knowing, an ordering of the soul to accord with the providential scheme; more important, it should result in well-doing, active deployment of that scheme in everyday affairs. To achieve this activist aim, it must be more experiential than meditational. So in Sidney's hands poetry becomes less an exercise in ritual worship and more an instrument of politics. While sharing with the earlier humanists their belief that the verbal arts are the most efficacious means of acculturating the populace, Sidney exploits the depictive potential of language to effect his plan for Protestant renewal.

For Sidney the right poets, those who truly deserve the name of maker, "do merely make to imitate, and imitate both to delight and teach" (*Defence* 81.10–11). That in brief is Sidney's poetic program. To "make" and to "imitate" are technical terms with specific meanings, and they point to the innovative techniques that Sidney advocates for poetry. Moreover, since poetry is an art of discourse, it falls within the bounds of rhetoric; so to "delight and teach" indicates the intent that Sidney imposes upon the poet, charting the course by which the poet achieves the purpose his making and imitating are designed for. With a sweeping amplitude of vision and a patriot's zeal, Sidney gives firm direction to English letters. He redefines the important role of the poet in society, contrary both to those who would give him privileged status and those who would castigate him, identifies a revitalized subject matter for poetry, bringing it down to earth, and delineates a new mechanism whereby the verbal artifact has its intended effect upon an audience.

This last consideration—the poetic mechanism itself—has gone largely unnoticed, despite Sidney's explicitness. Just what do "making" and "imitating" entail, and how does poetry "delight and teach" the reader? Until recently, the *Defence* has usually been read and praised as some sort of homage to poetry, a statement of poetic faith or testament to beauty.[3] Its effusive tone and talk about a golden world have been emphasized to the detriment of its sober and practical side, with the result that we have not asked the hard-nosed question of exactly how the arts of language are to be deployed in the serious business that Sidney proposes as poetry's best defence. How does the poet, restricted to the medium of words, produce poetic images which generate meaning that leads not only to architectonic knowledge, but to virtuous action? Sidney had pondered the question later posed by Wittgenstein: "What really comes before our mind when we *understand* a word?"; and he had reached a similar answer: "Isn't it something like a picture? Can't it *be* a picture?" This answer, of course, is itself a question, and in turn raises other questions—opening up possibilities, however, rather than terminating the discussion. Sidney explores these possibilities, starting from the assumption that language can produce images with semantic content, "speaking pictures." In this chapter we shall direct our attention toward that radical poetics which allowed development of the depictive potential of poetry.

Because of Sidney's concern with the transformation of verbal system into poetic image, *The defence of poesie* is a major event, if not *the* major event, in the development of literary theory in England. There is nothing before it that comes close to its scope and authority, nothing that even makes the attempt to identify poetry as a mature discipline separable from the rhetoric and grammar taught in the schools.

In its own day the *Defence* had reached a limited audience even before its printing, and was deferred to as the well-reasoned essay of a wise and witty man of letters.[4] Then in 1595, nine years after Sidney's death, there were two printed editions: one by William Ponsonby with the title *The defence of poesie,* and another by Henry Olney with the title *An apologie for poetrie.*[5] Since that time Sidney's treatise has been kept continuously in print. In the numerous editions of his complete works originally authorized by the Countess of Pembroke, starting with the folio of 1598[6] and continuing until 1674, the *Defence* holds a secure place in a central position following the *Arcadia* and *Certain sonnets,* but preceding *Astrophil and Stella* and what has come to be called *The Lady of May.* In E. Taylor's edition of Sidney's works,[7] which proved to be the format for the eighteenth century, the *Defence* was moved forward to second place, immediately following the *Arcadia* and heading the section subtitled "The Poetical Works of Sir Philip Sidney." The *Defence* regained its autonomy in 1752, when Robert Urie in Glasgow issued it independently of Sidney's other writings; and in 1787 Joseph Warton again published it in a separate volume, augmented by excerpts from Ben Jonson's *Discoveries.* Since then, the *Defence* has been regularly reprinted as a discrete tract. During a five-year period in the recent past it enjoyed no less than four scholarly editions.[8] Since its composition in winter 1579–80, it has remained, without abatement, a potent force in determining the course of English letters.[9]

Although inflated claims are self-defeating, the case for Sidney's *Defence* as the major event in English literary theory deserves a hearing. As an intelligent and well-educated humanist, Sidney was master of the discipline of rhetoric. Poetry was one of the arts of language, originating with invention and aimed at persuasion.[10] In this tradition, especially as conflated with the Horatian dictum that poets should delight and teach, Sidney saw literature as a means of encouraging the public and private virtues in his fellow Englishmen. This teleology for poetry was confirmed and abetted by his Platonism, particularly the civic humanism that the Florentines had extracted from the *Republic,* and it was given renewed urgency by his Protestantism. Literature, a message of words like the Gospel, could be applied in the task of raising fallen humanity from depravity and of obtaining for it, if not a state of eternal grace, at least a place in God's kingdom on earth. In the words of Sir John Harington, consciously echoing Sidney, the purpose of poetry is "to soften and polish the hard and rough dispositions of men, and make them capable of vertue and good discipline" (2:197).

None of this was other than commonplace, and it can be found at least piecemeal in other apologists for poetry in Elizabethan London.[11] What is new, however, is the charm and elegance of Sidney's argument; even more important, its solidity, comprehensiveness, and conviction; and most important of all, its introduction into England of a new depictive poetics based upon Aristotle without breaking continuity with the past. Sidney had carefully read the Continental critics—especially Scaliger, and probably Minturno and Castelvetro—and he had understood the issues in the raging debate over the *Poetics.* Furthermore, he had resolved several of those issues to his own satisfaction, especially those stemming from the concept of mimesis, and he published his solutions in a positive poetic program that underlay English literary theory well into the nineteenth century—when Shelley reconfirmed it and gave it renewed vitality as a Romantic poetics in his own *Defence of Poetry.*

With the original *Defence of poesie,* however, an Englishman for the first time, while having full knowledge of the Continental tradition, took off from that tradition and extended the range of poetic techniques. Like other neo-Aristotelians, Sidney departed from the age-old aesthetic of μουσική, where poetry was a product of divine inspiration expressed in meter, and placed it readily within the reach of human hands. He does not reduce poetry to an "art" in the Horatian sense of a skill learned by exercise—"A poet no industry can make," Sidney says, "if his own genius be not carried into it" (111.32–33). Nonetheless, in a brilliant adaptation of the empiricist bias of many neo-Aristotelians, Sidney makes the potential for poetic expression a distinctly human opportunity. In the *Defence* he explains how the poet, following the example of the heavenly maker, creates a fictive universe replete with characters, actions, and settings. The poet "makes" a verbal cosmos that mirrors the universe created by the deity.

Following Sidney, the English tradition separated from the Continent and took on a distinctly national character. In a direct way, he made it possible for Spenser, his contemporary, to multiply the valency of his genius, so *The Faerie Queene,* while retaining a similarity to the twelve-part form of *The Shepheardes Calender,* advances far beyond its predecessor to become not only the English national epic, but the picture gallery that so delighted Romantic critics. By legitimizing fiction and making it respectable, Sidney prepared also for the narrative poems of Shakespeare and Milton, so that *Venus and Adonis* and *Paradise Lost,* if alike in nothing else, flaunt a verbal self-assuredness that needs no further apology. By stressing the depictive potential of language, Sidney encouraged the word pictures that often passed for poetry in the seventeenth century. Perhaps most remarkable, by adding a visual dimension to verbal imagery, he extended the expressiveness of poetic language so it could develop into the composite art brought to such bountiful fruition by Elizabethan dramatists.

In the stricter discipline of literary theory, Sidney identified the problems that the critic must confront and instituted a vocabulary for the ensuing debate. He provided Jonson with a definition of the poet as maker and of poetry as an art of imitation,[12] and he certified those classical authors who could serve as the canon of models. After Jonson, Dryden acknowledged Sidney as his forebear, and took from him the concept of wit and what wit can accomplish. Throughout the eighteenth century, academic critics such as Joseph Trapp, though perhaps more mindful of Continental adversaries than of Sidney, continued to rehash the Sidneian themes of poet as maker, poem as imitation, and poetry as a musical and/or painterly art.[13] Even Fielding, that progenitor of the novel as parodic slice-of-life, harks back to the definition of poem propounded in the *Defence* and exemplified by the *Arcadia*. Long before then, poetry in England had become much more a feigning of images in narrative sequence than a metrical echo of celestial harmony. No doubt all of these changes would have eventually arrived in London, either imported from the Continent or produced at home, but without Sidney they would have taken much longer and would not have been so self-confidently English.

Sidney's literary accomplishment is prodigious, especially when the busyness and brevity of his life are considered. He worked against great odds, as he himself was aware. "I have just cause to make a pitiful defence of poor poetry," he says (and not wholly with the jestful humor of his opening remarks about horsemanship), "which from almost the highest estimation of learning is fallen to be the laughing-stock of children." Poetry, if not learning itself, was under attack. The enemies of poetry had renewed Plato's call for a ban against it, so that "even the names of philosophers [were] used to the defacing of it." The times were so hostile that there was "danger of civil war among the Muses" (73.34–74.6). These patronesses of learning were squabbling among themselves in an effort to preserve what they could of their favored disciplines. What was the difficulty? Who were these enemies of Apollo? Since Sidney's treatise is a "defence" of poetry, whom must he defend it against? And what is at stake?

Sidney speaks of the detractors of poetry in only a vague, general way: they are the "poet-whippers" (98.29), or the μισόμουσοι, meaning literally the "Muse-haters," although Sidney provides his own gloss of "poet-haters" (99.28). It has been argued that Sidney wrote in response to the attack on poetry launched by Stephen Gosson in his *Schoole of abuse* (1579),[14] a tract of sufficient popularity to warrant a second edition in 1587. But this, I think, is to assign too much importance to Gosson. His voice was only one among many who decried poetry as an abomination.[15] There had been an increasing number of literary works offered for recreation alone without even a pretense of moral instruction, and an increasing number of readers for writings of this sort.[16] Such idle minds, however, like idle hands, were easy marks for the devil.

The opprobrium under which poetry labored during Sidney's adolescence is exemplified by William Alley, the Cambridge-trained bishop of Exeter. Despite his own wide reading in several languages and genuine literary interests, Bishop Alley expressed a widespread proto-puritanical disapproval for any words other than the Lord's:

> I would to God that Christian Kinges, princes, noble, honourable, and men of worship were resolved, that thys perteyned principallye unto their office and dutie, I meane the reading of the holy scriptures. And that they would rather have in their houses Gods booke (out of the whiche they maye learne the will of God) then the booke of King Arthur, the booke of Troilous, & such other vayne, prophane vanities, and Wanton bookes, whereby God maye geve them a longer life, and a death and end lesse tragicall and troublous. (fol. 56)[17]

With the righteousness of an Old Testament prophet, Bishop Alley takes aim at the wantonness and prurience of poetry. According to him, secular tales are "prophane vanities." But behind this ostensible objection lurks another which is even more challenging for the apologist. "Gods booke" may be read trustingly, a forthright gospel; the poet's book, however, is "vayne"—not only empty, but puffed up and misleading.

The difficulty here, although it is unlikely the good Bishop thought of it in these terms, lay in the Protestants' insistence upon the literalness of the word. During the Middle Ages, despite the Church's suspicion of fictive narrative, a poet or his exegete could find excuse for a literary work in an allegorical meaning derived from it. The fascinating story was but a rind from which the kernel of truth could be extracted. So fiction was truth, when read in the proper fashion.[18] As late as 1589 a mind as energetic as that of Thomas Nashe still thought of literature in this way: "I account of Poetrie," he announced, "as of a more hidden & divine kinde of Philosophy, enwrapped in blinde Fables and darke stories, wherin the principles of more excellent Arts and morrall precepts of manners, illustrated with divers examples of other Kingdomes and Countries, are contained."[19] But Bishop Alley adhered narrowly to the reformed religion, and for him a primrose by a river's brim a yellow primrose was, and nothing more. He was one of those derided by Sidney who objected to calling chessmen "kings" or "knights"—who "would say we lied for giving a piece of wood the reverend title of a bishop" (*Defence* 103.25–26). According to these strict readers, words must be interpreted literally, without implied meanings. Fiction, therefore, is not a masked truth, but rather language used deceptively—probably for purposes of seduction, as the serpent and Eve had used it in Eden. For serious Protestants a medieval romance could no longer be read allegorically as a quest for heavenly beauty. Stories purportedly from history, such as "the booke of King Arthur" and "the booke of Troilous," were especially odious because they had some claim to authenticity, and consequently they required pointed condemnation if they record tales of illicit love.[20]

History itself was more generally tolerated,[21] especially if the episodes of history could be turned to a moral purpose, if kings and princes could be pointed out as models of approvable behavior or as negative examples of what to avoid. When Thomas Blundeville published *The true order and methode of wryting and reading hystories* (London, 1574), translated largely from Patrizi and Acontio, he dedicated it to Leicester, "knowynge youre Honor amongst other your good delyghtes, to delyght moste in reading of Hystories, the true Image and portrature of Mans lyfe, and that not as many doe, to passe away the tyme, but to gather thereof such judgement and knowledge as you may therby be the more able, as well to direct your private actions, as to give Counsell lyke a most prudent Counseller in publyke causes" (A2). Reading history led to probity in both private and public affairs. When in the heading of a chapter Blundeville poses the question, "Whose lyves ought to be chronicled," he answers in the opening sentence: "All those persons whose lyves have beene such as are to bee followed for their excellencie in vertue, or else to be fledde for their excellencie in vice" (C2).

To those of Blundeville's frame of mind, epic poetry, because of its affinities to history, was the most laudable literary genre—as Renaissance critics agreed, almost without exception. It offered a story with some historical basis and an exemplary hero. For Sidney, epic was "the best and most accomplished kind of poetry"; and he gives his reason for such praise: "As the image of each action stirreth and instructeth the mind, so the lofty image of such worthies most inflameth the mind with desire to be worthy, and informs with counsel how to be worthy" (*Defence* 119.24–30). The heroical poem with its concrete images was didactically effective.[22] But even the epic was vulnerable to corruption, because there was danger that love might intrude and seduce the hero. Bishop Alley deplored the medieval romances of Arthur and of Troilus for this very reason, and Ariosto and other Italian poets had wilfully corrupted the epic by making love rather than military glory the hero's motivation. As Sidney concedes, "Even to the heroical, Cupid has ambitiously climbed" (125.8).

The relation between history and poetry, between *historia* and story, between fact and fiction was very much the concern of Sidney.[23] Under the old dispensation, when ultimate reality lay among the essences in a platonist realm of being or among the attributes of God in a Christian heaven, poetry was validated by the truth of the heavenly beauty which it embodied. The poet sought his subject matter, like his authority and inspiration, from above. But in the modern world, reality lay among the palpable phenomena of physical nature. The validation of poetry under this new dispensation required that it be referred to the sense-perceptible world of facts rather than to an immaterial world of ideas. This relocation of reality inevitably caused a crisis in literary theory, as it did in all areas of human endeavor—science, theology, psychology, politics; and the retrieval of Aristotle's *Poetics* played a major role in the resolution of this crisis. A poetics based upon mimesis allowed an increasing reliance upon what the senses perceive in our phenomenal world, so that poetry attains the factual veracity ascribed to history. The new poet, like the historian, records the verifiable data of nature perceived. But Sidney was unwilling to forego his nostalgic allegiance to the antique poetics that optimistically directed our gaze toward heavenly beauty, and as a consequence he was forced to balance a platonist's ideality against an empiricist's materiality. He strove for syncretism, for a poetic artifact which embraces both the absoluteness of the idea and the immediacy of the actual. Often, however, inconsistencies and even contradictions seem to appear in the argument of the *Defence.*

In any case, Sidney wished to legitimize the golden world of the poet, despite its avowed fictitiousness, and to give it validity equal with—perhaps, even greater than—the realm of history, the brazen world we actually inhabit. "A feigned example," he avers, "hath as much force to teach as a true example" (*Defence* 89.9–10). So a basic problem that Sidney faced was how to certify poetic images so that they persuade in the cause of truth, but withstand the attack of literalists who believe only the facts of history or who insist that language has only one dimension or who take their morals only from God's book. In defence of poetry, Sidney pleads, "They that with quiet judgements will look a little deeper into it, shall find the end and working of it such as, being rightly applied, deserveth not to be scourged out of the Church of God" (*Defence* 77.27–30).

Sidney never joins issue with Bishop Alley's point of view on its own grounds of religiosity, however, and never addresses directly those who condemn fictive narrative as the way to perdition.[24] The closest he comes is in his response to the third of the four charges made against poets—viz., "that it [poetry] is the nurse of abuse, infecting us with many pestilent desires; with a siren's sweetness drawing the mind to the serpent's tale of sinful fancies" (101.30–33). But here his strategy is to shift the grounds of argument from religion to philosophy, taking it out of the church and into the academy. Sidney prefers to deal with the problem as Plato had formulated it in the *Republic* (pages 133–35). Later in the *Defence* he concedes that "Plato found fault that the poets of his time filled the world with wrong opinions of the gods, making light tales of that unspotted essence, and therefore would not have the youth depraved with such opinions" (108.7–10). For the nonce, though, Sidney prefers to recall the Plato who in Books 2 and 3 of the *Republic* assigned to poetry a responsible place in education of the young, that other Plato who in the *Phaedrus* and *Ion* situated the poet near the divine seat and favored him with celestial privilege. So Sidney argues for poetry's ability to instill "love of beauty" (104.2–3), rather than sinfulness; and he has an easy time of showing that the reader misled by poetry is weak-minded and cannot appreciate either love or beauty, the highest values in the Platonic system.

In the same vein, Sidney scorns those who claim that poetry

emasculates men of action, teaching them to read about glorious deeds rather than performing them. With the indignation of a φιλόμουσος, Sidney warns, "This argument, though it be levelled against poetry, yet is it a chainshot against all learning" (105.14–15); and with the snobbery of a humanist, he adds, "This indeed is the ordinary doctrine of ignorance" (105.23). So, he craftily concludes, we should "not say that poetry abuseth man's wit, but that man's wit abuseth poetry" (204.12–13). He turns the defence of poetry into a glorious offence, and overwhelms his opponents with a parade of examples demonstrating the high esteem that powerful patrons have always bestowed upon poets. From time immemorial, poets have provided sustenance for the noblest among us, and in return have been handsomely rewarded, "for poetry is the companion of the camps" (105.34)—and, Sidney goes on, "I dare undertake, Orlando Furioso, or honest King Arthur, will never displease a soldier" (105.34–106.1).[25] So much for the over-nice Bishop Alley and his ilk, who opposed poetry on moral grounds and used the arguments of a literalist.

Sidney's more difficult task lay in saving poetry from the dullards—from the "paper-blurrers" and "poet-apes," as he calls them (*Defence* 111.18, 120.34). Unlike the other arts, poetry had no firmly enunciated theory, no principles agreed upon by consensus, no undisputed place in the organization of learning. It was no clearly perceived discipline.[26] Furthermore, the enthusiasm so grandly expressed by the Italian humanists had suffered a period of decline. The echoes in England, most important in Wyatt and Surrey, were strongest in the songs and sonnets of Tottel's collection printed in 1557, and were still faintly audible in the gentlemen's miscellanies that followed.[27] But by the 1570s, the illustrious doctrine that the poet is inspired by the Muses and that poetry makes available the supernal beauty of celestial forms had degenerated to catalogues of metrical feet and stanzaic patterns. Englishmen, as evidenced by Gascoigne's "Certayne notes of instruction concerning the making of verse or ryme" (1575), were more concerned with their meters and tropes than with heavenly love. As Sidney complains, poetry was in the hands of "base men with servile wits . . . who think it enough if they can be rewarded of the printer" (111.3–5).

The vapidity of poetic theory in England, even among those who presumed to write on the topic, is revealed by William Webbe's definition:

> Poetry . . . is where any worke is learnedly compiled in measurable speeche, and framed in wordes contayning number or proportion of just syllables, delighting the readers or hearers as well by the apt and decent framing of wordes in equall resemblance of quantity, commonly called verse, as by the skyllfull handling of the matter whereof it is intreated. (1:247–48)

Here is a puerile version of the orthodox poetics of weighing syllables. Poetry is any discourse that has the pretence of learning and the polish of metrical smoothness. As for classification, poetry still lies in the domain of rhetoric: it is simply "measurable speeche," analyzed as *res* and *verba*—the "skyllfull handling" of some (any?) "matter." Overcoming this diffidence about poetry was Sidney's most formidable challenge.

Spenser's theory of poetry at this time was advanced not much farther than Webbe's, judging from the possibilities put forward in the October eclogue of *The Shepheardes Calender*. He still thought of poetry as an instrument for crude moral instruction or for praise of a patron, and the poet's scope lay in the progress toward poethood exemplified by Vergil's career. Cuddie is touted as "the perfecte paterne of a Poete," suggesting that he fits the mold of tradition; and he expresses the traditional lament of the poet that his art suffers neglect through indifference of the powerful.

Synthesizing the substance of the eclogue, E.K. in his Argument propounds a thesis which Sidney considers in the *Defence*, though ultimately rejects. E.K. has claimed that poetry is a worthy and commendable art—and for fear that his use of the word "art" may be interpreted in the Horatian sense of a skill with rules to be mastered, he scrupulously corrects himself: "or rather no arte, but a divine gift and heavenly instinct not to be gotten by laboure and learning, but adorned with both: and poured into the witte by a certaine ἐνθουσιασμὸς. and celestiall inspiration." An allegiance to the poetics dependent upon the Muses could not be more explicitly stated, with all the buzzwords dutifully repeated.

Moreover, the emblem assigned to Cuddie at the end—*Agitante calescimus illo &c.*—reminds us of the noble heritage and wondrous effects of poetry signaled in this tag from Ovid.[28] E.K. in his gloss clinches the point: "Hereby is meant, as also in the whole course of this Æglogue, that Poetry is a divine instinct and unnatural rage passing the reache of comen reason."

E.K. is right: throughout the eclogue there's a clear assumption that poetry—whatever the genre, from pastoral to epic—is dependent upon a divinely induced *furore*. There are audible echoes of the *Ion* as well as the *Phaedrus*. In his proem to Book 6 of *The Faerie Queene*, Spenser is still supplicating the "sacred imps, that on *Parnasso* dwell," and he prays for a visitation of the "goodly fury" which they alone can infuse "into the mindes of mortall men" (6.proem.2). Gabriel Harvey begins his commendatory verse for *The Faerie Queene* by recognizing Spenser's commitment to the orthodox poetics: "Collyn I see by thy new taken taske, / some sacred fury hath enricht thy braynes." There's at least the pretense that the poet is an inspired singer and his poem is divine. This view of poetry has a certain enforced nobility. It stands in a celebrated tradition.

But it would not do for Sidney. It was both too little and too much. Sidney aimed to resuscitate poetry, not merely to lament a longed-for past. He saw poetry as an instrument of social and political change, so it was too important to be left to the whim of an unpredictable and unapproachable Muse. On the other hand, Sidney felt the need to assign limits for the mortal poet—limits if not of knowledge, at least of aspiration. The mortal maker must not presume upon the godhead. Sidney hoped that poetry could move a reader toward a golden world of Platonic perfection, such as Spenser's Piers urges poesy to seek in retreat from hostile reality, but it cannot provide salvation. The poet cannot preempt this role of the Son or Holy Ghost. Furthermore, the poet is limited by other than the prohibitions of theology: his faculties are proscribed by the human condition. His mind, though capable of thought, can range no farther than the finite zodiac of human wit. He can't transcend the outer bounds of this world and soar beyond into the empyrean. Sidney was no mystic believing in neoplatonist ecstasy.

So Sidney set out to devise a poetics that was grounded in human experience and well within the domain of human knowledge. Modestly but firmly he gives advice to the "paper-blurrers" in England: "They that delight in poesy itself should seek to know what they do, and how they do; and especially look themselves in an unflattering glass of reason" (*Defence* 111.25–27). At the same time, however, Sidney sought a poetical theory which retained the exhilaration setting poetry apart from the humdrum existence that deadens the spirit. He sought a Protestant poetics without foregoing the richness of Augustinian harmonies,[29] without silencing that "planet-like music of poetry" (121.28).

As a consequence, Sidney is respectful toward the orthodox poetics. Early in the *Defence* he lauds poetry in neoplatonist terms: "For that same exquisite observing of number and measure in the words, and that high flying conceit proper to the poet, did seem to have some divine force in it" (77.5–8); and repeatedly he demonstrates his affectionate respect for "that numbrous kind of writing which is called verse" (81.23–24). Like Piers in the October eclogue, Sidney was given to praise of "pierlesse Poesye" in the best neoplatonist manner, coining epithets such as "graceful poesy" (111.9) and "ever-praiseworthy Poesy" (120.30). In the peroration of the *Defence* he cites a noted authority: Landino, Sidney recalls, believed that poets "are so beloved of the gods that whatsoever they write proceeds of a divine fury" (121.15–17).

But elsewhere in the *Defence* Sidney rejects any doctrine of a *divino furore*. He has considered it carefully, and firmly demurs. Although he speaks of Plato with the utmost reverence (and this is not mock reverence, it seems to me), Sidney feels compelled to take issue with him—"especially since he attributeth unto poesy more than myself do, namely, to be a very inspiring of a divine force, far above man's wit, as in the forenamed dialogue [the *Ion*] is apparent" (109.2–5).[30] By the time of writing *Astrophil and Stella* a few years later, Sidney is prepared to have Astrophil reject Landino's doctrine with some scorn: "Some do I heare of Poets' furie tell, / But (God wot) wot not what they meane by it" (74.5–6). Sidney with his Calvinistic bias, with his puritanical view of fallen humanity balanced against the humanist's view of humanity as God's image, could not assign to poetry qualities or effects that exceed a mortal's reach. Despite its ability to raise us from our earthbound condition and turn us toward the godly, poetry must not impinge upon divinity.

There was, of course, one important exception: religious poetry specifically validated as utterance inspired by Jehovah. In a prominent passage which comes early in the *Defence* Sidney classifies poets into "three general kinds." First are the religious poets, "they that did imitate the unconceivable excellencies of God" (80.4–5).[31] Second are those who "deal with matters philosophical" (80.19–20)—that is, who lay out the subject matter of a particular discipline, such as natural or moral philosophy. Third are the "right" poets, the genuine poets who "imitate to teach and delight" (81.3) and who require the defence of an extended explanation.[32] Religious poets are given pride of place because of their antiquity and sacredness, and of course "against these none will speak that hath the Holy Ghost in due holy reverence." The other poets, however, while sharing an almost equal responsibility for the well-being of their fellowmen, do not benefit from divine guidance other than the normal operation of providence. The didactic poetry of natural and moral philosophy, and also the third category of "right" poetry produced by Aristotelian mimesis, are unmitigatedly human efforts.

The "right" poet, then, the mimetic poet, unlike the divine poet, cannot rely upon inspiration from above. Nor, like the philosophical poet, does he simply repeat what nature has already prescribed as subject matter within the various disciplines. The right poet is a mortal maker, working within the confines of human reason though creating anew a fictive universe such as never was in nature (*Defence* 78.22–26). To aid in this distinctive task, the right poet relies upon the Aristotelian concept of mimesis. He makes to imitate. The poetic act of imitation becomes the means by which poetry is retained at the human level, grounded in the factual world, and yet is allowed to escape the confinement of any predetermined subject matter.

By the annus mirabilis when Spenser began his *Faerie Queene* and Sidney completed the first version of his *Arcadia,* the poetics of neoplatonic enthusiasm was long out of date on the Continent. The Pléiade had struggled to reformulate it and give it fresh vigor—and with considerable success, in France. But despite striking similarities in their aim,[33] Sidney's ear was surprisingly deaf toward the Pléiade.[34] Instead, he turned his attention to Italy, where the doctrine of divine inspiration from the Muses had been challenged and largely replaced by talk about Aristotle. The topic of mimesis had caught the attention of most commentators, coming as it does at the very beginning of the *Poetics* and working like leavening through the whole, and it provided a focus for intensive debate. Before Sidney's *Defence,* however, only a handful of references to Aristotle's *Poetics* had appeared in England, and those are scattered and misinformed.[35] It was Sidney who thrust Aristotle into the mainstream of English poetic theory and practice, and the concept of imitation was what made Aristotle of such great interest to Sidney.

In the *Defence* Sidney's debt to the *Poetics* is immediate, pervasive, and readily acknowledged. More references are made to Aristotle than to any other authority, with the single exception of Plato. Sidney confides, "Of all philosophers I have ever esteemed [Plato] most worthy of reverence"—"and with good reason," he adds, "since of all philosophers he is most poetical" (107.2–4). But he expresses almost equal respect for Aristotle. After explaining his theory of universals, for example, Sidney concludes, "Thus far Aristotle: which reason of his (as all his) is most full of reason" (88.8–9). Plato is the poetical philosopher; Aristotle, though, is the most reasonable.

Moreover, while most of Sidney's recollections of Plato are general, his allusions to Aristotle are direct, so that quite precise passages can be identified as the points of reference. We can bracket specific lines in the Aristotelian corpus as though Sidney had just read them. Often he adopts the Aristotelian vocabulary: *mimesis, metaphor, architectonike, gnosis* and *praxis, philosophoteron* and *spoudaioteron, katholon* and *kathekaston, energeia.* It is unlikely that Sidney read the *Poetics* in the original Greek; but the text was available in both Latin and Italian versions, and there were any number of paraphrases and digests. By the time Sidney was writing his own treatise on poetry, Aristotle's treatise had been annotated, explained, and amplified by almost a century of scholar-critics. Sidney was aware of this new criticism, and his *Defence of poesie* is a surprisingly mature contribution to the ongoing debate generated by the recovery and promulgation of Aristotle's text.

Sidney is most Aristotelian in his desire to analyze the nature of poetry and to differentiate its genres by systematic inquiry, just as he is most Platonic when extolling poetry as a vision of beauty.[36] Sidney first mentions Aristotle when he defines poetry as imitation (79.35–36), and at that point the *Defence* assumes a distinctly Aristotelian tenor. There immediately follows the classification of poetry into "three general kinds" (80.3), with Sidney concentrating attention upon the third kind of "right" poetry. And in turn the "right" poetry is soon broken down further into eight "more special denominations" (81.17–18). The *Poetics* provides a model for this definition of ποιητική and the anatomy of its species. Before long Sidney is citing Aristotle for "the mistress-knowledge, by the Greeks called ἀρχιτεκτονική" (82.35–36); and when he compares poetry to history, he adopts Aristotle's argument that poetry is more philosophical and serious (87.36–88.2). From this point, Aristotle maintains a continuing presence in the discussion.

Sidney, in fact, follows Aristotle's lead in the most important topics.[37] Aristotle had proposed that imitation is the distinctive feature of the poetical art, making it the cornerstone of his poetic theory, and Sidney does likewise. For the opening statement to introduce his methodical exposition, Sidney declares: "Poesy . . . is an art of imitation, for so Aristotle termeth it in the word μίμησις" (79.35–36). This pronouncement is unusually blunt for Sidney, with no trace of wit or equivocation, and it carries the full weight of Aristotle's authority. In the now-common division of the *Defence* into seven parts conforming to a classical oration, it is designated the *propositio*. All else flows from this seminal premise.

The most immediate result is that Sidney must reject versification as a requirement for poetry—which he does, vehemently, not long after declaring his allegiance to *mimesis*. Aristotle had decreed that Empedocles was no poet despite the fact he composed in meter; while Herodotus, even if revamped into verse, would still be no more than a historian (*Poetics* 1447b16–23, 1451a36–b5). And this contention over the interdependence of verse and poetry had flared sporadically ever since. During the Renaissance the debate had been revived with increased energy—arguments on both sides were strongly urged and the field was widened to include Romans such as Lucretius and Lucan.[38] This issue had been chosen as a keynote by Scaliger, who hoped to dominate the conflict by asserting with unrelenting hauteur that it is indeed the making of verses that identifies a poet (pages 202, 210–11).

Sidney, however, is at first more cautious. In the *Defence* after delineating his second kind of poets, those who use verse to write didactic poems (80.19–20)—all of whom, incidentally, by definition would fall under Aristotle's anathema—Sidney backs off from taking sides and leaves the decision to others. "Because this second sort is wrapped within the fold of the proposed subject," he observes, "and takes not the course of his own invention, whether they properly be poets or no let grammarians dispute" (80.25–28).[39] With a shrug, he turns to define his third category, who are "indeed right poets" without any question because they practice mimesis.

But shortly thereafter, when Sidney takes up the precise business of enumerating the several species of poetry, he is not so feckless. He is, in fact, far from indifferent about metrification. He must face the uncomfortable circumstance that poets had been classified according to two quite distinct criteria: according to the meters they use as well as the subjects they write about. Sidney carefully lists "the most notable" of the traditional kinds of poets ("the heroic, lyric, tragic, comic, satiric, iambic, elegiac, pastoral, and certain others"; 81.18–19);[40] then, applying the method of Aristotelian analysis which differentiates through the use of criteria, he adds, "some of these being termed according to the matter they deal with, some by the sorts of verses they liked best to write in." The first four categories, clearly, are the sorts that Aristotle chose to deal with in the *Poetics*. Since they practice mimesis, they are poets regardless of whether they compose in meter. But the others fall outside the Aristotelian pale.[41]

In order to continue with his generic analysis, therefore, Sidney must acknowledge this confusion and sort out the indiscriminate application of criteria. He does so boldly and firmly. He concedes that "the greatest part of poets have apparelled their poetical inventions in that numbrous kind of writing which is called verse." But this, he insists, is incidental to their poethood; and he continues with some scorn—"indeed but apparelled, verse being but an ornament and no cause to poetry, since there have been many most excellent poets that never versified, and now swarm many versifiers that need never answer to the name of poets." For Sidney the linkage of poetry and verse is severed.

Sidney pursues his argument by citing examples. The true poet is he who, like Xenophon in the *Cyropaedia,* uses the arts of language to fashion an image of the hero in action—"For Xenophon . . . did imitate so excellently as to give us . . . the portraiture of a just empire, under the name of Cyrus" (81.27–29). Heliodorus is similarly praised as a master of mimesis—"So did Heliodorus in his sugared invention of that picture of love in Theagenes and Chariclea." Although the much-admired *Aethiopica* takes us out of the domain of history and politics, and into the questionable realm of amatory romance, Sidney cagily associates Heliodorus's "sugared invention," acknowledged to be fictitious, with Xenophon's *Cyropaedia,* having some claim as history. Both authors are approved as poets—indeed, held to be exemplary—despite the fact they wrote in prose, as Sidney pointedly brings to our attention (81.32–33).

But Sidney has made his case; and with the unaccustomed bluntness that Aristotelian pronouncements bring over him, he insists: "It is not rhyming and versing that maketh a poet" (81.33–34). Metrification, as he has said, is but the apparel of poetry, just as in the rhetorical model the *verba* are the garb applied at a later stage to the *res;* and meter no more makes the poet than clothes ever make the man—"no more than a long gown maketh an advocate, who though he pleaded in armour should be an advocate, and no soldier." So rhyming and versing are extraneous to poetry, an ornament, perhaps, but no essential element. Even, some might say, they are an affectation of the would-be poet, the poet-ape.[42]

What, then, is the essential quality of poetry, the badge of the indisputable "right" poet? To answer this question, Sidney generalizes from the particular examples of Xenophon and Heliodorus, who had, respectively, given us "the *portraiture* of a just empire" and the "*picture* of love." In a positive vein, Sidney now makes his decisive statement about the poet being known by "that feigning notable images of virtues, vices, or what else." Sidney concedes that the most admirable poets have chosen to write in meter— "indeed the senate of poets hath chosen verse as their fittest raiment"—but his choice of words here echoes his earlier statement that verse is but an adornment. The "right" poet is the one who makes to imitate, who invents a fiction in implementation of Aristotle's doctrine of mimesis, producing "portraitures" and "pictures." Whether he versifies is incidental.[43]

In the opening pages of the *Defence* Sidney had found himself quite suddenly in the midst of this problem about versification, and it is interesting to observe how he extricates himself. In his eagerness to score points in poetry's defence, he draws attention to its antiquity and usefulness, and notes that the earliest men of learning professed their disciplines in poems—in fact, "the philosophers of Greece durst not a long time appear to the world but under the masks of poets" (75.1–3). In consequence, "Thales, Empedocles, and Parmenides sang their natural philosophy in verses; so did Pythagoras and Phocylides their moral counsels; so did Tyrtaeus in war matters, and Solon in matters of policy" (75.3–6). However, since these are poets of only the second category, those who deal with matters philosophical, Sidney grows uncomfortable in letting these versifiers represent the pantheon of poets. His endorsement of verse must not appear to be a definition of poetry. The fact that they "sang their natural philosophy in verses" is not a sufficient credential to merit the title "poet."

So Sidney must demonstrate that philosophers not only frame their statements in meter, but (more important) they express their thoughts in fiction. They are not mere versifiers, but makers. Solon, for example, devised the tale of Atlantis—"for that wise Solon was directly a poet it is manifest having written in verse the notable fable of the Atlantic Island" (75.8–10). Because of the *Timaeus,* mention of Atlantis brings to mind Plato, who of course never composed in meter, writing only in prose. But Sidney goes to great lengths to demonstrate that Plato is a poet. Indeed, he is the very prototype of a poet, for "whosoever well considereth shall find that in the body of his work, though the inside and strength were philosophy, the skin, as it were, and beauty depended most of poetry."

So lest the philosophical poets who wrote in verses be mistaken as the "right" poets, Sidney extolls Plato as the better poet and indicates in what ways he excells:

> For all standeth upon dialogues, wherein he feigneth many honest burgesses of Athens to speak of such matters, that, if they had been set on the rack, they would never have confessed them, besides his poetical describing the circumstances of their meetings, as the well ordering of a banquet, the delicacy of a walk, with interlacing mere tales, as Gyges' ring and others, which who knoweth not to be flowers of poetry did never walk into Apollo's garden. (75.11–21)[44]

Plato is a poet, and a good one, precisely because he creates fictions: "the well ordering of a banquet" in the *Symposium* and "the delicacy of a walk" in the *Phaedrus*. Elsewhere Sidney bestows the highest praise upon Plato, "since of all philosophers he is the most *poetical*" (107.4)—and in the passage here he repeats the epithet "poetical" (75.17), derived from Aristotelian ποιητική.[45] The definition of poetry is shifted, subtly but unmistakably, from the making of verses, as Scaliger would have it, to the making of fables. Even historians, Sidney goes on to observe, have borrowed of poets—not their verse, however, but their fiction, in the description of passions, in the reconstruction of battle scenes, and in reciting the supposed speeches of kings and captains (75.22–31).

In another passage of the *Defence* we can watch Sidney transfer his ground for the definition of poetry in a similar way. Near the end of the lengthy section where he demonstrates the superiority of poetry over both philosophy and history, Sidney draws to a conclusion: "Now therein of all sciences (I speak still of human, and according to the human conceit) is our poet the monarch" (91.35–36). Then in his most syncretistic mode, Sidney praises the poet, first as a musician/poet in the mold of the orthodox poetics of μουσική: "He cometh to you with words set in delightful proportion, either accompanied with, or prepared for, the well enchanting skill of music" (92.7–9). But this view of the poet is inadequate, so Sidney immediately revises it by making the poet again an irresistible author of fictions: "With a tale forsooth he cometh unto you, with a tale which holdeth children from play, and old men from the chimney corner" (92.9–11). In this instance the shift from poet as maker of verses to maker of fables is less drawn out, more sudden—but nonetheless complete. These lines encapsulate in briefest arc the metamorphosis of the poet from metrician to fictioneer.

Sidney brings up the question of versification on several other widely spaced occasions in the *Defence*. In his most extensive and explicit treatment of the topic, he softens his earlier stand, although he does not forsake it. Indeed, his prevarication is most informative, and betrays his uneasiness about the matter as well as the subtlety and profundity of his thought. After delineating his positive program for poetry, Sidney turns to "what objections be made against this art" (99.26), and eventually he enumerates four "imputations laid to the poor poets" (101.26–27). As a sort of prolegomenon to his defence of poetry against these specific charges by the μισόμουσοι, Sidney returns to the problem of metrification, because "that which giveth greatest scope to their scorning humour is rhyming and versing" (100.20–21).[46]

Sidney begins here by reiterating his earlier pronouncements: "It is already said (and, as I think, truly said), it is not rhyming and versing that maketh poesy." For emphasis, he repeats his previous bon mot: "One may be a poet without versing, and a versifier without poetry." He proceeds to examine this extreme position, however, and entertains substantive modifications of it. By way of self-rebuttal, he starts the next sentence, "But yet . . ."—and this will be a significant reservation. "But yet," he tentatively queries, "presuppose it were inseparable"—presuppose that verse and poetry *are* interdependent, mutually identifying; and he cites an imposing authority, "as indeed it seemeth Scaliger judgeth." What then? Always the philosophical optimist, seeking to syncretize rather than divide, Sidney concludes that such a circumstance could only redound to the credit of poetry, because the tradition for metrification is honorable, grounded in a venerable aesthetic. So if verse and poetry are inseparable, Sidney reasons (for the nonce adopting Scaliger's hypothesis), "truly it were an inseparable commendation."

This statement is followed by a full justification for such a position. Sidney starts with the Ciceronian dictum confirmed by Genesis that speech is the God-given talent by which man expresses his reason. Therefore, since speech is good, whatever enhances the effectiveness and beauty of speech must also be laudable: "For if *oratio* next to *ratio*, speech next to reason, be the greatest gift bestowed upon mortality, that cannot be praiseless which doth most polish that blessing of speech." Appropriating the Augustinian aesthetic, Sidney then explains how verse improves upon speech and turns it into poetry. Versification "considers each word, not only (as a man may say) by his most forcible quality, but by his best measured quantity, carrying even in themselves a harmony." To deny that meter embellishes language is to deny "number, measure, order, proportion"—in the universe, as well as in poetry. Such a choice, of course, would be barbarous, and perhaps heretical. After praising metrification as a mnemonic aid,[47] Sidney concludes, "Verse being in itself sweet and orderly, and being best for memory, the only handle of knowledge, it must be in jest that any man can speak against it" (101.23–25). Verse, then, is an admissible adjunct to a poem, but not necessary, and certainly not sufficient, to it.[48]

Yet, the problem of versification sticks in Sidney's mind, and he returns to it once more near the end of the *Defence.* By this point he has completed the exposition of his positive program for poetry, defended it against the most virulent charges laid at its door, and run through a brief exercise in applied criticism by surveying the state of letters in England. Now in rapid succession he touches upon a number of ancillary topics: the unities in drama, the need for decorum in respecting the genres, the difference between delight and laughter, the lack of *energia* in recent love poetry, the importance of diction, the suitability of the English language for poetry. As the last item in this list of miscellanea, immediately before his peroration, Sidney again brings up the topic of metrification.

But now his mood is practical rather than argumentative; and since the use of meter is an observed fact among poets, instead of decrying it Sidney offers information about its viability. With a mellowness perhaps born of resignation, he recognizes two sorts of versifying, one of which he calls "ancient" and the other "modern." These are the quantitative versifying, enjoying a revival according to what were thought to be classical precepts, and the accentual versifying usually accompanied by rhyme, which was native to vernaculars (119.30–34). Sidney describes both systems of metrification, but refuses to recommend one at the expense of the other:

> Whether of these be the more excellent, would bear many speeches: the ancient (no doubt) more fit for music, both words and time observing quantity, and more fit lively to express diverse passions, by the low or lofty sound of the well-weighed syllable; the latter likewise, with his rhyme, striketh a certain music to the ear, and, in fine, since it doth delight, though by another way, it obtains the same purpose.

By declining to prefer one over the other, Sidney condones both, "there being in either sweetness, and wanting in neither majesty." So Sidney seems to approve the use of metrification in poetry.[49] But the truth is that he had never denied the contribution that metrics could make to a poem. His strongest pronouncements against verse come when he is introducing his central thesis that imitation, the feigning of images, is the essential feature of the poetic art. And even there he admits that verse may be an ornament to poetry.

At first glance, the demotion of metrics in poetic theory may not seem of paramount importance. But what Sidney sets aside is nothing less than the revered definition of poetry which allied it with music through a shared aesthetic of formal properties. In this tradition, the poet *must* employ versification—not merely as an incidental nicety, but in compliance with the divine example. Sidney had found this poetics in Landino, and because of the vogue for "songs and sonnets" it had been a prominent feature of the literary scene for centuries.[50] In his survey of literature in England, Sidney sees the lyric as the only non-dramatic poetry worthy of note (116.27–35). So despite the newer cult of Aristotelianism, this was a formidable tradition for Sidney to engage as an adversary. And of course at almost every point in the argument, as we shall see, Sidney modified his Aristotelian position by concessions to it. Respect for the old neoplatonist aesthetic recurs as counterpoint to the dominant Aristotelian theme.

Aristotle's *Poetics,* nonetheless, provided the baseline for Sidney's theorizing about poetry, and the positive aspects of his program derive for the most part from it. Especially the concept of mimesis, so prominent in the *Poetics,* became a radical point of departure for Sidney. So how did he handle this, the most hotly debated issue in literary studies of the sixteenth century?

First, we should note that the text of Aristotle is anything but clear. Mimesis is unmistakably the quiddity of poetry, but how it is achieved is unspecified. Even so, we can draw certain conclusions. Aristotle is definite in prescribing what is appropriate to be imitated: the proper object of imitation, he decrees, is the actions of men. From this derives the notion of plot, a sequence of episodes presenting the actions of men as an integrated entity; and since someone must perform those actions, the notion of character follows in the wake of the necessity for plot. The other definite point which Aristotle makes is that the imitation need not reproduce events that have *actually* occurred in our phenomenal world. The poem, unlike history, does not faithfully record what men have already done. Rather, extrapolating from facts, it presents what is likely to occur according to probability or necessity (1451a36–38).

Aristotle here falls back upon his theory of the universal, a mental construct that derives from the particularities of physical nature but approaches the generality of a philosophical absolute.[51] From a large number of examples the common qualities are abstracted to arrive at a definition of the class, the "universal" description of each item in that class. The universal still partakes of physical reality because it is grounded in the data of the phenomenal world; it is a "concrete" universal. But since those data are generalized, submitted to inductive reasoning, the universal carries the weight of scientific hypothesis. So the universal readily assumes the authority of law. It becomes a norm, and any instance that contravenes the universal is discredited as an aberrancy.

By this process of self-confirmation, the universal rigidifies into an absolute and approaches a Platonic idea in its tyranny over temporal phenomena.[52] The universal acquires the power of what is true, good, and beautiful, the virtue of the noblest imperatives. Sir John Davies precisely delineates the process by which the soul derives its values from physical experience:

> From their grosse *matter* she abstracts the *formes,*
>   And drawes a kind of *Quintessence* from things;
>   Which to her proper nature she transformes,
>   To beare them light on her celestiall wings.
>
> This doth she when from things *particular,*
>   She doth abstract the *universall kinds;*

> Which bodilesse, and immateriall are,
> And can be lodg'd but onely in our minds.

> And thus from diverse *accidents* and *acts*
> Which do within her observation fall,
> She goddesses and powres divine abstracts,
> As *Nature, Fortune,* and the *Vertues* all.
> (*Nosce Teipsum* 541–52)[53]

"From diverse accidents and acts," as Davies puts it, the soul "draws a kind of quintessence from things," and these are "the universal kinds."

In poetry as Aristotle defines it, the universal serves as the object to be imitated. It provides the plot, which is then materialized in actual episodes. In consequence, since the object to be imitated has been arrived at by the mental process of induction, the poetic imitation does not present what has been—that is, the imitation is not a verisimilar reproduction of an instance that has already taken place. Rather, it presents the universal aspects of the action, what is likely to occur according to probability or even necessity. In theory, the imitation, like the universal, is valid to the same degree as any hypothesis arrived at inductively. Because the imitation derives ultimately from observed data, it maintains a direct relationship with the actual world that we experience with our senses.

In practice, however, the imitation based upon a universal pulls against its ties with actuality. It expatiates toward a realm of archetypes. In its broadest development, the abstraction drawn from human affairs becomes a cultural memory, the residue of communal experience; and as such, it transmutes to myth, serving directly as the subject matter for narrative. When a poem reflects such an object of imitation, it too acquires such virtue, achieving a veracity and pureness and power that exceeds the value of the experiential world. The poet sets forth this meta-reality; and consequently poetry, as Aristotle proposes, is more philosophical and serious than history. Sidney repeats this Aristotelian proposition and develops it as a major segment of his argument to prove the superiority of poetry over all the arts and sciences.[54]

But herein lies the weakness of this poetics: the meta-truth offered in the poem tends to dissociate from the reality of human experience. The poem tends to etherealize into speculation, tends to evaporate into idle thoughts of what should be or might be, tends to metamorphose into fantasies and misconceptions and delusions. The bond between the fictive world of the poem and the real world we inhabit is broken.[55] When this occurs, as Sidney notes, calling upon Plato as a corrective to Aristotle, the poetic faculty of εἰκαστική, which Sidney defines as "figuring forth good things," degenerates into φανταστική, the production of images that have no relation to truth. Such images may be perniciously misleading (*Defence* 125.24–26). The poet is then charged with lying, and the validity of his statement is undermined. The poet's "delivering forth," Sidney warns, then seems "wholly imaginative, as we are wont to say by them that build castles in the air" (79.10–12).

Sidney sought to devise a theory of poetry that would prevent this breach between the world of the poem and that of the audience, between the fiction that the poet contrives and the original nature that we observe, sometimes painfully, to lie about us.[56] The brazen world of nature must be the model for the golden world that the poet describes; it must be the original object of the poet's imitation. But somehow the poet must achieve the miracle of alchemy and turn what is dross into the most precious of materials. Sidney saw in the concept of mimesis the possibility of a poetics that would achieve this miracle:

> For whatsoever action, or faction [i.e., deed <L. *factus*], whatsoever counsel, policy, or war stratagem the historian is bound to recite, that may the poet (if he list) with his imitation make his own, beautifying it both for further teaching, and more delighting, as it please him. (89.27–31)

Although he must walk hand-in-hand with nature (78.28), the poet has the license, perhaps the directive, to beautify her data as a means of achieving his instructional purpose. The poet transforms his experiential world into a universal, perhaps *la belle nature,* which serves as model for his fictive world. By this theory of imitation, Sidney legitimizes the golden world of the poet so that it becomes a valid text for moral instruction.

There is abundant evidence that Sidney accepted Aristotle's

doctrine that poetry imitate not actual occurrence itself, but rather the universal abstracted from actual occurrence. Sidney forcefully declares for this option when he separates the "right" poets from their fellows. The didactic poets laying out their respective disciplines are like "the meaner sort of painters, who counterfeit only such faces as are set before them" (80.30–32). The authentic poets, however, do not slavishly reproduce a predetermined subject matter; rather, they are like "the more excellent [painters], who having no law but wit, bestow in colours upon you which is fittest for the eye to see" (80.32–34). The inference is clear: just as the good portrait painter passes over the minor blemishes of his subject and records what best represents the abiding identity of the person, so must the true poet avoid the accidental and disclose the everlasting verity of whatever subject he takes in hand.[57] The "right poets," Sidney counsels, "to imitate borrow nothing of what is, hath been, or shall be; but range, only reined with learned discretion, into the divine consideration of what may be and should be" (81.3–6). He who truly deserves the title of "poet" leaves behind the precise data of what actually *is* according to current perception, of what *has been* as recorded by history, and even of what *shall be* as reported in apocalyptic vision. Instead, by exercise of his imagination the poet ranges into the timeless consideration of what may be and should be. This is a search for what is probable or necessary—that is, for the universal.

Sidney's defence of the poet against the charge of lying is based on this very point. The second of the imputations laid against poetry bluntly charges "that it is the mother of lies" (101.30).[58] But the poet doesn't lie, Sidney argues, because he doesn't profess to be doing anything other than writing fiction. Indeed, "of all writers under the sun the poet is the least liar, and, though he would, as a poet can scarcely be a liar" (102.18). Those who practice the other arts—for example, the astronomer who measures the distances of the planets—can hardly escape lying, because they claim to be precise when at best they approximate. They claim to give particulars, which inevitably are erroneous. "For the poet," however, Sidney insists, "he nothing affirms, and therefore never lieth." He doesn't lie because, unlike the astronomer or the historian, he makes no attempt to give an accurate account of physical event. Instead the poet presents in Aristotelian fashion what is probable or necessary, "not labouring to tell you what is or is not, but what should or should not be." His fictions embody the universals arrived at by the mental process of abstraction and induction. Sidney repeats, "The poet's persons and doings are but pictures what should be, and not stories what have been." In consequence, the historian, by pretending to be accurate, necessarily misleads, at least in detail; but the poet, by transcending the particularity of actual occurrence and confessing a departure from fact, achieves a larger, overarching veracity. "As in history, looking for truth," Sidney warns in a balanced Latin construction, readers "may go away full fraught with falsehood, so in poesy, looking but for fiction, they shall use the narration but as an imaginative ground-plot of a profitable invention" (103.13–16). The reader of poetry, therefore, although concerned only with the fictive story, is likely to be instructed because the sequence of episodes in the narrative (the μῦθος or *fabula* or Aristotelian "plot") images forth by a literally "imaginative" (i.e., image-producing) mechanism the "profitable invention" of the poet/rhetorician. Thereby the *res* of the poet is revealed in the images of the story produced by the *verba,* and the rhetorical transfer from poet to audience is effected. The poet's narration serves as a ground-plot[59] of his invention, which though fictive carries the authority of probability.

For Sidney the search for universals affects especially the notion of character. The characters in a poem depict the actions appropriate for the type of person they essentially are. Just as the poet creates a golden world surpassing the brazen world of nature, so he creates exemplary people. Sidney asks "whether she [Nature] have brought forth so true a lover as Theagenes, so constant a friend as Pylades, so valiant a man as Orlando, so right a prince as Xenophon's Cyrus, so excellent a man every way as Virgil's Aeneas" (79.1–4)—and the answer, of course, is no. These fictional characters are the veritable embodiment of these abstract virtues. The poet, Sidney continues, describes not just the historically unique Cyrus produced by Nature, but the paragon Cyrus, so that poetry provides a model for others to emulate (79.12–15). It is by this process of universalizing that poetry teaches, as Sidney soon explains: "If the poet do his part aright, he will show you in Tantalus, Atreus, and such like, nothing that is not to be shunned; in Cyrus, Aeneas, Ulysses, each thing to be followed" (88.24–26).[60]

Even a precise name does not necessarily indicate individuality for a character. In his defence of the poet against the charge of lying, Sidney takes note of the fact that characters usually have individual names which suggest a particular identity; and since the name is, of course, a fiction, the validity of the entire poem is cast into doubt. In Sidney's words, "The poets give names to men they write of, which argueth a conceit of an actual truth, and so, not being true, proves a falsehood" (103.16–18). Sidney justifies this practice, however, by analogy to a lawyer who in court puts a case in the name of John-a-stiles or John-a-nokes—a fabricated name to accord with a hypothetical but likely situation. Such a practice is thoroughly acceptable, for "their naming of men is but to make their picture the more lively, and not to build any history" (103.21–22). The lawyer describes a hypothetical case in order to construct what is probable and render it lifelike, but he doesn't lie because he nothing affirms. He makes no pretense "to build any history." Sidney continues by likening the lawyer and the poet to painters, who must give a title to their subject once they have brought it into material existence on canvas: "Painting men, they cannot leave men nameless" (103.22–23). Just as the title in painting is applied post facto as a final act of definition, giving unmistakable identity to what the painter has already brought into being, so in poetry a name is bestowed after the character is identified by actions, as a shorthand for the sort of person that character is. As Sidney concludes, "The poet nameth Cyrus or Aeneas no other way than to show what men of their fames, fortunes, and estates should do" (103.26–28). The name is simply the codification of what the make-up of the character has predetermined. The name is generic, not individual: "The universal weighs what is fit to be said or done, either in likelihood or necessity (which the poesy considereth in his imposed names)" (88.5–7).

Sidney often takes the universal character so far that it becomes very much like a Platonic idea. For instance, he describes Xenophon's *Cyropaedia*, his favorite example, as "the portraiture of a just empire, under the name of Cyrus" (81.29–30). Here, as elsewhere, the historical Cyrus transubstantiates into the ideal of good governance. Later, Sidney gives a long list of characters with the dominant quality observable in each. Even the ignorant reader, he says, discerns "wisdom and temperance in Ulysses and Diomedes, valour in Achilles, friendship in Nisus and Euryalus . . . and, contrarily, the remorse of conscience in Oedipus, the soon repenting pride in Agamemnon, the self-devouring cruelty in his father Atreus, the violence of ambition in the two Theban brothers [i.e., Eteocles and Polynices], the sour-sweetness of revenge in Medea" (86.19–25). These are the actions of people interpreted like emblems or *imprese;* each character is simplified to a single virtue or vice. Again, Sidney speaks of the pleasure and profit that poems about heroes bring to even an anti-intellectual audience: "Glad will they be to hear the tales of Hercules, Achilles, Cyrus, Aeneas; and, hearing them, must needs hear the right description of wisdom, valour, and justice" (92.19–21). It is as though these characters represent certain qualities, much as the knights of *The Faerie Queene* represent holiness or temperance or chastity; and their tales display certain concepts, such as a book of friendship or justice or courtesy.

Nowhere does Sidney argue more vigorously for universals than in his preference for poetry over history, and nowhere is he closer to Aristotle. So eager is he to assert Aristotle's doctrine that he carries over certain vocabulary from the *Poetics.* Poetry, Sidney says, "is more philosophical and more studiously serious than history," and schoolboyishly he transcribes Aristotle's Greek words, φιλοσοφώτερον and σπουδαιότερον (87.36–88.2). Then he quotes Aristotle to justify this exaltation of poetry: "His reason is," Sidney parrots, "because poesy dealeth with καθόλου, this is to say, with the universal consideration, and the history with καθέκαστον, the particular." In this *paragone* between poetry and history, it is the ability to universalize that gives poetry its advantage. "Where the historian in his bare *Was* hath many times that which we call fortune to overrule the best wisdom," Sidney says, "the poet doth so far exceed him as he is to frame his example to that which is most reasonable" (89.2–6). The historian is hampered by the inexplicability of event: "Many times he must tell events whereof he can yield no cause; or if he do, it must be poetically" (89.6–8). In contrast, the poet, enjoying what came to be known as "poetic license," is never hobbled by irrationality or accident.

Whereas history reports countless examples of wickedness rewarded and goodness penalized, "poetry ever sets virtue so out in
her best colours, making Fortune her well-waiting handmaid, that
one must needs be enamoured of her" (90.4–6). In the golden
world of the poet, where the meta-truth of Aristotle's logic and
Plato's beauty coalesce, even the goddess Fortuna is subdued to
play a compliant role.

But Sidney goes beyond Aristotle. He is more daring, even
more sweeping in his claims for poetry. Perhaps responding to
Amyot,[61] Sidney declares a preference for poetry over philosophy
as well as over history. Not that he wishes to downplay philosophy—it is a laudable discipline, he notes amiably, and it teaches
what is right. Poetry, however, exceeds philosophy because poetry
not only demonstrates what is right, but also moves an audience
to perform it. "As Aristotle says," Sidney reminds us from reading
the *Ethics*, "it is not γνῶσις but πρᾶξις must be the fruit" (91.13–
14). Through observing the universals that poets present by their
imitation, we become aware of natural and moral philosophy of an
optimistic sort—what should be. It is true that philosophy ap-
prises us of this providential order. Poetry, however, goes further
and *moves* us to accord with it (cf. 91.25–34).

How poetry moves its audience to well-doing is a more difficult
question, requiring an increasingly sophisticated poetics. It is precisely here, though, that the concept of mimesis proves most useful. To meet his needs, Sidney gives Aristotle's theory of imitation
a practical application. What is one of several possibilities in Aristotle—that ποιητική is a verbal activity—becomes exclusive in
Sidney. He confines making to a verbal system, so that mimesis
becomes the use of language to produce imaginative fictions with
an immediate impact upon the reader. As an art of discourse, poetry shares in the suasiveness of rhetoric.

For Sidney poetry is superior both to philosophy and history
because one offers the precept and the other gives an example,
but only poetry embodies the precept in an example (85.8–22).
The example of poetry, of course, is not the particular of history,
which has no significance beyond its own locality of time and
place. Rather, the example of poetry is a universal, with general
applicability. Yet, although it approaches the absoluteness of a

Platonic idea, it avoids the tenuousness and elusiveness of a phil-osophical essence by being a concrete instance, a verbalized im-age. The poet, Sidney reiterates, "coupleth the general notion with the particular example" (85.25–26). So imitation, as Sidney refines it, involves both induction and deduction. By induction, the poet arrives at a universal, abstracting from actuality what is probable and necessary, conceptualizing to the extent of produc-ing a generality. And this generality serves as object of imitation for the fiction. But this generality, which is true for all cases, is then by deduction exemplified in a particular representative in-stance. The resultant poem is thereby validated by both inductive and deductive logic. Its object of imitation is grounded in the phe-nomenal world; but that universal is applied deductively to pro-duce a fictive though representative example whose verisimilitude can be confirmed by reference to our own experience.

To activate this model of mimesis, to render it efficacious in moving his readers to action, Sidney draws upon the time-honored theory of *enargeia* in rhetoric.[62] As Cicero and Quintilian had said, an orator not only delights and teaches, but also *moves,* and he achieves this purpose by several means, one of the most successful being the vivid description of a thing or event. By the use of lan-guage, the orator affects an audience as though the thing or event were actually present before their eyes. As Henry Peacham claims, "he may set forth any matter with a goodly perspecuitie, and paynt out any person, deede, or thing, so cunninglye with these couloures [of rhetoric], that it shall seeme rather a lyvely Image paynted in tables, then a reporte expressed with the tongue."[63] Although Sidney gets his mandate for such an effect of language from rhetoric, again his poetics is more sophisticated than the rhetorician's *enargeia.*

Sidney postulates that the poet, like the orator, uses language to produce an image, the imitation itself in concrete state. "Poesy is an art of imitation," Sidney says; and he continues by way of gloss, "that is to say, a representing, counterfeiting, or figuring forth" (101.33–35). He habitually speaks of poetry in terms of "figuring forth"—that is, producing a dimensional figure, an im-age—an artistic process that Sidney dignifies with the Platonic term εἰκαστική (104.15). This is the distinctive activity that iden-tifies a poet; as Sidney says soon afterwards: "It is that feigning notable images of virtues, vices, or what else, with that delightful teaching, which must be the right describing note to know a poet by" (81.36–82.1). These images, through the effects that language produces, cross the disjunction between the invisible and the visible worlds, between concept and sense datum. The image—verbally formulated, and therefore enjoying the amphibious nature of language—becomes palpable.

Since "feigning notable images" to achieve *enargeia* is the distinctive activity of a poet, we must now ask, how does a poet feign images? What is the mechanism that Sidney proposed for doing so? This question is central to Sidney's poetics. So what sort of images did Sidney have in mind?

To begin, we should pause over the word "feigning," which Elizabethans often paired with "counterfeiting" as a synonym,[64] and which I would gloss in addition with "imagining." The verb "to feign," like "to counterfeit," was ambiguous in Elizabethan usage: it meant "to produce by artifice," and could indicate an intent to deceive or not,[65] rather like the ambiguity in Spenser's favorite verb "to seem." The image that resulted as the end product of feigning might accurately reproduce the object of imitation in an exact replica or might seriously distort the original for the purpose of misleading the percipient. In Sidney's day, however, "feigning" and "counterfeiting" did not necessarily carry perjorative implications, any more than "artificial" did; and in fact all these words more often than not were terms of approbation that called attention to the creative talent and enterprise of the feigner, counterfeiter, or artificer. It is worth recalling that the etymology of "feigning" goes back to the Latin *fingere,* "to fashion, or make," whose past participle *fictus* provides the root as well for the term "fiction."[66] It is in this sense that Sidney speaks of "the *feigned* Cyrus in Xenophon" and "the *feigned* Aeneas in Virgil" (88.17–18; italics mine).

We should observe also that this feigning must be accompanied by "delightful teaching." The dictum of Horace, *utile dulci,* bears upon this passage;[67] certainly, Horace's statement accords with Sidney's general assumption that poetry should have a moralizing effect upon its audience. For this reason, to fulfill the didactic obligation, the poet feigns images of virtues and vices. But also Sidney casually adds "or what else," which opens the Sunday-school door to almost limitless possibilities. Images of almost anything may be presented so long as they are instructive.

The word that requires the most careful scrutiny, however, is the elusive term "image" itself. It comes directly from the Latin *imago* (= Gr. εἰϰών), which shares all the ambiguity of "feigning" and "counterfeiting."[68] An image may be a dependable representation of the original, conveying accurate information—an *imago mundi,* for example, is a map of the world; or an image may be dissemblative, a mere seeming—Arch*imago,* for example, is the source of deceit. All this is simply by way of saying that the ontology of an image is ambiguous: its reality should reside with its object of imitation in order to insure stability and value; but the particulars of its palpable phenomena are also undeniably "real," sense-perceptible, even though they may have become distorted in transmission and therefore may not be valid.

Finally, the verb "to imagine" means literally "to produce images," and the "imagination" is that mental faculty which is employed to such an end.[69] As Shakespeare concisely puts it, "Imagination bodies forth / The forms of things unknown . . . and gives to aery nothing / A local habitation and a name" (*MND* 5.1.14–17). The image, in Shakespeare's formulation, transfers the immaterial into some clearly defined bodily shape which is perceptible to the senses (at least, to the mind's eye), thereby reducing the ideal forms of the mental world to sensible data that the mortal faculties can process. The image is a metaphor,[70] translating meaning from the conceptual level to the physical, where it may be perceived as sense experience. And the activity of producing such images is "imagination" or "imitation."[71] This is actually so, not a word game. To follow the subtlety of Sidney's argument, we must remember the etymological linkage between "image," "imagination," and "imitation," a linkage which reveals the interdependency of the technical processes these terms signify.

But now to matters at once more fundamental and more complicated. Sidney claims that we recognize a poet by his ability to feign notable images which are ambiguous in their ontology. The image represents a previously existent object, physical or conceptual, which has been universalized; but once created, the image as an individual example also assumes an autonomous existence with its own phenomena. So what in the theory of language and in the arts of language would have allowed a poet to complete his assigned mission? How does language support the requisite ambiguity of the poetic image? How can a poet use words to produce images which will at once have universal application and yet will have the palpable effect on an audience that Sidney prescribes in his poetic program, moving them to virtuous action? To approach these questions, we must recall the theory of language as Sidney would have received it from the earlier Renaissance (pages 114–25).

The Florentine Platonists, drawing upon the *Cratylus* and thinking of Augustine, had placed great emphasis upon language, assigning words an important function as physical counters for the otherwise imponderable realm of essences. Words render ideas knowable. This mediating function of language as a bridge between an unchanging world of values and the mutable world of human affairs was seconded by the Hebraic-Christian tradition that Adam gave names to the other creatures. Once again, a verbal system allows knowledge of the absolute—in this instance, the attributes and intentions of Jehovah. These views of language were reinforced and somewhat exotically enhanced by the Hermetic philosophy, which saw words as hieroglyphs revealing the esoteric nature of things, and by the Cabalistic doctrine, which saw words as a divine vocabulary of sacred truth emanating from the otherwise ineffable tetragrammaton. In every instance, language is a semiotic system comprising two parts of an inviolable relationship, an immaterial set of signifieds and a concrete set of signifiers, and the relationship has been fixed by some holy power.

The art of rhetoric, and thence the art of poetry, exploited this dualistic nature of language that gave it an almost magical potency. As Agrippa carefully explains:

> A word is twofold, *viz.* internall, and uttered. An internall word is a conception of the mind, and motion of the soul, which is made without a voice. . . . But an uttered word hath a certain act in the voice, and properties of locution, and is brought forth with the breath of a man.[72]

This "act in the voice" realizes the latent effect of language, translating the verbal concept into physical fact. The word uttered by the poet impinges upon the bodily senses of the percipient with palpable force, with "properties of locution," as though it were a material object. When a word is conceived as a hieroglyph or as a Cabalistic vocable that commands the immediate presence of what it nominates, the physicality of language becomes even more apparent. Words are palpable counters for the invisible forms they represent. Language as physical experience when it impinges upon the ears or eyes is capable of conveying a prior non-sensible order of being. As Castiglione puts it, "Wrytyng is . . . an Image, or rather the life of the woordes" (64).

A word becomes a sign pointing in two directions at once—to use Platonic terminology, it points in the direction of intelligibility, where the soul is the faculty of response dealing with concepts, but also it points in the direction of sensibleness, where the bodily senses are the faculty of response dealing with percepts. In this fashion the word fulfills its function as mediating agent between mind and body, between world of thought and world of action, between that which abides and that which continually changes. Language is that cohesive factor in our universe which allows us to expatiate freely from the lowliest mundane corner to the most awesome heavenly expanse. It is, in fact, that gift which allows us to realize our godlike potential, to be human in the full biblical sense that although mortal we are created in the image of the infinite and eternal. After Cicero, there is no stint of praise for the arts of language, and the Renaissance revelled in it. What is most pertinent, though, is the dual nature of language, the amphibious life of the word. It inhabits both the realm of ideas, a *potentia* conceivable to the mind, and the world of fact, an *actus* perceptible to the senses.

When seen in this light, the nature of language explains why poetry wins in its competition with history and philosophy. The encompassing ambiguity of poetry which makes it superior both to history and to philosophy in terms of *what* it imitates is apparent also in its use of language, so that poetry is superior also in terms of *how* it imitates. History and philosophy can take advantage of one or the other half of a word, but not its full range. Only poetry exploits language to its uttermost, "so that truly neither philosopher nor historiographer could at the first have entered into the gates of popular judgements, if they had not taken a great passport of poetry" (*Defence* 75.32–34).

All three of these learned disciplines employ the arts of language. Because history deals with actual fact, however, historians use language only to produce a faithful account of what has happened—"their lips sound of things done, and verity be written in their foreheads" (*Defence* 75.22–23). In Sidney's scheme, a historian, such as Lucan, cannot rise above the second category of poets, along with the natural and moral philosophers who merely describe what is observed in nature. At least in Sidney's biased analysis, the historian is limited to particularities, and cannot implement the conceptual dimension of language or employ language to extrapolate conceptual possibilities. For him, words must be exact counters for precise facts, labels for the things of this world. "The historian," Sidney concludes, "is so tied, not to what should be but to what is, to the particular truth of things and not to the general reason of things, that his example draweth no necessary consequence" (85.17–21). The historian's vocabulary, like his statement, has no application beyond the particular instance.

In contrast, the philosopher suffers just the opposite limitation. He deals only with "definitions, divisions, and distinctions" (83.19–20), and never with the determinate data of individual case. So his language is perforce vague to the extent of being all speculation and no substance. "The philosopher," Sidney says, "is so hard of utterance and so misty to be conceived. . . . his knowledge standeth so upon the abstract and general, that happy is that man who may understand him" (85.10–16). The philosopher, of course, cannot use words as exact counters because what he wishes to express—such as "the quiddity of *ens* and *prima materia*" (106.1)—will not submit to specificity. Furthermore, for him, words should lead the mind away from concreteness toward further intellection. Rather than being definitive labels, words for the philosopher are mere pointers toward an immaterial reality of ideas.

The poet, however, projecting the palpable image of a universal concept, can utilize both components of language, both the physical and the conceptual. The physical component of words gives ontological validity to the phenomena of his image, while their conceptual component supports the existence of the image as an idea in the mind. Among those who depend upon the arts of language, in fact, only the poet brings into play the full range of linguistic potential, the range from mundane trivium to divine illimitability.

Finally, to tie up an earlier strand of our argument, we should note in passing that it is this ambiguousness of the word—and therefore of language, and consequently of the verbal image—which allows the poet to be true while admitting his fictitiousness on the physical level. This is how the poet never lies, while always lying. Whatever improbabilities and impossibilities his language may point to at the physical level of experience, whatever fantasies or paradoxes he may describe, the poet can use the other half of language to generate mental experience. His narration is but an imaginative ground-plot of a profitable invention (103.15–16). The poet straddles the fence that separates the experiential world from the world of art, keeping a foot on both sides. Just as the Aristotelian artificer depicts a wild beast or a cadaver and transmutes it into a pleasant event for the percipient, so the poet, because of the amphibious nature of language, can generate a rational meaning from what in reality would be an impossibility. The painter, incidentally, that other maker of images, benefits from no comparable ambiguousness in his medium.

The dual nature of language explains also how the rhetorician so readily achieves his aim of persuading an audience. In addition to the time-honored discipline reaching back through Quintilian and Cicero to Aristotle, he could call upon the authority of Agrippa for the near-magical potency of speech:

> Words therefore are the fittest medium betwixt the speaker and the hearer, carrying with them not only the conception of the mind, but also the vertue of the speaker with a certain efficacy unto the hearers, and this oftentimes with so great a power, that oftentimes they change not only the hearers, but also other bodies, and things that have no life.[73]

Like the magician, the rhetorician knew that words call forward what they signify, so they have a physical presence and an immediate force. Furthermore, through the use of *enargeia*, the orator creates a verbal image with the concreteness and impact of physical experience. Thereby the arts of language are the means of crossing from the conceptual realm inhabited by the will of the orator to the workaday world of the audience who feel and act as a result of the orator's skill.[74] Language bestows such power upon rhetoricians that Hercules became their unlikely emblem.[75]

And the orator's power to affect an audience was transferred wholesale to the poet. As Sidney comments about the end of the *Aeneid*, "Whom do not the words of Turnus move, the tale of Turnus having planted his image in the imagination" (*Defence* 114.14–16). The image of Turnus is implanted in the imagination of the reader by a verbal system which "moves" him, wreaking an effect upon his behavior. Vergil sways his audience by presenting the speaking picture of Turnus to the mind's eye. The verbal technique of *enargeia* coupled with the hypothesis of a mind's eye were ready means of influencing the reader.

To allow for this effect, Sidney, along with most of his era, hypothesized the existence of a quasi-sense faculty where this interchange between mental and sensible takes place in the psyche. This mind's eye is none other than what we—along with Sidney, as the quotation in the last paragraph indicates—have called the "imagination."[76] Not only is it the faculty by which poets *conceive* images, but also that by which we the readers *perceive* them. *Enargeia* is the technique of the imagining poet as he bodies forth the forms of things unknown; the *oculi mentis*, the reception equipment of his audience. So now we must consider how the mind's eye (or imagination) fits into the scheme of perception.[77]

"The mind's eye," in one formulation or another, occurs frequently in literary theory and in criticism, but the term is slippery because its meaning shifts according to the psychology which prevails in any period. In Sidney's day, however, the science of the soul and of how it receives and processes sense data was still determined largely by the faculty psychology set forth by Aristotle in two related treatises, *De anima* and *De sensu*.[78] According to Aristotle, the soul is distinct from the body, yet intimately interfused with it. Thereby the soul gives the body its individuality, its unique identification, just as form actualizes and identifies matter in any individuated entity. In return, the soul receives information of the outside world through the body, which possesses five senses for this purpose, the same five that we still enumerate: sight, hearing, smell, taste, and touch. Each of these *external* senses has its own province, receiving sense impressions of a certain sort. Furthermore, they are arranged in a scale of ascending order determined by the degree of physical contact between the sense and the object it is perceiving. Touch, for example, is at the bottom of the list because it requires complete physical contact with the object. Taste and smell follow in succession, each dependent upon contact with particles which emanate from the object, although the particles required by smell are less substantial than those required by taste. Hearing is next, which results from nothing more substantial than vibrations in the air that originate with the object. Finally there is sight,[79] the most tenuous and mysterious of all, involving nonmaterial radiations and light, which in Aristotelian physics is a disembodied medium rather than a substance.[80] The image which the sense of sight receives, therefore, is already divorced from materiality, rendered noncorporeal.

Since in many acts of perception several senses are concurrently active—for example, the perception of something in motion may involve touch, hearing, and sight—Aristotle proposed a "common sense" to deal with what he called "common sensibles"—that is, experiences reported upon by more than one sense (*De anima* 425a14–b12). The *sensus communis* collects the various data submitted to it by the several particular senses, all of which it recognizes as equivalent in kind;[81] and it has the ability to reduce the disparate impressions to a uniform state that can be utilized by the other mental faculties. The common sense, in fact, is an *internal* sense, a faculty of the soul, and it leads to further intellection. The congeries of impressions received by the common sense—comprising the various sense data, yet removed from the mutable coordinates of time and space—is now ready for immediate use in thinking, or it may be stored for future use.

What happens to the data received and processed by the common sense is well explained by Pierre de la Primaudaye. In the second part of his *French academie,* which advertises to be "a naturall historie of the bodie and soule of man" (title page), La Primaudaye begins piously with the creation of Adam and proceeds through those topics which were de rigueur for an encyclopedist of the human condition. He deals with the creation of woman, offers a detailed description of the human body, and soon arrives at a discussion of what he calls "the bodily and externall senses" (62). He covers each of the five senses in turn, and then comes to those chapters explaining "the nature, faculties, and powers of mans soule" (130), eventually arriving at "the internall senses . . . , which are farre more excellent and noble then the outward senses" (144). La Primaudaye operates within an overtly Christian context, specifically Protestant, and the Bible is the ultimate authority for any belief, although Aristotle and his followers have greatly colored its interpretation. Other authors such as Plato and Hippocrates are also infrequently mentioned.

When La Primaudaye comes to discuss "the Animal[82] vertues and powers in the internal senses" (146), he follows Aristotelian tradition as elaborated by Galen and identifies five different faculties: common sense, imagination, fantasy, reason, and memory. The first three, he observes, perform many of the same functions and are often grouped together, although he makes some attempt to distinguish them. He begins with the imagination:

> First there must bee some facultie and vertue that receiveth the images imprinted in the senses, the knowledge whereof is as single and plaine as may bee, because it is onely of thinges that are bodily and present, as I have alreadie declared. This vertue is called *Imagination,* or the *Imaginative* vertue, which is in the soule as the eye in the bodie, by beholding to receive the images that are offered unto it by the outward senses. (146)

Strictly speaking, the imagination is that faculty defined as the mind's eye—or, at least, it "is in the soule as the eye in the bodie." It produces images derived from sense data transmitted through the common sense. But La Primaudaye, according to prevalent practice, assimilates to the imagination functions of both the fantasy and the common sense. He continues:

> Nowe after that the *Imagination* hath received the images of the senses, singly and particularly as they are offered unto it, then doeth it as it were prepare and digest them, eyther by joyning them together, or by separating them according as their natures require.

The common sense, then, the lowest of the soul's faculties, receives the actual sense data from the physical world and transmits them indiscriminately to the imagination. It is the function of the imagination to sort and synthesize these data, producing a self-consistent composite image.

Again, strictly speaking, imagination is the coadunating faculty, to use Coleridge's vocabulary—the faculty of the soul which prepares and digests the sense data "by joyning them together." In contrast, briefly, the fantasy is a distributive faculty, "separating them [sense data] according as their natures require." As La Primaudaye notes of other authorities, "They that distinguish *Imagination* from *Fantasie*, attribute this office to *Fantasie*." While recording this differentiation, La Primaudaye does not insist upon it; and, in fact, he goes on to report that by some authorities these functions, that of joining and that of separating, are often assigned to the common sense:

> . . . the *Common sense,* under which they comprehend both the former faculties [i.e., imagination and fantasy], because the office thereof is to receive the images that are offered unto it, and to discerne the things as they are presented by all the externall senses, and to distinguish them as they doe. Afterwarde it is requisite, that all these things thus heaped together, shoulde bee distributed and compared one with another, to consider howe they may be conjoyned or severed, how one followeth another, or how farre asunder they are, that so a man may judge what is to be retained and what to be refused. (147)

So the imagination, fantasy, and common sense may all be subsumed into one faculty, one internal visualizing power of the soul that is likened to the eye of the body and that for convenience came to be called "the mind's eye."

In the last quotation, the functions of the common sense begin to merge with those of yet another animal faculty, with those of reason.[83] The reason is a judgmental agent, certifying the images, identifying what is true or false, and turning the results to further use in various mental processes. Those logical activities that have to do with evaluating the sense data—with considering "how one followeth another, or how farre asunder they are, that so a man may judge what is to be retained and what to be refused"—inhere, properly ascribed, in the rational faculty. And reason is followed by judgment, an ancillary activity attendant upon ratiocination, "whereby," La Primaudaye explains, "men chuse or refuse that which reason alloweth or disalloweth." Because of its evaluative component, judging right and wrong, the exercise of reason allows humanity to approach closest to deity.

There is still one more "animal virtue," and this is the memory, that internal sense which receives the images after they have been amalgamated by the imagination. The memory stores the images for future use. La Primaudaye characterizes the imagination as "the mouth of the vessell of memorie," while memory itself is "the facultie and vertue that retaineth and keepeth whatsoever is committed to the custody thereof by the other senses, that it may be found and brought forth when neede requireth." So the memory acts as a storage facility, preserving the images for further reference. It may be opened and utilized by the other animal faculties at will: "*Memorie* is as it were their treasurer to keepe that which they committe unto it, and to bring it foorth in due time and season." Sidney concurs that "memory . . . [is] the only treasurer of knowledge" (*Defence* 100.36–101.1).[84]

So the mind's eye incorporates several elements of a rather complex perceptual process. It is activated when a physical object is perceived by any one or several of the five bodily senses. The data impressed upon these external senses are in turn transmitted to the internal senses: the common sense, imagination, and fantasy. There a composite image is synthesized, validated with the aid of reason, and readied for use by the mind in the wide range of its rational functions. In addition, the mind's eye may call upon its ancillary, the memory, that residual inventory of ever-available images for comparison and contrast. It may, in fact, dismember images stored in the memory and re-member their component parts to construct such hybrids as gryphons, chimeras, and sphinxes (cf. *Defence* 78.22–30). The human imagination both receives and produces images.

We are now in a position to understand the full import of Sidney's *paragone* between the poet and the philosopher, and contingently we can appreciate his reason for making poetry superior to philosophy. Sidney acknowledges that both poet and philosopher use the arts of language, but the philosopher doesn't produce *images*, doesn't address the *imagination*. Only the poet *imitates*. "For whatsoever the philosopher saith should be done," Sidney argues, the poet "giveth a perfect picture of it in someone by whom he presupposeth it was done." Sidney continues to explain in terms that are now familiar to us: "A perfect picture I say, for he yieldeth to the powers of the mind an image of that whereof the philosopher bestoweth but a wordish description, which doth neither strike, pierce, nor possess the sight of the soul so much as that other doth" (*Defence* 85.22–29). The wordish description of the philosopher, while effective in teaching to some degree, doesn't *move* the reader (cf. 99.13–15). It doesn't "strike, pierce, nor possess the sight of the soul" with the same force as the quasi-physical image produced by the poet. So the mechanism by which poetic images are perceived and comprehended by an audience is basic to Sidney's poetics, setting poetry above philosophy. The mind must be able to visualize with a capacity approaching the sense of sight. In the reductive alembic of the mind's eye, the poet's imitation—the poetic image, the verbal picture—transmogrifies from mental concept to actual experience.[85]

Sidney's definition of poetry as a "speaking picture" hinges upon this point. It too attempts to explain how a verbal system becomes palpable, how speech becomes a picture. It implies the same sort of interchange between conceptual and sensible that the mind's eye permits. The Plutarchan phrase "speaking picture" is, of course, an oxymoron, joining together in paradox two terms that are mutually exclusive. In a Platonic context, a speaking picture encapsulates the incongruity that conceptual meaning can be known only through its ontological opposite, a sense-perceptible object. A picture speaks, expressing an idea. In an Aristotelian context, slightly different, a speaking picture encapsulates the incongruity that what is to be seen appears as something to be heard. Ordinarily, that which is addressed to the ear is discrete from what is to be perceived by the eye, but here these two sense faculties act as one. The humor of Bottom's speech when he awakens from his dream comes in part from his garbling of the biblical text (1 Corinthians 2:9), but even more from his confusion of the senses: "The eye of man hath not heard, the ear of man hath not seen . . . what my dream was" (*MND* 4.1.213–17). What we have in a speaking picture, then, is the scrambling of two sets of mutually exclusive paired terms: conceptual/sensible and aural/visual.

At least since the time of Boethius, though, a correspondence had been drawn between visual and auditory perception: "The ear is affected by sounds in the same way as the eye is by the appearance of things,"[86] no doubt by virtue of the common sense, which perceives and processes the shared formal properties of both the visual and aural objects. Moreover, to anneal the dichotomy between conceptual/sensible and between aural/visual there is language, which enjoys the ambiguousness of comprising both terms in either set. By the mechanism for perceiving language that operates within the psyche, this Plutarchan phrase assumes that the verbal, against all expectation, may be rendered visible. We have speech which is a picture. Language is a middle term which mediates between the two arts and conjoins them so that in the mind's eye poetry becomes painting. The word is rendered carnate, becoming an image that speaks.

The oxymoronic nature of the phrase is confirmed by its opposite formulation: not only is poetry a "speaking picture," but, as Sidney knew from the topos in Plutarch, a painting also is "dumb poesy," a nonverbal poem. Like poetry, painting presents a statement—although, paradoxically, expressed without words. Again, thanks to the ontological ambiguity of language, painting may become a semiotic system like speech but using only the physical component of its words, which therefore are silent—visual only, and not aurally addressed to the mind. Rather than having speech that is a picture, such as the poetic image, contrary to all expectations we have a picture that conveys conceptual meaning, like an illustration in an emblem. But the two formulations—speaking picture and silent poem—are exceedingly close and approach one another by intention. In practice, the two may converge upon the same truth, the same ontological *situs,* as do the woodblock and the verse of an emblem.

Painting and poetry, then, though one comprises visual data and the other verbal data, are equated in their ability to produce images and thereby to move a percipient.[87] They are interchangeable, at least as products of imitation, if not in the media of their expression. And the human faculty that permits this exchange between verbal and visual is the mind's eye, a shrewd hypothesis that assigns a sense faculty, that of sight, to the mind itself. Sidney brings this argument to a conclusion in favor of poetry by observ-

ing that the "learned definitions" of the philosopher "lie dark before the imaginative and judging power, if they be not illuminated
or figured forth by the speaking picture of poesy" (86.3–8). That
which is only conceptual remains unknown unless rendered efficacious in images directed to our "imaginative and judging
power"—that is, our mind's eye.

To substantiate his argument, Sidney cites many examples of
"the speaking picture of poesy" from Cicero, Vergil, Homer, and
others. "Tully," he begins, "taketh much pains, and many times
not without poetical[88] helps, to make us know the force love of our
country hath in us"; and he continues, "Let us but hear old An-
chises speaking in the midst of Troy's flames, or see Ulysses in the
fulness of all Calypso's delights bewail his absence from barren
and beggarly Ithaca" (86.9–13). These indeed are word pictures
that we *hear* and *see,* enunciating a devotion to homeland. There
are other examples of *picturae loquentes,* depicting a variety of
"virtues, vices, and passions so in their own natural seats laid to
the view, that we seem not to hear of [i.e., by means of] them, but
clearly to see through [i.e., by means of] them" (86.28–30). These
images may be addressed at first to the ear, but eventually they
make us "see." To clinch his point, Sidney notes that Christ himself chose to teach by parables rather than precepts because such
verbal images make indelible impressions upon the internal
senses. "Our Saviour Christ could as well have given the moral
commonplaces of uncharitableness and humbleness as the divine
narration of Dives and Lazarus," Sidney explains, "but that His
through-searching wisdom knew the estate of Dives burning in
hell, and of Lazarus in Abraham's bosom, would more constantly
(as it were) inhabit both the memory and judgment" (87.11–18).

In *The third part of the Countesse of Pembrokes Yvychurch*
(1592), Abraham Fraunce also explicates at some length Plutarch's topos of "speaking picture," expanding the equation to its
full palindromic formulation of "poetry, a speaking picture, and
paynting, a dumbe poetry" (fol. 3ᵛ). Fraunce, however, delineates
a quite different poetics from that of Sidney, by contrast highlighting the novelty of Sidney's proposition. Fraunce is strongly influenced by the tradition of allegorizing Ovid, and in fact uses this
Plutarchan topic as a starting-point for setting forth a poetics of

allegory reminiscent of Boccaccio.[89] The verbal system of the poem is a veil over a concealed truth, covering neoplatonist mysteries:

> Both poetry, a speaking picture, and paynting, a dumbe poetry, were like in this, that the one and the other did under an amyable figure and delightsome veyle, as it were, cover the most sacred mysteries of auncient philosophie. Nay, *Pythagoras* himselfe by his symbolicall kinde of teaching, as also *Plato* by his conceited parables and allegorical discourses in his bookes called, Phaedrus, Timaeus, and Symposium, may make any man beleeve, that as the learned Indians, Aethiopians, and Aegyptians kept their doctrine religiously secret for feare of prophanation, so the Grecians by their example, have wrapped up in tales, such sweete inventions, as of the learned unfolder may well be deemed wonderfull, though to a vulgar conceit, they seeme but frivolous imaginations.

This interpretation of Plutarch's dictum allies poetry with the emblem tradition, where the meaning of the woodcut is unfolded obliquely in the verse and stated directly in the motto. In such an artifact the ontological *situs* of the work resides in its implied truth, and its palpable components are sloughed off like chaff as the reader moves from the sensuous world of perceptible phenomena into an intellectual realm of ideas. The images, visual and verbal, are subservient to the conceptual essence of the emblem, which is its "mystery." They are mere prolegomena to comprehension of a wholly conceptual truth, which is the point of the exercise. The "picture," as Fraunce proceeds to demonstrate in a series of mythological examples, is incidental to the thought.

Aesop's fables were similarly printed and read in this way.[90] A Philostratian woodcut, capturing the climactic moment of the tale, stood at the head of the fable, while an extracted moral, an *affabulatio,* provided a conclusion. Each fable was organized and laid out rather like an emblem. These, Sidney agreed, should be regarded as allegories. In a Plutarchan mood, Sidney explains why young men should read these violent and indecorous fictions couched in the improbable mise en scène of the animal kingdom:

The poet is the food for the tenderest stomachs, the poet is indeed the right popular philosopher, whereof Aesop's tales give good proof: whose pretty allegories, stealing under the formal tales of beasts, make many, more beastly than beasts, begin to hear the sound of virtue from these dumb speakers. (*Defence* 87.24–28)[91]

The improbability of the fable as actual event, as Plutarch had argued, makes it inescapably apparent that the poet is lying. Prima facie, wolves and crows and pismires cannot speak. But from Aristotle, Sidney knew that even the most unlikely subjects, such as cadavers and wild animals, can be rendered pleasant by the mimetic art of poetry. When so transmuted, the gross episodes of Aesop become "pretty allegories," simple fare for the youngest stomachs. In this way, poetry teaches, and even the least intellectual of men—those who are "more beastly than beasts" because they lack all discourse of reason[92]—are taught the lessons of moral philosophy. They "begin to hear the sound of virtue from these dumb speakers"—that is, the animal characters in the fable are frozen in time to produce a permanent image (witness the woodcut), and they transmit a continuous message, an abstracted moral. The fable becomes an emblematic painting, a dumb poesy; and, to complete the analogy, the actors in it are "dumb speakers."

The "continued Allegory" of *The Faerie Queene* accords with this poetics. The reality of the poem lies not in the things which comprise the narrative; that fantastic story is a veil over the concealed truth. The poem's ontological *situs* lies in the ideas that reside behind the vestment of words. Jonson was aware of this dichotomy between *verba* and *res* in *The Faerie Queene:* disapproving of the archaic diction, he complains that Spenser "writ no Language"; "yet," Jonson continues, "I would have him read for his matter."[93] The true essence of the poem, in Spenser's phrase, is a "darke conceit." By Spenser's own account in his letter to Raleigh, he offers "good discipline" which is "clowdily enwrapped in Allegorical devises."[94] As a consequence, Spenser must distinguish between his verbal system and his meaning—for example, when speaking of Gloriana he says: "In that Faery Queene I meane glory in my generall intention, but in my particular I conceive the most excellent and glorious person of our soveraine the Queene." The word "Gloriana," then, or the phrase "Faery

Queene" means "glory" as a concept or the historical personage
"Queen Elizabeth." These are the meanings cloudily enwrapped
in the allegorical device coded as "Gloriana," and hence they are
the substance of the poem.

Spenser's reliance upon hidden meanings cautiously expressed
in verbal descriptions is attested by his penchant for poetic "visions." His first published work was an assigned exercise of this
sort, his translations for Jan van der Noot's *Theatre . . . [for] voluptuous worldlings* (1569), complete with woodblock illustrations
which visually reify the arcane meaning that the adept reader is
to comprehend. Spenser later translated additional visions of Du
Bellay and Petrarch, and compiled an original series of his own,
"Visions of the Worlds Vanitie"—all printed in the *Complaints* volume.[95] Much of the odysseylike voyage of Guyon and the Palmer
across the water to the Bower of Bliss is also handled in this visionary manner: after passing victims shipwrecked upon the vivid
Rock of Vile Reproach, for example, the Palmer says, "Behold
th'ensamples in our sights, / Of lustfull luxurie and thriftlesse
wast" (*Faerie Queene*, 2.12.9.2–3). Britomart has an even more
distended "wondrous vision" (5.7.12.8) in Isis Church which fore-
tells the outcome of her marriage to Artegall.

In his purest expression of the visionary mode, Spenser composed a dozen private visions as a final episode in "The Ruines of
Time." The female genius of Verulam in that poem comes into
sight (as a visionary presence, of course); and after her plaint and
disappearance, the poet sits transfixed by grief and horror, "deepe-
elie muzing at her doubtfull speach" (line 485). It is then that the
tendentious visions occur: "Before mine eis strange sights presented were, / Like tragicke Pageants seeming to appeare" (lines
489–90). There follow in succession a series of verbalized symbols: an idol on an altar, a stately tower, an earthly paradise, a
proud giant, a wide-arched bridge, two white bears, a dying swan,
a sounding harp, a rich coffer, a handsomely decorated bed and
virgin, a wounded knight, and a golden ark. Each of these visions
has some apocalyptic significance, rather in the manner of St.
John's Revelation or Solomon's Song of Songs.[96] Taken together,
they confirm the overall theme of the poem, at one point explicitly
stated: "All is vanitie and griefe of minde, / Ne other comfort in
this world can be, / But hope of heaven, and heart to God inclinde"

(lines 583–85). Although each is fantastic in and of itself, the visions body forth this moral.

Sidney recognized the validity and effectiveness of such a poetics of allegory that separates verbal system from implied meaning, although he tended to relegate such poems to child's play. They are food for only the tenderest stomachs, as he says about Aesop's fables. In a later passage of the *Defence,* when refuting the charge that poets lie, Sidney returns to the poetics of Aesop. He thinks no one so simple as to "say that Aesop lied in the tales of his beasts; for who thinks that Aesop wrote it for actually true were well worthy to have his name chronicled among the beasts he writeth of" (103.3–6)—that is, a reader so foolish has less than mature human reason and therefore belongs among the lower creatures on the chain of being. What is required to understand Aesop is nothing more sophisticated than the gullibility of the child who goes to a play, sees a sign "Thebes" written upon an old door, and takes the place to be indeed Thebes. "If then a man can arrive to that child's age to know that the poets' persons and doings are but pictures what should be, and not stories what have been," Sidney concludes, "they will never give the lie to things not affirmatively but allegorically and figuratively written" (103.8–12). So the fables of Aesop—like emblems, the speaking pictures of Fraunce, and the visions of Spenser—are valid, although they are "allegorically" written, "figuratively" (literally, by human or animal figures[97]) projected in a word picture that even a child can see through to the concealed truth.

Evidently, Sidney thinks that visions, emblems, and fables, being inferior poetic modes, are hardly worth arguing over. They are suitable, perhaps necessary, for childlike mentalities. They incidentally administer instruction in the very act of entertaining, and "pretending no more, doth intend the winning of the mind from wickedness to virtue—even as the child is often brought to take most wholesome things by hiding them in such other as have a pleasant taste" (92.12–15). This is the tacky poetics of the sugar-coated pill, the medieval version of Horace's *utile dulci.* "So is it in men," Sidney concludes condescendingly, "most of which are childish in the best things, till they be cradled in their graves" (92.17–19). For such minds, with their bias against learning, literature is a means of teaching unawares what they would boggle at learning from straightforward exposition: "Glad will they be to hear the tales of Hercules, Achilles, Cyrus, Aeneas; and, hearing them, must needs hear the right description of wisdom, valour, and justice; which, if they had been barely, that is to say philosophically, set out, they would swear they be brought to school again" (92.19–23). Poetry is superior to philosophy, particularly for the simple-minded—or for the inherently wicked, "those hard-hearted evil men who think virtue a school name" and who must be slyly dosed with the elixir of literature "ere themselves be aware, as if they took a medicine of cherries" (93.6–13).

As we gather from the peroration of the *Defence* with its mocking tone, however, Sidney himself was not given to the devious use of literature for such underhanded instruction. The best poetry instead should follow a forthright, reasonable mode of discourse. Sidney was not prone "to believe, with Clauserus, the translator of Cornutus, that it pleased the heavenly Deity, by Hesiod and Homer, under the veil of fables, to give us all knowledge, logic, rhetoric, philosophy natural and moral, and *quid non*" (121.9–13). What we need to know should be presented to our rational faculties in rational ways. Sidney's belittlement of allegory is further suggested by the playfulness with which we are "conjure[d] . . . , even in the name of the nine Muses, no more to scorn the sacred mysteries of poesy" (120.36–121.2). And he pokes fun at the esoteric interpreters of literature who in conspiratorial fashion insist "that there are many mysteries contained in poetry, which of purpose were written darkly, lest by prophane wits it should be abused" (121.13–15). Poetry is a more mature—that is, more consciously rational—activity than the unveiling of allegories. In Sonnet 28 of *Astrophil and Stella* the speaker expressly forbids the interpretation of the work within "allegorie's curious frame"; "when I say 'Stella,'" he insists, he means no more than Astrophil's mistress and does not seek "in hid ways to guide Philosophie."

In consequence, Sidney's speaking picture in its most serious formulation is something quite different from that of Fraunce. For the "right" poet, Sidney prescribes an Aristotelian mimesis that is *not* allegorical in the neoplatonist sense. For Sidney the ontological *situs* of the poem lies not in some concealed truth behind the veil of words. Rather, in the best poetry its ultimate being inheres in the verbal system itself, especially as that verbal system generates poetic images. The poem is its own reality instead of a counter for an anterior idea. This is not to deny meaning to the poem—in fact, quite the opposite. It is to recognize that meaning is inseparable from the poem, integral to it. The "*idea* or fore-conceit" is the poem's informing essence, its ever-present participle.

Nor does the ontological *situs* of a poem lie, as in a rhetorical model, in some predetermined subject matter which is subsequently clothed in words.[98] As one of his last topics in the *Defence,* Sidney looks at "diction," and he censures those poets who dress up their subject matter as though the externals of poetry were detachable ornaments. He has just denounced the love poets who profess their passions by bookish repetition of the sonneteering conventions and consequently lack *energeia.* From this point of rhetoric, he proceeds to other deficiencies of the same sort in contemporary poetry. "Now, for the outside of it, which is words, or (as I may term it) diction," he begins, "it is even well worse." In poetry composed according to the rhetorical model, there is an "outside of it, which is words," and an inside, which is subject matter, the familiar *verba* and *res* of the rhetor. But this dichotomization of poetry leads to abuses. Using the revered term of Cicero, *eloquentia,* Sidney exposes the folly of those who concentrate their efforts upon the externals of style:

> So is the honey-flowing matron Eloquence apparelled, or rather disguised, in a courtesan-like painted affectation: one time, with so far-fet words that may seem monsters but must seem strangers to any poor Englishman; another time, with coursing of a letter, as if they were bound to follow the method of a dictionary; another time, with figures and flowers, extremely winter-starved. (117.13–19)[99]

Sidney goes on to lament that these faults are rife not only among "versifiers," but also among "prose-printers" and "scholars," and even among "some preachers." In Sidney's view, this dissociation of subject matter and verbal system renders the discourse ineffectual. If poetry is to succeed in its mission of delighting, teaching, and moving, the rhetorician's *res* must merge with and emerge from his *verba* as a dynamic, uninterrupted event.

Therefore Sidney's model for mimetic poetry promotes the verbal system to a position of prime value.[100] The poetic image itself, rather than the idea it encodes, is supreme. This principle underlies the important reaffirmation of the poet's uniqueness which introduces Sidney's survey of poetry in England. Sidney recalls the old proverb, *Orator fit, poeta nascitur;*[101] and he comments, "A poet no industry can make, if his own genius be not carried into it" (111.32–34). Even so, the poet, regardless of native wit, can benefit from guidance, which Sidney specifies as the three components of Horatian poetics, "art, imitation, and exercise"—that is, learning the rules, following classical models, and practicing through exercises. But then Sidney minimizes the importance of such poetizing by rote—"But these, neither artificial rules nor imitative patterns, we much cumber ourselves withal." Although a poet with natural genius may benefit from training, as Horace had advocated, we needn't pay much attention to "artificial rules nor imitative patterns." The poet must practice his craft, of course, but not according to the sterile precepts of learning rules and imitating models. "Exercise indeed we do," Sidney concedes; although then he adds, admonishingly, "but that very fore-backwardly." And here Sidney makes a telling point. The Horatian poet's error lies in the dissociation of matter from manner, or in the rhetorician's assumption that knowledge (the noun) precedes knowing (the verb).[102] In contrast, the "right" poet recognizes that knowledge is an elusive truth, acquired only through experience. Even if "our degenerate souls, made worse by their clayey lodgings," frustrate our struggle toward "perfection" (82.15–16), this activity—as Camus said of Sisyphus toiling with his stone—is worthwhile within itself.

In any case, "right" poetry is more honestly a seeking than a having found. In Sidney's terse comment, to continue with the passage in hand, "For where we should exercise to know, we exercise as having known; and so is our brain delivered of much matter which never was begotten by knowledge" (112.4–8). So the poet "should exercise to know," the dynamics of *natura naturans,* rather than "exercise as having known," the static statement of *natura naturata.* True knowledge in poetry, as in life, derives only from such a continuous process. By way of further critique, Sidney goes on to excoriate the rhetorical model in its own terms: "For there being two principal parts, matter to be expressed by words and words to express the matter, in neither we use art of imitation rightly." If we separate poetry into *res* and *verba*—if, like the Horatian poet trained in rhetoric, we compose in two stages—we violate the conditions of "right" poetry. We destroy its integrity. We disrupt the vital relationship between verb and noun, between expression and concept, between signifier and signified. We abuse the art of poetry; we do not use imitation rightly.

Sidney had arrived at the same point earlier in the *Defence* when he summarizes his high commendation of the poet as maker:

> That name of making is fit for him, considering that where all other arts retain themselves within their subject, and receive as it were, their being from it, the poet only bringeth his own stuff, and doth not learn a conceit out of a matter, but maketh matter for a conceit. (99.5–9)

This statement, made cryptic by Sidney's playing with the words "conceit" and "matter," presents some difficulties to interpretation; but Sidney is, as usual, speaking precisely. First, practitioners of all the other disciplines, being limited to a prescribed subject matter, can only "learn a conceit out of a matter." Whatever conclusions they arrive at must arise from a predetermined set of principles and data; the "conceit" arises from a preexistent "matter." Even some poets, those of the second kind that deal with matters philosophical, similarly remain "wrapped within the fold of the proposed subject" (80.19–26) and do not extrapolate to freely imagined conceits.

To continue with the positive thrust of the quotation, "The [right] poet only bringeth his own stuff, and . . . maketh matter for a conceit." The poet as maker brings his own "stuff," the data of his own experience.[103] And rather than learning passively what a predetermined subject matter would constrain him to, he ranges boldly within the zodiac of his own wit to formulate a new subject matter, which like the rhetorician's *res* may be encoded in a verbal system. But unlike the rhetorician's *res,* which is merely clothed in words while retaining its own anterior identity, the poet's matter is completely transformed into a "conceit," a new imagining, a verbal image where language and picture are inseparable. Contrary to the rhetorician, who searches among preexistent topics for a *res*, which he then expresses in *verba*, Sidney's poet presents a universe of universals that is freshly invented and wholly transmogrified into a verbal image. The poet "maketh matter for a conceit." In fact, the matter[104] of the poetic maker has no existence apart from the conceit, the verbal system in which it inheres. Conceit is matter; in Sidney's poetics, *verba* are *res*. For that reason, the reader "shall use the narration"—that is, the verbal system of poetic images—"as an imaginative ground-plot of a profitable invention" (103.15–16). So Sidney restores integrity and dynamism to a poem, and once again poetry becomes ποιη-τική in the Aristotelian sense of a processive making.

An example will clarify the point, and we may as well take Sidney's favorite. "Xenophon," Sidney says, "who did imitate so excellently as to give us *effigiem justi imperii*, the portraiture of a just empire, under the name of Cyrus, (as Cicero saith of him) made therein an absolute heroical poem" (81.27–31).[105] As a poet, Xenophon "imitated"—that is, he universalized the historical Cyrus and provided us with a poetical image of the wise ruler, a "feigned Cyrus," as Sidney says twice elsewhere (86.33, 88.17). After completing the depiction of this general type, Xenophon appropriately reapplied to it the name of its original, so it appears "under the name of Cyrus," thereby insuring that the abstraction is in touch with historical reality. Since this portrait of Cyrus is universal, however, it expatiates in the direction of larger concepts, and becomes not merely the image of a man but the image of his action, "the portraiture of a just empire"—where "empire" should be read with a verblike sense (the business of governing) rather than as a local noun (a kingdom).[106] So Xenophon's imitation presents Cyrus in the act of ruling his empire. Through further extrapolation, it may become the idea of ruling, the very idea of justice. By such a process, quite different from writing static allegory, Xenophon "made therein an absolute heroical poem"— where "absolute" modifies the phrase "heroical poem," not "heroical" alone. The *Cyropaedia* is an absolute heroical-poem. Xenophon's poem is "absolute" both in the sense that it circumspectly follows the principles of imitation without contamination from other modes of discourse, and also in the sense that it provides an image so comprehensive as to approach a philosophical absolute.[107] Xenophon's poem is absolute in both manner and matter. Now evidently, as readers, we do not see through this image of a just empire (as though it were a veil) to uncover some concealed truth. Rather, we look directly at it. The poem, in the best Aristotelian manner, imitates the actions of Cyrus, and by means of the verbal description we watch him act. We watch the conceit that Xenophon has devised of his own making through mimesis.

Furthermore, by comprehending the image in our imagination we extend the poet's process of imitation. As Sidney explains elsewhere about Xenophon's poem, "so far substantially it worketh, not only to make a Cyrus, which had been but a particular excellency as nature might have done, but to bestow a Cyrus upon the world to make many Cyruses" (79.12–15). The poem produces not a single, one-shot image, such as Nature does when she projects an anterior idea by embodying it in a particular entity, an end-stopped process. Rather, the poet through his imitation produces an image that in turn produces myriad other images, because in our comprehension of Cyrus's significance and in our acting upon that knowledge each of us as a reader continues the imitative process of making. Just as Xenophon employed his imagination to make an image of the just governor named Cyrus in the act of governing, so we exercise our imagination in the perception of that image and carry on the imitation. So the readers of a poem carry the imaginative process to completion if they are properly apprised of the poetic mechanism: Xenophon "bestow[s] a Cyrus upon the world to make many Cyruses, if they will learn aright why and how that maker made him."

Here, in fact, is the major point. By reading the *Cyropaedia* we not only obtain information about the historical Cyrus and receive a verbal portrait of an idealized ruler in the act of empire. More important, we learn about the poetic process that has produced the literary Cyrus—we "learn aright why and how that maker made him." Reading poetry teaches us to imitate by watching the true poets at their task of making. We comprehend the purpose of poetic imitation and how to achieve it. We accept the validity of fiction and, as Plutarch urged, implement the doctrine implicit in its example. In fact, expertise in the activity of ποιητική is poetry's most valuable lesson. We come to appreciate the value of mimesis as a lifestyle, and gaining facility in the interpretation of mimetic artifacts becomes, as Margaret E. Dana phrases it, "the most humane response to life's riddling text." [108] Learning the why and how of poetry is more valuable than interpreting its what.

As the final reward of reading poetry, we recognize that imitating is the quintessential human activity, that the process of making places us in proper relationship to our heavenly maker and defines our position in the scheme of things. The purpose of knowledge is "to lift up the mind from the dungeon of the body to the enjoying his own divine essence" (82.26–27). While the other disciplines—astronomy, philosophy, music, mathematics—can lead to knowledge of certain sorts, they are merely "serving sciences," because they are wrapped within the fold of their proposed subject. They can teach only a prescribed subject matter. Poetry, alone, leads to "the highest end of the mistress-knowledge, by the Greeks called ἀρχιτεκτονική"—and Sidney adds, weightily, "which stands (as I think) in the knowledge of a man's self" (82.28–83.1). By repeating the act of poetic making, we participate in the vast design of *natura naturans* and come to realize most clearly who we are and why. We emulate our heavenly maker and come to realize those ways in which we are like Him, as well as the degree to which we are His inferior.

Xenophon's *Cyropaedia,* of course, is not the only text in which we discover this paramount lesson. For poetry to have its intended effect we may similarly learn aright why and how other makers have made Aeneas, Ulysses, Achilles, and so forth. "Only let Aeneas be worn in the tablet of your memory," Sidney advises, after extolling the heroical poem, "and I think, in a mind not prejudiced with a prejudicating humour, he will be found in excellency fruitful" (98.16, 25–27). As the end of the imitative process, the speaking picture of Aeneas carried in our mind's eye moves us to excellence not only in those actions which Vergil describes, but in every phase of our lives. It is fruitful in producing excellence in all our endeavors (cf. 102.7–15).

Contrary to Plato in the *Ion,* but in agreement with Aristotle, poetry leads to mastery of all subject matters. What we learn is an abstraction from the experience of reading itself. As Sidney claims, "It is manifest that all government of action is to be gotten by knowledge, and knowledge best by gathering many knowledges, which is reading" (105.28–30). What we gain from reading, then, is not the knowledge of specific subject matters, but the knowledge of how to read. Because it leads to mastery of this enabling skill, poetry is the purest expression of that architectonic knowledge which presides over all arts and sciences, and which Sidney defines as "knowledge of a man's self." Through the mimetic act discovered in poetry, we not only see into the life of things, but assume our active role in the cosmic plan. By mastering the verbal universe as Adam named its creatures, we take our place in the providential scheme.

Eventually, with such insight and the resultant conditioning of the psyche, we achieve the final end of learning, "the end of well-doing and not of well-knowing only." As Sidney remarks elsewhere with Aristotle in mind, "That imitation whereof poetry is, hath the most conveniency to nature of all other" (92.24–25), where "nature" is primarily "human nature." In consequence, "that imitation whereof poetry is," of all sciences, is most efficacious in ameliorating our state of being. Such knowledge is attainable only by watching the poet at his making, and then implementing that example in those numerous events in our own affairs where virtuous action requires the gathering, sorting, arranging, and interpreting of data. Each of us plots our life as though it were a narrative fiction based upon the probability of universals. When we confront our own "stuff," we must learn to make matter for a conceit, not take our conceit ready-made from the matter of our circumstance. Only in that way is well-knowing cut loose from the shackles of time and place, and well-doing without constraint can follow. It is this reward that Sidney offers as poetry's overwhelming apology.

To turn from the reception of poetic images to their production, we should note again that the mind's eye is a necessary faculty also in poetic composition. The imagination is the human faculty that produces images as well as receives them. As everyone from Aristotle through Quintilian to Erasmus had emphasized, the poet must "see" clearly what he wishes to express. So what role does the imagination play while the poet is writing his poem?

Here the memory, as La Primaudaye defined it (page 266), becomes an important resource. Drawing upon the rich treasury of information stored in the memory, the mind's eye can decompose those images and rejoin selected elements to produce hybrids such as centaurs and gryphons. Aristotle had stated (or so it was often averred): Nihil in intellectu quod non fuerit prius in sensu (Nothing exists in the mind which did not first appear to the senses). But these newfangled creatures of the mind's eye did not violate this dictum. Even though they had never been seen in nature and were not expected to be found, these denizens of the poetic bestiary enjoyed a more than merely fanciful existence because they are comprised of data actually observed by the external senses in one place or another. At least detail by detail, they may be empirically verified. They are "stuff" from which the poet contrives this "matter."

For that reason, as Sidney says, the poet has license to "grow in effect into another nature" of his own devising (100.22–23). By exercise of the mind's eye, he produces his own fictive world, "making things either better than Nature bringeth forth, or quite anew, forms such as never were in nature, as the heroes, demigods, Cyclops, Chimeras, Furies, and such like."[109] His only stricture is that nothing may occur in these fictional constructions which has not first appeared to the senses; it is imperative that "he goeth hand in hand with nature."

Insufficient attention has been paid to Sidney's empiricism, to his insistence that all thought must begin by observation of this "too much loved earth" (78.33)—too much loved, since the earthly pull is seductive to our senses. Nonetheless, our mundane home is worthy of approving scrutiny, and repeatedly in the *Defence* Sidney enjoins the poet to look about and keep in touch with nature. His culminating complaint against the devotee of euphuism is that he "flieth from nature, and indeed abuseth art" by doing so (119.3–4). Very early Sidney establishes the importance of observing nature and makes every discipline dependent upon the data gathered from it. Immediately after the description of the poet as a "maker" and in the opening of the familiar passage that culminates in the neoplatonist exaltation of the poet's golden world, Sidney pointedly asserts: "There is no art delivered to mankind that hath not the works of nature for his principal object, without which they [the various arts] could not consist, and on which they so depend, as they become actors and players, as it were, of what nature will have set forth" (78.1–5).[110] In this cosmology, nature is the determinant of each art, which merely expresses her preexistent data. Nature provides a script, a verbal cosmos, which practitioners of the various arts merely enact. As examples of the practitioners who perform nature's data, Sidney cites those who profess the quadrivium (the astronomer, geometrician, arithmetician, and musician), both the natural and the moral philosopher, the lawyer, the historian, those who profess the trivium (the grammarian, rhetorician, and logician), the physician, and even the metaphysician, who "though it be in the second and abstract notions, and therefore be counted supernatural, yet doth he indeed build upon the depth of nature" (78.20–22). Only the poet is exempt from strict adherence to observed data—but even he, it may be assumed, like the metaphysician must build upon the depth of nature because even he, though lifted up with the vigour of his own invention, is nonetheless required to walk hand in hand with nature. The poet's fiction must maintain a manifest relationship with our actuality.[111]

But the mind's eye looks inward as well as outward, and in counterthrust to the empirical impulse there was some attraction toward mysticism. Closely connected with the concept of the mind's eye is another notion that similarly derives from the Aristotelian theory of visual perception. In the Aristotelian system (pages 262–63), sight is the most admirable of the five senses (a sentiment, incidentally, to which Plato also lends support [*Timaeus* 47A]); and the reason for this exaltation of vision above the other senses lay in the simple fact that in visual perception there is no physical contact between the object being viewed and the bodily sense that it activates. Each of the other senses requires physical stimulation, either from the object itself, from particles issuing from the object, or from vibrations in the air which commence with the object. But for sight, physicality is reduced to an apparent nil. What the act of seeing does require is nothing more than an intermediary agent, something between the object and the perceiving subject; and this medium, wondrously effective although itself inert and insubstantial, consists of light. Rays of light in some fashion variously described carry the image from the observed object to the retina of the observing eye without any sort of material transfer. This miraculous arrangement had been ordained in the original scheme of creation, and indicates the near-divine status of sight.

Furthermore—and here we find the relevance of this doctrine to our topic—just as natural light permits the bodily eye to see those objects necessary for its instruction, so the divine light, God himself, illuminates those mental objects most pertinent to our inner life. *Dominus illuminatio mea*, proclaims the motto of Oxford University. This "inner light," often equated with religious knowledge, was the consummation devoutly to be wished by a Christian such as La Primaudaye, and it frequently engaged the mind's eye in introspection and meditation of a mystical sort.[112] At the very least, it endowed the mind's eye with a more than merely natural virtue. In La Primaudaye's enthusiastic words:

> Angelles and the spirites of men, which are spirituall and invisible creatures, are illuminated by the meanes of understanding, with that spirituall and heavenly light whereof God hath made them partakers: as the bodies of living creatures, and chiefely of man are illuminated with the corporall light of the Sunne by meanes of the eyes. For as bodies have their bodily eyes, so spirites have their spirituall eyes. For that understanding wherewith God hath indued them, is unto them as the eyes are to the body. Wherefore by that they see God, who is their heavenly Sunne, and the fountaine of all divine and spirituall light, as bodily eyes beholde the materiall sunne.[113]

Just as the bodily eye is rendered operable by light from the sun, the mind's eye is illuminated by an inner light from God. This inner light allows us to read the text of virtue imprinted on our souls. As Sidney says, "The inward light each mind hath in itself is as good as a philosopher's book" (91.27–29).[114]

David the psalmist was blessed with such vision, Sidney tells us, and he reported his experience in "a heavenly poesy," where more than any other place "he showeth himself a passionate lover of that unspeakable and everlasting beauty to be seen by the eyes of the mind" (77.10–24). Sidney offers this biblical example as a paradigm for the poet and as instruction in the art of reading. "The holy David's Psalms are a divine poem," Sidney begins, and he observes that the word "Psalms" means songs and that David composed in verse, although in Sidney's time the rules for understanding the metrics of Hebrew had not yet been reconstructed. "Lastly and principally," however, Sidney takes note of David's "handling his prophecy, which is merely poetical"—that is, which is wholly mimetic in the Aristotelian sense of fictionalizing,[115] as Sidney goes on to explain:

> For what else is the awaking his musical instruments, the often and free changing of persons, his notable *prosopopoeias,* when he maketh you, as it were, see God coming in His majesty, his telling of the beasts' joyfulness and hills leaping, but a heavenly poesy, wherein almost he showeth himself a passionate lover of that unspeakable and everlasting beauty to be seen by the eyes of the mind, only cleared by faith?[116]

Since David, like Orpheus and other notable poet/musicians, sang to his own accompaniment, his metrical performance begins by "awaking his musical instruments." More germane, he proceeds in poetical fashion to create fictions: there is "the often and free changing of persons," as in a Platonic dialogue, when the speaker is now one person and then another;[117] and there are "notable *prosopopoeias,*" when speeches of important characters are reported as though they had been overheard.[118] All is vivid and life-like.

The result of this dramatic personification is activation of our mind's eye: "he maketh you, as it were, see God coming in His majesty." And when God appears, we see also the blissful response of earth as well as heaven, "the beasts' joyfulness and hills leaping." This vision, engendered by poetic images, is "a heavenly poesy," wherein David realizes his "prophecy," his message of eternal truth. He makes us know that goodness whereunto we are moved (81.13–14). He "almost" (that is, "most of all") reveals "that unspeakable and everlasting beauty"—that conflation of the Platonic immortal beauty and the Hebraic-Christian Jehovah which is the object of his love and source of his inspiration. Unlike Sidney's "right" poet, who is confined to sublunary experience, David as religious poet benefits from direct communication with divinity. He witnesses God in the majesty of His heaven. That *sanctum sanctorum* is ineffable as well as everlasting, otherwise unknowable except through the privileged view enjoyed by David and shared with the faithful. But with David's help we see it in our *oculi mentis* and thereby comprehend its meaning—if (and here Sidney's Protestant bias intrudes) those "eyes of the mind . . . [are] cleared by faith." Then poetry becomes "heart-ravishing knowledge" (76.25), a Christianized version of the *divino furore* that rapt the soul of the humanist. All those pious Protestants who translated David's psalms, including Sidney and his sister Mary, sought to reproduce such an effect.

This in the nutshell of an example is the Protestant poetics pro-posed by Sidney in *A defence of poesie*. The "right" poet of Sid-ney's third category cannot hope to obtain the immediate access to divine knowledge allowed to David; but by following David in his devotion to God and by pursuit of that architectonic secular knowledge which reveals the glory of God in His handiwork, the poet can create a poesy which, if not heavenly like David's, none-theless can teach in the good cause of virtuous action. Later Sid-ney will be so bold as to suggest that the fictions of poets both in means and ends are similar to the "instructing parables" of the New Testament, such as those of Dives, of Lazarus, and of the lost child, which "meseems I see before mine eyes" (87.11–21).

In short, through imitation the poet exercises his imagination to produce a verbal image that has the palpability and efficacious-ness of experience itself. The poet uses the tractable medium of language to reformulate the stuff stored in his memory and makes a fictive universe which replicates God's poem. In turn, the reader in *his* imagination perceives that verbal image, inspects that fic-tional world. Through exercise of the mind's eye, the reader trans-forms verbal description into quasi-visible object, translating the poet's conceptual meaning into actual fact. The verbal images from poetry enjoy equal status with the sensible images from physical nature. Fiction takes precedence over actuality, however, because the mind's eye, perceiving the universal, sees with the myopia of an idealist. Furthermore, when cleared by faith, it sees farther and more perspicaciously than the external senses. When illuminated by the inner light of religious knowledge, it overlooks a rich and lively landscape—what the body's eye has never seen or ear heard.

We should now be prepared to comprehend the full implications of the passage that has provided the focus for this study:

> Poesie therefore, is an Art of *Imitation:* for so *Aristotle* termeth
> it in the word μίμησις, that is to say, a representing, counterfeit-
> ing, or figuring forth to speake Metaphorically. A speaking *Pic-
> ture,* with this end to teach and delight.[119]

When Sidney declares that poetry is an art of imitation, it is significant that he cites Aristotle as his authority and supplies the
Greek word μίμησις. Without question, Sidney wishes to place the
discussion in an Aristotelian context, making imitation the distinctive feature of the poetic art. To clarify his intention, since the
concept of *mimesis* would be strange to his English readers, Sidney emphasizes the term by glossing it with a series of three ger-
unds, and these three glosses when examined in turn reveal a
subtle but radical shift in meaning. The first gloss explains imitation as a "representing," a term that suggests the closest possible
relationship between the artifact and the imitated object.[120] The
artifact re-presents the object of imitation, offers a reasonable facsimile of it without prevarication. The second gloss explains imitation as a "counterfeiting," which may suggest, along with its synonym "feigning," some duplicity (pages 256–57). To use a Platonic
dialysis, a counterfeit is the same, and yet an other. It may enjoy
a valid relationship to the object of imitation, assimilating to it;
but then again it may not, separating from it. At least, an element
of doubt is introduced. Finally, the third gloss explains imitation
as a "figuring forth to speake Metaphorically." This last possibility,
which is the first to specify language as the medium of imitation,
opens to the poet the ample resources of the *ars dicendi* and
stretches the relationship between artifact and object of imitation
to its farthest extension.

"Figuring forth to speake Metaphorically" is a succinct and
careful formulation of Sidney's entire program for poetry. Each
word in this gerund phrase is pregnant with significance. Especially, we must recognize "metaphor" as a technical term with a
precise meaning and a long-standing, obligatory tradition which
would dictate its force here.[121] The locus classicus for μεταφορά
in literary theory, tellingly, is Aristotle's *Poetics* (1457b2), the
source also for the term μίμησις. So not surprisingly in this passage Sidney moves from one term to the other since, as Aristotle
proposes, metaphor is a prominent means by which the poet may
achieve the requisite mimesis.

Aristotle returns to this topic in the *Rhetoric,* confirms his definition of metaphor, and offers yet more examples (1404b1ff.). He also assigns to metaphor a function which may be implied in the *Poetics* but is not fully explained—that is, the ability to produce quasi-visual images by virtue of a quality that he calls ἐνέργεια, and that is variously translated as "forcibleness," "actuality," or "efficacy." As Aristotle says, metaphor has the ability "to create the matter before ones very eyes" (1405b12), and he links metaphor closely with the εἰκών or *icon* (1406b20). Because of its ἐνέργεια, the metaphor, like the *icon,* is successful in its "figuring forth," as Sidney claims.

From Aristotle, the concept of metaphor as an image-producing trope passed into the mainstream of the rhetorical discipline and became a staple of literary doctrine. Cicero repeats Aristotle's theory of such metaphors (*De oratore* 3.149–70) and postulates the mental faculty of a mind's eye to process them (3.160–63). Quintilian continues the tradition for promoting energeiac metaphor (8.6.1ff.) and broadens the term by confusing ἐνέργεια and ἐνάργεια, the notion of palpability. From Quintilian, Erasmus picks up the concept of ἐνάργεια, legitimizes its use for the creation of fictions in poetry, and makes it available to the Renaissance poet as well as the orator (pages 96–98). Sidney is thinking of mimesis in this tradition when he defines it in terms of "figuring forth *to speake* Metaphorically." Evidently, he regards poetry as one of the arts of discourse, using the technique of enargeiac metaphor and aiming at persuasion. By an established manipulation of language, the metaphor, a poet may figure forth his conceit in a fiction that successfully imitates the actions of men as Aristotle had decreed.

Aristotle defines μεταφορά quite precisely: "Metaphor is the transference of a name from the object to which it has a natural application" (*Poetics* 1457b6–7). As its etymology indicates, the Aristotelian metaphor in its origin was rather narrowly proscribed as a figure of speech that allows the transfer of a word specifying an attribute or quality from one thing to another.[122] As the metaphor flourished in the rhetorical tradition, it came to have two recognized purposes: to prove and to embellish.[123] Metaphor was useful as a component of argument and as an ornament of style. To assign an originating function, however, both Aristotle and Cicero cited metaphor as a means of explaining what is otherwise obscure. Its primary purpose is to compensate for the deficiencies of our denotative vocabulary by allowing the use of suggestive comparisons to extend the bounds of our knowledge by explaining an unknown in terms of something that is known.[124] The metaphor generates language.

When we recall Aristotle's notion of the *plenum*—that the universe is a vast system of contiguous levels arranged in a hierarchy—we can readily understand how the metaphor by its validation of comparison allows for the transfer of information from one level of being to another. Long ago Tillyard demonstrated how this belief in a network of correspondences underlay the Elizabethan worldview.[125] For example, just as a lion is primate of the animal realm and an eagle is primate among the birds, so on the level of men a king is the primate and may be described in terms of his correspondents: he is ferocious in battle and sharp-eyed in the surveillance of his kingdom. Metaphor allows for this transfer of information between the lower and higher orders of nature.

When we think in terms not of the Aristotelian *plenum,* however, but of the Platonic dichotomy between the ever-changing world of becoming and the immutable world of being, we can discern an even more expansive use of metaphor. It allows for a transfer of information between these two mutually exclusive areas of human experience. By means of metaphor a poet can use the properties of a physical object to describe the essence of an otherwise unknowable idea in the world of being—for example, the leaves and blossoms and bole of a chestnut tree give some notion of the leafiness, floweriness, and trunkness of the ideal tree that exists only as a concept in some platonist heaven. A transfer of information is effected from the physical level of mutable things to the immutable empyrean. Conversely, by means of metaphor a poet can use the inviolable authority of a Platonic idea to describe a physical object, thereby endowing it with meaning and assigning it an identity—for example, by calling that thing with leaves, blossoms, and trunk "a tree," the poet locates it in that vast network of correspondences that comprise our universe. Through language a transfer of information is effected from the conceptual level of ideas to the palpable level of human percepts.

This second direction for the metaphor, from world of being to world of becoming, proved of special importance to the poet. It made possible the neoplatonist aesthetic of divine inspiration, bestowing upon the poet a status approaching the deity and giving him a distinctive function in society. He acquired power over a verbal universe. Metaphor in this sense underlay the logocentric imperative.

The irrefutable analogue to the metaphor which encapsulates an idea in a physical object was the creation of our universe by God. Our world is God's poem, said Augustine, and Landino after him. By the metaphoric process of transferring His idea into actuality, God produced our multiplex environment, setting into motion the vast design of providence as it works out God's intention through the ages. The poet creates the universe of his fiction by an analogous metaphoric process, embodying his ideas in the actions of characters, and in this sense the poet is a maker in image of the heavenly maker. The poet figures forth to speak metaphorically, transferring information, whether privileged or self-derived, from the conceptual level of ideas to the physical level where his audience may perceive it with their sense faculties.

When metaphor is given the full play of the Platonic possibility, we can discern how greatly Sidney expands his license for poetry as he shifts in this definition of mimesis from "representing" to "counterfeiting" and finally to "figuring forth." The third gerundive gloss for mimesis endorses an activity that transfers an immaterial essence across the line of demarcation from conceptuality to physicality, so that a concrete image with intellective content results. Here the relationship between artifact and object of imitation is stretched to its uttermost. The imitated object is transformed from concept to palpable percept, and the dissimilarity between their modes of existence is at the greatest. This interpretation of "figuring forth" is reiterated and clarified by the infinitive phrase that follows: the "figuring forth" of the idea is accomplished in order "to speake Metaphorically."[126]

That is the definition of metaphor in a platonist aesthetic. However, even if we designate the object of imitation to be a universal in the Aristotelian sense of the term rather than a Platonic idea, it is still a mental construct, a bodiless entity rendered concrete by the figuring forth. Through metaphor, the poet "makes," almost "creates," an image.[127]

So in this series of glosses for μίμησις, Sidney progresses, stealthily but steadily, from a poetics of re-presenting what the poet has observed in nature to a poetics of metaphorically figuring forth ideas that exist only in his mind. Although the poet must begin with his own "stuff," he puts it through a process of generalization and "represents" it as Aristotelian universals. He "counterfeits" an image in which to "figure forth" his ideas. Sidney's poet makes by metaphorizing, and finally arrives at a poetics that must be referred to the *Ion, Phaedrus,* and *Timaeus* because it interrelates the phenomenal and ideal worlds of Plato's cosmology.[128] Sidney expands the basis of his poetics from empiricism to idealism. But this is not surprising, given his intention to provide the broadest possible defence for poetry.

The Plutarchan topos that continues the passage in hand, "a speaking picture," confirms the pertinence of this Platonic cosmology because an oxymoron can operate only in a system where a realm of ideas is correspondent to the world of things. In an oxymoron, the two items in tandem are patently dissimilar at the level of physical existence—as sensible percept, for example, what is spoken is manifestly different from what is seen. But at some ideational level there are congruences between the two items that allow the paradox to obtain—the conceptual meaning of both what is spoken and what is seen may be the same. In the world of sense, seeing and hearing are separate activities; in the realm of thought, they work to the same end.[129] An oxymoron survives its self-contradiction by virtue of this amphibious operation that interrelates the two levels of existence. It is this encompassing of the conceptual and the physical that distinguishes poetry as that architectonic knowledge which allows it to teach as well as delight, just as Horace had counseled.

Repeatedly in the *Defence* the efficacy of the rhetorician's *enargeia* is reinforced by the power of poetry to uplift the mind toward involvement with Platonic values. The lyric poet is engaged "in singing the praises of the immortal beauty . . . [and] the immortal goodness" (116.30–31). Just as the poet by the process of metaphor brings those values within our experiential range, so by a reverse process and as a result we are transported to witness goodness and truth and beauty in their original forms. We make the quantum leap from physicality to conceptuality, as the *Phaedrus* prescribes. As Sidney says, with the readers of poetry in mind, "To make them know that goodness whereunto they are moved . . . [is] the noblest scope to which ever any learning was directed" (81.13–16).

By noting this determined drift from an Aristotelian base toward Platonic coordinates, we can place within a more distinct framework the other most famous passage in the *Defence,* the passage that lies behind the subtitle of this study. As the greatest praise of the poet, Sidney derives his name from ποιεῖν and designates him a "maker." Sidney could have found this etymology in Landino (page 180), as well as in any number of other critics, including Scaliger (page 202). But generally speaking, it invoked a platonist context with reference to the *Timaeus,* where the creating demiurge is described by the epithet, "the poet and father of this universe" (page 130).

To elevate further the title of poet, Sidney compares him to other artificers in order to demonstrate that the poet alone has the unique ability of going beyond the physical data of the natural world. Those who practice the disciplines of the quadrivium—the astronomer, geometrician, arithmetician, and musician (78.5–9)—are at basis natural philosophers, as are also those who practice the disciplines of the trivium—the grammarian, rhetorician, and logician (78.13–18). Also, those arts other than the so-called liberal arts are in a proto-empiricist way based upon the works of nature. All "are compassed within the circle of a question according to the proposed matter" (78.17–18). The poet, however, through exercise of internal as well as external senses, can escape the confines of the natural world:

> Only the poet, disdaining to be tied to any such subjection, lifted up with the vigour of his own invention, doth grow in effect another nature, in making things either better than nature bringeth forth, or, quite anew, forms such as never were in nature, as the Heroes, Demigods, Cyclops, Chimeras, Furies, and such like: so as he goeth hand in hand with nature, not enclosed within the narrow warrant of her gifts, but freely ranging only within the zodiac of his own wit. Nature never set forth the earth in so rich tapestry as divers poets have done; neither with so pleasant riv-

ers, fruitful trees, sweet-smelling flowers, nor whatsoever else may make the too much loved earth more lovely. Her world is brazen, the poets only deliver a golden. (78.22–34)

Through use of his mental faculties—in terms of rhetoric, by "the vigour of his own invention"[130]—the poet enhances the data observed by his external senses, universalizes it, and produces poetic images which because of their universality have greater validity than the individual items of physical nature. He creates "another nature," a meta-reality, a world closer to God's design than the corporeal universe because it transcends the partiality and accidents of particular instance. The poet's creation is "better" than nature's. Or, by exercise of his imagination in conjunction with his memory, the poet may create "quite anew"—as Sidney explains and exemplifies, "forms such as never were in nature, as the Heroes, Demigods, Cyclops, Chimeras, Furies, and such like." The Heroes and Demigods are simply idealizations of humans like ourselves elevated to superhuman status, while the Cyclops, Chimeras, Furies and their sort of hybrids are reconstituted by the mind's eye from natural data stored in the memory. The poet, in fact, has an unbridled range in the search for material so long as he is not φανταστικός, "so as he goeth hand in hand with nature."

The poet refines nature, but does not separate from it by going beyond what the rational faculties can assimilate. He creates a golden world, but one that is a transformation of the brazen world rather than an arbitrary substitution for it. The poet's world incorporates that of nature while improving upon it. Active here is the topos of the four ages of the world—iron, brass, silver, and gold—with the poet's world corresponding to the last and noblest. But also operative is the alchemical context: the completed opus has sublimated the mutable (and therefore base) materials of physicality to arrive at a pure distillation of the timeless (and therefore golden).

Latent here is a comparison of poetry with painting—or, at least, with the depictive art of tapestry-making.[131] Nature as tapiser sets forth God's design in pleasing colors; but the poet in his imagining offers an even richer picture with the idyllic perfection of a pastoral setting (e.g., Sidney's *Arcadia*). Like the painterly rhetorician, the poet uses colors to ravish the souls of his audience.

Nature cannot match the seductive brilliance of his landscapes (78.32–34).

Furthermore, just as Nature brings into existence all those things that comprise our universe, so the poet must fill a canvas with God's plenty. By the mimesis of metaphorizing, he sets forth all the ideas derived from ranging within the zodiac of his wit, just as Nature lies under the charge to set forth God's intent in all its detail and completeness. The poem is a literary microcosm imaging the infinite variety of the macrocosm, though with heightened clarity because the dross of what is accidental or transient has been removed. As in the *Divina commedia,* that summation of human experience in its widest range, the poet has "all, from Dante's heaven to his hell, under the authority of his pen" (89.32–33).[132] He is the omnipotent ruler of a fictive universe in small.

After legitimizing the poet's golden world, validating his setting, Sidney provides the same service for his characters. "But let those things alone," he says, "and go to man." Again, the universals of the poet exceed in beauty and truth the particularities of nature. Nature has not "brought forth so true a lover as Theagenes, so constant a friend as Pylades, so valiant a man as Orlando, so right a prince as Xenophon's Cyrus, so excellent a man every way as Virgil's Aeneas." Sidney makes clear that he is not merely playing semantic games: "Neither let this be jestingly conceived, because the works of the one [i.e., nature] be essential [<L. *esse,* having actual existence[133]], the other [i.e., the poet] in imitation or fiction." The actual people who populate a scene recorded by historians may be attentive lovers, constant friends, and valiant knights, like Theagenes, Pylades, and Orlando. But the lovers, friends, or knights presented by the poet, even though the product of his "imitation or fiction," enjoy a greater validity because of their universality. They inhabit the meta-reality of the poem. The poet's characters have a veracity equal to that of his golden world.

As a conclusion to this argument for the validation of the poet's creatures, Sidney states forcefully: "For any understanding knoweth the skill of each artificer standeth in that *idea* or fore-conceit of the work, and not in the work itself." In context, this statement is offered as a sort of *probatum est,* a postscript that enforces the validity of the poet's "imitation or fiction." But various critics have removed this statement from its context and have interpreted it in several ways.[134] The term *idea* suggests a Platonic interpretation, and some, including myself,[135] have read it as an affirmation of a platonist aesthetic where the ontological *situs* of the artifact resides in an idea which antedates the artifact and is rendered palpable by it, by "the work itself." This at basis the poetics of metaphor, and it holds in this instance. The idea is figured or bodied forth by the palpable components of the poem.

This interpretation, though, is perhaps too narrow, too unrelenting in its platonizing, especially if it denies autonomy to the verbal system of the poem. True, the idea is antecedent to the work, anterior to its expression in the work; and the skill of the artificer lies largely in devising that idea, that *disegno,* that design. But the fore-conceit is objectified and reified in the verbal system of the work, and the resultant artifact has its own, even if derivative, existence. When the entire passage from the *Defence* is taken into account, Sidney's argument, it seems to me, runs something like this. The works of nature are individual humans, the acquaintances of our everyday experience, each a unique composition of faults and virtues. The works of poets, in contrast, are characters in poems, a verbalized "imitation or fiction." Admittedly, then, the works of nature have genuine existence, while the works of the poet are merely fictional. But nature's creatures are rigidly defined in their uniqueness, isolated, admitting no comparison; while the fictional characters of the poet are the product of his ability to universalize, and therefore typify an entire class. In consequence, as Sidney has just argued, they have a greater veracity than the people who walk our streets. And the skill of the poetic artificer, as opposed to nature, lies in that ability to universalize, to generate that "*idea* or fore-conceit" which underlies the poem. The "*idea* or fore-conceit of the work" is no more than that universalized lover, friend, or knight produced by "imitation or fiction" but not yet verbalized into a readable poem. It is the "matter" derived from the poet's "stuff" in preparation for producing the extended "conceit."

Without denying the Platonic underpinnings, then—and the platonist bias of Cicero allows us to recognize their pertinence here—we would probably be more just to read this cryptic statement in a rhetorical context. The "*idea* or fore-conceit" is the rhetorician's *res,* the product of *inventio,* the first step in the rhetorical exercise; and the poet proceeds to *elocutio*, apparelling *res* in words, producing "the work itself." [136] The fact that the word *idea* is given "fore-conceit" as a synonym modifies the Platonic context. The formulation becomes a neutral term, perhaps best glossed by the word *invention*.[137] According to the *OED*, in Elizabethan usage *conceit* meant no more than "that which is conceived in the mind, a conception, notion, idea, thought." [138]

If we place "fore-conceit" in the context of rhetorical "invention," the opening of Gascoigne's "Certayne notes of instruction" bears upon Sidney's statement. "The first and most necessarie poynt that ever I founde meete to be considered in making of a delectable poeme is this," Gascoigne says, "to grounde it upon some fine invention" (1:47).[139] It is essential, Gascoigne continues, that "the Invention have in it also *aliquid salis*." And by way of further elucidation, Gascoigne explains: "By this *aliquid salis* I meane some good and fine devise, shewing the quicke capacitie of a writer." Sidney's fore-conceit, I submit, is that basic element which Gascoigne looks for in the invention of a poet, that recessive but necessary form that demonstrates the poet's talent. Therein standeth the skill of each artificer, more than in the resultant verbal system of the work itself.

This poetics of fore-conceit in an unsophisticated state is demonstrated by the poems of Wyatt—for example, "The lover compareth his state to a shippe in perilous storme tossed on the sea," a paraphrase from Petrarch. The title (supplied apparently by Richard Tottel in his Miscellany of 1557) announces the conceit in the form of a comparison: the lover is like a storm-tossed ship. This *similitudo* is then developed into an *icon;* the conceit is given palpable extension in the body of the fiction that follows: "My galley charged with forgetfulnesse / Through sharpe seas, in winter nightes doth passe, / Twene rocke, and rocke. . . ." Poetry of this sort, however, follows a primarily rhetorical model, so that the *verba* are the expression of the pre-conceived *res,* the fore-conceit announced in the title. In this rhetorical model, the verbal system of a poem exists only as a projection of its conceit.

But just as Sidney downplays the metrification of poetry, removing it from the purview of musicians and grammarians, so also he extricates it from the rhetoricians. He does not conceive of the poet's idea as a topos to be located in another author, or, more creatively, as a solely intellectual object, a product of the mind abstracted from actual experience. Nor is the poetic act of making the simple act of apparelling such an idea in the material garb of words. Neither does Sidney maintain the strict Platonic dichotomy between the worlds of being and becoming. Rather, he wishes to interrelate the two, to nullify the boundaries between them. And he finds in language the means of doing so.

A word is amphibious, once again, with both conceptual and physical components. The word is both signified and signifier, both timeless idea and timely act, both inactive potential and immediate presence, both eternal cause and temporal effect. Although Sidney often seems to be thinking in terms of the rhetorician's quasi-Platonic dichotomy between *res* and *verba,* he is using the rhetorician's terminology for lack of anything better, and in fact he has tacitly revised the meaning of those terms. Sidney in his most advanced thinking about poetry bridges any discontinuity between conceptual and physical. The verbal system has ontological validity—indeed, the *verba* of the poem provide the sole existence for the *res.* Only through language can the conceit be realized. The artifact is the sole means by which the artificer produces his desired effect, so it is this ability to figure forth which justifies the imitation. Sidney offers a verbal model for imitation that has the palpability of a speaking picture and insures a poetry which delights and teaches and moves.

This qualified rhetorical interpretation of Sidney's statement about "*idea* or fore-conceit" is supported by what comes next. Sidney argues for the presence of the *idea* in the poet's mind on the grounds that it becomes evident through the poem: "That the poet hath that *idea* is manifest, by delivering them forth in such excellency as he had imagined them" (79.8–10), where the precise antecedent of the pronoun "them" is the poetical characters that Sidney has been talking about, and more generally the poet's imitations. Like the rhetorician employing *enargeia,* the poet delivers forth his ideas by imagining them.[140] Xenophon's Cyrus, judiciously fictionalized, accomplishes what an accurately historical account of Cyrus could never do. By imitation, the poet introduces the values of the ideal world into the forum of human affairs. As the ultimate aim of poetical making, the poet teaches us the virtues of imitation itself; we learn aright why and how Xenophon made the feigned Cyrus. We become makers ourselves.

This is a large claim for poetry, perhaps encroaching upon the spiritual prerogatives of the Gospel; and to say that the poet in his creatures is a better workman than Nature verges upon the impious, since by common account Nature is the immediate agent of God. Therefore Sidney grows wary. In his nervousness, he becomes crabbed, almost enigmatic; and, as he warns, great care must be taken to follow his argument:

> Neither let it be deemed too saucy a comparison to balance the highest point of man's wit with the efficacy of nature; but rather give right honour to the heavenly Maker of that maker, who having made man to His own likeness, set him beyond and over all the works of that second nature: which in nothing he showeth so much as in poetry, when with the force of a divine breath he bringeth things forth far surpassing her doings—with no small arguments to the incredulous[141] of that first accursed fall of Adam, since our erected wit maketh us know what perfection is, and yet our infected will keepeth us from reaching unto it. (79.17–26)

In this passage Sidney retreats from his overenthusiastic exaltation of the poet in the humanists' vein. More in line with the restraint of his Protestantism, he begins to praise not the poet, but the deity from whom poetic powers flow. It is God who has bestowed the gifts of reason and speech upon mankind, in order to make humans in His likeness. Therefore any acclaim for poetic greatness must redound to the beneficence of God, the heavenly maker of the poetical maker, who set him "over all the works of that second nature."

The phrase "second nature" requires attention because two variant interpretations are possible. It may have either of two referents. It may mean the sense-perceptible world that Nature oversees as the agent of God—it is "second" in the sense of *altera natura*, the physical world that projects the cosmic design everpresent in the mind of the deity.[142] Or it may be the fictional world created by the poet through exercise of his imagination—as Sidney has previously said, by virtue of his gifts of reason and speech the poet "doth grow in effect another nature" (78.24). This "second nature," then, may be either that which Nature supervises or that which the poet frames. But since the poem as literary microcosm must be correspondent to the macrocosm, there is no need to draw a distinction between these two possibilities and choose one to the exclusion of the other. Both meanings are operative. Since God made man in His likeness, he is lord of creation; and since God granted man the gifts of reason and speech, he alone among creatures can produce poems that reflect the providential design implied in the physical world, that "second nature." [143]

By such an argument, Sidney without impiety allows the poet to be placed above Nature as the purveyor of truth and goodness, as an instrument of the divine will. Not only the religious poets, but also the "right" poets speak with divine approval, if not with divine inspiration. God is designated by the distinctive act of creating the universe—He is "the heavenly Maker"; so making becomes the primary activity by which humanity might realize its godlike capacity. The poetic faculty is what allows mankind to approach nearest the status of divinity and fulfill its potential as an image of God. The heavenly Maker has made the mortal maker in His own likeness, Sidney reminds us, "which in nothing he showeth so much as in poetry." Now the analogy between poet as creator and God as creator is made explicit, with the poet, who is capable of initiative, taking precedence over Nature: "With the force of a divine breath he bringeth things forth surpassing her doings." [144] It was, of course, with the force of a divine breath that God created the heavens and earth, literally inspiring Adam; and similarly the poet produces a fictive universe and populates it with characters. The "divine breath" employed in this activity suggests also the faculty of speech that God has bestowed upon mankind alone among His creatures, in order that we may express our reason, God's greatest gift. By speech—in a mimetic act that syncretizes the Aristotelian, the Platonic, the Ciceronian, and the biblical—the poet brings forth his creatures, framing a poem that enjoys a privileged status above the flawed world of Nature and near the divine idea, a clear image of eternal providence.

But again, Sidney draws back from the humanists' impulse to exalt the poet in a purely platonist vein. Man is a fallen creature. [145] He has betrayed those gifts by which God designated him to be an image of divinity. Sidney's Calvinism restrains his neoplatonism, so he turns to address those who put no stock in original sin. "With no small arguments to the incredulous of that first accursed fall of Adam," Sidney says in one of the most cryptic passages of the *Defence*—that is, the argument must be made with particular care to those who are skeptical about the import of Adam's fall, because they might deny that man is depraved by sin and assume that we have unhindered access to divine wisdom. Admittedly, as the optimists would argue, we are created in the image of God, so "our erected wit maketh us know what perfection is." But we must remember that, even so, "our infected will keepeth us from reaching unto it." We must be mindful of the negation of reason perpetrated by Adam, thereby curtailing even the poet's perfectability. By our "erected wit"—by exercise of those internal faculties ruled by reason—we may perhaps reconstruct what God intended our behavior to be in His original scheme; but yet our will, corrupted by our parents' sin, prevents us from fulfilling this potential.

Almost unwittingly Sidney has wandered from poetics and philosophy onto the contiguous grounds of religion. But at this time he doesn't choose to venture there. He has gone too far, and so he retreats. Rather abruptly, he redirects his inquiry. "But these arguments will by few be understood," he says suddenly by way of breaking off, "and by fewer granted." It is noteworthy that Sidney feels so much in the minority. Not surprisingly, only a few will understand his sophisticated poetical program and the reasoning behind it; but those who do, one should think, would approve. Perhaps Sidney is recalling the English humanists' disapproval of romance (page 551 [n.20]), as well as Protestant strictures against fiction of any sort. In any case, he seems less than hopeful about gaining adherents; of those few who understand, fewer still will grant the validity of his arguments. So he returns to the opening of this segment of his treatise, the derivation of the name "poet" from ποιεῖν, and he trusts that at least he has made his case that this etymology is an honorable one. "This much (I hope) will be given me," he concludes, "that the Greeks with some probability of reason gave him the name above all names of learning" (79.27–29).

Sidney then proceeds to the "more ordinary opening" of the poet, the disclosure of the poetic art that will be less complicated and more readily apparent—as Sidney says, "that the truth may be more palpable." The poet will now be revealed in greatest clarity. "And so I hope," Sidney continues, "though we get not so unmatched a praise as the etymology of his names will grant, yet his very description, which no man will deny, shall not justly be barred from a principal commendation." With this stage direction, Sidney turns from his neoplatonist praise of the poet as maker to an Aristotelian analysis of the poetic art as mimesis.

To summarize, Sidney drew from the classical tradition—he knew Plato's *Republic* and *Ion* and *Phaedrus* in one state or another, and he dutifully read Cicero, Horace, and Plutarch; furthermore, he was aware of the medieval tradition, especially as it had been formulated by Augustine and revised by Landino. But Sidney's most pointed contribution to literary studies, the accomplishment that places him in the forefront of sixteenth-century critics and gives to English letters the surge of intellectual energy that pushed it ahead in new directions, is his interpretation of Aristotelian mimesis. Italian critics, especially Scaliger and Castelvetro, had already made much of Aristotle—indeed, had made the *Poetics* the reference for any serious literary discussion. But it is Sidney who develops the theory of imitation to its fullest potential, giving it a practical application that makes it acceptable to most Protestants and turning it to immediate use. He sought nothing less than the amalgamation of all the previous systems into one compendious poetics that would make poetry the supreme achievement of the human intellect. Without losing anything from the past—without foregoing any of the richness in the Platonic tradition, or in the Roman tradition that stemmed from Cicero— indeed, by maximizing what each had to offer—Sidney arrived at a synthetic poetics, essentially but not exclusively Aristotelian.

Although Sidney developed his poetical program in order to pursue immediate goals, his poetics introduced a literary revolution every bit as startling and long-lasting as that which took place concurrently in the natural sciences. Like the scientists, Sidney sought to take into account the new stirrings toward empiricism. The sense faculties, coopting new roles in the acquisition of human knowledge, were assuming greater authority; so, modernist that he was, Sidney wished to provide an empirical base for poetry. It deals with things of this world as perceived by human beings, and its images are sense-perceptible.

An empiricist interpretation of mimesis leads, of course, toward verisimilar description in poetry. The image must be palpable, or at least must give the illusion of being so, and the efforts of the poet must tend toward verbal pictures that are more and more realistic, more and more accurate and detailed. This development parallels the increasing illusionism in the sister art of painting, prompted by the same commitment to realism. The result is the nature poetry of the seventeenth century culminating in Thomson's *Seasons*. And beyond that we can trace the influence of this sort of mimesis in the sensuous imagery of the Romantics, especially Keats. Even Wordsworth, though he may not have been aware of any direct debt, is Sidney's heir when he asserts: "Poetry is the image of man and nature."[146]

Insistence that the mimetic image be lifelike, a tenable interpretation of Aristotle's *Poetics*, influenced also the theater—perhaps, even, accounts for the rapid rise of the drama in the decade after Sidney. Certainly it conditioned Sidney's conception of drama and led him to demand that it be as natural as possible. For this reason he insists, beyond Aristotle, that the play observe not only the unity of action, but even more carefully the unities of place and of time (*Defence* 112.35–114.29). If the two hours' traffic of a stage fails this test of verisimilitude, it violates what is probable, and the image it projects fails the test of genuine imitation.

The acceptance of Aristotelian mimesis had far-reaching results for all literary genres and even prepared the way for the novel. Since poetry imitates the actions of humans, implying the essentiality of plot and characters, and since this imitation must be true to life, transpiring within coordinates of time and place—well, all the elements of the novel are present, though it may take a century or so to put them together and produce a recognizably new genre. But from the vantage point of Sidney's *Defence*, echoing and amplifying Aristotle as it does, and from the way-station of the *Arcadia*, we can discern not too far down the road Fielding's *Joseph Andrews*, that "comic-epic poem in prose." Most evidently, perhaps, in the opening chapter of Book 3 we can see Fielding's residual concern about the relationship between history and fiction in a plot and between the particular and the universal in characterization. It is here that Fielding asserts, "I describe not Men, but Manners; not an Individual, but a Species."[147]

Finally, we should note again that this new poetics of imagery produced by imitation aligns poetry with painting. Since the time of Alberti, a painting was expected to have as its subject what he called a *historia,* an incident probably drawn from literature which implied a larger action.[148] So there had long been an incipient rapprochement between painting and poetry. Now with Sidney a poem produces quasi-visual images for perception by the mind's eye. Poetry leaves its intellectual base and approaches painting. The two arts become mutually assimilative. For at least a millenium before Sidney, poetry had been allied most closely with music as a formal art distinguished by metrification, but henceforth poetry will be closer to painting.

This realignment among the arts was completed by the time of Dryden, who proved most attentive to Sidney's theory of poetry.[149] The general poetical concerns of Dryden and his debt to Sidney are perhaps most evident in his early preface to *Annus Mirabilis,* an occasional poem that records the wondrous events of 1666, the English victories in the Dutch war as well as the Great Fire. Inherent in such a project are the poet's conflicting allegiances to history and to poetry, to fact and to fiction, and not surprisingly Dryden begins his preface by wrestling with this problem. He seems uncomfortably aware of the prevailing preference for poetry over history, and goes to some lengths to explain and justify his defection from this precious tradition. "I am apt to agree," he confides, "with those who rank Lucan rather among historians in verse, than epic poets" (*Essays* 1:11). Nonetheless, he is writing a historical poem instead of an epic; and consequently, with decorum in mind, he makes gestures in the direction of realism. He chooses a dignified yet simple metrical scheme of quatrains rhyming *a b a b,* appropriate for his martial subject matter (though obviously he considers verse but an ornament and no true cause to poetry); and he similarly adopts a suitable vocabulary—so that a naval battle, for example, is described in terms a seaman would use.

Much more remindful of Sidney are Dryden's comments on "wit," a term that assumes increasing prominence into the eighteenth century.[150] For Dryden (at least in this place), "wit" is the generic term for all those mental faculties involved in the composition of poems, and the way it functions recalls the faculty psychology as Sidney had interpreted it:

> The composition of all poems is, or ought to be, of wit; and wit in
> the poet, or *Wit writing,* (if you will give me leave to use a school-
> distinction), is no other than the faculty of imagination in the
> writer, which, like a nimble spaniel, beats over and ranges
> through the field of memory, till it springs the quarry it hunted
> after; or, without metaphor, which searches over all the memory
> for the species or ideas of those things which it designs to repre-
> sent. (1:14)

We can refer this passage to Sidney's statement that the poet
ranges within the zodiac of his own wit. According to Dryden, wit
should be equated with "the faculty of imagination in the writer,"
which ransacks the memory for elements to reassemble into ideas
it wishes to represent. In the far distance we can see this definition
of wit leading to the concept of original genius enunciated at the
end of the eighteenth century; and eventually to the concept of
the Romantic ego and the subjective self. In Dryden, with Sidney
behind him, wit is given a license to range; and in this admiration
for wit lies the seed of Romanticism.

Where Dryden goes from the definition of "wit" discovers an
even more interesting principle. From the notion of wit as it applies generally to poetry, Dryden proceeds to define wit as it operates in the particular case of the epic or the occasional poem:

> But to proceed from wit, in the general notion of it, to the proper
> wit of an Heroic or Historical Poem, I judge it chiefly to consist
> in the delightful imagining of persons, actions, passions, or things.
> (1:14)

Dryden echoes Aristotle here, perhaps from a distance; but at
least in the back of his mind Dryden recalls Aristotle's dictum that
poetry should imitate the actions of men. So wit consists chiefly in
the "imagining" or imaging forth of an episode. After telling us
what "the proper wit of an Heroic or Historical Poem" is *not* ("'Tis
not the jerk or sting of an epigram, nor the seeming contradiction
of a poor antithesis . . . , nor the jingle of a more poor paronoma-
sia; neither is it so much the morality of a grave sentence"; 1:14–
15), Dryden makes a positive statement of what wit *is:*

It is some lively and apt description, dressed in such colours of speech, that it sets before your eyes the absent object, as perfectly, and more delightfully than nature. (1:15)

Now here, it seems to me, we have an unequivocal statement of belief in the mind's eye, and the poet's task is to compose word pictures to be perceived by that quasi-sense faculty. If poetry is an art of imitation, as most theorists by this time agreed, we have a definition of imitation as the re-presentation of data from physical nature which the imagination finds stored in the memory. And through the poet's wit, art surpasses nature.

But there is one major difference between the poetics of Dryden and that of Sidney. These two critics have opposing views about the teleology of poetry. Sidney with his commitment to civic humanism tempered by Calvinistic piety insisted upon the instructional purpose of poetry. He acknowledged the Horatian dictum to the extent that a poem might be "delightful teaching" (*Defence* 81.37–38), but there is no question that teaching and not delight is the essential function of poetry (cf. 99.10–12, 116.2–5). To be justified, "delightfulness" must be "virtue-breeding" (120.30–31). Dryden, in contrast, plays down the didactic function of poetry and emphasizes its potential for pleasure. Indeed, the delight engendered by a poem becomes an end in itself and assumes an unwonted importance. The poem's superiority to the physical data it describes—art's advantage over nature—lies in this delight that the poem provides. A burgeoning aesthetic sees the justification of art as pleasure. A moral or social aim is no longer demanded.

From this position we see emerging a notion of the poet as one who prettifies nature and arrives at an idealized beauty. It is an image of this idealized beauty that the poet conveys by art. The cultural scene is set for the arrival of aesthetics as an intellectual discipline. Beauty is no longer the celestial idea of the neoplatonists, but rather something to be perceived by the senses; and the search for beauty is a science in its own right. Notice, however, the contradictory imperatives that now compel poetic imagery: an image can be simply a re-presentation of something in nature, an accurate description; or it may be the expression of an idealized beauty extracted Zeuxis-like from nature, but which exists nowhere but in the poet's imagination. The fruitful ambiguity of the Sidneian image has been rent into the contrarieties of its potential.

But Sidney himself holds a pivotal position in the development of literary theory as the neoplatonist aesthetic shifted toward an aesthetic grounded in empiricism, as the criterion of harmony acceded to verisimilitude. Being an author of sonnets and a humanist, he looks back nostalgically to a poetics with heavenly beauty as its subject and the Muses as its sponsor. Being a modern man of practical affairs, though, he introduces a new poetics where mimetic images direct their sensuous appeal to the mind's eye. Sidney stands at that node in our cultural history when poetry changed from an art of metrification to an art of imagery. As Jonson was to conclude under Sidney's influence, "The conceits of the mind are Pictures of things, and the tongue is the Interpreter of those Pictures." Even the concrete poets are distant heirs of Sidney. Their verbal images are yet another generation of mutants whose roots lie in Sidney's use of language for imitation. After his *Defence,* poetry became before all else a speaking picture.

6
Spenser: Imitation as Harmonious Form

> Take your entire poem and divide it into smaller sections in imitation of nature, which subdivides into ever smaller parts, and in that way you can create a self-consistent whole.[1]

We have only one comment that Sidney made about Spenser. Late in *The defence of poesie* Sidney surveys the state of English letters, and in the dreary prospect he sees only four works deserving of note. He praises Chaucer, who "did excellently in his *Troilus and Criseyde*"; he admires the *Mirror for Magistrates,* which is "meetly furnished of beautiful parts"; and he finds "in the Earl of Surrey's lyrics many things tasting of a noble birth, and worthy of a noble mind" (112.16–23). The single contemporary work he can approve, however, is one that had just appeared on the literary scene: "The *Shepherds' Calendar* hath much poetry in his eclogues, indeed worthy the reading, if I be not deceived" (112.23–25). It is unclear whether Spenser's poem had actually been printed when Sidney was writing this comment (*The Shepheardes Calender* was probably published in December 1579); he may have seen the work in manuscript.

What is at issue, though, is not the state in which Sidney read *The Shepheardes Calender,* but rather what Sidney might have meant by his statement about it. At first glance, Sidney's comment seems so vague as to appear noncommittal and even enigmatic.

This sense of uncertainty is aggravated by the fact that Sidney does not mention Spenser by name. Perhaps Sidney did not know the name of the author, or perhaps he complied with some plan to keep the authorship secret.[2] In any case, he speaks of *The Shepheardes Calender* as an anonymous work, and this failure to identify the poet lends a curiously detached air to Sidney's observations.

Even so, I think that what Sidney says submits to a reasonably precise interpretation—at least, to a more precise interpretation than is usually ascribed to it. When he says that "the *Shepherds' Calendar* hath much poetry in his eclogues," he means that it exhibits ποιητική in the Aristotelian sense. Sidney had earlier cited Plato as the prototypical poet—"whosoever well considereth shall find that in the body of his work, though the inside and strength were philosophy, the skin, as it were, and beauty depended most of poetry" (75.11–14). And Sidney goes on to explain that Plato's "poetry" is his fictioneering, his use of dialogue in direct discourse and his descriptions of men in action.[3] Just as Sidney claims that Plato is "poetical" when he produces his feigned images, so is *The Shepheardes Calender* "poetry" when it is fiction.

What Sidney has in mind as "poetry" in Spenser's poem are the monologues and dialogues reported as direct speech, which in accord with his rhetorical training he would have dubbed prosopopoeias (*Defence* 77.19). As poetry Sidney would also include the incidental fables that serve cameolike as speaking pictures, such as Thenot's tale of the Oak and the Brier in "February," a tale which, as E. K. notes in the Argument, "the olde man telleth . . . so lively and so feelingly, as if the thing were set forth in some Picture before our eyes, more plainly could not appeare." And of course the overarching story line of Colin Clout with his mistress Rosalind and his confidant Hobbinol would count as poetry. All these fictions, to repeat Sidney's parting shot in his effort to make Plato a poet, "who knoweth not to be flowers of poetry did never walk into Apollo's garden" (75.20–21).[4]

So what Sidney chooses to praise in *The Shepheardes Calender* is the "poetry," the fiction—exactly that feature of a poem which he makes paramount in his poetics. He is as generous as possible; it has "much poetry" in it. But there's disappointment, it seems to me, that there isn't *more* poetry, and that so many other things distract from the poetry—such as, probably, the fuss over metrical patterns, and perhaps even the obtrusive calendar form. Sidney feels the need to express disapproval of some sort, and what he finally settles upon is the fairly trivial matter of the archaic diction, which he faults on the neoclassical grounds that Theocritus and Vergil and Sannazaro did not affect "an old rustic language." But I suspect that Sidney objected as well to the old poetics that Spenser adhered to. Those who detect a begrudging note in Sidney's endorsement of *The Shepheardes Calender* are right.

Sidney's reservations about *The Shepheardes Calender* linger, and his disapproval breaks out again in the summarizing comment about the four works he has praised. "Besides these," he says rather severely, "I do not remember to have seen but few (to speak boldly) printed that have poetical sinews in them." He goes on to complain, "Let but most of the verses be put in prose, and then ask the meaning, and it will be found that one verse did but beget another." What is operative here is Sidney's rejection of metrics as the chief distinction of poetry and his emphasis upon fiction. A story, though in verse, can be reduced to prose without losing its significance. Its story line provides "poetical sinews" which endow it with coherence, identity, and meaning, that self-consistency of the Aristotelian plot. But poetry that has verse as its essential feature cannot be so translated into prose. When a poet is primarily a maker of verses rather than a maker of fictions, his poem "becomes a confused mass of words, with a tingling sound of rhyme, barely accompanied with reason." Sidney cannot approve such jingling rhymers. And there's at least a suspicion that Sidney might place Spenser in this category. *The Shepheardes Calender* would not submit to being put into prose without a debilitating loss of meaning. There is *much* poetry in it, but it isn't *all* poetry. It isn't an "absolute poem" (*Defence* 103.23, 108.26).

Nonetheless, Spenser was hailed as the "new poet" by many of his contemporaries, led by E. K.,[5] and *The Shepheardes Calender* is without question a notable achievement. In all fairness, it should be measured against Spenser's expectations of what a poem should be, rather than Sidney's as yet untested propositions. In the October eclogue, Spenser enunciates a poetics, if we allow Cuddie and Piers to be his spokesmen; and when we strip that poetics of the autumnal gloom appropriate to October, we find a

familiar aesthetic at work. The program adopted by Spenser is a
revitalization of the Augustinian aesthetic transmitted through the
Florentine Platonists (pages 182–96). A poem should be an echo
of the celestial harmony, a reflection of the heavenly beauty, made
palpable in the poem's formal properties, in its metrics and more
capacious forms; and the poet should seek guidance from the
Muses in order to accomplish this sacred mission. Despite being a
"new poet" in England, Spenser is quite orthodox in his views on
the purpose of poetry and on how the poet goes about achieving
that aim.

In the closing envoy to *The Shepheardes Calender,* which is the
sort of extramural comment that demands special attention and
merits special credence, Spenser states his intention with unusual
forthrightness:

> Loe I have made a Calender for every yeare,
> That steele in strength, and time in durance shall outweare:
> And if I marked well the starres revolution,
>   It shall continewe till the worlds dissolution.
> To teach the ruder shepheard how to feede his sheepe,
> And from the falsers fraud his folded flocke to keepe.

Spenser has made his calendar for the purpose of teaching, and
his pupils consist of "ruder shepheard[s]"—in the pastoral convention, his younger peers. Like Sidney, Spenser assigns to poetry a
didactic purpose. He assumes the stance of a *vates,* the experienced pastor who instructs his juniors in the care of their flocks—
that is, in the ethical management of their affairs.

As his vehicle of instruction, Spenser has chosen a calendar, the
twelve months that comprise the year. There are twelve eclogues
proportionable to those twelve months, as the title page declares,
with an implication of mathematical niceness in that word "proportionable"; and each eclogue is fitted to its month by appropriate notices about the weather. "January," for example, takes
place "when Winters wastful spight was almost spent" (line 2); in
"March," "the joyous time now nigheth fast, / That shall alegge
this bitter blast, / And slake the winters sorrowe" (lines 4–6); in
"May," Palinode opens the dialogue by asking, "Is not thilke the

mery moneth of May, / When love lads masken in fresh aray?"
(lines 1–2); "June" occurs on a summer day when Hobbinol lures
Colin to a shady dell where "the simple ayre" is "calme" and
"coole" (lines 1–5); and so forth. As we read through the poem, we
are kept aware of the progress of the seasons. Tempus fugit. This
passage of time, more than anything else, provides poetical sinews
for the work. Moreover, a variety of subject matter is also presented, which emphasizes the movement, the change, the mutability. From Colin's amorous complaint we pass to the débat on age
and youth between Thenot and Cuddie, to the coarse sexual jokes
between Thomalin and Willye, to Colin's encomium of Elisa, to
the serious theological issues raised by Palinode and Piers, and to
a wide range of other subject matters.

This welter of human experience centers on Colin Clout, directly or indirectly. Each eclogue comments upon his success or
failure as lover-poet-priest, the traditional threefold occupation of
the shepherd. It is he who moves through this calendar, providing
a continuity, however tenuous, by his unfulfillable devotion to
Rosalind.[6] He himself sings of this sadness in "January," "June,"
and "December," and we have reminders of it in other eclogues.
Colin is the typical shepherd who passes through the calendar;
and when he reaches its end—that is, when he exhausts the possibilities for experience—he has completed his life, and perforce
must die. As Agelastus sings in his lament for Basilius in the old
Arcadia, "Time ever old and young is still revolved / Within itself,
and never taketh end; / But mankind is for ay to naught resolved"
(ed. Robertson 347.10–12). This diachronic movement of Colin's
experience is salient.

But the calendar of Colin's experience may be viewed also synchronically. A well-known visual motif laid out the twelve months
in a continuous circle, each distinguished by a particular human
activity appropriate to it, and the whole calendar was coordinated
with the twelve signs of the zodiac similarly arranged in a circle.[7]
The calendar is a system composed of discrete parts, each carefully different; but yet these parts are so interrelated that they fit
together to make a seamless whole.[8] Furthermore, because these
parts exhaust all possibilities within the system—nothing can occur within the system which is not accounted for by the characteristics of one or another part—the whole is greater than the mere

sum of the parts. The whole itself is an absolute, a wholeness, and not simply a congeries of individual items. It is a perfection, enjoying a higher level of existence than that inhabited by the parts. The whole is an infinitude, even though within boundaries—the metaphor for infinity within the confines of that closed system. In his quadriplex humours, the shepherd repeats the pattern of the elements which comprise the universe; and in his sequence of infancy, youth, maturity, and old age, he reflects the seasonal cycle that governs macrocosmic nature. By completing the diachronic pattern of the calendar, by interiorizing that infinitude, Colin achieves the state of synchronic wholeness, the stasis of perfection.

According to the Christian reckoning, the year begins with January, as E. K. goes to great lengths to explain in "the generall argument of the whole booke." But according to the classical reckoning, which is more appropriate to pastoral, the year begins when the sun crosses the equator going northward in March—that is, at the vernal equinox. In the physical terms of astronomy, the calendar is a zodiac—perhaps even the zodiac of Spenser's own wit, for those who wish to give the poem a personal and intrapsychic reading similar to the reading that treats the *Divina commedia* as a psychological process recording Dante's despair, recovery, and beatitude.[9] By such a reading, Dante's poem becomes a compendium of the psychic states mythologized in the pattern of the fortunate fall. Dante suffers through hell and purgatory in order to arrive at the permanent bliss of paradise.

Whereas Dante's poem perfects the pattern, however, and ultimately brings the poet into the presence of God, Spenser's poem seems to end in despair without ameliorating hope, much less salvation. While Colin suffers, Hobbinol by "June" has achieved felicity. He inhabits a "place, whose pleasaunt syte / From other shades hath weand my wandring mynde" (lines 1–2); and he lacks nothing "to work delyte" (line 3). But Hobbinol's gratification by contrast accentuates the deprivation of Colin. "O happy *Hobbinoll,*" he exclaims, "that Paradise has found, whych *Adam* lost" (lines 9–10). Colin is painfully aware that beatitude is possible, though he, the progeny of sinful Adam, remains apart from such happiness. At the end of "December," he hangs his pipe upon a tree, saying farewell in turn to Rosalind, his flock, the forest, and

Hobbinol. Winter has come, with frightening finality, "and after Winter commeth timely death." There seems to be no *purgatorio* and *paradiso* in store for Colin. He has reached the end of his allotted time. Being mortal, he must die.

But we the readers must not limit our perception to what Colin perceives; we must not confine our insight to what he understands. Spenser arranges a series of shifting relationships between the reader and Colin by changing his own relationship to the persona. At the opening of *The Shepheardes Calender*, a clear and significant distinction is made between the poet Spenser and his surrogate, Colin Clout. In "January," the opening eclogue, two stanzas which set the scene are narrated by an impersonal voice, presumably that of the poet, before Colin begins his amorous complaint in the first person; and the same omniscient narrator resumes at line 72 to close the eclogue with a stanza describing the traditional pastoral scene of the shepherd driving his sheep to their fold at sunset. Again, in "December," the final eclogue, there is an introductory scene-setting stanza in which a narrator speaks in the third person before we hear Colin's first-person complaint. At both the beginning and the close of *The Shepheardes Calender* we recognize an intermediary between us and Colin's world. A disembodied author, presumably Spenser himself, speaks from the shadows, making that world available to us, and yet distancing us from it.

In the intervening ten eclogues, however, this interloping narrator does not appear, and we have an unmediated, direct view of Colin and his companions. Furthermore, as the omniscient poet recedes from our awareness, we are invited to conflate Spenser with the pastoral character he has created. Within the eclogues, Colin becomes Spenser's alter ego, as E. K.'s editorial paraphernalia repeatedly urges upon us. For the first item in his gloss on "January," for example, E. K. notes the soubriquet "Colin Cloute" and comments: "under which name this Poete secretly shadoweth himself, as sometime did Virgil under the name of Tityrus." This conflation of *auctor* and *persona* is a common practice among poets, perhaps the mark of the best poets—witness Dante, as well as his Vergil.

So while the eclogues unfold, Colin and Spenser appear as one. Even at the conclusion of "December," unlike "January," there is no final stanza narrated by an omniscient poet that shatters the illusion of unmediated experience for the reader. No impersonal voice intervenes, providing closure, distancing us from Colin's doleful circumstance. At the end of the twelve eclogues, Spenser and his increasingly presumptive persona are left unseparated, and we too remain in Colin's world, empathetically involved in Colin's fate. With Colin/Spenser, we too experience the finitude of man's allotted time on earth.

But after these eclogues have perfected the twelve months, Spenser abruptly eloigns himself from Colin. In the envoy Spenser speaks in his own voice. *The Shepheardes Calender* does not 'really close with Colin's demise in the last lines of "December." Rather, at this seemingly terminal point Spenser drops his persona, steps outside the dramatic illusion of the fiction, and in an envoy addresses his audience directly. The eclogues have been poetry of one sort, but now we are asked to respond to a different level of discourse. Artificer speaks openly and forthrightly to percipient, a rare and daring tactic. We too are therefore forced to disengage from Colin and to deal with his experience as a distanced object. The diachronic movement of the poem will now be viewed as a completed whole.

Spenser resorts to abruptness because he wishes to emphasize the importance of the envoy. It is not mere afterthought, tacked on to satisfy convention. In Spenser's hands, the envoy becomes a further means of instruction—not about moral matters only, but about how to interpret his poem. When Spenser casts aside the illusion of his identification with Colin, he posits a relationship between himself as poet and the protagonist of his poem, and also prepares a place for us, the readers, in his complex system of poet, persona, content, and form. We are invited to relate in different ways to the several components that make up the entity known as *The Shepheardes Calender*.

In the opening lines of the envoy Spenser claims to have framed a perennial calendar, and, as we have seen, in this calendrical form lies a dimension for Colin larger than his diachronic experience. Since the system of twelve months comprising the year exhausts all possibilities, it is a prototype, a paradigm not only for Colin/Spenser, but for all mankind. We respond to Colin as an object representing the microcosm.

Furthermore, a calendar for every year must be cyclical. As E. K. comments pointedly in his Argument for the December eclogue, "This Æglogue (even as the first beganne) is ended with a complaynte of Colin to God Pan," so the mode and subject matter of "December" repeats that of "January"; and the metrical scheme of "December" is likewise identical with the stanza of "January." In addition—a fact that is difficult to pass off as mere coincidence—the number of lines in "December" is exactly double the number of lines in "January," representing the ratio 2/1, in musical terms suggesting a diapason. Just as an octave on the musical scale begins where its predecessor leaves off, repeats the mathematical form of its predecessor, and provides the starting point for the octave that follows, ad infinitum, so Spenser's calendar represents a finite and self-consistent segment of an infinite scale. By its very nature, the calendar returns to its beginning and renews itself; it goes on and on, over and over. The one-year calendar, then, may be seen as the integer of eternity, the unity which reproduced an infinite number of times transcends its own finiteness to become eternity.

Augustine states the proposition exactly: "The course of the seasons following one another, the waning and waxing of the moon, the sun returning to the same position year by year, spring, summer, autumn and winter each passing away only to come round again—all this is a kind of imitation of eternity."[10] Repeated cycles of time such as these reduce eternity to a patterned magnitude within our mortal ken.[11] They become an ideogram for time itself, making knowable the otherwise inscrutable relationship between the timely and the timeless. The *content* of the annual calendar is concrete, time-bound, diachronic; but its *form* is abstract, immutable, synchronic. The metaphor of the calendar explains the relationship between these two levels of existence.

By such reasoning, Spenser can generalize his twelve eclogues proportionable to the twelve months. Since nothing can occur without happening during one of the twelve months, he has coopted all the potential of time. He has produced a description of time in its widest reaches. His poem will outwear the strongest steel, as he says; indeed, it will outlast time itself. It will continue unto eternity, where time no longer has meaning. Even death at that stage shall die.

So actually, Colin's apprehension at the end of "December" is groundless. Viewed from his mortal perspective, Colin approaches death. But viewed from the enlarged perspective that Spenser provides in the envoy, Colin will die only to lose selfhood, thereby rejoining, unhindered, the course of kind. One short sleep past, he wakes eternally. Seen from his perspective, *sub specie mortalitatis*, Colin has completed his life; but seen *sub specie aeternatitis*, the point of view that Spenser provides in the envoy, the death of Colin is a necessary and desirable prelude to integration within the providential scheme.

With the envoy, consequently, the *shepherd's* calendar becomes an absolutely plural *shepherds'* calendar.[12] Particular becomes universal, individual becomes archetypal, and Colin/Spenser becomes an everyman who represents the human race in its relation to time, and thence to deity. It is here that Colin's despair at reaching the end of his calendar transmutes to joy at our realization that, though his finite time is at an end, eternity stretches before him. In that end is his beginning. His relentless progress toward death in "December" bespeaks his mortality, the result of that fall which brought death into the world. But since this calendar is for every year—not just for now, but for always—there is continuing existence in some other than mortal state.

Colin's verbal emblem at the conclusion of Dido's dirge in "November" makes a punningly paradoxical promise: "La mort ny mord"—devouring time, despite the suitable epithet *tempus edax*,[13] brings on a death that does not bite. As the narrative voice at the end of the "Cantos of Mutabilitie" explains:

> . . . all that moveth, doth in *Change* delight:
> But thence-forth all shall rest eternally
> With Him that is the God of Sabbaoth hight.
> (*Faerie Queene* 8.1.2.6–8)

The optimistic message is clear: the vicissitude of things leads inexorably to the sabbath. So the cyclical form of *The Shepheardes Calender*, although the poem itself does not contain a *purgatorio* and *paradiso*, points resolutely beyond winter/death to everlasting bliss. "If I marked well the starres revolution," Spenser claims somewhat grandly, "it shall continewe till the worlds dissolution." Spenser's poem, coterminous with the calendar, is, to borrow a phrase from Plato, "a movable image of Eternity" (*Timaeus* 37D).

So, Spenser thought, *The Shepheardes Calender* provides an emblem of human life in both its mortal and sacred aspects. This fulfills the exalted mission that humanists assigned to poets. There's but one proviso: "If I marked well the starres revolution." His poem is valid, Spenser says, if he read aright the signs in the heavens, and he's concerned to reassure his readers that he has.

Spenser is here acknowledging an old topos that can be traced ultimately to Plato's *Timaeus* (47A–D), but which received its most fulsome expression by Augustine. Jean de Serres in his edition of Plato, which Sidney certainly knew and which Spenser is likely to have seen, quotes the relevant passage:

> It is far from vain or useless to observe the beauty of the heavens, the order of the stars, the brightness of celestial light, the alteration of days and nights, the monthly courses of the moon, the fourfold division of the year, the consonance of the four elements, the great force of seeds, the variety and number of creatures, and all things preserving in their kind the measure and rhythm of nature. In such contemplation, curiosity is not emptily or dangerously employed, but rather it is the pathway to the immortal and to what abides forever.[14]

Augustine gives a long heading to the chapter where this passage appears: "About another aid to well-being—that is, reason; how man is drawn to God by this guide; and reason is seen to operate first in our sense faculties." So the orderly movements of nature are like the *verbum Dei,* displayed to view for our edification. We should read the *liber de natura* with the eyes of reason, which "is seen to operate first in our sense faculties." By exercising our reason in the observation of nature, we shall be "drawn to God by this guide," and shall ascend "the pathway to the immortal and to what abides forever."[15]

In the *Phaedrus* Plato complains that "the region above the heaven was never worthily sung by any poet, nor will it ever be" (247C); and yet this is the only worthwhile subject matter for poetry, because the "truly existing essence, with which all true knowledge is concerned, holds this region and is visible only to the mind, the pilot of the soul." Despite Plato's dim view of what poets might achieve, or perhaps because of it, many of them sought to write a heavenly poetry. Poets who compose in this spirit are the special minions of Urania, muse of astronomy, and legions claimed her patronage.[16]

Spenser was well acquainted with the lore surrounding the nine wards of Apollo, and in "The Teares of the Muses" he presents Urania as the sister who "professe[s] the skill / To make men heavenly wise, through humbled will" (lines 521–22). Urania explains the purpose and the course of her discipline in considerable detail:

> Through knowledge we behold the worlds creation,
> How in his cradle first he fostred was;
> And judge of Natures cunning operation,
> How things she formed of a formelesse mas:
> By knowledge wee do learne our selves to knowe,
> And what to man, and what to God wee owe.
>
> From hence wee mount aloft unto the skie,
> And looke into the Christall firmament,
> There we behold the heavens great *Hierarchie,*
> The starres pure light, the Spheres swift movement,
> The Spirites and Intelligences fayre,
> And Angels waighting on th'Almighties chayre.
>
> And there, with humble minde and high insight,
> Th'eternall Makers majestie wee viewe,
> His love, his truth, his glorie, and his might,
> And mercie more than mortall men can vew.
> O soveraigne Lord, O soveraigne happinesse
> To see thee, and thy mercie measurelesse.
>
> (lines 499–516)

Here is the rationale behind the vogue for astronomical poetry, which shaded off into philosophical and theological ("divine") poetry. Urania encouragingly concludes: "Such happines have they, that doo embrace / The precepts of my heavenlie discipline" (lines 517–18). With an intent of that sort, Spenser "marked well the starres revolution," where the stars are, at least in part, the constellations that provide signs for the zodiac.

The old and oft-reprinted kitchen almanack, *The kalender of sheepehardes*—from which, as E. K. tells us, Spenser lifted the title for his poem—took its cue from this discipline, and the title page of those editions current in Spenser's time display a large woodcut showing a shepherd observing the stars in their wheeling courses. And Palingenius wrote the *Zodiacus vitae* to exemplify these Uranian principles. When Barnabe Googe translated this popular didactic poem, he entitled it *The zodiake of life;* and the title page continues: "Wherein are conteined twelve severall labours, painting out most lively, the whole compasse of the world, the reformation of manners, the miseries of mankinde, the pathway to vertue and vice, the eternitie of the Soule, the course of the Heavens, the mysteries of nature, and divers other circumstances of great learning, and no lesse judgement." [17] *The Shepheardes Calender* is similarly a reworking of this familiar motif, albeit a much more refined and elegant version of it. [18] As Augustine advises, "It is far from vain or useless to observe the beauty of the heavens, [and] the order of the stars," because such observation provides the encyclopedic knowledge prerequisite to that introspective quest for the divine in each of us.

This Augustinian advice explains the presence of the calendar in Spenser's poem. The significance of its cosmic form is pointed out in the final envoy, after we have completed the twelve eclogues proportionable to the twelve months and at the moment when we should stand back and regard the work as a whole—that is, after we have sequentially assimilated the *content* of the poem, and are ready to translate that metaphor into its *form*.

What we see in retrospect, of course, is an entity composed of discrete but interrelated parts, a clear expression of the Augustinian esthetic of multeity in unity (pages 190–92). There are internal pairings and oppositions, summations and divisions, a highly articulated system. The eclogues follow one another in orderly succession, as the months do in the course of a year; but also each is individualized, distinct unto itself, a defined unit. And each relates as an aliquot part not only to its neighbors before and after, but perhaps even more immediately to the bounded infinitude which is the whole greater than the sum of the parts. The year as the annual unit of time, the integer of eternity, is greater than twelve months or four seasons. The poem thereby realizes Augus-

tine's aesthetic of *concordia discors,* of the reconciliation of opposites, and of typology. Through its form it overcomes the limitations of space and time, and achieves that overarching knowledge
that Sidney called, with Aristotle, ἀρχιτεκτονική, "the knowledge
of a man's self." [19]

From this example, it is easy to extrapolate a poetics for Spenser. The poet with the eyes of reason reads the book of nature;
and using that universal harmony as the object of imitation, he
produces an artifact that displays its fecundity and at the same
time demonstrates its coherence. As Scaliger in the epigraph to
this chapter advised the poet, "Take your entire poem and divide
it into smaller sections in imitation of nature, which subdivides
into ever smaller parts, and in that way you can create a self-
consistent whole." In the instance of *The Shepheardes Calender,*
the stately progress of twelve months bodies forth the infinite variety of the macrocosm. Each month in turn divulges its appropriate content. But meaning is generated not only by the subject
matter of the eclogues—not only by the monologues, dialogues,
fables, tales, encomia, dirges, etc. In addition, the exhaustive variety is meaningful in itself; the all-inclusiveness is itself a metaphor for God's plenty, His infinitude. [20] The diachronic movement
results in a synchronic stasis—indeed, the diachronic has been a
metaphor for the synchronic, a figuring forth in concrete detail of
the inclusive idea. It is content revealing the semantically significant form. In the final analysis, in fact, the subtext of the calendrical form is the poem's major means of signifying.

Conversely, in this poetics the form of a poem is an inclusive
absolute to which each detail must be referred for its interpretation. Each aliquot part exists within the total system and gains its
definition from the function it performs within that system—not
just in the orderly sequence of items as the form is generated diachronically through the passage of time, but in the more fundamental relationship of part to whole synchronically. In *The Shepheardes Calender* there are twelve eclogues *proportionable* to the
twelve months. So at its most mechanical, this poetics encourages
the reconstruction of a quasi-mathematical cosmos: the twelve
months or four seasons of the calendar, the six days plus the sabbath of the heptaemeron (such as Du Bartas's *Sepmaine*), the
duality of the daily alternation between daylight and darkness

(such as Milton's "L'Allegro" and "Il Penseroso"). Each part inheres in the whole as a *ratio* (see page 542 [n. 92]).

In this instance, the calendar provides the idealized pattern, an optimistic framework of twelve parts within which Colin lives out his despair. The perfection of the calendar, of course, is what Colin longs for, but cannot obtain. It is that infinitude and eternity denied to mankind in the mortal state. Just as paradise stands behind Beatrice, so the calendar's idea stands behind Rosalind, and it both measures how far Colin falls short of achieving that ideal and endows his suffering with poignancy. As Hobbinol comments, he "loves the thing, he cannot purchase" ("April" 159). The calendar taken in full represents that perfection which our erected wit maketh us know, and yet our infected will keepeth us from reaching unto.

This inadequacy, needless to say, is the source of Colin's despondency even at the beginning of the poem. Even in "January" he languishes for the impossible ideal of cosmic completeness, embodied in Rosalind: "May seeme he lovd, or els some care he tooke" (line 9). In his verbal emblem at the end of "January"— the religious motif of *Anchora speme*—Colin finds some hope, as E. K. notes in his gloss.[21] Spenser's model here is clearly Dante's love for Beatrice, the avowed genetrix of the *Divina commedia*.[22] As a love poem, *The Shepheardes Calender* is unmistakably in the neoplatonist tradition of praise for a lady, *la mia donna*, unattainable in this world though still longed for and looked forward to in the hereafter. Spenser's later poetry will continue to pay homage to *madonna* in a series of transformations culminating in the most ambitious of all, the Fairy Queen.[23]

Within the cosmos of *The Shepheardes Calender*, however, Colin's immortal longings are concentrated in Rosalind, and his faint hope gives way to abject hopelessness in "June." Halfway through the calendar, Rosalind actively rejects his suit in favor of another, and Colin's emblem changes to *Gia speme spenta*. As E. K. carefully explains in his gloss: "In the fyrst Æglogue, Colins Poesie was Anchora speme: for that as then there was hope of favour to be found in tyme. But nowe being cleane forlorne and rejected of her, as whose hope, that was, is cleane extinguished and turned into despeyre, he renounceth all comfort and hope of goodnesse to come." At this midpoint in his progress between the Christian joy in a new year and the promise of an afterlife through Christ's birth in December, Colin falters at the bottom of a Dantesque descent, farthest from love, and therefore hope. It has been Colin's inadequacy as disciple of Tityrus that has allowed Menalcas to distract Rosalind. It has been his failure as poet—and, metonymically, his failure as lover and priest, the other two roles of the shepherd—that Colin blames for losing what he most desired ("June" 81–112).

In "August," however, Cuddie rehearses an elegant sestina composed by Colin, and this literary tour de force is much praised. Moreover, although "October" is devoted to the decayed state of poetry at the present time, in "November" Colin sings a hopeful elegy in commemoration of Dido, a reprise of the blazon in praise of Elisa in "April." Both these ladies are disguises of *la mia donna*, just as both these songs are striking evidence of Colin's poetic ability. His facility at making has returned. And it will be this poetic talent, this ability to sing like David in praise of sacred values, that ultimately permits Colin to transcend the limits of human life and achieve some sort of immortality by joining the never-dying company of poets. "December," a graceful monologue addressed to Pan, is final proof of Colin's lyric genius. Significantly, at the end of "December" (unlike at the end of "January," when he *breaks* his pipe[24]), Colin hangs his pipe upon a tree, honoring the tradition while laying it aside, preserving it intact for those who follow.

In "December," as E. K. aptly observes in the Argument, Colin "proportioneth his life to the foure seasons of the yeare," an abridged calendar form. The final eclogue serves as pandect for the whole. As Colin says concisely:

> So now my yeare drawes to his latter terme,
> My spring is spent, my sommer burnt up quite:
> My harveste hasts to stirre up winter sterne.
>
> (lines 127–29)

Colin completes the pattern of the calendar, realizing its perfection by exhausting the last of its possibilities. Though he remains unaware of it, he activates the potential of hope implicit in "January." Colin, with Dante, has demonstrated the necessity of despair as a sort of humility. It is the loveless pit from which hope must start, the foul rag and bone shop of the heart that serves as workshop for the poet.

Even Colin, who does not enjoy the benefit of our overview, reaches a state of resignation, if not of understanding. Rosalind may be unattainable in this world, a fact already recognized in "January" and confirmed in "June." But when the cosmic pattern is completed in "December," she becomes available as *la mia donna* in the encompassing abstraction of the calendar's wholeness, and Colin becomes the ever-singing voiceless shepherd. At the end, though bereft of all, Colin remains true to Rosalind. In the *content* of the poem, Colin dies. But paradoxically, la mort ny mord. In the optimistic *form* of the shepherds' calendar he lives forever.

Finally, the cyclical pattern of the calendar indicates a continuation, an endless repetition. Although the form is determinate, the poem does not result in closure. After "December," "January" brings a new beginning. The calendar form promises an ongoing existence not just for Colin, but for the poem itself. This continuous and continuing vitality insures an eternal life not just for humankind, but for our artifacts—perhaps, even for art in general as our highest, architectonic achievement. As E. K. purports to explain Colin's final emblem, citing passages from Horace and Ovid, "The meaning wherof is that all thinges perish and come to theyr last end, but workes of learned wits and monuments of Poetry abide for ever."

This, in fact, is the most comprehensive and profound meaning for *The Shepheardes Calender*. It demonstrates the mechanism of *ars aeterna,* of how mundane experience, even that of lowly shepherds, transubstantiates into heavenly beauty. The poem provides an abstract of motion itself, a paradigm for mutability. It teaches the lesson of repetitious change: pessimistically, each of us learns that he must die, like Colin; but optimistically, we understand that death is but the return to an everlasting beneficence, the completion of the pattern of perfection, an ordained prelude to immortality. It images in capsule the consciousness of time as a durational period, and yet as an inexhaustible beatitude.

In Spenser's poetics, then, the macrocosm is the object of imitation, which is imaged forth in some cosmic form; and it is this form that becomes the poet's chief vehicle of expression. Poetic meaning is conveyed primarily through form rather than subject matter. The content of the poem, in fact, is largely a metaphor for the form—and seen in toto, after the reading of the aliquot parts, the poem is that metaphor. In consequence, the poet must take great care in the arrangement and in the metrification of parts. His poetizing is largely an exploitation of formal properties, in the manner of μουσική. This is, of course, the orthodox poetics of proportion and harmony expounded by Augustine and Landino. But Spenser casts it in the more capacious mold of cosmic forms such as the zodiac, rather than leaving it to the flimsy devices of versification alone. The poem turns out to be a substantial world, not merely an ornate lyric.

Although these are not the only poetical principles we find in Spenser, he implements this poetics in poem after poem. It is, in fact, the most persistent feature of his poetizing and the surest basis for plotting the course of his career. It is evident in most of his major works from *The Shepheardes Calender* to *The Faerie Queene;* and in those works where it is conspicuously absent— such as "Mother Hubberds Tale," "Muiopotmos," and *Colin Clouts Come Home Againe*—it throws light on Spenser's intention by suggesting a conscious choice to produce something other than a literary microcosm. But more of these matters as we turn to Spenser's other poems.

Perhaps the second most egregious instance of Spenser's "making" through the imitation of cosmic forms is "The Teares of the Muses." Although not published until the *Complaints* volume of 1591, this poem was probably composed about the time of *The Shepheardes Calendar.* For its metrical scheme, Spenser resorted to the six-line stanza used by Colin Clout in both "January" and "December," and the poem deplores the decline of the arts in doleful tones reminiscent of "October." It bears the mark of youthful work—in its use of the old-fashioned genre of a lament, in the stilted artificiality of its language, and in the clumsy supplication to the Queen at the end. Most important for our purposes, "The Teares of the Muses" shares the poetics demonstrated by *The*

Shepheardes Calender, and the dynamics of its form can best be understood as an analogue to that poem.

The symphony of the Muses, a topos stretching back to antiquity, was a familiar motif in the Renaissance.[25] In this heavenly concert, each Muse plays a different instrument or sounds a different note, though together under the direction of Apollo all are harmonious. None is discordant—in fact, the beauty of the total effect depends upon the contribution that each Muse makes to the whole.[26] In addition, according to an ancillary topos, each Muse was assigned a note in the music of the spheres and was positioned to preside over a planet,[27] so the motif was geared to physical nature and endowed with a correspondent exactitude and concreteness. In its full elaboration, the symphony of the Muses served as a synecdoche for universal harmony and impinged upon much cosmological thinking of the period. When induced into an artifact, as here, it is a clear example of Augustine's aesthetic of multeity in unity. In fact, it enjoyed a definite numerological significance. The nine Muses plus their leader, Apollo, add up to 10, the number that represented the universe in its heavenly aspect as a unified system.

In "The Teares of the Muses" a narrating first person, presumably the poet himself, opens the poem by inviting the Muses to voice the complaints they are accustomed to rehearse in their native land, "beside the silver Springs of *Helicone*" (line 5). Each Muse then sings in turn, beginning with Clio and running right through the directory of nine, and each laments the decay of her particular discipline. By this plan, the poem notes the decline of all the arts—in fact, the decline of learning and civilization in general, under attack from Ignorance and his crew. As Urania frames the problem, "What difference twixt man and beast is left, / When th'heavenlie light of knowledge is put out" (lines 487–88). According to the first eight Muses, mankind seems destined to a bestial state devoid of reason, because of "fleshes frailtie and deceipt of sin" (line 492). In the final complaint, however, Polyhymnia, while recognizing the general abuse of learning, suddenly points to Elizabeth, "her ages ornament, / And myrrour of her Makers majestie" (lines 571–72). The poem culminates in an effusive compliment to the Queen, presented as a patroness of poetry and a princely hope for its continuance. There is at least a glance toward the future, though a rather modest one compared to the vision of cosmic perfection held out to the reader in *The Shepheardes Calender*.

This clear-cut scheme for the poem is rendered even more mechanical by its metrical arrangement. Each Muse sings the same number of six-line stanzas. After the introductory passage in which the poet sets up the scheme, each Muse is allotted nine stanzas for her performance plus one stanza as transition to the next Muse, making a total of ten. The poet, though, being mortal rather than divine, takes only nine stanzas for the introduction, so Euterpe's section is padded by an extra stanza to reach the total of exactly one hundred. This number has numerological significance, as we know from the *Divina commedia:* it is the square of the celestial number, 10. Because 10 incorporates the first four integers $(1 + 2 + 3 + 4 = 10)$, exhausting the possibilities for physical extension in nature, it was considered the number of perfection, a summation of earthly experience.[28]

Once again, as in *The Shepheardes Calender,* a cosmic pattern of completeness and perfection is used as a norm, a framework wherein to measure the inadequacies of this world. Each Muse mourns the attack upon her particular discipline and the resultant danger to the community as an integrated whole. At the same time, this pattern of perfection as a durable form holds out hope for an improved future, especially under the kindly ministrations of Elizabeth. While acknowledging the wretchedness that lies about us, the poet affirms eternal values. The meaning of the poem is largely a function of form, a longing for the sort of supernal beauty echoed in the content of the Muses' performance and reflected in the form of their harmonious symphony.

This form is so glaringly evident, however, and so relentlessly enforced, that it becomes a detriment rather than a graceful ornament (at least, to modern tastes). It distracts by its prominence and generates monotony through a sense of sameness. Although each Muse sings individualistically about those matters dearest to her, so that considerable variety is introduced into the poem, the lugubrious tone is constant and the length of each performance is the same. Furthermore, the transitional stanzas from one Muse to the next are all but identical, bringing us back repeatedly and insistently to the basic scheme. The result is a stately movement through the one hundred stanzas in a series of epicycles, but hardly a lively or memorable one. The formal features of the poem become obtrusive, and eventually deadening. In consequence, modern readers tend to be more embarrassed by "The Teares of the Muses" than edified by it, and largely overlook it as juvenilia. Spenser's contemporaries, however, may have responded more favorably to the elegance of its arrangement and diction, and may have comprehended more readily its movement as a Uranian poem from the baseness of this world to a holy presence, "divine *Elisa,* sacred Emperesse" (line 579).

The purest example of Uranian poetry in Spenser's canon is *Fowre Hymnes,* a progress in four stages from the nether regions of creation, where the pandemic love of Plato's *Symposium* prevails, to the supreme presence of Jehovah, where the immortal beauty of Plato's *Phaedrus* resides. In this work Spenser perfectly fulfills the role of poet as *vates,* which, as Sidney says, "is as much as a diviner, foreseer, or prophet" (*Defence* 76.22–23). Like David, Spenser "showeth himself a passionate lover of that unspeakable and everlasting beauty to be seen by the eyes of the mind, only cleared by faith" (77.22–24). Spenser openly aspires to such a role in the proem to the final hymn, "An Hymne of Heavenly Beautie" (lines 1–21; cf. lines 134–40).

The date of composition for these poems is open to question, the doubt being raised by the poet himself. Spenser says that the first two, the earthly rather than the heavenly two, were written in the greener times of his youth (ded., lines 1–3). This may be only a pretence, however, to excuse the indiscretions (mild though they are) of describing sexual passion,[29] what is called "loose desyre" and "sinfull lust" ("Hymne in Honour of Love" 175, 179). Or perhaps Spenser hoped to forestall adverse criticism of some disjunction that he himself might have felt between the earthly and heavenly halves of his scheme. In any case, *Fowre Hymnes* was published as a separate volume in 1596 (along with a second edition of *Daphnaida*); and whatever the composition date for any particular hymn, they deserve to be dealt with as a self-consistent entity comprising four quasi-autonomous parts. All four hymns are of one piece with regard to style, and with regard to subject matter they complement one another to produce a continuous course of instruction and a sequential argument.

As the title of the work indicates, Spenser is following the classical model of a literary hymn addressed to a powerful god, such as those presumably by Orpheus and Homer.[30] Each of Spenser's hymns is appropriately addressed to a deity, and the four are arranged hierarchically in a scale of increasing authority and dominion. The hymn of earthly love is dedicated to Cupid (though not so named), of earthly beauty to Venus, of heavenly love to Christ (though, again, not named), and of heavenly beauty to God the Father. Evidently there is a shift from the pagan to the Christian at the midway point of this arrangement, although both religious doctrines are syncretistically applicable throughout the poem. The same sort of syncretism is suggested also by the term "hymn," which covers not only the ancient literary genre but as well the song of praise in current Christian worship. Indeed, the title *Fowre Hymnes* accurately indicates the inextricable fusion of classical and Christian sentiment that characterizes the work.

The movement of the work closely follows Urania's injunction in "Teares of the Muses" to "behold the worlds creation" and "judge of Natures cunning operation," and thence to "mount aloft unto the skie, / And looke into the Christall firmament" (lines 499–506). We, the readers, are guided by the poet, who speaks in first person and puts very little distance between himself and his persona. With him, we follow a mystic's route of regression from the physical things of this world and an ascent into some interior world where essences are organized into a perfect order representing Platonic beauty and Christian providence. At the juncture between the second and third hymns, we pass in this introspective quest from the earthly to the heavenly, from the sensible to the intelligible. These Platonic terms are appropriate, because the substance of the work—vocabulary, subject matter, thought, form—derives from the Platonic system as a Christian would have interpreted it.[31]

Being a Uranian poem, *Fowre Hymnes* has affinities with the philosophical treatises in verse that learned Elizabethans frequently wrote to popularize their beliefs. The content of these poems is philosophy pressed into the service of theology. In this particular work Spenser takes up the perennial metaphysical problem of the relation between physicality and spirit, and argues in terms of Greek thought as it had been Christianized by Renaissance neoplatonists. Underlying all four hymns as an unstated premise is Plato's theory of ideas, an assumption that things of the physical world are imperfect replicas of the essential ideas which persist as immutable archetypes in a world of spirit beyond human sense perception (pages 129–30).

This relationship of physical example to archetype was established by the neoplatonist account of the world's creation. The divine Creator had used the perfect pattern of the archetypes, what Spenser most comprehensively calls "heavenly beauty," as his model for the cosmos at large. Particular ideas, such as justice or treeness, were projected into inchoate matter, literally informing that matter and imposing identity upon separate portions of it to produce the individual items of physical nature. Spenser acknowledges this theory of creation at the opening of "An Hymne in Honour of Beautie":

> What time this worlds great workmaister did cast
> To make al things, such as we now behold,
> It seemes that he before his eyes had plast
> A goodly Paterne, to whose perfect mould
> He fashiond them as comely as he could.
>
> (lines 29–33)

Through his benevolence, the divine architect insures a considerable degree of accuracy in his material reproduction of the cosmic pattern.

Since the physical is a crude manifestation of the essences, however, mankind's search for truth necessitates a progressive movement from sense experience with physical things to more and more refined experiences until we perceive the essential ideas themselves. The aim of the reflective mind is to proceed from the particular thing with its concrete physicality to more and more abstract and more and more inclusive versions of the thing until the mind arrives at some perception of the archetypal essence. The movement is from participation of body in the physical world to participation of soul in the spiritual realm. In the chain of being, humanity provides the nexus between the physicality of beasts, plants, and stones on one side and the spirituality of angels and God on the other, and in this movement the mind ascends this scale. The soul is eventually freed from the encumbering flesh, and with the senses sloughed off, it perceives directly the eternal verities.[32] This is the literal definition of ecstasy.

In Platonist doctrine the experience of essential reality, the contact with and assimilation into the spiritual realm, is love, the experience of harmony with the universe. The Church Fathers had early taken over this tenet, applying the term *caritas* to such circumambient love. Despite our present-day notion of Platonic love, however, such charity must originate with sense impressions. The entire range of human potential, from stones through angels, must be activated in order to arrive at the consummation known as *caritas*. Because this scale of love necessarily starts at the physical level, sexuality is a purposeful first phase of the process. Hence the indispensable role of women in the scheme. They are the inciters of love. But since the lady is an agent of heaven, the vessel of celestial values, she provides the means not only for sexual gratification, but also, more importantly, for the heavenward ascent. The lover's desire for her becomes his first step toward beatitude. Such was Beatrice for Dante, as her name implies. In Christian thought the level of essential reality, the abode of the archetypes, was equated with heaven, and arrival there was equated with acceptance into the presence of God. The stages of Platonic love, from sense experience to mystic ecstasy, then become an ascent from love of a woman through the planetary spheres and the empyrean to the throne of God—the route of Dante.

Fowre Hymnes provides one of the most explicit and detailed accounts of this process whereby the lover is raised from brutish sexuality and prepared for assimilation into Christian charity.[33] In "An Hymne in Honour of Love," after Cupid is invoked in the proem, he is addressed reverentially: "Great god of might, that reignest in the mynd, / And all the bodie to thy hest doest frame" (lines 43–44). Immediately follow two more epithets that emphasize the wide scope of this cosmic force which prevails in both heaven and earth: "Victor of gods, subduer of mankynd"; and finally an adjective clause that designates love at this point to be a bestial passion: "That doest the Lions and fell Tigers tame." Man in his loving is first associated with the gods, a possibility of coalescing with the deity that eventually will be realized, although for the present it is held in abeyance. More nearly, though, man is aligned with wild beasts in their violent mating, and the scale of love is firmly anchored in physical nature.

After the parentage and infancy of Cupid are recounted in accord with the conventions of a classical hymn, his attributes and effects are set forth. As his initial and most consequential act, Cupid creates cosmos out of the chaotic abyss. By instituting the pattern of the elemental tetrad, Love establishes order throughout nature (lines 78–98).[34] All creatures live within this beneficent order and gain their sustenance from it; and warmed by the heat of this desire to couple in love, they "multiply the likenesse of their kynd" (line 100). While the lower orders of the animal kingdom indulge in sex to relieve their burning desire, man procreates for the purpose of insuring a future for his race—"Not for lusts sake, but for eternitie, / [He] seekes to enlarge his lasting progenie" (lines 104–5). So in his sexuality it is an awareness of time and a wish to persist that sets mankind apart from the brutes.

As a lingering memory of his heavenly origin, man retains a recollection of beauty, and therefore in his aspirations toward eternity he seeks to marry the beautiful. This is accomplished under the aegis of Cupid, who shoots his darts through the eyes of the lover and pierces his heart (lines 120–26). The resultant pain is extreme—and the course of action and concurrent psychological states of the lover are given in considerable detail. The fleshly lover, with "his dunghill thoughts," is consigned "to dirtie drosse," and he dare presume no higher (lines 183–86). But the devoted lover is rewarded and raised by "the powre of that sweet passion," which "all sordid basenesse doth expell, / And the refyned mynd doth newly fashion / Unto a fairer forme." This "fairer forme" is the beauty of the lady, which serves as "the mirrour of so heavenly light" (lines 191–96). Fixing his eye upon that beauty reflected from above, the lover undergoes the struggle of proving his worthiness and the torments of doubt and jealousy.

Eventually, however, by loyal service to love and after suffering "through paines of Purgatorie," the lover gains "heavens glorie" (lines 278–79). He reaches the earthly paradise in company with his mistress, and there, purged of base lust and instructed in true

love, he may endlessly indulge his sexual appetite "without rebuke or blame" (line 288). Spenser paints an elysian picture of
passionate but licensed love. This is the upper limit of Cupid's
domain, a region of "hurtlesse sports . . . devoyd of guilty shame"
(lines 288–90). It is the happy residence of "*Venus* dearlings" (line
284), with a hint of what is to follow in the next hymn.

The first hymn then ends in two quick stanzas with the poet
wishing to gain "that happie port" of Cupid's paradise. Such bliss
would make worthwhile his pain in loving and his effort in making
verses. If Love grants this wish, Spenser says, "Then would I sing
of thine immortall praise / An heavenly Hymne" (lines 301–2)—a
promise fulfilled in the third hymn and looking forward to that
further stage in love's ascension heavenward.

"An Hymne in Honour of Beautie" is prefaced by a proem recognizing that we have progressed past Cupid's realm and invoking
his mother, Venus, a "great Goddesse, queene of Beauty" (line
15). It too begins with an account of creation, though now cosmos
is seen as the beneficent act of a divine creator reproducing the
pattern of his own goodness rather than as the result of a natural
force organizing the elements. A heavenly influence, "perfect
Beautie," is introduced into the scheme (line 40). Under the ministrations of Venus, every earthly thing partakes of this celestial
quality, especially humankind. Idle wits contend that beauty is
physical and transient—"Beautie is nought else, but mixture
made / Of colours faire, and goodly temp'rament / Of pure com-
plexions, that shall quickly fade / And passe away, like to a som-
mers shade" (lines 65–68). But the true lover knows "that Beautie
is not, as fond men misdeede, / An outward shew of things, that
onely seeme" (lines 91–92). Rather, it is "that faire lampe" which
"shal never be extinguisht nor decay" (lines 99–101). It is a light
brought from heaven by the soul, and it still burns in the soul.
Naturally, those souls which bear the strongest heavenly light inhabit the most beautiful women. A soul informs its body with this
beauty, "for of the soule the bodie forme doth take: / For soule is
forme, and doth the bodie make" (lines 132–33). Therefore,
comes the obvious conclusion, "a comely corpse" bespeaks "a
beauteous soule," and a man's desire for beautiful women is justified, even encouraged (lines 135–40).

Yet there are those who abuse this innate beauty and thwart its hallowed influence. So the poet pauses for condemnation of the lechers who debauch it and for some warning to the "faire Dames" who use it shamefully for reprehensible ends. For the benefit of the weaker sex, he intones, "Loath that foul blot, that hellish fier-brand, / Disloiall lust, faire beauties foulest blame" (lines 169–70). Eschew "disloiall lust," but participate in "gentle Love, that loiall is and trew" (line 176), because it is through love that beauty is made manifest. In consequence, the poet advises the ladies to re-veal their beauty to a lover who can appreciate that "celestiall ray" (line 187). The lover should be one who recognizes "your forms first source" and who "with like beauties parts be inly deckt" (lines 192–93). The poet rises to a paean of love as the marriage of true minds: "For love is a celestiall harmonie, / Of likely harts composed of starres concent" (lines 197–98).

In his pursuit of beauty, the lover must operate within these guidelines prescribed by heaven, and the poem proceeds to de-lineate in step-by-step detail how the lover advances from percep-tion of his lady's physical beauty to a recognition of her "inmost faire" (line 237). First, those who love indeed look to their ladies "with pure regard and spotlesse true intent." Then, "drawing out of the object of their eyes, / A more refyned forme," they present this image abstracted from sense data and purified of flaws "unto their mind, voide of all blemishment."[35] Finally, lovers match this abstraction with the idea of beauty which they carry innately in their souls, discerning the "first perfection" which originally in-formed the body of the mistress. Now, though, the "refyned forme" of her beauty is released from the limitations that the body imposes, so a lover sees it "free from fleshes frayle infection" (lines 211–17). But the lover goes even beyond this stage—from love of this particular beautiful woman to love of beauty as an abstract quality, and eventually to love of the heavenly source of beauty: "Thereof he fashions in his higher skill, / An heavenly beautie to his fancies will" (lines 221–22). Once more, this hymn, like "An Hymne in Honour of Love," looks forward to a later stage in love's ascension, to its heavenly counterpart in "An Hymne of Heavenly Beautie." And again, this second hymn, similar to the first, con-cludes quickly in two stanzas with a supplication to Venus that she soften the heart of the poet's mistress.

Christ is the dedicatee of "An Hymne of Heavenly Love," although He is not called upon by name. He, like Cupid, is addressed only as Love. But clearly the love of this third hymn has moved to a more advanced stage than that of the first, because it is now enhanced with beauty. The deity who presides over this realm has an unmistakably larger dominion than the god whose precinct terminated with the earthly paradise. In the proem He is prayed to as "the god of Love, high heavens king" (line 7), and supplicated to raise the poet across the dividing line between physical and spiritual: "Love," begs the poet, "lift me up upon thy golden wings, / From this base world unto thy heavens hight" (lines 1–2). We have progressed to heavenly love. Moreover, we have entered the region of the mind, "farre above feeble reach of earthly sight" (line 5), where the soul, not the bodily senses, is the appropriate faculty of perception.

After the proem, the body of this hymn, like its two predecessors, begins with an account of creation, but now this momentous event is seen with the added dimension of Christ's love for mankind. Even before creation, God was moved by love to beget a "sonne and heire, / Eternall, pure, and voide of sinfull blot" (lines 31–32). Even before time began, Christ reigned with God and with the Holy Spirit. After invoking the aid of his dedicatee, the poet recounts the events in heaven leading up to the bringing forth of man: God's creation of the angels, their glorious abode, their arrangement in "trinall triplicities" and their service to God, their seduction by Lucifer into the sinful way of pride, their expulsion from heaven and damnation to hell (lines 50–98).

To fill the breach in the holy plan left by the fallen angels, God created man in His own image: "Such he him made, that he resemble might / Himselfe, as mortall thing immortall could" (lines 113–14). But Adam too proved disobedient and fell from grace. To save man from "that deepe horror of despeyred hell" (line 130), to retrieve him from "the mouth of death to sinners dew" (line 123), Christ came as redeemer: "Out of the bosome of eternall blisse, / In which he reigned with his glorious syre, / He downe descended" (lines 134–36). Christ's life on earth and His passion are recalled with religious fervor, and this passage culminates in a rapturous stanza of apostrophe to the "blessed well of love" (line 169). What Christ asks in return for His sacrifice is nothing more than acceptance of the gift of love; he asks only that we participate in *caritas:* "Him first to love, that us so dearly bought, / And next, our brethren to his image wrought" (lines 118–19). Such is the definition of "heavenly love."

This third hymn, not surprisingly, is the most overtly and exclusively Christian. Spenser makes little effort to interpret Christ in ambiguous terms that accommodate the classical tradition. There is no treatment, for example, of Christ as Pan, such as Spenser resorted to in "May" (lines 54, 111) and "July" (lines 49–54). Carrying on the strongly religious tone, "An Hymne of Heavenly Love" proceeds with a sketch of Christ's life, beginning "from first, where he encradled was / In simple cratch, wrapt in a wad of hay" (lines 225–26), and ending "lastly how twixt robbers crucifyde" (line 244). The hymn concludes with an injunction to worship Christ, and the final lines make a feeble gesture of platonizing Him by a reference to "th'Idee of his pure glorie" (line 284). The message of this hymn, though, is clearly the moralistic one to love Christ as He loves mankind, because this experience of heavenly love is uplifting to the spirit: "Then shall thy ravisht soule inspired bee / With heavenly thoughts, farre above humane skil" (lines 281–82).

The final hymn carries on from the high level of rapture achieved in the closing lines of its predecessor. The "sweete enragement of celestiall love, / Kindled through sight of those faire things above" prepares the poet for his ultimate experience. In the proem to "An Hymne of Heavenly Beautie," he invokes the Holy Ghost and prays for the ability to express for his fellow mortals some small portion of the "eternall Truth" that he has been privileged to witness in this introspective quest:

> Vouchsafe then, O thou most almightie Spright,
> From whom all guifts of wit and knowledge flow,
> To shed into my breast some sparkling light
> Of thine eternall Truth, that I may show
> Some little beames to mortall eyes below,
> Of that immortall beautie, there with thee,
> Which in my weake distraughted mynd I see.
>
> (lines 8–14)

Thereby "the hearts of men, which fondly here admyre / Faire seeming shewes, and feed on vaine delight," will be "transported with celestiall desyre / Of those faire formes." They will be raised aloft, "and learne to love with zealous humble dewty / Th'eternall fountaine of that heavenly beauty" (lines 15–21). The purpose of this Uranian enterprise will be accomplished by Uranian means.

The body of this concluding hymn begins, like each of its antecedents, by a look at creation, but now our world is seen as a vast and inexhaustible plenitude. "Looke on the frame / Of this wyde *universe*," we are instructed, "and therein reed / The endlesse kinds of creatures, which by name / Thou canst not count, much lesse their natures aime" (lines 30–33). The ubiquitous beauty comes, of course, from the bounteous hand of the Creator. Our gaze is directed first to the region of the four elements, arranged in layers from earth and water through air to fire as they traditionally appeared in diagrams of the universe. They are enclosed by a crystalline sphere, a conflation of the sphere of fixed stars and the primum mobile that becomes the lower boundary of heaven— "that mightie shining Christall wall, / Wherewith he hath encompassed this All" (lines 39–40). The orderly movements of the planets are seen as evidence of heavenly beauty, and spheres beyond mortal sight are postulated to extend this eternal beauty beyond the limits of our finitude (lines 64–70).

This brings us in our ascent to the upper reaches of heaven, arranged in a hierarchy of different levels (lines 78–98). All are fair, though some are fairer than others. First comes the residence of "happy soules" who continuously "behold the glorious face / Of the divine eternall Majestie." Next comes the realm of Platonic essences; and "more faire," we are told, "is that, where those *Idees* on hie / Enraunged be, which Plato so admired." Then come the angels, arranged in the traditional ranks of nine orders, each more fair than the other, and leading to those who immediately attend upon God. "That Highest," of course, is "farre beyond all telling, / Fairer than all the rest, which there appeare" (lines 101–2). This essence of heavenly beauty, this "endlesse perfectnesse" (line 105), is beyond description, so the poet settles for an enumeration of His attributes as they impinge upon our natural world: "His truth, his love, his wisedome, and his blis, / His grace, his doome, his mercy and his might, / By which he lends us of himselfe a sight" (lines 111–12). In phrases reminiscent of the Old Testament, we're enjoined to fall before His throne and plead for mercy (lines 141–82).

Beside God on His throne sits a female figure called by the name of Sapience, "the soveraigne dearling of the *Deity*" (line 134). She is regally clad, in the manner of a queen from the Book of Revelation, "and on her head a crowne of purest gold / Is set, in signe of highest sovereignty" (lines 190–91). Sapience reigns beside God the Father, although she does not possess His commanding absoluteness. Her sway is far-reaching, but delimited. She holds a scepter, "with which she rules the house of God on hy, / And menageth the ever-moving sky, / And in the same these lower creatures all" (lines 192–95). But her rule extends no farther than the bounds of the finite universe: "Both heaven and earth obey unto her will, / And all the creatures which they both containe" (lines 197–98).

The significance of Sapience has been much debated by scholars, and her prototypes have been traced to numerous sources, most frequently to those grounded in mysticism.[36] She has affinities with Dame Nature, with the Virgin Mary, with Solomon's Wisdom, and with the Cabbalistic Schekina. To me, as to Quitslund, she seems a genuinely syncretistic figure, coalescing the benign qualities traditionally assigned to her sex. She is the essence of heavenly beauty in female form, especially its potential for fecundity. Her face, like God's, is beautiful beyond description; so with purposeful vagueness the poet declines to characterize her further and leaves her praise to the angels. What seems most important are the marriage of Sapience to God, her power and beauty, and the riches she has at her disposal to bestow upon her worshippers. Once they see the "glorious sight" of her seat in heaven, "in nought else on earth they can delight, / But in th'aspect of that felicitie, / Which they have written in their inward ey" (lines 283–85). They are carried "into an extasy" (line 261): such "sweete contentment . . . doth bereave / Their soule of sense, through infinite delight, / And them transport from flesh into the spright" (lines 257–79).

This final hymn then closes quickly, as have the earlier ones, with two stanzas of personal application. The poet enjoins his "hungry soule" to turn away from "this vile world, and these gay seeming things," and instead to "looke at last up to that soveraine light, / From whose pure beams al perfect beauty springs, / That kindleth love in every godly spright" (lines 288–301). The poet hopes to become a worshipper of Sapience, the source of beauty and thence of love in this world. The upward movement of this introspective quest, coterminous with the poem, has come to rest in the image of her seated beside God in heaven. The closing lines of the hymn record the transformation of motion into stasis: "With whose sweete pleasures being so possest, / Thy straying thoughts henceforth for ever rest." Spenser has shared his vision and his aspirations, and he brings us to a synchronic conclusion.

Such is the content of *Fowre Hymnes.* I am not suggesting that Spenser's poem merely versifies an established philosophical or theological dogma, because the work is fully individualized as an artistic object. But it is important to see the content of the poem displayed in full metaphysical dimension since, as always in the neoplatonist aesthetic, content is a metaphor for form. Form emerges into our consciousness through the content of a poem; or conversely, we perceive form by means of an analysis of content. Since meaning ultimately resides with form, however, the revelation of form must be the interpreter's governing objective.[37] So our concern will now be to discover the form that underlies the discursive philosophico-theological content. In *The Shepheardes Calender,* form emerged from a temporal movement as each month passed in sequence; in *Fowre Hymnes,* by contrast, form emerges from a movement through space as the mind of the lover ascends from earth to heaven. Since movement requires both time and space, however, there is an interdependency between the two, and the ascent in *Fowre Hymnes* implies a temporal factor.

To look at each of the four hymns as an autonomous entity, we should note that each has a definite internal structure. Each begins with a few stanzas of introduction identifying the deity to whom it is addressed, then proceeds to a discourse of his/her attributes and effects, and finally concludes in Spenser's personal expression of hope or praise. This internal structure gives identity to each poem and sets it apart from its fellows. But in addition, this structure, which all share, posits a relationship between them as equal and coordinate entities. They are correspondent elements, each making its equitable contribution to the system, just as each of the twelve months holds its necessary place in the calendar and each Muse plays her distinctive instrument in the universal symphony. These four poems are therefore a multeity, although at the crudest level of interpretation, in the most mechanical way, they are held together in unity by virtue of the fact that they share an identical structure.

More important, by virtue of their content the four hymns interrelate to form a carefully ordered whole. The progress from confrontation with Cupid in the "Hymne in Honour of Love" to confrontation with Jehovah in the "Hymne of Heavenly Beautie" charts the continuous transition of the human mind in the ascent from physical to spiritual. The opening stanza of each hymn reports on the stage of this motion under the impetus of love. So not only are the four hymns correspondent to one another as elements in a horizontal system, but also they relate as consecutive segments in an ascension. They are four steps on a scale. There is a vertical, even hierarchical, arrangement. The effect is cumulative.

Within this fourfold system, there are also significant relationships between certain pairs of hymns. Obviously, for example, the "Hymne of Heavenly Love" is a reprise of the "Hymne in Honour of Love" at a higher level, and similarly the "Hymne of Heavenly Beautie" is a more exalted statement of the "Hymne in Honour of Beautie." As we have noted, at the end of each earthly hymn, Spenser glances forward to its heavenly counterpart.[38] Moreover, and of equal significance, there are two son-parent relationships among the dedicatees. Cupid is the son of Venus, and Christ is the son of God, thereby positing a special relationship between the "Hymne in Honour of Love" and the "Hymne in Honour of Beautie," and between the "Hymne of Heavenly Love" and the "Hymne of Heavenly Beautie." Interpreted, these relationships indicate that in each instance love is subordinate to beauty—an effect of it, a response to it; and therefore love belongs to a lower order than beauty. Just as earthly love is a response to earthly beauty, so is heavenly love an effect of heavenly beauty. The four-stage ascent is thereby broken into two halves, where the second half repeats in a finer tone the arrangement of the first half. The two halves are nonetheless correspondent, though, so that earthly love remains analogous to heavenly love, and the inclusive order of *caritas* is maintained.

Even so, since Cupid is Venus's son and Christ is God's, these two relationships break down the fourfold system into two halves. These two relationships delineate the dichotomy between physical and spiritual, so that within the fourfold movement there is the subdivision of two parts, earthly and heavenly. The ascent from lowest to highest, first distributed among four stages, can be further reduced—schematized and abstracted—to two correspondent (though not equivalent) halves. The disjunction between the pagan hymn to Venus in honor of beauty and the moralistic hymn to Christ in honor of heavenly love indicates the discontinuity between these two parts of the whole. The earthly is a different level of being, a different level of experience, from the heavenly.

But Spenser has made this distinction in order to exploit the opportunity of obliterating it. He separates earthly from heavenly in order to indicate the juncture where physical and spiritual come together and to demonstrate how smoothly the physical transmutes to spiritual. Both Venus and Christ in their significance cross this juncture, each coming from her/his appropriate territory but crossing the border into the alien terrain. Christ descends into the mortal flesh of man to make heavenly love known on earth ("Hymne of Heavenly Love" 134–40). In an exactly contrary, compensating movement Venus reaches above to the empyrean for the heavenly pattern imprinted in matter to give it beauty ("Hymne in Honour of Beautie" 43–56).[39] The two halves of the dichotomy, therefore, the earthly and the heavenly, readily interpenetrate across this midway line. The emphasis is not upon their separation, though that is recognized, but upon their integration.

The final hymn, "An Hymne of Heavenly Beautie," displays the attributes of God the Father. He is supreme and eternal, the progenitor of everything that Christ, Venus, and Cupid preside over. Their power is vested in His omnipotence, which by a calculus of integration subsumes the powers of the lower deities. He is the consummation of both space and time. Paradoxically, He is the One that is also immeasurable, boundless—the circle with center everywhere and circumference nowhere. Somehow this final hymn must climax the other three, providing the apex of the fourfold movement toward beatitude. But it must do more. Not only must it comprehend the first three hymns, but it must transcend them and suggest the limitless significance of the deity. No circumference can proscribe God. The form of the poem, though integrated, must expand beyond all-inclusiveness.

Spenser accomplishes this architectural feat by instating a female figure, Sapience, to be co-regnant with God. She is God's helpmeet, as Eve was to Adam, although of course exempt from the imperfections that brought about humanity's fall. She is the female counterpart of God, complementing His being and thereby, if it were necessary, completing His infinitude. In any case, she removes any doubt of His completeness or stability. Together they represent a self-sufficient and indestructible two-phase system, the concept crudely depicted by the alchemical hermaphrodite,[40] hinted at early in the hymn when the Sun and Moon are labelled the King and Queen of heaven's empire who rule night and day (lines 55–56). As Sun and Moon, they govern time, the movable image of eternity.

More precisely, in her own right Sapience controls "both heaven and earth" (line 197), a fit mate for God, His partner in governance if not His equal in power and longevity. Her limitations are suggested by her analogy with Venus, the goddess of earthly beauty, with whom she is pointedly compared—but whom she surpasses in every way (lines 211–24). By dominating Sapience, God subsumes also what Venus represents; indeed, He incorporates the female principle in whatever state it may appear. He thereby attains the indestructible completeness that derives from self-sufficiency, the immutable soundness depicted by the alchemical hermaphrodite. As King and Queen of heaven, as Sun and Moon, God and Sapience are conjoined in a union that represents time as the ceaseless alternation of day and night.[41] Together, they form an icon for the daily unit of time, another integer of eternity. The upward movement of *Fowre Hymnes* terminates in the stasis of their marriage, as the final couplet of the poem announces. The temporal factor in the poem is thereby resolved into permanence. Time rests in them.

Moreover, this marriage of God and Sapience demonstrates in terms of cosmic love the mystic union of man and woman, of spiritual and physical, of eternal and temporal.[42] So the fourfold structure of the work (four autonomous hymns) coalesces into two parts (earthly and heavenly), and finally culminates in this comprehensive union of God and Sapience. Perception of this unity out of the multeity of Creation is the truth that Spenser has sought to disclose, the spiritual awareness that he wishes to share with his reader. The work closes with description of the celestial delights that contemplation of this vision brings.

The form of the work is based, then, on the divisions and summations which are possible within the number 4. There are four components that relate to one another in various permutations, each of which generates meaning; and the four components integrate to form a whole that exceeds in significance the sum of the parts. That wholeness of the whole transcends the finiteness of particulars and stretches outward to suggest the imponderable magnitude of deity. The multeity of the poem's content is imaged forth as a rich metaphor for this infinitude, which though boundless is by definition a unity because nothing can exist outside it.

Furthermore, we should not overlook the numerological significance of the number 4. It is the mundane number, being the number of the elements and of the bodily humours. It is also the number of the seasons, gaining an additional dimension as an ideogram for time. The number 4 is simply a reduction of 12, a schematized, abstracted form of the annual calendar; and just as the twelve months are the integer of eternity, so are the four seasons. Actually, the number 4 when presented as the Pythagorean tetrad offers a highly articulated system of tensions and attractions,[43] just the sort of contrarieties and assimilations that comprise the totality of *Fowre Hymnes*. Early in the first hymn Spenser details the construction and implications of the creative tetrad:

> The earth, the ayre, the water, and the fyre,
> Then gan to raunge them selves in huge array,
> And with contrary forces to conspyre
> Each against other, by all meanes they may,
> Threatning their owne confusion and decay:
> Ayre hated earth, and water hated fyre,
> Till Love relented their rebellious yre.
>
> He then them tooke, and tempering goodly well
> Their contrary dislikes with loved meanes,
> Did place them all in order, and compell
> To keepe them selves within their sundrie raines,
> Together linkt with Adamantine chaines;
> Yet so, as that in every living wight
> They mixe themselves, and shew their kindly might.
>   (lines 78–91)

When it is remembered that in the *Timaeus* the tetrad is the basic arrangement of items inhering in every level of creation and informing each creature, we can appreciate what the fourfold form of the poem contributes to its cosmic significance. While 4 is the mundane number, it readily expands indefinitely and by endless repetition abstracts to divinity.

There is significance also in the metrical scheme of each stanza. Spenser composes in a seven-line stanza of iambic pentameter rhyming *a b a b b c c*. There is precedence for this stanza in rime royal—most notably for Spenser, perhaps, in the tale of patient Griselda related by Chaucer's sententious Clerk or in his tale of *Troilus and Criseyde*. Spenser uses this stanza also in "The Ruines of Time," although nowhere else.[44] As usual with Spenser, this choice of metrics is not casual, so we are compelled to look for special significance in it. As Sidney noted, "The senate of poets have chosen verse as their fittest raiment, . . . peising each syllable of each word by just proportion *according to the dignity of the subject*" (*Defence* 82.1–6; italics mine).

The sort of significance we might expect in the metrics is indicated by Michael Drayton, who first composed his *Mortimeriados* (1596) in the seven-line stanza of rime royal. But this stanza form proved unsatisfactory, as Drayton explains, because "the often harmonie thereof softned the verse more then the majestie of the subject would permit."[45] In consequence, he recast his poem in the eight-line stanza of *Orlando Furioso* and retitled it *The barrons wars*. Drayton is quite clear in his reasons for resorting to ottava rima:

> I chose Ariostos stanza of all other the most complete, and best proportioned, . . . [because it] both holds the tune cleane through to the base of the columne (which is the couplet at the foote or bottom) & closeth not but with a full satisfaction to the eare for so long retention.
>
> Briefely, this sort of stanza hath in it majestie, perfection, & soliditie, resembling the pillar which in Architecture is called the Tuscan, whose shaft is of six diameters, & bases of two.

What Drayton is taking into account resides in the relationships between the lines of the stanza forms as these relationships are dictated by the respective rhyme schemes. In rime royal, as Drayton forcefully illustrates by a diagram in his text, the first four lines establish a pattern of alternating rhymes, *a b a b*. The fifth line, however, another *b* rhyme, modulates this pattern. Added to the fourth line, also a *b* rhyme, it produces a rhymed couplet, *b b,* and thereby prepares for the rhymed couplet of lines 6 and 7, *c c.* The *a b a B* of the first four lines, a quatrain of alternating rhymes, is elided with the *B b c c* of the last four lines, a quatrain of two rhymed couplets. Drayton found such a smooth transition objectionable because, as he says, "the often harmonie thereof softned the verse more then the majestie of the subject would permit."[46]

In ottava rima, however, Drayton discovered the less mellifluous stanza form that he thought generated the "majestie, perfection, & soliditie" appropriate to his subject matter.[47] The ottava rima stanza rhymes *a b a b a b c c.* The alternating rhyme scheme of the first six lines, again as Drayton illustrates by a diagram,[48] is preserved intact, pristine, without modulation; and the concluding couplet comes without preparation, unheralded, with undiminished finality. As Drayton shrewdly observes, using a visual comparison, "This . . . holds the tune cleane through to the base of the columne (which is the couplet at the foote or bottom)." He sees this stanza form as a column of six lines resting upon a base provided by the concluding couplet, which "closeth not but with a full satisfaction to the eare for so long detention." This arrangement, more architectural than harmoniously musical, produces the effects that he deems appropriate to his historical/epic poem. We must conclude from Drayton's comments that he expected the metrics of a poem to evoke certain qualities, such as harmoniousness, majesty, perfection, solidity; that these qualities may be generated by the grouping of lines related by rhyme, so that rhyme unifies some lines while it distinguishes them from other lines, and thereby the stanza becomes an arrangement of distinct parts comprising a whole; that in the perception of this arrangement both the eye and the ear are involved; and finally, that the expectation of and search for significant forms in this arrangement most likely presumes a platonist aesthetic (especially as Augustine had professed it; pages 182–95), where sense data are the clues that reveal underlying forms, ideal qualities.

The rationale for assigning such significance to metrical schemes is explicitly laid out by Puttenham in the opening chapter of his second book, entitled "Of proportion poeticall." Placing himself in the direct line of the quadrivium, with Plato's Academy (and its emphasis upon mathematics) behind Boethius, Puttenham begins with a general statement: "It is said by such as professe the Mathematicall sciences, that all things stand by proportion, and that without it nothing could stand to be good or beautiful." In the next sentence Puttenham, as he often does, adds a quasi-biblical authority to his argument, recalling the topos of God as archgeometer: "The Doctors of our Theologie to the same effect, but in other termes, say: that God made the world by number, measure and weight." The inference is clear: the mortal poet, in emulation of the heavenly maker, composes in meter and endows his creation with comparable proportions in order to simulate the proportions evidenced by cosmic harmonies. Puttenham refers knowingly to the three types of proportion utilized in the quadrivial sciences—"the Arithmeticall, the Geometricall, and the Musical"[49]—and he proceeds by adapting his thesis to the mode of perception appropriate to each of the five senses:

> By one of these three is every other proportion guided of the things that have conveniencie by relation, as the visible by light colour and shadow: the audible by stirres, times and accents: the odorable by smelles of sundry temperaments: the tastible by savours to the rate: the tangible by his objectes in this or that regard.

Proportion in poetry is aimed at the similar effect of conveying to the percipient a sense of order, an echo of the supernal beauty. And all artifacts in this aesthetic, regardless of the medium by which they are expressed, may be compared on the basis of the mathematical ratios embodied in their proportions, on the basis of their formal properties. It is this platonist dispensation that joins music and poetry as sisters.

"Returning to our poeticall proportion," Puttenham concludes, "Poesie is a skill to speake & write harmonically: and verses or rime be a kind of Musicall utterance, by reason of a certaine congruitie in sounds pleasing the eare." The rhythms of a line, then, and the divisions of a stanza occasioned by rhyme result in proportions that recall the proportions in our universe created according to number, weight, and measure, and consequently they have significance as counters for these cosmic facts. Puttenham contin-

ues by demonstrating this thesis at considerable length—at a
length so considerable, in fact, that most modern readers out of
boredom or indifference skip over this portion of his *Arte of English poesie,* which comprises a third of it.

To miss the significance of metrical forms, however, is to overlook an important mode of expressing meaning, a mode that is
distinctively characteristic of the Renaissance in general and of
Spenser's poetics in particular. We must therefore pay close attention to his "poetical proportions." The numbers of his poetry are
saying something of central importance.[50]

Like all platonist forms, the metrical patterns put forward here
as significant relationships in the stanza of *Fowre Hymnes* should
emerge gradually in our consciousness rather than hitting us in
the eye and pummelling our ear, so what I propose may not be
readily granted. Nonetheless—without insisting upon the certainty of any of these suggestions, and with apologies for the
simple-mindedness of their concreteness—I think it is worth noting that the first four lines of this seven-line stanza rhyming $a^1\ b^1$
$a^2\ b^2$ confirm the sort of son-parent relationships that exist in the
four hymns.

$$a^1\colon b^1 \ = \ a^2\colon b^2$$

Cupid is the son of Venus just as Christ is the son of God the
father. Similarly, these first four lines reflect the relationship between the two hymns on love and the two on beauty.

$$a^1\colon a^2 \ = \ b^1\colon b^2$$

Earthly love is to heavenly love as earthly beauty is to heavenly
beauty. Furthermore, the fourth line of the stanza, which is the
middle line, is ambiguous in the rhyme scheme, belonging either
to a system comprising the first four lines, *a b a B,* or a system
comprising the last four lines, *B b c c.* It therefore marks the disjunction between the earthly and the heavenly halves of the total
work, so the division between the first two earthly poems and the
last two heavenly poems is reflected in the organization of any
individual stanza by the divisiveness of this anomalous line. If the
last four lines of the stanza are taken as a system, rhyming *b b c*

c, we see repeated even more clearly the division into two distinct halves, *b b* and c c. Finally, the concluding rhymed couplet of c c is the sort of culmination and summation that suggests the inclusiveness of the deity and the completeness of the marriage between God and Sapience. Each stanza eventuates in the sort of firm closure that characterizes the total work.

In addition, there is cosmological pertinence in the total number of lines in each stanza. Seven is the number of the planets, and even more significantly the number of days in the week. Not only does 7 suggest the flux of time through the orderly movements of the planetary spheres and the passage of a weekly unit, however, but it also brings to mind the seven days of creation, that extravagant unfolding of the divine will which eventuates in the joyous hallelujah of the sabbath.[51] Spenser's poem is a comparable revelation of God's vast design and of our place within it. *Fowre Hymnes* is a similar feast of love and praise of beauty. So Spenser's intention as *vates* is perhaps most clearly and fundamentally revealed in these permutations of 7 and 4 and 2 and 1—or rather, in the cosmic forms abstractable from these numbers. In accordance with Augustine's advice, Spenser has trod "the pathway to the immortal" and has recorded his vision of "what abides forever." The omnipresence of multeity in unity makes *Fowre Hymnes* a celebration of God's inexhaustible plenty at every level of Creation.

The doctrine of love and beauty propounded in *Fowre Hymnes* is shown in practical application in *Amoretti* and *Epithalamion*,[52] by genre a sequence of sonnets and a marriage hymn. The historical element in these poems comes from the events leading to Spenser's second marriage on 11 June 1594, so again the narrative voice is a first-person lover who coalesces readily with Spenser himself.[53] But like Colin Clout, the protagonist here becomes the typical lover. In Sonnet 3, at the earliest convenient moment in the sequence, he tells us about his mistress and his relation to her:

> The soverayne beauty which I doo admyre,
>> witnesse the world how worthy to be prayzed:
>> the light whereof hath kindled heavenly fyre,
>> in my fraile spirit by her from basenesse raysed.
>
>> (lines 1–4)

In terms reminiscent of *Fowre Hymnes,* the "soverayne beauty" of the mistress has kindled love in the speaking "I," and the remainder of the poem recounts the consequences. The lady is *la mia donna,* very much in the manner of Dante—in Sonnet 61, for example, she is "the glorious image of the makers beautie, / My soverayne saynt" (lines 1–2), and the couplet concludes: "Such heavenly formes ought rather worshipt be / then dare be lov'd by men of meane degree." At the close of *Amoretti,* in accordance with the conventions of sonneteering, the lover has not attained the mistress, because she inhabits a sphere beyond the reach of mortal man. In *Epithalamion,* however, their marriage is celebrated, a consummation of love that is contrary to the sonnet tradition but in keeping with the doctrine of *Fowre Hymnes.*

So the content of *Amoretti* and *Epithalamion* demonstrates the course of true love, which admittedly does not run smooth. Uranian intentions and principles also determine the form of these two works, although this fact might not be immediately apparent. Like the segments of *Fowre Hymnes,* however, *Amoretti* and *Epithalamion* should be taken together as a single, self-consistent poem. They deal with the same personal events in Spenser's life (his courtship and marriage of Elizabeth Boyle), and they were published in a separate volume in 1595 with nothing else except a few insignificant anacreontics to serve as a marker between them.[54] But quite apart from these historical facts, the two works comprise a single artistic and intellectual whole. Neither is complete without the other. The sequence of sonnets is a necessary prelude to explain the vitality of the marriage hymn, just as the marriage hymn is a sequel that completes the sonnet sequence and appropriately reorients it toward happiness. *Amoretti* comprises the temporal, while *Epithalamion* results in stasis.

Certainly the sonnet sequence charts the passage of time. *Amoretti* comprises eighty-nine sonnets, and once again, as in *The Shepheardes Calender,* the lover acts out his despair within a seasonal framework. At the start, Sonnet 4 specifies the season as the beginning of January, a "new yeare forth looking out of Janus gate" and "calling forth out of sad Winters night, / fresh love." In Sonnet 19 the cuckoo appears as the "messenger of Spring" and the herald of Cupid. Sonnet 22 takes place in the "holy season" of Lent, perhaps on the "holy day" of Ash Wednesday, so in his mind the lover builds a temple to his "sweet Saynt" in order to worship her chastely. On the day of Sonnet 28 the mistress wears a laurel leaf, suggesting a day in spring or early summer. In Sonnet 40 summer has arrived—or, at least, the lady's smile is compared to "the fayre sunshine in somers day," and the lover feels appropriately warmed. The "hideous stormes" of Sonnet 46 which impede the lover's departure from his mistress's house most likely occur in the autumn or early winter. By Sonnet 60, a year has passed. Soon after, Sonnet 62 recognizes a new year according to the pagan calendar, when the sun passes the equator in a northward direction at the vernal equinox,[55] so the lover hopes that his fortunes will take a new turn for the better—and encouragingly, two sonnets later he is rewarded by a kiss. Sonnet 68 celebrates Easter, with the appropriate prayer that we might live in accord with heavenly love, while Sonnet 70 is a paean to spring as the season of natural, earthly love and of gathering rosebuds. The day at the seashore in Sonnet 75 implies summer, with emphasis on the evanescence of its pleasures. In the final sonnet, the barren bough on which the culver sits, the darkness of the day, and the general desolation predicate winter. So references to the changing seasons clock the passage of two years between Sonnet 4 and Sonnet 89.[56] The calendar rolls around twice. When viewed as an analogue to *The Shepheards Calender*, *Amoretti* necessarily ends in the lover's despair and his spiritual death in winter. Separated from his mistress, he laments in the final line of the poem, "Dead my life that wants such lively blis."

But when viewed optimistically in the ongoing life of the calendar, love, like the cycle of the seasons, renews itself, so the despair of the closing sonnet is the prelude to the joy of *Epithalamion*. As the poet/lover writes earlier when saying goodnight to his mistress, "I her absens will my penaunce make, / that of her presens I my meed may take" (52.13–14). So the separation at the end of *Amoretti* is contrived to express metonymically the humility from which true love springs. After the consummation of love in the marriage hymn, the temporal events recounted in *Amoretti* are properly seen as preliminary phases of a larger scheme: "The wished day is come at last, / That shall for al the paynes and sorrowes past, / Pay to her usury of long delight" (lines 31–33). In *Amoretti* the passage of time, perhaps, not the amount of time passed, is the important thing. In *Epithalamion,* by contrast, time is abridged, approaching the static. *Amoretti* gives a durational account of the relationship to *la mia donna,* while *Epithalamion* gives an account compressed to the essentials, the culmination, the limit before passing over into the nondurational—the ecstasy of rapprochement with *la mia donna,* the idea of *la mia donna.*

In *Epithalamion* the integer of eternity is not the stretched-out annual calendar, but rather time is collapsed into the ecstatic events of a single day. Those events, like those in *Fowre Hymnes,* lead inexorably to a union in marriage between male and female. The stability attained at the end of *Fowre Hymnes* in the union of God and Sapience is repeated at the human level in the "lasting happinesse" (line 419) of the bride and groom. The process of loving, detailed in *Amoretti,* reaches its consummation in the wedded bliss of *Epithalamion.* And the poem itself, a record of that process, shares in the completeness and durability of that perfect union; it is "for short time an endlesse moniment" (line 433).[57] The multeity of the loving experience has been subsumed into a timeless unity.[58]

In also another sense *Amoretti* and *Epithalamion* demonstrate the aesthetics of multeity in unity. In a sequence of sonnets, the lady is a Platonic absolute, a constant: in Sonnet 3, for example, the lover praises her as "the soverayne beauty which I do admire," and in Sonnet 45 he claims that his heart retains "the fayre Idea of your celestiall hew." In Sonnet 88, the next to last, the lover, though separated from his mistress, sustains himself by contemplating the "image of that heavenly ray" that persists in his inner eye; he remains faithful in his love by "beholding the Idaea playne, / through contemplation of my purest part" (lines 7–10). The lady in her ultimate significance is the heavenly beauty of *Fowre Hymnes,* a Platonic idea of loveness. She has this unchanging identity.

The lover, however, undergoes a variety of experience in response to her. Each sonnet, in fact, records a particular reaction to the lady at a particular point in time. While the lady remains above vicissitude, the lover in each sonnet succumbs to a momentary, fleeting sensation. And his responses, significantly, cover the extremes of possibilities. As Petrarch says, "Love, though I have been tardy in seeing it, wishes me to be untuned between two contraries" (55.13–14).[59] Most crudely, love is likened to ice and fire, in the hackneyed Petrarchan manner, so the lover alternately freezes and fries (cf. *Amoretti* 30 and 32). In more religious terms, he despairs and hopes (cf. *Amoretti* 25). In one self-conscious mood, the lover sees himself as a pitiable actor on the stage of "this worlds Theatre," observed by the mistress as "the Spectator" who beholds him "with constant eye":

> Sometimes I joy when glad occasion fits,
>   and mask in myrth lyke to a Comedy:
> soone after when my joy to sorrow flits,
>   I waile and make my woes a Tragedy.
>   (Sonnet 54.5–8)

Whatever the vocabulary—Petrarchan, religious, or theatrical—the lover runs the gamut of emotions and incorporates the extremes. He reconciles opposites. It is through this assimilation of multeity and arrival at unity that he hopes to know the mistress in her full capacity, and hopes thereby to arrive at the worthiness to be her peer. Each sonnet is an aliquot part within this whole dominated by the mistress. Each sonnet is a separate experience for the lover (and the reader), although it contributes to the wholeness that represents her perfection.[60]

So the mistress is a first cause which precedes all the rest, which generates and sustains all the rest, and to which all the rest must be referred. She is the unity that produces the paradoxical contrary states of love best expressed by oxymoron: "O living death, O delightful harm."[61] She is the system within which all the rest inheres. Nonetheless, the essence of the system, which is the lady, is made known to us only through the lover's variable reactions to her. The essence of the system is available only by means of its transformations as evanescent experience in the transitory individual sonnets. As in *Fowre Hymnes,* content is a metaphor for the underlying unity embodied in the lady.

Therefore reading a sequence of sonnets involves the comprehension of each sonnet in turn as a particular significant experience for the lover (and vicariously for us, since for didactic purposes we are attached to him[62]). We read the sonnets one by one, diachronically, as the poet/lover has ordered them, so they take on the semblance of fictive narrative. The sequence records the course of the lover's wooing. The purpose of the poem, however, is not to tell a story, but to reveal the nature of the mistress. As Spenser explains in Sonnet 69, his sonnets are an "immortall moniment . . . in which I may record the memory / of my loves conquest, peerelesse beauties prise." Their purpose is "to tell her prayse to all posterity." At first we recognize her physical attractiveness, her pride, her aloofness and even cruelty; but these are gradually reinterpreted as over-hasty evaluations of her heavenly beauty, her integrity as a servant of God, and her purity.[63] At the end, as in Sonnet 84, we are sent to "visit her in her chast bowre of rest," where we may "behold her rare perfection." Eventually, under instruction from the poet/lover we penetrate to the lady's essence. Through his eyes, as Spenser puts it in the final sonnet of the Amoretti, we behold "the Idaea playne."[64] The poet/lover fulfills his Uranian role as vates, and we are instructed in the heavenly discipline of caritas.

The form of the quatorzain, the metrical unit of Amoretti, has cosmological significance of a highly sophisticated sort that supports its Uranian purpose. The sonnet of fourteen lines is a nonclassical form, an innovation of the late medieval period,[65] and no cultural phenomenon better illustrates the continuity between Middle Ages and Renaissance. The fourteen-line arrangement reflects directly the Augustinian aesthetic of number, weight, and measure. In its original state it comprised an octet and a sestet, which may be abstracted to the ratio 4/3. The sonnet expresses a relationship between what is represented by 4, the mundane number, and what is represented by 3, the holy number of the Trinity—that is, it demonstrates how the earthly transmutes to the heavenly, the process made explicit in Fowre Hymnes.

So the mathematics of the sonnet moves faithfully heavenward. By its form, the sonnet affirms the existence of heaven and assures the reader that he, like the lover, may arrive at it, participate in it. The form is resolutely optimistic, signifying the persistence of this providential order. In consequence, regardless of the rhetorical division of the sonnet and regardless of its subject matter, the 4/3 ratio inherent in its form is a comforting reminder that a vast design is in place.[66] The rhetorical arrangement of the sonnet (as distinct from its metrical arrangement) might obscure this ratio;

and the subject matter, as in many of Shakespeare's sonnets, may even question, denounce, or deny a divine plan. But the durable form of octet-sestet insists that rhetorical deviations and skeptical defiance are but temporary anomalies. In fact, the significance of such content, like the significance of any aberration, may be determined only by measuring the degree of its divergence from the constant represented by the form of the sonnet. The formal design insists upon the concept of order and acts as a norm, while the content becomes meaningful only as a variation of or deviation from that norm. As always in the neoplatonist aesthetic, the ontological *situs* of the poem lies in its form.

In Spenser's distinctive adaptation of the quatorzain in *Amoretti,* the octet-sestet arrangement is obscured, but the original 4/3 ratio that characterizes the fourteen-line sonnet is not entirely obliterated. It persists beneath an overlay of another significant form. Spenser's rhyme scheme and his variable rhetorical divisions are appropriately seen as a sophisticated adaptation of the traditional quatorzain. Metrically speaking, with a single exception[67] Spenser composed his sonnets as an arrangement of three quatrains and a concluding couplet, with the quatrains interlinked by rhyme:

$$a\ b\ a\ b\ /\ b\ c\ b\ c\ /\ c\ d\ c\ d\ /\ e\ e\ ^{68}$$

It is easy to see a continuous progression in such a scheme as *a* transmutes to *b* (in the second quatrain the position held by *a* in the first is filled by *b*), as *b* transmutes to *c*, and as *d* appears as a potential fulfillment of *c*. It is an intricate and dynamic system of likenesses and contrarieties and transformations. All the variety comes to rest in a final couplet, however, which is both an entity apart from and a consummation of all that has gone before. The rhyming couplet is both a culmination (the end term in a sequence) and a finality (the inclusive term that delimits the whole). The form that emerges in our consciousness, then, is exactly analogous to that in the fourfold arrangement of *Fowre Hymnes,* and with comparable cosmological significance. There are four parts, quasi-autonomous but linked in a continuous progression, and the fourth part both caps and comprehends its antecedents.

The metrical unit of *Epithalamion* is even more pliant than that of *Amoretti*. Although reminiscent of the canzoni of Dante and Petrarch, it is in fact a sophistication of the fourteen-line sonnet. The metrics of *Epithalamion* are notable for their intricacy and have been much praised for their fluency and grace. Viewed simply as a metrical construction, this poem ranks among the greatest virtuoso performances in English, and rightly so. Spenser deploys in it a stunning array of metrical statements.

For one thing, unlike every other poem by Spenser, the stanzas of *Epithalamion* are not uniform.[69] They range in length from seventeen to nineteen lines, with the final truncated stanza, serving as envoy, having only seven lines.[70] There seems to be no pattern to the arrangement of stanzas containing the same number of lines; rather, the effect is simply a slight modulation of form, a minor variation within distinct limits. The fact that modulation occurs is the point, rather than the extent of that modulation.

Furthermore, within each stanza Spenser uses long lines and short lines, iambic pentameters and trimeters;[71] and the final line in every stanza (except the last) is a hexameter. Usually, there are three short lines in each stanza.[72] For the eighteen-line stanzas, the normal pattern for the number of feet in the lines is as follows:[73]

$$5\ 5\ 5\ 5\ 5\ 3\ 5\ 5\ 5\ 5\ 3\ 5\ 5\ 5\ 5\ 3\ 5\ 6$$

For the nineteen-line stanzas, without exception, the pattern for the number of feet in the lines is as follows:

$$5\ 5\ 5\ 5\ 5\ 3\ 5\ 5\ 5\ 5\ 3\ 5\ 5\ 5\ 5\ 5\ 3\ 5\ 6$$

Again, the effect is a strong one of minor variation within firmly established limits. Every stanza has an opening section of six lines, comprising five pentameters and a final trimeter, and rhyming *a b a b c c*.[74] This opening section is followed by two more sections of pentameters delimited by a concluding trimeter, and the fourth section is a rhymed couplet comprising a pentameter and a hexameter. If the trimeter lines are taken to be markers or boundaries between sections (and this function is made salient by the fact that each short line rhymes with the immediately preceding line), we see that this pattern is congruous with the form of

Spenser's sonnet as three quatrains and a concluding couplet. Each full stanza of his *Epithalamion* is similarly an arrangement of four sections, a variation of the *Amoretti* sonnet. It has approximately the same number of lines as a quatorzain, although a few more; in addition, it begins with a quatrain rhyming *a b a b,* and it ends with a rhymed couplet. The stanza of *Epithalamion,* then, is simply an exuberant quatorzain, a sonnet that threatens to get out of hand. It begins with the expected quatrain—but then it breaks the quatorzain form; it violates the rigid mold of the 4/3 ratio and attenuates toward a larger, less confining form, until firmly brought under control again by the concluding couplet. So the stanza of *Epithalamion* repeats the metrical unit of *Amoretti,* although with greater freedom and variety. It contributes markedly to the liveliness of *Epithalamion,* and links it to *Amoretti* as a companion piece.

Of equal importance, the metrical unit of *Epithalamion* produces a system of repetitions. It confirms the underlying sonnet form by opening repeatedly with the expected *a b a b* rhyme; and though it moves beyond the quatrain in an adaptation of the sonnet that verges upon the evaporation of form, it restricts finally to a rhymed couplet. And then this process begins again in the next stanza. Like the sonnets of *Amoretti,* the stanzas of *Epithalamion* provide a succession of near-identical forms. Moreover, the final line in every stanza is virtually the same (although a significant modulation which exactly reverses the content occurs in stanza 17 and thereafter), and the rhyme words of the final couplet are consistently "sing" and "ring." Finally, in the original publication of 1595 each sonnet of *Amoretti* and each stanza of *Epithalamion* is printed on a separate page; each metrical unit has an equal amount of physical space, and turning the pages reproduces this same space over and over. There is a sameness in the dimension of each unit in the sequence. Identical units are perceived in orderly progression.

So despite the minor variations within each stanza, the repetition of form is strongly accentuated in the arrangement of *Epithalamion.* The reiterated return to an established pattern is emphasized by the repeated rhyme of every concluding couplet—indeed, by the almost identical wording of each concluding couplet. And the conclusiveness of this return is settled by the extra foot of the alexandrine that closes each stanza. The result is a distinctly measured effect as each stanza concludes, like the ticking of a metronome. The alexandrine refrain recurs with a time-marking certainty.

Only the final seven-line stanza is liberated from this metrical scheme quickly established as a norm in *Epithalamion*. The final stanza eludes any pattern of line lengths or of rhymes, and it stands exempt from the closing alexandrine. The absence of these constrictions indicates an escape from the measured passage of time. A long-standing tradition had interpreted the biblical account of creation in just this way. According to La Primaudaye, who is drawing ultimately if not directly upon Augustine,[75] the alternation of light and darkness during the six days of activity dissolved into perpetual light on the seventh day:

> Whereas also the prophet having made mention in each of the six precedent daies of the creation, of evening and morning, doth mention no such matter of the seventh day: it seemeth hee woulde signifie, that this Sabbaoth day was ordained to represent the great and last day of everlasting rest, wherein there should be no more anie such distinction of evening and morning, nor of day and night, as now is: but altogither light, by which we shall contemplate God face to face in true and perfect felicitie, such as eie hath never seene, eare never heard, nor ever hath entred into the hart of man.[76]

The last stanza of *Epithalamion*, innocent of any indication that time passes, completes a perfection that will be an "endlesse moniment" not subject to mutability. It brings the poem to a synchronic wholeness, to an everlasting sabbath. This transcendence of time and space is confirmed by the number of lines in the final stanza, which is the number of days in the heptaemeron of creation. The poem ends in a hosanna of seven lines.

In its overall construction, then, *Epithalamion* is perhaps the most obviously ordered of Spenser's poems. Indeed, many different systems of ordering are in effect. In addition to the metrical order and its significance, even a casual reading reveals a progression from early morning through the nuptial activities and the connubial night to the next morning. A count of the stanzas comes to twenty-four, suggesting that each one may represent an hour in the wedding day. A. Kent Hieatt has, in fact, discovered a complex number symbolism in the structure of *Epithalamion,* involving not only the twenty-four hours of the day, but also the 365 days of the year, the time of sunset on 11 June 1594 (the date of Spenser's marriage), and the division of the zodiac into 360°.[77] This number symbolism for the poem is now widely accepted in its general configuration if not in all its minute details.

So once again in *Amoretti* and *Epithalamion* Spenser exemplifies the Augustinian aesthetic of multeity in unity. Following the dictates of Uranian poetry he takes the everlasting beauty of God's design as his object of imitation and leads his reader to an awareness of it. In such analysis, of course, we are subject to the danger of reducing every poem to the same cosmic forms, to the imitation of an identical cosmos. But that danger is inherent in Augustinian poetics, where the end of all purposes is praise of God and appreciation of His attributes.[78] There is an additional limitation in such analysis which we should acknowledge, even if in this study I do not overcome it. We must not forget the linguistic surface of Spenser's poems. My primary aim, however, has been to look behind the surface elements for his forms. Because the language of a Spenserian poem encodes the idea anterior to it, I have so far felt justified in giving priority to that idea while relegating analysis of the verbal system itself to an ancillary role.[79]

In other poems, though, Spenser follows a different poetics, where form is not fundamental. In "Mother Hubberds Tale,"[80] for instance, he expressly shuns the neoplatonist aesthetic that had been the legacy of Landino. To repeat the tale of that "good old woman," Spenser says at the end of the introductory paragraph, "No Muses aide me needes heretoo to call" (line 43).[81] This is merely a beast fable, so the poet need not call upon heavenly inspiration. The poem doesn't herald what the erected wit of man may achieve, but rather it specifies what the infected will of man has actually wrought.

On the face of it, "Mother Hubberds Tale" is a child's story from the large-print book of Reynard the Fox. As Sidney described such poetry, these are "pretty allegories, stealing under the formal tales of beasts," and therefore "food for the tenderest stomachs" (*Defence* 87.25–29). After line 942, "Mother Hubberds Tale" becomes also an occasional poem, commenting upon contemporary political events. The poem grows precisely satirical, even propagandistic. Spenser is writing close to history, directed away from Uranian poetry.

Nonetheless, the persona who speaks in this poem is aware of the traditional poetics imported from Italy. His refusal to call upon the Muses is an acknowledgment of their designated powers, not a denial of their existence. Later in the poem, in that idealistic portrait of the perfect courtier whom tradition identifies as Sidney, we learn of the important role the Muses should play in the courtier's life. For his recreation when tired in body, "his minde unto the Muses he withdrawes; / . . . With whom he close confers with wise discourse, / Of Natures workes, of heavens continuall course" (lines 760–64). In brief, he reads Uranian poetry. He reads also "of dreadfull battailes of renowmed Knights"—that is, heroical poetry—"with which he kindleth his ambitious sprights / To like desire and praise of noble fame" (lines 767–69). High-minded poetry plays a large part in both the active and the contemplative life of the ideal courtier. When the Ape, however, an imposter, assumes the trappings of a courtier and perverts courtship, he abuses poetry. He writes love poems of a salacious sort and provides his younger peers with the means of seducing the ladies of the court:

> Thereto he could fine loving verses frame,
> And play the Poet oft. But ah, for shame,
> Let not sweete Poets praise, whose onely pride
> Is vertue to advaunce, and vice deride,
> Be with the worke of losels wit defamed,
> Ne let such verses Poetrie be named:
> Yet he the name on him would rashly take,
> Maugre the sacred Muses, and it make
> A servant to the vile affection
> Of such, as he depended most upon,
> And with the sugrie sweete thereof allure
> Chast Ladies eares to fantasies impure.
>
> (lines 809–20)

In his satiric mood, Spenser recognizes the current debasement of the amorous poetry deriving from Dante and Petrarch, an offence to "the sacred Muses." But this is to the shame of scoundrel poets, and not of poetry itself. Rather, Spenser's concern here is to defend poetry, largely on the grounds of its moralistic purpose, "vertue to advaunce, and vice deride."

But "Mother Hubberds Tale" is neither amorous poetry nor heroical poetry nor Uranian poetry. The site of its activity is far from any haunt of the Muses. It recounts the adventures of a reprehensible Fox and Ape as they traverse the three estates of society (common folk, clergy, and nobility), exposing the silliness and sometimes the wickedness in each rank; and it concludes in a pointed comment on the intrigue surrounding Anjou's proposal of marriage to Elizabeth. This content conceals no underlying form; it simply relates in temporal sequence a series of episodes held together by nothing stronger than the continual presence of the Fox and Ape. For this poetic performance, Spenser devises no metrical scheme that echoes celestial harmony; instead, he satisfies himself with rhymed pentameter couplets, the modest verse that Chaucer had relied upon for the prologue that set his Canterbury tales in motion.

This is not to say that "Mother Hubberds Tale" is artless. Quite the contrary. But it is primitivistic art, self-consciously simple, rather than the sophisticated poetics of making that we have seen heretofore in Spenser's poems. It is the art of Chaucer, rather than of Dante, and throughout we see evidence of Chaucer's wit and irony, and hear the echo of his language. The poem displays a shrewd yet humorous knowledge of the world that appears here alone in the corpus of Spenser's work.

Another quality sets "Mother Hubberds Tale" apart from the poetry of Spenser we have looked at: the wealth of depictive particulars. Early in the work, for example, when the Ape assumes his first disguise as a discharged soldier, his appearance is described with the empiricist's taste for realism and with the raconteur's eye for significant detail:

> The Ape clad Souldierlike, fit for th'intent,
> In a blew jacket with a crosse of redd
> And manie slits, as if that he had shedd
> Much blood throgh many wounds therein receaved,
> Which had the use of his right arme bereaved;

> Upon his head an old Scotch cap he wore,
> With a plume feather all to peeces tore:
> His breeches were made after the new cut,
> *Al Portugese,* loose like an emptie gut;
> And his hose broken high above the heeling,
> And his shooes beaten out with traveling.
> But neither sword nor dagger he did beare,
> Seemes that no foes revengement he did feare;
> In stead of them a handsome bat he held,
> On which he leaned, as one farre in elde.
>
> (lines 204–18)

Here we have a genuine word picture, an example of the rhetorician's *prosopographia,* a technique we have not seen before in Spenser. Not only the Ape and Fox, but also minor characters are sharply drawn—the ignorant parish priest, for instance, and the snobbish courtier (lines 361–550 and 580–654).

Sidney would have called these "poetical descriptions," approving their *energeia.* He would have approved also the sprightly dialogue that frequently breaks out in "Mother Hubberds Tale," the best example occurring between the Fox and Ape and the Mule when our rascal-heroes first arrive at the court (lines 580–654). Although this dialogue, admittedly, recalls the self-revealing conversation of Chanticleer and Pertelote rather than the artificial maunderings of Pyrocles and Musidorus, this is the mimetic "right" poetry that Sidney proposes in the *Defence.* It is the flip side of the golden world, a grotesque vision of the pastoral landscape.

In *Colin Clouts Come Home Againe,* Spenser reverts after sixteen years to the pastoral pretense of *The Shepheardes Calender.*[82] The opening line of the poem echoes the opening line of the January eclogue and reminds us of "the shepheards boy" known as Colin Clout. In both poems, Spenser exploits the well-established tradition for commenting upon the contemporary scene under the guise of pastoral, an aspect of *The Shepheardes Calender* that we largely neglected in our discussion of the work. In my zeal to demonstrate the principles of Uranian poetry, I minimized the historical content of the poem with its immediate reference to current events. Nonetheless, *The Shepheardes Calender* is a distinctly oc-

casional poem, prompted by religious and political controversy;
and in its topicality, it serves as a necessary point of reference for
Colin Clouts Come Home Againe.

In form, however, the later poem is nothing like its predecessor.[83] There are no discrete parts proportionable to anything. Urania does not supervise the poetics that govern *Colin Clouts Come
Home Againe,* despite Colin's call upon her to awake (line 48).
Actually, the work of Spenser most similar to it in poetic principles
is "Mother Hubberds Tale," which likewise deals exclusively with
the contemporary scene and comments upon specific events. In
the dedicatory epistle of *Colin Clouts Come Home Againe* addressed to Raleigh, Spenser apologizes for "the meanesse of the
stile," but insists that the poem agrees "with the truth in circumstance and matter"—that is, it faithfully records the facts of Raleigh's visit with Spenser in Ireland and of their return together to
London. It too is closer to history than to Uranian poetry, and
consequently exhibits the "simplicitie and meannesse" required
by decorum. Spenser chose to compose in an appropriately simple
metrical scheme, a pentameter quatrain rhyming *a b a b.*

Furthermore, *Colin Clouts Come Home Againe,* like "Mother
Hubberds Tale," is fictive narrative—at least, of sorts. The narrative design of the work is based upon the familiar motif, indigenous to pastoral, of the shepherd who returns from a visit to the
city and reports his observations to the innocent stay-at-homes.
What moves the narrative forward is a series of questions by Colin's impressionable peers, to which he responds with fulsome answers. So there is dialogue—but again, only of sorts. The effect is
more the stilted exchange between *magister* and *discipulus* than
the lively give-and-take of a dramatic scene. The narrative development is not continuous and smooth, but rather an impromptu
succession of set pieces: the tale of Mulla and Bregog (lines 104–
55), the description of crossing the ocean (lines 196–289), the
praise of Cynthia (lines 332–51, 596–615), the catalog of her
poets (lines 380–455), another catalog of her ladies-in-waiting
(lines 485–583), the didactic satire of malfeasance at court (lines
680–794), a reprise of *Fowre Hymnes* in honor of Love (lines
835–94), the homage to Rosalind (lines 931–51).

Sidney, I think, would have been pleased by the dramatic opening of *Colin Clouts Come Home Againe,* where Colin sits down

with his pipe and draws his peers to listen. And there is one inset of true fictive narrative: the tale of the river Bregog's wooing of the Mulla, an example of the popular topographical poetry. In this story some of the childish delight of "Mother Hubberds Tale" returns and a great deal of the allegorized morality. As a result of his illicit passion, the Bregog lost his own identity: he was "scattred all to nought, / . . . [and] Did lose his name: so deare his love he bought" (lines 153–55). Sidney would have seen this incident as "poetry," perhaps the only right poetry in the entire poem. He would also have seen the praise of Cynthia as a "pretty allegory," in manner like Solomon's Song of Songs: "Her words were like a streame of honny fleeting, /. . . . Her deeds were like great clusters of ripe grapes, /. . . . Her lookes were like beames of the morning Sun, /. . . . Her thoughts are like the fume of Franckincence" (lines 596–608).

For the most part, however, this is poetry of Sidney's second category; and while it sometimes seeks the platonist heights of *Fowre Hymnes,* it more usually inhabits the flat plains of forthright exposition. In fact, when Colin soars too far aloft in praise of Cynthia, Cuddy rudely calls him back. "Thou has forgot / Thy selfe, me seemes, too much, to mount so hie," Cuddy chides; and he sets the limits for such poetry: "Such loftie flight, base shepheard seemeth not, / From flocks and fields, to Angels and to skie" (lines 616–19). Colin is denied the wings of poesy. Despite the thin veneer of pastoral in this poem, Spenser himself remains "wrapped within the fold of the proposed subject, and takes not the course of his own invention" (Sidney, *Defence* 80.25–27).

Spenser's most successful exercise in Sidney's sort of right poetry is "Muiopotmos," where he gives his invention the freest rein.[84] Although by analogy with Spenser's other poems many scholars have assumed that the work contains covert allusion to historical persons and events, no one has proposed an allegorical reading that has gained acceptance.[85] Given the lack of success in unlocking any secrets of the poem, despite persistent and ingenious efforts, I'm inclined to agree with William Wells that the poem is no roman à clef recording some gossip at court or some conflict of personalities in the larger arena of national politics.[86] Furthermore, despite the frequent philosophizing in the vein of medieval tragedy, I minimize the sententiousness of the moral allegory in the work. "Muiopotmos" cannot be dismissed as a blunt parable. Rather, I take at face value Spenser's request to Lady Carey, the dedicatee, to see it as a "smal Poeme" and "to make a milde construction" of it. While not merely a jeu d'esprit, as De Selincourt called it (xxxiv), "Muiopotmos" is an effort to implement Sidney's poetics of a fictive narrative that leads us gently and divertingly to well-doing.

The point of reference for "Muiopotmos," then, is not history, neither particular event nor some malpractice at large in Elizabethan England, but rather the literary tradition for telling tales. The poem is unadulterated fiction with negligible topicality, and it demonstrates how a work generates meaning when literature is taken as a system. "Muiopotmos" assumes its place among and derives its meaning from the ancient monuments of fictive narrative. Long before the Elizabethans, the main body of fiction had differentiated itself into such diverse kinds as the beast-fable, the epic, the epyllion, and the nondramatic tragedy; and at one point or another Spenser activates each of these genres and invites us to interpret the poem as an example of it. There are abrupt shifts in reference from one genre to another, however, and the resulting inconsistencies give the work a kaleidoscopic changeableness that prevents us from taking any of it as actual or from assigning anything a lasting significance. The final effect is one of amused bedazzlement, exactly the effect that forces us to make a mild construction of it and precludes a reading that is too ponderous as allegory of either a precisely historical or stridently moral sort.

"Muiopotmos," like "Mother Hubberds Tale," its companion in the *Complaints* volume, is first and foremost a beast-fable. It does not derive from current events, however, or even indirectly from the contemporary scene. Rather, it is the reworking of an oft-told tale,[87] relating how a handsome and talented butterfly, Clarion, is trapped and destroyed by a wicked and despicable spider, Aragnoll. There is natural enmity between these species, as so often occurs in the fabulous kingdom of animals, and much of the action and emotion is described nursery-fashion in terms of these inferior creatures. We often hear echoes of Mother Hubberd's voice. Moreover, much of the imagery comes from the world of beast-fable, such as the descriptions of Aragnoll's malice (lines 249–56,

393–400), and the similes based upon the "wily Foxe" (lines 401–8) and the "grimme Lyon" (lines 434–35).

Basically, "Muiopotmos" is by genre a beast-fable. But contrary to that mode, it is elegantly wrought. It transpires in the "gay gardins" of the court (line 161), rather than in the barnyard or forest. The piece, in fact, is most often praised for its delicate and elaborate details, especially with regard to the butterfly. Clarion's comeliness and sensuous pleasures are delineated with a doting fondness. The metrical unit is also highly mannered, the Italians' ottava rima. This is a sonorous metrical scheme, with its music drawn out into a long echo of three rhymes terminated only by the couplet, but it has no explicit cosmological significance. Its meaning lies in the contribution it makes to the overall sense of elegance and beauty.

Nor does the action of "Muiopotmos" unfold with the naive directness of a beast-fable. Although there is only one complete action, in keeping with tragedy as well as the Aesopic fable, the story is not told with the rapid delivery of a Mother Hubberd. The plot itself is filled with suspense: Where is Clarion flying? What will he do in the gardens? Who is the spiteful creature lurking in the shadows? Furthermore, there are diversions from the main narrative—most disruptively, the tale of Astery and the account of the weaving contest between Minerva and Arachne; and there are philosophical digressions about the fickleness of fortune. What is notable about the expository technique of "Muiopotmos" is the leisureliness in telling a fundamentally simple and familiar story. The narrative meanders amiably, pausing here to glance at the flirtatious ladies of the court (lines 105–12), stopping there to admire the equally lovely flowers in the garden (lines 185–200). All is gracefully unhurried.

All is unhurried, that is, until the gruesome death of the protagonist. Aragnoll kills Clarion with a single thrust that spills his heart's blood. The ending of the poem is so abrupt, in fact, that it does not perform the storyteller's duty of satisfying our curiosity and rounding off our emotional response. Aragnoll slays Clarion, and that's that. The cruelty and finality of the last stanza unexpectedly reneges against the often playful, often sentimental tone that prevails in the rest of the poem. The poet offers no summarizing words of explanation or of comfort or of admonition. Although we might expect some lengthy moralizing about Clarion's folly, we get no comment or interpretation whatsoever. Aragnoll strikes him under the left wing "into his heart," just as Aeneas slew Turnus,[88] and the poem is suddenly over. While the main body of the narrative is full of incidentals and ornaments, the end is unsettling by its abruptness.

So "Muiopotmos" is not a common beast-fable. Not only does the elegance of the piece and the artfulness of its narrative raise it above this category, but from the beginning another genre is operative. The title—Spenser's coinage, derived from μυῖα, fly + πότμος, evil destiny, death—is exactly translated by the portentous subtitle, "The Fate of the Butterflie," and it suggests the defeat of a mighty hero with ancient lineage. The persona of the poem is the singing voice of the ancient bard, and the opening line—"I sing of deadly dolorous debate"—recalls the opening of the *Iliad* and the *Aeneid*. From the outset the entire epic tradition is brought to bear upon the fate of this insect. The *propositio, invocatio,* and *narratio* of the next two stanzas confirm that we are in the heroic world of "mightie ones of great estate, / Drawne into armes, and proofe of mortall fight" (lines 3–4), and epic formulae continue to reverberate throughout the poem (cf., for instance, the reiterated *invocatio* of lines 409–16). The action itself is often related in heroic terms that echo famous passages in Homer and Vergil, such as the arming of Clarion (lines 57–96) and his swift death (lines 436–440). There are similes drawn in the epic manner (e.g., lines 84–87, 401–8), and much of the phraseology recalls the oblique, extraordinary language of the classics, what the rhetorician would call *antonomasia:* the sun, for example, is "*Hyperions* fierie childe" (line 51), the peacock is "*Junoes* bird" (line 95), and Minerva is "the *Tritonian* Goddesse" (line 265). Allusions to several Greek champions—Achilles (lines 63–64), Hercules (lines 71–72), Odysseus (lines 419–20)—repeatedly remind us that Clarion belongs among the illustrious heroes of our literary past. When we recall that Ariosto composed the *Orlando Furioso* in ottava rima, the eight-line stanza of "Muiopotmos" lends the tale a certain epic seriousness—"majesty, perfection, and solidity," to apply the attributes that Drayton ascribed to this verseform (pages 343–44).

But "Muiopotmos" is not lengthy enough nor sufficiently complex to be an epic poem. Such an identification rapidly becomes untenable and, though urged by the poet, must be modified. Perhaps, then, the poem can be more immediately compared to the epyllion, that Hellenistic distillation from the legendary lore of classical Greece. The short narrative that the Alexandrian school of poets had brought to its brightest lustre was highly regarded in the Renaissance. Spenser had himself translated the pseudo-Vergilian *Culex.* It was Ovid's *Metamorphoses,* however, that provided the best-known examples of the tradition and showed it to best advantage: the polished language, the penchant for concrete detail, the focus on exotic narrative, but with a willingness to digress in description of an object, a person, a scene, or a sentiment. "Muiopotmos" also shows these characteristics. The main business of the poem is the narrative of Clarion's defeat, though the style often seems more important than the event. Throughout, a recurrent tone of Ovidian sophistication plays to the reader's courtliness and entices the reader to enjoy the artistry of the tale without too much concern for the tragic consequences. Moreover, much of the subject matter comes from the *Metamorphoses:* the love of Cupid and Psyche (lines 131–33), the contention between Arachne and Minerva (lines 257–352), the rivalry between Minerva and Neptune for the governance of Athens (lines 305–28), Vulcan's embarrassment of Venus and Mars (lines 369–74). The narrative digression about the sad fate of Astery, a fabrication by Spenser, is itself a metamorphosis according to the Ovidian pattern.[89]

Nonetheless, the sophistication of the epyllion, the pomposity of the epic, and the homeliness of the beast-fable are undercut by the activation of yet a fourth genre. In his fall from highest place, Clarion's tale imitates the pattern of medieval tragedy. The Muse invoked in the second stanza of "Muiopotmos" is neither Clio nor Calliope, but Melpomene, "the mournfulst Muse of nyne, / That wontst the tragick stage for to direct" (lines 10–11; cf. line 413). It is tragedy that demands the emphasis upon Clarion's magnificence and high rank, his expectation of the crown after Muscaroll, the envy he generates, his hedonism, his precipitous and complete demise. In the midst of his splendor and his pleasure, "in the pride of his freedome" (line 380), Clarion "fall[s] into mischaunce" (line 383). The tale of Clarion belongs among all those tragedies so lugubriously recounted by Chaucer's Monk.

The doleful message of tragedy, however, is garbled by the elegance and lushness of "Muiopotmos."[90] Clarion's fall seems accidental in an otherwise beautiful world. No cause is given; although several suggestions are offered, none is confirmed (lines 417–24). Of course, there is evil in the garden, as in Eden, but no ugliness. Aragnoll is the sleek instrument of "wrathfull *Nemesis* despight" (line 2); and once in the spider's web, Clarion struggles heroically and then nobly resigns himself to death. His fate is no grubby decline into depravity or fearfulness or remorse. Clarion's spirit never darkens. His tragedy per se is never explained.

Actually, the genres of tragedy and epic are juxtaposed at the beginning of "Muiopotmos" and continue in counterpoint to confront one another throughout the poem. In the first stanza, the poet announces with great fanfare that he sings of heroes in the epic strain; but in the second stanza, he invokes Melpomene and talks about the "tragicall effect" of these heroic actions. In the second stanza the "mightie ones" of the first stanza are reduced to "lowest wretchednes" under direction of the tragic muse. In epic, the hero triumphs; in tragedy, the rash man falls. So if "Muiopotmos" is an epic, Clarion must be praised for his vivacity and virility, his "brave courage and bold hardyhed" (line 27), virtues that he actively affirms and that continue to prevail despite his unwarranted death. But if the poem is a tragedian's warning against self-advancement, it may be readily turned to a mockery of the heroic stance, to a deprecation of epic values. *Sic transit gloria mundi*— or even, "Oh, how the mighty are fallen, through the error of their ways." The fate of the butterfly becomes a cautionary tale for the confident and celebrated. In short, epic and tragedy are immediately juxtaposed in the first two stanzas of "Muiopotmos" in order to accentuate their contrariety as worldviews. Although mutually contradictory, however, they are counterbalanced in the narrative of the poem as two equally plausible interpretations of the same occurrence. Clarion's death is noble when viewed in the context of epic battle, but lamentable when viewed as the result of human failure.[91] With equal plausibility our view of life, as the literary tradition affirms, may be either heroic or tragic.

So the tragic elements in "Muiopotmos" modify the heroic, just as the epic and epyllic elements lift the beast-fable far above the intellectual level of the nursery or the artistic level of Mother Hubberd. "Muiopotmos" is generically conditioned, but not generically contained.[92] Although we are urged to consider the poem within the framework of at least four different genres, no one of them is adequate to accommodate all aspects of its narrative. In fact, the various generic conventions contradict one another, undermine one another, so in the end we are disappointed in our efforts to classify the work. "Muiopotmos" defies the literary system. We are called upon to read according to a barrage of generic instructions fussily issued by the poet, but our efforts are continually frustrated. By the final scene, none of the generic instructions has proved workable—or, perhaps, the same thing, all are shown to be equally valid. The poet has activated a number of genres which are in turn qualified and then disqualified as acceptable norms of action and belief. In consequence, the conclusions we draw as we read are repeatedly challenged and shown to have been too hasty, ill-advised. In Clarion's world no prefabricated set of literary conventions or of moral values can be assumed.

The indecisiveness of expository method in "Muiopotmos" adds to this sense of indeterminacy. The poem changes back and forth between several modes of discourse, between authorial addresses to the reader, straightforward narrative, lingering description, apostrophes to various entities both inside and outside the story, interruptive ekphrasis, and outright preaching. And the attitude toward Clarion ranges shiftily between the frivolous and the earnest, between the condemnatory and the sympathetic, between the ridiculous and the sublime. There is no fixed framework, no constant perspective. In the end, no single answer or simple interpretation is offered. As aids to understanding, the poet has methodically rejected everything outside the poem itself, the literary tradition as well as the phenomenal world. Of all Spenser's poems, "Muiopotmos" has proved the most resistant to interpretation because there is no topical allusion to unlock a doorway to its meaning and no ready resolution to either the moral or the literary issues that it raises. We are left questioning, turned loose to find our own explanation.

In this quandary, our easier methods of literary analysis are manifestly inapplicable. We cannot deal with "Muiopotmos" as the sort of fictive narrative that eventuated in the novel. The plot is too simple and too obvious to be taken seriously as a meaningful arrangement of episodes, and its outcome is given away as soon as we recognize that this is the well-known tale of the spider and the fly. Nor can we rely upon plot in the usual sense as a sequence of episodes to be explained as cause and effect. Clarion does not fall because of his own mistaken choices; he did not bring Aragnoll into existence or elicit his malevolence. The action cannot be perceived as a re-presentation of any possible events from the phenomenal world we know by experience. The events are not particular, but archetypal. However, neither is "Muiopotmos" allegory or a similarly simplistic poetic mode. Interpretation is not the easy matter of disclosing a veiled meaning or drawing a conclusion from a vision or deriving a moral from a fable. The poem resolutely resists any such reductive analysis.

Rather, "Muiopotmos" exemplifies the poetic mode that Sidney defined as a "speaking picture" (pages 286–91), where the ontological *situs* lies not outside the poem but immediately in it. Interpreting the poem involves the comprehension of a verbal system that produces quasi-visual imagery. We read the verbal system and perceive the verbal images directed to our mind's eye in order to discover the profitable invention, the fore-conceit, inherent in it but not separable from it. The verbal system that produces the images is the *res* of the poem, both the material of which it is made and the idea which it expresses. Here the rhetorician's *res* and *verba* not only enjoy comparable ontological status, but coalesce.

So what is "Muiopotmos" a poetical image of? At the literal level, it is the image of Clarion, the butterfly whose fate the poem depicts. After the first two preliminary stanzas, essential to the generic orientation of the poem, the poet introduces Clarion with the unmistakable flourishes of an experienced storyteller presenting his central character. The butterfly's rank and his magnificence, as well as our intended attitude toward him, are clearly indicated. He is a princely fly, handsomely adorned with gorgeous wings, flitting in the air betwixt earth and heaven—a vivid and vital image. After four stanzas describing Clarion, the action of this narrative begins with line 49—"So on a summer's day . . . ," when our hero decides to venture forth from a sheltered adolescence and explore the farther reaches of his father's domain. He attires himself for the journey, and the description of his furnishings—the breastplate, the cloak of a wild beast's hide, the helmet, the two spears protruding from the helmet—takes up four stanzas, one for each of the pieces of equipment passed before our view. The copiousness of detail is enriched by overt reference to the arming of Achilles in Homer, the most painterly of poets.

Clarion's preparations conclude with the attachment of his wings—"his shinie wings as silver bright, / Painted with thousand colours, passing farre / All Painters skill" (lines 89–91). And it is here that the initial description of Clarion comes to rest. The wings are emphasized and given visual forcefulness by comparisons to Iris's rainbow, the night sky filled with twinkling stars, and the tail of Juno's peacock. These wings are many times more beautiful than those of Cupid himself; and by a sort of hyperbole through admiration—such as Homer devises to suggest the matchless beauty of Helen when the old men lust after her on the walls of Troy—the ladies of the court, above all else, envy these wings of Clarion, "so silken soft, / And golden faire" (lines 107–8). Clarion's wings are the center of attention.

The storyline is abruptly interrupted here by the first narrative digression, by the inserted tale of Astery and her sad fate: "Report is that dame *Venus* on a day . . ." (line 113). The storyteller, much in the manner of Ovid, diverges to relate a tale within a tale. The description of Astery and of this particular event which changed her life is given in colorful detail, and again the narrative comes to rest on a pair of wings—in this case, on those of the nymph: "All those flowres, with which so plenteouslie / Her lap she filled had, that bred her spight, / She [Venus] placed in her wings" (lines 140–42). Astery's wings, like Clarion's, are noted for their many colors and their brightness. Astery, in fact, stands behind Clarion as a predecessor in wingship; her tale is a prolegomenon to his. In language of the nursery (and of the epyllion), her tale explains how butterflies, including Clarion, got their beautiful wings. From this martyred heroine, butterflies derive their gentleness and fragility, their industry, their ability to ply the air, and especially the unique beauty of their characteristic feature, their bright wings.

The story of our hero resumes in line 145: "Thus the fresh *Clarion* being readie dight, / Unto his journey did himself addresse." Then the course of his flight and the variety of his pleasures are delineated for eight detail-packed stanzas. We watch him soaring over "the woods, the rivers, and the medowes green" (line 153), and eventually entering the "gay gardins" with their "sweete odors, / And alluring sights" (lines 161–64). He busily flies over the flower beds, whose plants are catalogued in two stanzas of distinctive epithets; and finally, sated with delight, he preens in the warm sunshine.

Clarion's story is again interrupted at this point, in this instance by three stanzas of musing by the poet for the edification of his readers. Word pictures give way to preaching. The poet first rhapsodizes about the joys of freedom and about the privileged position of man as lord of creation. In lines that Keats recalled on the title page of his 1817 volume of *Poems,* he asks: "What more felicitie can fall to creature, / Than to enjoy delight with libertie, / And to be Lord of all the workes of Nature" (lines 209–11). By way of indirect answer, the poet concludes seductively: "Who rests not pleased with such happines, / Well worthie he to taste of wretchednes" (lines 214–16). Not to feast on this world's pleasures is an affront to Nature's bounty and calls down retribution. This is a hero's thinking. But implicit in these lines is also a warning: to seek more than this world's pleasures is to defy the lot of mankind and impinge upon the godhead. With a quick shift of attitude, therefore, in the next stanza the poet bewails our vulnerability: "But what on earth can long abide in state? / Or who can him assure of happie day" (lines 217–18).[93] He warns about the slipperiness of prosperity and the unpredictability of fortune, "for thousand perills lie in close awaite / About us daylie, to worke our decay" (lines 221–22). Our future, he reminds us, rests in the hands of the gods. In this philosophical discussion, we have moved from the heroic to the tragic view of life.

The story of Clarion resumes once more with the announcement, full of foreboding, that his "cruell fate is woven even now / Of *Joves* owne hand" (lines 235–36). Aragnoll is introduced, though as yet we're not told his name or lineage. "As heavens had behight" (line 241), however, this garden is inhabited by an ugly spider, the epitome of evil described in a string of satanic epithets: "the foe of faire things, th'author of confusion, / The shame of Nature, the bondslave of spight" (lines 244–45). There is no doubt that of the "two mightie ones" mentioned in the opening stanzas, this is the character identified by his "hartswelling hate" (line 5), the predestined adversary of Clarion.

To predicate the ill will that consumes Aragnoll, we are treated to another lively narrative digression that explains "the cause why he this Flie so maliced" (line 257). There follows a lively account of the contention between Arachne and Minerva when the mortal nymph, too proud of her own ability at weaving, rashly challenged the goddess to a contest. The event is related at considerable length for twelve stanzas, and the tapestries that each of the contestants produced are presented to our view in remarkable examples of ekphrasis. We see in Arachne's work the rape of Europa, and in that of Minerva we see the council of the gods which made her (rather than Neptune) the patron deity of Athens. Arachne, of course, must concede defeat, and for punishment she changes into a spider. As in the case of Astery, we have another Ovidian metamorphosis. Arachne, in fact, stands behind Aragnoll and typifies his dominant characteristic just as Astery stands behind Clarion. She explains how Aragnoll came to embody envious wickedness. His name is a derivative of Arachne; she too, like Astery, is the eponymous heroine of a distinctive breed.

After the introduction of Aragnoll and the extended explanation of his spitefulness, the account of Clarion's fate recommences in line 353. Aragnoll weaves his web, which is described in depictive detail (lines 357–60) and is further substantiated by a complicated hyperbole (lines 361–68) and a classical allusion (lines 369–74). Now the crafty spider waits for his victim, and Clarion, "the foolish Flie without foresight" (line 389), soon appears. The epic genre is reactivated by means of a simile in the manner of Homer; while in the next stanza, tragedy is renewed as an operative genre by another invocation of the "Tragick Muse" (lines 401–16). Clarion then flies into the web; and after struggling valiantly but counterproductively until his "yougthly forces" are spent (line 431), he is swiftly slain by Aragnoll. In a final image which remains as a persistent residue of the poem, the poet presents the corpse of Clarion, "his bodie left the spectacle of care" (line 440). Unlike Astery, Clarion undergoes no metamorphosis into a continuing, if changed, existence.

What we have in "Muiopotmos," then, is a series of lively scenes imaging forth the major events of Clarion's life: the preparations for his journey, focusing on his wings; his experience in the gardens, especially his unstinted enjoyment of its sensual pleasures; and his cruel death, resulting from the machinations of Aragnoll.

These three episodes are interspersed with two narrative digressions, which separate and define them—to wit, the tale of Astery and the tale of Arachne. In the midst of the poem, as an intrusive centerpiece when Clarion rests in the gardens after satisfying his appetite, a philosophical digression debates the appropriate attitude toward Clarion's behavior in particular and toward the human condition in general. The shift from a scene depicting the "prowd ambition" of Clarion to a scene depicting his "lowest wretchednes" occurs in this philosophical digression, where the heroic view of mankind as "Lord of all the workes of Nature" gives way to a tragic view of mankind as a "fraile fleshly wight." The main fiction of the poem images this shift, projecting it into the three busy episodes that we have identified.

To raise the fiction of "Muiopotmos" above the level of insect life and make it worthy of the philosophical digression at its center, we need only recall that "butterfly" in Greek is ψυχή, which also means "soul."[94] Ever since Plato's *Phaedrus* (246A–247C), the soul appears iconographically as a winged creature striving to reach heaven—hence the emphasis on the wings of Astery and of Clarion, the two butterflies in the poem. It is the ability to fly that allows Clarion "to mount aloft unto the Christall skie" (line 44)— that is, to transcend the state of ordinary men, to aspire to bliss, to realize his heroic potential. But such an obsession violates the limits allowed to mortals. His wings are also what bring Clarion to the gardens, to temptation, to sensuality and even pride. The wings that put heaven within his reach also lead him to actions that call forth retribution, hence tragedy. So wings are both a blessing and a danger. They allow for activity beyond the lot of unwinged creatures, but they make the soul susceptible to excess. In any case, the fate of the butterfly in "Muiopotmos" figures forth the fate of the soul, led hither and yon by the gift of wings, by its aspiring thoughts of heaven. What happens to this butterfly presages what happens to the human soul when it leaves its empyreal home and sojourns in the physical world, all the while maintaining citizenship in the celestial realm though absent from it.[95]

The tale of Astery also supports this interpretation of the poem. Her name, from Latin *aster,* means "starry," and according to an ancient tradition taken over by poets, the souls of the very good are regularly apotheosized as stars. Her tale is an account of just such an ascent. Astery is accused of sensual love and, though guiltless, pays the penalty of death. Her industry and honesty do not protect her from the enmity of peers and the anger of Venus, from Aragnollian malice. Despite her gentleness and unmatched beauty—indeed, because of them—she suffers an undeserved fate. But her conduct is approved and memorialized. As soul and star, Astery reverts to her native element: she is "turn'd into a winged Butterflie, / In the wide aire to make her wandring flight" (lines 138–39). Since then, every butterfly has benefitted from her virtue, commemorated in those wings, the means by which the climb to heaven is accomplished. Astery exemplifies the soul in its unblemished, wholly blameless state—too good for this world.

In comparison, though, Clarion is much less innocent and his fate much more harsh. At first, the poet appears sympathetic to Clarion's wish to experience the world. His urge to travel abroad is seen as a natural impulse, "the kindly fire / Of lustfull yougth," and his adventurousness is preferred over the "loathsome sloth" of staying at home (lines 33–36). But once out of his father's house, Clarion develops rapidly into a figure of "prowd ambition." Already in his preparations for flight there is something of the hero's swagger with hints of impiety. He wears a breastplate like Achilles's, throws a lion's skin like Hercules's around his shoulders, and dons a helmet of the strongest metals in case he encounters "th'hayling darts of heaven beating hard" (line 80). He seeks to protect himself from the will of the gods, even "from yron death" (line 59). Most audacious of all, especially for a young hero, he flaunts his wings, which for magnificence surpass those of Cupid (lines 89–104). Wings that should be used in the search for heaven are used instead to challenge the god of earthly love.

As Clarion flits here and there, the poet grows increasingly censorious. He disapproves of Clarion's fickleness (lines 157–60), chides his "unstaid desire" (line 161), and exposes his insatiable appetite: "Evermore with most varietie, / And change of sweetnesse (for all change is sweete) / He casts his glutton sense to satisfie" (lines 177–79). Gluttony is a deadly sin; but Clarion gluts, then rests—only to compound his self-indulgence: "Againe he turneth to his play, / To spoyle the pleasures of that Paradise" (lines 185–86). Like our first parents, "whatso else of vertue good or ill / Grewe in this Gardin, fetcht from farre away, / Of everie one he takes, and tastes at will" (lines 201–3). Finally, fully sated, "when he hath both plaid and fed his fill" (line 205), Clarion luxuriates in the caressing heat of the sun.

The narrative also pauses at this climax of Clarion's "riotous suffisaunce" and "kingly joyaunce" (lines 207–8). Three stanzas of medieval didacticism moralize that mankind, though apparently blessed with freedom, may also be a hapless pawn of fortune. We are offered two distinct views of the human condition, which we have characterized generically as the heroic and the tragic. But which is more appropriate? more valid? Is Clarion to be admired as a hero or reprimanded as a sinner? The answer, of course, is ambiguous. Like Thenot at the end of Colin's dirge for Dido we are so baffled by the inextricable fusion of the doleful and the hopeful that we "ne wotte, / Whether rejoyce or weepe" ("November" 204–5). So we make no choice. The poetic image allows this equivocality. The fiction of Clarion's fate provides an overview of our mortal state that incorporates both the heroic and the tragic, where either is not only possible, but likely.

Spenser encapsulates this holistic view of life in one stunning word picture which stands out even among the vivid images of "Muiopotmos." For his second narrative digression, devoted to Arachne, Spenser went to Ovid and lifted wholesale the episode of the weaving contest between the mortal nymph and Minerva.[96] Nowhere is Spenser closer to an earlier text. In "Muiopotmos," as in Ovid, Arachne frames her tapestry "with a faire border wrought of sundrie flowres, / Enwoven with an Yvie trayle" (lines 298–99); and Minerva overgoes the maiden even in this detail—after completing her tapestry, "then all the storie / She compast with a wreathe of Olyves hoarie" (lines 327–28). But then Spenser makes a notable addition to his source in Ovid. Among those leaves, reflecting much that has already transpired in Spenser's poem, Minerva depicts a butterfly lifelike in its accurate detail. A self-contained stanza dwells upon the liveliness and handsomeness of this creature, which seems a sure analogue to Clarion:

> Emongst those leaves she made a Butterflie,
> With excellent device and wondrous slight,
> Fluttring among the Olives wantonly,
> That seem'd to live, so like it was in sight;
> The velvet nap which on his wings doth lie,

> The silken downe with which his backe is dight,
> His broad outstretched hornes, his hayrie thies,
> His glorious colours, and his glistering eies.
>
> (lines 329–36)

The description of this artificial butterfly is strongly reminiscent of Clarion in the attire which he had donned in preparation for his journey. It emblematizes his condition at the moment, "fluttring . . . wantonly" in the gardens.

But in Minerva's tapestry is Clarion at liberty to fly where he wishes, or is he ensnared among the leaves of the goddess's border? Is he a self-determined agent, or an unwitting victim of some fate already decreed? Free will, or predestination? Carefree spirit, or sodden flesh? Whatever his status, Arachne concedes victory to Minerva only when she sees this embroidered image of a butterfly resembling Clarion. This image brings her to an epiphanic recognition of some uncontestable circumstance. It seals her doom and leads to her transformation into a spider. For this reason, Clarion is blamed for Arachne's defeat; at the beginning of her tale, we are told that Aragnoll detests Clarion because "*Arachne, by his meanes was vanquished / Of Pallas*" (lines 261–62). Given the fact that Spenser invented this butterfly in Minerva's border and that it provides the immediate occasion for Arachne's submission to Minerva, the image assumes unusual importance for the interpretation of "Muiopotmos." It seems, however, to be a *signifiant* with a perplexingly uncertain *signifié*. The poet emphasizes the astonishing effect the image has upon Arachne, but offers no clue to any precise meaning for it.

Spenser again encapsulates the ambiguous view of Clarion's life in one memorable figure of speech. In the philosophical digression that serves as centerpiece for "Muiopotmos," the image of Clarion as one who "mount[s] aloft unto the Christall skie" (line 44) transmutes to an image of one whom "nought may . . . save from heavens avengement" (line 240). At the crux of this transmutation, Spenser apostrophizes Clarion in a daring oxymoron: "unhappie happie Flie" (line 234). The "hap" in this phrase is an Anglo-Saxon word that survives in such compounds as "hapless" and "haphazard," and that means approximately what "fortune" means in "fortunate" and "unfortunate" (cf. line 421). Clarion is "happie" because he is fortunate in his birth, his resources, his pleasures—in his position as hero. But he is also "unhappie," being marked for "heavens avengement," the fate of the tragic victim. That both these states are simultaneous is indicated by the tight construction of the oxymoron: Clarion is at once happy and unhappy. The generations of mankind are condensed into this prototypical creature, Clarion, and the human condition is contracted into this figure of speech, with its violent contrariety and yet with an inner resonance that allows for coexistence of the contraries if not their reconciliation.[97] This oxymoron embodies the tension between the tragic and the heroic in the poem. More economically than Pope, it shows that man is both the glory and the jest, but finally the riddle of the world.

An oxymoron, like the image of Minerva's butterfly with no specified meaning, throws us into a paroxysm of interpretative frenzy. It calls attention to itself as an extraordinary ploy, a teasing clue to the poet's meaning; and yet it refuses resolution. To force a reconciliation between the contraries within the oxymoron is simply to intensify its self-contradiction. So we are caught in a spiral of indeterminacy. From the start, however, to inveigle us into this activity has been the ulterior aim of "Muiopotmos."

From its title and opening stanzas, "Muiopotmos" activates certain expectations through its generic signals, but these signals are systematically jammed. Furthermore, we get no help from outside the text, such as references to historical events or persons. As our initial expectations from the text are challenged and discarded, we grow increasingly uncertain, wary, and alert. We read more and more critically. In our effort to understand, we concentrate upon the verbal system provided by the poet. With utmost heed, we watch him at his making, proposing and disposing. We observe how he manipulates his materials to produce both tragic and heroic effects. The indeterminacy of many passages, the inconclusiveness of many images, requires our participation in the assignment of meaning. By such apprenticeship, we acquire that most characteristic and necessary of human skills, the ability to imitate.

The Faerie Queene bears a considerable resemblance to *The Shepheardes Calender,* which is not surprising since Spenser was busily at work on both in the winter 1579. In the longer poem he retains the emphasis on formal properties; indeed, he retains the form of twelve semiautonomous parts conjoined into a whole. As we know from the "Letter of the Authors" addressed to Raleigh, Spenser planned twelve books in which twelve knights pursue their individual quests, setting out from and returning to the court of Gloriana.[98] However, the story line of *The Faerie Queene* is more highly articulated than that of *The Shepheardes Calender*, often so richly developed that we lose the thread.

An even more radical departure appears in painterly features of *The Faerie Queene*. Individual characters and events persist in our mind as vital images. The epic, of course, not only allows but demands a greater dependence upon pictorial elements, and the Italian romance reinforces the expectation of vividness. In addition, however, Spenser had become more keenly aware of the effectiveness of depictive poetry. I would suggest that this willingness to explore poetry's depictive potential came in considerable part from an acquaintance with Sidney's literary theory in the *Defence* and probably to an equal degree with his literary example in the *Arcadia*.[99]

Spenser begins his letter to Raleigh somewhat defensively, by explaining the obvious: he has written an allegory. Knowing how readily allegories are misconstrued, he has thought it prudent to provide some guidance for interpreting his *Faerie Queene*. He will therefore in this letter "discover" to his reader "the general intention and meaning" of the work at large. Perhaps recalling Sidney's disparagement of allegories, Spenser is also apologetic, it seems to me, embarrassed by the clumsiness and obsolescence of his allegorical method. He closes this letter with another round of defensive concern: "Thus much Sir, I have briefly overronne to direct your understanding to the wel-head of the History, that from thence gathering the whole intention of the conceit, ye may as in a handfull gripe al the discourse, which otherwise may happily seeme tedious and confused." Uncomfortably aware of the new poetics that Sidney had proposed, Spenser hopes to protect himself from the charge that his work lacks poetical sinews.

In any case, Spenser hastens to assert that his purpose in *The Faerie Queene* is "to fashion a gentleman or noble person in vertuous and gentle discipline," a purpose in line with the cult of the gentleman that by the 1570s had been imported wholesale from

Italy. Sidney had similarly insisted that the aim of literature must be to encourage virtue, so *The Faerie Queene* falls in with such a program for poetry according to the principles of civic humanism. It may be construed as a courtesy book leading not only to well-knowing, but to well-doing, as Spenser is quick to claim.

In order to achieve this purpose, Spenser has chosen to present his doctrine in what he calls "an historicall fiction." We must look at this phrase carefully, though, because it implies an allegiance to poetical practices that are at odds with the tradition of allegory. The word "fiction" derives from *fictus,* past participle of *fingere,* and it indicates the product of poetical making. In the *Defence* Sidney uses the word three times (79.6, 89.24, 103.14), in two instances in immediate conjunction with "imitation," giving the word an Aristotelian cast. "Fiction" was a new and quasi-technical term called into use by the poetics of making (pages 60–61).

The word "historical" is of course the adjectival form of "history," a word Spenser uses several times in his letter. In Elizabethan usage, "history" does not necessarily imply a record of actual events, as we might assume. Rather, the word derives from the Latin *historia,* which means little more than our modern "story," a narrative comprising a sequence of episodes that may be either true or feigned.[100] "An historicall fiction," then, is a story which has been made by an author as opposed to the accurate account of an actual occurrence, with Aristotle's differentiation between poetry and history as the basis for the distinction. Later in the Letter, Spenser will differentiate between the method of "a Poet historical" and that of "an Historiographer" in exactly these terms. In writing *The Faerie Queene,* in fact, Spenser claims to "have followed all the antique Poets historicall," and he lists Homer and Vergil and Ariosto and Tasso—exactly the sort of makers whom Sidney advocates as models. They are authors of fictive narratives.

When we scrutinize Spenser's comments about his own poetical method, we come to suspect that he may not have fully accepted or completely understood Sidney's program for poetry. After announcing that his general intention is to fashion a gentleman, Spenser confides that he will follow the rhetorical principle of garbing his *res* in *verba.* Because he is rather feckless about the syntax, we need to examine his exact statement: "The general end therefore of all the booke is to fashion a gentleman or noble person in vertuous and gentle discipline: Which for that I conceived shoulde be most plausible and pleasing, being coloured with an historicall fiction." To accomplish his disciplinary aim, Spenser says, he will present the doctrine in story form, "being coloured with an historicall fiction." The word "coloured" here is telling; it belongs to the jargon of the schoolroom and implies that the "colours" of rhetoric will be used to paint a vivid sequence of episodes in the manner of epic poets.

This is, I suppose, a reasonable approximation of Sidney's program for a poetry of enargeiac images. But Spenser proves to be uncomfortable and impatient with it, feeling as though he must comply with this poetics out of deference to a debased popular taste. Rather dourly, he says that he will use the colours of rhetoric to paint "an historicall fiction, the which the most part of men delight to read, rather for a variety of matter, then for profite of the ensample." The sage and serious Spenser would prefer to preach rather than poetize. But remembering Sidney's advice that the platitudes of the philosopher "lie dark before the imaginative and judging power, if they be not illuminated or figured forth by the speaking picture of poesy" (*Defence* 86.6–8), Spenser grudgingly decides to adopt Sidney's precepts for a mimetic poetry. The new poetics of image-making was not easy for Spenser, however, given his particular talent and expertise. Only "Muiopotmos" augurs well for success in this endeavor.

Later in the letter to Raleigh, the malaise Spenser felt with the method of a poet historical again surfaces. "To some I know this Methode will seeme displeasaunt," he says, "which had rather have good discipline delivered plainly in way of precepts, or sermoned at large." Spenser appears in sympathy with this conservative group, the parishioners of Bishop Alley (pages 229–30), who want their doctrine stated forthrightly, as they were accustomed to have it, or maybe expressed in the familiar fable or parable they knew from the pulpit—but not stated in fiction. Reluctantly, though, he defers to the changing times: "But such, me seeme, should be satisfide with the use of these dayes, seeing all things accounted by their showes, and nothing esteemed of, that is not delightfull and pleasing to commune sence." The newfangledness of the times gives preference to the glitter of superficial appearance, Spenser complains, while unadorned truth goes unnoticed. In the new empiricist aesthetic, nothing is deemed delightful or pleasing except that which presents itself to the common sense, that faculty of the soul which receives sense data from the phenomenal world and transmits it wholesale to the imagination. Spenser himself would prefer a more direct mode of presenting his doctrine. He could state his meaning forthrightly without the aid of poetical fictions, or he could write in the customary vein of allegory where appeal is made to the intelligent soul rather than to the faculties of sense. But since all things are now judged by their visibilia, "their showes," he reluctantly adopts a depictive poetics. And he exhorts his readers to bear with him, to be "satisfide with the use of these dayes." His conciliatory reasoning, taken over from Sidney, is forthright: "So much more profitable and gratious is doctrine by ensample, then by rule."

The uncertainty and discontent displayed here by Spenser suggest that he was not wholly at ease with his expository method—indeed, that his modus operandi, if not his intention, may well have changed over the ten years that elapsed between his inception of *The Faerie Queene* and the publication of a first installment. He began as an allegorist, purveying "good discipline . . . clowdily enwrapped in Allegoricall devises," as he says in the Letter, but wound up a poet historical.

It's true that as late as the 1570s the classical poets whom Spenser mentions, Homer and Vergil in particular, were still regularly allegorized. Tasso also had provided an allegorical interpretation for the *Gerusalemme Liberata,* and Ariosto was often read in a similar way into the 1590s, as Harington's comments before his translation of the *Orlando Furioso* indicate. Even the most famous among the poets historical had been perverted to allegorical ends. But Xenophon's *Cyropaedia,* now taken as an exemplary text, was not to be read with the same expectations and according to the same principles, as Sidney and others well knew. The *Cyropaedia* did not submit to a polysemous layering that imposed level upon level of meaning, as Landino had interpreted the *Aeneid* in Books 3 and 4 of the *Disputationes Camaldulenses.* Rather, Xenophon's work was seen in Aristotelian light as "the portraiture of a just empire," to use Sidney's phrase lifted from Cicero (*Defence* 81.29); or in the echoing words of Spenser in this letter to Raleigh,

Xenophon "in the person of Cyrus and the Persians fashioned a governement such as might best be." Spenser, like Sidney, recognized that the *Cyropaedia* required a new order of reading. Cyrus under the new dispensation was an imitation, an image of good government in action as it might be or should be. Spenser framed the coadunating figure of his narrative according to this model: "I labour to pourtraict in Arthure, before he was king, the image of a brave knight." Similarly Spenser speaks of "portraiture" when he presents the first three books of his *Faerie Queene* and their respective heroes: "The first of the knight of the Redcrosse, in whome I expresse Holynes: The seconde of Sir Guyon, in whome I sette forth Temperaunce: The third of Britomartis a Lady knight, in whome I picture Chastity."

What we perceive in this letter, I propose, is a sequence of developmental phases in the composition of *The Faerie Queene*. Spenser first desired to write a nationalistic epic that would demonstrate the literary maturity of the English language, approve certain codes of behavior for his Protestant countrymen, flatter Elizabeth and the more important members of her court, and incidentally further his own career according to the Vergilian pattern. The October eclogue touches upon all these matters. So in the winter 1579–80, flush with the hope of Leicester's patronage and Sidney's encouragement, Spenser launched an ambitious project that would submit to an allegorical interpretation such as Landino had devised for Vergil's *Aeneid* and Dante's *Divina commedia*. Following this model, he naturally devised a complex plan in compliance with the Augustinian aesthetic of multeity in unity. Spenser the artificer chose as his object of imitation the form of supernal beauty as it is manifested in the harmonies that resonate within the cosmic number 12.[101] This initial plan, which Spenser refers to as the "conceit" of the poem, is openly alluded to in several passages of the letter to Raleigh (indeed, it dominates the letter), and it survives on the title page in the descriptive phrase which announces that *The Faerie Queene* is "disposed into twelve bookes, Fashioning XII. Morall vertues." This plan would have invited the sort of polysemous analysis to which epic poems were then subjected.[102] It is essentially a neoplatonist scheme, expressing idea as palpable artifact and deploying content as metaphor for form. In such a poem, parts correspond to other parts and interrelate to produce larger wholes—just the sort of harmonious form that characterizes Spenser's early work. Spenser may have thought in terms of perceiving this plan as a vision—just as Arthur in a vision becomes aware of the heavenly beauty that is Gloriana, and Britomart in a similar transcendence first feels the heavenly love vested in Artegall. And Spenser may have thought in terms of inducing a *divino furore* in his audience in order to share this vision, so that his reader too might experience directly the platonist values of goodness and truth and beauty.[103]

That is where Spenser began. But in the fateful year 1579–80 he became aware of Sidney and learned of the neo-Aristotelian poetics that Sidney meddles with platonist principles in the *Defence*. So willy-nilly and over a period of time, Spenser revised his expository method for *The Faerie Queene,* if not his overall plan—and produced a much more sophisticated poem as a result. He expanded his repertoire of poetic techniques, experimenting with a "Mother Hubberds Tale" and a "Muiopotmos" as well as playing it safe with a "Teares of the Muses." In time he learned to produce speaking pictures of a suasive sort. For this reason he was hailed by readers in his own day for his effectiveness as a Protestant moralist. He was to Drayton, for example, "grave morall *Spencer.*"[104] And he continued to be praised by readers in the seventeenth century, who enjoyed gossipy narrative,[105] and honored by readers in the eighteenth century, who searched the world of letters for platitudinous tales;[106] and he was enshrined by readers in the nineteenth century, who adored beautiful things. In any case, the chameleonlike quality of *The Faerie Queene,* which appeals to every taste (including that of present-day theorists who are fascinated by the poem because it deconstructs so readily), is due to Spenser's gradual relinquishment of allegorism and his emergence over time as a poet historical under the tutelage of Sidney's *Defence.*[107]

I would like now to turn from what Spenser became and revert to his starting point, concentrating upon those formal properties of *The Faerie Queene* that he insists upon in the letter to Raleigh. These incipient patterns and the resultant network of correspondences emanate from Spenser's initial scheme of writing twelve books to represent the twelve private virtues of Arthur before he was king.[108] As a significant form, according to the neoplatonist aesthetic of Augustine, this scheme generates meaning in its own right, so no comprehensive interpretation of the poem can afford to ignore it. Actually, it provides an encompassing whole in which each of the parts inheres, so no particular episode can be properly interpreted without reference to the total system which contains that episode and regulates the conditions which allow it to exist. To ignore the form of *The Faerie Queene* is to obliterate the centrality of Gloriana's court, and incidentally to remove Queen Elizabeth as a continuous factor in the poem.

Returning to the "Letter of the Authors," we soon are told that Spenser "chose the historye of king Arthure, as most fitte for the excellency of his person, being made famous by many mens former workes." Defying the humanists' censure of the Arthurian matter for its frequent licentiousness (page 551 [n. 20]), Spenser selected Arthur for his hero because he belonged to the English past and furthered Spenser's nationalistic aims. He also was progenitor of the Tudor line, and therefore served Spenser's more precise purpose of flattering the Queen. But Spenser's use of Arthur satisfies a much more subtle aim than that. He is content that discloses form.

Many scholars have noted the difficulty of writing a national epic when a queen is on the throne, even when that queen is so doughty as Elizabeth.[109] According to the canons of the day, a queen, being female, should be fixed and passive, like Aeneas's Dido or like a sonneteer's mistress. Only men roam the seas or the countryside. So Spenser hit upon the ruse of idealizing his queen as a personification, Gloriana, who (as he pointedly explains in the Letter) represents in polysemous fashion every sort of glory from the most mundane to the most celestial. She is the summation of glory: feminine, military, heavenly, etc. And he fixes her at a court from which she never moves, as befits an absolute (Gloriana's constancy is the ultimate compliment to Elizabeth). Yet, a continuous cavalcade of males set out from this court and return to it. As Spenser explains in his next to last sentence of the Letter, Gloriana's court is "the wel-head of the History."[110] According to Spenser's original plan, twelve knights venture forth successively at Gloriana's bidding, complete their assigned quests, and return to take their place in the stable system that she centers. So Gloriana, like great Nature herself in the "Mutabilitie Cantos," is "still mooving, yet unmoved from her sted; / Unseene of any, yet of all beheld" (7.7.13.3–4). Her court is the φύσις that animates Fairyland and produces the context that makes its existence possible.

Furthermore, Arthur moves inexorably toward that court, having seen Gloriana in a vision. He travels the seemingly endless byways of Fairyland in search of the lady whom he knows at this point only in concept, as heavenly beauty. In the course of these travels he appears and disappears in the narrative, and interweaves the twelve books of the poem into a continuous discourse. At his destination he will arrive in the actual presence of his lady and claim her for his bride, just as the lover in *Amoretti* achieves wedded bliss in *Epithalamion*. Arthur, then, is Gloriana's potential mate, her intended counterpart. The epic poet, by honoring and revealing him, can coordinately honor and reveal Gloriana, and consequently the historical Elizabeth.

But how to insure that Arthur is worthy to be the mate, the male counterpart, of that permanence and completeness, that perfection, represented by Gloriana? This is where the aesthetic of multeity in unity is most helpful, or perhaps where the full complexity of that paradox is best revealed. As Spenser states in his letter to Raleigh, just as he uses Gloriana to represent glory of every sort, so he uses Arthur to represent the inclusive male virtue, magnificence. "So in the person of Prince Arthure," he says, "I sette forth magnificence in particular, which vertue for that (according to Aristotle and the rest) it is the perfection of all the rest, and conteineth in it them all." Spenser's narrative strategy, quite simply, will be to use a separate knight to exemplify each of the twelve subsidiary virtues that he identifies as the constituents of the inclusive virtue, magnificence. Spenser will demonstrate one of the subsidiary virtues in each of twelve books—in his words, "Of the xii. other vertues, I make xii. other knights the patrones, for the more variety of the history." But between Arthur and the other twelve knights there is a relation of whole to parts, corresponding to the relation between magnificence and its constituent virtues. Arthur infolds the other twelve knights. Or conversely, they unfold him.[111] They are the content of his form, the palpable manifestation of the idea that he recessively represents. Their activities are a demonstration of how the inclusive virtue of magnificence "is the perfection of all the rest, and conteineth in it them all."

So when Arthur appears in each book to aid the exemplar of

that book's virtue, he acquires that virtue. As Spenser explains, "In the whole course I mention the deedes of Arthur applyable to that vertue, which I write of in that booke." And while Arthur rides through the total of twelve books (as projected), he accumulates the constituent virtues of which magnificence is comprised, thereby perfecting his own virtue. He will literally "perfect" (<L. perficere) his wholeness, working through its constituent parts and assimilating them. Eventually, like Gloriana, he becomes perfection personified.

Moreover, the narrative of how Arthur enfolds the twelve other knights serves as a metaphor for the paradox of multeity in unity, disclosing that sacred form. Abstracted, the speaking pictures of the history reveal the form of that supernal beauty which Spenser set out to imitate. So Arthur, as exemplar of the inclusive virtue, magnificence, subsumes his knightly peers and becomes a whole greater than the sum of its twelve parts. As the perfected unity arising out of that multeity, he fulfills the pattern of heavenly beauty that qualifies him to be a fit mate for Gloriana. And to go yet one step farther in clinching his perfection, the two in their marriage will produce the exhaustiveness and self-sufficiency of the alchemical hermaphrodite, imaging the eternality and beatitude of the marriage between God and Sapience at the conclusion of *Fowre Hymnes*. Arthur's superquest should eventuate in an image of cosmic love forever joining the male and female principles in stable yet fruitful union.

There is one point yet to be made about the comprehensive scheme of *The Faerie Queene* as Spenser projected it, a form essential to Spenser's plan from his inception of the poem. The prominence given to the number 12 must be explored. Spenser in the Letter is thinking of his artifact as a whole: his purpose announced at the beginning is "to discover unto you the general intention and meaning which in the whole course therof I have fashioned, without expressing of any particular purposes or by-accidents therein occasioned." Nonetheless, he stresses the fact that there are twelve parts to this whole. Repeatedly in the Letter, Spenser speaks of "twelve bookes," and the title page, as we have noticed, immediately calls attention to the fact that the poem is "disposed into twelve bookes, Fashioning XII. Morall vertues." This emphasis upon the number 12 takes on special significance when we read in the Letter that in point of *chronological* time the events of the story should actually begin where in point of *narrative* time the poem ends. "The beginning therefore of my history," Spenser advises, "if it were to be told by an Historiographer, should be the twelfth booke, which is the last." And he continues to anatomize this projected twelfth book, "where I devise that the Faery Queene kept her Annuall feaste xii. dayes, uppon which xii. severall dayes, the occasions of the xii. severall adventures hapned, which being undertaken by xii. several knights, are in those xii. books severally handled and discoursed."

The repetition of the number 12 is so obtrusive that it cries out for interpretation, and of course it has to do with the "Annuall feaste" held by Gloriana.[112] The annual feast comprises twelve days, so it has duration, just as the year is unfolded in twelve months. Gloriana's feast is an analogue for the annual calendar. Like the calendar, it is repeated annually, when the same pattern recurs; while there is continual motion, there is also a sameness, a stasis. Like the twelve-part calendar that Colin Clout enacts, it becomes an integer of eternity.

This image of time as simultaneously durational and static is fleshed out, figured forth, by the twelve knights who depart from Gloriana's court to do her bidding, and yet who inevitably return—indeed, never manage to completely leave her sphere of influence, which is Fairyland. Dame Nature in her final judgment in the "Mutabilitie Cantos" explains the delicate mechanism at work. "I well consider all that ye have sayd," she assures the disruptive challenger, Change,

> And find that all things stedfastnes doe hate
> And changed be: yet being rightly wayd
> They are not changed from their first estate;
> But by their change their being doe dilate:
> And turning to themselves at length againe,
> Doe worke their owne perfection so by fate:
> Then over them Change doth not rule and raigne;
> But they raigne over change, and doe their states maintaine.
>
> (7.7.58)

Change is necessary, concludes Dame Nature, for the completion of a pattern, for "perfecting" it. So each knight sets out from Glo-

riana's court in order to "dilate his being," to "work his own perfection," as prescribed by a beneficent fate.[113] Orderly change in
accord with divine decree is essential to realizing an ordained end.
The ordered passage of time—the four seasons of the year, the
twelve months, the seven ages of a man's life, the shepherd's calendar—each in its form of moving pattern that eventuates in
stasis verifies the providential plan. To demonstrate this truth, in
The Faerie Queene as in *The Shepheardes Calender,* was one of
Spenser's overriding aims. The beginning of his history, as he
points out, resides in his twelfth book. His beginning and end coincide. In the end, perhaps, is his beginning.[114] As in the "Mutabilitie Cantos" he leads us to the Sabbath's sight.

This ambiguity in the time frame of *The Faerie Queene*—time
is ever-moving, and yet forever still—accounts for the confusion
in the sequence of quests by the individual knights. According to
the letter to Raleigh, the annual feast of Gloriana lasts for twelve
days, and one knight sets out on his adventure on each of those
days. But clearly, as we read the poem, the quest of each knight
goes on for more than one day, so several of the knights (and perhaps all of them) are abroad at once. Yet in the course of the poem
itself the quest of one knight seems to finish when the quest of
another begins, almost as though one must finish in order to make
way for his successor. This phenomenon is especially evident at
the end of Book 1 and the beginning of Book 2, when Red Crosse
meets Guyon and speeds him on his way: "God guide thee, *Guyon,* well to end thy warke" (2.1.32.8), says the knight of holiness
as he gives over to the knight exemplifying temperance. This end-
to-end joining of quests at this initial point in the narrative establishes an expectation of how the remaining quests are tandemly
arranged in sequence. But this sequentiality of quests, and yet
their simultaneity, are a reflection of the double coordinates of
time in the poem, a pattern that we have explained as a calendar
which constantly evolves through its twelve months, and yet as a
totality is the integer of eternity. There is both a diachronic movement and a synchronic stability in the narrative.

This same form governs the arrangement of episodes in the narrative. The episodes of *The Faerie Queene* are not related like the
episodes in an Aristotelian plot.[115] One episode does not arise out
of what comes before and prepare for what follows; there's no

frame of cause and effect. There is, in fact, an obvious lack of any unity in the action. Rather, the narrative is governed by some principle of fecundity, just the opposite to unity of action. There is no beginning, middle, and end in this narrative construction, no concern about a plot of appropriate magnitude that can be readily comprehended. Disregarding Aristotelian prescriptions, in *The Faerie Queene* each episode is related to the total form in which it inheres, as part is related to whole. To be specific, each episode occurs within the sphere of Gloriana's court and must acquire its meaning within that system of values, just as each eclogue of *The Shepheardes Calender* acquires meaning by virtue of its participation in the year (pages 319–21). And the reward of reading *The Faerie Queene*, the means by which it fashions gentlemen, is perception of this form that demonstrates the relation between wandering knights and eternal glory, between fragmented multeity and comprehensive unity, between erring mortal and beatific deity. Despite the confusing welter of apparently haphazard events in our phenomenal world, the poem assures us that there is an underlying order—a mighty maze, admittedly, but not without a plan.

In *The Faerie Queene,* as in poems so dissimilar as *The Shepheardes Calender* and "Muiopotmos," Spenser performs the duty of the Christian poet to assert eternal providence. But Spenser's optimism had been undercut between the time of beginning *The Faerie Queene* at the start of his career and the publication of the poem as we know it. Several scholars have noted the darkening of Spenser's spirit in the later books.[116] No doubt personal circumstances had a great deal to do with his loss of simple faith in the providential scheme which the poem originally would have touted. His separation from Leicester's employ, the hardship of life in Ireland, his isolation from kindred spirits in London—all this and more inevitably had a sobering effect on Spenser's initial plan.[117] Any poem that's still a-writing after sixteen years is bound to meander from what the poet had in mind at the start. Whatever the extraneous circumstances to which Spenser was responding, however, the poetics of Sidney gave him a means of accommodating his original scheme to a revised intention. Increasingly, he became a maker in order to imitate, as Sidney had advised.

Spenser frequently heeds Sidney's prescription for a mimetic poetry of images, and many passages of *The Faerie Queene* have a visual component that turns the verbal system into a speaking picture. Not only are there notable instances of ekphrasis and set pieces of emblematic writing, but often an episode speaks eloquently to the mind's eye. In his letter to Raleigh, Spenser gives several examples of "adventures," which, he explains, "are intermedled [in the whole], but rather as Accidents, then intendments"; and he proceeds to offer a list: "the love of Britomart, the overthrow of Marinell, the misery of Florimell, the vertuousnes of Belphoebe, the lasciviounes of Hellenora, and many the like." To paraphrase Sidney (*Defence* 79.1–4), Nature never brought forth so true a lover as Britomart, so proud a knight as Marinell, so miserable a lady as Florimell, so virtuous a virgin as Belphoebe, or so lascivious a matron as Hellenore. These figures are presented as some sort of Philostratian icon in their characteristic activity; as summarized here, they function as emblems for their respective vice or virtue. The vividness of these actions, which remain in our memory as images, led the Romantics to view *The Faerie Queene* as a gallery of pictures.[118]

But in his use of language, Spenser is not so far advanced as Sidney. In *The Faerie Queene* his *res* and *verba* do not often coalesce into an indissoluble compound. Like the rhetorician, Spenser still thinks in terms of clothing his invention in words, of coloring his doctrine with the brushes of rhetoric. If his fiction is a speaking picture, it is because he has painted it with the generous palette of schemes and tropes. At least one informed seventeenth-century reader complained about the separability of Spenser's meaning from his fiction. "His Moral lay so bare," grumbles Sir William Temple, "that it lost the Effect."[119] After a century of Sidney's sort of fictioneering, Spenser seemed too obvious to a man of taste. His doctrine could be too easily extracted from its fictive vehicle.

The actual language that Spenser uses, in fact, is notably unnotable. His vocabulary is disappointingly bland, a transparent veil which he lays over his meaning as undistortingly as possible and through which the reader is invited to peer without distraction to perceive the underlying meaning. With few exceptions—"blatant" being the one that proves the rule—Spenser's language is ordinary, trite, careful not to call attention to itself. Analysis of a passage will demonstrate my point.

One of the most memorable passages in *The Faerie Queene* recounts Calidore's vision of Colin Clout piping on Mount Acidale while a hundred damsels dance around the Graces, who in turn encircle Rosalind. Most readers agree that this episode is the high point of Book 6, if not of the entire poem.[120] If Spenser were indeed a painterly poet, this opportunity should exercise his visual imagination and descriptive skills. Yet what does Acidale look like? How does Spenser describe it? He devotes five stanzas to this setting, and they typify his impoverished lexicon:

> One day as he did raunge the fields abroad,
>   Whilest his faire *Pastorella* was elsewhere,
>   He chaunst to come, far from all peoples troad,
>   Vnto a place, whose pleasaunce did appere
>   To passe all others, on the earth which were:
>   For all that euer was by natures skill
>   Deuized to worke delight, was gathered there,
>   And there by her were poured forth at fill,
> As if this to adorne, she all the rest did pill.
>
> It was an hill plaste in an open plaine,
>   That round about was bordered with a wood
>   Of matchlesse hight, that seem'd th'earth to disdaine,
>   In which all trees of honour stately stood,
>   And did all winter as in sommer bud,
>   Spredding pavilions for the birds to bowre,
>   Which in their lower braunches sung aloud;
>   And in their tops the soring hauke did towre,
> Sitting like King of fowles in maiesty and powre.
>
> And at the foote thereof, a gentle flud
>   His siluer waues did softly tumble downe,
>   Vnmard with ragged mosse or filthy mud,
>   Ne mote wylde beastes, ne mote the ruder clowne
>   Thereto approch, ne filth mote therein drowne:
>   But Nymphes and Faeries by the bancks did sit,
>   In the woods shade, which did the waters crowne,
>   Keeping all noysome things away from it,
> And to the waters fall tuning their accents fit.
>
> And on the top thereof a spacious plaine
>   Did spred it selfe, to serue to all delight,
>   Either to daunce, when they to daunce would faine,

> Or else to course about their bases light;
> Ne ought there wanted, which for pleasure might
> Desired be, or thence to banish bale:
> So pleasauntly the hill with equall hight,
> Did seeme to ouerlooke the lowly vale;
> Therefore it rightly cleeped was mount *Acidale.*

> They say that *Venus,* when she did dispose
> Her selfe to pleasaunce, vsed to resort
> Vnto this place, and therein to repose
> And rest her selfe, as in a gladsome port,
> Or with the Graces there to play and sport;
> That euen her owne Cytheron, though in it
> She vsed most to keepe her royall court,
> And in her soueraine Maiesty to sit,
> She in regard hereof refusde and thought vnfit.
>
> (6.10.5–9)

This presentation of Acidale offers little more than a pastiche of literary clichés. Whereas Spenser's characters often persist in the mind's eye because he describes their distinctive actions, his settings rarely display any particularity or vividness. The antipictorial quality of such passages, as here, is due largely to a jaded vocabulary.

Spenser begins this passage with the storyteller's formula: "One day as he did raunge the fields . . ."; and he continues to rely heavily upon a series of formulaic devices, opening the last stanza with the impersonal *On dit* borrowed from French romance. On infrequent occasions Spenser resorts to metaphors: the trees "spread pavilions to bower the birds," the hawk "towers" in the tree tops, a stream flows at the "foot" of Mount Acidale, and the woods "crown" the banks of the stream. Less frequently he employs what we call similes: the hawk sits "like King of fowles," and Venus reposes on the hillside "as in a gladsome port." But none of this calls for or submits to close scrutiny. Expectedly, Spenser provides an etymology for "Acidale" (8.7–9), although its relevance is anything but clear; and he introduces conventional alliteration—for example, "place" and "pleasaunce" (5.4), "devized" and "delight" (5.7), and "banish bale" (8.6).

Spenser often joins adjective to noun and produces a number of epithets—"faire *Pastorella,*" "an open plaine," "the soring hauke," "a gentle flud," "silver waves," "ragged mosse," "filthy mud," "wylde beastes," "the ruder clowne," "a spacious plaine," "the lowly vale," "royall court," "soveraine Majesty"—none of them with the slightest glimmer of originality. But other than these colorless epithets, there is a paucity of descriptive modifiers, of graphic adjectives and adverbs—almost, it seems to me, as though Spenser were intentionally avoiding them. Those that do occur are the most ordinary among the possibilities, flattening the picture rather than particularizing and highlighting it. For instance, in the opening lines of stanza 7 (where, incidentally, we have the highest concentration of adjectives and adverbs), Spenser describes the stream that runs at the foot of Acidale as "a gentle flud" with "silver waves" that "softly tumble downe." "Gentle" and "silver" and "softly" are hardly novel words to excite the reader to imagine a distinct picture. Furthermore, Spenser describes the purity of the stream in terms of what is not present, which is counterproductive if he wants us to see it. The stream is "unmard with ragged mosse or filthy mud"—again, "ragged" and "filthy" are only so-so as depictive modifiers.

Finally, the association of this place with Venus and the Graces in stanza 9 adds nothing to the graphic description of the scene, but rather undermines it by turning the account into legend. The appropriate referent is not some hill that we might know from our own experience; instead, it is those fabled hills in Vergil and Ovid. The appropriate milieu of this passage is not natural, what the eye *per*ceives, but literary, what the mind *con*ceives.[121]

Actually, this passage, for those well-read in the classical poets (as Spenser's audience certainly were), is a literary topos: the easily recognized *locus amoenus,* the earthly paradise of both pastoral and epic. We have the familiar trees and birds and stream, devoid of "all noysome things" (7.8). There is no need to visualize it; from our reading we know where we are. The significance of the passage is immediately apparent without violating the integrity of its own medium, without converting from verbal to visual. How *can* we visualize it, at least adequately, since this place beggars description. The point of the *locus amoenus* is that only heroes find it, because it exists beyond what you and I can ever know except as an intellectual construct in a literary context. That is what Calidore learns at the top of Acidale.

But there may be method in Spenser's indifference to language.

By being transparent the verbal system offers no resistance to our entering into Fairyland. We look through the verbal veil—go through it without hindrance, like Alice through the looking-glass—and, linguistically lulled, we emerge into a world of concepts. In his pose as storyteller, Spenser perforce suggests an illusion of concrete detail. He allows us to extrapolate to a visual image if we (like the Romantics) are so inclined, thereby resorting to the sense-perceptible, feeling the poem along our pulses. To do so, however, is to wander aimlessly in a picture gallery. And significantly, *The Faerie Queene* did not carry illustrations when it first appeared, despite the fact that Spenser's avowed models— Vergil, Ovid, Ariosto, and Tasso—were regularly illustrated.[122] With Spenser, though, as with the fabulist, it is the moral that finally counts, not the pictures, or even the tale. Those readers of sturdier intellect will proceed directly from verbal image to meaning, without recourse to the slower and less certain route via the visual image. They will go directly from Acidale to the fragileness of courtesy. The invisibility of the actual vocabulary acts as an invitation to speculate immediately upon the inventions—the conceits, the ideas, the forms—that are modestly apparelled in Spenser's words.

Spenser began his poetic career, then, not surprisingly under the influence of neoplatonist principles that he could have found in Landino's paraphernalia before his edition of Dante's *Divina commedia*. Spenser's allegiance to a fundamentally Augustinian aesthetic accounts for the initial plan of twelve books for *The Faerie Queene*. After acquaintance with Sidney, however, Spenser modified his expository technique and sought to follow the new poetics of fictioneering, of "representing, counterfeiting, or figuring forth to speak metaphorically." But his initial plan was so intractable that he never managed to produce a plot in any sense acceptable to an Aristotelian. So his "historical fiction" for the most part retains the dichotomization of verbal and visual that we find in the emblem. It rarely achieves that exact convertibility between verbal and visual that we expect of speaking pictures.

Nonetheless, some of Spenser's individual episodes achieve a vivacity that appeals to the mind's eye and affects the memory. Following Sidney's prescription, he adopts a mode of characterization that reveals a character as virtuous or vicious by means of what he or she does. Character flows from action. Although no one is likely to claim that Spenser's characters portray any of the psychological realism that motivates action in the later novel, they do make an advance over the static characters of allegory who merely personify this or that quality. They are, again to use Sidney's words, "notable images of virtues, vices, or what else"; and the most complex of them, such as Britomart or Amoret, are just as individual and lifelike, no more nor less, than the denizens of *Arcadia*. They inhabit the same poetical intermundum between fantasy and the phenomenal world.

As his career progressed, Spenser was groping toward an art of poetry based upon Aristotelian imitation. Hampered by his neoplatonist aesthetic, though, and hobbled by the rhetorician's breach between *res* and *verba,* he never completely mastered the new poetics of mimesis. Judged as a Sidneian maker, Spenser is not wholly successful. Perhaps he realized this himself and therefore could not finish *The Faerie Queene.* Just as the prospect of Sidney's approval had set him to the task, his failure to fulfill Sidney's poetical program led him to lay it aside. But Spenser nevertheless produced a wondrously accommodating verbal artifact, as generations of admiring readers attest. Perhaps the richness and resiliency of *The Faerie Queene* are best explained by his change of plans, his lack of consistency in expository technique—by his refusal to remain a simple allegorist, and yet his inability to become wholeheartedly a poet historical as Sidney had prescribed.

7

Sidney: Imitation as Image

> In all these creatures of his making, his intent, and scope was, to turn the barren Philosophy precepts into pregnant Images of life.[1]

Sidney composed his poetical works in a relatively brief span of time, beginning late and dying young. He was not a precocious poet, and nothing in his adolescence suggested that he would become a major literary figure. His first completed work was an entertainment for the Queen, *The Lady of May*, written to accommodate his uncle, the earl of Leicester, and performed in May of either 1578 or 1579.[2] There is a report that as early as 1577 he had begun writing what eventually became the *Arcadia*, but sound evidence indicates that for the most part the old *Arcadia* was composed during 1580.[3] By this time Sidney was in his mid-twenties. Scholarly opinion about the date of *The defence of poesie* has varied—and indeed, it is an open question; but van Dorsten, the most careful editor of the *Defence*, suggests that it was written in winter 1579–80[4] (and I concur, largely on the evidence of the topical references to *The Shepheardes Calender* and the clear echoes of Jean de Serres's edition of Plato which Sidney had received shortly after publication in 1578[5]). The *Certain Sonnets* also belong to this period. The dates and even the order of composition of those miscellanea are impossible to ascertain, but Ringler concludes "that all except the first two *Certain Sonnets* were written in 1581 or earlier, and that the first two were added to the collection late in 1581 or in 1582."[6] Ringler also argues that

Astrophil and Stella was composed after Penelope Devereux's marriage on 1 November 1581, probably during the summer of 1582, although it contains some earlier work assimilated into this larger project.[7] It appears that Sidney began to revise the *Arcadia* after that date,[8] and of course he never completed the revision. His metrification of the Psalms, also left unfinished, defies dating: while Ringler hypothesizes that Sidney did not begin it until late in his career, perhaps during the last year of his life (500–501), Rudenstine counters with a suggestion of 1580–81 (284–86 and 287 [n. 4]). What is notable about the corpus of Sidney's poetry is its inchoate state and the rapidity with which he produced it. The entire canon falls between 1577 and 1585, with a heavy concentration in the years 1579–82.

It is therefore appropriate to think of Sidney's writings as a body of closely interrelated work rather than a sequence of discrete items composed seriatim. At any given time Sidney was likely to be working on two or more of these items, and at all times he was likely to have most of them in mind at once, either in the planning or compositional stage. With the exception of *The Lady of May,* which was occasional, there is no evidence that Sidney considered any of his works completed. Quite the contrary. None of them was printed during his lifetime. Judging by the number of extant manuscripts, he allowed the old *Arcadia* to circulate among friends, but he subjected the text to continuous revision; and within a few years he launched into a major rewriting of it. Since no extant manuscript of *Astrophil and Stella* antedates Sidney's death, it is arguable that he did not circulate this poem.[9] *Certain Sonnets* was an open-ended miscellany, and its makeup did not stabilize until the Countess of Pembroke provided printer's copy for the 1598 folio of Sidney's collected works.

We are justified in dealing with the writings, then, not in some dubiously arrived at chronological order, but rather as more or less simultaneous products of a single teeming brain. *The defence of poesie* applies equally to each, and all comment upon one another. As Rudenstine has eloquently put it, "Taken together, Sidney's various writings resemble the dialogues of the *Arcadia*: they qualify, correct, and debate with one another, turning over and over again the same issues and tensions, never resolving them, yet always placing them in fresh perspectives" (52). The *Arcadia,* how-

ever, both old and new, was Sidney's preoccupation from start to
finish of his literary career, so it will furnish the focus of this discussion. After a nod at *The Lady of May*, I shall turn to the old
Arcadia, Sidney's most sustained literary effort, followed by *Astrophil and Stella*, a sophisticated but incidental diversion; and I
shall conclude with the new *Arcadia*, his most advanced and challenging work and the one upon which until this century his reputation rested.

The Lady of May, as it has been called since the 1724–25 edition
of Sidney, was an outdoor entertainment prepared for Elizabeth's
visit to Leicester's recently acquired estate, Wanstead. The text as
we know it, though, has come from Sidney's hand by a circuitous
and uncharted route. What we have is an account of the event
recorded by an unidentified witness, and therefore of indeterminate accuracy. The text was first printed in the 1598 folio of Sidney's works, but we know little of its provenance other than that
neither the printed text nor the sole extant manuscript represents
exactly what Sidney composed for the occasion. There is a likelihood that much of the action and some of the dialogue was impromptu, and an equal likelihood that something has been lost.

Nonetheless, *The Lady of May* displays many qualities that are
characteristic of Sidney's more mature and protracted work. It is,
for example, a prose narrative interspersed with verse recited or
sung by appropriate characters. This mixture of verse and prose
was a popular mode, and Sidney could have found an immediate
instance in Gascoigne's "Adventures of Master F.J." (1573). The
gentlemen's miscellanies of the 1560s and 70s, including Gascoigne's *Hundreth sundrie flowres*, often employed it. Early in the
century Sannazaro had made it fashionable with his *Arcadia*, and
in the far background was Dante's *Vita nuova* (although it is improbable that Sidney and his generation knew this work firsthand). The unlikely prototype for this mingling of what the classical grammarians had so severely kept apart was Boethius's *De
Philosophiae consolatione*, as Sidney specifically recalled (*Defence* 94.25–26). While prose and verse are intermixed in *The
Lady of May*, each serves a different function: the prose moves the
plot along, while the verse is used expressively to elaborate a character's state of mind. Sidney follows this pattern in the *Arcadia*.

The Lady of May is also, of course, in a playlike mode, with addresses to an audience and characters engaged in dialogue, as well as costuming, stage props, and pantomimic scenes. Even before the action begins to unfold, there are speaking pictures, prosopopoeias of the "honest man's wife of the country" (21.3),[10] who supplicates for the Queen's attention; of "Lalus the old shepherd" (22.27), who introduces Master Rombus, "a substantial schoolmaster" (23.2); and of Rombus himself, who acts as a sort of major domo for the performance. The dramatic mode is the most objective of narrative techniques, as Aristotle had postulated; the poet in his own person has no place in the presentation.

While this witty jeu d'esprit was ostensibly aimed at amusing the Queen, there is also a didactic or even propagandistic strain. The assumption that the May Lady must select one of her two suitors for a husband makes a cheeky comment on Elizabeth's unmarried state, and the contrast between the ethos of the shepherd Espilus and that of the forester Therion delineates two extremes between which the Queen might choose a consort. Some readers have seen quite pointed allusions in the text and have read *The Lady of May* as highly political.[11] Certainly in his final speech Rombus resorts to naming names, and those present were not excepted. Politics aside, at the least this courtly entertainment must be read as socio-philosophical discourse about the relative merits of the contemplative life vs. the active life, another round in the continuing humanistic debate.

Perhaps what is most characteristic, and therefore most significant, is Sidney's careful attention to language in *The Lady of May*. Each speaker employs a vocabulary and abides by a style appropriate to his or her station and pretentions. Each character is most tellingly individuated, in fact, by a distinctive manner of speaking. The country wife speaks honestly in straightforward sentences and in an all but monosyllabic vocabulary. "Old father Lalus," as he is described, "one of the substantiallest shepherds" (22.24–25), makes some effort to rise to the august occasion and adopts the style of a courtier; but his inaccurate Latinisms ("minsical countenance" [22.31], "fransical malady" [22.34]), his simple-minded double epithets ("she-creature, which we shepherds call a woman" [22.30–31]), and bumpkinish oaths ("by my white lamb" [22.31–32], "by my mother Kit's soul" [22.30]) reveal him to be unschooled, as he himself readily admits.

The pedagogue Rombus, on the other hand, "being fully persuaded of his own learned wisdom" (22.20), makes a great pretense of scholarship—and in the process makes a fool of himself, albeit a loveable fool. By his folly he also invites the audience to poke gentle fun at the rhetorical tradition which he so ineptly employs. In the speeches of Master Rombus we see in plenty the excesses of the schoolboy style that lent itself so readily to parody: the Latinate multi-syllabic vocabulary and the clumsy neologisms, the unending alliteration, the farfetched mythological allusions, the mangled Latin tags from Cicero and Vergil, the *copia* of synonyms strung out in boring profusion, the tortured enthymemes and syllogisms. These excesses reveal the weaknesses and faults of the inkhorn style, which Sidney wishes to expose for the sake of humor, much as Shakespeare does in *Love's Labor's Lost* through the stilted language of Don Armado and the affected conversations of Holofernes with Sir Nathaniel.

So a prevalent rhetoricism in *The Lady of May* separates the characters from their maker. As always, Sidney is a heedful author, deliberate in his poetical making, artfully formulating his verbal system.[12] The inhabitants of rural Wanstead are other than the young aristocrat who frequented Elizabeth's court. But while Sidney separates his characters from himself, as the self-effacing playwright must do, he also projects his own thought through the variety of speakers who comprise his cast of characters. The text is rife with secondary meanings, political and personal.

In fact, although the dramatic is the most objective of literary modes, relegating the author to the tiring-house, Sidney may have maneuvered himself into the playing area through the character of Rombus, the garrulous pedant surrounded by simple folk whom he takes to be intellectual inferiors. Certainly Sidney gives to Rombus an unwarranted prominence. Within the world of the play, it is he who accepts the poet's responsibility for the performance and keeps things moving. It is also he who is entrusted with presenting a gift to the Queen, concluding the entertainment with a comically inflated speech of exaggerated deference. Rombus takes liberties with his betters, Leicester as well as Elizabeth, that Sidney in propria persona could not afford. Through Rombus, Sidney manages to make mischievous observations about the royal favor. In addition, Sidney may have seen Rombus as a caricature of his own bookishness, so there's an element of self-mockery as the intellectual superiority assumed by Rombus is revealed to be unmerited. With gentle irony Sidney sets up himself, alongside his uncle and his queen, as the butt of verbal wit. Sidney generates a great deal of humor as Rombus abuses language.

We should remember this pointed, if playful, exploitation of language when we read the passionate speeches of Pyrocles and Musidorus in the *Arcadia,* and indeed of all the other characters, male and female, shepherds and kings. While drawing a clear distinction between the poet and his creatures, Sidney cleverly deploys his verbal wit to speak through his dramatis personae, giving each a personal style that identifies his or her individual nature. Sidney himself is fragmented in his multifarious characters, appearing in each by partial and distorted reflection, although not contained by any—rather in the way that light is refracted by a prism into its constituent colors, no one of which is light per se, but all of which taken together reproduce luminescence.

So reading the *Arcadia,* like reading *The Lady of May,* becomes an exercise in the analysis of styles, in discerning the art of the poet in the presentation of men and women. Sidney stands behind his magistrates and his lovers, and through them promulgates his views about governance and justice and honor and passion. He images virtues and vices in what they do. In these ground-plots we shall look for Sidney's profitable invention. We shall search out those fore-conceits in which lies the true skill of the artificer. We shall seek to observe the maker at his making in order to learn how and why he made his creatures as he did.

Sidney took considerable pains to draw attention to the literary traditions lying behind the *Arcadia.*[13] The very title points to the pastoral with its division between rural and urban, forest and court—with its platonist assumptions about an isolated, perfect world which our erected wit is aware of, but which our infected will renders inaccessible. Arcadia is an ideal in contradistinction to the actual. That ideal, however, is itself subject to the limitation of time, and death dwells even in Arcadia. According to the Hebraic-Christian scheme, it was Adam's error that brought death into the world with all our woe, so Arcadia readily transmutes to Eden with its willful sin. Arcadia, opposing rustic ease and metropolitan turmoil, provides also a site for the weighing of the active against the contemplative life, a debate that continued to occupy the humanists as the ruling class was increasingly torn between the demands of practical politics and the call for personal piety. These issues hang in the air above Basilius's sylvan retreat and condition the atmosphere that he and his fellow Arcadians breathe.

More particularly, the title of Sidney's fiction points to Sannazaro's *Arcadia,* a work that had retained popularity since the beginning of the century. In this elegant if aimless recitation, Sannazaro intermixes prose and verse, although the prose is subservient to the verse, providing a tenuous narrative thread upon which to string the glittering eclogues. Following Sannazaro, it became modish to affect a dissatisfaction with the world as it is, a secular world-weariness that leads to melancholy rather than contemptus mundi and induces an effete longing for what is not attainable. This attitude is epitomized in Sincero, a lovesick shepherd who stands for Sannazaro in a direct and acknowledged way.

Sannazaro's arrangement of prose and verse is clearly reflected in the sets of eclogues that intersperse the books of Sidney's old *Arcadia.* These largely lyrical interludes are assigned such prominence that they acquire a certain independence from the prose narrative, enticing some readers to deal with them as an autonomous body of verse.[14] Tellingly, this is the residence of Philisides, the abject lover of Mira, who has scornfully rejected him. Sidney found in Sincero, the self-absorbed persona of Sannazaro, a model for Philisides, the love-bereft shepherd who most evidently represents Sidney.

The literariness of Sidney's *Arcadia* is intensified by the omnipresent and archaic motifs of medieval romance, by the knights and ladies, the assumptions of courtly love, and the constant discourse about virtue and honor. Moreover, the complicated plot—with its accidents, coincidences, crises, and surprises—owes something to the rapid series of events that characterizes chivalric tales such as *Amadis of Gaul,* from which Sidney drew extensive narrative materials. Other prominent reference points in this line of vision include classical romance such as Heliodorus's *Aethiopica,* which provided Sidney with an opening episode when he rewrote the *Arcadia,* and Renaissance romance such as Montemayor's

Diana, which like Sidney's *Arcadia* punctuates its racy narrative with incidental songs.

With equal obviousness Sidney associates his fiction with the rich tradition for storytelling by repeated echoes of the epic, especially in the delineation of acceptable male behavior. Particularly for Pyrocles and Musidorus, "virtue" is defined in classical terms of manliness as well as in Christian terms of morality. These princes fight like Homeric warriors, taking pride in their lineage and seeking to become national heroes. Even at the nadir of their fortunes, their advocate Kerxenes notes these qualities: "'Such,' said he, 'heroical greatness shines in their eyes, such an extraordinary majesty in all their actions, as surely either fortune by parentage or nature in creation hath made them princes'" (*Old Arcadia* 325.29–31). At the conclusion of the *Arcadia,* the manifold accomplishments of Pyrocles and Musidorus, including the classical virtue of friendship, are conjoined and perpetuated in dynastic marriages that assure a prosperous future for all of Greece. In the second eclogues, Histor's odyssey of the princes' exploits (152.22–158.29) recalls even more explicitly the heroical genre, especially as it had been transformed into the collection of *gesta.*

Sidney carefully positions his work in the existing order of these acknowledged monuments and establishes its intertextuality, its artifice. His early readers recognized this strategy and were unanimous in calling the *Arcadia* a "poem," applying the term, like Sidney, as a cognate of "fiction." They well knew that the *Arcadia* is prose narrative interspersed with songs and segmented by sets of eclogues, but they called it a "poem" in the context of Sidney's application of the term to the *Cyropaedia* of Xenophon and the *Aethiopica* of Heliodorus even though "both these wrote in prose" (*Defence* 81.27–36), not verse.

Fulke Greville, for example, referred to Sidney's *Arcadia* as "his *Matchless Poem*" (ded. epist.). Francis Meres, writing with the *Defence* open before him, turned Sidney's commendation of Xenophon and Heliodorus into a commendation of Sidney himself:

> As *Xenophon,* who did imitate so excellently, as to give us *effigiem justi imperii,* the portraiture of a just Empyre under the name of *Cyrus* (as *Cicero* saieth of him) made therein an absolute

heroicall Poem; and as *Heliodorus* writ in prose his sugred invention of that picture of Love in *Theagines* and *Cariclea*, and yet
both excellent admired Poets: so Sir *Philip Sidney* writ his immortal Poem, *The Countesse of Pembrokes Arcadia*, in Prose,
and yet our rarest Poet. (fols. 280–280ᵛ)

Milton in a strident and impatient moment denigrated the *Arcadia* with the epithet "vain amatorious Poem."[15] But Thomas
Fuller, writing more sympathetically as Sidney's biographer, characterized it as a "rare piece of prose-poetrie" (b2ᵛ). Edward Phillips, voicing the prevalent opinion of the seventeenth century,
praised Sidney, "the Glory of the English Nation in his time," and
commented that "in his own Writings [he was] chiefly if not wholly
Poetical" (using the word "poetical" in the Aristotelian sense, as
Sidney himself had used it; page 243). And Phillips goes on: "his
Arcadia being a Poem in design, though for the most part in solute
Oration" ([Part 2] 152).

So the *Arcadia* is a "poem," a "fiction." But we would be going
too far, I think, to give it much credit as a proto-novel. In accordance with Aristotle's precept that plot is primary in poetical making, it has a meticulously constructed plot, particularly evident in
the old *Arcadia*. It differs from the novel, however, in its conception of character. The old *Arcadia* is pristine in following the Aristotelian dictum that poetry should imitate the actions of men, so
that character is an outgrowth of plot.[16] The novel, though,
adapted that dictum to mean that fiction should portray men in
action, both physical and psychological. The novel as it developed
became obsessed with characterization—with motivation, inner
conflict, and personal identity. While there is a great deal of that
in the *Arcadia*, it is never an end in itself, but only ancillary to
plot. Among all the Arcadians, only Gynecia has a substantial inner life. *Astrophil and Stella* is the more novelistic work, with its
revelations of Astrophil's mental states and its intimations of a sensual Stella repressed by the social order.

In the old *Arcadia*, Sidney seems to be following fairly closely
his pronouncement that a poet be known by the feigning of notable images (*Defence* 81.36–37). He deploys his characters to
represent virtues and vices pertaining to governance and love,
and perhaps a few "what elses," a few amusing foibles that belong

to a grey area between unmitigated right and wrong.[17] Only to increase their didactic effectiveness does Sidney endow his characters with a certain vraisemblance. Greville speaks with authority in a passage that I have used as epigraph for this chapter. Sidney's aim was to promulgate certain moral precepts; his images of life were means toward that end.

We may also distinguish the *Arcadia's* mode of characterization from that of Spenser's comparable poem, *The Faerie Queene*. While Sidney's characters are images of vices and virtues and so forth, he is not writing "a continued allegory," as Spenser identified his work. Basilius does not represent kingship in the way that Red Crosse Knight represents holiness. And the difference, I believe, is this. Spenser began with a concept, holiness, which he wished to express by means of a character in action. The purpose of the tale is to convey the concept of holiness, and the narrative is merely the means by which the concept is conveyed. To the reader, the verbal system is a husk or a veil that conceals the truth. This is the way allegory works. The ontological *situs* of the literary work resides in a preexistent system of values, not in its language. While, admittedly, such an anatomy of *The Faerie Queene* is reductive of Spenser's actual achievement, that is a reasonable résumé of Spenser's narrative theory when he planned to write "twelve bookes, fashioning XII. morall vertues." Spenser employs his characters as metaphors in the platonist sense, as a mechanism for translating an idea from a transcendent world of essences into the time-bound world of mortals.

In contrast, Sidney begins with a plot in the best Aristotelian fashion, imitating the actions of men; and characters are determined by how they act, interact, and react in this plot. Only after characters are fully fashioned by what they do may they be assigned an appropriate name: Philanax or Philoclea. The name is a confirmatory seal, not an introductory label. The name is not an essence which the character is predestined to realize. We know a character by what he or she does and says, empirically observed, not by deduction from a fixed identity.

Reading the *Arcadia*, then, requires a strategy different from reading *The Faerie Queene*. We mustn't peer through the language of the *Arcadia*, expecting to uncover some prefabricated truth, some system of values already formulated—for example, "twelve private morall vertues, as Aristotle hath devised." It's not so simple as that. Although there is morality in the *Arcadia*, it doesn't teach a preconceived discipline. Rather, it teaches by offering a literary experience, an experience encoded in language. The reader engages a text. The verbal system is a self-contained object, embodying its own reality; and while it may make reference to anterior items in the order of literary monuments and to actual practices in Elizabethan England, it transforms and assimilates those contexts into a new system sui generis.

Furthermore, to achieve its end of societal reform, the work must have an effect upon a widespread audience. In accord with this rhetorical function, the raison d'être of the work resides in the active and processive encounter between its verbal system and the reader. Engagement with the text is the essence of the poem, by Sidney's design. And in addition to the moral instruction, the art of engaging a text is what an astute reader eventually learns. Reading the *Arcadia*, therefore, is not an exercise in decoding an extraneous system of signs, or of comprehending a prior set of concepts, or of completing a predetermined paradigm. There is no quest limited to a single topic and defined by a knight travelling between two termini. What one learns is not a homily, but a method—the why and the how of the maker's art. To accomplish this aim, the poet must grant autonomy to the language of his work. Its mode of existence must lie in the fiction, in the unfolding of the text itself. A poem is *natura naturans*, not *natura naturata*.

It is in this fundamental way that Sidney separates from his contemporaries and becomes a forerunner of the novel. He legitimizes the act of making and validates the art of fiction. In the eyes of Thomas Fuller, an early critic of the *Arcadia*, Sidney's achievement lies exactly here: "The invention is wholly spun out of phansie, but conformable to possibilitie of truth in all particulars" (b2ᵛ). Poetry carries a truth of its own, inherent in its very language. The fiction is sufficiently lifelike to give an illusion of actuality; the poet must walk hand in hand with nature—certainly, with human nature—and he may not build castles in the air. But since his objects of imitation are universals, since his tale recounts what might be or should be, the fiction avoids evanescence and acquires authority. Consequently, the truth of poetry is more generally applicable than the particular facts of history, while its images are also more immediately efficacious than the tenuous precepts of philosophy.

In the old *Arcadia* Sidney uses a verbal medium to give us "images" and "portraitures" of actions—what he encapsulates in the Plutarchan tag, "speaking pictures." He brings his own "stuff" to make the "matter" for this "conceit" (pages 277–78)—that is, he draws from his own observation for his depictions. But by universalizing these data, by ranging within the zodiac of his wit, he elevates his fiction to the realm of art, where perfection insures that all is constant, all is true—a golden world. Since we can identify a poet by the ability to feign images of human actions, both virtuous and vicious, we are right to concern ourselves with those techniques that induce visualization so that images can materialize. Just as we interpret Xenophon's Cyrus as a portrayal of just governance and Heliodorus's Theagenes and Chariclea as a picture of true love, so we should perceive the characters in the old *Arcadia* as realizations of actions that give substance to universals and make them knowable. To paraphrase Greville, Sidney takes the precepts of philosophy, which are "barren" because their immateriality renders them ineffectual, and turns them into lifelike images which are "pregnant" because they result in issue.

On many occasions Sidney resorts to forthright visual effects and produces word pictures. The rhetoricians had delineated several figures to create the impression that what they describe is an immediate presence, to produce the forcibleness and vividness known as *enargeia,* and Sidney would have been trained in these at school. Erasmus in the *De copia,* to cite an authority of particular importance for the curriculum in England, had devoted a lengthy section to enargeia as a means of enriching subject matter, and under this topic he had included the description of things (hypotyposis), the description of persons (prosopographia, dialogismos, and prosopopoeia), the description of places (topographia), and the description of times, such as twilight or spring (chronographia).[18] Even more than most writing of the period, the old *Arcadia* displays a remarkable number of these setpieces which are formally introduced into the text.

For instance, Sidney sometimes uses the figure of *hypotyposis,* the detailed description of an object or action.[19] In the old *Arca-*

dia, Sidney is more concerned with actions than with things, and therefore he tends to depict objects by a few decisive attributes rather than by the formal figure of hypotyposis. The vessel in which Gynecia carries the sleep-inducing potion drunk by Basilius, for example, is described simply as a "cup of gold" (278.19). Actions, though, tend to be represented in greater detail, and Basilius's ingestion of the liquor with its subsequent effects is exposed to view in a full-blown hypotyposis:

> The duke, whose belly had no ears, and much drought kept from the desiring a taster, finding it not unpleasant to his palate, drank it almost off, leaving very little to cover the cup's bottom. But within a while that from his stomach the drink had delivered to his principal veins his noisome vapours, first with a painful stretching and forced yawning, then with a dark yellowness dyeing his skin and a cold deadly sweat principally about his temples, his body by natural course longing to deliver his heavy burden to his earthly dam, wanting force in his knees (which utterly abandoned him), with heavy fall gave soon proof whither the operation of that unknown potion tended. For, with pang-like groans and ghastly turning of his eyes, immediately all his limbs stiffened and his eyes fixed, he having had time to declare his case only in these words: "O Gynecia, I die! Have care—." (278.26–279.3)

The concrete details of this scene are directed to the mind's ear as well as eye, and a sharp image results. Again, when Musidorus fights off the rabble of Phagonians who surround him and Pamela in flight, there is an initial similitude: they "straight (like so many swine when a hardy mastiff sets upon them) dispersed themselves"; and then follows a *copia* of hypotyposes:

> But the first he overtook as he ran away, carrying his head as far before him as those manner of runnings are wont to do, with one blow strake it so clean off that, it falling betwixt the hands, and the body falling upon it, it made a show as though the fellow had had great haste to gather up his head again. Another, the speed he made to run for the best game bare him full butt against a tree, so that tumbling back with a bruised face and a dreadful expectation, Musidorus was straight upon him, and parting with his sword one of his legs from him, left him to make a roaring

lamentation that his mortar-treading was marred for ever. A third, finding his feet too slow as well as his hands too weak, suddenly turned back, beginning to open his lips for mercy, but before he had well entered a rudely compiled oration, Musidorus's blade was come betwixt his jaws into his throat; and so the poor man rested there for ever with a very ill mouthful of an answer. (308.2–17)

These images of Musidorus's aggressiveness exhibit a hypotypotic force probably stronger than the modern sensibility cares to register.

To lend importance to a particular scene, Sidney sometimes resorts to *topographia,* which Puttenham dubs "the counterfait place" (239). In Book 1, for example, to highlight the culminating action when the ferocious lion and ravenous bear charge out of the forest and attack the princesses, Sidney offers a detailed description of the meadow in which the royal party sits, waiting for the eclogues to begin: "It was, indeed, a place of great delight," replete with brook and flowers, and surrounded by "pleasant arbours" (46.2–15). The reader is invited to visualize the scene. In Book 3 when Cleophila comes upon the cave that will provide a locale for several amorous trysts, Sidney offers a graphic description from "the rich growing marble [which] serve[d] to beautify the vault of the first entry" to "a little sweet river which had left the face of the earth to drown herself for a small way in this dark, but pleasant, mansion" (179.19–28). This description is achieved, it seems to me, not facilely by a few well-chosen adjectives; rather, it is the product of Sidney's active realization of the scene in his imagination. The result is not static, but affectively dynamic.

When appropriate, at moments of crisis in a character's history, Sidney makes use of the figure known as *prosopographia,* the description of a person.[20] He describes the demeanor and attire of the character in telling detail, so that his or her total appearance materializes. It is as though the character were being costumed for a dramatic entrance, and the court masque with its gorgeous accoutrements inevitably comes to mind.

An excellent example of this technique occurs early in the old *Arcadia* when Pyrocles puts on the womanish apparel disguising him as Cleophila (26.20–27.17). The text gives the proper signal that a prosopographia is to follow: "To begin with his head, thus was he dressed." Sidney does indeed begin with Cleophila's head, noting the coiffure and the coronet of gold, pearl, and varicolored feathers, and methodically he moves downward to the "little short pair of crimson velvet buskins" which cover Cleophila's feet. When the prosopographia is completed, the text formally indicates the conclusion of the figure: "Thus was this Amazon's attire." Narrative time is officially stopped to allow this feast for the mind's eye of the reader. Other instances of prosopographia occur at scattered places in the old *Arcadia*[21]—most notably, in the last book when Gynecia, Pyrocles, and Musidorus appear before Euarchus for their trial (376.6–377.13).

On some few occasions Sidney resorts to a more recondite kind of word picture, to the image with occluded but evident significance that we are most familiar with in the emblem book. For example, in the description of Cleophila just noted, the ends of her mantle are fastened on her left shoulder "with a very rich jewel, the device whereof was this: an eagle covered with the feathers of a dove, and yet lying under another dove, in such sort as it seemed the dove preyed upon the eagle, the eagle casting up such a look as though the state he was in liked him, though the pain grieved him" (27.9–14). While the reader visualizes this small ornament with its precise and intricate device, he must also go beyond the visual image and penetrate its implied significance. In this case, the meaning is clear: through the power of love Pyrocles has been transformed from eaglelike valor to dovelike docility, and indeed has become subservient to the very personification of docility, Philoclea. Most vivid here, and certainly most amusing, is the look on the face of the eagle, expressing the exquisite masochism of the Petrarchan lover, who feels pleasure only when suffering the pangs of passion. A similar jewel is worn by Pamela on a chain around her neck, bearing the device of a white lamb tied to a stake, an emblem of both Pamela's virtue and her detention (37.14–20). Also Dicus, the anti-erotic shepherd, in the first set of eclogues bears before him "a painted table, wherein he had given Cupid a quite new form, making him sit upon a pair of gallows, like a hangman"; and there follows an elaborate emblem of Cupid exposed as death-dealing lust (64.18–29).

Much more frequently Sidney visualizes his text by the figure of *prosopopoeia*. Strictly speaking, as the rhetoricians had defined it, prosopopoeia involves the assignment of speech to dumb creatures, such as a fox or an ape, or to an abstraction, such as Fame or an apparition representing the city of Verulam, or to someone who is dead or absent, such as Homer. Quintilian offers the gloss *fictiones personarum* (9.2.29), a fiction that produces vocal personifications. More simply defined by actual practice, prosopopoeias are "fictitious speeches supposed to be uttered," again to cite Quintilian (6.1.25). So prosopopoeia required the preparation of an extended speech that projected a character presenting a certain point of view—literally, a "figuring forth to speak metaphorically." As the orator used it, prosopopoeia usually consisted of an acknowledged mimicking of someone under discussion, a lengthy and studiously crafted utterance purportedly in the person's own words recited in order to expose his or her true nature. To vivify the subject and intensify immediacy for the audience, the orator simulates the person being held up for praise or blame, using the appropriate voice and gestures and facial expressions. As Quintilian says, "We may draw a parallel from the stage, where the actor's voice and delivery produce greater emotional effect when he is speaking in an assumed role than when he speaks in his own character" (6.1.26). Transferring the practice of orators to the needs of poets, Erasmus identified prosopopoeia as "the technical term for the realistic presentation of persons" (*Copia* 582), and he saw it as a handy way of describing people (586).

Writers of fiction readily adapted the figure of prosopopoeia to their need for overheard utterance, and they drew upon their rhetorical training to construct the overwrought speeches that characterize Elizabethan narrative. Certainly in his fiction Sidney depends heavily upon the technique of prosopopoeia. There is a notable example soon after the action of the old *Arcadia* begins. When Basilius comes to Philanax in order to charge him with care of the government while Basilius is in retirement from Mantinea, Philanax responds in a lengthy performance setting forth his reservations about the oracle and his disapproval of Basilius's abdication (6.36–8.32). Through his style as much as his subject matter, Philanax reveals to the audience his complete devotion to the king, so the prosopopoeia of Philanax is an image of an action, a portraiture of a loyal courtier performing his duties.[22] The name

Philanax is evidently the only name worthy of this admirable character, as his deeds indicate.

Another notable example of prosopopoeia soon occurs after Pyrocles has seen the painting of Philoclea but before Musidorus lays eyes upon Pamela. The well-known debate between the two princes as they argue the pros and cons of love may be fruitfully analyzed as two intersecting prosopopoeias, what the rhetoricians called *dialogismos*.[23] In such an exchange each speaker is defined not only positively by what he says, but also in contradistinction by the statement of his adversary. This mode of discourse finds a respected precedent in the medieval débat, where two equally matched disputants define one another by the exact expression of contrary views, and the resolution of the débat, difficult though it may be, is implied by the reconciliation of these opposites. Perhaps more immediately, the princes' debate on love looks to the Platonic dialogue for its model. In that mode, well known to Sidney, several differing points of view are offered, each of which is valid on at least its own grounds. Sidney recognized that prosopopoeiac dialogues such as the *Symposium* and *Phaedrus,* where each disputant speaks in turn and in character and at length, are a legitimate means of producing speaking pictures.

Textbook examples of dialogismos enliven the old *Arcadia* throughout. Most memorable, perhaps, are the debate between Pyrocles and Philoclea on suicide after being apprehended in flagrante delicto (291.20–300.15), Philanax's plea with Euarchus to assume the magistracy after the apparent death of Basilius (360.8–361.20) and Euarchus's response (362.14–363.14), and the stilted exchange between Pyrocles and Musidorus in prison affirming their friendship (370.21–373.21). As modern readers, we're attuned to the repartee of the novel, which tries to replicate the naturalness of the voice overheard, so we are likely to respond negatively to the stylized exchanges between Sidney's characters. But he looked to dialogismos as a showcase for revealing their true nature.

In fact, the prosopopoeiac utterance becomes a major mode of narration in the old *Arcadia*.[24] Character after character, in monologue as well as dialogue, discloses himself or herself in an extended speech that has none of the naturalism of actual speech, none of the interchange of conversation, none of the simplicity of forthright expression. Speech whenever it occurs in the *Arcadia*—from the mouth of Basilius or Dametas, from Gynecia or Miso, from Pamela or Mopsa—is always carefully crafted to expose the character who speaks. Speech, the language he or she uses, *is* character, the image of the action this character performs in the plot.

It may be supererogatory to cite further examples of prosopopoeia in the old *Arcadia* since they are so numerous and so visible. But we should note their especial contribution to depicting the character of Gynecia, that worthy matron who is suddenly and devastatingly smitten with passion and, perhaps even more tormenting, with a self-loathing because of it. There are several remarkable incidences when Gynecia reveals her conflicting emotions in stunning prosopopoeias. Book 2 opens with a wretched monologue by Gynecia—punctuated by apostrophes to the sun, to the heavens, to the desolate forest, to virtue—in which she acknowledges her hopeless passion for Cleophila, recognizes the unlikelihood of its requittal, and bemoans a future of shameful behavior (91.23–92.23). In this formal lament she speaks for all the lovers and typifies their plight. Not long after, Gynecia prays in bed and tears her hair: " 'Take here, O forgotten virtue,' said she, 'this miserable sacrifice' " (112.35–113.5)—but her noise awakens Basilius and this prosopopoeia is aborted. In Book 3, however, when Cleophila by chance overhears Gynecia in the cave, she is given ample opportunity to express her longing, her frustration, and her feelings of guilt (182.27–183.22). In Book 4, immediately following the collapse of Basilius after drinking the potion, Gynecia magnifies the tragedy by a formal expression of her remorse and sorrow (279.27–280.12). Finally, Gynecia's interruption of Philanax at the trial and her public confession (381.24–382.22) affectingly portray the eventual degradation of a virtuous lady betrayed by carnality, and the assembled populace responds accordingly with pity. It is largely due to these prosopopoeiac images that Gynecia remains in our consciousness as the most full-bodied of the Arcadians.

In the actual forum of human affairs, the efficacy of prosopopoeia, especially as it was used forensically, derives from the fact that the person whom the orator purports to portray is unaware of the implications of his words and does not comprehend the extent to which the speech discovers what in his own interests he might wish to conceal. So there is often an implied self-betrayal in the prosopopoeia, and an opportunity for dramatic irony. The imputed speaker thinks the speech creates one impression, but the perceptive audience sees through the sham of the speech and interprets it quite differently. For example, the orator might present an adversary as a braggadochio who affects the soldier's language, thereby exposing him as an ignoble pretender. Similarly, the lover who activates the Petrarchist system by using the conventional vocabulary and motifs may be suspected as someone hiding a carnal desire. In a prosopopoeia the purported speaker is likely to use words in a sophistical way, with an intent to mislead; and the audience must listen critically, with an ear for nuances that give away the deception, with an awareness that the pretense must be dispelled for the truth to appear.

Not only in its masterful deployment of language to simulate a performance, then, but also in this multivalency of meanings the prosopopoeia is remarkable for its literariness. The verbal system induces a literary moment that is patently artificial, and in fact invites analysis of its artifice. With particular reference to the debate on love between Pyrocles and Musidorus, but with general application to the entire text, Lanham comments on the rhetoricism that prevails in the old *Arcadia*: "Here at the beginning of the romance Sidney takes pains to indicate the spirit in which we are to read. He alerts us to the constant rhetorical maneuver in which his characters are engaged, and if we ignore the warning we shall constantly misread the *Arcadia*."[25] The prosopopoeia is especially adaptable to the purpose of sophisticated narrative of this self-conscious sort, and not surprisingly the best storytellers exploited its potential. Even before Sidney's *Arcadia*, Gascoigne in "Master F.J." and Lyly in *Euphues* had employed prosopopoeia for much the same purposes and to similar effects.

Of course, Sidney would have been trained in the composition of rhetorical figures, including the prosopopoeia, from his earliest school days, and he would have known the definitions and examples of it in Quintilian and Erasmus. For instruction he also would have looked to David the psalmist, whose "notable *prosopopoeias*" were capable of making even the deity appear to the mind's eye as a carnate being (*Defence* 77.19). Probably his most compelling authority for the use of speaking characters in this way, however, was Aristotle, who in the *Poetics* had indicated two distinct modes of narration: an account related in retrospect by the author, and a dramatic presentation in the present tense during which the characters speak in their own voices (pages 150–51). Aristotle had noted as well that a poet may deploy these two narrative modes in combination, citing Homer as a poet who used both modes alternately to good effect. The prosopopoeia clearly lends itself to such poetic use in a dramatic setting, and many speeches in the Homeric epics have the autonomy, artificiality, and extensiveness that characterize it. The councils of war in the *Iliad*, where each statesman rises in turn and argues for a strategic plan (thereby revealing his "character"), provide prime examples of prosopopoeiac images interacting in the sort of conflict that moves drama forward. Milton recognized this technique as the epitome of the high style, and he employed it generously in *Paradise Lost*—most notably, perhaps, in the council of fallen angels in Pandemonium that dominates Book 2.

Sidney exploits Aristotle's license that authorial narrative be enlivened by histrionic scenes in which characters speak for themselves; and the narrative virtuosity of Homer, who was after all acclaimed as the father of both comedy and tragedy, served as at least a distant model for the *Arcadia*. Its characters, whether reported upon or heard in action, have a certain heroic stature. In any case, the old *Arcadia* is conceived as a highly dramatic work, and this large element of drama also contributes to the visualization of its verbal system.

Most evidently, the old *Arcadia* is divided into "five books or acts," and this generic signal conditions the reader's first encounter with the text. Before the tale itself begins, a division head announces: "The First Book or Act of the Countess of Pembroke's Arcadia." The initial lines set the scene (in Arcadia), and we are introduced to the dramatis personae (Basilius, Gynecia, and their two fair daughters). The opening situation is efficiently presented: Basilius, moved by uncertainty about the future, has gone to Delphos and has returned with a puzzling oracle—all within a scant two pages. The action begins when Basilius, now even more uncertain and increasingly fearful, goes to Philanax to turn over the government so the royal family can retire from court and elude the dangers which the oracle has darkly hinted at. The curtain has risen, and the reader should settle back for the presentation.

The ease with which the prosopopoeiac image lends itself to dramaturgy is well illustrated in this opening episode of Basilius's conference with Philanax. The scene is introduced by expository narrative in which the author describes Basilius's dismay upon receiving the oracle, his relationship to Philanax, the course of action he has decided upon, and his reasons for coming to Philanax. All of this is accomplished within one more page of text. At this point, however, the mode of narration abruptly changes. The text gives a clear signal of this change: "Philanax, having forthwith taken into the depth of his consideration both what the duke said and with what mind he spake it, with a true heart and humble countenance in this sort answered" (6.32–35); and then Philanax proceeds with a prosopopoeiac response that extends to over two pages (6.36–8.32). The loyal counselor—indeed, the entire scene—springs to vivid life as we hear his exact and revealing words. With deference, but also with firmness and reason, he sets out his objections to Basilius's proposal. When Philanax concludes his lengthy speech, the authorial narrator intrudes and insists upon the visibility of what is taking place: "Whilst Philanax used these words, a man might see in the duke's face that, as he was wholly wedded to his own opinion, so was he grieved to have any man say that which he had not seen" (8.33–35). Basilius then replies to Philanax, prosopopoeia gives over to dramatic dialogue, and the scene ends in a passage of stichomythia (9.11–17), a convention that emphasizes the literariness of the text. So this opening scene has given us an instructive lesson in how to read the old *Arcadia*. Our mind's eye and ear must be alert.

After this opening encounter between Basilius and Philanax, the author resumes the narrative in his own voice, confirms Basilius's resolve to take up residence in the sylvan lodge, and introduces the comic trio of the dramatis personae—Dametas, Miso, and Mopsa (9.32–34). With a storyteller's "now" (9.35), to change the subject and to insure the immediacy of the narration, the author brings on stage the two princely counterparts of Basilius's daughters, Pyrocles and Musidorus; and after informing us of their background and present circumstances, he prepares for the next scene. In the house of Kerxenus, the gentleman who has of-

fered them hospitality, Pyrocles sees a picture of Philoclea and
according to the conventions of sonneteering immediately falls in
love with her. This activity, which consumes a bit more than three
pages of text (9.35–13.8), introduces the two handsome heroes
necessary to complete the quartet of young lovers and moves the
plot along. But it also functions as preparation for the next set
piece, the debate between Pyrocles and Musidorus on the topic of
love which is carried out, as we have noted, in a prosopopoeiac
exchange. This scene, with its incidental incursions into the im-
propriety of solitariness ("the sly enemy that doth most separate a
man from well-doing," 14.5–6) and the merits of friendship (the
"extremity of love," 14.15–16), consumes no less than thirteen
pages of text (13.9–26.11).

By its prominence and length, this dialogismos becomes a centerpiece for Book 1. Like the exchange between Basilius and Philanax, it includes an extended passage of stichomythia (23.6–28),
and it ends in dialogue (25.17–26.11). Our first experience of Pyrocles and Musidorus therefore confirms the earlier instruction on
how to read the old *Arcadia:* it is a combination of authorial narrative and dramatic presentation, rather as Aristotle had predicated for the most admired sort of poetry; and the few pages of
authorial narrative serve as scaffolding to support the extended
dramatic scene between the two princes that culminates the episode. Throughout the old *Arcadia,* in fact, the passages related by
the author are primarily links to provide coherence for theatrical
set pieces, largely exposition to provide context for the more important images addressed to the mind's eye of an audience.[26] The
authorial narrative is written with grace and wit; but the center of
gravity, as the distribution of text indicates, lies in the dramatized
scenes.

In any case, the dramatic structuring of the old *Arcadia* in "five
books or acts" is not gratuitous or superficial. Scholars are fairly
well agreed that the narrative follows the five-act arrangement
widely known from the school texts of Terence's plays. As Robertson rightly observes, echoing Ringler, the old *Arcadia* "is a tragicomedy, with a serious double plot and a comic underplot, based
on a Terentian structure of exposition, action, complication, rever-
sal, and catastrophe."[27] She also notes the presence of "an unexpected anagnorisis and peripateia at the end," dramatic elements

that Sidney would have known from his reading of Aristotle's *Po-etics*. Robertson further recalls that in the Italian theater musical diversions were often performed between the acts of a play, and the sets of eclogues in the old *Arcadia* serve a similar function. At the end of Book 1 the eclogues are recited "to ease . . . the tedi-ousness of this long discourse" (55.14–15). When viewed as inter-mezzi, the eclogues placed between contiguous books also contrib-ute to the theatricality of the text. Finally, the old *Arcadia* is dramatized by the carefully prescribed settings for every action. Each episode is precisely located in a particular time and place; the stage is carefully set before the characters appear to play their parts.

The theatricality of the old *Arcadia* is further brought to our attention by the characters who repeatedly speak of themselves as actors in a play. When Musidorus attempts to dissuade Pyrocles from his fit of loving, he warns his impassioned friend against such folly, lest "like an ill player [he] should mar the last act of his tragedy" (19.12–13). By the end of Book I, "Fortune had framed a very stage-play of love among these few folks" (54.24–25). It is Gynecia, however, who is most persistently conceived as a theat-rical figure, perhaps because in accord with Aristotelian principles she most completely bears the blame for her own downfall and suffers the most painful self-knowledge. When Cleophila proves unresponsive to her advances, Gynecia warns that "she would stir up terrible tragedies rather than fail of her intent" (96.17–18). Later, she threatens outright: "I will not be the only actor of this tragedy!" (184.21–22). When the narrator turns to report the in-cident of Basilius's unknowing tryst with Gynecia in the cave and its unfortunate aftermath, he conditions the reader by referring to the events as "tragedies" (274.12), and Gynecia reinforces this conditioning by speaking of the "scene" in which her own "tragical end" will be presented (280.11). Throughout the last several books we are exhorted to do what Philanax asks of Euarchus: "Imagine, vouchsafe to imagine, most wise and good king, that here is before your eyes the pitiful spectacle of a most dolorously ending tragedy" (360.18–20).[28]

The old *Arcadia* is so highly visualized, in fact, that the reader is often invited to participate in a vicarious voyeurism, especially when the virtue of the princesses is in jeopardy (which is most of the time). At least the males in the readership are expected to smirk at the early descriptions of Philoclea in her see-through garments, and even the ladies have a right to wonder whether someone so careless about modesty might not be equally careless about her honor. Philoclea's first appearance is in answer to Dametas's knocking at the lodge, summoning the duke to inquire how to deal with the recently discovered Cleophila: "The fair Philoclea came down in such loose apparel as was enough to have bound any man's fancies, and with a sweet look asking him what he would have" (33.27–30). But Dametas is such a clod, so far beneath a manly response, that he does not notice her negligence. When Philoclea next appears (the first time that Cleophila sees her), she is even more seductively deshabillée: she "appeared in her nymphlike apparel, so near nakedness as one might well discern part of her perfections . . . her body covered with a light taffeta garment, so cut as the wrought smock came through it in many places (enough to have made a very restrained imagination have thought what was under it)" (37.21–29). Shortly after, when Philoclea runs from the lion, she is not surprisingly ogled by Cleophila (47.29–48.1).

The voyeurism, however, is not confined to Philoclea. When Musidorus contemplates rape of the sleeping Pamela, we are encouraged to view the scene with the eyes of peeping Tom: "The sweet Pamela was brought into a sweet sleep with this song, which gave Musidorus opportunity at leisure to behold her excellent beauties"; and there follows a catalog of those beauties reminiscent of the Song of Solomon (201.7–202.6). In just a few pages when Gynecia offers herself to Cleophila in the cave, "under a feigned rage tearing her clothes," she uncovers "some parts of her fair body" (205.21–22), and we are invited to imagine which parts.

It was the ultra-innocent Philoclea, though, who most piqued Sidney's prurient imagination. When Pyrocles finally arrives at Philoclea's bedroom, he pauses before the open door:

—for the duke at his parting had left the chamber open, and she at that time lay (as the heat of that country did well suffer) upon the top of her bed, having her beauties eclipsed with nothing but with a fair smock (wrought all in flames of ash-colour silk and gold), lying so upon her right side that the left thigh down to the

foot yielded his delightful proportion to the full view, which was
seen by the help of a rich lamp which, through the curtains a little
drawn, cast such a light upon her as the moon doth when it shines
into a thin wood. (230.30–231.7)

A golden world, indeed. Oh, newfound land! The ensuing seduction is highly erotic, a license for prurience, since lewdness, like
beauty, lies in the eye of the beholder. The language is delicate—
just as Gascoigne resorts to the most seemly of terms when F.J.
and Elinor fall to the floor for their sexual consummation[29]—but
the action is coarse. And the disjunction between language and
actuality highlights the coarseness of what is in fact taking place.
The sensuality of the scene is heightened by Pyrocles's recollection of Philisides's luscious blazon of Mira, indicating his own
mental state of idolatrous obsession, and Book 3 closes with the
two young lovers blissfully entwined—left there wittily, as though
on some roué's Grecian urn, to perpetuate the ecstatic moment of
satiety. The third set of eclogues that immediately follows celebrates the marriage of Lalus and Kala, the reenactment in idyllic
terms of the sexual union simultaneously occurring in Philoclea's
bed.

Nor is the voyeurism confined to the ladies, as the scene of Philoclea's seduction makes clear. Pyrocles—the more bashful of the
two princes (408.15), the one who can pass for a woman—comes
in for his share. After he, disguised as Cleophila, is wounded by
the lion in Book 1, both Philoclea and Gynecia apply their surgi-
cal arts; and the narrator observes wryly, "In which doing, I know
not whether Gynecia took some greater conjectures of Cleophila's
sex" (50.14–15). We giggle as we look through Gynecia's eyes and
scrutinize Pyrocles's body, and we wonder if Philoclea has also
joined in this titillating sport. One of the more delicious occasions
of such voyeurism occurs when Dametas walks through the open
door of Philoclea's bedroom to discover her and Pyrocles asleep in
one another's arms. With something of the same bisexuality that
characterizes Marlowe's *Hero and Leander,* the narrator reports
archly: "Dametas . . . did not only perceive it was Cleophila . . . ,
but that this same Cleophila did more differ from the Cleophila
he and others had ever taken her for" (273.11–17). Later Dametas
announces to the other shepherds "that Cleophila, whom they had

taken all that while to be a woman, was as arrant a man as himself was, whereof he had seen sufficient signs and tokens; and that he was as close as a butterfly with the lady Philoclea" (273.33–274.3). Even in the midst of their debate on suicide, Pyrocles cops a few feels of Philoclea (295.8–9). Young love, no matter how raunchy, is a thing of beauty, a joy forever—or, perhaps, young love, no matter how beautiful, is always a raunchy joy.

Anyway, the extent to which the old *Arcadia* is visualized through its fictive text is well demonstrated by Book 5, which is presented with close to the objectivity of drama. As Edward Phillips rightly observed, the *Arcadia* is "a Poem in design, though for the most part *in solute Oration*" (page 404). Of the 2,253 lines comprising Book 5 in the Robertson edition, over half (to be exact, 53%) are devoted to direct discourse, to the actual words spoken or written by a character,[30] while many more lines are devoted to indirect discourse, to a narrator's report of what was said. This culmination to the series of increasingly serious events is staged with vividness and forcibleness—and with a sense of anticipation, of excitement, of suspense, of all those dramatic qualities that sharpen the reader's perception.[31] There is even an audience within the fiction who maintain the stance of concerned onlookers and serve as surrogates for our stake in what happens, rather like the chorus in a Greek tragedy. The Arcadian populace are gathered in convocation, addressed by would-be leaders, movingly appealed to by a procession of the central characters—and in every instance they respond simply but actively, providing an unhindered perspective that we are invited to share.

When "the last book or act" begins, the loss of Basilius has plunged Arcadia into political chaos. Philanax rapidly emerges as the most powerful man in the realm, however, and Euarchus fortunately appears to serve as interim ruler. First, Philanax convenes the Arcadians and in a prosopopoeiac address (353.3–354.12) obtains their agreement to accept Euarchus as the judge of those implicated in Basilius's death. Next, Philanax goes to Euarchus and, after an authorial intrusion which assures us of Euarchus's good intentions (357.3–359.28), issues the invitation that he become temporary regent (360.8–361.20). Euarchus accepts in an equally careful speech (362.14–363.14). The two politicos then return to the lodges, where the populace is waiting for them despite the late hour, and Euarchus addresses the convocation in a suitable prosopopoeia (364.34–366.7).

Before the actual day of judgment begins, and in preparation for it, the narrator intrudes, because "first it shall be well to know how the poor and princely prisoners passed this tedious night" (366.27–28). So we are treated to individual vignettes of Gynecia, of Pamela and Philoclea, and of Pyrocles and Musidorus. In their closely guarded confinement the princes are of course concerned about the safety of their ladies; what we hear, however, is an extended dialogismic exchange avowing mutual friendship and confirming their noble love for the princesses (370.31–373.21). This overheard conversation is followed by a stoical quatorzain sung to Pyrocles by Musidorus (373.25–374.4).

But soon the day of judgment dawns, and this last, long-awaited scene takes us to the end of the work. The stage is carefully set:

> Euarchus called unto him Philanax, and willed him to draw out into the midst of the green (before the chief lodge) the throne of judgement seat in which Basilius was wont to sit. . . . and therein Euarchus did sit himself, all clothed in black, with the principal men who could in that suddenness provide themselves of such mourning raiments, the whole people commanded to keep an orderly silence of each side. . . . Then, the duke's body being laid upon a table just before Euarchus, and all covered over with black, the prisoners (namely the duchess and two young princes) were sent for to appear in the protector's name. (374.33–375.34)

Into this assembly "first was Gynecia led forth in the same weeds that the day and night before she had worn, saving that, instead of Cleophila's garment, in which she was found, she had cast on a long cloak which reached to the ground, of russet coarse cloth, with a poor felt hat which almost covered all her face"—and we have a prosopographia of the wretched Gynecia (376.6–17). Next, "Pyrocles came out, led by Sympathus, clothed after the Greek manner in a long coat of white velvet reaching to the small of his leg, with great buttons of diamonds all along upon it"—and we are offered another prosopographia which emphasizes the elegant simplicity of Pyrocles's attire (376.22–36). Finally, we see "the noble Musidorus who had upon him a long cloak after the fashion of that which we call the apostle's mantle, made of purple satin"— and his accompanying prosopographia accentuates his nobility

(377.1–9). The prisoners stand vividly before the bar of justice (377.10–36).

Musidorus, "the more goodly" (while Pyrocles is "the more lovely"), seizes the initiative and speaks purposefully to the assembly, calling attention to Pamela's rights as "the just inheritrix of this country" and absolving her of any wrongdoing (378.6–379.7). This forceful prosopopoeia is immediately matched by another when Pyrocles addresses a plea to Euarchus on Philoclea's behalf (379.26–380.22). But Euarchus does not totally exonerate Philoclea. He pronounces that she must spend the remainder of her life chastely in a religious house.

Euarchus then proceeds with the trial of Gynecia. Philanax eagerly begins a prepared condemnation of her, which is not quoted—"But Gynecia, standing up before the judge, casting abroad her arms, with her eyes hidden under the breadth of her unseemly hat, laying open in all her gestures the despairful affliction to which all the might of her reason was converted, with suchlike words stopped Philanax as he was entering into his invective oration" (381.18–23). The prosopopoeiac confession and self-flagellation that follows is worthy of the melodramatic stage directions which set it up. After the pitying response of the populace is duly noted, Euarchus again speaks at length, elaborating his reasons and issuing a formal sentence: "She should be buried quick in the same tomb with him, that so his murder might be a murder to herself, and she forced to keep company with the body from which she had made so detestable a severance" (383.22–25). The assembly responds with approving, though sorrowful, consent.

The trial now builds in intensity as the two princes are brought forward to be charged. There is a brief legal scuffle as they stand upon their regality and question the jurisdiction of an Arcadian court to try "absolute princes" according to local laws, but this technicality is soon resolved against them on the grounds that a foreigner must abide by the laws of whatever country he might visit. So the trial of the princes proceeds. First, Pyrocles. Philanax steps forward to make the charge against him, and the stage directions are explicit:

> Philanax, that was even short-breathed at the first with the extreme vehemency he had to speak against them, stroking once or twice his forehead, and wiping his eyes (which either wept, or he

would at that time have them seem to weep), looking first upon Pyrocles as if he had proclaimed all hatefulness against him, humbly turning to Euarchus (who with quiet gravity showed great attention), he thus began his oration. (386.7–13)

Philanax's speech (386.14–391.21)—a masterful oration of five pages, brilliantly displaying Sidney's forensic skill—is answered by Pyrocles's defence (391.35–395.20), almost as long and equally masterful.

At this point, to complicate the moral issues and to deepen the suspense, two letters written by the princesses are introduced and quoted in full—first, Philoclea's on behalf of Pyrocles, then Pamela's more imperious letter on behalf of Musidorus (395.34–398.6).[32] Philanax craftily suppresses these letters, however, so the trial continues with none of the others being aware of the sentiments that Philoclea and Pamela have expressed.

Pyrocles, angered by the virulence of Philanax, has challenged him to a trial by single combat. But Euarchus forbids it, on the proper grounds that "since bodily strength is but a servant to the mind, it were very barbarous and preposterous that force should be made judge over reason" (398.30–32). So the trial of Musidorus takes center stage. In an oration that parallels his charge against Pyrocles, Philanax makes the formal accusation against Musidorus (399.5–400.22). And Musidorus immediately replies, as had Pyrocles, in an angry rebuttal (400.30–403.2). After a brief authorial report on the attitudes of Sympathus, of Kerxenus, and of the populace, the climactic moment has come: Euarchus will make his judgment in the case of the two princes. He does so in a lengthy proclamation which shows him to be the wisest of judges (403.21–408.7). He painstakingly discloses the rational basis for his judgment, and then pronounces sentence on the defendants: Pyrocles "shall be thrown out of a high tower to receive his death by his fall," and Musidorus "shall be beheaded" (408.2–4).

Once the sentence by Euarchus is uttered, and as though it were a signal, a clamorous stranger is thrust into the scene by Kerxenus. This is Kalodoulus, a servant of Musidorus from Thessalia, and we are told by authorial narrative how he had become concerned for the welfare of the long-absent princes and how he identifies them as the son and nephew of Euarchus. In the light of this recognition, everyone expects the judge to recant his harsh sentences. But Euarchus, inflexibly committed to what he calls "the never-changing justice" (411.28), cannot renege against the eternal law in order to accommodate his personal wishes. So he stands a tragic figure; and in a moving prosopopoeia he expresses his sorrow, though reconfirming the death sentences of the princes (411.5–412.8). Euarchus and everyone lament, "dolefully to record that pitiful spectacle" (412.12). In a bitter speech Musidorus angrily attacks Euarchus as an inhuman father responsible for the death of his own son (412.20–413.5). Pyrocles interrupts, and in a matching speech pleads more submissively for Euarchus to spare the life of Musidorus (413.14–414.25). The princes prove their selfless friendship for one another, but Euarchus remains unmoved in his dedication to unbending justice. The problem, brought about by all-too-human failings and exacerbated by the rigidity of Euarchus seems irresoluble. All these mortals are fools, and no Puck hovers over them.

It is at this point that Basilius begins to groan and his body stirs beneath the black velvet coverlet. As though risen from the dead, he returns to life. No murder has been committed. The assumption upon which the plot was built has proved erroneous. Once the artificer reveals this mendacity, he had best pack his bag of tricks and skip out. So the authorial narrator again smartly takes over; and in case any members of the audience are growing restive, he defensively promises: "How it fell out in few words shall be declared" (415.13). He explains that what Basilius had drunk was not actually poison, but only a sleeping potion. And after one more good yarn to account for its magical properties, he rapidly ties up all the loose ends into a jubilant denouement where everyone gets his fondest wish. Just when all seems hopeless, the tragedy turns to comedy.

The point of this résumé of Book 5 has been to accentuate the compelling dramatic quality of the old *Arcadia*, a quality that acquires increasing force as the work draws toward its close. Every page is filled with lively scenes, with vivacious characters in sprightly speech, with enargeiac figures, with speaking pictures. The verbal system produces a highly visual and auditory cavalcade of mortal creatures interacting busily and moving toward a seeming impasse in their multiple relationships. The meticulously contrived plot seems to be moving ineluctably toward tragedy. But at its nadir, suddenly, the story transmutes to comedy.

The old *Arcadia* is a comedy in the Aristotelian vein: it imitates the actions of men and women morally inferior. The sins of Basilius and of Gynecia especially, though of the others as well, are heinous and must be disapproved. But these are sins that all flesh is heir to, so the old *Arcadia* is a comedy also in the Dantesque mode: it has a happy rather than horrible ending. Indeed, it reveals the divine presence.[33]

In any case, when the old *Arcadia* is considered a comedy—or a tragicomedy, as Robertson suggests—Sidney's comments on the comic genre in the *Defence* are applicable. In his survey of the several kinds of poetry, Sidney eventually comes to "the Comic, whom naughty play-makers and stage-keepers have justly made odious" (95.30–31); but he will defend comedy, along with the rest of poetry, and assign it a useful purpose. Sidney begins with a straightforward statement that aligns comedy with satire in its purpose of reforming individual behavior: "The comedy is an imitation of the common errors of our life, which he representeth in the most ridiculous and scornful sort that may be, so as it is impossible that any beholder can be content to be such a one." The comic poet works by mimesis to figure forth the common errors of mankind so the beholder can use these fictional characters as negative exempla. As Sidney continues, "Now, as in geometry the oblique must be known as well as the right, and in arithmetic the odd as well as the even, so in the actions of our life who seeth not the filthiness of evil wanteth a great foil to perceive the beauty of virtue." The comic poet is enjoined to make in order to imitate, and he imitates in order to delight and teach. Furthermore, the means by which his comedy achieves this end is prescribed by the next sentence: "This doth the comedy handle so in our private and domestical matters as with hearing it we get as it were an experience what is to be looked for of a niggardly Demea, of a crafty Davus, of a flattering Gnatho, of a vainglorious Thraso; and not only to know what effects are to be expected, but to know who be such, by the signifying badge given them by the comedian." So the comic poet accomplishes his reformative mission by creating characters who by their actions represent certain types. To deter readers from niggardliness, for example, the poet produces a character who by what he says and does demonstrates what it means to be niggardly. To teach about craftiness, the poet produces another character who by his actions exemplifies that reprehensible quality. And so too for sycophancy and boasting. In a familiar word, the poet produces images of vices, virtues, and what else.

Moreover, "with hearing it we [the readers] get as it were an experience." And this experience is spelled out. It consists not only of learning "what effects are to be expected" of niggardliness and other depicted vices, but also of learning "to know who be such." By applying "the signifying badge" which the comic poet gives to each of the vicious characters—by ascertaining how and why the poet made these creatures—we too become adepts at the comic business of reform "in our private and domestical matters." The emphasis upon intimate relationships suggests that comedy is primarily a corrective for personal behavior, and the reader is the primary target of reform.

How well the characters in the old *Arcadia* fulfill these expectations for satiric comedy is so obvious that it would be tedious to belabor the point. Each of them cries out for analysis in these terms and readily submits to such treatment. As Sidney says of Aeneas, only let these characters be worn in the tablet of your memory—how Pyrocles and Musidorus loved, how Philoclea and Pamela were worthy of being loved, how Gynecia succumbed to illicit passion, how Basilius pursued an improper object of desire—and they will be found in excellency fruitful (*Defence* 98.16–27). Even Philanax in his fanatical loyalty to the prince and Euarchus in his narrow interpretation of justice offer valuable lessons to the discerning reader. Although the tale delights, we learn from each of the characters that unfolds it.

All these techniques whereby Sidney turns his text into "speaking pictures" are subsumed under what we may succinctly call enargeiac metaphors. By this I mean the use of fictional characters who are lifelike (and therefore enargeiac), but yet who exemplify concepts and introduce them effectively into human affairs (so that they are metaphors). "For whatsoever the philosopher saith should be done," says Sidney, "the peerless poet . . . giveth a perfect picture of it in someone by whom he presupposeth it was done" (*Defence* 85.22–24). Cyrus, the portraiture of just empire, is an enargeiac metaphor, and so are Theagenes and Chariclea,

the picture of love. Characters in the old *Arcadia,* like those of
Xenophon and Heliodorus, are imitations of the universalized actions involved in governing and loving, inclusively covering all
those human relationships of both a public and private sort. But
they are not allegorical, since their definition is provided within
the text itself and not by reference to some anterior system of
values. Just as the *Aeneid* plants the image of Turnus in our imagination, so that we can visualize it and be moved by it (*Defence*
92.33–37), so the fiction of the old *Arcadia* serves as the effective
agent of instruction. It is the tale of Basilius and of Gynecia, of
the four young lovers, of Dametas and his family, of Philanax and
Euarchus and all the rest, that plants their images in our imagination so that, willy-nilly, we are moved to well-doing. That is the
work of enargeiac metaphor.

Despite the intensified objectivity that heightens the vividness
and forcibleness of the last book, the old *Arcadia* is not "absolute"
drama, not fully realized as visible data. Despite the animated
images directed to the mind's eye of the reader, the old *Arcadia* is
still a literary event rather than a physical experience, and the
reader undergoes a mental response to verbal phenomena without
benefit of stage presentation. So far we have examined how these
verbal phenomena (the text) affect the reader through those mental faculties posited by Renaissance psychology and rhetoric. But
a literary event involves not only the relationship between artifact
and percipient, but also the relationship of artificer to artifact, and
through that relationship the equally important one (at least in
Sidney's poetics) between artificer and percipient. From the beginning a narrating voice asserts itself in the old *Arcadia,* and this
authorial presence is maintained throughout. How does this in-
truder condition the text and affect how the reader engages with
it?

At the outset we should note that Sidney, as a disciple of Aristotle, did not draw the qualitative difference between drama and
poetry that we have come to insist upon. "Drama," in fact, was not
a word in his vocabulary (nor, for that matter, in Spenser's or
Shakespeare's). There were plays, of course, but no "dramas" in
England until Aristotle's principle of mimesis as the imitation of
the actions of men was widely accepted and put into practice in

its perverted formulation: the imitation of men in action. Certainly, Sidney was interested in plays—he had been to the theater in Italy as well as at home, and he had thought about dramatic theory, as his extensive comments on the unities of place, time, and action clearly indicate (*Defence* 112.35–114.29). But for him, as for Aristotle, playwrighting was simply a species of ποιητική— or, in Sidney's metaphor, a daughter of Poesy (*Defence* 116.24– 26). In consequence, shifting between authorial narrative and direct conversation occurs smoothly in the old *Arcadia* and does not disrupt the overall poetical mode of discourse. As in the Homeric poems, the bardic voice is present, at least latently, even in those extended scenes where characters speak in their own persons.

With the Homeric model in mind—and the Xenophonic and Heliodoran, as well—we should not be surprised to find an omnipresent narrator in the old *Arcadia*. A story implies a storyteller. What is remarkable, though, is the degree to which this imputed narrator is developed as a participating entity. He proves far more assertive than an authorial presence need be. He is so obstreperous and persistent, in fact, that he achieves a distinct ethos of his own. Sidney puts the tale into the mouth of an officious persona who feels free to proclaim his presence at any time, who gratuitously offers his opinion about almost everything, and who presumes to identify a specific audience for the work. He patronizingly addresses his supposed readership as "fair ladies." Obviously this narrator participates in the fiction and controls to a large extent the effect of the text. It is impossible to ignore him. Furthermore, there is reason to believe—increasingly, as the tale progresses—that the imputed narrator is not Sidney himself.[34]

From the opening lines of the old *Arcadia*, readers feel that they are in the hands of a skillful storyteller. The setting, the major characters, the opening situation—all are given with brisk efficiency in little more than a page. And this sense of efficiency, which implies a knowing narrator, continues throughout the work. It is evident in the purposiveness with which the plot unfolds. Each episode makes a deliberate contribution, moving the plot forward, and the scenes are strung together in a remarkably smooth sequence, often by means of an intrusion by the narrator. The plot, especially in retrospect, is laid with extreme canniness. The characters needed in Book 5—particularly, Philanax and

Euarchus—are carefully introduced in Book 1, and their reappearance on cue for the final scene is reasonably accounted for. The arrival of Kalodoulus essential to the anagnoresis, reminiscent of the appearance of the old servant in *Oedipus Rex*,[35] is also foresightedly arranged for in Book 1. Even the costumes for the eye-catching entrance of the princes when they are called up for trial are readied during their early visit with Kerxenus. There are no unmet needs of the plot, and no loose ends (other than those incidentals listed in the final sentence which the narrator expressly leaves to the pens of others). The exact economy of the plot makes us continually aware of an artful maker.

This author frequently steps out into the playing area and speaks to the readership in his own voice. He makes a point of reminding us that he controls the narrative, intruding abruptly and without concealment to move us from one episode to another. For example, when he is ready for the young princes and wishes to introduce Pyrocles and Musidorus into the plot, he announces: "Because this matter runs principally of them, a few more words how they came hither will not be superfluous" (10.2–4); and his account of their background follows. Later in Book 1, after Gynecia sees through Cleophila's disguise when he slays the lion, the narrator hints at Gynecia's infatuation—"but of that you shall after hear" (48.27–28), he teases, and proceeds instead with the business of Cleophila presenting the lion's head to Philoclea. When Gynecia finally in Book 3 has Cleophila cornered in the cave, she presses her suit upon the perplexed transvestite, and one or the other must capitulate; but the narrator coyly breaks off, and with a snicker diverts our attention elsewhere: "But methinks I hear the shepherd Dorus calling me to tell you something of his hopeful adventures" (185.20–21). After we are told of Dorus's affairs and just as his rape of Pamela is thwarted by the villainous rebels, our narrator, again snickering, intervenes and returns to the plight of Cleophila hard-pressed by Gynecia: "But Cleophila (whom I left in the cave hardly bested) makes me lend her my pen awhile to see with what dexterity she could put by her dangers" (202.17–19). And so it goes. Perhaps these stratagems are no more than the games good storytellers usually play, but our narrator is notable for the openness with which he makes his moves.

Actually, this imputed author makes his presence felt from the opening of the text. No sooner is Arcadia established as the setting of the tale and its royal family designated as the central characters than he ventures to appear. He intrudes to offer his opinion about what Basilius is doing, and makes it clear who is telling this story. The opening situation, the terminus à quo for the plot, is presented in this fashion:

> And thus grew they on in each good increase till Pamela, a year older than Philoclea, came to the point of seventeen years of age. At which time the duke Basilius—not so much stirred with the care for his country and children as with the vanity which possesseth many who, making a perpetual mansion of this poor baiting place of man's life, are desirous to know the certainty of things to come, wherein there is nothing so certain as our continual uncertainty—Basilius, I say, would needs undertake a journey to Delphos, there by the oracle to inform himself whether the rest of his life should be continued in like tenor of happiness as thitherunto it had been. (5.1–11)

The narrator slips into the text with no fanfare, so he can offer his opinion of Basilius without disturbing the receptiveness of the reader, and he goes on to generalize about the unpredictability of what lies ahead for any of us. He is quite willing to hold up the narrative for a bit of blather even at this initial point. But once these moralistic sentiments are expressed, there is a break in the text indicated by the dash, and the narrator then steps forward into full view, appearing as a first-person speaker, insisting that his voice be recognized as the sole begetter of this tale. All this is so because "I say" it.

This officious narrator is a prominent and complicating feature throughout the work. Continually he intrudes with an "I say" or "I think," or he reminds us, "As I told you." Like a cough behind an arras, such gestures serve no purpose other than letting the audience know that he is there. By this means, though, an agent of narration is identified, and thereby a line of demarcation is drawn between the world of the fiction and the space inhabited by the narrator. The universe of the poem is hypostatized, set apart from that of the narrator. Even as Arcadia comes into being, the narrator eloigns himself from it. He is not himself an Arcadian. But at the same time he mediates between the story and us. He regularly addresses the reader with an intimate "you" or a conspiratorial "we," making us cohabitants of his space so that we share his perspective. Perforce we must look where he looks, dependent upon him for our point of view.

Given his importance, we must ask, who is this fellow looming so large in our engagement with the text? In addition to his bumptiousness and ubiquity, we are not allowed to overlook the frequent sanctimoniousness which our narrator assumes toward the human behavior that he reports. We have already noted his readiness to sermonize upon the folly of mankind when Basilius expresses uneasiness about the future, and he stops just short of warning against a lack of faith. Not only does he presume to judge specific actions, but he is handy with platitudinous generalizations as well. When Musidorus enters the service of Dametas as a simple shepherd in order to be near Pamela, our narrator sententiously opines: "The greatest point outward things can bring a man unto is the contentment of the mind, which once obtained, no state is miserable; and without that, no prince's seat restful" (44.36–45.4). Even true love such as that of Musidorus is not exempt from reprimand, and on occasion our narrator apostrophizes it in feigned rebuke: "O feminine love, what power thou holdest in men's hearts!" (174.2–3). Especially the passions of Gynecia elicit strong reproof, and he denounces her jealousy in a high-sounding string of Ciceronian epithets and oxymorons and parallelisms: "O jealousy, the frenzy of wise folks, the well wishing spite and unkind carefulness, the self-punishment for other's fault and self-misery in other's happiness, the sister of envy, daughter of love, and mother of hate, how couldst thou so quickly get thee a seat in the unquiet heart of Gynecia?" (122.14–18). But passion of any sort is decried, even the recklessness of a rebellious rabble, "so much easier is it to inflame than to quench, to tie than to loose knots" (131.14–15). Not even the virtuous Philoclea escapes censure: when Pyrocles at last has the opportunity of expressing his love and finds Philoclea eagerly compliant despite some hesitation because of honor, our narrator knowingly observes, "Such contradictions there must needs grow in those minds which neither absolutely embrace goodness nor freely yield to evil" (120.33–121.2).

This knowingness on the part of the narrator suggests a degree of experience in human duplicity, and sometimes he speaks with a worldliness that discloses an underlying disillusionment with his fellow mortals, especially the weaker sex. On occasion he sounds very much like a jaded wit in a Restoration comedy. In Book 1, for example, when Cleophila concentrates her attention upon Philoclea to the exclusion of the other ladies, Gynecia and Pamela quite naturally feel twinges of envy; but with a pretended innocence that is actually a petty wickedness, our narrator comments brightly to his audience: "You ladies know best whether sometimes you feel impression of that passion; for my part, I would hardly think that the affection of a mother and the noble mind of Pamela could be overthrown with so base a thing as envy is" (39.17–20). Sometimes our narrator speaks with an archness that verges upon sarcasm. When reporting the passion that both Gynecia and Basilius feel for Cleophila, he frets: "It seems to myself I use not words enough to make you see how they could in one moment be so overtaken"; then, however, he tauntingly adds: "But you, worthy ladies, that have at any time feelingly known what it means, will easily believe the possibility of it" (49.24–27). And sometimes, we must admit, our narrator indulges in prurience. We have already noted the repeated instances of voyeurism. They may delight the naughty boys in the readership, but just as certainly they violate the sensibility of the gentle ladies for whose benefit, supposedly, this tale is being told.

Our narrator is never loath to offer a judgment or a generality, frequently praising virtue, but more often smirking at the vice that undercuts it. He is far from consistent in his professed attitude toward human behavior, though, vacillating in wide swings between apparent pietism and equally apparent cynicism. Given this capriciousness of the narrator, we must guard against his facile opinions, especially his blatant moralizing. Can we accept it without evaluation, without revision? Can even fair ladies (if we *were* ladies) be expected to prove so trusting? Perhaps his professed morality, as so often in prosopopoeia, is a pretense, a cover-up for a basic amorality, a sham that by its presence calls attention to what it hopes to conceal. Or perhaps his glib comments reveal an inadequacy in making moral judgments, a shallowness, a silliness. Either circumstance would fundamentally affect the way we read what if taken at face value would be the serious musings of the narrator. Can we accept without adjustment his mediation between the story and us?

A crucial case in point is the pontificating about "the everlasting justice" that opens the fourth book. By this time in the fiction each of the major characters has committed some grave crime, and Book 4 begins portentously with the phrase "the everlasting justice." Before uttering another word, however, the narrator increases the weightiness of this phrase by adding parenthetically: "using ourselves to be the punishment of our faults, and making our own actions the beginning of our chastisement, that our shame may be the more manifest, and our repentance follow the sooner." Some recent readers have taken this pronouncement to be the bald statement of what Sidney means to teach in the old *Arcadia*. This is a Calvinistic universe. During the climactic trial of Book 5 this same narrator, with a Gloucester-like pessimism, observes gloomily: "In such a shadow or rather pit of darkness the wormish mankind lives that neither they know how to foresee nor what to fear, and are but like tennis balls tossed by the racket of the higher powers" (385.31–386.2).

But at the beginning of Book 4 when the voluble narrator intrudes this ponderous—and gratuitous—remark about "the everlasting justice," we must note that it is grossly out of place. The passage is in essence a comic one, describing how Dametas was disabused of his expectations of great treasure after Dorus tricked him into leaving Pamela unattended. The incongruity between the subject matter and the pious remarks of the narrator is flagrant. And it continues. Finally, a predicate is supplied for the opening phrase in order for the sentence to proceed. Without the interruption of the narrator the sentence runs: "The everlasting justice . . . took Dametas at this present (by whose folly the others' wisdom might receive the greater overthrow) to be the instrument of revealing the secretest cunning [i.e., Dorus's trickery]." Perhaps God is working here in mysterious ways, using weak vessels to manifest His will. But the irrepressible narrator again butts in with a devout, and misplaced, platitude: "So evil a ground doth evil stand upon, and so manifest it is that nothing remains strongly but that which hath the good foundation of goodness." Such sentiments are glaringly inappropriate to the comedy at hand; and given the deliciousness of the moment we are led to expect when

the clown Dametas awakens to his catastrophe, we are in no mood
to entertain them.

As the fiction proceeds, the decorum of the narrator, and therefore his credibility, is irreparably impugned. He is exposed as a
busybody who can be tolerated only by being laughed at. He himself becomes a comic figure by expressing a piety that we by this
time know he does not practice and probably does not believe in.
So, distrusting the narrator, we distance ourselves from him despite his autocratic attempts to corral us under his authority, and
we come to see him as part of the fun.

We arrive at a similar conclusion after another passage in which
the narrator takes an equally comprehensive (and dim) view of
the human condition. In Book 3 after Cleophila has deceived Gynecia into believing that her love will finally be requited during a
tryst in the cave, the narrator reports on Gynecia's willingness to
accept what her loved one says: "Gynecia [was] already half persuaded in herself (O weakness of human conceit!) that Cleophila's
affection was turned toward her" (206.75–77). The narrator proceeds to posit Gynecia's condition as a common denominator in
human behavior: "For such, alas, are we all! In such a mould are
we cast that, with the too much love we bear ourselves being first
our own flatterers, we are easily hooked with others' flattery, we
are easily persuaded of others' love" (206.27–30). In this passage
the sentiments of our narrator at first glance seem appropriate to
the subject matter. The plight of Gynecia might well call forth a
plangent outburst such as this. His melodramatic exclamations,
however, activate our doubts about his sincerity and dependability; and upon closer examination we see that Gynecia is being
charged with perhaps the only sin she has avoided. Her crime is
not self-love, the "love we bear ourselves," but self-loathing. So
again the narrator is wrong in his commentary, and we distance
ourselves from him. His wholesale and inaccurate condemnation
of Gynecia only increases our sympathy for her. As we turn away
from his posturing, we explore our alliance with Gynecia, as he
suggests, but we come to pity her weakness and honestly lament
her folly.

From what we have said, it should be obvious that we cannot
equate the imputed narrator with Sidney himself in any simplistic
way.[36] The narrator is not Sidney per se. Of course, the narrator *is*

Sidney in some sense, just as a persona always represents the author to some degree or in some fashion. The persona is the means by which the author tells his tale, the dummy on the ventriloquist's knee. The imputed narrator in the old *Arcadia* represents Sidney in the same way and to the same extent that Rombus, the major domo, represents him in *The Lady of May*. The narrator, like Rombus, keeps things moving. And there is a comparable intention of self-parody, self-mockery, self-apology. Sidney confesses that in his own judgment of human behavior he is as vagarious as our narrator, and just as likely to be in error. By encouraging us to laugh at the narrator, he invites us to laugh at himself, who ludicrously presumes to the omniscience of a poet; and we should admire Sidney's humility in standing before us clothed only in human shortcomings.

But in another more important sense, our narrator is not Sidney. Nor could Sidney allow his persona, guilty of caprice and blunder, to represent that serious maker who poetized in order to move men to take that goodness in hand which would lead to well-doing (*Defence* 81.11). The young aristocrat with societal reform on his mind could not afford to project himself into the playing area as the obstreperous finger-wagging hypocrite that the narrator proves to be, a persona whom the reader learns to distrust. Such a characterization of the actual author (as opposed to the imputed author) would undermine the serious purpose that Sidney assigned to poetry.

Nor can we argue that Sidney assumed such a supercilious attitude toward his material because he considered the *Arcadia* to be only a trifle, recreation for himself while composing it and amusement for his sister when she read it. He spent many years working on the *Arcadia*, both in and out of favor at court, and he was too busy a man—too committed and ambitious a politician—to have wasted so much time on a trifle. This is not to say that Sidney was always serious, relentlessly dour; he can be playful and purposeful at once, as the continual sunniness of the *Defence* demonstrates. To apply his own phrase, he was a "good-fellow poet" (93.10). He was well aware of Horace's dictum about delightfulness as well as teaching, and he knew that "the philosophers, as they scorn to delight, so must they be content little to move" (93.1–2). This *is* to say, however, that Sidney would not have been simple-mindedly playful in his fiction, and he would not have jeopardized the good he wished to accomplish by presenting himself as a waggish narrator. It is therefore imperative that we separate Sidney from the imputed narrator, who is of course part of the fiction—or, perhaps more accurately, the fictive mediator between us and the story.

By the same token, it is imperative to separate the imputed readership of the old *Arcadia,* the "fair ladies," from the Countess of Pembroke. We have already noted how the narrator coerces his audience by using the second-person pronouns "you" and "your," and by including us in his first-person plural pronouns "we" and "us" and "our." He gathers us under his wing. He also at the beginning addresses his readership as "fair ladies," another gesture of containment. Such a relationship between an all-knowing narrator and an innocent and immature but refined female audience may suggest the actual relationship between Sidney and his younger sister Mary in the late 1570s. He had returned from his studies at Oxford and his travels abroad, a worldly man, while she had remained in the shelter of the family. It is improbable, however, that Sidney was so patronizing toward his much loved sister, and especially after her marriage in 1577 it is unlikely that he could have gotten away with so superior an attitude.[37] Such an assertion of authority would have been insulting and quite contrary to all we know about their relationship. Therefore we should not use this evidence to argue that Sidney himself is the narrator and that "fair ladies" is a collective noun representing the Countess of Pembroke as a presumed audience. Rather, the supercilious narrator as well as his docile (if eager) female listeners are all part of the fiction.

Creating an imputed audience is the obverse of creating an imputed narrator, and it confirms the same narrative strategy of establishing the artificiality of the fictional enterprise. Imputing an audience similarly hypostatizes the story. And Sidney goes about it with a comparable zest, so appeals to the "fair ladies" begin early in the old *Arcadia.* The first instance accompanies the important moment when Pyrocles transforms into Cleophila (27.18–22), and others soon follow. Such asides to "fair ladies" do not occur throughout the work—they are concentrated in Book 1, and a few appear again in Book 3;[38] but they are a definite feature of our early engagement with the text and they must be taken into account.

Their immediate effect may be to sharpen our attention. They personalize the readership, establishing eye contact, as it were. But their overall effect is quite different. Eventually, if taken seriously, they trivialize the text since they assume that decorative "ladies" are the only fit audience for this story. It is suitable for passing otherwise idle time and perhaps for moralizing in a mildly reproving manner, but it isn't meant to waste the time of busy men who have better things to do and who probably don't require moral instruction anyway. We're no more fair ladies, however, than Sidney is a pietistic parablist, as we are the first to know; and ultimately we resent our inclusion in a group characterized by the traditional female vices, ranging from the relatively innocuous infirmity of envy to the venal sin of unrestrained lust. We dissociate ourselves from this group just as we draw apart from the narrator. Even if some men in the readership smile indulgently at its feminine foibles, including gullibility, the women in the audience may not take so kindly to the spoofing.[39] Again, though, we must remember that it is the imputed narrator, and not Sidney, who addresses the readership as "fair ladies." These objectionable asides to a fictionalized readership are yet another way that Sidney establishes the artifice of his text.

So once more we are forced to recognize a line between the actual world and the world of the fiction. We must dissociate the Countess of Pembroke, as well as ourselves, from the fair ladies who comprise the imputed audience, just as we separate Sidney from the narrator. Although the narrator is Sidney's persona, he is not Sidney. But we must also note the ambiguous stance of the narrator in his role as purveyor of the text. On the one hand, he objectifies the story, viewing it from a privileged, superior position; on the other, he knows the Arcadians with a congenial intimacy. On the one hand, he hypostatizes the fiction, setting it apart from our time and space; on the other, he introduces it to us, mediating between us and text. The narrator belongs to a fictive world at the same time that he offers that world to us, so he bridges the discontinuity between our reality and Arcadia.

The role of Sidney's narrator, then, is more significant than simply making the fictive world of Arcadia available to the reader.

And it is even more sophisticated than the usual role of the unreliable narrator who forces the reader to evaluate the subject
matter because it is being provided by a biased reporter, or a narrator who reveals his own personality by reporting only those facts
that are relevant to his own inner life. Sidney did not intrude a
narrator between us and the story simply to illustrate the partiality of human perception in distorting what it sees or the power of
human personality to bend everything to its likeness. So why did
Sidney create a fictive narrator (and a fictive audience), and what
are the effects of that narrative strategy? To answer this question,
we shall do well to look at another character who represents the
author in the text.

How about Philisides? While we conclude that Sidney should
not be placed in exact equation with the narrator, can we so readily separate *Philip Sidney* from a character named Philisides?
The answer is, again, both yes and no. Philisides clearly is, but
also is not, Sidney.[40] In fact, since Philisides has no relevance to
the plot of the story, the major reason for his existence is to demonstrate that a character can indeed be both actual and fictional,
"real" and not real, outside and inside the text. With Philisides,
Sidney's own circumstances are intruded into Arcadia. The world
of fact and the world of fiction intersect, interact. And the presence of Philisides forces an examination of that exchange. This is
why his maker made him. Furthermore, Philisides reveals *how* a
character bridges the discontinuity between fact and fiction,
thereby disclosing the means by which our world and the world of
fiction are related. Philisides, who is otherwise gratuitous, exists
to give us further instruction in how to read the old *Arcadia*.

So let's take a closer look at Philisides. Sidney got the idea for
such a character from Sannazaro's *Arcadia,* where Sincero is the
same sort of person and represents the author in exactly the same
way. Nowhere is Sidney's debt to Sannazaro more immediate or
more evident. Sincero is a world-weary cosmopolite, not a native
of Arcadia, although he is sympathetic to their ethos; and he is
hopelessly in love with an unattainable mistress. He activates both
the pastoral and the Petrarchist codes.

And, of course, so does Philisides. After the dissatisfying experience of love, Philisides has retired to Arcadia. He implements
the pastoral pattern of foregoing the urban life for the country,

and even there he eloigns himself from human relationships—as we have noted, he doesn't participate in the plot but rather inhabits only the lyric world of the eclogues. Because of his inescapable identification with the historical personage Philip Sidney, though, Philisides (like the narrator) bridges the discontinuity between the real world and Arcadia, between the affairs of men and the pastoral ideal, between the active life and the life of leisurely contemplation. Quite naturally, leisurely contemplation leads to melancholy, as the crying philosopher, Heraclitus, well knew; and from Philisides's perspective, this is a Heraclitean universe, in constant flux and always for the worse. Inevitably we lose what we love—to death if not to a rival. That is the point of Philisides's loss of Mira. *Et in Arcadia ego.* The death of Basilius (until divine providence manifests itself at the last possible moment) confirms the point, which the fourth set of eclogues is devoted to iterating. So Philisides in the very act of exemplifying the pastoral code offers a negative critique of it, with its debilitating langor and grief and resignation.

In addition, Philisides offers a negative critique of the Petrarchist code. Since *sides* in Latin means "star," he is a star-lover like Astrophil. The image of his actions in the fiction provides a speaking picture of the Petrarchan lover, the identity that Pyrocles and Musidorus have chosen but cannot successfully achieve. Philisides is the hopeless devotee of Mira, the wondrous one, and he exemplifies the Petrarchan system pushed to its ineluctable conclusion. If the lady is a heavenly being, she cannot be engaged on earth; since she is essentially spiritual, she cannot meet fleshly needs. Philisides is the hapless product of such an impractical system.[41]

But this is to get into interpretation of the text, and perhaps we are not yet ready for that. First we must deal more carefully with the question of why Sidney introduces into the Arcadian fiction a stranger shepherd who inevitably recalls his own circumstances. As a prolegomenon to that, we need to have the full-length portrait of Philisides in view.

When Philisides makes his earliest appearance in the first set of eclogues, he is described as a disengaged malcontent, "another young shepherd . . . who neither had danced nor sung with them, and had all this time lain upon the ground at the foot of a cypress tree, leaning upon his elbow with so deep a melancholy that his

senses carried to his mind no delight from any of their objects"
(71.31–35). On this occasion he reluctantly participates in a three-
way eclogue with Geron and Histor. Philisides is next called upon
in Book 2 to sing a highly mannered amorous complaint in answer
to Dorus, who has just sung in a similar vein (125.13–29). And he
appears in the second set of eclogues. After Histor narrates the
"worthy acts" of Pyrocles and Musidorus, Basilius "willed Philisides to declare the discourse of his own fortunes, unknown to
them as being a stranger in that country"; but Philisides demurs
on the grounds that "the rehearsal of his miseries" would be out
of place at this joyful time, and he sings instead a dolorous duet
with the echo (159.30–162.28). Philisides shows up again in Book
3, at least at one remove. When Pyrocles places the compliant
Philoclea upon her bed, he pauses to relish her outstretched
beauty (and to tease the readership), "having so free scope of his
serviceable sight that there came into his mind a song the shepherd Philisides had in his hearing sung of the beauties of his unkind mistress" (238.1–4)—and there follows Philisides's anatomical blazon of Mira, a highly erotic poem that was taken out of
context and printed in anthologies as well as subjected to a round
of equally erotic imitations.[42] It suggests a lover not always given
to indolence.

"The melancholy Philisides" again turns up among the wedding
guests at the marriage of Lalus and Kala in the third set of eclogues, and on this occasion he sings the song about watching his
flock on the banks of the Ister in which Languet is mentioned by
name (254.21–259.23). Also in the fourth set of eclogues, Philisides is included by brief mention among the mourning shepherds
(328.3); and after the lament for the departed Urania by Strephon
and Claius, he goes on at considerable length to "impart some part
of his sorrow" (334.8). In actual fact, he gives a brief account of
his own life in prose,[43] which scholarly consensus interprets as
autobiographical on Sidney's part; and then in verse he recites
"how love first took me" (335.10) by showing him a vision of Mira
in a dream, and he also includes an elegiacal poem which he had
sent Mira by way of despairing farewell. This is the last we see of
Philisides, although in the final paragraph of the old *Arcadia* the
narrator includes "the poor hopes of the poor Philisides" (417.19)
among the topics that another pen may wish to pursue. We must

note that Philisides maintains a consistent and continual presence from the first set of eclogues to the last page.

We must also reiterate that there are strong ties which link Philisides with the historical person of Philip Sidney. Not only is there a personal signature in the name itself, but there are also other tokens that point directly to the youthful courtier. In the song "As I my little flock on Ister bank," Philisides mentions places, people, and politics that were particular to Sidney; and in the prose account of his life, Philisides describes an upbringing and adolescence that exactly match those of Sidney.[44] In ways that cannot be ignored, Sidney insists that Philisides be seen as a projection of his own circumstances.

Yet at the time of writing the old *Arcadia,* Sidney was engaged in no amorous liaisons. If he were melancholy, it was not because of unrequited love. Mira and the lovesickness of Philisides are fictitious. There is no evidence (Astrophil apart) that Sidney was susceptible to affairs of the heart; in fact, it seems to me, there is a telling lack of such evidence. At most, his family was considering a few carefully selected young ladies, any one of whom would have made a suitable bride in terms of the wealth, social prestige, and political advantage she brought to the marriage, and Sidney seems to have been agreeable to what his family decided. He made no amorous choices for himself, and when the time came, he dutifully married Frances Walsingham. There was no real-life counterpart of Mira[45]—of all those wraithlike mistresses who animate love lyrics, she is one of the more noumenal. How, then, do we reconcile Sidney's inescapable hints that Philisides represents him with the incontrovertible fact that Philisides is at best an extremely partial and grossly distorted representation?

What we have, I would argue, is a case of Sidney bringing his own stuff and making matter for a conceit. Philisides evolves out of portions of Sidney's own experience, as the references to Languet, Vienna, and a schooling which parallels Sidney's indicate. Since Sidney's stuff pertaining to love was meager, he relied heavily upon the model of Sannazaro's Sincero; but with that supplement he extrapolated from what he knew of love to create a type of the melancholy Petrarchan lover in a pastoral setting. Philisides as a familiar type then becomes matter for a conceit, and Sidney can set him in action in the Arcadian fiction. Sidney imagines what a Petrarchan lover would be like, what it would be like to be a Petrarchan lover. So eventually this act of making Philisides, imitating the actions of a Petrarchan lover, is an act of testing the Petrarchist code. Is it viable? Philisides's melancholy and his unfulfilled longing are strong deterrents to following his example. Sidney has made to imitate, and has imitated to teach, and has wisely delighted while teaching so that we swallow our instruction as though it were a medicine of cherries.

But this moral didacticism was not Sidney's only purpose in creating Philisides. He had a larger aim. Philisides as object lesson for would-be Petrarchists does not account for his firm grounding in Sidney's own experience. Sidney could have accomplished his purpose of warning against the debilities of Petrarchan love without resorting to a character connected so directly to himself. In fact, by using a character that unmistakably recalls his own name, Sidney opened himself to the charge of obsessive passion—a charge that has regularly been levelled against him as a result of *Astrophil and Stella* (though with equal inappropriateness, as we shall see).

So why did Sidney take the risk of having Philisides interpreted in a simplistic way as merely a counter for himself? Because he was playing for high stakes, for nothing less than the unqualified justification of poetry itself. Sidney arranged for Philisides, like the imputed narrator, to bridge the gap between the real world and the world of fiction to prove that commerce between these two worlds is possible. Philisides, like the narrator, provides a conduit through which an interchange between our world and Arcadia takes place. In effect, Philisides validates the fiction and legitimizes the art of fiction. The poetical artifact is based upon the phenomena of actual occurrence and re-presents these phenomena, just as Philisides re-presents Sidney. Philisides in *praxis* confirms the theory of poetry that Sidney had proposed in its defence.

The most important role for Philisides arises from the fact that he cannot be confined to the function of serving as a simple counter for Sidney. He is the product of active mimesis by a right poet. He does not remain wrapped within the fold of a proposed subject; rather, he addresses speculatively the vital questions that Sidney faced: what if, like a Petrarchist, I become a lover? what if, like a pastoralist, I forego the active life? In this speculation the fictive creature is an extrapolation from the maker, made from his stuff, and yet the creature is clearly set apart from the maker. A space appears between the maker and his fictional counterpart, between the maker and his artifact. And it is in this space, in this no-man's-land between fact and fiction, that we can watch the maker at his making. This intermundum between what is and what is not provides a natural habitat for the imputed narrator, who claims it for his own. Through the narrator, Sidney creates a Philisides, not only bestowing a Philisides upon the world, but also revealing why and how he made him so that we the readers may learn aright the art of making.

Further important consequences stem from the how of making Philisides, because he demonstrates the multivalency of meaning that arises from fiction as a re-presentation of nature.[46] Since Philisides is a conceit made from a matter abstracted from Sidney's own experience, he generates meaning at each of these levels of his existence. His character comprises not a single, simple meaning, but a field of probable meanings. As imaginative conceit, Philisides is a speaking picture, an enargeiac metaphor, and in the durational fiction we watch his actions to learn about love through vicarious experience, just as we watch Xenophon's Cyrus to witness good governance. As a rhetorician's matter, Philisides is a type, a topos, an atemporal and aspatial concept, the Petrarchan lover who warns against such love because our mutable world is inimical to its presuppositions. As Sidney's stuff, Philisides is personal fact, actual occurrence as Sidney experienced it, and he incorporates those issues of consequence to Sidney and discloses how Sidney viewed them. Like the narrator, who also represents Sidney and similarly manifests this multivalency of meaning, Philisides is a key term in the semantics of the old Arcadia.

For Philisides demonstrates how fiction arises from fact, how fiction explores the potential of fact, how it speculates upon what might be or should be given certain circumstances. Fiction bestows the eternal life of natura naturans upon what would otherwise be only the dead past of natura naturata. It creates a continuous present. With an alchemist's magic, it produces an everlasting golden world from the brazen world of history. By ranging from actual existence through derived type to imagined story, fiction defines a continuous scale of being, combining the

static, the abstract, and the kinetic. By encompassing the extremes of this scale, it illustrates the multeity that comprises our
universe, and yet its unity. Fiction shows how each of the infinite
points along this scale has its own identity—defined crudely in
terms of the static fact, the abstract universal, and the kinetic possibility; and yet each of these innumerable points is interrelated
to all other points to form a self-consistent whole. Consequently,
the meaning of each point is not simple, but multivalent, implying
all the rest. Philisides, who embraces the extremes from hard fact
to fanciful fiction, is the paradigm that Sidney provides to apprise
us of such a system.

Sidney inserts himself into the fictional world of Arcadia by means
of Philisides as well as a quite different personality, the imputed
narrator. It is notable how dissimilar these two characters are, and
we shall shortly consider how and why the two characters that
most immediately represent Sidney contrast one another so
neatly. For the moment, though, I shall generalize from the cases
of Philisides and the imputed narrator and argue that all the characters in the old *Arcadia* represent Sidney to some degree. Each
character is a creature of his making. Each is a conceit that originates with his stuff, since an author perforce can write only out of
his own experience.

The point is probably best substantiated by Pyrocles and Musidorus.[47] In age, station, and temperament these young aristo-
crats quite obviously accord with what we know of Sidney himself.
They are virile youths, active in what they consider to be noble
causes. When the narrator first introduces them, he notes that
they "gave themselves wholly over to those knowledges which
might in the course of their life be ministers to well doing" (10.29–
30); so they are motivated students. They are also—or, perhaps,
especially—lovers. In Pyrocles's words to Philoclea, he is "a living
image and a present story of the best pattern love hath ever
showed of his workmanship" (120.6–7). Pyrocles is open and susceptible to love, while Musidorus is resistant but equally vulnerable. In part to satisfy sexual urgings, but also to meet dynastic
pressures, both feel the need to marry. Tellingly, they have been
reared to abide by the platonist code of courtship, and they exemplify its principles with their talk of servitude, their disavowal

of carnality, and their songs in ritual worship of a mistress. But in the end the platonist code serves to measure how far their sensuality causes them to fall from their noble natures. They find themselves unable to succeed as purely Petrarchan lovers. In this, they are often compared to and contrasted with Philisides. In Book 2, for example, to celebrate his engagement to Pamela, Musidorus participates in a pair of companion poems with Philisides (124.22–125.29); while in Book 3, just before his seduction of Philoclea, Pyrocles recalls Philisides's blazon of Mira. Each of these young lovers acts out some attitude toward love that we are justified in saying occupied the mind of Sidney. Each in his own way addresses a different question, what if the lover . . . ?

Gynecia also is a lover, though a degenerate one. She makes no pretense of honoring the platonist imperatives, and she violates as well the rules of marriage and of motherhood. Viewed more charitably, Gynecia is the fallen woman who proceeds from sin to self-loathing, and eventually to despair.[48] In her fiction we see the plight of the mature and worthy person who submits to illicit passion, and the fact that she cannot by her own resources resist this passion is not incidental. We are all fallen creatures, Sidney would say with the Calvinists, and we are all dependent upon God's mercy. Gynecia's despair is not the least of her sins, just as her self-awareness is not the least of her torments.

Nor is it incidental that this abject creature is a woman, like Eve. Her name is indicative of her archetypal status. All of the female characters in the old *Arcadia*—including the princesses, Mopsa, and even Cleophila—are willing to abandon their virtue to achieve more tangible ends. Only Miso is chaste; but her ungiving nature, rather than high principles, enforces her honesty. In presenting this unflattering view of womankind, Sidney appears to be a misogynist, and the most we can say to mitigate this charge is to note that he reflected the prevailing attitudes of his time.

Perhaps most disturbing, Pamela and Philoclea come nowhere near the perfection that Musidorus and Pyrocles imagine them to possess. They repeatedly belie the idealized portraits that the young men carry in their hearts. The princesses display envy, jealousy, vanity, haughtiness, and suspicion, and they practice disobedience and deceit—all in the name of a love which derives from body chemistry.[49] They are no more Petrarchan mistresses than

Pyrocles and Musidorus are genuine Petrarchan lovers. They are flawed, outwardly seeming very much like the "fair ladies" who comprise the imputed readership of their story. On the opening page of the old *Arcadia*, when the narrator introduces Pamela and Philoclea as the daughters of Basilius and Gynecia, he reports that they were "both so excellent in all those gifts which are allotted to reasonable creatures as they seemed to be born for a sufficient proof that nature is no stepmother to that sex, how much soever the rugged disposition of some men, sharp-witted only in evil speaking, hath sought to disgrace them" (4.30–5.1). But like much that the narrator tells us, this statement subverts what it purports to affirm.

Finally, Basilius is a lover—but one who is so unsuited to the role and who has chosen so improper an object of affection that we can never take his wooing seriously. To implement the distinction between laughter and delight that Sidney takes over from Aristotle (*Defence* 115.12ff.), we find Basilius in his pursuit of Cleophila to be a lunatic buffoon at whom we laugh, but in whose amatory activities we take no pleasure. Neither Sidney nor we feel much identity with Basilius as a lover. Instead, we consider him seriously only in his role as ruler. As his name indicates, he has the responsibility of governing; and with Cyrus as our benchmark, we view him as a portraiture of just empire.

As a sovereign, Basilius reigns in the dukedom of Arcadia. As a husband, he is chief partner in his marriage with Gynecia. As a father, he is charged with the upbringing of Pamela and Philoclea. But he fails wretchedly in all these magisterial roles. In the Renaissance view, since each of these duties is correspondent with the others and all are interdependent, he fails wretchedly as a man created in the image of God, the ruler of the universe. Gynecia neatly details the several levels of his wrongdoing when she confronts him in the cave after his attempted infidelity in marriage. "Remember the wrong you do me is not only to me," she scolds after disabusing Basilius of the notion that he has spent the night with Cleophila, "but to your children, whom you had of me; to your country when they shall find they are commanded by him that cannot command his own undecent appetites; lastly to yourself, since with these pains you do but build up a house of shame to dwell in" (277.12–16). The folly of his passion has brought shame to Basilius on all scores. Worst of all, he has not been true to himself as a man, God's best-loved creature. He is acting in an unmanly—what the Elizabethans would have called an "unkindly"—fashion. In the *Defence* Sidney notes that philosophers teach how virtue "extendeth itself out of the limits of a man's own little world to the government of families and maintaining of public societies" (83.28–29). Just the opposite, Basilius exemplifies how man allows his own corruption to infect his family and the commonwealth.

We must look more closely into Basilius's case, however, since he is the focal figure of the plot, providing both its initial impetus and its conclusion. The plot is bracketed by his decision to retire to the wooded retreat and by his revival from a deathlike sleep. When we examine his actions more carefully, we find that the folly of an inappropriate love is not the only crime of Basilius. In fact, his infatuation with Cleophila is at most ancillary, an incidental that occurs after his retirement to the sylvan lodge. His misdirected pursuit of Cleophila is a result of his retreat; an effect, not a cause of anything else. It manifests a deeper malady. The abdication of his royal responsibilities is the more heinous crime, certainly as the Elizabethans would have viewed it. So why does Basilius leave his throne? Because of the oracle. And why does he seek the oracle? Because he is uncertain about the future. And why is he suddenly fearful of what lies ahead for him and his family? Because his daughters have reached marriageable age. And why should this inevitable (and hoped for) consummation cause him concern? Because he realizes that the old order is changing, and his roles as father, husband, and sovereign are being threatened by the imminent arrival of two virile sons-in-law.[50] Basilius, who so far has been the unchallenged male in his domain, must make adjustments in all his roles. This circumstance is the opening situation in the old *Arcadia*, given with irreducible economy in the first page of the text.

If Basilius were a sanguine man, confident in himself and his fortune, he would not have gone to the oracle. If he had faith in a benign and almighty deity, he would leave himself and his family in the unquestioned hands of that power. But despite his strict observance of the ritual worship of Apollo (note the beautiful hymn that closes Book 2),[51] Basilius does not understand that religion must be based upon faith. In his uncertainty, therefore, which is a breach of faith, he applies to the oracle. He attempts to ascertain the future. He seeks to know that which man cannot know. He presumes to transcend the limits of human knowledge. In fine, he reenacts the sin of Adam. And as in the case of Adam, carnal lust complements the lust for forbidden knowledge. Basilius's infatuation with Cleophila follows in natural consequence; his unrestrained desire metonymically represents his fall.

The folly of Basilius's actions also metonymically represents his lack of understanding. His rejection of Gynecia, the wife sanctioned by holy matrimony, in favor of the unattainable Cleophila indicates his inability to make appropriate choices. Despite his assertiveness, Basilius regularly misinterprets his circumstances, a failing evident also first in his bewilderment upon receipt of the oracle (5.22–28) and later in his utter misreading of it (133.15– 134.1). Actually, when read aright, the oracle is reassuring, an optimistic message; but Basilius lacks the wisdom to interpret it correctly. He takes it to be threatening. In his panic to elude what he thinks he knows to be the future, he flees to the country. Oedipus-like, by trying to escape his fate, he precipitates it.[52]

Also like Oedipus, whose lack of insight is eventually made manifest by physical blindness, Basilius cannot see the truth in the verses from the oracle. Basilius's error can be identified as a blunder in reading, an inability to interpret a metrified text. Basilius makes the empiricist's assumption that the primary meaning of a text resides in its material phenomena, its verbal signifiers, rather than in its underlying form, as the neoplatonist would know (pages 186–89)—an error that parallels his need to have conscious reassurance about the future rather than being satisfied with an unseen providence. In any case, its verbal system aside, the oracle contains a positive statement of benevolent order that if read aright would have provided Basilius with the reassurance he was seeking. In the *Defence,* in connection with his definition of the poet as *vates* and just before his citation of David as the typical vatic poet, Sidney recalls that "both the oracles of Delphos and Sibylla's prophecies were wholly delivered in verses." By way of explanation, he continues: "For that same exquisite observing of number and measure in the words, and that high flying liberty of conceit proper to the poet, did seem to have some divine force in it" (77.4–9). The versification implies "some divine force"; and while this is the *divino furore* of Landino, a man of faith would listen for that echo of heavenly love in the metrics.

This optimistic message is quite apparent in the metrical system of the oracle when looked for. There are seven lines rhyming *a b a b c c c:*

> Thy elder care shall from they careful face
> By princely mean be stolen and yet not lost;
> Thy younger shall with nature's bliss embrace
> An uncouth love, which nature hateth most.
> Thou with thy wife adult'ry shalt commit,
> And in thy throne a foreign state shall sit.
> All this on thee this fatal year shall hit.

The first two lines pertain to Basilius's "elder" daughter, Pamela; the next two lines pertain to his "younger" daughter. Taken together, the four lines form a quatrain, as the rhyme scheme indicates, and they pertain to Basilius's duties as father. The last three lines respectively cover his duties to his wife, to his kingdom, and to himself, so that all his various roles as governor are covered. Furthermore, the last three lines through their rhymes form a triplet. The versified oracle, then, comprises a quatrain and a triplet. The two parts in relation exhibit the proportion 4/3, the same proportion that relates the octet and sestet in a sonnet (pages 352–53). As in the sonnet, the movement is from 4, the mundane number, to 3, a sacred number. The form moves optimistically from this world to heaven, confidently pointing to the spiritual haven toward which our life is directed. This microcosmic system displays the comprehensiveness, the completeness, the perfection, of the divine scheme. The joyous message is confirmed by the total number of lines: the heptaemeral number 7 represents creation, recalls God's goodness in this manifestation of His benevolence and omnipotence, and echoes the paeans of hallelujah on the sabbath.[53] As a heavenly poesy should, these verses make us see God coming in His majesty, for they show us that unspeakable and everlasting beauty to be seen by the eyes of the mind, only cleared by faith (*Defence* 77.19–24).

But the inward sight of Basilius is not cleared by faith, so he misses all of this. He is too much of this world and not sufficiently attuned to things spiritual. We no doubt miss it, too—but at least we have the excuse that our cultural conditioning has deadened our souls in their response to numerical forms and consequently we do not easily detect the planetlike music in poetry that recalls the sacred cosmic scheme. But Sidney's readers, especially in retrospect after being told that "all had fallen out by the highest providence" (416.18), should have recognized the hint of that providence in this oracle which Basilius so perversely misinterprets.

Anyway, in his folly—in his lack of faith, in his inability to read a metrified text, in his misperception of Cleophila—in his blindness, Basilius falls. And he undergoes the death that Adam brought into the world. He pays the usual wages of sin. Miraculously, however, he is not left among the dead. He is resurrected, although through no human act or agency. When the assembled Arcadians hear his groans and observe his body to stir beneath the black coverlet, "some began to fear spirits"; but others, the faithful rather than the superstitious, began "to look for a miracle" (415.8). Truly, a miracle has occurred. Basilius with all his sins upon his head rises from the dead, redeemed from permanent death through the intervention of an unseen power. Moreover, Pyrocles and Musidorus, and Gynecia—and everyone—are brought to happiness by the same divine love and mercy. The "highest providence" has worked in this mysterious way. Through no other means, in fact, could the folly of Basilius (and the others) have been cured. The optimistic message concealed in the verses from Delphos has come to pass. The old *Arcadia*, like the days of creation, concludes in celebration of an all-loving and almighty deity.

Through Basilius, then, Sidney expresses his strong sense of original sin, but also his strong belief in salvation through divine mercy. Mankind, though fallen, must have faith in God's benevolence. Basilius, as the core of Sidney's fiction, offers his most complete image of the human condition. Basilius is archetypal man, and his name should be read in an ironical way, with the same inversion that is implied in the sign above the crucified Christ: Jesus Nazarenus *Rex* Judeorum. He is paradoxically both the highest and the lowest.

Most interestingly, perhaps, Basilius looks forward to Shakespeare's Lear, another king who precipitates a crisis in the realm at the very moment that his youngest daughter has reached the age of marriage. Shakespeare took the subplot of Gloucester and his two sons from the story of the Paphlagonian king, an episode in the new *Arcadia*. But in all probability he would have known the *Arcadia* from the composite 1593 edition, and therefore would have read the last three books of the old *Arcadia* as well. In the 1593 text Shakespeare would have found the complete story of Basilius—how he reprehensibly assigned away his regal authority, how civil war ensued as a result, how he underwent the loss of identity through his loss of reason, then a deathlike sleep, then a resurrection from this purifying period of helplessness, and how in the end he became a sober and generous man, at last worthy of being father, husband, and sovereign. Lear, like Basilius, shows how the lack of virtue "extendeth itself out of the limits of a man's own little world to the government of families and maintaining of public societies."[54]

King Lear, of course, is a tragedy—that is the way Shakespeare chose to retell the story. The old *Arcadia,* in contrast, is a comedy—or, more accurately, a tragicomedy, because the plot is heading for catastrophe until the unexpected revival of Basilius. While unexpected, though, this event is not surprising to the thoughtful, especially to those who (unlike Basilius) could properly interpret the oracle. All along the providential scheme has been in place, even if working in undetected ways. To the blessed, in any case, death is but a beginning. One short sleep past, they wake eternally. And so Basilius does, to the everlasting bliss of a happy ending.

There is, however, one genuinely tragic figure in the old *Arcadia:* Euarchus, another sovereign. Basilius and Euarchus are old friends, longtime allies. They have much in common and are compared at several points. Within the time frame of this story, however, a contrast between the two is drawn, and their contrariety is significant. At the outset, Basilius is an adequate ruler, "a prince of sufficient skill to govern so quiet a country where the good minds of the former princes had set down good laws, and the well bringing up of the people did serve as a most sure bond to keep them" (4.20–23). But upon receipt of the oracle, he blemishes his

thirty-year record of successful governance by abdicating his responsibilities, and upon the arrival of Cleophila, he lapses into
total folly. With his limitations and weaknesses, Basilius readily
becomes a figure representing the infirmity of mankind. In contrast, Euarchus is at once a more powerful potentate and a more
admirable governor. When he is mentioned early in the story as
the father of the newly introduced Pyrocles, the narrator goes out
of his way to describe and praise him: "Euarchus, king of Macedon, a prince of such justice that he never thought himself privileged by being a prince, nor did measure greatness by anything
but by goodness" (10.4–6). As his name confirms, he is the very
source of goodness in his kingdom.

In Book 5 Euarchus assumes the position of command, arriving
fortuitously to become the regent of Arcadia and replacing Basilius as its sovereign. The opening lines of this last book, preparing
for his appearance, reiterate his reputation for wisdom and justice,
impressing the reader with the impeccable credentials of this
model monarch. He is "the renowned Euarchus, king of Macedon" (351.9); and Philanax (a shrewd observer of kingship, as his
sound advice to Basilius repeatedly shows) remembers "the excellent trials of his equity which made him more famous than his
victories" (351.26–27). In his address to the assembled Arcadians,
Philanax proposes to place the affairs of the realm in the hands of
"that just prince, Euarchus, king of Macedon" (353.29–30), and
he argues that the arrival of this best of all possible regents must
have been divinely sanctioned: "Surely, surely, the heavenly powers have in so full a time bestowed him on us to unite our dis-
unions" (353.34–354.1). When Philanax makes the formal request that he assume the duties of judge in the case of Basilius's
murderers, Euarchus accepts out of a sense of duty, though with
commendable humility and self-knowledge, adding: "But remember I am a man; that is to say, a creature whose reason is often
darkened with error" (364.13–15).

And it is here that the astute reader may gather a premonition
of what lies in store for Euarchus. He is a wise and effective ruler,
known for his just application of reason, the faculty which distinguishes man from the lower orders of nature and allies us with the
angels. But at the same time, Euarchus is mortal; and to adapt the
familiar syllogism, since all men err, Euarchus, despite his ad-

vanced capacity to reason, is still subject to error. To err is human, a condition that in the end Euarchus forgets. Nonetheless, as the trial proceeds and as Euarchus passes his sentences upon Philoclea and Gynecia, and then upon Pyrocles and Musidorus, he judges with the wisdom and justice that we have been led to expect, always offering a full explanation for his decisions based upon reason.[55]

Even after the arrival of Kalodoulus and after knowing that he has sentenced to death his only child and his beloved sister's only child, Euarchus refuses to deviate from what he takes to be the absolutely rational course of the impartial judge:

> Euarchus stayed a good while upon himself, like a valiant man that should receive a notable encounter, being vehemently stricken with the fatherly love of so excellent children, and studying with his best reason what his office required. At length, with such a kind of gravity as was near to sorrow, he thus uttered his mind. (410.35–411.4)

His utterance, despite the intensity of his inner conflict, repeats the earlier sentence of death, claiming that it is necessitated by "the never-changing justice" (411.28). It is at this point that Euarchus reaches full tragic stature. He seals his own doom in the doom of his only son and heir. Like the best tragic heroes, he has brought about his own demise. He has presumed to judge, presumed to know how "the never-changing justice" works, presumed to transcend the limits of human initiative. Therefore he too falls, another Adam.

Those of us who recall the opening of Book 4 and the narrator's inappropriate remarks about "the everlasting justice" know that the providential plan does not submit to facile moralizing. So the Arcadian populace, horrified at his unbending inhumanity (and representing our attitude), turn from Euarchus. He is finally "an obstinate-hearted man, and such a one, who being pitiless, his dominion must needs be insupportable" (414.32–34). He is denounced and dethroned as an overbearing monster who presumes to know the divine will and presumes to act as the sole arbiter of that will. We are reminded of the biblical injunction: Judge not, that ye be not judged.

But in the end, Euarchus too is saved from a miserable fate by the resurrection of Basilius. He too participates in the providence that has overseen all these otherwise unbelievable events, and he too is preserved from the self-destruction of a tragic hero, from the error that darkens reason, from the common fate of the fallen— from the oxymoronic human condition of "unjust justice" (287.23). In the best of all possible worlds, presided over by a benevolent and omnipotent power, even the fallible judge is forgiven. "Justice" applied without compassion and humility, as the oxymoron states, is likely to be "unjust." To judge in the rigorous way attempted by Euarchus—or by us, when we denounce Euarchus— must be deferred to the all-knowing deity.

With a remarkable generosity of spirit, Sidney acknowledges the equivocality of human motive and the fallibility of human judgment in detecting it. And he most concisely expresses this sentiment through the enargeiac figure of Euarchus. The sage and serious Euarchus represents Sidney's projection of himself as judge. Euarchus performs solemnly what the narrator undertakes in a superficial manner. Both presume to castigate their fellow-men, and both are found wanting. Given the incompleteness of human knowledge and the limitations on human reason, neither can actually make wise judgments. No mortal can, not even the poet. That must be left to the heavenly maker.

Underlying all that we have said about the old *Arcadia* is the assumption that the poet is a maker who emulates the heavenly maker. Just as the Timaean godhead produced the cosmos or the Hebraic-Christian deity created the heavens and earth, so the poet invents a fictive universe that reflects the providential order. The poet simulates a durational and extended continuum, comparable to what we know from looking at the world around us, and he populates it with creatures universalized from the men and women whom we know from our acquaintance. By a sort of alchemical magic, the poet transforms the brazen world of actual occurrence into a golden world of immutable forms.

The poet sets this fiction apart from his own reality by relating it to earlier fiction such as Sannazaro's *Arcadia*, the *Amadis of Gaul*, and Heliodorus's *Aethiopica*—that is, by emphasizing its literariness. He further indicates its poeticality by using highly artificial language and by contriving an obviously controlled plot, which generate a distinctly theatrical effect. He puts the story in the mouth of a gregarious but foolish persona who improperly directs it to fair ladies, a narrative strategy that forces the reader to become dissociated from both imputed narrator and imputed audience, further distancing the fiction. Just as the heavenly maker circumscribed a portion of his infinitude and created our universe, so Sidney sets Arcadia apart as an autonomous and explorable entity.

But just as our universe has its limits in the primum mobile yet resides in the larger being of the deity, so Arcadia is set apart as fiction yet resides in the larger experience of Sidney. Fiction allows this ambiguity by being both self-consistent and relational. The artifact as product is autonomously identifiable, but it derives from a context which is still discernible within it. Indeed, the residual value of the art of making lies in this fictionality, in this ability to relate the speculative and the actual. The character Philisides provides a template that teaches us to appreciate this ambivalence of fiction, which is both real and not real.

A further paradox. The deity existed before the creation, and He continues to exist above and beyond it, a transcendent being; and yet He is immanent, present in each of his creatures. Just so, the poetical maker. He is the author of his artifact, with a prior existence and a continuing identity separate from it; and yet each of his creatures in the fiction is a projection of himself, a representation of himself. He ultimately provides the unity for that multeity. It is this paradoxical transcendence/immanence of the poet which in the long run allows a relationship between the real world and the world of fiction. The act of making becomes perforce the paradigm of fictionality.

The immanence of Sidney in the *Arcadia* is most evident through the characters of Philisides and the imputed narrator. The one is his acronym; the other, his persona. Now we must deal with the question raised before: Why does Sidney represent himself by two such distinctly different personalities? Philisides is indolent and reluctant to speak; the narrator is hyperactive and garrulous. Two enargeiac figures could hardly be more different. If both represent Sidney—and unmistakably they do—doesn't this undermine the fictional enterprise by calling its truth into question? Doesn't this strain our credulity to the point of disbelief?

The answer is, of course, yes. But Sidney was aware of this likelihood; in fact, he set it up as a straw man to topple over. In his refutation of the charge that poets are liars, Sidney repeated the accusation "that the poets give names to men they write of, which argueth a conceit of an actual truth, and so, not being true, proves a falsehood" (*Defence* 103.16–18). Sidney ostentatiously represents himself in the fiction by one character named Philisides and by another identified as the "I" of a first-person speaker. In a verisimilitudinous manner he gives individualized personalities to these characters. But since they both represent the same historical personage, they belie the veracity of the fiction; not being true, this proves the falsehood of the entire fictional pretense. So goes the argument in disproof of the poem. By this daring strategy, however, Sidney strives for sublime effects. Again, he gambles for high stakes.

First, we have already noted how these two characters taken singly validate the fiction of the text. Since each obviously derives from Sidney's own circumstances, they show how the fictional world relates to the actual, derives its substance from the actual. Each character is an evident instance of fiction at work.

Sidney could have achieved this purpose, of course, by using either character alone, as we showed in an earlier section. By placing the two in contrast, however, he accomplishes something further: he denies the possibility that either is a forthright representation of his own self. Thereby he insists upon the fictionality of the text. No reader is allowed to make the easy assumption that either Philisides or the narrator is simply Sidney, and therefore that the text is simply fact.

By this strategy Sidney forces the reader to acknowledge that the story is "made up," detailing a fictive universe created by a self-conscious artificer. The necessity for an author is established and a space between artificer and artifact is recognized. By assuming two such different guises within the fiction, Sidney raises questions about the definitiveness of any one of the characters and directs attention to the creator of this artificial world. Behind Philisides and the narrator—and the other inhabitants of Arcadia—stands a maker. Behind the multeity of the fiction remains the *mens poetae*.

Moreover, by representing himself in characters so widely apart, Sidney suggests the range of choice enjoyed by the poet and extended to the reader. Which of these mutually exclusive options represents the author himself? Since the answer is both and neither, Sidney indicates the boundless choices the poetical maker is forced to resolve. The fictive universe of the poet reflects the fullness of God's art, so the poem must represent all possibilities and permutations. Like the heavenly maker on the first day of creation, the poetical maker faces innumerable decisions. He chooses from a bottomless abyss, making judgments in order to manifest that goodness he would have his reader take in hand. Making in essence becomes this act of judging.

Finally, by representing himself by two characters exactly contrary in nature, Sidney demonstrates that his fiction encompasses the extremes, runs the gamut of examples, exhausts the possibilities. His fiction is all-inclusive, complete, perfect. It incorporates multeity and reduces it to the unity of the transcendent/immanent poet. By being both Philisides and the narrator, Sidney shows that his fiction reconciles discordant elements.

So the importance of the narrator and of Philisides lies not so much in their individual significances—not so much in the fact that one cautions against affectation and cynicism while the other warns against melancholy withdrawal and idealistic love. Their greater importance lies in their relationship. They demonstrate that in a poem the form inherent in the relationships between elements is more important than the content of those elements. Judgment consists in recognizing and evaluating this form.

Here it is essential to delineate the model for the choice that Sidney has designed in his contrariety between Philisides and the narrator. The paradigm is not the choice between two mutually destructive possibilities, one precluding the other. Nor is it the singleness of a mean between two extremes, where each loses its identity by mergence into a third mediating entity. Rather, the paradigm aims for the inclusiveness which reconciles opposites without the eradication of their respective identities, making them compatible by their complimentariness, by their exact otherness. Paradoxically, by being exactly the other's opposite in every precise detail, two counterparts can represent one another. In this closed system, each determines the status of the other by providing the conditions of its existence, as in the well-known symbol of yin and yang from another culture. Yin is not yang, but yin is exactly like yang; and yin defines yang just as yang defines yin. While perfectly opposite, by their interdependence the two counterparts become the same. The result is a field of meaning (as we suggested pages 444–45) rather than a single point. A multivalent field is embodied in a particular circumstance, but the full range of valences remains intact. All possibilities continue to be viable. The result is dynamism rather than stasis.

Reading a poem of this sort consists of reconstructing this field of meaning, discerning the forms that comprise it, and evaluating the choices it presents. Reading involves judging. As Plutarch revised Aristotle (pages 175–76), the way we should read poetry is first to delineate the parameters of motive, and then within those coordinates to explain why characters act as they do. When all the characters are considered, there emerges a network of balanced contrarieties, of confirmative correspondences, of mutually sustaining identities. The distance between maker and his creatures, that intermundum between fact and fiction, provides the space for this activity; it is there that we can watch the poet at his task and learn the art of making as judgment. The model of behavior that Sidney proposes as a societal norm is exemplified by this activity which the text induces in the reader as he acquires the art of judging. This activity alone realizes the field of meaning to the fullest and moves the reader beyond a passive virtue, well-knowing, to well-doing, an active virtue.

Now we see the topic addressed by the old *Arcadia* in its largest dimension. It becomes an exercise in analyzing ambiguities and assessing alternatives. The activity induced in the reader ultimately involves "judgment,"[56] a word which appears with but slightly less frequency than "virtue" or "reason."

And now we can understand why Book 5 concentrates our attention elsewhere than Basilius, who otherwise is the linchpin of the plot. Act 5 of this human comedy moves Euarchus to center stage, displacing Basilius from his central position. The story refocuses upon a character who has been mentioned previously, but who only at this point appears upon the scene. From the opening of Book 5, though, the old *Arcadia* becomes largely the story of Euarchus, the judge. Through Basilius, Sidney provides us with instruction in the human condition, a subject matter, a noun; but more important, through Euarchus he provides us with instruction in judging, an action, a verb. After all, behind the quintessential human fact, original sin, lies prideful disobedience, an active choice.

Because we have been swayed by Euarchus's impeccable credentials and his irrefutable logic, but yet have found ourselves on the side of error, we have undergone a practical exercise in the act of judging. We have vicariously participated in the judgment of others by Euarchus, persuaded by his reasoning; moreover, we have independently made a judgment of Eurarchus himself. So we have had the experience of judging, and know firsthand the pitfalls that beset the judge and the likelihood of error. By the closing episode, most important, we have seen that never-ending justice cannot be circumscribed by human laws or fathomed by human reason. But we are surprised by the goodness of the providential scheme, so our faith is strengthened, and we face the future without the fear that unnerved Basilius at the beginning of this story.

There is one character, however, whose sphere of judgment is wider even than Euarchus's. While Euarchus is regent of Arcadia, the imputed narrator is sole regent of this entire text. While Euarchus judges what has already taken place and while he is bound by the preexisting laws of Arcadia, the narrator takes into account human weakness and failure as well as the eternal law. The narrator attempts to reconcile what should be with what is, a task that accounts for his vacillation between sanctimoniousness and cynicism, for the equivocality that manifests itself as insouciance. Placed in this compromised position between the ideal and the actual, and burdened with revealing the truth of what is happening, our narrator occupies the seat of judgment from start to finish.

Not only does the narrator judge the behavior of other characters, praising or blaming what they do, but he chooses what to tell us. Although the narrator may not have the power of inventing the story—in one place (but one place only), he intimates that he is indebted to how "the ancient records of Arcadia say it fell out" (51.25)—he does determine the order in which the episodes are presented. He controls the plot; and in Aristotelian poetics, it is the plot, the interrelation of episodes, that generates meaning. So the narrator plays the role of the poetical maker in this fictive universe, making those choices and decisions—those judg-

ments—which produce a fiction displaying what might be or
should be according to the principles of poetry as an art of imitation. In his role as such a maker, the narrator exemplifies the task
of the judge.

In the final analysis, therefore, it is the imputed narrator who
has the most to teach us. In him—the poetical maker, the archetypal fictioneer, the universalized storyteller that Sidney invents
from his own narrative impulse—in that daring re-presentation of
himself, hopeful while disillusioned, Sidney shows us most explicitly the maker at his making. By watching him, we can learn the
complexities involved in making, the difficulties involved in judging. By diligent engagement with the verbal system provided by
our narrator/Sidney, we arrive at the wisdom of his final pronouncement (which, like all his pronouncements, is equivocally
true): "So uncertain are mortal judgments, the same person most
infamous and most famous, and neither justly" (416.34–35).[57]

That in the broadest view is what the old *Arcadia* is mostly
about, as its culmination in the trial scene indicates. The issue is
not whether Pyrocles and Musidorus—or any of the other characters—are guilty or innocent. Strong arguments can be made on
both sides of that question, and neither position is unassailable, as
recent criticism of the work has shown.[58] What is irrefutable,
though, is the necessity of judging them. We cannot avoid the fact
that judgment is called for. This is an imperfect world, and mortals
are fallen creatures—indeed, that is what "mortal" signifies. But
in the case of Pyrocles and Musidorus, as in all cases, there is
redemptive virtue as well as guilt, a coexistence of opposites occasioned by the paradox that Adam's fall, while evil in itself,
proves to be fortunate within the comprehensive scheme of providence. Mankind, though tainted with original sin, retains a hope
of salvation. In consequence, there is an equivocality of motive in
all our actions, in all our choices, in all our judgments.

But we must remember that all falls out by the highest providence. This is not a hopelessly Heraclitean universe, as Philisides
views it. Although time passes and change occurs, and death is
inevitable, there is a beneficent intelligence behind the cycles of
mutability; so death is not an end, but a beginning. Nor is this a
harsh Calvinistic universe as the narrator would have us assume.
Admittedly, man is a fallen creature, and our infected will seri-

ously impairs our erected wit; but we may still discern goodness and even proceed to well-doing. Whatever the shortcomings of nature, including human nature, divine love and mercy—the true everlasting justice—prevail. This is Arcadia, which has ever been had in singular reputation, partly for the sweetness of the air and other natural benefits, but principally for the moderate and well-tempered minds of the people.

Early in 1591 Thomas Newman, one of the more enterprising if less scrupulous of the London stationers, published the work which after this came to be known as *Astrophil and Stella*. Sidney's sequence of love lyrics, which he apparently left untitled,[59] first appeared in Newman's slim quarto with a supplement of other amorous verse by Samuel Daniel, Thomas Campion, and Fulke Greville, printed also without the knowledge or approval of those poets. The text is corrupt as well as unauthorized. There are numerous errors in particular words, suggesting that Newman had an inferior manuscript as printer's copy; Sonnet 37 is omitted entirely, and Sonnets 55 and 56 are transposed; whole lines and even longer passages have been dropped from several quatorzains and songs; and the ten songs that do appear (Song xi is missing) are, inexplicably, grouped together after the quatorzains.[60] Newman put together this little volume for sale to the fashionable set who bought gentlemen's miscellanies and maintained a demand for Tottel's *Songes and Sonettes,* the prototype in English for this sort of thing first published in 1557; and he rushed it into print to capitalize on the success of the (new) *Arcadia* published the year before. The more nearly complete text of *Astrophil and Stella,* and the one with which we are most familiar, was supplied by the Countess of Pembroke for the 1598 folio of Sidney's works.

Nonetheless, Newman's pirated volume is of consummate interest not only for the textual variants it provides, but perhaps even more for a preface prepared by Thomas Nashe. Here we have exactly contemporary remarks by an especially perceptive and articulate reader. At this time Nashe was approaching his mid-twenties, down from Cambridge a few years before, already a published prose writer and an unpublished pornographic versifier, and now enjoying a helter-skelter life in London. He was a bright and brash "university wit," no doubt having recently read the *Ar-*

cadia, soon to try his own hand at fictive narrative with *The Unfortunate Traveller* (1594), and probably already thinking about similar literary ventures. His comments are therefore not only timely, but especially cogent. They constitute, in fact, the kind of stringent and witty observation that has earned Nashe a prominent place in the history of literary realism.

In his prefatory essay, which with characteristic breeziness he entitled "Somewhat to read for them that list," Nashe begins by linking Sidney with Ovid. He opens with a quote from the *Amores:* Tempus adest plausus, aurea pompa venit (The time for applause is here—the golden procession is coming, 3.2.44); and he comments: "So endes the Sceane of Idiots, and enter *Astrophel* in pompe" (329.3–4).[61] Ovid's *Amores* is a sprawling collection of anecdotes told by a first-person narrator in a lively manner and recounting his exploits (not always successful) in love. In them Corinna makes a frequent appearance, though she is by no means the only mistress. The passion of the lover is ardent, but superficial and inconstant, and we are invited to be amused by him. The style of the poet, in fact, seems of greater consequence than any suffering of the persona. Suavity and light-heartedness provide the measure of excellence in this poetry, which flaunts its literariness by echoing previous love poets. It is not surprising that *Astrophil and Stella* called the *Amores* to Nashe's mind.

Ovid's eighty-four-line poem from which Nashe quotes is a dramatic monologue in the mouth of a man who has come to the circus for the races because he is working on a sexual prospect who in turn has her eye on one of the charioteers. It is typically Ovidian in its wittiness, its eroticism, and its innuendo. Despite the fervency with which the lover professes his passion, he achieves no more than a promise, which might even be self-delusory: "She smiled, and with speaking eyes promised—I know not what" (3.2.83). The lover is left unfulfilled, but still in attendance, hanging onto distant hopes. The line that Nashe quotes at the beginning of his preface occurs midway through the poem when the procession enters the circus preparatory to the race, and it is clear that Nashe views Astrophil as another in the long line of amorous fools who compete for reward in love but without success. Though the parade of love scenes depicted by Ovid has ended, now enters Astrophil in full regalia to replay the same scenario.

Nashe assumes a mocking attitude toward both love and Sidney's silly lover.

Nashe then turns to his audience, whom he addresses as "Gentlemen" and whom he conceives as readers jaded by inferior poetry—they "have seene a thousand lines of folly drawn forth *ex uno puncto impudentiae,* & two famous Mountains to goe to the conception of one Mouse," etc., etc. Nonetheless, he entreats them: "Let not your surfeted sight, new come from such puppet play, think scorne to turn aside into this Theater of pleasure." In Nashe's view earlier lyrics are childish, an infantile playing with dolls ("puppets"). He thinks that *Astrophil and Stella* is far superior to what has gone before, and he invites his audience to attend it. The "pleasure" that identifies this theater is Astrophil's pleasure, his illicit love; but also, I think, the pleasure of the reader as he witnesses Astrophil's performance. Nashe's pitch for the reader's attention is commonplace, but his mode of expression exhibits a special inventiveness that characterizes his style.

Furthermore, the particular vocabulary that Nashe employs in making this statement is significant. "Scene," "enter," and finally "theater of pleasure"—all language of the stage. Nashe conceives of *Astrophil and Stella* in dramatic terms, as mimetic representation, as speaking pictures. His next sentence crystallizes this concept; "for here you shall find a paper stage," he advises his audience—"paper" because the work is printed and to be read, and "stage" because we shall hear and see human figures in action. So Nashe goes on to deck this stage and provide a setting that colors the interpretation of what takes place upon it: ". . . a paper stage," he says, "streud with pearle, an artificial heav'n to overshadow the faire frame, & christal wals to encounter your curious eyes, whiles the tragicommody of love is performed by starlight." Nashe stresses the opulence and artificiality of this stage, suitable to the high station of Astrophil and his lady, but also appropriate for the elegance of Petrarchism. And what we shall witness is a tragicomedy performed by "starlight," with a macaronic pun upon "Stella," the source of love (and therefore of light) in this story. In accordance with the Petrarchist code, the mistress is celestialized. But also, I think, there is an implication that Astrophil's love belongs in an idealized, magical world, like that of the forest in *A*

Midsummer Night's Dream, where moonlight and starlight always shine, and where this ideality shades into illusion.

So Nashe assumes a rather derisive attitude toward Astrophil. He is another idiotic lover whose rashness necessarily ends in grief, and he brings it on himself by adopting the lover's code of behavior. Poets have made us familiar with this sort of tragicomedy. But we are to be more amused than pained by the lover's lamentations, which display a prosopopoeiac duplicity. The wailing is largely for literary effect; and besides, there are other mistresses.

Nashe does not use the word "tragicomedy" lightly, however, and he continues to make more of it. In company with Ringler and Robertson, we have applied this dramatic term to the old *Arcadia* (page 417). But while the protagonists in that poem seem headed for tragedy until divine providence asserts itself and prevents the catastrophe, Astrophil benefits from no such intercession. Rather, his story ends tragically, with him in despairing resignation to the loss of Stella. For it to be a tragicomedy, therefore, requires further explanation. Having noted that *Astrophil and Stella* is a tragicomedy of love, Nashe proceeds to the comment that "the chiefe Actor here is Melpomene"; and, given the sad state of Astrophil in the concluding sonnet, this is a valid observation. The muse of tragedy holds the stage. But upon second glance, upon further consideration—after objectifying his story and gaining some distance from it—the reader perceives that comedy rather than tragedy prevails. Astrophil has been a fool. As Nashe puts it, Melpomene's "dusky robes, dipt in the ynke of teares, as yet seeme to drop when I view them neere."

Nashe's shrewd perception that Melpomene's robes, like the emperor's clothes, disappear when really looked at, is useful in the interpretation of Astrophil's tale. It is more comedy than tragedy. But also Nashe's comment implies a way to read the poem. We should not read it simplistically, as merely a sad story, a tragedy. That would be taking a fiction literally, as though it were something the poet affirms—like a naive child, to believe that a door is Thebes because "Thebes" is written upon it (*Defence* 103.6–8). When Astrophil's tale is examined more closely, analyzed more keenly, thought about more inventively, we clearly discern the character Astrophil, but also we become aware of a maker who has made that creature. While to Astrophil within his fictive universe the outcome of the tale may be tragic, to the author (and therefore to us, who look over his shoulder) the net effect may be comic. The layering of meaning is similar to that of the play within a play in the last scene of *A Midsummer Night's Dream*. To Bottom and the other menials who act it out, the tale of Pyramus and Thisbe is tragic; but to the lords and ladies of the court watching from the sidelines, the interlude is comic. And to us, invited to view it from both perspectives simultaneously while keeping also in mind its unstable metamorphic context, the Ovidian tale is a tragicomedy—neither tragic nor comic, but wondrously both. Philostrate has already given it an oxymoronic billing as "tragical mirth" (5.1.57).

In any case, as Nashe goes on to interpret *Astrophil and Stella,* "The argument [is] cruell Chastitie, the Prologue hope, the Epilogue dispaire." This seems a fair enough, if somewhat reductive, analysis. The poem does depict the outcome of cruel chastity, although that epithet oversimplifies Stella and her role.[62] Furthermore, Astrophil begins in hope, but ends in despair, so once again comic and tragic elements are integrated into the same tale. Then Nashe adapts the line which precedes the one already quoted from Ovid's *Amores,* and we are told to be quiet and see for ourselves, for the drama is about to start: Videte, queso, et linguis animisque favete.

Nashe was an appreciative and sensitive reader of *Astrophil and Stella,* and the laudatory comments about Sidney which follow amply demonstrate the deference he felt toward "so excellent a Poet, (the least sillable of whose name, sounded in the eares of judgement, is able to give the meanest line he writes a dowry of immortality)." The name "Astrophil" repeats a syllable of Sidney's name; sounded in the ears of those capable of judging correctly, it will insure the immortality of the work. To Nashe, though, an urbane and literate young man of the kind that became the rake of a century later, *Astrophil and Stella* was to be enjoyed as a witty jeu d'esprit. It was a spoof of love in the Ovidian tradition, a send-up of the sonneteer. Nashe tried his own hand at this sort of thing when the earl of Surrey and his Geraldine appear in *The Unfortunate Traveller* and turn Petrarchan platitudes into farce. While we may not wish to adopt Nashe's interpretation as the definitive reading of *Astrophil and Stella,* his facetious remarks deserve consideration.

What most significantly emerges from Nashe's preface are three points that bear directly upon how we read *Astrophil and Stella.* First, there is an awareness that the poem is essentially a dramatic work comprised of speaking pictures—a theater of pleasure, a paper stage. It describes actions to be visualized, like the fiction of the old *Arcadia.* But unlike the old *Arcadia* this fiction has been stripped of authorial narrative and comment; with few exceptions, Astrophil narrates his own tale in first-person monologue, like Ovid's lover in the *Amores.* Nashe's metaphor of the theater is highly appropriate because it implies that the text is a performance, and also that the reader attends that performance and provides the circumstance for allowing it to come alive once again. Reading the text is a performative act, a reenactment of the text. Second, there is an argument or fore-conceit to the work. It displays the meaning of cruel chastity; and in the beginning Astrophil represents hope, while in the end he emblematizes despair. By means of the fiction, though—as also in the instance of the old *Arcadia,* according to Greville—Sidney turns those barren precepts into pregnant images of life. Third, a distinction must be made between poet and persona with a different perspective upon the fictive universe of Astrophil for each.

This last point requires careful elaboration because it bears upon the crucial question of personal reference in the work. To what extent and in what ways is *Astrophil and Stella* an autobiographical poem? The answer to this question conditions our reading of the text in a fundamental manner. If we link Astrophil too closely to Sidney, insisting upon the veracity of every incident and the accuracy of every detail, we will read the work as a record of actual occurrence, and thereby, according to Sidney's poetics, we limit its general applicability. Astrophil's world coincides with the brazen world of history. If, on the other hand, we completely sever Astrophil from Sidney, in addition to ignoring conspicuous evidence, we will read the work as a fantasy with no discernible basis in fact, and thereby, according to Sidney's poetics, we undermine its validity. Astrophil's world, though recognizable as the golden one of platonist sentiment, becomes as evanescent and elusive as castles in the air. So what is the appropriate relationship between the fictive character Astrophil and the historical personage Philip Sidney?

To begin, we must note the unmistakable signs which identify Astrophil with Sidney. As in the case of Philisides, there is a personal signature in the name itself. Moreover, there are details in the story which coincide with the circumstances of Sidney's own life, most tellingly the fact that Astrophil says his father has been governor of Ireland (Sonnet 30) and that his family's coat of arms exhibits an arrowhead (Sonnet 65). We must also take into account the allusions which identify Stella as Penelope née Devereux, now the wife of Lord Rich (Sonnets 13, 24, 35, 37), because they support a historical reading of the text.[63] Perhaps what carries the most weight is the overwhelming evidence that his contemporaries thought of Astrophil as representing Sidney and after his death regularly used that name, at least in a literary context.

We must conclude that Astrophil does in some way represent Sidney. But I shall argue, of course, that he does so only to the extent and in the same fashion that Philisides represents him in the old *Arcadia*. Astrophil is yet another conceit made from the matter of the Petrarchan lover which Sidney had extracted from his own stuff. Therefore, while Astrophil derives from Sidney's experience, he is not confined to those facts. Sidney ranges within the zodiac of his wit and uses Astrophil, as he uses Philisides (and Pyrocles and Musidorus), to speculate upon how a young man deals with sexual love.[64]

I shall even suggest that *Astrophil and Stella* had its genesis in the same impulse that drove Sidney in the first place to write poems in the persona of Philisides. Astrophil and Philisides are the same sort of acronym—indeed, are linguistic cognates; and Stella and Mira are all but interchangeable names for a sonneteer's mistress. It is probable that the Philisides poems in praise of Mira antedate both the old *Arcadia* and *Astrophil and Stella,* a probability that textual evidence supports. Ringler shows that Song v of *Astrophil and Stella* is an adaptation of an earlier piece, with "Stella" conveniently substituted for "Mira."[65] And in the old *Arcadia,* when Philisides appears elsewhere than in the sets of eclogues—that is, when he sings a companion piece with Musidorus (125.12–29), and when Pyrocles recalls his erotic blazon of Mira (238.1–242.32)—the circumstance is awkwardly contrived, as though a place was being made for material already on hand. Most suspicious is the 146-line blazon of Mira which runs through Pyrocles's mind on the way to his thalamic initiation with Philoclea in his arms. The intrusive blazon is so disruptive that the narrator feels the need to make some apology: "But do not think, fair ladies, his thoughts had such leisure as to run over so long a ditty; the only general fancy of it came into his mind." Moreover, the vivacity of this inventory of Mira's anatomical delights is so out of character for the morose Philisides as he appears elsewhere in the fiction that it must have been composed without the Arcadian narrative in mind.[66]

What I'm proposing is a kind of Ur-text comprising the Philisides poems to Mira which underlies both the old *Arcadia* and *Astrophil and Stella*, and which survives piecemeal in them. Such a hypothesis would explain the prominence and central importance of Philisides in the Arcadian text (pages 439–42). It also would explain why Sidney composed a sequence of quatorzains and songs even though the poetics of rhyming and versing by this time was anathema to him, a point to which I shall return. Most important, it would explain why both works focus upon love and its effects; or, put another way, why there is such a close resemblance between Philisides and Pyrocles and Musidorus and Astrophil. All derive from the same stuff, which originated with Sidney, who first projected himself into an enargeiac figure named Philisides, the most obvious acronym for the poet himself. We probably have the earliest incarnation of Philisides preserved in the song that Ringler places as #5 among the "Other Poems" of Sidney, a song which the editor of the 1593 *Arcadia* found somewhere and intruded into the third set of eclogues. Evidently, he thought that any ready-to-hand piece by Philisides belonged in the Arcadian text. Finally, in the last paragraph of the old *Arcadia*, when the narrator signs off by pointing to fictional material that other authors may wish to develop, he includes "the poor hopes of the poor Philisides" (417.19); and it is tempting to suggest that Sidney already had an embryo of Astrophil in mind—or at least that *Astrophil and Stella* fulfills what is proposed for Philisides at the end of the old *Arcadia*.[67]

When we turn to the text with these remarks in mind, we find that *Astrophil and Stella* is a lively, multivalent, and sophisticated work that fully accords with the principles of poetry set forth by Sidney in the *Defence* and exemplified in the old *Arcadia*. The Philisides poems provide a communal base from which to approach both works, an approach dictated by the *Defence*. Following his cardinal tenet that poetry is an art of Aristotelian imitation, Sidney produces speaking pictures directed to the mind's eye of the reader. A good example of the technique is provided by Song viii, the first time that Astrophil is named in the sequence and a cameo of the entire action of the story.

The eighth song meets the criteria for mimetic fiction in every way. There is a vivid (if conventional) woodland setting, which the opening stanza details:

> In a grove most rich of shade,
> Where birds wanton musicke made,
> May then yong his pide weedes showing,
> New perfumed with flowers fresh growing . . .

In the shepherds' calendar, May is the traditional month for courtship, so this setting is populated with lovers in the next stanza, where grammatically the sentence is completed. The second stanza presents characters and an opening situation:

> *Astrophil* with *Stella* sweete,
> Did for mutuall comfort meete,
> Both within themselves oppressed,
> But each in the other blessed.

And there is conspicuous action. Despite their sorrows—"Him great harmes had taught much care, / Her faire necke a foule yoke bare" (8–9)—they take comfort in one another's company. First they weep in mutual grief, each for the other; but these tears change to smiles as they look in one another's eyes and see their love reflected. They sigh; but sighs of woe transmute to sighs of joy. Their lovesick state is manifested by the position of their arms crossed upon their breasts, and the conflicting emotions of the Petrarchan lover are revealed by the oxymoronic formulation of their state of mind: "restelesse rest and living dying" (20). They are hungry for conversation, but do not speak "till their harts had ended talking" (24). The details are precise and graphic.

Eventually, from the pressure of his passion Astrophil breaks the silence: "Love did set his lips asunder, / Thus to speake in love and wonder" (27–28). Then the dialogue begins. Astrophil speaks first, addressing Stella with a string of epithets that define her role as the sonneteer's mistress:

> *Stella* soveraigne of my joy,
> Faire triumpher of annoy,
> *Stella* starre of heavenly fier,
> *Stella* loadstar of desier.
>   (29–32)

Astrophil continues in this vein for three more stanzas, beseeching her favor and using the vocabulary and arguments of the Petrarchist code. Stella has shining eyes that serve as stars in Cupid's heaven. She has a voice that overwhelms the senses when she speaks and sounds like the angels when she sings. Her body is inscribed with "each character of blisse" (42). Her face is the epitome of beauty, and yet her mind surpasses it. Before such beauty Astrophil is awed, tongue-tied. But he gathers his courage, thinking "no fault there is in praying" (48), and kneels on the ground before Stella. He also calls upon the motif of *Carpe diem*, increasingly popular in the Renaissance as sonneteering turned from its religious attitude toward *madonna* and secularized the mistress as an object of sexual desire. "Now use the season" (56), he pleads with Stella; and he concludes that since all nature submits to the power of love, so should they, because "if dumbe things be so witty, / Shall a heavenly grace want pitty?" (63–64).

At this point, having perfected his argument, Astrophil resorts to direct action. The narrating voice describes it with utmost delicacy, but also with rare wit:

> There his hands in their speech, faine
> Would have made tongue's language plaine;
> But her hands his hands repelling,
> Gave repulse all grace excelling.
>   (65–68)

With Stella's rebuff to Astrophil's grappling also comes her chance to speak. She is rent by inner conflict. At once she dearly loves Astrophil, but a sense of shame restrains her from openly joining him. While Stella professes a deeply felt and abiding passion for Astrophil, she resigns herself to "hellish anguish" (80) and rejects him. Since she cannot compromise her virtue, Stella tells Astrophil that "tyran honour doth thus use thee" (95). As Nashe observed, the argument here is cruel chastity.

But the scene is over. All that can be done has been done; all that can be said has been said. So a narrator, the same anonymous voice that set the stage in the opening stanza and provided the transition from Astrophil's speech to Stella's (65–72), steps in and draws the curtain:

> Therewithall away she went,
> Leaving him so passion rent,
> With what she had done and spoken,
> That therewith my song is broken.
>
> (101–4)

Stella leaves. Astrophil remains love-stricken and unsatisfied, with only the memory of "what she had done and spoken."

As a final act of comprehension required of the reader, we must note that in this last stanza the narrator makes a more definite appearance. He is no longer a disembodied voice reciting from the wings, as in the first seven stanzas. Rather, he steps more clearly into our view with the use of the first-person "my" in the last line. The last line, in fact, announces unmistakably the presence of a maker who has composed this song. And while he pretends that he lacks the power to extend this literary event—the departure of Stella and the resultant grief of Astrophil break off his song—at the least he is the purveyor of this fiction, just as the narrator in the old *Arcadia* is the mediator between that story and us. Note that an unmistakable distinction is drawn between Astrophil, a character within the fiction, and the narrator. They cannot be the same entity; they cannot both be Sidney. This narrator appears nowhere else in *Astrophil and Stella,* and consequently never becomes an intrusive presence or a powerful personality like the imputed narrator of the old *Arcadia.* Therefore it is easier to equate the narrator of *Astrophil and Stella* and its author, Sidney, without equivocation. But the important point is that the ending of Song viii makes it evident that in this poem we have in clear relief a narrator imposed upon the fiction. We have in obvious distinction both a maker and his creation, with the same sort of objectifying and distancing of the fictive world that we saw in the old *Arcadia*.

There is yet one other point about Song viii, a small but, I think, significant one. For the first time in the work—that is, when the sequence is about three-fourths finished—the lover is given a name. Moreover, he is called "Astrophil" twice: once by the narrator (5), and once by Stella (73). Astrophil is called by name once by someone within his fictive world, and once by someone who stands outside it. Thereby attention is drawn to the discontinuity that sets the circumscribed vignette of Astrophil and Stella apart from the space that the narrator shares with us; and yet, since both Stella and the narrator use the same name, there is manifestation of a relationship between Astrophil's world and ours. Fiction and fact interpenetrate.

The name "Astrophil" occurs in the work only once more, in the immediately adjacent poem, Song ix. There is no narrator in this piece, no intermediary between the reader and Astrophil's world. He speaks in his own voice without introduction or farewell, and he refers to himself as "Astrophil" (27). This is a conventional amorous complaint, with Astrophil lamenting his lack of success with Stella, and the pastoral milieu is even more prominently and consistently developed. Almost by formula, Astrophil opens by addressing his sheep:

> Go my flocke, go get you hence,
> Seeke a better place of feeding.

Astrophil appears here in the traditional guise of lover and poet as well as shepherd, and the unkindness of Stella has impaired his ability to fulfill his duties—hence the advice to his flock to desert him, as Stella has. But before they leave, he repeats for their instruction the cold fact that "Stella hath refused me" (26), and consequently he longs for death. It is altogether an artificial performance, in both subject matter and language. The last stanza begins: "Then adieu, deere flocke adieu" (46), sounding more like the winter-ravaged Colin Clout than Astrophil. Nowhere else does Astrophil's voice bear these bucolic accents.

Nowhere else, in fact, does the pastoral mode intrude into the otherwise courtly world of Astrophil. These adjacent pieces, Songs viii and ix, are exceptional, quite out of keeping with the urbane and aristocratic ambiance that prevails on all other occasions. They form an anomalous fragment, an archeological shard embedded in the text. I suggest, in fact, that if they are not remnants of the Ur-text comprising the Philisides lyrics, these songs belong to approximately the same period. They preserve the first embodiment of Astrophil and represent the initial work from which the remainder of *Astrophil and Stella* evolved.

There are several reasons for thinking that Songs viii and ix are premature and aberrant, vestiges from his earliest poethood when Sidney was engaged largely in pastoral exercises in the manner of Sannazaro. Song ix, for instance, which begins, "Go my flocke, go get you hence," closely echoes the song that Philisides sings in reply to Musidorus, which begins, "Leave off my sheep; it is no time to feed." Both are amorous complaints sung to a flock by a deserted shepherd. They are alike in subject matter, genre, rhetorical organization, and narrative strategy. We have already noted that Song v is an actual revision of a piece originally assigned to Philisides. Song ix is a more thorough reworking of early material, but nonetheless it seems out of place.

In addition, Song viii bears resemblances, particularly in structure, to #5 among the "Other Poems," where Philisides laments his unrequited love for Mira. "Other Poems" 5 opens with a stanza recited by an anonymous narrator who sets and populates the scene:

> The ladd *Philisides*
> Lay by a river's side,
> In flowry fielde a gladder eye to please:
> His pipe was at his foote,
> His lambs were him beside,
> A widdow turtle neere on bared root
> Sate wailing without boot.
> Each thing both sweet and sadd
> Did draw his boyling braine

> To thinke, and thinke with paine
> Of *Mira's* beames eclipst by absence bad.
> And thus, with eyes made dimme
> With teares, he said, or sorrow said for him.

There follows Philisides's lament in seven thirteen-line stanzas with the same intricate metrics and a final truncated nine-line stanza with complementary metrics. In separate stanzas the love-bereft shepherd apostrophizes the earth, the "wanton brooke," the "flowers faire," his "seely pipe," his "lamb of gold," and the nearby turtledove, which he then gathers together formulaically to make his inclusive statement:

> Earth, brooke, flowrs, pipe, lambe, Dove
> Say all, and I with them,
> "Absence is death, or worse, to them that love."
> (92–94)

The piece ends in a thirteen-line stanza in which the anonymous voice again assumes its narrating function: "This said, at length he ended / His oft sigh-broken dittie" (114–15). The rhetorical organization—opening and closing with a narrator's recital which brackets the intervening dramatic presentation—is the same as that for Song viii.[68]

The rhetorical organization of Song viii and "Other Poems" 5 is also the same as that for Spenser's January eclogue. There too Colin's amorous complaint is framed by opening and closing remarks offered by an unidentified authorial voice, a voice not otherwise heard in *The Shepheardes Calender* except at the opening of the December eclogue. Furthermore, in both of Colin's complaints he similarly uses a series of apostrophes to structure his lamentations. While I do not wish to exaggerate the similarities of these several pastoral pieces by two individualistic poets, their resemblance does seem more than coincidental. To my mind they provide the most suggestive evidence for a poetical exchange between Sidney and Spenser during that year before Spenser's departure for Ireland when both young men frequented Leicester House. These poems indicate shared interests about subject matter, genres, metrification, and not least the rhetorical strategy for relating fictive narrative to a readership.

The question inevitably arises: who borrowed from whom? I admit that there is no hard evidence in answering this question, only opinion. But in my opinion, Sidney was the leader in the poetical activity in Leicester House, and not only because of his rank. He was more committed to poetic theory, as the *Defence* shows. He also gave much consideration to generic definition and potential, recognizing the pastoral as the easiest place for an aspiring poet to start—"for perchance where the hedge is lowest they will soonest leap over" (*Defence* 33–34). Most telling, he gave more conscious consideration to the relationship of artificer to artifact, and thence to percipient. Sidney more than Spenser was experimenting with narrative strategies. But the main point of this digression into the January and December eclogues is to argue that if the similarities with "Other Poems" 5 and Songs viii and ix are other than coincidental, as I believe, Spenser must have known Sidney's pieces by mid-year 1579, when he was completing *The Shepheardes Calender.* So they are early works of Sidney, antecedent to the quatorzains and the other songs of *Astrophil and Stella.*

What we have done, then, is to isolate in Sidney's canon a number of lyrics that are similar in subject matter, genre, and narrative strategy. This group comprises "Other Poems" 5, Philisides's song in the old *Arcadia* beginning "Leave off my sheep," Song viii of *Astrophil and Stella,* and Song ix. We can add Song v of *Astrophil and Stella,* a slight recasting of an earlier piece of Philisides addressed to Mira, and Philisides's blazon of Mira in the old *Arcadia* beginning, "What tongue can her perfections tell." To this group of Sidney's poems we have also allied Spenser's January and December eclogues, the only two to rely upon a narrative voice from outside Colin's world; and as a new addition to the group we can include Greville's *Caelica* 76, reporting a failed tryst between Philocell and his Caelica, which is recognized as a companion piece to Sidney's Song viii. All of this is early work, dating to the days of the so-called Areopagus in Leicester House.

In *Astrophil and Stella,* only Songs viii and ix are pastoral, only in these songs is Astrophil called by name, and only in Song viii does an authorial narrator appear anywhere in the work. I conclude that these songs represent an embryonic stage from which *Astrophil and Stella* as we have it developed.[69] They contain in gist the entire action of the extended sequence of quatorzains and songs. They fossilize the matrix out of which Astrophil and Stella evolved. Perhaps we should think of them as the fore-conceit of the work itself, or the ground-plot of the narrative.

It is possible that this argument would shed some light upon the relationship between the songs and the quatorzains in *Astrophil and Stella,* and also upon the placement of the songs in the text, which is far from certain.[70] Why are the songs identified as different in substance from the quatorzains and numbered independently? Why are the songs separated from the quatorzains in some manuscripts (and in Newman's two printed editions) and collected together as a supplement at the end? How likely is it that the placement of the songs in the 1598 folio, the copy text that Ringler chose for his edition, represents Sidney's intention of where the songs should appear? Even, had Sidney made a decision about distributing the songs? At this time I will not pursue those lines of inquiry, although they are relevant—perhaps, fundamental—to our understanding of the work. I will pursue, however, a line of inquiry that examines the rhetorical assumptions underlying Song viii because it throws light upon Sidney's modification of narrative strategies as *Astrophil and Stella* evolved, and consequently it is informative about how we should read the work.

In Song viii Sidney employs a narrator to introduce, propel, and conclude the story. This authorial presence controls the text and makes it available to the reader, a technique that Sidney exploited so brilliantly in the old *Arcadia.* There is also a lengthy passage of dialogue in which first Astrophil and then Stella speak prosopopoeia-like in their own voices. We read Song viii, then, as we read the old *Arcadia*—although of course it is not so expansive a work, and therefore it doesn't provide so rich a reading experience. But the reading strategy for the two narratives is the same. The reader suffers under the authority of an imputed narrator, who fully materializes, and it is he who makes the story accessible.

As work on *Astrophil and Stella* proceeded, however, Sidney decided, consciously or unconsciously, to eliminate the narrator (in the new *Arcadia* also the narrator disappears). At some point after composing Song viii he decided to render the text more objective by removing the narrator and letting the characters speak wholly in their own voices. Song ix is such an unmediated lyric sung by

Astrophil, but its pastoral milieu and strong reliance upon literary convention peg it as nonetheless very early work.

Song iv better represents the intermediate stage in the transition to a purely dramatic mode. Like Song viii, Song iv is another vignette, replete with action, although no visible narrator appears. Astrophil and Stella in a dramatic dialogue act out a vivid scene. In each six-line stanza Astrophil speaks the first four lines plus a fifth line, which serves as a refrain: "Take me to thee, and thee to me";[71] and Stella finishes with another refrain: "No, no, no, no, my Deare, let be." Astrophil sets the scene himself at the beginning of the second stanza: "Night hath closd all in her cloke, / Twinckling starres Love-thoughts provoke" (7–8); and he implies the course of the action by what he says. What happens is a reprise of what takes place in Song viii: the two lovers have met for a prearranged tryst; Astrophil expresses his love and attempts to seduce Stella; when Stella continues reluctant, he resorts to the theme of *Carpe diem* ("Take time while you may," 28); that argument also proves ineffective, so he begins to fondle her; but she resists with "force of hands" (45), and eventually leaves in a huff, to Astrophil's chagrin. At no point is there any hint of an authorial presence. Song iv is Song viii removed from its authorial frame.

As in Songs viii and ix, nothing in Song iv identifies Stella with Penelope Devereux.[72] In the fiction the human obstacle to Astrophil's satisfaction is not a husband, but Stella's mother (37–39), who is not otherwise mentioned. It seems as though at this stage of composing *Astrophil and Stella* Sidney had not yet decided to assign any historical reference to Stella, so Song iv also is an early piece. But unlike Song viii, Song iv is fully realized in dramatic terms. There is no narrator, no mediator of the text; the verbal system includes nothing other than lines spoken by the two lovers, the direct discourse of overheard conversation.

As Ringler notes, there seems to be "clumsy joinery" in this portion of the sequence between Sonnets 85 and 87. As the text stands in the 1598 folio, there is only one quatorzain, but six of the eleven songs. Such a concentration of songs is uncharacteristic and disruptive, so this section required further attention on Sidney's part. What he intended to do, however, or even if he had a plan in mind, is indeterminate.

What we can be more sure of, though, is how Sidney expected

the opening quatorzains to be read. They are polished work and some of the most successful pieces in the collection. The initial sonnet is a good example of the narrative strategy that Sidney eventually arrived at, and it exemplifies the sophisticated story-telling that results. The lines come wholly from the mouth of Astrophil; and though he speaks in the past tense, like a storyteller, the liveliness of his utterance lends it immediacy.[73] The audience is unspecified—certainly not Stella, since she is spoken of in the third person (what we have are not the sonnets that Astrophil sent to Stella, but his account of the courtship). Nor is the audience some artificially homogeneous group of "fair ladies," as we found in the old *Arcadia*. The imputed audience as well as an imputed narrator has been firmly removed. It is Astrophil who juxtaposes the fictional world with ours. We are spectators in his theater of pleasure; we watch him perform upon a paper stage of his construction.

The persona of the sequence, whom we do not learn to call "Astrophil" until Song viii, is a complex and fascinating personality. In the first phrase of the opening sonnet he tells us that he is a lover, "loving in truth"—although with Pyrocles and Musidorus in mind, we may already have some doubts about the sincerity (or, at least, the purity) of this love. We should be wary of someone who professes his love so readily. He next tells us that he is a poet, wishing to express his love in verse; and that the purpose of his lyrics, quite naturally, has been to win his mistress's favor. He hopes his poetry will have a suasive effect upon the lady, moving her to accept his advances, and upon us, the readers, moving us to approve his poetizing. He delineates this rhetorical purpose in an extended *gradatio,* a textbook figure that begins with the persona's profession of love and ends with Stella's acquiescence. So Astrophil is more than a piece of a rhetorician. He is also more than a novice in love, since he fully displays the Petrarchist code, especially its religious dimension. The lady is a "deare She" who has the capacity of dispensing "grace" once she is moved to "pity."

After the *gradatio* of the first quatrain, in which the persona reveals himself as a Petrarchan lover and an accomplished speaker, he purports to describe his ends and means. He will entertain Stella's "wits" by "paint[ing] the blackest face of woe." Sonneteers before Sidney, including Turbervile and Gascoigne,[74] had used the colors of rhetoric to paint facial expressions, so this conceit had become commonplace. Yet it seems particularly appropriate in a poetics of speaking pictures, and on several other occasions Astrophil resorts to the conceit of painting with words.[75] In this instance the face of woe portrayed by Astrophil is a verbal image addressed to the mind's eye of Stella, and also to ours. Moreover, as we should expect of a trained rhetorician, Astrophil seeks for the suitable phrases of love by looking for topoi in the writings of previous poets, by "studying inventions fine." Note that "inventions" here has the rather strict meaning of the rhetorician's *inventio,* looking for useful subject matter in approved authors; "inventions" means topoi. So he laboriously turns the pages of other poets, hoping for stimulation. At this point Astrophil resorts to a proportional metaphor as Aristotle had defined the figure (pages 288–89):

a shower : a sun-burned field = others' poems : his brain

Reading other poets might bring "some fresh and fruitfull showers" that fall upon his "sunne-burn'd braine"—further evidence of Astrophil's prowess as an image-maker.

The third quatrain, introducing the sestet, opens with a "but" to indicate a change in the direction of thought: "But words came halting forth." Now begins another proportional metaphor:

inventio : *elocutio* = a crutch : a cripple

Consequently, since the persona's efforts at *inventio* have failed, "words came halting forth, wanting Invention's stay." Note that now the word "invention" has shifted slightly in meaning. It is no longer confined to topics in already existent writings; rather it is the rhetorician's *inventio* in the process of composition, requiring some initiative on the author's part as he formulates his argument. Invention comprises not merely the locating of topoi, but also the framing of a fore-conceit so that it can be dressed in words. Invention that merely restates prefabricated topics, in fact, is no more than a crutch; and while it supports elocution, the third step in the traditional five-step exercise, it nevertheless hobbles the verbal expression so that words are halting.

To demonstrate further his expertise as a rhetorician, Astrophil develops this last metaphor into an *allegoria*, a figure regularly defined as an extended metaphor.[76] Since his "invention" has proved inadequate to its assignment, he sends it to school. But it is a recalcitrant scholar, despite the harsh discipline imposed by the schoolmistress, personified as "Study," so "Invention, Nature's child, fled step-dame Studie's blowes." Note that here "invention" is "Nature's child," a product of nature, a natural gift.[77] Actually, during the three instances in which he uses "invention" Astrophil transforms the word from meaning the faculty for searching out topics in the writings of others to something close to the Romantics' natural genius. There is distinct slippage in the word "invention." Astrophil proves to be a subtle manipulator of language.

He continues to play with words in the next line: "Others' feete still seem'd but strangers in my way." Picking up the notion of the cripple leaning upon a crutch introduced in line 9, Astrophil makes a pun about the "feet" of other poets—their *metrical* feet, of course; but also he asserts that his way does not coincide with the path of others. So once again, while calling attention to his poetical predecessors, Astrophil claims that his poetry is sui generis, original.

In the next line Astrophil changes the metaphor in a dazzling mélange of imagery. Now he switches to the language of child-birth:

a poem : a poet = the infant : a woman in labor

As Astrophil puts it, he was "great with child to speake, and help-lesse in my throes."[78] This vivid image gives way to an equally lively dramatic scene described straightforwardly in the concluding couplet:

Biting my trewand pen, beating my selfe for spite,
"Foole," said my Muse to me, "looke in thy heart and write."

Astrophil's pen is "truant" since it has fled the classroom of the schoolmistress Study. So he clenches it in his teeth, pounding his breast or forehead (or both), until his Muse intervenes. This Muse is the vaunted inspiration of the neoplatonist poetics that Sidney rejects in the *Defence,* and therefore provides further necessity for distinguishing between Sidney and Astrophil, who accepts her advice. She counsels Astrophil to look into his heart, where he carries an image of Stella, and this abiding presence of the Petrarchan mistress will be a sufficient source of inspiration.

In this opening quatorzain, as in all the rest, we hear only Astrophil.[79] And in the course of the sequence we see him pursuing a variety of actions and expressing a range of moods. He apostrophizes a number of different addressees, some of whom are immediate presences, including Stella and an unnamed friend who has chastized him for amatory excess (Sonnets 14, 21); some of whom are personifications of objects, such as the moon (Sonnet 31) and his bed (Sonnet 98); some of whom are mythological such as Cupid (Sonnet 11) and Morpheus (Sonnet 32); and others of whom are personifications of concepts, such as virtue (Sonnet 4) and reason (Sonnet 10). Astrophil surrounds himself with a full corps de ballet, but he remains at center stage, a vivacious performer.[80]

Ringler comments, "The mode of presentation is essentially dramatic,"[81] and most readers, I think, would agree. It is this dramatic quality, in fact, that holds the work together and provides a subliminal coherence. The storyline is not continuous; at best, from the disconnected episodes we can piece out a simple narrative. Rather than a seamless plot, we have a series of autonomous vignettes, sometimes encompassing more than one quatorzain, as in the *baiser* group or the series lamenting Stella's absence. This discontinuity in the work generates a spontaneity similar to that which characterizes Eliot's *Waste Land:* except in the songs, settings are unspecified and Astrophil speaks unheralded, so in each instance we surmise the circumstances only from the gradual discovery of incidental information. Rather than being led passively through a story with a narrator at our side, the reader is forced to engage actively with the verbal system, asking questions, sorting information, making judgments. *Astrophil and Stella* is Sidney's *Fragments d'un discours amoreux,* a Barthesian history of tears. And other than a single vestige in the early work of Song viii, the author stays well hidden from our view.

As we watch Astrophil's performance in the opening quatorzain, we are made aware of a masterful wordsmith producing a plethora of imagery. He excites us with intricate figures of speech, including *gradatio, metaphora,* and *allegoria.* He teases us with amusing plays upon words, such as "invention" and "feet." He can write wittily when he wishes, as well as graphically and economically. In his chosen task of persuading a mistress, Astrophil has at his disposal the considerable resources of the skilled rhetorician.

By his actions, as well as his vocabulary and attitude, Astrophil insistently calls the familiar Petrarchist tradition to our attention. He begins as an overtly Petrarchan lover. But just as quickly he denies adherence to those tenets. Astrophil states that he has read the lyrics of other love poets; however, he finds their practice dissatisfying and therefore departs from it. At once Astrophil brings the Petrarchist code to bear upon the text, and at the same time announces that the text is not confined by it.[82] Through this strategy a norm is introduced, but only to be contravened. The reader must have the Petrarchist system in mind as a terminus à quo; meaning is generated, though, by deviation from this reference.

In the platonist poetics of the Petrarchists, for example, the poet receives his inspiration from a divine Muse and transcends his human limitation. Often inspiration comes from the mistress as surrogate for the Muse, a point that Astrophil iterates and elaborates in Sonnets 3, 55, 74, and 90. Stella becomes the means by which the poet-lover attains his near-divine status; love should be uplifting in the poetical enterprise as well as in matters of the heart. But Astrophil's inspiration is also the object of his sexual pursuit. So how sincere is Astrophil in addressing Stella in Petrarchist terms? Within the strict Petrarchist system, Stella is his mistress and therefore his means of achieving beatitude. But since Astrophil abjures this norm, the mistress may well be a cause of carnality, diverting the lover from any heavenly course; and the claim that she is inspirational may represent a sly perversion of the code, a witty testimonial to her sexual attractiveness.[83] By Sonnet 4 Astrophil confesses to the conflict between passion and reason that rages within his soul, so the Petrarchist system does not prevail unchallenged in the story line itself. Astrophil may be voicing the clichés in an insouciant way. And we as readers must comprehend this potential for duplicity, these double and contrasting possibilities.

The truth lies not in their mutual cancellation, however, as a deconstructionist would have it, but rather in their reconciliation.

What is stable and permanent—that is, golden—can come only from the reconciliation of such opposites. Astrophil is honestly devoted to Stella and consequently sincere in his profession of love; but also, perhaps because of self-delusion, like Pyrocles and Musidorus he is duplicitous. He is simultaneously innocent and insidious, and Sidney must reveal both aspects of his nature. As a true portraiture of the act of loving, Astrophil must display how love itself is both uplifting and debasing, both selfless and selfish.

Sidney accomplishes this ambiguity by manipulating the relationship between poet and persona. We are allowed to see Astrophil's world objectively through the eyes of its maker, but also we can feel vicariously the experience of Astrophil as we look from his vantage point. While reading the unmediated quatorzains, we share Astrophil's world and empathize with him. When we look from the unrestricted perspective of his maker, however, we conclude that Astrophil professes an impossible ideal, like Pyrocles and Musidorus, and is equally self-deluded. As Nashe observed, therefore, in this larger context Melpomene gives way to Thalia. When neatly framed and distanced, the behavior of Astrophil appears foolish, and tragedy is tempered by the comic. But Melpomene refuses to submit entirely; and in the end, *Astrophil and Stella* pays homage to both Muses. Put another way, Astrophil straddles the worlds of Ovid and of Dante.

The net response of the reader is indeterminate in one sense: it cannot be fixed, but rather ranges within a field of valences.[84] We both weep and scoff, and sometimes simultaneously. Our response, though, is not meaningless. The work is far from nihilistic. The two contrasting perspectives offered the reader, the despairing one of Astrophil and the supercilious one of his maker, do not negate one another. Instead, we benefit from the multiple sightings, rather as in a cubist painting, and we gain new insights into the life of things, into the ontology that allows opposites to coexist.

With this multivalency in mind, we can read *Astrophil and Stella* as Sidney's analysis of Petrarchism and of the assumptions about language implied in that cultural code. We might even say that Sidney created the space between himself and Astrophil in order to facilitate these subversive speculations.

As a critique of the Petrarchist code, *Astrophil and Stella* demonstrates that the idealized love of the neoplatonists is not practicable. Without equivocation Sonnet 25 directs the argument to Plato and cites the reason: man is susceptible to sensual appetites. Astrophil, like Pyrocles and Musidorus, struggles against his desire; yet, like them, he succumbs to carnal pleasure. As in the old *Arcadia,* where love is a demeaning and destructive force, so also in this collection of lyrics the lover feels the continual conflict between passion and reason, and never reaches a stable resolution of the problem. Although Astrophil professes to accept the servitude of the Petrarchist, he nevertheless moves aggressively to steal a kiss in violation of the lady's wishes, a contradiction inherent in the code itself. So *Astrophil and Stella* discloses the inconsistency and impossibility of the Petrarchan ideal.

As a critique of the Petrarchist's use of language, *Astrophil and Stella* demonstrates also how readily words may be abused. Astrophil applies his considerable skill to win Stella's acquiescence, and he is continually concerned not only with what he will say, but with how he will say it.[85] However, despite repeated claims of speaking forthrightly—at one point, he asserts, "My words I know do well set forth my mind" (44.1)—Astrophil is regularly devious.[86] His assertion of directness and honesty, in fact, may be part of the deceit. Astrophil is not to be trusted as lover or speaker, so once more we are placed in the position of judging. Is he innocently sincere, but incompetent? or does he knowingly prevaricate? The indeterminacy of human motive is neatly inscribed in the multivalency of language itself.

In the end, Sidney redefines love, modifying the prevalent platonist assumptions, and he rejects the sonnet tradition. In fact, the aesthetic of multeity in unity implied by the Timaean cosmology is rendered invalid. Celestial love is not only dissipated in its earthly translation, but metamorphosed into the sensual. The beauty that sonnets seek to praise and preserve is sullied in the palpable moniment, and thereby destroyed. To reify is to annihilate. So Astrophil's loss of Stella may be seen metonymically as Sidney's farewell to platonist idealism—a farewell suffused with sorrow and regret, but nonetheless inevitable and final. In the closing couplet of the work Astrophil complains to Stella lost: "In my woes for thee thou art my joy, / And in my joyes for thee my only annoy." It is as though Sidney were lamenting an irretrievable innocence.

Moreover, Astrophil's loss of Stella represents metonymically Sidney's rejection of the theory of language implied by platonist philosophy and presented most concisely in the *Cratylus* (pages 114–16). Sidney could no longer believe that an abiding world of ideas determines our verbal universe. A word is not dictated by what it designates; there is no inviolable bond between signifier and signified. Perhaps, even, Adam in his naming of the creatures had no clear directive. So *Astrophil and Stella* represents an important phase in the development of Sidney's attitude toward the poet's medium. Language is an inexact mode of expression, and it permits (even induces) prevarication. Poetry, like painting, thrives on illusion.

We have now gone some way toward answering a question raised earlier: why did Sidney compose a sequence of songs and sonnets after he so firmly renounced the poetics of rhyming and versing in the *Defence?* Why did he choose to implement the Augustinian aesthetic of multeity in unity after proclaiming his allegiance to Aristotelian imitation? I propose that *Astrophil and Stella* is his final, nostalgic analysis of platonist assumptions. As a humanist, Sidney had been conditioned by his training to revere those traditions, and quite naturally they dominate his early work. The songs of Philisides, his experiments in quantitative verse, and the miscellany known as *Certain Sonnets*—all of which he finished before beginning protracted work on *Astrophil and Stella*—attest to his initial view of poetry as metrified language echoing the heavenly harmony, what he himself called "the planet-like music of poetry" (*Defence* 121.27–28). Certainly he should not relinquish the old order without a careful assessment of it, before a respectful trial. Hence *Astrophil and Stella,* a full-scale exercise in implementing the aesthetics of sonneteering.

As a Protestant and proto-empiricist, however, Sidney reluctantly admitted that platonist assumptions were not adequate to the changing times. Politics demanded a revised worldview, and literature, the discourse of politics, called for a new poetics to comply with the changes in how men saw themselves in relation to the world and to the deity. In his own writing Sidney had already begun to implement the new Aristotelianism in the fiction of the *Arcadia,* developing a modern narrative strategy from the early poems of Philisides to Mira. So he laid aside the allegoricism im-

plicit in the sonnet tradition, where service to the lady is an analogue for mankind's duty to God, and turned to revising the *Arcadia*.

For all of his interest in Elizabethan drama and metaphysical poetry, T. S. Eliot proved to be a quirky reader of Renaissance literature. His favorite plays by Shakespeare were chosen for curious reasons, and his strictures against Milton were so eccentric as
to require recantation. But his readings of those poets appear
charitable and enlightened when compared to his attack on Sidney. In the second of his Norton lectures delivered at Harvard on
25 November 1935, Eliot reached this slashing conclusion:

> The works of Sir Philip Sidney, excepting a few sonnets, are not
> among those to which one can return for perpetual refreshment;
> the *Arcadia* is a monument of dulness.[87]

The arbiter of postwar taste who enthusiastically responded to
Donne and Herbert could find a few items in *Astrophil and Stella*
to salvage from oblivion. But the *Arcadia*? A monument of dull-
ness!

Eliot had read the composite *Arcadia*, one must assume, as it
had been patched together in Ponsonby's edition of 1593—"The
book which lived," as C. S. Lewis reminds us: "Shakespeare's
book, Charles I's book, Milton's book, Lamb's book, our own book
long before we heard of textual criticism" (333). The old *Arcadia*,
but recently recovered[88] and printed in 1926 for the first time,[89]
was still a literary curiosity.[90] One must ask, though, why did a
work that had commanded such reverence in its own time appear
so misguided to a modern sensibility like Eliot?

The answer, I believe, lies in Eliot's commitment to formalism
and his belief that a poem should be self-contained. In the works
he lectures on, Eliot looks for a quality that he coyly and quaintly
calls "unity of sentiment"; and although he never gets around to
saying it, the *Arcadia* in his view lacks this essential wholeness.
To Eliot, the *Arcadia* must have seemed sprawling and disjointed,
violating the need for organicism, lacking in objective correlatives,
silly in both its artificial language and fictitious story. Especially
the poorly seamed version of the *Arcadia* which had come down

to the twentieth century is vulnerable to the sort of attack that Eliot waged against it.

But what a pity Eliot never reread Sidney as he reread Milton, because upon reflection he would have found in the revised *Arcadia* many of those qualities that a modernist looked for. In the new *Arcadia* Sidney continued the collation of poetry with rhetoric that he had propounded in the *Defence*. He found further ways of hypostatizing the text, giving additional independence to the verbal system of a poem. He devised innovative narrative strategies whereby the reader is involved even more intimately and actively in the performative act of assimilating disparate episodes. In technique and in subject matter, *Astrophil and Stella* bears comparison with *The Waste Land,* and so does the new *Arcadia*. It is a collage of the debilitating attitudes that Sidney witnessed in his society. I suspect, in fact, that Sidney would have been a more successful reader of Eliot's poem than Eliot proved to be of his.

The new *Arcadia* was made available to the public early in 1590, when William Ponsonby published a compact quarto containing the first printed version of the *Arcadia* in any state. Sidney had begun extensive rewriting of the old *Arcadia* as early as 1582; and when he departed for the Low Countries in 1585, he left a manuscript of the revision with Fulke Greville. Sidney had not allowed this revision to circulate because it was so far from finished; in fact, there is only one manuscript of it, a copy deriving in some way from the manuscript that Sidney left with Greville. After Sidney's death, Greville became Sidney's literary executor, acting under instructions from the Countess of Pembroke; and eventually Greville's manuscript of the new *Arcadia* found its way into the hands of Ponsonby, a rising London bookseller who had begun angling for it as far back as November 1586.[91] Ponsonby entered the *Arcadia* in the Stationers' Register on 23 August 1588, and the printed volume duly appeared less than two years later, with the blessing of the Countess of Pembroke. This is the text we shall now consider.[92]

At the outset, however, we must recognize the inherent limitations of this text. Not only is it a far from complete revision of the old *Arcadia,* but also hands other than Sidney's have tampered with it. In a headnote by someone who identifies himself as "the over-seer of the print," we're warned that "the division and summing of the Chapters was not of Sir *Philip Sidneis* dooing" (A4ᵛ). Rather, the overseer of the print—Greville, or more likely one of his agents, Matthew Gwinne or perhaps John Florio—divided the work into chapters and provided headpieces that summarize the action in each. While the division into chapters is therefore an editorial decision without authority from Sidney, the division into three books follows the division of the first three books of the old *Arcadia* and therefore seems authentic. The sets of eclogues which appear between Books 1 and 2 and between Books 2 and 3, however, have been selected, arranged, and augmented by an unwarranted editorial hand. Again in his headnote the overseer of the print reveals that although the eclogues "were of Sir *Phillip Sidneis* writing, yet were they not perused by him"; and he openly admits, "They have bene chosen and disposed as the over-seer thought best."

We must be aware, then, that the new *Arcadia* is but a fragment, and even that fragment has been altered by officious (albeit reverent) editors. In the telling of the story as it stands in the new *Arcadia,* there are lacunae, discontinuities, and interpolations, not to mention the abrupt breaking-off in mid-sentence halfway through Book 3. Necessarily, therefore, anything we say about this text is tentative.[93] But it is irresistible to speculate, and some things of relevance might be proposed. The importance of the work demands that we study it.

I think it safe to conclude that in the new *Arcadia* Sidney continued to visualize the action, and perhaps took steps to intensify its vividness.[94] The techniques of visualization that we identified in the old *Arcadia* are abundantly evident. Prosopographias (the description of persons) occur more frequently and more casually than before, and there are more topographias (the description of places), and even a few chronographias (the description of a particular time). Prosopopoeiac speeches abound, although in the expanded narrative there is not so heavy a reliance upon them. There is a notable increase in the number of emblematic elements, usually in the form of *imprese* borne by warrior-knights. Among the highly visualized moments of the text, in fact, only the voyeurism decreases (pages 418–21); but there is no longer a smirking narrator to leer at Philoclea and Pyrocles. Finally, the characters in their speech continually refer to their circumstances in terms of playing in a drama,[95] usually a tragedy, continuing and augmenting a technique of the old *Arcadia* for suggesting a visualized action.

The overall dramatic effect, however, is probably diminished—certainly, the highly charged Book 5 is missing. But even beyond that omission, there is less frequent use of dialogue, a lower proportion of episodes presented as an exchange between speakers. As the dominant mode, dramatic presentation gives way to narration by an all but invisible storyteller.

This lessening of dramatic effect and greater reliance upon storytelling is due in large part to fundamental changes in the narrative strategy that Sidney adopted in the revision. Whereas in the old *Arcadia* an evident narrator officiously presides over the proceedings, in the new *Arcadia* that narrator has disappeared. And along with that imputed narrator, the imputed audience of "fair ladies" has likewise vanished. The mediating agents between text and reader have been removed. In the new *Arcadia* the implied readership is undefined in any way, and the fiction is placed in the charge of an omniscient narrator. Furthermore, despite the omniscience and authority of this narrator, he remains an indistinct figure, self-effacing, hiding along the margins of the discourse. Only rarely, if at all, does he achieve any personality as a prude or a wit; instead, he reports impartially what the reader needs to know.

The reticence of the narrator, his reluctance to assert himself and take control, is manifest also in the looseness of construction. In the old *Arcadia* the plot is planned and executed with utmost economy, but in the new *Arcadia* the plot is overwhelmed by a plethora of incidentals and digressions. Many readers feel, like Eliot, that the center does not hold. Rather than moving smoothly along a clearly demarcated route, the plot in the revised version lurches along, energized more by the surprising turn of events and by the promise of more surprises than by any sequence of cause-and-effect. The text is self-determining, operating under its own momentum but without discernible direction.

Moreover, other characters within the fiction often take over from this reticent narrator, replacing him as storyteller, sometimes telling their own story. Whereas in the old *Arcadia* the narrator opens the work by describing the setting, the royal family, and the oracle, in the revision this necessary information is delayed until the third chapter and then is supplied by Kalander (fols. 11ff.). The omniscient narrator resumes at the very end of chapter 4, but he is soon interrupted by Kalander's steward, who fills chapter 5 with the marvelous tale of Argalus and Parthenia as incidental to the plight of Clitophon, Kalander's son. The narrator again picks up at the beginning of chapter 6 and holds forth for a few chapters. But shortly into chapter 8, Pyrocles takes over briefly to relate to Musidorus his experience during their shipwreck. Soon, though, the narration is returned to the narrator, who continues to the end of chapter 10, when Queen Helen of Corinth arrives on the scene. Queen Helen preempts most of chapter 11 to tell her own tale of being courted by Philoxenus while she loved Amphialus; and although the narrator intrudes on folios 44^v–45, she does not conclude until folio 48. The narrator then resumes for the next chapter, but Pyrocles takes over at the beginning of chapter 13 to relate the circumstances of his falling in love with Philoclea, of his gaining entrance to Basilius's forest retreat, etc. The narrator recovers the narrative near the end of chapter 14 and continues through the remainder of Book 1, although Basilius intrudes in chapter 15 first by indirect discourse and then by direct discourse to relate the story of Phalantus (fols. 66–68^v).

In Book 2 of the new *Arcadia* the chore of storytelling is passed around with equal liberality. The book opens, as in the old *Arcadia*, with the narrator revealing the state of Gynecia, of Pyrocles, and of Basilius in love. Early in chapter 2 Musidorus takes over to report to Pyrocles his progress in wooing Pamela, and in the process repeats his own history for the benefit of Pamela. The narrator recommences with chapter 4 and continues until midway chapter 5, when Pamela reports to Philoclea how Musidorus has wooed her. The narrator takes over smoothly at the end of the chapter and begins chapter 6, but Musidorus soon interrupts to relate to Pamela the adventures of Pyrocles, in which he also appears prominently. Musidorus continues for several chapters, despite a brief interruption by Pamela (fol. 128^v), a short intrusion by the narrator (fol. 137), and a tale within Musidorus's tale when the Paphlagonian king tells his story of mistakenly believing his wicked son, Plexirtus, to the detriment of his loyal son, Leonatus (fols. 143–144^v). At the end of chapter 10 Musidorus is interrupted, and the narrator recommences with the beginning of chapter 11. He continues until chapter 13, when Philoclea takes over to recount the history of Erona as Plangus had related it. The narrator intrudes briefly on folio 160, but does not resume the storytelling until early in chapter 14. Soon Miso breaks in (fol. 163), however, and insists upon telling a story; and then Mopsa begins a silly tale (fols. 165ᵛ–166), though she is stopped by Philoclea (as reported by the narrator). With chapter 15 Pamela picks up from where Philoclea had left off in the history of Erona and Plangus, but after several pages she is interrupted when Basilius appears at the end of the chapter (fol. 172), and the narrator again takes over. He continues in chapter 16 with material about Basilius, Gynecia, Zelmane, and Philoclea taken directly from the old *Arcadia*. At the end of chapter 17 Philoclea asks Pyrocles to relate what happened to him and Musidorus after they left Erona, and he complies, filling the next seven chapters. In chapter 18, however, the much- abused Dido is allowed to tell in her own words the wrongdoing of Pamphilus (fols. 182ᵛ–185); the narrator intrudes very briefly in chapter 20 (fol. 192), and again at the end of chapter 21 (fol. 198ᵛ) so that Pyrocles and Philoclea can kiss; and in chapter 22 the story of Tydeus and Telenor is embedded in Pyrocles's narrative when the villain tells it (fols. 201ᵛ–203ᵛ). Although Philoclea wishes to hear still more from Pyrocles at the end of chapter 24, the narrator assumes control (fol. 211) and the plot is moved forward by more material from the old *Arcadia*. The original explanation of the rebellion against Basilius is adapted and put in the mouth of Clinias (fols. 221ᵛ–223ᵛ), and Basilius is allowed to continue the history of Erona (fols. 227ᵛ–233ᵛ), which consumes most of chapter 29. But the omniscient narrator returns hurriedly at the end of the chapter to wind up Book 2 and announce the eclogues.

The ease with which the responsibility for narration passes from the omniscient narrator to characters within the fiction produces a certain independence for the text. It is not attached to one storyteller, emanating from one source. Rather, it circulates among several. The text is thereby destabilized, informed with a vitality of its own divorced from any narrator—or, indeed, from any author. It enjoys a freedom, a sprightliness, an unpredictability, a vagariousness that focuses attention upon the story rather than the storyteller. The appropriate analogue might be the *Metamorphoses* of Ovid, where the role of narrator passes from one person to another, creating an unsettling effect of tales within tales within tales.

A good example of this layered effect is provided in chapter 8 of Book 2, while Musidorus recounts the past of himself and Pyrocles for the edification of Pamela. At this point in the plot Musidorus has revealed his true identity to Pamela, but he must continue his disguise as a shepherd in order to lay plans for their escape. He therefore is faced with the tricky task of telling Pamela about himself without raising the suspicions of those who keep watch over her. Predictably, he hits upon the ruse of telling his own story while disguised as Dorus, who pretends to be talking about a third party. It is important to the plot for Sidney to make clear that Pamela understands this role-playing, and also to indicate the sentimental communication, necessarily concealed, that passes between the lovers. In consequence, at a high point in Dorus's narration, when Pyrocles at the last moment rescues Musidorus from public execution on a scaffold, Sidney has Dorus commit a faux pas and speak of the incident in the first person: "In truth, never man betweene joy before knowledge what to be glad of, and feare after considering his case, had such a confusion of thoughts, as I had, when I saw *Pyrocles,* so neare me" (fol. 137). And to make the narrative strategy fully evident, Sidney has the omniscient narrator break in at this point to describe the response of both Musidorus and Pamela to this slip that reveals the disguised storyteller's true identity:

> But with that *Dorus* blushed, and *Pamela* smiled: and *Dorus* the more blushed at her smiling, and she the more smiled at his blushing; because he had (with the remembraunce of that plight he was in) forgotten in speaking of him selfe to use the third person.

What we have is the narrator commenting upon Musidorus and Pamela's response to Dorus's tale of Musidorus and Pyrocles. We watch the narrator, who reports upon Musidorus and Pamela, who in turn are listening to Dorus telling a tale of himself. By having Musidorus appear simultaneously in two fictive worlds, as both first- and third-person players, Sidney reminds us that the laudable feats of Pyrocles and Musidorus are part of a larger tapestry, and that their history is currently employed in Musidorus's ulterior purpose of winning Pamela.

Without this intrusion by the narrator to report the sympathetic exchange between Musidorus and Pamela it is likely that fascination with the inner story would have become an end in itself, obfuscating the main narrative of the young lovers. But Sidney is careful here so that both layers of narrative remain operative in our minds. In this instance, his strategy is fully developed and successful. Perhaps, had he completed the revised *Arcadia,* he would have taken precautions to insure that incidental tales did not obscure the main plot. As the unfinished text stands, however, the plot about Basilius and the oracle which provides the occasion for all else is almost lost in the profusion of episodes. In its present state the text often seems to wander off down a side path—usually beguiling enough in its own right, but digressive and disintegrative.

There is no way of telling if Sidney would have eventually consolidated the narrative point of view in further revision of the *Arcadia,* or if having multiple storytellers and a weak chief narrator were part of his calculated strategy. We can say for certain only that in the text we have, because of the distribution of authorial prerogative, emphasis tends to be shifted to individual episodes and the plot is dispersed. The text is decentered—although we must be careful here, since the effect is no doubt heightened by the unfinished state of the work. Without question, however, the structure of the revised *Arcadia* is more episodic and less well integrated than that of the original version.

Because of this episodic structure, many readers see the new *Arcadia* as an heroical poem, while disregarding its pastoral aspects.[96] They point to its rewritten opening, which begins the narrative *in medias res* according to the best examples of epic. They also point to the seeming rehabilitation of the two princes, Pyrocles and Musidorus. There are now lengthy accounts of their valiant feats, so they easily fill the role of heroes; and their sexual misconduct is greatly toned down, if not eliminated. In the revised text as we have it, they become the protagonists in the action, and the story of Basilius and the oracle is pushed aside. The recasting of the oracle into a ten-line verse that includes an extended reference to the lovers of Pamela and Philoclea (fol. 225^v) further supports the supposition that Sidney proposed to amplify the roles of Musidorus and Pyrocles. But as the text stands, it is impossible to say whether Sidney intended to elevate the princes and their history at the expense of Basilius. The evidence is inconclusive because the revision is so far from finished. At most, we are justified in saying that in the new *Arcadia* the plot is episodic, and therefore like the epic, and that the story in Books 1 and 2 is assigned among a variety of narrators. Both these techniques are effective means of hypostatizing a text, since frequently changed venues and multiple narrators subvert the authority of author over text and consequently tend to liberate it.

By Book 3 of the new *Arcadia*—by which time the reader has had considerable opportunity to adjust properly to the demands of an increasingly autonomous text—the task of storytelling is assigned exclusively to the omniscient narrator. No other voice intervenes. Even the dialogue is reported rather than overheard. Because of the indistinctness of the narrator, however, the resultant verbal system is even further objectified, presented without the benefit of any noticeable narrator. Book 3 is pure fiction, unmediated to an extreme. It exists independently, *in vacuo,* unrelated to author or context, freed from antecedent. The sufferings of Pamela and Philoclea in the grip of Cecropia, and the tribulations of those who fight for their release, have the stark reality of brute nature. The text achieves the objectivity of direct experience, and the reader must grapple with it unaided, instructed by no more than his engagement with Books 1 and 2. The reader, in fact, is invited to deal with it without interference from its source, without reference to its origin. This invitation to experiment and play is at once a challenge to the reader and a license to make anew according to our own predilections. It is this sophisticated strategy of reader involvement that makes the new *Arcadia* an irresistible work. Our ability to engage with a text is continually tested.

Finally, just as the officious narrator disappears from the new *Arcadia,* so also does the other character who most evidently represents Sidney in the old *Arcadia.* In the earlier version, Philisides is a persistent and important presence, providing a bridge between the Arcadian world and our reality, demonstrating how fiction grows out of and relates back to fact. In the new *Arcadia*, however, Philisides appears only once, briefly and insignificantly. He appears but incidentally, to swell a progress of jousting knights assembled to do honor to Andromana, Queen of Iberia. Moreover, though he is still a knight masquerading in the guise of a shepherd, there are no attempts to confirm the significance of his name by assigning him other qualities or experiences that would identify him as Sidney. There is reference to a lady named "the *Star*, whereby his course was only directed" (fol. 196), so this Philisides has affinities to Astrophil; but that is a roundabout and tenuous link with Sidney.

While Philisides was a major means by which Sidney projected himself into the fiction of the old *Arcadia*, in the new *Arcadia* the role of Philisides is so constricted and the identification with Sidney so remote that the character has negligible effect. It seems likely that Sidney eventually would have eliminated Philisides completely. In the text as it stands, his materials have been deleted or distributed among other lovers. The blazon of Mira is assigned to Zelmane (fols. 150^v–152^v), the dream of Mira is assigned to Amphialus (fols. 246^v–247^v), and the elegiacs saying farewell to Mira are assigned to Dorus (fols. 272^v–275^v)—all without any reference to Philisides.[97] In effect, Philisides has been written out of the new *Arcadia*. But this elimination of the figure that most insistently links the old *Arcadia* to Sidney himself is a further weakening of the tie between fiction and author, a further means of freeing the text.

To summarize, in the old *Arcadia* Sidney inserts himself into the text by means of Philisides, thereby validating the fiction by giving it the vraisemblance of autobiography; and he uses the rather obvious instruments of an imputed narrator and an imputed audience to mediate the fiction, to relate the text and the reader. In *Astrophil and Stella* Sidney moves toward an unmediated text: although the trace of a narrator survives in Song viii, a vestige from earlier work, Sidney fully implements the Aristotelian poetics of mimesis and places Astrophil upon a paper stage to perform his tragedy/comedy. In the new *Arcadia* Sidney continues to work toward a fully hypostatized text, an autonomous verbal system, where the narrator is first displaced by characters who tell the story and eventually obscured. By Book 3 the story is as authorless as possible.

In his brief career Sidney steadily evolved toward a poetics of self-justifying images. To use Foucault's term,[98] his text becomes a "monument" in the public domain, severed from its origins while preserving them, facing the future rather than the past. To confirm the argument of Barthes, by the end of the revised fragment of *Arcadia* the author has slain himself in order to license the reader. To accomplish his program of societal reform, Sidney obliterated himself, committing his presence to the neutral medium of language, the medium of public discourse. With something of the same belief in the efficacy of the word shared by Elizabethan preachers bringing their parishioners to godliness, Sidney applied his remarkable talents to a literary artifact that involved the reader in an ever more performative act of making.

In 1593 Gabriel Harvey, Spenser's friend and Sidney's admirer, wrote an open letter to John Wolfe, the eminent London printer. Harvey displayed an unwonted ebullience, full of hope for the English language as a literary medium and full of commendation for those who had used it. At the top of his list of praiseworthy authors, not surprisingly, are the two with whom he most wished to be associated:

> Is not the Prose of *Sir Philip Sidney* in his sweet Arcadia the embrodery of finest *Art* and daintiest *Witt*? Or is not the Verse of M. *Spencer* in his brave Faery Queene the Virginall of the divinest Muses and gentlest Graces? Both delicate Writers, alwayes gallant, often brave, continually delectable, sometimes admirable. What sweeter tast of Suada then the Prose of the One; or what pleasanter relish of the Muses then the Verse of the Other?[99]

While Sidney and Spenser exist in the mind of Harvey side by side (or, at least, in tandem according to their rank), he also takes pains to particularize the genius of each. Sidney is admired as a writer of prose, and his major work is naturally the *Arcadia,* which is called "sweet" out of deference to its pastoral setting. It is the embrodery of finest art and daintiest wit because a mortal artificer exercised his human talent to produce it, and no artificer ever set forth the earth in so rich tapestry (*Defence* 78.30–31). In contrast, Spenser is admired as a writer of verse, and his major work is of course *The Faerie Queene,* which is called "brave" in recognition of its epic style. It is the virginal of the divinest Muses and gentlest Graces because inspiration from above filled the poet with an enthusiasm that manifests itself as the harmony of heavenly beauty. Both are estimable writers—but again, a telling differentiation. The prose of Sidney offers the sweetest taste of Suada, the goddess of persuasion; by his rhetoric he leads his readers to adopt that goodness he would have them take in hand. In contrast, the verse of Spenser provides the pleasantest relish of the Muses; by his μουσική he leads his readers to experience the rapture he himself has felt in the poetic frenzy.

It is reassuring that our view of Sidney and Spenser squares so nicely with that of Harvey. He too saw them as belonging to an age, but yet interpreting that age in quite distinctive ways. One was progressive; the other, orthodox. One persisted in writing poetry that echoed the music of the spheres; the other transformed poetry into primarily an image-producing exercise. Both were makers with highly individualized skills, applying the arts of language to create fictive worlds that still delight and teach.

Notes

Preface

1. For perhaps the most incisive discussion, see Jacques Derrida, *Positions*, trans. Alan Bass (Chicago: University of Chicago Press, 1981).

2. Roland Barthes, *S/Z*, trans. Richard Miller (New York: Hill and Wang, Farrar, Straus and Giroux, 1974), 5.

3. Paul de Man, *Allegories of Reading: Figural Language in Rousseau, Nietzsche, Rilke, and Proust* (New Haven: Yale University Press, 1979).

4. Jonathan Culler, *On Deconstruction: Theory and Criticism after Structuralism* (Ithaca: Cornell University Press, 1982), 182.

Chapter 1

1. William Lisle (?), Commendatory Verses with *The Faerie Queene* (1590), *The Works of Edmund Spenser: A Variorum Edition,* ed. Edwin Greenlaw et al., 11 vols. (Baltimore: Johns Hopkins University Press, 1932–57), 3:188. In subsequent footnotes this text is cited as *Spenser: Variorum.* All quotations from Spenser's works are taken from this edition, and all line references are made to it.

2. In 1590 Lisle was a twenty-year-old scholar at Cambridge, where he continued to reside, spending most of his adult life working on Anglo-Saxon manuscripts. He had entered King's College in 1584, after Eton, and he received an M.A. in 1592, at which time he became a fellow of his college.

3. *The Life of Edmund Spenser* (1945) by Alexander C. Judson is still the authoritative biography, and little has been added to it (*Spenser: Variorum,* vol. 10). For a stringent reexamination of this period in Spenser's life, see my "Sidney and Spenser at Leicester House," *Spenser Studies* (forthcoming).

4. For an assessment of Leicester's political career, see Wallace T. MacCaffrey, *Queen Elizabeth and the Making of Policy, 1572–1588* (Princeton: Princeton University Press, 1981), 440–48.

5. François, duc d'Anjou, was the youngest of Catherine de' Medici's four sons. The eldest had ruled France briefly as François II from 1559 to 1560. The next son had ruled as Charles IX from 1560 to 1574. The third son, who until 1574 had held the title of duc d'Anjou, ruled as Henri III from 1574 to 1589. The fourth son, while still the duc d'Alençon, had wooed Elizabeth as early as 1572; in 1576 he acquired the more prestigious title of duc d'Anjou.

6. The classic account of these events is given by Conyers Read, *Mr. Secretary Walsingham and the Policy of Queen Elizabeth*, 3 vols. (Oxford: Clarendon, 1925), 2:1–117. The most recent extended account, especially good for its context of international politics, is given by MacCaffrey 243–66. See also Patrick Collinson, *The Elizabethan Puritan Movement* (Berkeley: University of California Press, 1967), 191–201; and Roger Howell, *Sir Philip Sidney: The Shepherd Knight* (Boston: Little, Brown, 1968), 61–74. The importance of these events for Spenser's career was first elucidated by Edwin A. Greenlaw, "Spenser and the Earl of Leicester," *PMLA* 25 (1910): 535–61; cf. Alexander C. Judson, "Mother Hubberd's Ape," *Modern Language Notes* 63 (1948): 145–49.

Sidney was very much involved in this protest over the French marriage, writing his famous letter to Elizabeth advising strongly against it (*Miscellaneous Prose of Sir Philip Sidney*, ed. Katherine Duncan-Jones and Jan van Dorsten [Oxford: Clarendon, 1973], 33–57). His objection was so vocal and well-known that by March 1580 he had incurred the active dislike of Anjou; see *The Correspondence of Sir Philip Sidney and Hubert Languet*, ed. and trans. Steuart A. Pears (London, 1845), 177; cf. ibid. 170 and 187.

7. In contrast, the career of Arthur Atey, who was Leicester's secretary by late summer 1580, is well-documented; see Eleanor Rosenberg, *Leicester: Patron of Letters* (New York: Columbia University Press, 1955), 150 (n. 61).

8. *Spenser: Variorum* 9:12. Harvey also records an occasion when he anticipated foreign service for Leicester, but which similarly never came to pass and proved a royal joke; see Rosenberg 324–26.

9. For a suggestive reconstruction of Spenser's attitude toward poetry at this time, see Richard Helgerson, "The New Poet Presents Himself: Spenser and the Idea of a Literary Career," *PMLA* 93 (1978): 893–911.

10. See Alexander C. Judson, *A Biographical Sketch of John Young, Bishop of Rochester, with Emphasis on His Relations with Edmund Spenser* (Bloomington: Indiana University Press, 1934), 20–24.

11. The relation of *The Shepheardes Calender* to political and religious controversy has been most relentlessly studied by Paul E. McLane, *Spenser's Shepheardes Calender* (Notre Dame: University of Notre Dame Press, 1961). For broader sociopolitical implications, see Nancy Jo Hoffman, *Spenser's Pastorals: "The Shepheardes Calender" and "Colin Clout"* (Baltimore: Johns Hopkins University Press, 1977), esp. chap. 4. MacCaffrey suggests that, although the evidence is incomplete, *The Shepheardes Calender* was part of an "organized campaign" which Leicester mobilized and directed toward "exciting public opinion against the Anjou match" (446).

12. See Judson, *Life of Spenser, Spenser: Variorum* 10:68–71; but cf. Rosenberg 336–43.

13. For these and other "lost works" of Spenser, see the headpiece that the publisher William Ponsonby placed before *Complaints* (*Spenser: Variorum* 8:33). For an outdated summary discussion of the "lost works," see *Spenser: Variorum* 8:510–20.

14. *Spenser: Variorum* 9:6. The closest Spenser came to making Leicester a dedicatee during Leicester's lifetime was his overt reference to Leicester as a fit personage for heroical poetry in "October" 46–48; cf. E.K.'s gloss. Arguing from evidence based upon terms of address, William A. Ringler, Jr., concludes "that earlier in 1579 Spenser intended to dedicate his *Calender* to the Earl of Leicester, but that sometime after the middle of October he changed the dedication to Sidney" ("Spenser, Shakespeare, Honor, and Worship," *Renaissance News*, 14 [1961]: 160). Ringler does not speculate upon the reasons for such a change.

In "The Ruines of Time" Spenser berates himself in his persona as Colin Clout for being neglectful of Leicester, now dead (lines 225–31). "Virgils Gnat" is "long since dedicated to the most noble and excellent Lord, the Earle of Leicester, late deceased"; but this work was not published until the *Complaints* volume of 1591, and it is unlikely that Leicester was ever aware of it. Greenlaw's account of the events surrounding the composition and dedication of "Virgils Gnat" may well be true ("Spenser and Leicester" 557–59). This reluctance to dedicate his work to Leicester while Leicester was alive suggests to me that Spenser feared it would be construed as presumptuous to claim publicly an association with Leicester and that Spenser was not a member of Leicester's inner circle.

15. *Spenser: Variorum* 9:17, 18, 459–60, 471.

16. *Spenser: Variorum* 9:17, 470.

17. *Spenser: Variorum* 9:17, 471–72.

18. See "The Typographical Layout of Spenser's *Shepheardes Calender*," *The Word and the Visual Imagination*, ed. Karl Josef Höltgen and Peter M. Daly (Erlangen: University of Erlangen Press, 1988), forthcoming.

19. *A Discourse of English Poetrie, Elizabethan Critical Essays*, ed. G. Gregory Smith, 2 vols. (London: Oxford University Press, 1904), 1:232, 246.

20. For the irresponsible speculation about the contents of *The English poete* and about its relation to Sidney's *Defence of poesie*, see *Spenser: Variorum* 7:377–78. The scholars there quoted, while admitting the lack of evidence, invariably assume that Sidney was acquainted with and drew upon Spenser's lost treatise. For skepticism about the actuality of Spenser's treatise, see Theodore L. Steinberg, "*The English Poete* and the English Poet," *Spenser at Kalamazoo, 1979* (Cleveland: Cleveland State University, 1979), 35–53.

21. By far the fullest account of these travels is provided by James M. Osborn, *Young Philip Sidney, 1572–1577* (New Haven: Yale University Press, 1972), chaps. 2–16.

22. But see Richard A. Lanham, "Sidney: The Ornament of His Age," *Southern Review: An Australian Journal of Literary Studies* 2 (1966–67): 319–40; and Katherine Duncan-Jones, "Philip Sidney's Toys," *Proceedings of the British Academy* 66 (1980): 161–78.

23. For reasonable speculation on this question, see F. J. Levy, "Philip Sidney Reconsidered," *English Literary Renaissance* 2 (1972): 5–18.

24. There is some evidence, however, that this mission was a personal success for Sidney. The anonymous author of "The Life and Death of Sir Philip Sidney," first printed in the 1655 edition of Sidney's works, reports: "This yong Gentleman so acquitted himself, that the Lord *Burleigh* (our English Nestor) otherwise disaffected to the Lecestrian partie, gave him the especial commendation of industrie and discretion; which made him return with a doubled reputation" (Sidney, *Countess of Pembrokes Arcadia*, 10th ed. [London, 1655], b1ᵛ). Cf. Osborn 493–95. Daniel H. Woodward argues convincingly that Thomas Fuller is the author of the 1655 biography cited above ("Thomas Fuller, William Dugard, and the Pseudonymous Life of Sidney [1655]," *Publications of the Bibliographical Society of America* 62 [1968]: 501–10).

25. See Osborn 491.

26. The fullest report of any personal encounter between Sidney and the Queen results from his notorious challenge to the earl of Oxford in 1579 after Oxford's insult to Sidney on the tennis court; see Arthur Collins, *Letters and Memorials of State, in the Reigns of Queen Mary, Queen Elizabeth, King James, King Charles the First, Part of the Reign of King Charles the Second, and Oliver's Usurpation*, 2 vols. (London, 1746), 1:101–2. This incident must have convinced Elizabeth that while Sidney was a young man of spirit and integrity, he was also difficult to control.

27. A. C. Hamilton develops this thesis; see *Sir Philip Sidney: A Study of His Life and Works* (Cambridge: Cambridge University Press, 1977), 28–32. See also William A. Ringler, Jr., ed., *The Poems of Sir Philip Sidney* (Oxford: Clarendon, 1962), xxvii–xxviii. Annabel Patterson places Sidney's literary career in a larger political context (*Censorship and Interpretation: The Conditions of Writing and Reading in Early Modern England* [Madi-

son: University of Wisconsin Press, 1984], 24–43). In the opening paragraph of *The defence of poesie*, Sidney comments that he is writing in his "idlest times having slipped into the title of a poet," a career which he refers to in the next line as his "unelected vocation" (73.29–31). Unless specifically noted otherwise, references to Sidney's *Defence* will be given, as here, according to page and line numbers of the text printed in *Miscellaneous Prose of Sidney*, ed. Duncan-Jones and van Dorsten.

In a passage that had served as reference for the traditional dichotomy between the active life and the contemplative life, Cicero describes rather accurately Sidney's situation:

> Persons usually engaged in constant daily employment, when . . . [they] have been debarred from their work of politics by the circumstances of the time or have chosen to take a vacation, some of them have devoted themselves entirely to poetry, others to mathematics and others to music, and others also have created for themselves a new interest and amusement as dialecticians, and have spent the whole of their time and their lives in the sciences that were invented for the purpose of moulding the minds of the young on the lines of culture and of virtue. (*De oratore* 3.58)

Sidney's recourse to literary creation as an adjunct to an active political career was in keeping with the prevalent view of Cicero's own life established by Leonardo Bruni in his *Cicero novus*, the seminal biography of Cicero in the Renaissance.

28. See Ringler, ed., *Poems of Sidney* 365, 423.

29. *Spenser: Variorum* 9:6.

30. Harvey was seeking the post of Public Orator at Cambridge; see Virginia F. Stern, *Gabriel Harvey: His Life, Marginalia and Library* (Oxford: Clarendon, 1979), 53ff.

31. For a summary of arguments on this topic, see *Spenser: Variorum* 9:479–80, extended by Derek Attridge, *Well-Weighed Syllables: Elizabethan Verse in Classical Metres* (London: Cambridge University Press, 1974), 130 (n. 2).

32. *Spenser: Variorum* 9:442.

33. For an account of the spate of elegies commemorating Sidney's death and of their conventionality, see Berta Siebeck, *Das Bild Sir Philip Sidneys in der englischen Renaissance* (Weimar: Böhlaus, 1939), 72–83.

34. *Spenser: Variorum* 3:197.

35. "The Ruines of Time" contains an extended eulogy of Sidney (lines 281–343) following the laments for Leicester, Warwick, and Sidney's mother—all recently dead. Sidney appears again later in the poem as a wraithlike dying swan on the banks of the Thames, singing "of his owne death in dolefull Elegie" (lines 589–602); and his poetic faculty, "th'Harpe of *Philisides*," is the object of the next vision (lines 603–16). Carl J. Rasmussen is certainly right when he says, "The second set of six visions represents the death and resurrection of Sir Philip Sidney" ("'How Weak Be the Passions of Woefulness': Spenser's *Ruines of Time*," *Spenser Studies* 2 [1981]: 175).

36. *The Poetical Works of Edmund Spenser*, ed. J. C. Smith and Ernest de Selincourt (London: Oxford University Press, 1912), xiii.

37. *The Works of . . . Mr. Edmond Spenser* (London, 1679), A1.

38. See also William Wells, ed., *Spenser Allusions: In the Sixteenth and Seventeenth Centuries*, *Studies in Philology*, Extra Series (Chapel Hill: University of North Carolina Press, 1971–72), 136, 143, 269, 271, 281–82, 296, 300; and Edward Phillips, *Theatrum poetarum* (London, 1675), 35. John Aubrey picked up the anecdote of Sidney's reading the Despair canto; see Oliver Lawson Dick, ed., *Aubrey's Brief Lives* (London: Martin Secker, 1949), 279. It continued to be viable well into the eighteenth century: cf. John Hughes, ed., *The Works of Mr. Edmund Spenser*, 6 vols. (London, 1715), 1:iii–vi; Thomas Birch, "The Life of Mr. Edmund Spenser," *The Faerie Queene*, 3 vols. (London, 1751), 1:vii–viii; Theophilus Cibber, *The Lives of the Poets of Great Britain and Ireland*, 5 vols. (London,

1753), 1:92–93; and John Upton, ed., *Spenser's Faerie Queene,* 2 vols. (London, 1758), 1:v–vi.

39. Wells, *Spenser Allusions* 143.

40. It seems to me likely that by autumn 1579 Spenser and E.K./Harvey were familiar with Sidney's *Defence* in some state of completeness which included his comments about the archaic diction of *The Shepheardes Calender*—hence E.K.'s apologetic opening of the dedicatory epistle in which he defends at length the use of "such olde and obsolete words."

41. A possible reference to Spenser has been suggested in a letter from Sidney to Edward Denny dated 22 May 1580; see Osborn 535. This possibility has been effectively refuted, however, by John Buxton, *Times Literary Supplement,* 24 March 1972: 344 (n. 16); cf. Roy L. Davids, *Times Literary Supplement,* 7 April 1972: 394.

42. Ringler, ed., *Poems of Sidney* 413. Actually, the appropriate reference for Philisides' performance is the seventh prosa and eclogue of Jacopo Sannazaro, *Arcadia,* ed. Francesco Sansovino (Venice, 1571), fols. 49ᵛ–56. Cf. Sannazaro, *Arcadia & Piscatorial Eclogues,* trans. Ralph Nash (Detroit: Wayne State University Press, 1966), 69–76.

43. See Jean Robertson, ed., *Sir Philip Sidney: The Countess of Pembroke's Arcadia (The Old Arcadia)* (Oxford: Clarendon, 1973), xv–xix. Citations of the old *Arcadia* will be made by reference to page and line numbers in this edition.

44. See Ringler, ed., *Poems of Sidney* 423–24. All of the *Certain Sonnets* were completed by 1582.

45. Ringler, ed., *Poems of Sidney,* 438.

46. See Duncan-Jones and van Dorsten, eds., *Miscellaneous Prose* 59–63.

47. The most judicious discussion of this question remains T. P. Harrison, Jr., "The Relations of Spenser and Sidney," *PMLA* 45 (1930): 712–31. The nature and extent of any exchange between Spenser and Sidney, however, have been studied by a long line of diligent scholars: see Frederic I. Carpenter, *A Reference Guide to Edmund Spenser* (Chicago: University of Chicago Press, 1923), 95–98; Dorothy F. Atkinson, *Edmund Spenser: A Bibliographical Supplement* (Baltimore: Johns Hopkins University Press, 1937), 39–42; Waldo F. McNeir and Foster Provost, *Edmund Spenser: An Annotated Bibliography 1937– 1972,* 2d ed. (Pittsburgh: Duquesne University Press, 1975), 481–82 ("Sidney"). For a summary of the results to 1943, see *Spenser: Variorum* 7:487–90. See also Ralph M. Sargent, *At the Court of Queen Elizabeth* (London: Oxford University Press, 1935), 58– 64; Judson, *Life of Spenser, Spenser: Variorum* 10:54–72; Rosenberg 329–48; Jean Robertson, "Sir Philip Sidney and His Poetry," *Elizabethan Poetry,* ed. John R. Brown and Bernard Harris (London: Edward Arnold, 1960), 114; A. C. Hamilton, *The Structure of Allegory in "The Faerie Queene"* (Oxford: Clarendon, 1961), 29 (n. 1); McLane 22–26, 30, 286–87; Ringler, ed., *Poems of Sidney* xxix–xxxiv; William Nelson, *The Poetry of Edmund Spenser* (New York: Columbia University Press, 1963), 18–20; John Buxton, *Sir Philip Sidney and the English Renaissance,* 2d ed. (New York: St. Martin's Press, 1964), esp. 126–32; Roger Howell 157–58; Osborn 504, 536–37; Robertson, ed., *Old Arcadia* xix.

The most rigid argument for minimizing the exchange between Spenser and Sidney has been mounted by Ringler in the introduction to his edition of Sidney's poems. In his strong words, "The two men do not appear to have become intimately acquainted" (xxxi); and on the next page, "The two men had only occasional opportunities for meeting one another during a period of less than six months" (xxxii). Although Ringler understates the length of time during which they might have come together in London, I am inclined to agree, as Ringler urges, "that the two men never became well acquainted and never had any really serious discussions of the technicalities of their craft" (xxxiii–xxxiv).

48. *Spenser's Shepherd's Calender in Relation to Contemporary Affairs* (New York: Columbia University Press, 1912), 251.

49. "The Function of Criticism," *Selected Essays 1917–1932* (New York: Harcourt Brace Jovanovich, 1932), 13.

50. *The Renaissance: Studies in Art and Poetry*, 4th ed. (London, 1893), xv–xvi.

51. "Tradition and the Individual Talent," *Selected Essays* 4.

Chapter 2

1. Omnes artes, quae ad humanitatem pertinent, habent quoddam commune vinculum et quasi cognatione quadam inter se continentur (Cicero, *Pro Archia poeta*, 1; my translation). Quoted by Antonio Mancinello, "De poetica virtute, et studio humanitatis impellente ad bonum," *Sententiae veterum poetarum, per locos communes digestae*, by Georg Major (Lyons, 1551), 271. As Franciscus Junius translated this passage, "All Arts, sayth Tullie, that doe belong to humanitie, have a common band, and are ally'd one to another, as by a kind of parentage" (*The painting of the ancients, in three books* [London, 1638], 44).

2. By "imitation" I do not mean simply the making of a copy, or even the representation of physical reality, as a modern reader might assume. For development of this Romantic notion of artistic imitation, see M. H. Abrams, *The Mirror and the Lamp* (New York: Oxford University Press, 1953), esp. 11–14. "Imitation" in other periods has meant much more than the replication of objective nature. The concept is so complex, in fact, that it requires this entire chapter to suggest the possibilities.

For an informed discussion of the term in Italian criticism, see Ferruccio Ulivi, *L'Imitazione nella poetica del Rinascimento* (Milan: Marzorati, 1959). For two distinct interpretations of the term during the Renaissance, neither of which is appropriate to Sidney, see A. J. Smith, "Theory and Practice in Renaissance Poetry: Two Kinds of Imitation," *Bulletin of the John Rylands Library* 47 (1964–65): 212–43. For a brief statement of Sidney's theory of imitation, see Geoffrey Shepherd, ed., *An Apology for Poetry or The Defence of Poesy* (London: Thomas Nelson, 1965), 47–50.

For a detailed analysis of what "imitation" and its derivatives might have meant to Plato and Aristotle, the progenitors of an art theory based upon *mimesis*, see Göran Sörbom, *Mimesis and Art: Studies in the Origin and Early Development of an Aesthetic Vocabulary* (Stockholm: Bonniers, 1966). For an influential and still valuable discussion of the term in Aristotle, see S. H. Butcher, ed. and trans., *Aristotle's Theory of Poetry and Fine Art*, 4th ed. (London: Macmillan, 1927), 121–62; cf. also Aristotle, *Poetics*, ed. D. W. Lucas (Oxford: Clarendon, 1968), 258–72.

3. The earliest extant commentary on the *Defence* comes about 1584 from William Temple, a protegé of Sidney. Temple has the following to say about this statement:

> This is the definition, most illustrious Philip, which contains the whole controversy, and upon which like a basis rests almost entirely the treatise on poetics which you have devised. Therefore let's see if it properly unfolds and defines the problem. For you wish the nature of poetry to lie in a sort of fiction.

(Temple, "Analysis tractationis de poesi contextae a nobilissimo viro Philippo Sidneio equite aurato," De L'Isle and Dudley MS 1095; my translation). I am indebted to William A. Ringler, Jr., for making available to me a photostat of this ms. An excellent edition and translation with a most informative introduction has now been prepared by John Webster, *William Temple's "Analysis" of Sir Philip Sidney's "Apology for Poetry"* (Binghamton, NY: Center for Medieval and Early Renaissance Studies, 1984).

4. For a sweeping view of this movement, see Harry Levin, "What Is Realism?" *Comparative Literature* 3 (1951): 193–99.

5. For a penetrating (yet sympathetic) look at "program music," see Albert Wellek, "The Relationship between Music and Poetry," *Journal of Aesthetics and Art Criticism* 21 (1962–63): 149–56. See also Edward F. Kravitt, "The Impact of Naturalism on Music and

the Other Arts during the Romantic Era," *Journal of Aesthetics and Art Criticism* 30 (1971–72): 537–43.

6. *Art and Illusion: A Study in the Psychology of Pictorial Representation,* 2d ed. (New York: Pantheon Books, 1961), 16. For a wide-ranging discussion of the many ways in which art may be said to imitate nature, see A. J. Close, "Commonplace Theories of Art and Nature in Classical Antiquity and in the Renaissance," *Journal of the History of Ideas* 30 (1969): 467–86.

7. In the last half-century "the author" has been systematically annihilated by a succession of theorists reacting against the cult of the artistic ego that flourished in the nineteenth century. For milestones along this path, see W. K. Wimsatt, Jr., and Monroe C. Beardsley, "The Intentional Fallacy," *The Verbal Icon* (Lexington: University of Kentucky Press, 1954), 3–18; Roland Barthes, "The Death of the Author," *Image/Music/Text,* trans. Stephen Heath (New York: Hill and Wang, Farrar, Straus and Giroux, 1977), 142–48; and Michel Foucault, "What Is an Author?" *Textual Strategies: Perspectives in Post-Structuralist Criticism,* ed. Josué V. Harari (Ithaca: Cornell University Press, 1979), 141–60.

8. By "poetry" I do not mean only metrified literary works, a definition arising from the classical distinction between poetic and rhetoric, but rather what we with a post-Romantic bias are likely to call "creative" or "imaginative" literature, including both prose and verse. Sidney used "poetry" in this sense, casually interchanging this term with its cognate derivative from Greek, "poesy" (see page 514 [n. 5]). In a paragraph defining "poet," Jonson was careful to note that versifying is not the poet's distinctive occupation: "*A Poet* . . . [is] not hee which writeth in measure only; but that fayneth and formeth a fable" (*Timber: or, Discoveries, Ben Jonson,* ed. C. H. Herford and Percy and Evelyn Simpson, 11 vols. [Oxford: Clarendon, 1925–52], 8:635). In *The advancement of learning,* Francis Bacon similarly pronounced that "Poesy . . . is nothing else but Feigned History, which may be styled as well in prose as in verse"—and by "history," he meant *historia* or "story" or "narrative" (*Works,* ed. James Spedding et al., 7 vols. [London, 1857–59], 3:343). "Prose" and "verse," then, are both species of poetry, distinguished from one another by their formal properties. If we exclude prose from the genus we designate as "poetry," we are tacitly defining poetry as an art characterized solely by the formal properties of verse. Sidney, Jonson, and Bacon, following Aristotle, rejected this simplistic definition of poetry and instead defined it as an art dependent upon a potential for depiction and narrative—that is, the potential for producing a "fable," to use Jonson's term, or a "feigned history," to use Bacon's.

Symptomatic of a residual confusion is the fact that we have no single term to cover all the products of the creative art which uses words as its medium. Aristotle felt this embarrassment (cf. *Poetics* 1447a27–b48), and so still does Murray Krieger (cf. *Poetic Presence and Illusion* [Baltimore: Johns Hopkins University Press, 1979], xiii). For an intelligent response to the confusion over "poetry," "verse," and "prose," see Graham Hough, *An Essay on Criticism* (London: Gerald Duckworth, 1966), 97–104. For an influential modern attempt to separate poems from prose, see Jean-Paul Sartre, *Qu'est-ce que la littérature?* (Paris: Gallimard, 1948), 11–48.

9. For an important essay on the significance of how we determine membership in this class, see Paul Oskar Kristeller, "The Modern System of the Arts," *Journal of the History of Ideas* 12 (1951): 496–527 (reprinted in Kristeller, *Renaissance Thought II: Papers on Humanism and the Arts* [New York: Torchbooks, Harper and Row, 1965], 163–227).

10. For a well-voiced similar concern, see Grahame Castor, *Pléiade Poetics* (Cambridge: Cambridge University Press, 1964), 4–6, 184–85.

11. See Thomas Munro, *The Arts and Their Interrelations* (New York: Liberal Arts, 1949), 26–30, 56–60.

12. Cf. *Defence* 78.1–22, 82.18–83.9, 102.19–25.

13. For the scholar with a historical bent, John Dee's academic definition of the term might be pertinent here: "I define an Arte, to be a Methodicall complete Doctrine, having abundancy of sufficient, and peculier matter to deale with, by the allowance of the Metaphisicall Philosopher: the knowledge whereof, to humaine state is necessarye" ("Mathematicall praeface" to Euclid, *The elements of geometrie*, trans. Henry Billingsley [London, 1570], aiii); cf. also William Alley, Πτωχομουσεῖον: *The poore mans librarie* (London, 1565), fol. 29ᵛ. This, of course, is the meaning that Sidney ascribed to the word "art."

14. Abrams similarly resorts to a diagram (6), which he labels "some co-ordinates of art criticism," and he offers valuable historical perspective on many topics that appear in this chapter (3–29). I take it as reassurance that we begin with the same elements. His focus of interest is Romanticism, however, quite different from mine; and therefore our arguments develop along different lines.

For a theoretical discussion that in many ways is analogous to what follows, see Elder Olson, "An Outline of Poetic Theory," *Critiques and Essays in Criticism 1920–1948*, ed. Robert W. Stallman (New York: Ronald Press, 1949), 264–88.

15. See Ludwig Wittgenstein, *Lectures & Conversations on Aesthetics, Psychology and Religious Belief*, ed. Cyril Barrett (Berkeley: University of California Press, 1966), 8–9.

16. But see Nicholas Wolterstorff, "Worlds of Works of Art," *Journal of Aesthetics and Art Criticism* 35 (1976–77): 121–32.

17. Northrop Frye has made perhaps the strongest plea for a clear distinction between the "direct experience" of a literary work and "criticism" of it (*Anatomy of Criticism* [Princeton: Princeton University Press, 1957], 27–29). By "criticism," however, he means a disciplined analysis according to recognizable critical principles—primarily an in-house exercise. He is wary of making value judgments on aesthetic grounds, and warns against using our "subjective background of experience" (i.e., our cumulative emotional life, unique for each individual) as a context for evaluating or even interpreting a literary work. While I subscribe to his theory, I suspect that our practice is otherwise, as he himself is aware (cf. 6–7).

Contrary to Frye, some critics, such as Arnold and Leavis, so nearly conflate art and life that the two become indistinguishable. Others go farther and view art as compensation or substitution for a reality too grim to face. Nietzsche in *The Birth of Tragedy* develops this latter thesis. Tragedy, he says, is the art devised by the Apollonian mind to contain and control the discordance, wildness, cruelty, and ugliness of the Dionysiac spirit: "Art is not an imitation of nature but its metaphysical supplement, raised up beside it in order to overcome it" (*The Birth of Tragedy and The Genealogy of Morals*, trans. Francis Golffing [New York: Anchor, Doubleday Publishing, 1956], 142). By turning from the grimness of actuality, art becomes a purely aesthetic activity. Across the Channel this way of thinking took on refinement and led to the frivolousness of "art for art's sake."

18. Again, Wittgenstein is cogent here, especially his picture theory of the proposition. Cf. Anthony Kenny, *Wittgenstein* (London: Penguin Books, 1973):

> Every picture represents a possible state of affairs, which may be called its sense; it is a true picture if its sense agrees with reality, and otherwise a false picture. No picture will itself show whether it is true or false: for this it must be compared with reality. (58)

By "picture" Wittgenstein means any representation, a musical score or a verbal description as well as a painting. He is, in fact, dealing with a theory of representation as broad as the concept of mimesis which we are examining in this chapter.

19. Cogent here are Derrida's notions of the frame, which is both inside and outside, and of "invagination"; see Jonathan Culler, *On Deconstruction: Theory and Criticism after Structuralism* (Ithaca: Cornell University Press, 1982), 193–99.

20. *Lectures on Aesthetics* 8.

21. The most relentless and fundamental exposition of this point is contained in the work of Stephen C. Pepper, especially *The Basis of Criticism in the Arts* (Cambridge: Harvard University Press, 1945).

22. *S/Z*, trans. Richard Miller (New York: Hill and Wang, Farrar, Straus and Giroux, 1974), 4.

23. 3d ed. (New York: Harvest, Harcourt Brace Jovanovich, 1956), 139.

24. See Worringer, *Abstraction and Empathy: A Contribution to the Psychology of Style* [1908], trans. Michael Bullock (London: Routledge and Kegan Paul, 1953), 9. See also Erwin Panofsky, "The Concept of Artistic Volition," *Critical Inquiry* 8 (1981–82): 17–33.

25. See *Reason in Art* (New York: Charles Scribner's Sons, 1905), 4–5.

26. See Monroe C. Beardsley, *Aesthetics: Problems in the Philosophy of Criticism* (New York: Harcourt Brace Jovanovich, 1958), 6–7.

27. "Death of Author."

28. "Yet say I, and say again, I speak of the art, and not of the artificer" (*Defence* 89.34–35); cf. also 79.6–8. In his use of "artificer" Sidney may well be following rhetorical practice as exemplified by Quintilian; cf., "I promised that I would speak of the art, the *artifex*, and the work" (Promiseram me de arte, de artifice, de opere dicturum; *Institutio oratoria* 12.10.1).

29. We must be very careful about this word "real." I am using it here in its modern meaning, which is quite different from its meaning in earlier cultural contexts. It comes from L. *res*, "thing"; and to us, "real" means the palpable as opposed to the conceptual— "reality" is physical, objectified nature. In modern times, *res* implies *res objecta sensibus*, a "thing presented to the senses." But in a preempiricist culture, *res* meant not a physical thing, but a conceptual thing, more like what we would call an "idea." For example, in the tradition of classical rhetoric, a distinction is made regularly between *res* and *verba*, between an idea and the words that express it. For the Platonist, then, an ἰδέα was a *res*, a conceptual object, to be contemplated by the mind and rendered knowable by language. And "reality" for a Platonist implies an ontology exactly opposite to that implied by "reality" as it means today.

30. See "What Is Poetry" [1833], *Essays on Poetry by John Stuart Mill*, ed. F. Parvin Sharpless (Columbia: University of South Carolina Press, 1976), 12.

31. R. G. Collingwood has argued most consistently that art is expressionism, and the rigidity of his logic demands that the artificer be thoroughly spontaneous and unselective:

> If art means the expression of emotion, the artist as such must be absolutely candid; his speech must be absolutely free. This is not a precept, it is a statement. It does not mean that the artist ought to be candid, it means that he is an artist only in so far as he is candid. Any kind of selection, any decision to express this emotion and not that, is inartistic not in the sense that it damages the perfect sincerity which distinguishes good art from bad, but in the sense that it represents a further process of a non-artistic kind.

(*The Principles of Art* [Oxford: Clarendon, 1938], 115). Even an aesthetic of expressionism so rationally defined as that, however, presupposes an audience (see 110–11, 147–51, 308–15, 321–24).

32. In recent literary theory, two independent developments in this direction are the critical school centered in Geneva that we might call the recorders of consciousness, best represented by Georges Poulet (cf., for example, "Phenomenology of Reading," *New Literary History* 1 [1969–70]: 53–68; see also Sarah N. Lawall, *Critics of Consciousness: The Existential Structures of Literature* [Cambridge: Harvard University Press, 1968]); and the critical school centered in America that calls itself affective stylistics, best represented by Stanley E. Fish (cf. *Self-Consuming Artifacts* [Berkeley: University of California Press,

1972], esp. 383–427; for a devastating critique of Fish's methodology, see Jonathan Culler, *The Pursuit of Signs: Semiotics, Literature, Deconstruction* [Ithaca: Cornell University Press, 1981], 119–31). This phenomenological approach to literature has culminated in two distinguished books by Wolfgang Iser: *The Implied Reader: Patterns of Communication in Prose Fiction from Bunyan to Beckett* (Baltimore: Johns Hopkins University Press, 1974); and *The Act of Reading: A Theory of Aesthetic Response* (Baltimore: Johns Hopkins University Press, 1978). On Iser, see Rudolf E. Kuenzli, "The Intersubjective Structure of the Reading Process: A Communication-Oriented Theory of Literature," *Diacritics* 10.2 (1980): 47–56. The work of Barthes has also been influential in focusing critical attention upon the reader—most provocatively, perhaps, in *Le Plaisir du texte* (Paris: Seuil, 1973). For a survey of the various ways of dealing with the reader at the present time, see Susan R. Suleiman, "Introduction: Varieties of Audience-Oriented Criticism," *The Reader in the Text: Essays on Audience and Interpretation,* ed. Suleiman and Inge Crosman (Princeton: Princeton University Press, 1980), 3–45; and Culler, *On Deconstruction* 31–43, 69–83.

33. Some would make a further significant distinction between the art event as a dynamic happening to be dealt with temporally while it is affecting the percipient, and the art event viewed retrospectively after the percipient assimilates it; see esp. Iser, *Act of Reading* 107–59.

34. See *Philosophical Investigations,* trans. G. E. M. Anscombe (Oxford: Basil Blackwell, 1953), 32.

35. The efforts of Roman Ingarden to define the mode of existence of the literary artifact have been highly influential; see *The Literary Work of Art,* trans. George G. Grabowicz (Evanston: Northwestern University Press, 1973), esp. 9–19, 331–55. Ingarden philosophizes within a phenomenological framework and in gist argues that the literary work is constituted by the infinite number of readings which comprise the Wittgensteinian family of perceptions by individual percipients ("concretizations"). His ingenious analysis was introduced into the mainstream of English studies by Wellek and Warren, who in their own right argue in a somewhat circular fashion: "A poem, we have to conclude, is not an individual experience or a sum of experiences, but only a potential cause of experiences. . . . Thus, the real poem must be conceived as a structure of norms, realized only partially in the actual experience of its many readers. . . . The norms we have in mind are implicit norms which have to be extracted from every individual experience of a work of art and together make up the genuine work of art as a whole" (150–51). See also Earl Miner, "The Objective Fallacy and the Real Existence of Literature," *PTL: A Journal for Descriptive Poetics and Theory of Literature* 1 (1976): 11–31.

36. For a statement of this point from the Renaissance, see the opening chapter of Giovanni Pietro Capriano, *Della vera poetica libro uno* (Venice, 1555), A3–A3ᵛ. For the efforts of an eighteenth-century aesthete to deal with this point, see Joseph Trapp, *Lectures on Poetry* (London, 1742), 13–16.

37. For a compelling demonstration of this fact in terms of the Platonic corpus, see Sörbom 133–45.

38. In his dedicatory epistle for *The Courtier,* Castiglione expresses allegiance to a theory of imitation like this. His treatise, he says, will provide the image of an ideal courtier, just as major works by Plato, Xenophon, and Cicero image forth "the Idea or figure conceyved in imagination of a perfect commune weale, and of a perfect king, and of a perfect Oratour" (Baldassare Castiglione, *The Book of the Courtier* [1561], trans. Sir Thomas Hoby, ed. Walter Raleigh [London: Nutt, 1900], 22). Castiglione has in mind Plato's *Republic,* Xenophon's *Cyropaedia,* and Cicero's *De oratore.*

39. "A Defence of Poetry," *Shelley's Critical Prose,* ed. Bruce R. McElderry, Jr. (Lincoln: University of Nebraska Press, 1967), 12. For Shelley, of course, "Poets are the unac-

knowledged legislators of the world" (36) because they can convey ideas in a pleasurable medium. Elsewhere in his treatise, Shelley makes a revealing statement which is highly pertinent here: "All the authors of revolutions in opinion are . . . necessarily poets . . . [since] their words unveil the permanent analogy of things by images which participate in the life of truth" (10).

40. I use "intellectual" for lack of a better term. By it, I mean what transpires in the mind without a direct counterpart in sense response. My use of the term harks back to Plato's dichotomy between the "intelligible" and the "sensible" worlds.

41. It should be remembered that music is based upon mathematical laws, and that at least for the ancients and their medieval and Renaissance followers it consists in ratios between simple integers—what is known as the Pythagorean tuning system; see my *Touches of Sweet Harmony: Pythagorean Cosmology and Renaissance Poetics* (San Marino: Huntington Library, 1974), 93–97. The point of the music is the representation of these abstract relationships, not the expression or arousal of emotion.

42. Note that the process of abstracting is different from making a composite—e.g., a sculptor who molds a beautiful head by reproducing the nose of one woman, the lips of another, the brow of a third, and so forth. An example of making a composite appears in Lucian's *Eikones* 6, when Lycinus describes a statue put together from discrete parts. Cicero's account of Zeuxis (see n. 44, below) is also sometimes (erroneously) interpreted in this fashion. A composite involves little more than the replication of physical objects, however, and remains at the level of total physicality.

43. For an explanation of Leonardo's "grotesque heads" according to this dichotomy between ideal and grotesque, see E. H. Gombrich, *The Heritage of Apelles* (Ithaca: Cornell University Press, 1976), 57–75.

44. *De inventione* 2.1. Aristotle also mentions Zeuxis in the *Poetics* (1461b12). Leon Battista Alberti recalled this tale (*On Painting and On Sculpture*, ed. and trans. Cecil Grayson [London: Phaidon, 1972], 99; cf. 15). Giovanni della Casa referred to it (*Galateo*, trans. Robert Peterson [London, 1576], 103), and Spenser was familiar with it (*Faerie Queene*, Ded. Sonnet, "To . . . Ladies in the Court," *Spenser: Variorum* 3:198). Roger Ascham in *Toxophilus* recounts the topos with utmost succinctness:

> The noble paynter Zeuxes in payntyng Helena . . . to make his Image bewtifull dyd chose out .v. of the fayrest maydes in al the countrie aboute, and in beholdynge them conceyved & drewe out suche an Image that it far exceded al other, bycause the comelinesse of them al was broughte in to one moost perfyte comelinesse.

(*English Works*, ed. William Aldis Wright [Cambridge: Cambridge University Press, 1904], 100).

Cicero's story of Zeuxis and the maidens of Croton became a commonplace in art theory of the Renaissance; see Erwin Panofsky, *Idea: A Concept in Art Theory*, trans. Joseph J. S. Peake (Columbia: University of South Carolina Press, 1968), 48–49, 57–68, 157; Rensselaer W. Lee, *Ut pictura poesis: The Humanistic Theory of Painting* (New York: W. W. Norton, 1967), 11, 14–15; Mark W. Roskill, *Dolce's "Aretino" and Venetian Art Theory of the Cinquecento* (New York: New York University Press, 1968), 11, 288–89; and cf. Shakespeare, *WT* 5.1.14–16. This is the same Zeuxis who in his contest with Parrhasius to see who could most accurately depict an inanimate object drew a bunch of grapes so natural that birds flew at the picture to eat the fruit (Pliny, *Historia naturalis* 35.9.36.3; cf. Francis Meres, *Palladis tamia: Wits treasury* [London, 1598], fol. 287). Painting as accurate representation and also as idealization are both old topoi.

45. *Petrarch's "Africa,"* trans. Thomas G. Bergin and Alice S. Wilson (New Haven: Yale University Press, 1977), 125 [6.597–605]. Cf. Torquato Tasso: "By considering the good in various particular goodnesses, we form the idea of the good, just as Zeuxis formed the

idea of the beautiful when he wished to paint Helen in Croton" (*Discourses on the Heroic Poem,* trans. Mariella Cavalchini and Irene Samuel [Oxford: Clarendon, 1973], 6).

46. For the progenitor of this view, see Charles Batteux, *Les beaux arts réduits à un même principe* (Paris, 1746). Already by the end of the seventeenth century, however, the notion of *la belle nature* was incipient in Giovanni Pietro Bellori, as Dryden extracted him: "The artful painter and the sculptor, imitating the Divine Maker, form to themselves, as well as they are able, a model of the superior beauties; and reflecting on them, endeavour to correct and amend the common nature, and to represent it as it was at first created, without fault. . . . This idea . . . descends upon the marble and the cloth, and becomes the original of those arts" ("A Parallel of Poetry and Painting," *Essays,* ed. W. P. Ker, 2 vols. [Oxford: Clarendon, 1900], 2:118).

47. See Abrams 12–13, 35–36; Monroe C. Beardsley, *Aesthetics from Classical Greece to the Present* (New York: Macmillan, 1966), 160; Kristeller, "Modern System of Arts" passim; and Lawrence Lipking, *The Ordering of the Arts in Eighteenth-Century England* (Princeton: Princeton University Press, 1970), 4 (n. 1).

48. *Observations on the 22. stanza in the 9th. canto of the 2d. book of Spencers Faery Queen* (London, 1644), 10 (italics mine).

49. In *The Lamb and the Elephant* (San Marino: Huntington Library, 1974), John M. Steadman investigates what he calls "ideal imitation"; see esp. chaps. 4–6. Ben Jonson's epigram "On Lucy Countesse of Bedford" records an experience of this sort of poetizing.

50. William Alley, a bookish prelate who enjoyed Elizabeth's favor, gives the proper definition of "type" using a Platonic vocabulary:

> Typus doth properly signifie a forme, a figure, an example, a shadow, and an image of an other thing. . . . Typus also is a figure and symboll of the veritie and truth, in whiche signification we say, the old Testament to be a type of the new, and the Sacrifices of the same to be types of the Sacrifice of Christ. (fol. 179ᵛ)

For the "difference betwene a type and an allegory," see Alley fol. 252. For a discussion of typology as Augustine practiced it, see pages 192–95.

51. Shelley, for example, claims that "Milton conceived the Paradise Lost as a whole before he executed it in portions" (31).

52. *A Portrait of the Artist as a Young Man* (New York: Viking Penguin, 1964), 215.

53. For an entrée to this point of view, see Harold Osborne, *Aesthetics and Art Theory: An Historical Introduction* (New York: E. P. Dutton, 1970), 306–7.

54. This essay serves as the opening chapter of their book, *The Verbal Icon.* See also Beardsley, *Aesthetics: Problems* 17–29, 456–60. A useful epitome of the resultant controversy over the intentional fallacy is offered by John Kemp, "The Work of Art and the Artist's Intentions," *British Journal of Aesthetics* 4 (1964): 146–54.

55. Frye reasons in a similar way in order to argue the necessity for critics and criticism; see *Anatomy of Criticism* 5–6.

56. Robert M. Durling develops this principle into a methodology for comparing Renaissance epic poets, including a valuable chapter on Spenser; see *The Figure of the Poet in Renaissance Epic* (Cambridge: Harvard University Press, 1965).

57. Jacques Derrida adopts this point and develops its implications in an important way; cf. "Signature Event Context" [1971], *Margins of Philosophy,* trans. Alan Bass (Chicago: University of Chicago Press, 1982), 307–30. Olson, however, was an early objector. Following the analytical method of Aristotle, he differentiates "diction" from the other elements of a literary work and considers it least important. Language, he argues, is merely the medium of poetry:

> Just as we should not define a chair as wood which has such and such characteristics—for a chair is not a kind of wood but a kind of furniture—so we ought not to define poetry as a kind of language. The chair is not wood but wooden; poetry is not words but verbal. . . . [Words] are the least important element in the poem, for

they do not determine the character of anything else in the poem; on the contrary, they are determined by everything else. (281 [n. 3])

The issue in contention, of course, is whether the words of a poem are its substance or merely its medium. Olson differentiates substance and medium (as he does, following Aristotle, cause and effect); Wimsatt and Beardsley conflate the two.

58. On the aesthetic quality of nature and natural objects, see Theodore Meyer Greene, *The Arts and the Art of Criticism* (Princeton: Princeton University Press, 1940), 8–11. Worringer, who following Riegl argues for the primacy of the artist's volition to create, begins with the premise that the aesthetics of artifacts must be clearly separated from the aesthetics of natural beauty (3).

A pleasing configuration chanced upon in actual experience—such as Thomas Browne's quincunxes or Wordsworth's daffodils—does not itself constitute an artifact. It might stimulate profound thought in its percipient, as indeed it does in both Browne and Wordsworth, but it does not *represent* profound thought. It might cause us to speculate, ascribing meaning to it, but we do not search it for its own hidden meaning. To do so would be to treat nature like a congeries of hieroglyphs—which of course has been done, perhaps most systematically and memorably by Jakob Boehme.

59. *Validity in Interpretation* (New Haven: Yale University Press, 1967), esp. chap. 1. See also Helen Gardner, *The Business of Criticism* (Oxford: Clarendon, 1959), esp. 75.

60. "*Meaning* is that which is represented by a text; it is what the author meant by his use of a particular sign sequence. . . . *Significance*, on the other hand, names a relationship between that meaning and a person" (8; cf. 38–39). Paralleling this distinction between "meaning" and "significance" is the distinction between "interpretation" and "criticism": "Significance is the proper object of criticism, not of interpretation, whose exclusive object is verbal meaning" (57). "Interpretation," then, is the determination of the verbal meaning of a text, while "criticism" allows the individual to pursue what the verbal meaning might suggest to himself.

61. Donne wittily employs this argument in "A Valediction: of the Booke," *The Elegies, and The Songs and Sonnets,* ed. Helen Gardner (Oxford: Clarendon, 1965).

62. For the structuralist version of this argument, see Jonathan Culler, *Structuralist Poetics: Structuralism, Linguistics and the Study of Literature* (Ithaca: Cornell University Press, 1975), 116–17, 131–33.

63. For a brilliant analysis of "style" in these terms, see Worringer esp. 26–48.

64. See *OED*, "artist," 3.7. Oddly enough, the earliest instance of this usage (and the only one before 1853) comes from Sidney's *Defence of poesie* (102.28), where the meaning is clearly "one who practices some art or skill in contradistinction to poetry, which allows some freedom of invention." The *OED* misinterprets Sidney's sentence.

65. Cf. *The Enneads*, trans. Stephen MacKenna, 4th ed. (London: Faber and Faber, 1969), 1.6.9. In this passage Plotinus is explaining how we should free ourselves from sense experience so that the soul may come into the presence of (and comprehend the beauty of) essential forms: "Withdraw into yourself and look. And if you do not find yourself beautiful yet, act as does the creator of a statue that is to be made beautiful: he cuts away here, he smoothes there, he makes this line lighter, this other purer, until a lovely face [i.e., exterior] has grown upon his work." This theory drew sustenance also from Aristotle, *De anima* 2.1, in which the relation between soul and body is explained in terms of the individuality the sculptor bestows upon a block of stone when he carves a statue.

66. See Anthony Blunt, *Artistic Theory in Italy 1450–1600* (Oxford: Clarendon, 1940), 73–74. Cf. also this opening of a sonnet by Michelangelo:

> The best of artists never has a concept
> A single marble block does not contain
> Inside its husk, but to it may attain
> Only if hand follows the intellect.

(*Complete Poems and Selected Letters,* ed. Robert N. Linscott, trans. Creighton Gilbert [New York: Modern Library, 1965], 100). See also Robert J. Clements, *The Peregrine Muse: Studies in Comparative Renaissance Literature* (Chapel Hill: University of North Carolina Press, 1959), 24–25.

Not surprisingly, this theory has been most compelling in the art of sculpture. Giorgio Vasari defined sculpture as "an art which by removing all that is superfluous from the material under treatment reduces it to that form designed in the artist's mind" (*On Technique,* trans. Louisa S. Maclehose [London: Dent, 1907], 143)—a definition which hedges between a theory of inherent form and mimesis of a form in the artificer's mind. Maclehose (180) traces the theory of inherent form in sculpture to Cicero, *De divinatione* 1.13 and 2.21. For a critique of this theory, which radically modifies it, see Worringer 81–92.

67. Cf. Sidney Geist, *Brancusi/The Kiss* (New York: Harper and Row, 1978).

68. *Philosophy in a New Key,* 3d ed. (Cambridge: Harvard University Press, 1957), esp. chaps. 2, 3, and 9. See also Herbert Read, *The Forms of Things Unknown* (London: Faber and Faber, 1960), 110–11, where it is argued that poetry is an affective response to experience resulting in mythmaking.

69. For a theoretical discussion of this point, see Nelson Goodman, *Languages of Art: An Approach to a Theory of Symbols* (Indianapolis: Bobbs-Merrill, 1968), esp. chap. 1. In the *Tractatus Logico-Philosophicus,* a major concern of Wittgenstein was to describe the relationship between a representation and what it represents, and the results are the most cogent analysis in this century; see George Pitcher, *The Philosophy of Wittgenstein* (Englewood Cliffs: Prentice-Hall, 1964), 75–98, and Kenny 54–60.

70. Of particular pertinence to our concerns are Wellek and Warren 226–37; and Rosalie L. Colie, *The Resources of Kind: Genre-Theory in the Renaissance* (Berkeley: University of California Press, 1973), esp. chap. 1.

71. Roman Jakobson has expressed a correlative view; see "On Realism in Art" and "The Dominant," *Readings in Russian Poetics: Formalist and Structuralist Views,* ed. Ladislav Matejka and Krystyna Pomorska (Cambridge: Massachusetts Institute of Technology Press, 1971), 38–46, 82–87, respectively. Don Cameron Allen has demonstrated a methodology for explicating literary motifs as they accumulate meaning through repeated use by poets; see *Image and Meaning: Metaphoric Traditions in Renaissance Poetry,* rev. ed. (Baltimore: Johns Hopkins University Press, 1968). Thomas M. Greene has explored how Renaissance poets both emulate and modify the authors of the classical world; see *The Light in Troy: Imitation and Discovery in Renaissance Poetry* (New Haven: Yale University Press, 1982).

72. "Poetry: A Note in Ontology," *The World's Body* (New York: Charles Scribner's Sons, 1938), 111.

73. Gombrich sees impressionism as a turning point in art history for the very reason that it leaves the object of imitation inchoate and gives the percipient a role in the creative process. "It is the point of impressionist painting that the direction of the brushstroke is no longer an aid to the reading of forms. It is without any support from structure that the beholder must mobilize his memory of the visible world and project it into the mosaic of strokes and dabs on the canvas before him" (*Art and Illusion* 202). Gombrich's study is based upon the assumption that the artifact in painting is at least ambiguous, if not largely undefined, and the percipient is called upon to exercise options; see esp. 313.

In his analysis of reading, Umberto Eco speaks in terms of "open texts," which require the active participation of a percipient, and "closed texts," which preclude contributions from an audience (*L'Oeuvre ouverte,* trans. Chantal Roux de Bézieux [Paris: Seuil, 1965]; see also *The Role of the Reader: Explorations in the Semiotics of Texts* [Bloomington: Indiana University Press, 1979], 3–65). Barthes similarly distinguishes texts which are *lisible* (i.e., easily interpreted according to recognized conventions) from those which are *scriptible* (i.e., difficult to interpret because of omissions, contradictions, ambiguities, etc., which frustrate the reader and require his active participation); see esp. *S/Z* 4.

74. Of particular importance here is the work of Ingarden (see n. 35, above), who sees the artifact as a stimulus which allows a wide range of responses, all of which are valid unless specifically ruled out by the determinate qualities of the artifact; cf. Osborne 267–68. Of course, many of the most recent theorists would argue that the artifact has no existence apart from the percipient's experience of it. The tree in the forest makes no noise when it falls unless some one hears it. These theorists deny any ontological substance to the text itself.

75. For seminal works on this topic, see Frank Kermode, *The Sense of an Ending: Studies in the Theory of Fiction* (New York: Oxford University Press, 1967); and Barbara Herrnstein Smith, *Poetic Closure: A Study of How Poems End* (Chicago: University of Chicago Press, 1968).

76. See G. E. Lessing, *Laocoön* [1766], trans. Ellen Frothingham (New York: Farrar, Straus and Giroux, 1961), esp. 89–117.

77. For a theoretical start in answering this question, see Pepper 69–71. Barthes glances at this problem, but with shifty eyes. He of course advocates multiple readings because they generate the multiple meanings (at least, "old" and "new") that he proposes for a text. But he also maintains that no text can be reread because each reading of the text is spontaneous (see *S/Z* 15–16).

78. *Anatomy of Criticism* 28.

79. Most influentially, perhaps, Tolstoy—see Munro 80–81; most methodically, perhaps, Jakobson—see Robert Scholes, *Structuralism in Literature* (New Haven: Yale University Press, 1974), 24–31, and Culler, *Structuralist Poetics* 55–57. The underlying assumption of most rhetorical analysis, of course, is that literature is communication between orator and audience—e.g., Wayne Booth, *The Rhetoric of Fiction* (Chicago: University of Chicago Press, 1961). Semiotic analysis also assumes that literature is some sort of sign system which operates between a sender and a receiver; see, for example, Scholes, "Toward a Semiotics of Literature," *Critical Inquiry* 4 (1977–78): 105–20. For the taxonomy of the relationship between Renaissance author and reader, see William J. Kennedy, *Rhetorical Norms in Renaissance Literature* (New Haven: Yale University Press, 1978), chap. 1.

The tenuousness of the assumption that literature is communication, however, is indicated by the stance, reflective of phenomenology, taken by Eliot at the end of his first Norton lecture on criticism:

> *If* poetry is a form of "communication," yet that which is to be communicated is the poem itself, and only incidentally the experience and the thought which have gone into it. The poem's existence is somewhere between the writer and the reader; it has a reality which is not simply the reality of what the writer is trying to "express," or of his experiences of writing it, or of the experience of the reader or of the writer as reader.

(*The Use of Poetry and the Use of Criticism* [Cambridge: Harvard University Press, 1933], 21). For a suggestive essay correlating the communication between author and reader with the concept of mimesis, see Lowry Nelson, Jr., "The Fictive Reader and Literary Self-Reflexiveness," *The Disciplines of Criticism*, ed. Peter Demetz et al. (New Haven: Yale University Press, 1968), 173–91.

80. *Painting and Sculpture in Europe 1880–1940*, rev. ed. (Baltimore: Penguin Books, 1972), 19.

81. "Preface to *Lyrical Ballads*" [1802], *Literary Criticism of William Wordsworth*, ed. Paul M. Zall (Lincoln: University of Nebraska Press, 1966), 48.

82. *Anatomy of Criticism* 4.

83. For an important essay on how the poet coerces his reader into playing a predetermined role, see Walter J. Ong, S.J., "The Writer's Audience Is Always a Fiction," *PMLA* 90 (1975): 9–21.

84. An interesting case of the percipient's search for the artificer is Caroline F. E. Spurgeon's *Shakespeare's Imagery, and What It Tells Us* (Cambridge: Cambridge University Press, 1935). By compiling lists of what Shakespeare talks about in his plays, Spurgeon sought to reconstruct his mental profile. Because of its emphasis upon "imagery," her methods were seized upon by the New Critics, who resolutely ignored her motives; and her study has been lately subjected to scorn, if recalled at all. The new school of scholars who reconstruct an author's mental world out of his vocabulary and even his syntax looks to Freud and Lacan.

85. See *Essays from the "Guardian"* (London, 1896), 111.

86. "Apology for Heroic Poetry," *Essays* 2:179.

87. See *Self-Consuming Artifacts* 406; and again, *Is There a Text in This Class? The Authority of Interpretive Communities* (Cambridge: Harvard University Press, 1980), 48–49.

88. On the subjective fallacy, see Theodore Meyer Greene 4–5 ("The Objectivity of Aesthetic Quality").

89. Actually, the phrase "significant form" was popularized by Clive Bell in *Art* (London: Chatto and Windus, 1914), though in using the term Bell had in mind only the visual arts.

90. "An Essay on Criticism" 73; *The Poems*, ed. John Butt (New Haven: Yale University Press, 1963).

91. See Beardsley, *Aesthetics from Greece to Present* 363–76; and Ransom, *New Criticism* 281–94.

Chapter 3

1. John Addington Symonds, "The Provinces of the Several Arts," *Essays: Speculative and Suggestive*, 2 vols. (London, 1890), 1:143.

2. There is, of course, a difference between the experience of hearing a poem and reading it. But in the late sixteenth century this difference was not yet insisted upon by poets because it was a period of transition between the time when poems were more commonly heard in recitation and the time when poems were more commonly read on a printed page without benefit of performance. Most poems were designed to be either heard or read, indifferently. The ingenuous use of homonyms in printed poetry—such as "sun/son"—attest to this practice; in the poetry of Donne, for example, while printed "sun," the word may polysemously mean "son" as well. Although we *read* Donne's poem, we respond as though we *hear* its language.

3. Julius Caesar Scaliger compared a poem to a statue at some length (see pages 212–13). Sir John Davies composed a dancelike poem in *Orchestra*, and George Herbert composed a buildinglike poem in *The Temple*.

4. See page 505 (n. 8).

5. "Poesy" is the direct derivative from Latin *poesis*, which in turn comes from Greek ποίησις. "Poetry" derives from a late Latin form, *poetria*. In Elizabethan usage there seems to have been little commonly accepted distinction between "poetry" and "poesy." Sir John Harington in the "Preface" (1591) to his *Orlando Furioso* uses the two terms frequently and interchangeably.

In his edition of Sidney's *Apology for Poetry*, Shepherd attempts to separate the two terms as Sidney uses them, suggesting (after Ben Jonson; see below) that "poesy" means "the poet's 'skill or crafte of making,'" while "poetry" is "the more general term for the product of the art" (152 [n. 18]; cf. 19). Duncan-Jones and van Dorsten accept Shepherd's hypothesis (*Miscellaneous Prose of Sidney* 189 [n. 77.21]). Although Shepherd's distinction happens to hold for the five instances which he cites from the first fourth of Sidney's *Defence,* it breaks down in the many more instances he leaves unexamined, and therefore the distinction is not valid. It seems to me that Sidney uses the two terms quite indiscriminately, often in adjacent sentences: e.g., cf. Shepherd 109.23–33, 114.5–12, 121.32–35, 125.20–27, 129.36–130.10, 133.37–134.7, 137.19–25. And of course *The defence of poesie* was published by William Ponsonby the same year that Henry Olney published *An apologie for poetrie.*

Spenser seems to have preferred the form "poesy" (which, according to Osgood's concordance, he used seven times) to "poetry" (which he used only three times). In the one instance where the two forms appear adjacently, there is no distinction between them ("Teares of Muses" 555–57).

Jonson does not discuss "poetry" in conjunction with "poesy," but he goes to some effort to distinguish between "poem" and "poesy": "A *Poeme* . . . is the worke of the Poet; the end, and fruit of his labour, and studye," while "*Poesy* is his skill, or Crafte of making" (*Timber* 8:636). He is probably drawing upon Julius Caesar Scaliger, *Poetices libri septem* (Lyons, 1561), 5–6. According to these two critics, as I likewise suggest, a "poem" is that which has been made, while "poesy" retains a gerundlike sense.

After the sixteenth century, the term "poetry" quickly subsumed both "poem" and "poesy." Since the eighteenth century, the word "poesy" has been archaic and is patronizing in tone; cf. Trapp 22.

6. For a comprehensive study of the word ποιεῖν and these derivatives in the Platonic dialogues, see Paul Vicaire, *Recherches sur les mots désignant la poésie et le poète dans l'oeuvre de Platon* (Paris: Presses Universitaires, 1964), passim.

7. George Turbervile illustrates the precise use of this word in his preface "To the Reader" which introduces his *Epitaphes, epigrams, songs and sonets* (London, 1567): "Whatsoever I have penned, I write not to this purpose, that any youthlie head shoulde folow or pursue such fraile affections, or taste of amorous bait: but by meere *fiction* of these Fantasies, I would warne (if I myghte) all tender age to flee that fonde and filthie affection of poysoned & unlawful love" (*6–*6ᵛ; italics mine). Sidney uses the word in this sense when Plangus speaks of "poet's fiction" (*Old Arcadia,* ed. Robertson 151.4).

Spenser uses "poem" as a synonym for "fiction" in *Faerie Queene* 4.proem.1.9. Jonson also uses "poem" in this sense when he argues in an Aristotelian vein that "a *Poeme* is not alone any worke, or composition of the Poets in many, or few verses," but rather the abstract quality that distinguishes poetry from other discourse, so that "even one alone verse sometimes makes a perfect *Poeme*" (*Timber* 8:635).

8. *The metamorphosis of Pigmalion's image and certain satyres* (London, 1598), E5. Behind Marston's lines is Aristotle's statement that plot is the "soul" of tragedy (*Poetics* 1450b40), and Marston is using "fiction" here to mean what came more commonly to be called the "fable." Cf. Jonson: "The Fable and Fiction is (as it were) the forme and Soule of any Poeticall worke, or *Poeme*" (*Timber* 8:635).

In this passage, Jonson has just previously cited Aristotle, and he is using "fable" from the Latin *fabula,* the term often employed for Aristotle's μῦθος, which today we customarily translate as "plot." He has also just previously cited the etymology of poet from ποιεῖν. By "fiction," then, it is clear that Jonson means the "fable" (or plot) that the poet contrives as his act of "making" (cf. *Timber* 8:645). His phrase "Poeticall worke" echoes the Aristotelian term ποιητική, which we translate as "poetics," but which means "the activity of making." By using "Poeme" as a synonym for "Poeticall worke," Jonson confirms my definition of "poem" as "that which has been made," and he supports my reading it as a cognate with "fiction."

Lodovico Castelvetro, following Aristotle, had earlier insisted that fiction is the sine qua non of poetry: "Fable enters into all poems, and without it they would not be able to exist, for it is the prime feature of poetry—as it were, its soul" (Favola entra in tutte le poeese, le quali senza lei non possono havere l'essere, ed e la principale, e come anima della poesia; *Poetica d'Aristotele volgarizzata et sposta* [Basle, 1576], 11). On the term *fabula,* see William Nelson, *Fact or Fiction: The Dilemma of the Renaissance Storyteller* (Cambridge: Harvard University Press, 1973), 5. Marvin T. Herrick observes that "the commentators that follow Aristotle use *imitatio, fictio, inventio,* and *fabula* interchangeably" (*The Fusion of Horatian and Aristotelian Literary Criticism, 1531–1555* [Urbana: University of Illinois Press, 1946], 36).

In the rhetorical tradition, as Herrick notes (34), the closest synonym of "fiction" would be "invention," just as Marston uses the two terms. "Invention" means literally "that which has been discovered" (< L. *inventus,* past participle of *invenire)*—"discovered" in the ambiguous sense of being either "revealed" or "invented/created," or perhaps both. This ambiguity of *inventio* allows the rhetorician the same range of inventiveness as the poet—all the way from merely uncovering a topos which is already existent in earlier authors, to creating something entirely new. For a useful summary of *inventio* in Renaissance rhetoric, see Brian Vickers, *Classical Rhetoric in English Poetry* (London: Macmillan, 1970), 61–65.

9. The literary work is viewed, in fact, as an analogue to the interdependency between soul and body expounded in Aristotle's *De anima* 412a3–413a10.

10. "The Author's Apology for Heroic Poetry and Poetic License," *Essays* 1:188.

11. See Trapp 19–21.

12. G. W. F. Hegel, *The Philosophy of Fine Art,* trans. F. P. B. Osmaston, 4 vols. (London: Bell and Hyman, 1916–20), 4:21.

13. Note the difficulty that even so expert an aesthetician as Beardsley has in maintaining this distinction (*Aesthetics: Problems* 126–27, 233–35).

Structuralists have been most active in nullifying the distinction between prose and poetry through the use of linguistic models for both literary theory and applied criticism; note esp. Tzvetan Todorov, *Poétique de la prose* (Paris: Seuil, 1971). The tendency to remove this distinction, however, was already operative by the beginning of the nineteenth century: it receives clear expression by Wordsworth in the preface to the second edition of *Lyrical Ballads* (*Criticism of Wordsworth,* ed. Zall 24–25); and Shelley states flatly, "The distinction between poets and prose writers is a vulgar error" ("Defence of Poetry," *Critical Prose* 9). See also Munro 487–90.

14. For the turning point in this meaning of the term "fiction," see Richard Hurd, "Dissertation I. On the Idea of Universal Poetry," *Works,* 8 vols. (London, 1811), 2:8–11. Hurd argues that the aim of poetry is "to *gratify the desires of the mind*" (3), and one of the requisites to this end is "*that licence of representation,* which we call *fiction*" (10–11). This meaning of the word, however, was already implicit in Dryden's criticism; cf., for example: "You are not obliged, as in History, to a literal belief of what the poet says; but you are pleased with the image, without being cozened by the fiction" ("Apology for Heroic Poetry," *Essays* 1:185).

15. To suggest the tightness in the web of interrelated meanings among these terms, Sidney used "fiction" as a synonym for "imitation" (*Defence* 79.6); cf. *Temple's "Analysis" of Sidney's "Apology,"* ed. Webster 80. Sir John Harington treated the terms "fiction," "imitation," and "invention" as though they were synonymous ("A Preface," *Elizabethan Critical Essays,* ed. G. Gregory Smith, 2 vols. [London: Oxford University Press, 1904], 2:204). As late as 1789, Thomas Twining in his commentary on Aristotle's *Poetics* could say:

> The word *imitation* is also . . . applied to Poetry when considered as FICTION—
> to stories, actions, incidents, and characters, as far as they are *feigned* or *invented*
> by the Poet *in imitation* . . . of nature, of real life, of truth, in *general,* as opposed
> to that individual reality of things which is the province of the historian.

("Dissertation I: On Poetry Considered as an Imitative Art," *Aristotle's Treatise on Poetry,* trans. Twining [London, 1789], 19). Following Aristotle, the distinction is not between prose and verse, or between fiction and truth, but rather between the general truth of a poetic fiction and the particular truth of a historical fact.

16. *Timber* 8:635.

17. Many, historians both of ideas and of the physical sciences, have charted this ontological shift. For a recent study, notable for conciseness as well as its balance, see Allen G. Debus, *Man and Nature in the Renaissance* (Cambridge: Cambridge University Press, 1978).

18. Letter 7, "On divine frenzy," *The Letters of Marsilio Ficino,* ed. Paul O. Kristeller, 3 vols. to date (London: Shepheard-Walwyn, 1975–), 1:43; cf. Ficino, *Opera* (Basle, 1561), 613. This letter contains a complete theory of art. For the general views of Ficino on art, see Kristeller, *The Philosophy of Marsilio Ficino,* trans. Virginia Conant (New York: Columbia University Press, 1943), 304–9; and André Chastel, *Marsile Ficin et l'art* (Geneva: Droz, 1954). For the transmission of this theory of art to Baïf and others in France, see Frances A. Yates, *The French Academies of the Sixteenth Century* (London: Warburg Institute, 1947), 4–6. The death of the notion that Creation and our knowledge of it has been predetermined by a divine mind is not finally recorded until Thomas S. Kuhn, *The Structure of Scientific Revolutions* (Chicago: University of Chicago Press, 1962), 170–72.

19. "Metaphor" < Gr. μετά, beyond, across + φέρειν, to carry. The term is a cognate with "translate" < L. *trans* + *latus* (past participle of *ferre*, to carry), and with "transfer." See pages 288–89.

20. *On Technique* 205.

21. "Rose-cheekt Lawra" 5–6; *Works,* ed. Percival Vivian (Oxford: Clarendon, 1909).

22. The most recent study of early experiments with and writings about perspective is Samuel Y. Edgerton, Jr., *The Renaissance Rediscovery of Linear Perspective* (New York: Basic Books, 1975). Edgerton demonstrates convincingly that the sudden and complete success with perspective in quattrocento Florence was made possible by the classical and medieval science of optics, which of course was basically mathematical, and that the initial impetus behind the practice of perspective was theological rather than naturalistic: "Perspective rules were accepted by these early artists because it gave their depicted scenes a sense of harmony with natural law, thereby underscoring man's moral responsibility within God's geometrically ordered universe" (56; cf. 24, 162–63). Nevertheless, when Brunelleschi painted his epoch-making first perspective picture of the Baptistry in Florence, his aim was to reproduce exactly what someone actually saw upon walking through the central portal of the Duomo and looking from the inside toward the outside (see esp. 143–52). For him, the ontological *situs* of the painting lay to an equal degree in the things it portrayed as well as in some concept of cosmos whose mathematics the painting disclosed by its symmetry and proportion. See also Rudolf Wittkower, "Brunelleschi and 'Proportion in Perspective,'" *Journal of the Warburg and Courtauld Institutes* 16 (1953): 275–91; Carroll W. Westfall, "Painting and the Liberal Arts: Alberti's View," *Journal of the History of Ideas* 30 (1969): 487–506; and A. C. Crombie, "Science and the Arts in the Renaissance: The Search for Truth and Certainty, Old and New," *History of Science* 18 (1980): 233–46.

23. See, for example, Girolamo Fracastoro, *Naugerius, sive de poetica dialogus,* ed. Murray W. Bundy, trans. Ruth Kelso (Urbana: University of Illinois Press, 1924), 56–60, 66. Dryden in his later thought neatly illustrates the compromises that a realist was prepared to make to retain beauty in art. In his essay "A Parallel of Poetry and Painting," which served as preface to his translation of Du Fresnoy's *De arte graphica* (1695), Dryden comments negatively on Aristotle's observation that we delight in the mimesis of natural objects, even unpleasant ones:

> Since a true knowledge of Nature gives us pleasure, a lively imitation of it, either in Poetry or Painting, must of necessity produce a much greater: for both these

arts, as I said before, are not only true imitations of Nature, but of the best Nature, of that which is wrought up to a nobler pitch. They present us with images more perfect than the life in any individual; and we have the pleasure to see all the scattered beauties of Nature united by a happy chemistry, without its deformities or faults.

(*Essays* 2:137). Dryden's "best nature," "that which is wrought up to a nobler pitch," is of course *la belle nature* of the French theorists.

For the persistence of neoplatonist aesthetics in Augustan England and its permutations in order to remain viable, see Martin C. Battestin, *The Providence of Wit: Aspects of Form in Augustan Literature and the Arts* (Oxford: Clarendon, 1974), esp. 1–57, 270–72.

24. See Joan Gadol, *Leon Battista Alberti: Universal Man of the Early Renaissance* (Chicago: University of Chicago Press, 1969), esp. 100–108.

25. Although in what follows I offer a taxonomy of the so-called fine arts in the late sixteenth century, which implies stasis, we must keep in mind that the relocation of reality was in process over a considerable length of time as platonist assumptions gave over gradually to empiricist demands. The decade of the 1580s, however, was the period of greatest tension, when the conservative forces and the forces of change were evenly matched. Consequently, it is worthwhile supposing that we can catch them at some convenient moment when they are poised in balance.

26. For a comprehensive look at the widespread practice of music in sixteenth-century England, see Bruce Pattison, *Music and Poetry of the English Renaissance* (London: Methuen, 1948), chap. 1. For most of the topoi appropriate to music at the beginning of the century, see Richard Pace, *De fructu qui ex doctrina percipitur* [1517], ed. and trans. Frank Manley and Richard S. Sylvester (New York: Renaissance Society, 1967), 39–47.

27. See James Hutton, "Some English Poems in Praise of Music," *English Miscellany* 2 (1951), 1–28; Nan C. Carpenter, *Music in the Medieval and Renaissance Universities* (Norman: University of Oklahoma Press, 1958), 6–14; and Warren D. Anderson, *Ethos and Education in Greek Music* (Cambridge: Harvard University Press, 1966), 67–70, 122–46. See also Kristeller, "Modern System of Arts" 113. For Quintilian's profuse praise of music, see *Institutio oratoria* 1.10.9–33.

28. "*Plato* calleth it, *A divine and heavenly practise,* profitable for the seeking out of that which is good and honest. . . . *Aristotle* averreth Musicke to be the onely disposer of the mind to Vertue and Goodnesse" (*The compleat gentleman* [London, 1622], 98).

29. For the humanists' reservations about teaching music, however, see William H. Woodward, *Vittorino da Feltre and Other Humanist Educators,* ed. Eugene F. Rice, Jr. (New York: Columbia University Press, 1963), 239–41.

30. See Theodore C. Karp, "Music," *The Seven Liberal Arts in the Middle Ages,* ed. David L. Wagner (Bloomington: Indiana University Press, 1983), 169–95. For a comprehensive example, see Franchino Gafuri, *Practica musicae* [1496], ed. and trans. Clement A. Miller (Neuhausen-Stuttgart: American Institute of Musicology, 1968), esp. the dedicatory epistle addressed to Lodovico Sforza, duke of Milan, 14–17.

31. See my *Touches of Sweet Harmony* 95–97; and Richard L. Crocker, "Pythagorean Mathematics and Music," *Journal of Aesthetics and Art Criticism* 22 (1963–64): 189–98, 325–35.

32. See Manfred F. Bukofzer, "Speculative Thinking in Mediaeval Music," *Speculum* 17 (1942): 177–80; Edward E. Lowinsky, "Music in the Culture of the Renaissance," *Renaissance Essays: From the "Journal of the History of Ideas,"* ed. Paul O. Kristeller and Philip P. Wiener (New York: Torchbooks, Harper and Row, 1968), 371–72; and Gilbert Reaney, "The Irrational and Late Medieval Music," *The Darker Vision of the Renaissance,* ed. Robert S. Kinsman (Berkeley: University of California Press, 1974), 201ff.

33. For the currency of this Boethian lore in Spenser's Cambridge, see Everard Digby, *Theoria analytica* (London, 1579), 369. For its currency in twelfth-century France, see Otto

Notes 519

Georg von Simson, *The Gothic Cathedral: Origins of Gothic Architecture and the Medieval Concept of Order,* 2d ed. (New York: Pantheon Books, 1962), 190–92. For its currency among the most learned men of mid-seventeenth-century Europe, see Athanasius Kircher, *Musurgia universalis sive Ars magna consoni et dissoni in X. libros digesta,* 2 vols. (Rome, 1650), 1:47.

34. See Leo Schrade, "Music in the Philosophy of Boethius," *Musical Quarterly* 33 (1947): 188–200.

35. "On divine frenzy," *Letters* 1:45; cf. *Opera* 614.

36. "On music," *Letters* 1:143; cf. *Opera* 651.

37. For the reference to Plato, see *Republic* 530D.

38. See my *Cosmographical Glass: Renaissance Diagrams of the Universe* (San Marino: Huntington Library, 1977), 134–42.

39. *The second part of the French academie,* trans. Thomas Bowes (London, 1594), 83. For the place of music in the Elizabethan grammar school, see Richard Mulcaster, *Positions* (London, 1581), 36–40.

40. *Compleat gentleman* 103.

41. John Stevens argues knowledgeably that to ascribe this sort of nebulous expressiveness to medieval and Renaissance musicians is an anachronism. With a somewhat debilitating rigidity, he asserts: "It was never the first duty of music to express emotion" (*Music & Poetry in the Early Tudor Court* [London: Methuen, 1961], 59; cf. 74).

42. See Theodore Meyer Greene 332–38; and the "Supplementary Essay" (487–506) by Roy D. Welch analyzing in detail Beethoven's Eroica symphony. See also Langer 204–45; Victor Zuckerkandl, *Sound and Symbol: Music and the External World,* trans. Willard R. Trask (New York: Pantheon Books, 1956); and Van Meter Ames, "What Is Music?" *Journal of Aesthetics and Art Criticism* 26 (1967–68): 241–49. The initial document in the freedom of music from imitative demands was Eduard Hanslick, *Vom Musikalisch-Schönen* (Leipzig, 1854).

43. The locus classicus for this tradition is Aristotle's *Politics* (1342a8–b35), augmented by Plutarch's *De musica* (1136B–1137A). It was well known in the Renaissance: cf., e.g., Scaliger, *Poetice* 30–31; and John Case, *The praise of musicke* (Oxford, 1586), 54–56. For a technical exposition of it, see Franchino Gafuri, *De harmonia musicorum instrumentorum opus* [1518], ed. and trans. Clement A. Miller (Neuhausen-Stuttgart: American Institute of Musicology, 1977), 179–89; or Kircher 1:151–54.

44. See Edward E. Lowinsky, "Music of the Renaissance as Viewed by Renaissance Musicians," *The Renaissance Image of Man and the World,* ed. Bernard O'Kelly (Columbus: Ohio State University Press, 1966), 150–52. See also page 525 (n. 98).

45. Case repeats the familiar tale of Timotheus and Alexander, as well as many more of the same sort (59–62). Cf. Heinrich Cornelius Agrippa, *Three books of occult philosophy,* trans. John Freake (London, 1651), 255–57; and E.K.'s gloss on "October" 27. See also S. F. Johnson, "Spenser's 'Shepherd's Calendar,'" *Times Literary Supplement* 7 Sept. 1951: 565; and John M. Steadman, "Timotheus in Dryden, E.K., and Gafori," *Times Literary Supplement* 16 Dec. 1960: 819. For a medical account of how music restores harmony to the soul, see Ficino, *Letters* 1:142–43; cf. Kircher 2:213–30.

46. The reason for David's restorative effect upon Saul is fully explained by John Brown, "The Cure of Saul: A Sacred Ode," prefixed to *A Dissertation on the Rise, Union, and Power . . . of Poetry and Music* (London, 1763), 5–19. To dispel Saul's despair, according to the Argument, "David is sent for, to cure him by the Power of Music"; and David "sings the Creation of the World, and the happy Estate of our first Parents in Paradise" (3). Brown may well be recalling Abraham Cowley's treatment of this episode in *Davideis* (*Poems,* ed. A. R. Waller [Cambridge: Cambridge University Press, 1905], 253–55). Spenser recalls this biblical incident in *Faerie Queene* 4.2.2.1–6.

47. Cf. Theodor Zwinger, *Theatrum vitae humanae* (Basle, 1571), 3196. The other

"mechanical" arts, according to Zwinger, include such occupations as agriculture, animal husbandry, metallurgy, armor-making, coinage, painting and sculpture, printing, and the making of clothes.

48. See von Simson 25ff.

49. Cf. Giorgio Valla, *De expetendis, et fugiendis rebus opus* (Venice, 1501), LL3ᵛ–LL4. See also Leonard Barkan, *Nature's Work of Art: The Human Body as Image of the World* (New Haven: Yale University Press, 1975), esp. 136–43.

50. Marin Mersenne compels this argument to its logical extreme. Since the Temple of Solomon was the most excellent building ever constructed, it must have been modelled upon the body of Christ:

> Car supposé que toute la symmetrie de l'architecture ait esté prise sur les mesures du corps humain, comme Vitruve assevre, il est raisonnable que la plus excellente architecture de l'univers, telle qu'a esté celle du Temple de Jerusalem, ait esté prise sur le corps le plus parfait, & le mieux composé & temperé qui fut jamais, tel qu'a esté le corps de Nostre Sauveur.

(*Traité de l'harmonie universelle* [Paris, 1627], 476).

51. This is the basic assumption, for example, of Alberti, who thinks of architecture as the imposition of design upon inchoate building materials. In the opening chapter of *De re aedificatoria,* the cornerstone of Renaissance architectural theory, he states: "It is the Property and Business of the Design to appoint to the Edifice and all its Parts their proper Places, determinate Number, just Proportion and beautiful Order; so that the whole Form of the Structure be proportionable. . . . We shall call the Design a firm and graceful preordering of the Lines and Angles, conceived in the Mind, and contrived by an ingenious Artist" (*Ten Books on Architecture,* trans. James Leoni [1726], ed. Joseph Rykwert [London: Alec Tiranti, 1955], 1–2). Incidentally, this also was at basis the assumption of Hegel, who gives architecture the primacy of place among the fine arts (1:112ff. and 3:25ff.). Dee summarizes Alberti's views in his "Mathematicall praeface" d4. On Alberti, see also Edward E. Lowinsky, "The Concept of Physical and Musical Space in the Renaissance," *Papers of the American Musicological Society: Annual Meeting, 1941,* ed. Gustave Reese (Minneapolis: American Musicological Society, 1946), 82–83; and Joan Gadol, "The Unity of the Renaissance: Humanism, Natural Science, and Art," *From the Renaissance to the Counter-Reformation: Essays in Honor of Garrett Mattingly,* ed. Charles H. Carter (New York: Random House, 1965), 37–39.

52. *Letters* 1:85.

53. This was the clearly expressed view of the sixteenth-century French architect, Philibert de L'Orme; see von Simson 227–28. L'Orme's *Le premier tome de l'architecture* (Paris, 1568) resided in several Elizabethan libraries; see Lucy Gent, *Picture and Poetry 1560–1620: Relations between Literature and the Visual Arts in the English Renaissance* (Leamington Spa: Hall, 1981), 83.

54. *On Architecture,* trans. Leoni 197.

55. *The elements of architecture* (London, 1624), 53.

56. Cf. Alberti, *On Architecture,* trans. Leoni 197–200. For a full exposition of this technique, see Rudolf Wittkower, *Architectural Principles in the Age of Humanism* (New York: Random House, 1965), esp. part 4.

57. See Munro 32.

58. *Phisicke against Fortune, as well prosperous, as adverse,* trans. Thomas Twyne (London, 1579), fol. 57–58.

In his sonnet on the painting of Laura by his friend Simone Martini, Petrarch indicates what a theory of the depictive arts in a Platonic context would be. The ancient Polyclitus, Petrarch says, could never capture Laura's beauty, because he reproduced only what he saw with his eyes in the phenomenal world. Simone, however, in a *furor divinus* had been privileged to see the beauty of Laura's soul in heaven, where he sketched that essence and gave it sufficiently substantial form to be witnessed by mortal senses:

> Even though Polyclitus should for a thousand years compete in looking with all the others who were famous in that art, they would never see the smallest part of the beauty that has conquered my heart.

> But certainly my Simon was in Paradise, whence comes this noble lady; there he saw her and portrayed her on paper, to attest down here to her lovely face.

> The work is one of those which can be imagined only in Heaven, not here among us, where the body is a veil to the soul;

> it was a gracious act, nor could he have done it after he came down to feel heat and cold and his eyes took on mortality.

(*Petrarch's Lyric Poems: The "Rime sparse" and Other Lyrics*, ed. and trans. Robert M. Durling [Cambridge: Harvard University Press, 1976], 176 [*Canzoniere* 77]). Cf. *Canzoniere* 78, 130, 159. See also Spenser, *Faerie Queene* 3.proem.1–2.

59. As late as 1624 Wotton was saying, "There are two *Arts* attending on *Architecture*, like two of her principall *Gentlewomen*, to *dresse* and *trimme* their *Mistresse*, PICTURE & SCULPTURE" (82–83).

60. Rudolf Arnheim discusses the effects of this development in *Art and Visual Perception: A Psychology of the Creative Eye*, rev. ed. (Berkeley: University of California Press, 1974), 239–40.

61. *Canterbury Tales*, "General Prologue" 96; *Works*, ed. F. N. Robinson, 2d ed. (Boston: Houghton Mifflin, 1957).

62. Ed. Henry H. S. Croft, 2 vols. (London, 1883), 1:43. Cf. Alberti, *On Painting*, trans. Grayson 63–64.

63. *Positions* 34–36. See also Foster Watson, *The Beginnings of the Teaching of Modern Subjects in England* (London: Pitman Books, 1909), 136–42.

64. On the retardation of the visual arts by religious controversy in Elizabethan England, see Karl J. Höltgen, "The Reformation of Images and Some Jacobean Writers on Art," *Functions of Literature: Essays Presented to Erwin Wolff on His Sixtieth Birthday* (Tübingen: Niemeyer, 1984), 119–46.

65. See Herbert Weisinger, "Renaissance Theories of the Revival of the Fine Arts," *Italica* 20 (1943): 163–70; Arnold Hauser, *The Social History of Art*, 2 vols. (London: Routledge and Kegan Paul, 1951), 1:266–68; and André Chastel, *The Myth of the Renaissance 1420–1520* (Geneva: Skira, 1969), 7–8, 71–77.

66. *Lives of Seventy of the Most Eminent Painters, Sculptors and Architects*, ed. and trans. E. H. and E. W. Blashfield and A. A. Hopkins, 4 vols. (New York: Charles Scribner's Sons, 1926), 1:229. For a similar view of Masaccio as the "ottimo imitatore di natura," see Cristoforo Landino, ed., [Dante's] *Divina commedia* (Florence, 1481), [*]5ᵛ; reprinted in Landino, *Scritti critici e teorici*, ed. Roberto Cardini, 2 vols. (Rome: Bulzoni, 1974), 1:124. See also E. H. Gombrich, *Norm and Form: Studies in the Art of the Renaissance* (London: Phaidon Press, 1966), 2.

67. *The artes of curious paintinge, carvinge & buildinge*, trans. Richard Haydocke (Oxford, 1598), 4. This work was first published in Italian in 1584.

68. For a conservative view of painting's dependence upon mathematical proportion, see Gafuri, *De harmonia* 204.

69.   The first part from the toppe of the heade to the nose, answereth to the space
      betwixt that, and the chinne, in a triple proportion, which maketh a *Diapente* and

a *Diapason.* That betweene the chinne and the throat-pit, answereth to that be-twixt the nose and the chinne in a double proportion, which makes a *diapason:* whereunto the head answereth in the same proportion. The three faces [i.e., the length of three heads] betweene the throat pit and the *privities* answere to the second, betwixt them & the knee in a *sesquialter proportion;* whence ariseth a *Diapente:* but with the legge they are *Unisones,* for it hath the same proportion with the *thigh.*

(*Artes of painting* 33). Cf. Lomazzo, *Idea del tempio della pittura* (Milan, 1590), 128–42; and Gafuri, *De harmonia* 207–8.

70. *Paragone: A Comparison of the Arts,* ed. and trans. Irma A. Richter (London: Oxford University Press, 1949), esp. 52–64.

71. For the most that could be said by way of approval for dancing, see Thoinot Arbeau, *Orchesography* [1589], trans. Mary Stewart Evans (New York: Dover Publications, 1967), 12–17. For the place of dance in the scheme of things, see Zwinger 2511–12. For an early history, see Jacques Bonnet, *Histoire générale de la danse, sacrée et prophane* (Paris, 1724).

72. *Laws,* Book 2 passim; cf. *Alcibiades I* 108B–D; *Republic* 441E. For a learned and handsomely illustrated treatise on gymnastics as practiced by the ancients, see Girolamo Mercuriale, *De arte gymnastica libri sex,* 2d ed. (Venice, 1573). See also John M. Major, "The Moralization of the Dance in Elyot's *Governour,*" *Studies in the Renaissance* 5 (1958): 27–37. At the beginning of the first set of eclogues in the old *Arcadia,* Sidney assumes the platonist relation of gymnastics to music and associates it with pastoral: "The manner of the Arcadian shepherds was, when they met together, to pass their time, either in such music as their rural education could afford them, or in exercise of their body" (56.1–3).

73. *Positions* 74.

74. For the case against dancing, see Heinrich Cornelius Agrippa, *Of the vanitie and uncertaintie of artes and sciences,* trans. James Sanford (London, 1569), fol. 30–31^v.

75. *Phisicke against Fortune* fol. 32^v.

76. For a classical example, see Lucian, *The Dance* 7. At an early date this topos had been endowed with concrete details by Philostratus the Elder, *Imagines* 2.34. Cf. Du Bartas, *Devine weekes & workes,* trans. Joshua Sylvester (London, 1605), 42; and Mersenne esp. 69–70. Sidney alludes to it in *Astrophil and Stella* 26.7–8.

77. See Yates, *French Academies* 60–62, 236–74. For an excellent example of *danse figurée* in the proper context, offered by Sidney, see "the skirmish betwixt Reason and Passion" that opens the Second Eclogues in the *Old Arcadia,* ed. Robertson 135–36.

78. *The Poems,* ed. Robert Krueger (Oxford: Clarendon, 1975). For a well-informed discussion, see Sarah Thesiger, "The *Orchestra* of Sir John Davies and the Image of the Dance," *Journal of the Warburg and Courtauld Institutes* 36 (1973): 277–304.

79. For a quick survey of several theories of poetry in the Renaissance, see O. B. Hardison, Jr., *The Enduring Monument: A Study of the Idea of Praise in Renaissance Literary Theory and Practice* (Chapel Hill: University of North Carolina Press, 1962), 5–23. See also Bernard Weinberg, *A History of Literary Criticism in the Italian Renaissance,* 2 vols. (Chicago: University of Chicago Press, 1961), 1:1–13, where poetry is located among "the arts of discourse" and associated most closely with rhetoric. For the place of poetry in a comprehensive scheme of all the arts and sciences, see Zwinger 8–9; cf. 160–61.

80. *The Arte of English Poesie* [1589], ed. Gladys Doidge Willcock and Alice Walker (Cambridge: Cambridge University Press, 1936), 4.

81. "There are just as many opinions as there are individuals, especially about poetry" ("Certayne notes of instruction concerning the making of verse or ryme in English," *Elizabethan Critical Essays,* ed. G. Gregory Smith, 2 vols. [London: Oxford University Press, 1904], 1:46–47).

82. See, for example, the long-lived *Doctrinale* (chap. 10) by Alexander of Villadei, composed in 1199 (ed. Dietrich Reichling, 1893 [New York: Burt Franklin, 1974], 100–52). For an example even more cogent for the late Renaissance, see Gregor Reisch, *Margarita philosophica,* ed. Oronce Finé (Basle, 1583), 101–22. This encyclopedia of the liberal arts, initially published at Freiburg in 1503, incorporates the traditional curriculum as it was passed on to the Renaissance. First edited by Finé in 1535, it was reprinted several times throughout the sixteenth century. For a thorough account of metrics in their grammatical context, see Henricus Glareanus, *De ratione syllabarum brevis isagoge* (Paris, 1555), which follows the disposition of the subject as laid out by Henricus Bebelius, *Ars versificandi et carminum condendorum cum quantitatibus syllabarum* (Strasbourg, 1513). On the relation of poetry to grammar at this time, see Foster Watson, *The English Grammar Schools to 1660: Their Curriculum and Practice* (Cambridge: Cambridge University Press, 1908), 468–74; and Elizabeth J. Sweeting, *Early Tudor Criticism: Linguistic & Literary* (Oxford: Basil Blackwell, 1940), 65–74.

83. See, for example, Reisch 241–66. See also Donald L. Clark, *Rhetoric and Poetry in the Renaissance* (New York: Columbia University Press, 1922), esp. 43–100; Marvin T. Herrick, "The Place of Rhetoric in Poetic Theory," *Quarterly Journal of Speech* 34 (1948): 1–22; Ian Sowton, "Hidden Persuaders as a Means of Literary Grace: Sixteenth-Century Poetics and Rhetoric in England," *University of Toronto Quarterly* 32 (1962–63): 55–69; Marcia L. Colish, *The Mirror of Language: A Study in the Medieval Theory of Knowledge* (New Haven: Yale University Press, 1968), 228–37; Castor 14–23; Walter J. Ong, S.J., "The Province of Rhetoric and Poetic," *The Province of Rhetoric,* ed. Joseph Schwartz and John A. Rycenga (New York: Ronald Press, 1965), 48–56; Thomas O. Sloan, "The Crossing of Rhetoric and Poetry in the English Renaissance," *The Rhetoric of Renaissance Poetry: From Wyatt to Milton,* ed. Sloan and Raymond B. Waddington (Berkeley: University of California Press, 1974), 212–42; and George A. Kennedy, *Classical Rhetoric and Its Christian and Secular Tradition from Ancient to Modern Times* (Chapel Hill: University of North Carolina Press, 1980), 108–16. With particular reference to Sidney, see Robert L. Montgomery, *Symmetry and Sense: The Poetry of Sir Philip Sidney* (Austin: University of Texas Press, 1961).

84. See Joel E. Spingarn, *A History of Literary Criticism in the Renaissance* (New York, 1899), 24–27; and Wilbur S. Howell, *Logic and Rhetoric in England, 1500–1700* (Princeton: Princeton University Press, 1956), 3–6, 39–40, 75–77.

85. Cf. Jonson: "The Study of it [poetry] (if wee will trust *Aristotle*) offers to mankinde a certaine rule, and Patterne of living well, and happily; disposing us to all Civill offices of Society" (*Timber* 8:636; cf. also 8:640).

86. La poesia presuppone tutto il trivio, il quadrivio, e tutta la filosofia, e il sapere umano e divino, e tutte le scienze (Eugenio Garin, ed., *L'Educazione umanistica in Italia: Testi scelti e illustrati* [Bari: Laterza, 1949], 25). See also William H. Woodward 212–15; and Garin, *L'Educazione in Europa, 1400–1600: Problemi e programmi,* rev. ed. (Bari: Laterza, 1976), 87–89.

87. In this addition of poetry to the three traditional language arts Valla is followed by Zwinger (160ff.).

88. The bibliography of works dealing with the relation between music and poetry in the Renaissance is long and diverse. The studies that I have found most useful include Daniel Webb, *Observations on the Correspondence between Poetry and Music* (London, 1769); Thomas Robertson, *An Inquiry into the Fine Arts* (London, 1784); Bruce Pattison, "Literature and Music," *The English Renaissance 1510–1688,* ed. Vivian de Sola Pinto (London: Cresset, 1938), 120–38; Paul Oskar Kristeller, "Music and Learning in the Early Italian Renaissance," *Journal of Renaissance and Baroque Music* 1 (1946–47): 255–74; Pattison, *Music and Poetry of the English Renaissance* (London: Methuen, 1948); Catherine Ing, *Elizabethan Lyrics* (London: Chatto and Windus, 1951), chap. 5; James E. Phil-

lips, "Poetry and Music in the Seventeenth Century," *Music & Literature in England in the Seventeenth and Eighteenth Centuries* (Los Angeles: Clark Library, 1953), 1–21; John Hollander, *The Untuning of the Sky: Ideas of Music in English Poetry 1500–1700* (Princeton: Princeton University Press, 1961); John Stevens, *Music & Poetry in the Early Tudor Court* (London: Methuen, 1961); Gretchen L. Finney, *Musical Backgrounds for English Literature: 1580–1650* (New Brunswick: Rutgers University Press, 1962), esp. chaps. 1–7; Dean Tolle Mace, "Marin Mersenne on Language and Music," *Journal of Music Theory* 14 (1970): 2–34; Jerome Mazzaro, *Transformations in the Renaissance English Lyric* (Ithaca: Cornell University Press, 1970), esp. chap. 4; Elizabeth W. Pomeroy, *The Elizabethan Miscellanies: Their Development and Conventions* (Berkeley: University of California Press, 1973), chap. 6; Hollander, *Vision and Resonance: Two Senses of Poetic Form* (New York: Oxford University Press, 1975), esp. 3–22; and Arthur Wayne Glowka, "The Function of Meter According to Ancient and Medieval Theory," *Allegorica* 7 (1982): 100–109. For theoretical discussion of the linkage between poetry and music, and for a survey of the exploitation of this linkage, see Calvin S. Brown, *Music and Literature: A Comparison of the Arts* (Athens: University of Georgia Press, 1948); Hollander, "The Music of Poetry," *Journal of Aesthetics and Art Criticism* 15 (1956–57): 232–44; Brown, "The Relations between Music and Literature as a Field of Study," *Comparative Literature* 22 (1970): 97–107; James A. Winn, *Unsuspected Eloquence: A History of the Relations between Poetry and Music* (New Haven: Yale University Press, 1981); and Steven P. Scher, "Literature and Music," *Interrelations of Literature*, ed. Jean-Pierre Barricelli and Joseph Gibaldi (New York: Modern Language Association, 1982), 225–50. For general views on the relation between music and poetry, see T. S. Eliot, "The Music of Poetry," *Selected Prose*, ed. John Hayward (Harmondsworth: Penguin Books, 1953), 56–67; George P. Springer, "Language and Music: Parallels and Divergencies," *For Roman Jakobson: Essays on the Occasion of His Sixtieth Birthday*, ed. Morris Halle et al. (The Hague: Mouton, 1956), 504–13; Northrop Frye, "Introduction: Lexis and Melos," *Sound and Poetry*, ed. Frye (New York: Columbia University Press, 1957), ix–xxvii; and Donald Davie, *Articulate Energy: An Inquiry into the Syntax of English Poetry* [1955] (London: Routledge and Kegan Paul, 1976), esp. 14–23. For a more technical consideration of the similarities between poetry and music, see Wilfrid Mellers, *Harmonious Meeting: A Study of the Relationship between English Music, Poetry and Theatre, c.1600–1900* (London: Dobson, 1965); Bertrand H. Bronson, "Literature and Music," *Relations of Literary Study: Essays on Interdisciplinary Contributions*, ed. James Thorpe (New York: Modern Language Association, 1967), 127–50; Monroe C. Beardsley, "Verse and Music," *Versification: Major Language Types*, ed. W. K. Wimsatt, Jr. (New York: Modern Language Association, 1972), 238–52; Seth Weiner, "Renaissance Prosodic Thought as a Branch of Musica Speculativa," diss., Princeton, 1981; and Elise Bickford Jorgens, *The Well-Tun'd Word: Musical Interpretations of English Poetry 1597–1651* (Minneapolis: University of Minnesota Press, 1982). For an innovative study of the formal properties that allow a comparison of music and poetry in Elizabethan England, see Paula Johnson, *Form and Transformation in Music and Poetry of the English Renaissance* (New Haven: Yale University Press, 1972). For an exhaustive bibliography on the relation between music and poetry, see T. V. F. Brogan, *English Versification, 1570–1980* (Baltimore: Johns Hopkins University Press, 1981), 209–25, 725–41.

89. Most importantly *Phaedo* 60E–61B, *Alcibiades I* 108C–D, *Republic* 376E, and *Laws* 669B–D.

The Greeks had also another word for music, μέλος. This is the term usually translated as "music" in Aristotle's *Poetics*, although "song" might be preferable. Like μουσική, μέλος also implies a verbal component; see Gerald F. Else, ed. and trans., *Aristotle's Poetics: The Argument* (Cambridge: Harvard University Press, 1957), 61–66.

90. An influential treatise, Περὶ μουσικῆς, appeared in the Renaissance canon of Plutarch's *Moralia*, although modern scholarship doubts the attribution to Plutarch. At one

point, this treatise specifies the three components of μουσική that the listener must attend to: "Three smallest components must always simultaneously strike the ear: the note, the time, and the syllable or sound. From the course of the notes we recognize the structure of the scale [i.e., harmony]; from that of the times, the rhythm; and from that of the sounds or syllables, the words of the song" (De musica 1144A).

91. Faerie Queene 4.2.2.5.

92. "On Music," trans. Robert C. Taliaferro, Writings of St. Augustine, Fathers of the Church, 6 vols. (Washington, D.C.: Catholic University of America Press, 1947), 2:324; cf. 2:331–33. On the priority of Augustine in medieval aesthetics, see von Simson 21–50.

93. See Marianne Shapiro, Hieroglyph of Time: The Petrarchan Sestina (Minneapolis: University of Minnesota Press, 1980), esp. 3–90.

94. See D. P. Walker, "Musical Humanism in the 16th and Early 17th Centuries," Music Review 2 (1941): 1–13, 111–21, 220–27, 288–308, and 3 (1942): 55–71; Lowinsky, "Music in Culture of Renaissance" 375–78, 380; Howard M. Brown, Music in the Renaissance (Englewood Cliffs: Prentice-Hall, 1976), 3, 337–43, 371–72; and Winn 163–79.

95. Howard M. Brown, Music in Renaissance 231–32. For another German who set classical texts (Vergil, Ovid, Martial, Horace et al.) in order to demonstrate the interchangeable rhythms of music and poetry, see Lucas Lossius, Erotemata musicae practicae (Nuremberg, 1563). Thomas Morley was familiar with Lossius; see A plaine and easie introduction to practicall musicke (London, 1597), *3, *3ᵛ, pages 13, 28, 30. For the prototype in this exercise of setting classical meters to musical notes, see Francesco Negri, Grammatica (Venice, 1480). For the theory which suggested this practice, see Gafuri, Practica musicae 69–72. For Sidney's awareness of this practice, see Old Arcadia, ed. Robertson 89.

96. See Hermann Zenck, "Zarlino's 'Istitutioni harmoniche' als Quelle zur Musikanschauung der italienischen Renaissance," Zeitschrift für Musikwissenschaft 12 (1929–30): 540–78; and Lowinsky, "Music in Culture of Renaissance" 363–68. The peculiar potency of song is explained in careful physiological detail by Agrippa:

> Singing can do more then the sound of an Instrument, in as much as it arising by an Harmonial consent, from the conceit of the minde, and imperious affection of the phantasie and heart, easily penetrateth by motion, with the refracted and well tempered Air, the aerious spirit of the hearer, which is the bond of soul and body; and transferring the affection and minde of the Singer with it, it moveth the affection of the hearer by his affection, and the hearers phantasie by his phantasie, and minde by his minde, and striketh the minde, and striketh the heart, and pierceth even to the inwards of the soul. (Of occult philosophy 257)

97. This statement glosses over the furious argument about whether the madrigal—or, indeed, any setting for a text—should be polyphonic or have a single melodic line. The more rigorous humanists objected to the fashionable polyphonic setting with several voices singing different words of the text at once; such complexity, they justly observed, rendered the verbal system unintelligible. They therefore argued for plainsong as opposed to partsong. According to the purest theory as enunciated by Vincenzo Galilei, one note and one alone should be set to each syllable of the text (see Lowinsky, "Music in Culture of Renaissance" 377). See also Dorothy Koenigsberger, Renaissance Man and Creative Thinking: A History of Concepts of Harmony 1400–1700 (Atlantic Highlands: Humanities Press, 1979), 188–203. The bone of this contention was the humanists' insistence that a work of art have rational meaning; and the meaning, of course, would be more readily conveyed by the verbal system than by the musical setting. Lalus in the old Arcadia makes this point in his contention with Dicus over quantitative measure vs. rhyme: "Dicus did much abuse the dignity of poetry to apply it to music, since rather music is a servant to poetry, for by the one the ear only, by the other the mind, was pleased" (Old Arcadia, ed. Robertson 89.39–90.2).

98. The history of opera as we know it begins with the experiments of the Camerata

meeting in Florence in the last quarter of the sixteenth century under the patronage of Giovanni de' Bardi. Its chief theoreticians were Girolamo Mei and Vincenzo Galilei, father of the famous Galileo. Behind these experiments lay a desire to reproduce the so-called "effects" attributed to the various musical modes in classical times (page 70). Among the extensive musical activities of this Camerata, which included many of the most accomplished musicians of the day, some wrote dramas to be declaimed to music—which they pointedly called *melodrammi*—in emulation of what they thought Greek drama to have been. So far as we know, the first of this genre was a work entitled *Dafne,* performed about 1597, with libretto by Ottavio Rinuccini and musical score by Jacopo Peri and Jacopo Corsi. For the philosophical context of this group, see Yates, *French Academies* 9–10. See also Claude V. Palisca, ed., *Girolamo Mei: Letters on Ancient and Modern Music to Vincenzo Galilei and Giovanni Bardi* (Rome: American Institute of Musicology, 1960); Howard M. Brown, "How Opera Began: An Introduction to Jacopo Peri's *Euridice* (1600)," *The Late Italian Renaissance 1525–1630,* ed. Eric Cochrane (New York: Torchbooks, Harper and Row, 1970), 401–43; and Barbara R. Hanning, *Of Poetry and Music's Power: Humanism and the Creation of Opera* (Ann Arbor: University Microfilms International Research Press, 1980).

99. See Howard M. Brown, *Music in Renaissance* 340–41; and, for greater detail, Isidore Silver, "Ronsard on the Marriage of Poetry, Music, and the Dance," *Studies in the Continental Background of Renaissance English Literature: Essays Presented to John L. Lievsay,* ed. Dale B. J. Randall and George W. Williams (Durham: Duke University Press, 1977), 155–69.

100. *Étrènes de poézie fransoeze an vers mesurés* et al. (Paris, 1574). See D. P. Walker, "The Aims of Baïf's Académie de Poésie et de Musique," *Journal of Renaissance and Baroque Music* 1 (1946): 91–100; Yates, *French Academies* 19–25, 36–46, 52–58; and Beverly Jeanne Davis, "Antoine de Bertrand: A View into the Aesthetics of Music in Sixteenth Century France," *Journal of Aesthetics and Art Criticism* 21 (1962–63): 189–200.

101. See Pattison, *Music and Poetry* 62–68; James E. Phillips 2–7; Hollander, *Untuning of Sky* 141–43; Attridge 122; and Anne Lake Prescott, *French Poets and the English Renaissance* (New Haven: Yale University Press, 1978), 91–95.

102. For a comprehensive study of the word μουσική and its derivatives in the Platonic dialogues, see Vicaire passim. In the *Politics* Aristotle offers a stringent critique of Plato's emphasis upon music in education (1339a11–1340b19). Aristotle rather grudgingly condones music (like Plato, he uses the word μουσική) because it gives pleasure to both performer and auditor, and induces a moral character.

103. *Commentary on the Dream of Scipio,* trans. William Harris Stahl (New York: Columbia University Press, 1952), 194.

104. *Letters* 1:46; cf. *Opera* 614. See also my *Cosmographical Glass* 136–38. Cf. Case 52–53.

105. *Works,* ed. Vivian 35.

106. *Disputationes Camaldulenses,* opening of Book 3, trans. Thomas H. Stahel, S. J., "Cristoforo Landino's Allegorization of the *Aeneid:* Books III and IV of the *Camaldolese Disputations,*" diss., Johns Hopkins, 1968, 42.

107. Plato animam nostram musicis proportionibus compactam affirmabat (*Margarita philosophica* 343). See *Phaedo* 100C–105E and *Phaedrus* 245C–246A. Cf. Reisch 828, 868–69; and Kenelm Digby 21–23.

108. *Spenser: Variorum* 7:100. Cf. Gafuri, *De harmonia* 206–7.

109. Several Renaissance books deal extensively with this topic. Three especially cogent to our interests are Francesco Giorgio, *De harmonia mundi totius cantica tria* (Venice, 1525), reprinted (Paris, 1545), and translated by Guy le Fèvre de la Boderie as *L'Harmonie du monde* (Paris, 1579); Pontus de Tyard, *Solitaire second* (Lyons, 1552), often reprinted; and Marin Mersenne, *Traité de l'harmonie universelle* (Paris, 1627).

110. Stahel 42.

111. *De re poetica,* ed. and trans. Alastair D. S. Fowler (Oxford: Blackwell, 1958), 89.

112. See esp. Hallett Smith, *Elizabethan Poetry: A Study in Conventions, Meaning and Expression* (Cambridge: Harvard University Press, 1952), chap. 5.

113. *Practicall musicke* ¶1. The last book of Augustine's *De musica* is devoted to music as an aid to religious love (i.e., caritas), so the soul is not seduced by the sensuousness of music, but instead uses the musical experience as a prelude to divine love and a place in heaven; see esp. chaps. 16–27. Sidney makes a joke of this platonist lore in the discourse on love between Pyrocles and Musidorus in the first book of the old *Arcadia* (ed. Robertson, 17.4–9).

114. *Adagiorum chiliades quatuor, et sesquicenturia* [4.5.15] (Lyons, 1559), col. 1071.

115. *TN* 1.1.1. Cleopatra also calls for "music, moody food / Of us that trade in love" (*Ant.* 2.5.1–2).

116. Milton, "Il Penseroso" 62.

117. See Henry J. Chaytor, *From Script to Print* (Cambridge: Cambridge University Press, 1945), esp. chap. 2.

118. *The Arte of Rhetorique* [1553], ed. Robert H. Bowers (Gainesville, FL: Scholars' Facsimiles and Reprints, 1962), fol. 108ᵛ.

119. Although one of those most influential in establishing Aristotle as a dominant authority, Julius Caesar Scaliger curiously persisted in the requirement of verse for poetry; cf. *Poetice* [1.2], 3; and see page 208.

120. The crisis in quantitative vs. accentual versification at the beginning of the seventeenth century is neatly delineated by the exchange between Thomas Campion, *Observations in the art of English poesie* (London, 1602), and Samuel Daniel, *A defence of ryme* (London, 1603). For the confusion, though, that reigned in England during the last half of the sixteenth century, see Weiner, "Renaissance Prosodic Thought," esp. chap. 3. For the sort of compromise a metrician of the eighteenth century was prepared to make, see John Mason, *An Essay on the Power of Numbers, and the Principles of Harmony in Poetical Compositions* (London, 1749).

121. See Lowinsky, "Music as Viewed by Renaissance Musicians" 136–38.

122. In the Jesus College (Oxford) manuscript of the old *Arcadia,* Sidney returns to the distinction between quantitative and accentual verse in musical terms. There again Sidney is thinking of accentual meter as an experience for the ear (cf. William A. Ringler, Jr., "Master Drant's Rules," *Philological Quarterly* 29 [1950]: 72). See also *Old Arcadia,* ed. Robertson 89.35–90.18.

123. *Compendium of musick,* trans. anon. (London, 1653), 1. This treatise, although written in 1618, was not published until 1650, when it was printed at Utrecht in Latin. For a cogent discussion of this treatise, see Bertrand Augst, "Descartes's Compendium on Music," *Journal of the History of Ideas* 26 (1965): 119–32. For Descartes's effect on Mersenne in the separation of music and poetry, see Mace, "Mersenne on Language and Music" 4–10, 23–26. For a landmark in the development of music as an expressive art preparing for Romanticism, see Charles Avison, *An Essay on Musical Expression* (London, 1752).

124. Cf. Claude V. Palisca, "Scientific Empiricism in Musical Thought," *Seventeenth Century Science and Arts,* ed. Hedley Howell Rhys (Princeton: Princeton University Press, 1961), 91–137.

125. See Battestin 58–102.

126. *Essai sur l'origine des langues,* chap. 12; see Jean-Jacques Rousseau, *Essay on the Origin of Languages* et al., trans. John H. Moran and Alexander Gode (New York: Frederick Ungar, 1966), esp. 50–52.

127. Cf. Abrams 88–94.

128. *Die Welt als Wille und Vorstellung* 3.42–52; see Arthur Schopenhauer, *The World as Will and Idea,* trans. R. B. Haldane and J. Kemp, 7th ed., 2 vols. (London: Kegan Paul,

c.1914), 1:274–346. Hegel also should be recognized in the background of this movement to remove the constraint of particularity from music (cf. 3:338–58).

129. *Renaissance* 141. Pater's essay first appeared in *The Fortnightly Review* ns 22.2 (1877): 526–38. Nietzsche confirmed this trend: cf. *Birth of Tragedy* esp. 43–46; or, "Amidst our degenerate culture music is the only pure and purifying flame, towards which and away from which all things move in a Heraclitean double motion" (120). The most stringent critique of this conflation of the arts in music, perhaps because closest to the movement, is Irving Babbitt, *The New Laokoon: An Essay on the Confusion of the Arts* (Boston: Houghton Mifflin, 1910), esp. 115–85. For a curious fin-de-siècle fad which conflated music, poetry, and painting, see Calvin S. Brown, "The Color Symphony before and after Gautier," *Comparative Literature* 5 (1953): 289–309.

130. *Renaissance* 144.

131. See Wendell Stacy Johnson, "Browning's Music," *Journal of Aesthetics and Art Criticism* 22 (1963–64): 203–7.

132. See, for example, Stéphane Mallarmé, "La Musique et les lettres" [1893], *Studies in European Literature: Being the Taylorian Lectures 1889–1899* (Oxford: Clarendon, 1900), esp. 138–45.

133. *The Science of English Verse* [1880], ed. Paull F. Baum, *Sidney Lanier*, ed. Charles R. Anderson et al., 10 vols. (Baltimore: Johns Hopkins University Press, 1945), 2:39.

134. See Charmenz S. Lenhart, *Musical Influence on American Poetry* (Athens: University of Georgia Press, 1956), 290–91; and Helen Hagenbuechle, "Epistemology and Musical Form in Conrad Aiken's Poetry," *Studies in the Literary Imagination* 13.2 (1980): 7–25.

135. *Timber* 8:635. That Jonson is not thinking of versifying when he uses these musical terms is clear in the next sentence, where he is careful to state that a poet is "not hee which writeth in measure only."

136. Like the writings on "poetry and music" in the Renaissance, the studies on "poetry and painting" are extensive. I have found the following to be most useful: Jacques Bonnet, "Paralele de la peinture et de la poésie," *Histoire générale de la danse, sacrée et prophane* (Paris, 1724), 213–69; Hildebrand Jacob, *Of the Sister Arts: An Essay* (London, 1734); William Guild Howard, "Ut Pictura Poesis," *PMLA* 24 (1909): 40–123; Rensselaer W. Lee, "*Ut Pictura Poesis:* The Humanistic Theory of Painting," *Art Bulletin* 22 (1940): 197–269; Rudolph Gottfried, "The Pictorial Element in Spenser's Poetry," *ELH* 19 (1952): 203–13; Walter J. Ong, S. J., "System, Space, and Intellect in Renaissance Symbolism," *Bibliothèque d'Humanisme et Renaissance* 18 (1956): 222–39; John R. Spencer, "*Ut Rhetorica Pictura:* A Study in Quattrocento Theory of Painting," *Journal of the Warburg and Courtauld Institutes* 20 (1957): 26–44; Walter Sutton, "The Literary Image and the Reader: A Consideration of the Theory of Spatial Form," *Journal of Aesthetics and Art Criticism* 16 (1957–58): 112–23; Jean H. Hagstrum, *The Sister Arts: The Tradition of Literary Pictorialism and English Poetry from Dryden to Gray* (Chicago: University of Chicago Press, 1958), esp. chap. 3; Ong, "From Allegory to Diagram in the Renaissance Mind: A Study in the Significance of the Allegorical Tableau," *Journal of Aesthetics and Art Criticism* 17 (1958–59): 423–40; Robert J. Clements, *The Peregrine Muse: Studies in Comparative Renaissance Literature* (Chapel Hill: University of North Carolina Press, 1959), esp. chap. 1; Clements, *Picta Poesis: Literary and Humanistic Theory in Renaissance Emblem Books* (Rome: Storia e Letteratura, 1960); Mark W. Roskill, ed. and trans., *Dolce's "Aretino" and Venetian Art Theory of the Cinquecento* (New York: New York University Press, 1968); Murray Krieger, "*Ekphrasis* and the Still Movement of Poetry; or, *Laokoön* Revisited," *Perspectives on Poetry,* ed. James L. Calderwood and Harold E. Toliver (New York: Oxford University Press, 1968), 323–48; Carroll W. Westfall, "Painting and the Liberal Arts: Alberti's View," *Journal of the History of Ideas* 30 (1969): 487–506; Mario Praz, *Mnemosyne:*

The Parallel between Literature and the Visual Arts (Princeton: Princeton University Press, 1970); Dean Tolle Mace, "Ut pictura poesis: Dryden, Poussin, and the Parallel of Poetry and Painting in the Seventeenth Century," *Encounters: Essays on Literature and the Visual Arts,* ed. John Dixon Hunt (New York: W. W. Norton, 1971), 58–81; John B. Bender, *Spenser and Literary Pictorialism* (Princeton: Princeton University Press, 1972); Lucy Gent, *Picture and Poetry 1560–1620: Relations between Literature and the Visual Arts in the English Renaissance* (Leamington Spa: Hall, 1981); Norman K. Farmer, Jr., *Poets and the Visual Arts in Renaissance England* (Austin: University of Texas Press, 1984); and Mason Tung, "Spenser's 'Emblematic' Imagery: A Study in Emblematics," *Spenser Studies* 5 (1984): 185–207.

137. See, for example, Michel Benamou, "Wallace Stevens: Some Relations between Poetry and Painting," *Comparative Literature* 11 (1959): 47–60.

138. On shaped poems, see Puttenham 91–101; Margaret Church, "The First English Pattern Poems," *PMLA* 61 (1946): 636–50; A. L. Korn, "Puttenham and the Oriental Pattern-Poem," *Comparative Literature* 6 (1954): 289–303; Hollander, *Vision and Resonance* 252–68; and Elizabeth Cook, "Figured Poetry," *Journal of the Warburg and Courtauld Institutes* 42 (1979): 1–15. See also John Sparrow, *Visible Words: A Study of Inscriptions in and as Books and Works of Art* (Cambridge: Cambridge University Press, 1969), 140–44. For additional bibliography, see Brogan 463–68.

139. For an anthology of shaped poems in several languages and periods, see Dick Higgins, *George Herbert's Pattern Poems: In Their Tradition* (West Glover, VT: Unpublished Editions, 1977). For a selection of shaped poems in Latin, see the volume of "tears" for Sidney, *Exequiae illustrissimi equitis, D. Philippi Sidnaei,* ed. William Gager (Oxford, 1587), C2^v, E4, E4^v, G4 [STC 22551]; for a shaped poem in English with theoretical explanation, see Thomas Watson, *The Hekatompathia* [1582], ed. S. K. Heninger, Jr. (Gainesville, FL: Scholars' Facsimiles and Reprints, 1964), 94–95.

140. See Nina S. Hellerstein, "Paul Claudel and Guillaume Apollinaire as Visual Poets: *Idéogrammes occidentaux* and *Calligrammes,*" *Visible Language* 11 (1977): 245–70; and Willard Bohn, "Circular Poem-Paintings by Apollinaire and Carrà," *Comparative Literature* 31 (1979): 246–71. Ferdinand de Saussure provided theoretical underpinning for these poets: "The signs comprising a language are not abstractions, but real objects" (*Course in General Linguistics,* trans. Roy Harris [London: Gerald Duckworth, 1983], 101).

141. See W. K. Wimsatt, Jr., "In Search of Verbal Mimesis," *Day of the Leopards* (New Haven: Yale University Press, 1976), 57–73.

142. For an illuminating study of Williams's alliance with avant-garde painters, see Bram Dijkstra, *The Hieroglyphics of a New Speech: Cubism, Stieglitz, and the Early Poetry of William Carlos Williams* (Princeton: Princeton University Press, 1969).

143. *Hudson Review* 16 (1963–64) 516.

144. Jonson quotes this passage and paraphrases what follows; cf. *Timber* 8:610.

145. The locus classicus of the actual phrase *mentis oculi* is, I believe, Cicero, *De oratore* 3.163; cf. *Orator* 29.

146. For definitions and examples of these terms, see Lee A. Sonnino, *A Handbook to Sixteenth-Century Rhetoric* (London: Routledge and Kegan Paul, 1968). To illustrate one of these terms, typical of all, E.K. in his gloss on Spenser's February eclogue identifies the fable of the oak and brier as an "Icon or Hypotyposis." Henry Peacham offers this definition of the term: "*Hypotiposis,* a discription of persons, things, places, and tymes, and it is, when by a diligent gathering togeather of circumstaunces, we expresse & set forth a thing so plainely, that it seemeth rather paynted in tables, then expressed with wordes, and the hearer shall rather thincke he see it, then heare it" (*The garden of eloquence* [London, 1577], O2). For Peacham's sources in Quintilian and Erasmus, see immediately below.

147. Cf., for example, Joannes Susenbrotus, *Epitome troporum ac schematum et gram-*

maticorum et rhetoricorum (London, 1621), 75–76 [first edition in England: 1562]; see Joseph X. Brennan, "The *Epitome troporum ac schematum* of Joannes Susenbrotus: Text, Translation, and Commentary," diss., University of Illinois, 1953, 83. See also Scaliger, *Poetice* [3.33] 122.

148. Puttenham includes an extended passage which attests to the continued viability of this comparison between rhetoric and painting (138). A century later, Dryden was still espousing it: "Expression, and all that belongs to words, is that in a poem which colouring is in a picture" (*Essays* 2:147). Cf. also Ascham, *Scholemaster* 282–83. Quintilian had devoted a section of his final book to painting and painters and to sculpture and sculptors (12.10.7–9).

149. Cf. Quintilian 4.2.63, 6.2.32, 9.2.40–44; cf. also pseudo-Cicero, *Ad C. Herennium* 4.68.

150. In Renaissance usage it is impossible to extricate the terms ἐνάργεια and ἐνέργεια. Aristotle uses ἐνέργεια (*Rhetoric* 1411b) to characterize a figure of speech that produces a strong quasi-visual image in accord with actuality (his example: "A man has the prime of his life in full bloom"). Quintilian seems to draw some distinction between ἐνέργεια, the forcefulness that makes the orator effective (8.3.89), and ἐνάργεια, the vivid representation of something which activates the mind's eye (8.3.61–62). When Erasmus paraphrases Quintilian, he bases his statement upon the passage on ἐνάργεια although the edition of *De duplici copia verborum, et rerum, commentarii duo* printed at London in 1569 by John Kingston spells the term ἐνέργεια (110). The same is true for the edition printed at Antwerp in 1553 by Johannes Loeus (135). Scaliger uses ἐνέργεια where ἐνάργεια is the proper word, and further confuses the two terms. He gives ἐνέργεια as a synonym for *efficacia* and supplies a rather nondescript definition: "This is the power of speech representing something in an excellent fashion" (Ea est vis orationis repraesentatis rem excellenti modo; *Poetice* [3.27] 116).

By Sidney's time ἐνάργεια and ἐνέργεια had become inextricably combined: see Richard Sherry, *A treatise of schemes and tropes* (London, 1550), E1ᵛ, where "Energia" appears as a marginal gloss for a paragraph defining the term "Enargia"; and cf. Puttenham 142–43. Therefore when Sidney uses *energia* (*Defence* 117.9), the term implies ἐνάργεια as well. See my "'Metaphor' and Sidney's *Defence of Poesie*," *John Donne Journal* 1 (1982): 136–44.

This term has been frequently discussed in modern Sidney criticism, most importantly by Neil L. Rudenstine, *Sidney's Poetic Development* (Cambridge: Harvard University Press, 1967), 149–71; and Lewis Soens, ed., *Sir Philip Sidney's Defense of Poesy* (Lincoln: University of Nebraska Press, 1970), xxvi–xxvii. Despite his valuable insights, however, Rudenstine insists upon distinguishing ἐνέργεια from ἐνάργεια (305 [n. 13]). For a critique of Rudenstine, see Forrest G. Robinson, *The Shape of Things Known: Sidney's "Apology" in Its Philosophical Tradition* (Cambridge: Harvard University Press, 1972), 131–35.

Longinus offers a cogent critique of Aristotelian ἐνέργεια (*On the Sublime* 15.1–11); and although neither Sidney nor Spenser is likely to have been familiar with Longinus, he had a high impact on English letters in the seventeenth century and later. For Dryden's citation of this passage, see "The Author's Apology for Heroic Poetry and Poetic Licence," *Essays* 1:186.

151. *"Copia": Foundations of the Abundant Style*, trans. Betty I. Knott, *Collected Works of Erasmus*, ed. Craig R. Thompson, 10 vols. to date (Toronto: University of Toronto Press, 1974–), 24:577.

152. *Tusculanarum disputationes* 5.39.114. Cicero was later confirmed by Lucian, who called Homer "the best of all painters" (*Icones* 8).

153. *Paragone* 50.

154. Quoted by H. B. Charlton, *Castelvetro's Theory of Poetry* (Manchester: Manchester University Press, 1913), 36.

155. For the importance of *enargeia* in later poetic theory, see Hagstrum 11–12, 29, 34–36, etc.

156. Note the similarity to the definition of *efficacia* given by Scaliger in n. 150 above.

157. *Religio Medici and Other Works*, ed. L. C. Martin (Oxford: Clarendon, 1964), 12.

158. Pictura autem est imago exprimens speciem rei alicuius, quae dum visa fuerit ad recordationem mentem reducit. Pictura autem dicta quasi fictura; est enim imago ficta, non veritas (*Etymologiarum sive Originum libri XX*, ed. W. M. Lindsay, 2 vols. [Oxford: Clarendon, 1962], 19.16.1). The translation is mine.

159. *Artes and sciences* 35.

160. *Artes of curious paintinge* 185.

161. *Poetae graeci principes heroici carminis, & alii nonnulli*, ed. Estienne (Geneva, 1566), 9–10.

162. For a similar sentiment in the seventeenth century, cf. Henry Reynolds, *Mythomystes* (London, 1632), 28–34. In a passage of the *Phaedrus* (275D), Plato compares writing to painting, though to the detriment of both.

163. See George Boas, trans., *The Hieroglyphics of Horapollo* (New York: Pantheon Books, 1950).

164. For an architectural facade (Palladio's S. Francesco della Vigna in Venice) designed as "silent poetry," see Sparrow 41–46.

165. See Elizabeth K. Hill, "What Is an Emblem?" *Journal of Aesthetics and Art Criticism* 29 (1970–71): 261–65.

166. For a ménage à trois involving poetry, painting, and music, see Michael Maier, *Atalanta fugiens* (Oppenheim, 1618). Consider also the court masque, where the three are even more lavishly domiciled.

167. This original use of the epigram is perfectly exemplified in the old *Arcadia* when Philoclea before the arrival of Pyrocles inscribes her vows of chastity in verse upon "a fair white marble stone that should seem had been dedicated in ancient time to the sylvan gods" (109.24–110.12).

168. Cf. Alberti, *On Architecture*, trans. Leoni 169.

169. For the intimate relation between epigram and emblem, see Peter M. Daly, *Literature in the Light of the Emblem* (Toronto: University of Toronto Press, 1979), 9.

170. *Cebes' Tablet*, intro. by Sandra Sider (New York: Renaissance Society, 1979).

171. See George Kurman, "Ecphrasis in Epic Poetry," *Comparative Literature* 26 (1974): 1–13. For outstanding examples in Spenser, see "August" 26–34, "Muiopotmos" 277–336, and *Faerie Queene* 2.12.44–45, 3.1.34–38, 3.11.29–46. Sidney did not employ ekphrasis.

172. See pseudo-Cicero, *Ad C. Herennium* 4.28. Sidney found both the Horatian and the Plutarchan phrases juxtaposed in Estienne's preface to *Poetae graeci* (10). But they were to be found everywhere.

173. This is the same Simonides who is credited with having invented the art of memory, the fourth division of classical rhetoric: cf. Cicero, *De oratore* 2.86; Thomas Wilson fol. 113ᵛ–114; and Frances A. Yates, *The Art of Memory* (London: Routledge and Kegan Paul, 1966), 1–2, 27–29.

174. *The philosophie, commonlie called, the morals*, trans. Holland (London, 1603), 983. Plutarch repeats this dictum in another famous essay, "How the Young Man Should Study Poetry" (18A); cf. also "How To Tell a Flatterer from a Friend" (58B). Hagstrum (58) found no example of this dictum in English before 1586. The earliest that I've found appears in James Sanford's translation of Agrippa printed in 1569: "*Paintinge* is nothing els, but a silente *Poesie, & Poesie* a speakinge Picture" (*Artes and sciences* 35). Cf. also the quotation from Leonardo page 102; Spingarn 270 (n. 1); G. Gregory Smith 1:386 (n. to 158.8); and Aristotle, *Poetics*, ed. Lucas 269–70. With Du Bartas in mind, Gabriel Harvey formulated this dictum in familiar Latin: "Pictura, tacita Poesis. Poesis, loquens

Pictura" (see Eleanor Relle, "Some New Marginalia and Poems of Gabriel Harvey," *Review of English Studies* ns 23 [1972]: 413).

175. Hagstrum is especially helpful in understanding the history and interpretation of this phrase (59–62). For a painstaking reconstruction of what the phrase means in its original position in Horace, see Wesley Trimpi, "The Meaning of Horace's *Ut pictura poesis*," *Journal of the Warburg and Courtauld Institutes* 36 (1973): 1–34.

176. *Horace His Arte of Poetrie, Pistles, and Satyrs Englished,* ed. Peter E. Medine (Delmar, NY: Scholars' Facsimiles and Reprints, 1972), 35.

177. *Boccaccio on Poetry,* trans. Charles G. Osgood (Princeton: Princeton University Press, 1930), 79–80.

178. Commenting on the semantic capacity of dance, Plutarch had also said: "Dancing is . . . silent poetry and poetry articulate dance" (*Table-Talk* 748A).

179. For our purposes, the most systematic and comprehensive investigation of these topics is Theodore Meyer Greene, *The Arts and the Art of Criticism* (Princeton: Princeton University Press, 1940).

180. See pages 149–50. The argument of this paragraph is repeated essentially by Tasso:

> Poetry is nothing other than imitation. But painting, sculpture, and other similar arts also imitate; and hence the necessity of clarifying the differences that separate poetry from the other imitative arts. Clearly they do not differ because of the subjects imitated, since the same subject—the Trojan war or the wanderings of Ulysses—may be taken by painter or poet; it is not then a difference in the actions imitated that makes the arts different, but rather that one uses colours and the other words, either with or without meter. (*Discourses on Heroic Poem* 7)

181. *Renaissance* 136.

182. For studies especially germane to our interest in the epistemology of perceiving concrete poetry, see Mike Weaver, "Concrete Poetry," *Visible Language* 1 (1967): 293–326; Mary Ellen Solt, ed., *Concrete Poetry: A World View* (Bloomington: Indiana University Press, 1970); and Aaron Marcus, "An Introduction to the Visual Syntax of Concrete Poetry," *Visible Language* 8 (1974): 333–55.

183. The bibliography of materials on the separation of the arts is lengthy. Especially helpful, though in different ways, are Lessing, *Laocoön;* Babbitt, *New Laokoon;* Theodore Meyer Greene esp. 35–39, 46–119; Wellek and Warren 125–35; Ulrich Weisstein, *Comparative Literature and Literary Theory: Survey and Introduction,* trans. William Riggan (Bloomington: Indiana University Press, 1968), 150–66; Niklaus R. Schweizer, *The Ut pictura poesis Controversy in Eighteenth-Century England and Germany* (Bern: Lang, 1972); Svetlana and Paul Alpers, *"Ut Pictura Noesis?* Criticism in Literary Studies and Art History," *New Literary History* 3 (1971–72): 437–58; James D. Merriman, "The Parallel of the Arts: Some Misgivings and a Faint Affirmation," *Journal of Aesthetics and Art Criticism* 31 (1972–73): 153–64, 309–21; Judith Dundas, "Illusion and the Poetic Image," *Journal of Aesthetics and Art Criticism* 32 (1973–74): 197–203; Gerard LeCoat, *The Rhetoric of the Arts, 1550–1650* (Bern: Lang, 1975); and Dundas, "Style and the Mind's Eye," *Journal of Aesthetics and Art Criticism* 37 (1978–79): 325–34.

184. See Kingsley Price, "The Performing and the Non-Performing Arts," *Journal of Aesthetics and Art Criticism* 29 (1970–71): 53–62.

185. See Paula Johnson 2.

186. Ficino's commentary on the *Cratylus* is a concise survey of the linguistic discipline in the late fifteenth century, indicating the major sources of linguistic theory; see *Omnia divini Platonis opera,* trans. Marsilio Ficino (Basle, 1546), 302–6. On familiarity with the *Cratylus* and Ficino's commentary in Elizabethan England, see Martha Craig, "The Secret Wit of Spenser's Language," *Elizabethan Poetry: Modern Essays in Criticism,* ed. Paul J. Alpers (New York: Oxford University Press, 1967), 449. The best Renaissance critique of

the *Cratylus* is provided by Jean de Serres (Joannes Serranus) in his monumental Greek and Latin edition of Plato printed by Henri Estienne, *Platonis opera quae extant omnia,* 3 vols. (Geneva, 1578), 1:378–82. See also Louis LeRoy, *Of the interchangeable course, or variety of things in the whole world,* trans. Robert Ashley (London, 1594), fol. 18ᵛ–19. For a short bibliography of other classical writers on language recommended by a humanist, see Pietro Crinito, *De honesta disciplina* et al. (Basle, 1532), 42.

187. Joachim du Bellay is one of the earliest to express this same conviction; see the opening chapter of his *Deffence et illustration de la langue francoyse,* ed. Henri Chamard (Paris: Didier, 1948), 11–15; cf. esp. 13 (n. 2).

188. Cf. Plato, *Theaetetus* 201A–202E; *Phaedrus* 276A.

189. In the *Phaedrus* also, Plato underscores the speciousness of language in order to denigrate rhetoric, and he compares writing to painting as deceptive arts (274C–275E). The cleavage between words and what they signify underlies as well Plato's caustic observation in the *Ion* that being able to recite the *Iliad* does not make one a great general on the battlefield (540D–541E).

190. If the physical scientist began with the assumption that experimental data were unavoidably unreliable—which they are, at least to some degree, as Sidney well knew (see *Defence* 102.16–26)—he could never reach a hypothesis. He would end up with nothing more than (to use the terminology of Barthes) the pleasure of the experiment. The fact that experimental data are unreliable but the scientist uses them anyway suggests the reason why literary analysis cannot be reduced to a science.

191. In the myth of Prometheus also, according to Plato, the earliest men put to immediate use the gift of fire and invented the arts, the first of which was "articulate speech and names" (*Protagoras* 322).

192. *A hyve full of hunnye* (London, 1578), fol. 4.

193. La Primaudaye expounds this biblical passage at great length; see *Second part of French academie* 23–24.

194. *Second part of French academie* 23.

195. *Of occult philosophy* 153. The original Latin version of this influential text appeared at Antwerp in 1531. See also Arnold Williams, *The Common Expositor: An Account of the Commentaries on Genesis 1527–1633* (Chapel Hill: University of North Carolina Press, 1948), 80–81, 228–29.

196. This dual authority from both classical and biblical sources gave license for the persistent practice of literary etymologizing; see Ernst R. Curtius, *European Literature and the Latin Middle Ages,* trans. Willard R. Trask (New York: Pantheon Books, 1953), 405–500. See also Martha Craig 450–51; Frank L. Borchardt, "Etymology in Tradition and in the Northern Renaissance," *Journal of the History of Ideas* 29 (1968): 415–29; and K. K. Ruthven, "The Poet as Etymologist," *Critical Quarterly* 11 (1969): 9–37.

197. Cf. Richard Mulcaster's argument for teaching the language arts:

> We nede not to prove by *Platoes Cratylus* . . . that words be voluntarie [i.e., express volition], and appointed upon cause, seing we have better warrant. For even God himself, who brought the creatures, which he had made, unto that first man, whom he had also made, that he might name them, according to their properties, doth planelie declare by his so doing, what a cunning thing it is to give right names, and how necessarie it is, to know their forces, which be allredie given, bycause the word being knowen, which implyeth the propertie the thing is half known, whose propertie is emplyed.

(*The first part of the elementarie* [London, 1582], 167–68).

198. For a popular treatment of the Tower of Babel, see Pedro Mexia, *The foreste,* trans. Thomas Fortescue (London, 1571), fol. 21–23. For an even better-known account, see Guillaume Saluste du Bartas, "Babylon: The second part of the second of the II.

weeke, " *Divine weeks and workes,* trans. Joshua Sylvester (London, 1633), 120–21, where Nimrod's perfidious speech is reported verbatim in a prosopopoeia. For a seventeenth-century learned account of how all languages derived from Hebrew, see Theophilus Gale, *The court of the gentiles* (Oxford, 1669), 60–102. Behind all these accounts of Babel lies Genesis 10:8–10 and 11:1–9. Cf. also Augustine, *De civitate Dei* 16.4; and *De doctrina Christiana* 2.4–5. For Sidney's awareness of this lore, see *Defence* 119.17–23.

199. The motif of Christ as λόγος drew its greatest sustenance from the Gospel according to St. John 1.1; cf. Augustine, *De doctrina Christiana* 1.13; and Thomas Palfreyman, *The treatise of heavenly philosophie* (London, 1578), 14–15. It was supported also by the thrice-great Hermes: "The Workman made this Universal World, not with his Hands, but his Word" (Hermes Trismegistus, *The divine Pymander,* trans. John Everard [London, 1650], 159); cf. ibid. 16–18.

200. For a statement of the "great providence of God, which appeareth in the framing of the voyce and speach of man, and in the nature and use thereof," see La Primaudaye, *Second part of French academie* 90–91. Cf. also Colish ix–x, 33–35. For the demise of this theory, see Margreta de Grazia, "The Secularization of Language in the Seventeenth Century," *Journal of the History of Ideas* 41 (1980): 319–29.

201. This argument provides the gist of the Preface before Thomas Wilson's *Arte of rhetorique* 9–12.

202. *A woorke concerning the trewnesse of the Christian religion* [1587], trans. Philip Sidney and Arthur Golding, *The Complete Works of Sir Philip Sidney,* ed. Albert Feuillerat, 2d ed., 4 vols. (Cambridge: Cambridge University Press, 1962), 3:266; cf. ibid. 3: 291. Behind Mornay is Agrippa, *Of occult philosophy* 152.

203. Cf., for example, Mornay 3:283. See also John G. Burke, "Hermetism as a Renaissance World View," *The Darker Vision of the Renaissance,* ed. Robert S. Kinsman (Berkeley: University of California Press, 1974), 102–3.

204. A brief theory and history of Renaissance hieroglyphs is offered by an anonymous N.W. in a prefatory letter in Samuel Daniel's translation of Paolo Giovio, *Dialogo dell' imprese militari et amorose* (Lyons, 1574):

> Concerning the arte of *Imprese,* I neede not draw the petigree of it, sith it is knowne that it descended from the auncient *Ægiptians,* and *Chaldeans,* in the Schoole of *Memphis:* who devised meanes before Characters were founde out, to utter their conceiptes by formes of Beastes, Starres, Hearbes, (as you have declared) and these notes were called ἱερογλυφικά à. *sacrae notae.* This Philosophie was increased by *Orus Niliacus,* and *Pythagoras:* & was more plainely revealed by *Clemens, Pausanias, Atheneus:* & in this last age revived by *Pierius Valerian.* But to what end served this? to shadow suerly their purposes and intents by figures. So counsayled *Plato:* So practised the first parents of Philosophie. As by the picture of a Stork they signified Ἀντιπελαργίαν. By a Serpent pollicie. By an olive peace. By a Gote lust: drawing these Characters from the world, as from a volume wherein was written the wonders of nature. Thus was the first foundations layd of *Imprese:* From hence were derived by succession of pregnant wittes *Stemmata* Coates of Armes, *Insignia* Ensignes, and the olde Images which the *Romaines* used as witnesses of their Auncestors, *Emblemes* and *Devises.* Then what was the intent of these Ensignes and *Devises?* What cause can bee pretended for them? What did they import? *Iamblicus* saieth that they were conceiptes, by an externall forme representing an inward purpose.

(Daniel, trans., *The worthy tract of Paulus Jovius, contayning a discourse of rare inventions, both militarie and amorous called imprese* [London, 1585], *5–*5ᵛ); cf. ibid. A1ᵛ–A2. Cf. Pierre L'Anglois, *Discours des hieroglyphes Aegyptiens, emblemes, devises, et armoiries* (Paris, 1583). See also Liselotte Dieckmann, *Hieroglyphics: The History of a Literary Sym-*

bol (St. Louis: Washington University Press, 1970), 1–99; and Don Cameron Allen, *Mysteriously Meant: The Rediscovery of Pagan Symbolism and Allegorical Interpretation in the Renaissance* (Baltimore: Johns Hopkins University Press, 1970), 107–19.

205. *The third volume of the French academie,* trans. R. Dolman (London, 1601), A2. Cf. Ramón Sabunde, *La théologie naturelle,* trans. Michel de Montaigne [preface], *Oeuvres complètes,* by Montaigne, 12 vols. (Paris: Conard, 1924–41), 9:x–xii; and Spenser, "Hymne of Heavenly Beautie" 127–33. For a historical survey of the motif of nature as a book, see Rensselaer W. Lee, *Names on Trees: Ariosto into Art* (Princeton: Princeton University Press, 1977), 3–7; cf. William G. Madsen, *From Shadowy Types to Truth: Studies in Milton's Symbolism* (New Haven: Yale University Press, 1968), 124–27. For the medieval origin of this motif, see Georg Horn, *Historiae philosophiae libri septem* (Leiden, 1655), 333; and Beardsley, *Aesthetics from Greece to Present* 113–14. See also Gordon K. Chalmers, "'That Universal and Publick Manuscript,'" *Virginia Quarterly Review* 26 (1950): 414–30.

206. *The history of the world* (London, 1614), 2.

207. *Religio Medici* 12; cf. ibid. 57.

208. See Gershom G. Scholem, *On the Kabbalah and Its Symbolism,* trans. Ralph Manheim (New York: Schocken Books, 1965), 35–36; and Claude-Gilbert Dubois, *Mythe et langage au seizième siècle* (Bordeaux: Ducros, 1970), 76–81.

209. See Joseph Leon Blau, *The Christian Interpretation of the Cabala in the Renaissance* (New York: Columbia University Press, 1944), 41–49.

210. *Of occult philosophy* 162. A fundamentalist belief in the gist of this quotation persisted until the end of the seventeenth century and culminated in John Wilkins's *Essay towards a real character, and a philosophical language* (London, 1668). For an application of the principle, see A. J. Turner, "Andrew Paschall's Tables of Plants for the Universal Language, 1678," *Bodleian Library Record* 9 (1978): 346–50.

211. *De vulgari eloquentia* 1.3, *Literary Criticism of Dante Alighieri,* ed. and trans. Robert S. Haller (Lincoln: University of Nebraska Press, 1973), 5–6.

212. Admittedly, this is the conservative view of language theory in the Renaissance, coming to it from the medieval perspective. As Colish summarizes: "Medieval thinkers conceded that a word might signify truly, if partially, a really existing thing [i.e., a res or ἰδέα]. According to this theory, a real relation may obtain between the word and the thing, although significance and identity, meaning and being, are by no means to be confused" (4). This, I believe, remained the basic tenet of language theory as long as Christ was held to be the incarnation of God's word. There is a prior and nonsensible knowledge which, with God's help, may be expressible in a verbal system. And just as the verbal disciplines of the trivium persisted out of the Middle Ages and far into the Renaissance, providing the unexamined premises of pedagogy, so also did this conservative theory of language. It permeated the schools, the Church in its numerous ramifications, and the arts—not only verbal discourse, but music and the plastic arts as well. Because signs were assumed to convey meaning, both music and painting were expected to have a semantic (usually verbal) component.

In this century, of course, Saussure also insisted upon the amphibious nature of language, arguing that it is a system of signs each of which comprises a *signifié* and a *signifiant* (cf. Saussure 65–67, 101–2). As Jonathan Culler paraphrases Saussure, "Noises count as language only when they serve to express or communicate ideas" (*Saussure* [Hassocks: Harvester, 1976], 19). The obvious difference between Saussure and the conservative Renaissance view is that language for the modern linguist is merely a set of social conventions rather than some natural or divinely arranged code, so the relation between signifier and what is signified is arbitrary (culturally determined) rather than absolute (divinely or naturally determined); but see also Culler, *Saussure* 19–29.

213. For an excellent discussion of the importance of language in Augustine's theology, what the author calls a "new covenant between speech and knowledge" (20), see Colish, chap. 1.

214. For an opposite opinion in keeping with his skepticism, see Montaigne, *Essais* 1.51.

215. *De officiis* 1.16. As usual, Cicero is thinking in a cultural context, looking for the basis of human society—in the words of his Tudor translator, Nicholas Grimald, "natures principles of neiborhod, and the felowship of man." The passage continues: "The bond whereof is reason [ratio], and speache [oratio], which by teachinge, learning, conferring, reasoning, and judging, winneth one man to an other, & joineth them in a certaine naturall felowship" (*Marcus Tullius Ciceroes three bookes of dueties*, 2d ed. [London, 1558], fol. 23). In this same passage, Cicero makes his famous distinction between humans and brutes on the basis of *ratio et oratio:* humans use speech to express their reason, while brutes cannot. Cf. Quintilian 2.16.11–15.

For the assimilation of this topos to the Platonic tradition, see Jean de Serres's preface to *Phaedrus,* which is given the Latin subtitle *De pulchro,* "On the Beautiful": "The true beauty is Reason, by which man is conjoined with God, Who is the source of goodness. . . . Speech is the palpable agent of reason, as it were, its interpreter. . . . So the true beauty of man is contained in this combination of reason and speech. . . . It is therefore the thesis of this dialogue that the true beauty of man shines forth in reason and speech" (Illa autem vera pulchritudo, est Ratio, qua cum Deo, qui est αὐτόκαλον, homo conjungitur. . . . Rationis autem & σύμβολον & interpres est oratio. . . . Ita & in ratione & in oratione vera illa pulchritudo hominis versatur. . . . Est igitur huius dialogi θέσις, de vera hominis pulchritudine, quae in ratione & oratione elucet; 3:224). Cf. also Serres's preface to *Ion* (1;528–29).

Scaliger with his customary certainty proclaims the Ciceronian assumption that language is a dependable vehicle for meaning: Orationis igitur proprium est significare (*Poetice* [7.2] 347).

For a different theory of language, however, deriving from the rhetorical tradition based upon the Sophists, see Nancy S. Struever, *The Language of History in the Renaissance: Rhetoric and Historical Consciousness in Florentine Humanism* (Princeton: Princeton University Press, 1970), esp. chap. 1. While Struever's book has been widely employed, especially by those like the deconstructionists who wish to emphasize the relativism or instability or contingency of language, it should be remembered that Cicero was a much stronger influence upon the humanists (and therefore the Renaissance) than were the Sophists. Although Struever is helpful in pointing to "the rehabilitation of the Sophists," as she puts it (3), Ciceronian rhetoric assumed fixed values, linguistic norms, and a motivated vocabulary. For Struever on Cicero, see Struever 27–31. For a reasonable advocacy of Struever's position, see Nancy Lindheim, *The Structures of Sidney's* "Arcadia" (Toronto: University of Toronto Press, 1982), esp. 7–9.

Marion Trousdale takes a more moderate position on the nature of language as Renaissance rhetoricians assumed it to be. While arguing for "a disjunction between words and things," she does not suggest that language was considered invalid or even suspect. "Such disjunction," she concludes, "meant that language use was by definition a conscious endeavor and that there was always a recognized gap between the thought or the *res* and the words on the page" (*Shakespeare and the Rhetoricians* [Chapel Hill: University of North Carolina Press, 1982], 24–31). On the inseparability of *verba* and *res,* however, see Cicero, *De oratore* 3.19; cf. also Augustine, *De doctrina Christiana* 1.2, 2.1–4, 4.28.

216. *Of occult philosophy* 463.

217. The rich tradition of *oratio/ratio* in both its humanistic and Christian contexts is encapsulated by La Primaudaye:

> We ought to acknowledge the great nobility and dignity of speech, with which
> God hath indued & honored man above al other creatures. For he hath not given
> it to any of them, but to him only, & by that he hath put a difference betweene
> him & the beasts, as also by reason and understanding, whereof he hath made
> him partaker, & in respect wherof he hath given him speech, which is as naturall
> unto him as reason, which is the spring head thereof, and from whence it proceed-
> eth, as a river from his fountaine.

(*Second part of French academie* 87). Cf. Juan Luis Vives, "De tradendis disciplinis libri
quinque" [1531], *Vives: On Education,* trans. Foster Watson (Cambridge: Cambridge University Press, 1913), 90–92; Thomas Wilson A3–A4^v; Peacham, *Garden of eloquence* A2;
Mornay 3:267–68; Tasso 139–40; and LeRoy fol. 17^v.

218. See, for example, Capriano, chap. 2, "La Poetica esser la suprema & assoluta, &
perchè" (A3^v–B1).

Chapter 4

1. Petrarch, *Phisicke against Fortune* ¶3^v–4.

2. For an overview of Sidney's education, see Roger Howell 125–52.

3. There is no dearth of studies dealing with Plato's theory of art. The one most germane to our interests is James A. Coulter, *The Literary Microcosm: Theories of Interpretation of the Later Neoplatonists* (Leiden: E. J. Brill, 1976), 32–39.

4. For Ficino's summary of the *Timaeus,* see his *Letters* 1:85–88. See also Serres
3:11–15.

5. Cf., for example, *Timaeus* 35A, and *Phaedrus* 246A. Under "Idea" in his *Thesaurus
linguae Romanae & Britannicae* (London, 1578), Thomas Cooper gives several Latin synonyms for the term: *forma, figura, species;* and a definition: "The figure conceyved in
Imagination, as it were a substance perpetuall, being as paterne of al other sorts or kind,
as of one seale procedeth many prints, so of one *Idea* of man proceede many thousandes
of men" (Nnn4).

6. Cf. *Phaedrus* 250B–C.

7. See my *Touches of Sweet Harmony* 160–76.

8. See my *Touches of Sweet Harmony* 210–12, and *Cosmographical Glass* 97–98.

9. Cf. *Laws* 659D–660E. Aristotle picks up this point in his well-known definition of
the tragic hero (*Poetics* 1452b34–53a22).

10. The distinction between ἐικαστική and φανταστική became an important topos of
art theory in the sixteenth century; cf. Serres's preface to *Ion* in Serres 1:528. Sidney
adopts this distinction and appropriates these very terms (*Defence* 104.14–17). For Tasso's
sensitive critique of this passage from *Sophist,* see Tasso 32–33.

11. Cf. Sidney, *Defence* 107.7–17. In *Cratylus* Socrates argues in similar fashion that a
word is an unreliable imitation of what it designates, and therefore the knowledge of things
may not be deduced from their names (439B); cf. *Phaedrus* 274C–277A. Plutarch attempted to heal the breach between philosophy and poetry (page 176). For the status of
the problem in the Renaissance, see Jerrold E. Seigel, *Rhetoric and Philosophy in Renaissance Humanism: The Union of Eloquence and Wisdom, Petrarch to Valla* (Princeton:
Princeton University Press, 1968). For the present stage of the ongoing debate about Book
10 of the *Republic,* see Robert W. Hall, "Plato's Theory of Art: A Reassessment," *Journal
of Aesthetics and Art Criticism* 33 (1974–75): 75–82.

12. See my "Sidney and Serranus' *Plato,*" *English Literary Renaissance* 13 (1983):
146–61.

13. Shakespeare closely echoes Socrates in Theseus's famous speech about the poet whose "imagination bodies forth / The forms of things unknown" (*MND* 5.1.2–17).

14. "Plato's Philosophy of Art," *Mind* 34 (1925): 154; reprinted in Collingwood, *Essays in the Philosophy of Art* (Bloomington: Indiana University Press, 1964).

15. For example, *Republic* 377E, 603B; *Laws* 668D–669B; *Cratylus* 424A–425A, 429A–B, 430B–434B; *Phaedrus* 275D–E. For a useful article on Plato's "dialectic of the visual arts," see George K. Plochmann, "Plato, Visual Perception, and Art," *Journal of Aesthetics and Art Criticism* 35 (1976–77): 189–200.

16. For example, *Republic* 373B, 376E–377A, 398C–401A, 601A–B; *Symposium* 205B–C; *Laws* 668A–671A.

17. See, for example, Else xi, 11, 133, 637–38. The choice of an English translation of the *Poetics* is difficult, and none is wholly satisfactory. I quote from the translation in Else's volume, however, because he displays most evidently the many uncertainties, both textual and interpretative, about the language of the treatise. Furthermore, I draw upon his commentary in my discussion of Aristotle.

18. For a summary of the widely divergent scholarly opinion on the relation between Aristotle's *Poetics* and Platonic doctrine, see Sörbom 176–77, 207. For a classic comparison of how Plato and Aristotle use the term *mimesis*, see Richard McKeon, "Literary Criticism and the Concept of Imitation in Antiquity," *Modern Philology* 34 (1936–37): 1–35.

19. But see Butcher 116–20.

20. See Panofsky, *Idea* esp. 83–121.

21. Else neatly discloses the incipient equivocality in this passage:

> There is a potential discrepancy, or at least an ambiguity, between the concepts of the poetic art as "making" and as "imitating." The two terms glance past each other; and this asymmetry is grounded in their history, since ποιεῖν originally referred to the verses or the poem, that is, the thing that the poet actually produces (ποίημα, thing made), while μιμεῖσθαι inherently referred to what was represented in or by the product. The one seems to assign the dominant role to the *poet,* the other to his *object.* (13)

Sidney falls heir to this ambiguity when in the *Defence* he defines the poet as a "maker" (77.32–36); but soon thereafter he repeats the platitude, "Poesy . . . is an art of imitation" (79.35).

22. See Else 37.

23. Sidney refers specifically to this passage: "That imitation whereof poetry is, hath the most conveniency to nature of all other, insomuch that, as Aristotle saith, those things which in themselves are horrible, as cruel battles, unnatural monsters, are made in poetical imitation delightful" (*Defence* 92.24–27). Cf. also *Astrophil and Stella:* "Oft cruell fights well pictured forth do please" (34.4). For Sidney's application of this principle, see Maurice Evans, ed., *The Countess of Pembroke's Arcadia* (Harmondsworth: Penguin Books, 1977), 18–19.

24. Aristotle expands and clarifies this point in *Rhetoric* 1371b4–10.

25. For a variety of opinions about the Aristotelian universal, though all essentially agree, see Butcher 163–84; Else 304–6, 320–22; Sörbom 192–99; Hough 42–44; Baxter Hathaway, *The Age of Criticism: The Late Renaissance in Italy* (Ithaca: Cornell University Press, 1962), 189–97; and John O. Hayden, *Polestar of the Ancients: The Aristotelian Tradition in Classical and English Literary Criticism* (Newark: University of Delaware Press, 1979), 44.

26. See, for example, 1447a8–11, 1450a4–5, 1450a15–b3, 1450b21–23, 1453b1–3.

27. For an important discussion of the original meaning of μῦθος, see Else 242–44.

28. For Coleridge's strong affirmation of this passage, see *Biographia Literaria,* 2 vols. (London, 1817), 2:41–42.

29. It is worthwhile here to recall the etymology of the term "character": < Gr. χαϱάσσειν, "to engrave"—i.e., to mark by a distinctive sign.

30. Francis Bacon considers these two opposing possibilities in *The Advancement of Learning,* ed. Thomas Case (London: Oxford University Press, 1974), 99.

31. For other passages that compare poets to painters in this ability to produce images, see 1448a4–18, 1450a32–34, 1454b8–18, 1460b8–10, 1461b12–14. But cf. Else 25–29.

32. This is the vocabulary of Sidney; see page 257.

33. See pages 96–100, and pages 262–66.

34. Cf. also 1459b23–30. For the effect that Aristotle's endorsement of the marvelous had on Renaissance criticism, see Baxter Hathaway, *Marvels and Commonplaces: Renaissance Literary Criticism* (New York: Random House, 1968), esp. 54–87.

35. During the decade before and the decade after Sidney wrote the *Defence,* Weinberg concludes, "Increasingly, writers see as one of the necessary components of imitation a kind of heightened and vivid portrayal which appeals to the senses rather than to the intellect" (1:633).

36. For a more extended discussion of these three styles, see *Orator* 5–6; cf. also *De oratore* 3.52. In addition, see pseudo-Cicero, *Ad C. Herennium* 4.11–14; Quintilian 12.10.58–67; and Puttenham 152–53.

37. Erit Poetae sic dicere versibus, ut doceat, ut delectet, ut moveat (Antonio Sebastiano Minturno, *De poeta* [Venice, 1559], 102).

38. Enim eo tantum spectandum est, ut spectatores vel admirentur vel percellantur . . . sed & docendi & movendi & delectandi (*Poetice* [3.97] 145).

39. Cf. the relatively late example taken from English criticism: "Men were first withdrawne from a wylde and savadge kinde of life to civility and gentlenes and the right knowledge of humanity by the force of this measurable or tunable speaking" (Webbe 1:227). See also Thomas Wilson A3–A4, and Puttenham 6–7. On the importance of this topos in Renaissance poetic theory, see O. B. Hardison, Jr., "The Orator and the Poet: The Dilemma of Humanist Literature," *Journal of Medieval and Renaissance Studies* 1 (1971): 33–38.

40. See esp. *Pro Archia poeta* 6.

41. See esp. *Orator* 19, 29.

42. See page 123. Cf. also Quintilian 2.16.12–19.

43. Cf. *De inventione* 1.4. A seconding authority for this privileged position of humanity could be found in the book of Genesis, where Adam assumes his lordship over creation by naming the other creatures (see pages 116–17).

44. For a more thorough comparison of poet and orator, see *Orator* 20. Cf. Quintilian 10.1.27–30. Landino greatly extends the comparison of poetry and rhetoric, to the advantage of the former; see *Scritti critici* 1:146.29–147.7. For useful notes on the relations between poetry and rhetoric in the time of Boccaccio, see Osgood 160 [n.25].

45. Cf. *De oratore* 1.5–6, 1.14, 2.2.

46. Quintilian at great length develops Cicero's course of training for the orator/poet (10.2). In Book 1 Quintilian lays out his general program of education.

47. This passage is replicated in the spurious Ciceronian treatise, *Ad C. Herennium* 1.3. On these five divisions of rhetoric, see also Cicero, *De oratore* 1.31. Cicero's treatise entitled the *Orator* is in effect an extended discussion of these divisions of rhetoric, especially *elocutio* or "style." Cicero's rhetoric, at least in gist, was early rendered into English by Thomas Wilson in his *Arte of rhetorique* (1553, and several later editions); see esp. a1–a4.

48. For Cicero's familiarity with and approval of Plato's theory of ideas, see *Orator* 2–3, 29.

49. Cf. Jonson, *Timber* 8:640.

50. Weinberg 1:71–72, 150–55. See also Herrick, *Fusion of Horatian and Aristotelian Criticism.*

51. At the end of his *Discourse of English Poetrie,* Webbe translates the "Cannons or generall cautions of Poetry" that Georgius Fabricius had drawn from the *Ars poetica* (1:290–98).

52. See Medine ix.

53. See Valla KK3; Scaliger, *Poetice* [5.1] 214; Jonson, *Timber* 8:638–39; Castor 64–65. Although Sidney does not cite Horace, he mentions imitation of this sort (*Defence* 112.3–10).

54. Cf. Thomas Wilson fol. 3; Ascham, *Scholemaster* 264ff.; and Gabriel Harvey, *Ciceronianus,* ed. Harold S. Wilson, trans. Clarence A. Forbes (Lincoln: University of Nebraska Press, 1945), passim, e.g. 58.33, 64.13, 68.19, 72.30, 76.26, 78.5, 84.29. Cf. also du Bellay 45–48, 103–7. See also Marvin T. Herrick, *The Poetics of Aristotle in England* (New Haven: Yale University Press, 1930), 18; Harold O. White, *Plagiarism and Imitation during the English Renaissance* (Cambridge: Harvard University Press, 1935), chap. 2; and G. W. Pigman III, "Versions of Imitation in the Renaissance," *Renaissance Quarterly* 33 (1980): 1–32. The definitive study of this sort of imitation, wide ranging and densely argued, is Thomas M. Greene, *The Light in Troy: Imitation and Discovery in Renaissance Poetry* (New Haven: Yale University Press, 1982).

55. See Ralph G. Williams, ed. and trans., *The "De arte poetica" of Marco Girolamo Vida* (New York: Columbia University Press, 1976), esp. xli.

56. See, for example, Quintilian 10.2.1–28.

57. Cf. 14–23, 99–118, 156–78, 240–47.

58. Cf. 83, 324, 407.

59. A full and dependable Renaissance biography of Plutarch is provided by Simon Goulart among the lives added to Plutarch's *Lives of the noble Grecians and Romaines,* trans. Thomas North (London, 1603), 76–98.

60. *The philosophie, commonlie called, the morals,* trans. Holland (London, 1603), 17.

61. Sidney aims to refute this maxim (*Defence* 102.16–103.28). Harington, citing Plutarch, follows Sidney without fully understanding him (2:198–204).

62. See page 105–7.

63. See McKeon 29, and Hagstrum 10–11.

64. Plutarch was popular as a storyteller, and James Sanford published a collection of moral tales under his aegis with the title: *The amorous and tragicall tales of Plutarch whereunto is annexed the hystorie of Cariclea & Theagenes, and the sayings of the Greeke philosophers* (London, 1567) [STC 20072].

65. See J. A. Symonds, *Renaissance in Italy,* 2 vols. (New York: Modern Library, n.d.), 1:484–85. The locus for modern accounts of Landino is Angelo Maria Bandini, *Specimen literaturae florentinae saeculi XV,* 2 vols. (Florence, 1747), which is devoted in large part to the life and writings of Landino. For an abbreviated account of Landino, with bibliography, see Kristeller, ed., *Letters of Ficino* 2:109. For the best supplement to this information, consult William Roscoe, *The Life of Lorenzo de' Medici, Called the Magnificent,* rev. Thomas Roscoe, 9th ed. (London, 1847), 83, 91–92, 241; Michele Barbi, *Della fortuna di Dante nel secolo XVI* (Pisa, 1890), 150–79; Chastel, *Ficin et l'art* 25–26, 193–94; Chastel, *Art et humanisme à Florence au temps de Laurent le Magnifique* (Paris: Presses Universitaires, 1959), passim; Frank J. Fata, "Landino on Dante," diss., Johns Hopkins, 1966, esp. 2–29 (plus a useful bibliography); Thomas H. Stahel, S. J., "Cristoforo Landino's

Allegorization of the *Aeneid:* Books III and IV of the *Camaldolese Disputations*," diss., Johns Hopkins, 1968; and Allen, *Mysteriously Meant* 142–54. Weinberg mislocates Landino by placing him among the Horatian critics and gives him very short shrift (1:79–81). For the proper placement of Landino in the broad spectrum of humanist thought as the "theologia poetica" evolved into the "theologia platonica," see Charles Trinkaus, *In Our Image and Likeness: Humanity and Divinity in Italian Humanist Thought,* 2 vols. (London: Constable, 1970), 2:712–21.

66. For a concise account of the Florentine Academy centering on Ficino, see Paul Oskar Kristeller, "The Platonic Academy of Florence," *Renaissance Thought II: Papers on Humanism and the Arts* (New York: Torchbooks, Harper and Row, 1965), 89–101.

67. Cf., for example, *De civitate Dei* 12.22.

68. Francesco Sansovino assimilated the lavish commentary of Alessandro Vellutello to that of Landino, adding considerable annotation of his own, to produce *Dante con l'espositione di Christoforo Landino, et di Alessandro Vellutello, sopra la sua Comedia dell' Inferno, del Purgatorio, & del Paradiso* (Venice, 1564).

69. For a modern text of this material in the original Italian, see Landino, *Scritti critici e teorici,* ed. Roberto Cardini, 2 vols. (Rome: Bulzoni, 1974), 1:140–48. Citations of Landino in the paragraphs that follow are made to this text by page number and line number. All translations into English are my own.

70. In the editio princeps of Landino's edition of the *Divina commedia* (Florence, 1481), this material appears on [*]8ᵛ–[*]10. In Sansovino's edition printed at Venice in 1578, the one most likely known to Sidney, these essays are printed together as a separate item on b3ᵛ–b5, under the running title, "Laudi della poesia, et de poeti." In the edition printed at Venice in 1564, they are printed together on **3ᵛ–**5, under the same running title.

As an introduction to Book 3 of his *Disputationes Camaldulenses,* Landino offers a digest of views on poets and poetry extracted from these three essays. For a translation into English, see Stahel 40–46.

71. This is Landino's only reference to Aristotle in these essays (except for a reprise of the same point in 142.14–16). It does not indicate knowledge of the *Poetics,* although Landino says: "[Aristotle] valued them [poets] so highly that he wrote two books about the poetic faculty and three about poets" (140.34–141.1). Most likely, Landino picked up this information from Boccaccio, *Genealogia deorum gentilium* 14.8 and 15.8; see Osgood 46, 122. Cf. Aristotle, *Metaphysics* 1000a9–14.

72. Cf. "Democritus," fragment 18, in Kathleen Freeman, trans., *Ancilla to "The Pre-Socratic Philosophers"* (Cambridge: Harvard University Press, 1957), 97.

73. This etymology may be found in Isidore 8.7.3.

74. See pages 130–31. For a sixteenth-century disquisition on this important difference, see Serres 3:5–11.

75. See my *Touches of Sweet Harmony* 71–78.

76. Cf. Kings 6.1–38; 2 Chronicles 3.1–17; Ezekial 41.1–26.

77. Cf. Exodus 25.8–26.37.

78. For a survey of Augustine's influence upon Landino's contemporaries, though not Landino himself, see Paul Oskar Kristeller, "Augustine and the Early Renaissance," *Studies in Renaissance Thought and Letters* (Rome: Storia e Letteratura, 1956), 360–72.

79. *De civitate Dei* 8.9.

80. Cf. *Confessions* 4.12, 11.5.

81. Augustine makes a great deal of this point in *De fide et symbolo,* esp. chaps. 2–3; see "Faith and the Creed," trans. Robert P. Russell, *Treatises on Marriage and Other Subjects,* ed. Roy J. Deferrari, *Fathers of the Church* (New York: Fathers of the Church, 1955), 15:319–20. Cf. *Confessions* 7.9, 11.6–7, 12.20.

82. See Colish chap. 1. This respect for the word, incidentally, did not carry over to stage plays. Augustine was quite strong in his disapproval of the theater, largely because it was given to bawdy comedy (cf. *De civitate Dei* 1.32, 2.8–14; *Confessions* 3.2).

83. For the final and incredibly full development of this tradition (in Hebrew, Arabic, Greek and several other languages as well as Latin), see Kircher 2:27–184.

84. The *De civitate Dei* was one of the earliest printed books and one of those most frequently published in the early years of printing. Sidney probably knew it in the important edition prepared by Juan Luis Vives and first published by Froben at Basle in 1522, reprinted in 1555 and 1570. This edition, with Vives's lengthy and very learned commentary, was translated into English by John Healey, *Of the citie of God* (London, 1610). In reconstructing Augustine's aesthetics, I draw primarily upon the *De civitate Dei* because it was the Augustinian text best known outside the circle of professional theologians.

For a critique of Augustine's aesthetics more broadly based in all his writings, see D. W. Robertson, Jr., *A Preface to Chaucer: Studies in Medieval Perspectives* (Princeton: Princeton University Press, 1962), 52–137. See also Maren-Sofie Røstvig, "*Ars Aeterna:* Renaissance Poetics and Theories of Divine Creation," *Mosaic* 3.2 (1970): 40–61. For a concise account of the epistemology that conditions Augustine's aesthetics, see Robert L. Montgomery, *The Reader's Eye: Studies in Didactic Literary Theory from Dante to Tasso* (Berkeley: University of California Press, 1979), 29–39.

85. "Faith and Creed" 318. Cf. *Confessions* 12.8.

86. This assumption underlies *De civitate Dei;* but see esp. 11.22, 12.7, 14.11, and 22.1. Cf. *Confessions* 7.12. The point is well made by Mornay:

> *Plato, Plotin,* and other great Philosophers of all Sexts, are of opinion that *Evill* is not a thing of itselfe, nor can bee imagined but in the absence of all goodnes, as a deprivation of the good which ought to be naturally in every thing. (3:231)

87. Cf. Mornay 3:226–30.

88. Cf. *Confessions* 13.22.

89. For the exposition of this aesthetics in Augustine's *De musica,* see my *Touches of Sweet Harmony* 388. Cf. *Confessions* 11.26. See also von Simson 21–25. For the mindless cacophony that results when "sweet numbers and melodious measures" are allowed "to runne at libertie," see Spenser, "Teares of Muses" 547–58.

90. See *De civitate Dei* 22.24, quoted page 188.

91. See my "The Semantics of Symmetry in the Arts of the Renaissance," *Hebrew University Studies in Literature and the Arts* 11 (1983): 284–303.

92. The word "ratio" may need a Renaissance gloss. *Ratio* in Latin means "plan or scheme," rather like the blueprint drawing for a house, and implies the use of numbers. Bede, for instance, writing in the wake of Augustine, uses the term to emphasize the formal properties of art: "It should be noted that all art operates by virtue of *ratio*. Music also consists in and is contained in the *ratio* of numbers" (Notandum est, quod omnis ars in ratione continetur. Musica quoque in ratione numerorum consistit atque versatur; "Musica theorica," *Opera,* 8 vols. [Basle, 1563], 1:403). The "ratio" is itself a concept, and therefore immaterial, although it may be reified as an extended and quantified structure. After the rise of empiricism the reified ratio became the norm, so we tend to think of it as a relationship between numbers as quantities. We should distinguish, however, between a proportion and a ratio. A proportion involves quantities; a ratio, in contrast, is an abstracted relationship divorced from actual quantity. For example, the *proportions* 8/6, 12/9, and 16/12 may all be represented by the *ratio* 4/3. A "ratio" is the schema for a thing, instead of the thing itself, as the plot is the schema for a drama instead of the actual presentation of durational scenes.

93. These are what Shakespeare's Lear calls "germains" when he enters deranged in

Act 3 and summons the elements to destroy the world: "Crack nature's moulds, all germains spill at once / That makes ingrateful man" (*Lr.* 3.2.8–9).

94. Augustine here, as in many places, seems to be echoing Plotinus: "The excellence, the power, and the goodness of the intelligible realm is revealed in what is most excellent in the realm of sense, for the realms are linked together. From the one, self-existent, the other eternally draws its existence by participation and to the extent it reproduces the intelligible by imitation" (*Enneads* 4.8.6).

95. Ficino is quite definite on this point:

> Nature has so ordained that he who seeks anything should also delight in its image; but Plato holds it the mark of a dull mind and corrupt state if a man desires no more than the shadows of that ["supernal"] beauty nor looks for anything beyond the form his eyes can see. For he believes that such a man is afflicted with the kind of love that is the companion of wantonness and lust. And he defines as irrational and heedless the love of that pleasure in physical form which is enjoyed by the senses. (*Letters* 1:44–45)

96. *Enneads* 1.6. For this definition of beauty, reference is sometimes made also to Cicero, *Tusculanorum disputationes* 4.13.30–31.

97. Cf. Wittkower, *Architectural Principles* 33.

98. A more sophisticated example is the seven-note tuning system defining the octave in music; see my *Touches of Sweet Harmony* 95–97.

99. Cowley based the poetics for his *Davideis* on this passage from Augustine; see *Poems* 276 (n. 34).

100. The prototype for such a system is the Pythagorean tetrad; see my *Touches of Sweet Harmony* 160–68; and my *Cosmographical Glass* 99–110.

101. Spenser expounds this cosmology when Nature pronounces her final judgment on Mutabilitie (*Faerie Queene* 7.7.58).

102. "It's certain because it's impossible" (*Religio Medici* 9).

103. For this general theory, cf. *De civitate Dei* 7.32. See also Augustine, *De fide rerum quae non videntur* esp. chaps. 3–5. For an interesting argument that the invention of polyphony in music was a similarly polysemous sort of allegorical typology (music actually permits the simultaneous performance of two or more melodies), see Winn 87–91.

104. For Augustine's similar treatment of the story of Paradise, see *De civitate Dei* 13.21.

105. "Urania, or the heavenly Muse," *Devine weekes* (1605) 533. For two other French versions of the *divino furore*, which Sidney may well have known, see Pontus de Tyard, *Solitaire premier, ou, Prose des Muses et de la fureur poétique* (Lyons, 1552); and Pierre de Ronsard, "La Lyre," *Les Oeuvres . . . Texte de 1587*, ed. Isidore Silver, 8 vols. (Abbeville, Somme: Washington University Press, 1966–70), 7:53–65.

106. Cf. Marsilio Ficino, *Théologie Platonicienne de l'immortalité des âmes*, ed. and trans. Raymond Marcel, 3 vols. (Paris: Belles Lettres, 1964–70), 1:154–55.

107. *Saturnalia*, ed. Jakob Willis, 2 vols. (Leipzig: Teubner, 1963), 1.17.7ff.

108. For the identification of the Muses with the planetary spheres, see page 83.

109. Landino unblushingly cribs this essay from a letter written by Ficino to a young poet, Peregrino Agli, in 1457; see *Letters of Ficino* 1:42–48. Ficino himself began ordering his letters about 1470, and they circulated in manuscript before being printed at Venice in 1495. Evidently, Landino knew Ficino's letter in manuscript.

In his seminal Latin translation of Plato's works, Ficino gives each dialogue a subtitle, and he calls the *Ion* "de furore poetico." In his famous preface to this dialogue, Ficino identifies four sorts of divine frenzy: the poetic, from the Muses; the mystic, from Dionysius; the prophetic, from Apollo; and the amorous, from Venus (Ficino, ed. and trans.,

Platonis opera 167). Landino, however, does not seem to know this preface by Ficino; the first edition of Ficino's translation of Plato was not printed until 1484.

For earlier versions of the *furor poeticus,* see Curtius 474–75. For the importance of the divine frenzy in poetic theory of the Pléiade, see Castor 24–36.

110. In this passage Landino may be summarizing Boccaccio, *Genealogia deorum gentilium* 14.8 and 15.8; cf. Osgood 42–47, 121–23.

111. 100.25, 108.24, 110.19, 121.7.

112. Cf. Rudenstine 154–58 and 304 (n. 10); also J. R. Brink, "Philosophical Poetry: The Contrasting Poetics of Sidney and Scaliger," *Explorations in Renaissance Culture* 8–9 (1982–83): 45–53.

113. A sound critical biography is provided by Vernon Hall, Jr., "Life of Julius Caesar Scaliger," *Transactions of the American Philosophical Society* 40 (1950): 85–170.

114. For a concise history of the rediscovery and publication of Aristotle's *Poetics* in the Renaissance, see Clark 70. For the detailed history, see Weinberg 1:349–423. Cf. Hathaway, *Marvels and Commonplaces* 9–26. On the survival of the text from classical times and its transmission to the Western world, see Lucas xxii–xxv.

115. See Lane Cooper, *The Poetics of Aristotle: Its Meaning and Influence* (New York: Longmans, 1927), 100.

116. On this important volume, see Weinberg 1:361–66.

117. See *De expetendis rebus opus* EE6ᵛ, FF1ᵛ.

118. *In libros duos, qui inscribuntur de plantis, Aristotele autore, libri duo* (Paris, 1556); and *Aristotelis historia de animalibus, Julio Caesare Scaligero interprete, cum eiusdem commentariis,* ed. Philippus J. Maussacus (Toulouse, 1619).

119. Frederick M. Padelford, *Select Translations from Scaliger's Poetics* (New York: Holt, Rinehart and Winston, 1905), 8–9. There is no complete translation of Scaliger's *Poetice* in English. A small portion of the total has been rendered by Padelford in the slim volume just cited. Wherever possible, I quote from that translation. For those passages not translated by Padelford, however, I use my own translations, giving in a footnote the original Latin, a reference in brackets to the book and chapter numbers of the *Poetice,* and a reference to the page number of the 1561 edition.

120. Scaliger's choice of words is highly significant: Poetae igitur nomen non à fingendo, ut putarunt, quia fictis uteretur: sed initio à faciendo versu ductum est (*Poetice* [1.2] 3). The word *fictis* is the parsed past participle of *fingere.*

121. Cf. also Scaliger's epilogue addressed to Sylvius at the end of the *Poetice* 364.

122. The phrase in Latin is *aurium pictura,* "a picture for the ears." This is probably, as Padelford has translated it, Scaliger's contrived paraphrase for Plutarch's more common *pictura loquens.*

123. Cf. Sidney, *Defence* 78.1–5. For a broad view of Sidney's debt to this passage, see A. C. Hamilton, "Sidney's Idea of the 'Right Poet,'" *Comparative Literature* 9 (1957): 51–59.

124. Scaliger's word is *condere,* which Padelford has exaggerated by translating "to create."

125. In another passage of the *Poetice,* Scaliger further explains our proclivity for versifying: "Rhythmical utterance seems to have been learned in the field, either through an impulse caught from nature, or through imitation of the songs of little birds, or of the sighing of the trees" (*Translations* 21).

126. Cf. Sidney, *Defence* 74.16–23.

127. Cf. *Defence* 80.3–22. For a redaction of this passage, see Serres 1:529, from which Sidney most likely took his information; see my "Sidney and Serranus' *Plato*" 157–58.

128. Cf. Herrick, *Horatian and Aristotelian Criticism* 34–38.

129. The quotations in the next several paragraphs come from the following passage of

Scaliger's *Poetice*, which because of its length and difficulty I offer in my translation as well as in the original Latin:

> Now that we have confirmed that poetry consists of two basic parts, substance [materia] and form [forma], we must discuss both of them. Accordingly, what is commonly said by everyone might seem to be true, that the very thing [res] which is written of is the substance of the poem. For they call the subjects and the materials of poetry two sides of the same coin, and not without cause, since the Greeks have said they lie close together. But this is far from the truth. For in the same way that a statue of Caesar is Caesar's image [imago], so also the poem that describes him is his physical representation. But bronze or marble is the substance of the statue, not Caesar. Caesar is the object [objectum], as the philosophers say, and the ultimate referent [finis]. What is more, if we follow Plato, we shall make the opposite judgment, for Plato distributed the order of things in this way. First, there is an absolute and incorruptible form [idea]. In the second place, from that form a corruptible thing [res] may be produced, which is the image of that form. In the third position, Plato puts the picture or literary work [oratio]—they are produced in the same way. Since they are derived from the projected images of the original forms, they are merely the images of appearances [species]. And so, just as an idea provides a form for each thing that exists in our universe, so there must be something to provide the form for each picture, statue, or literary work. I subscribe to this opinion, for it accords with the Aristotelian demonstration by which we understand the design [species] of a bath to be in an architect's mind before he constructs the bath, where the same would be both form and ultimate referent.

> Nunc quum Poesis duabus constet partibus substantialibus, materia & forma: de utraque nobis dicendum est. Igitur quod ab omnibus vulgo jactatum est, fortasse verum videatur: Rem ipsam quae scribitur, Poematis ipsius esse materiam. Sic enim argumenta, & περιοχὰς, & ὑποδέσεις, & materias vocant, neque sine causa, quippe etiam ὑποκείμενα à Graecis dicta sunt. Caeterum à veritate longe absunt. Nam quemadmodum statua Caesaris, est Caesaris imago: ita & poema quod ipsum describet. At statuae materia aes est, aut marmor, non autem Caesar. Caesar autem objectum, ut vocant Philosophi, & finis. Quin potius, si Platonem sequamur, è contrario judicemus. Plato enim rerum ordinem ita digessit. Idean incorruptibilem separatam. Rem ab ea depromptam corruptibilem, quae ipsius Ideae imago existat. Tertio loco picturam aut orationem: eodem enim modo referuntur: & sunt imagines specierum. Quare sicuti Idea erit forma rei nostratis, ita res debuerit haberi pro forma picturae, & statuae, & orationis. A qua sententia neutiquam discedendum censeo. Est enim consentanea eo ipso Aristotelicae demonstrationi: qua intelligimus balnei speciem esse in animo architecti, antequam balneum aedificet, ubi idem sit & forma & finis. ([2.1] 55)

130. For example, "Every speech [oratio] however consists at once of that which is expressed and that which expresses, that is to say of matter [res] and words [verba]" (Quintilian 3.5.1). Cf. Cicero, *De inventione* 1.7, quoted page 166. For background to this commonplace about the two components of oratory, see A. C. Howell, "*Res et verba:* Words and Things," *ELH* 13 (1946): 131–34.

131. The Aristotelian argument is incompatible with Plato's system. For Aristotle, form is imposed upon the content from the outside, a mold imprinting wax; for Plato, form

impregnates content from the inside and literally informs it. For Aristotle, form is quantifiable and palpable from the beginning; for Plato, form gradually emerges into palpability.

132. Quotations in this paragraph are translated from the following passage:

> Orationis autem materia quid aliud sit quam litera, syllaba & dictio? Id est aer, aut membrana, aut mens, in quibus ea sint tanquam in subjecto. Quare in Caesaris statua aes erit materia: in Poesi, dictio. In statua forma exprimens vigorem aut motum, aut statum, aut sessionem, aut eiusmodi: in Poesi eadem omnia in lineamentis ac dispositionibus dictionum. In statua, toga aut arma pro ornamentis atque accessionibus: in Poesi rhythmi, sive numeri, figurae, pigmenta dictionum. Quocirca de Poeseos materia in hoc libro scribendum erit, in tertio de forma, in quarto de ornamentis. ([2.1] 55)

133. Quotations in this paragraph are translated from the following passage:

> Quum igitur Poema, quemadmodum dictum est, imitatio quaedam sit: quatuor quaerenda fuere: primum, quod imitemur: alterum, quare imitemur: tertium, quo imitemur: quartum, quomodo imitemur. Sic enim etiam acutius quam Aristoteles. Atque in primo quidem libro Poetices usum ostendimus, atque eius originem simul & finem: quare imitaremur, ut scilicet humana vita compositior fiat. Quomodo autem imitemur, dicemus libro sequenti. Nam in superiore digesta sunt versuum genera, ac rationes quibus imitaremur. Nunc quid imitandum nobis sit, videamus. ([3.1] 80)

134. Quotations in this paragraph are translated from the following passage, which is continuous with the passage in the preceding footnote:

> Igitur universum negotium nostrum in Res & Verba quum dividatur, verba ipsa & partes sunt & materia orationis, quae iam à nobis explicata est: verborum autem dispositio atque apparatus, qua si forma quaedam, de qua postea dicemus. Res autem ipsae finis sunt orationis, quarum verba notae sunt. Quamobrem ab ipsis rebus formam illam accipiunt, qua hoc ipsum sunt, quod sunt. Iccirco liber hic Idea est à nobis inscriptus, non iccirco quia cum Platonicis eo verser in errore, ut putem à rebus ipsis verba natura sua concreata esse: sed quia res ipsae quales quantaeque sunt, talem tantamque non illae, sed nos efficimus orationem. ([3.1] 80)

135. Numerus est anima poeseos. . . . Nullam sane dicendi genus sine numero est ([4.7] 185).

136. Iudicium igitur duplex adhibendum est: primum, quo optima quaeque seligamus ad imitandum; alterum quo ea, quae à nobis confecta fuerint, quasi peregrina perpendamus, atque etiam exagitemur ([5.1] 214).

137. This quotation and the summarized argument in this paragraph come from the following passage:

> Everything that exists is designated by the term "thing" [res]. Some of these things, however, are primary, while others are images [imagines] of the primary things. An ox, a man, an oak tree—all these are primary things, while pictures and other sorts of expression are images of the primary things. If one makes a sharper and more subtle examination, one will see that some of these images exist entirely by art, though others belong entirely to nature. There are some that are mixed, in which art adds something to nature. Let's give some examples. The imitations [imitationes] which are without material substance exist by art alone, such as the leaps and bounds in tumbling; for these are produced only by the position and movement of the body. Nature provides no concrete material [materia] for them. In contrast, an ape belongs entirely to nature, for it is fashioned in the shape of a man. The mixed imitations are those whose materials are borrowed

from nature. A shape [facies] is imposed upon them, and art makes them her own. This happens in many ways. Some are clear enough, such as pictures, things that are molded, objects of marble, things cast in metal. Others are less clear to the general public, but are not hidden to the wise. For if the horse was produced by nature for bearing burdens, threshers imitate the horse when lines of them carry straw to the hay-lofts. Moreover, the house appears to be a sort of imitation [imago] of the cave. When the first mortals had noticed the empty caverns, they made use of the conveniences they offered; first they excavated rock for themselves, but soon they thought of assembled structures. Evidently, imitation is the most important feature of the arts. Cork shoes came from the happy use of bark after shoemakers had observed the protection afforded by the hoofs of animals. The cork was used to make rough boots and sandals, though after shoemakers acquired more skill, they improved the appearance of their product. The shoemaker's art produced also coverings for the head. Both the threads and knottings of weaving were developed from the work of spiders.

Omne quod est, Rei appellatione demonstratur. At harum rerum quaedam primariae sunt, quaedam illarum sunt imagines. Primariae bos, homo, quercus: horum imagines, picturae aut aliusmodi expressiones. Subtilius atque acrius intuenti, harum imaginum aliae sunt ab arte tota: alias totas sibi Natura vindicat: nonnullae mistae sunt, in quibus ars addidit aliquid Naturae. Exempli gratia, quae imitationes sunt immateriales, eae solae constant arte: veluti saltationes, quoniam solo corporis habitu motuque conficiuntur. His nullam suppeditat Natura materiam: simia tota est in Naturae censu, hominis enim ibi efficta forma est. Mistae vero sunt: quarum materias à Natura mutuatas, imposita facie quapiam, suas facit ars. Hoc multis ad eo modis fit. Ac quaedam sane manifestae sunt, ut pictura, plastae, marmoraria, fusoria. Quaedam vulgo obscuriora, non tamen latuere sapientes. Nam si equus ad gestationem fuit à Natura comparatus, equum profecto trituratores imitantur, ubi phalangibus paleas gerunt ad foenilia. Quin etiam domus imago quaepiam videtur antri. Vacuas natura specus ubi primi mortales animadvertissent, earumque commoditatibus usi essent: principio ipsi quoque rupes excavarunt sibi: mox etiam contignationes excogitarunt. Maxima ergo artium pars imitatio est; quippe etiam Cerdonica ex corticum fortuiti utilitatibus, spectatis in animalium genere munimentis ungularum, sese comparavit ad perones & carbatinas conficiendas: quarum rudimentis adjunxerunt facies elegantiores post ingenia commodiora. Sutrina quoque frontium expressit operimenta. Textrina ab aranearum operis tum fila, tum interconnexiones meditata est. ([7.2] 346)

138. The quotations and summarized argument in this paragraph come from the following passage, which is continuous with the passage quoted in the preceding footnote:

Caeterum huiuscemodi inventorum rationes alibi tractandae sunt. Quod vero ad Rem pertinet: illud imprimis considerandum, omnem imitationem cuiuspiam finis causa institui. Nanque honoris ergo statuae positae sunt ab antiquis ad eorum memoriam qui praeclare gessissent rem: ut talibus exemplis ipsi quoque posteri ad paria edenda facinora inflammarentur. Nulla igitur imitatio propter se. Nempe ars omnis extra se prospectat quod alicui conducibile sit. Non enim ensis sui causa fabricatus est, sed propter domini tuitionem. ([7.2] 346)

139. His ita constitutis, satis patet omnem sermonem nostrum nihil aliud esse quam imaginem. Rerum nanque sunt notiones ipsa nomina ([7.2] 346). This passage is continuous with the passages in the last two footnotes.

140. Quotations in this paragraph are translated from this passage:

Verba igitur nuda ac singularia significant hoc, id est, quod quidque est: ut homi-
nem aut album. Composita vero significant sic: ut homo albus. Quarum igitur artium instrumentum oratio est, eae omnes imitatione constituuntur. At imitatio non
uno modo: quando ne res quidem. Alia nanque est simplex designatio, ut Æneas
pugnat: alia modos addit atque circunstantias. Verbi gratia: Ense, armatus, in
equo, iratus. Iam hic est pugnantis etiam facies, non solum actio. Ita adjunctae
circunstantiae, loci, affectus, occasionis; temporis, orationis, eventus, pleniorem
adhuc atque torosiorem efficiunt imitationem: qua oritur, praeter aequabilitatem
atque tenuitatem delineationis, umbra, lux, recessus, partium promotio, vigor, efficacia. Haec igitur omnia quum poetae opera effingantur. ([7.2] 347)

141. Eius finem totum fecit Aristoteles imitationem, quam omnium animantium soli
homini attribuit tanquam peculiarem. Eiusmodi vero sententiam quum semel positam,
saepe repetitam perpetuo foueret: in duas nos abduxit absurditates. Altera est, ubi non
solum poesim in genere: sed ipsam quoque speciem Epopoeiam communem fecit & So-
phronis mimis, & Alexamenis Teii dialogis, soluta conscriptis oratione, de Philosophia. Altera, quum ait, Herodoti historiam, si pedum legibus astringatur, nihilo secius historiam
futuram. Quorum primum adeo est absurdum, ut ἔπος fecerit genus solutae orationis. De
historia vero haud ita est. Erit enim non historia, sed poesis historica ([7.2] 347). Cf. Aristotle, *Poetics* 1447b9–23.

142. Propterea quod non est poetices finis, imitatio: sed doctrina jucunda, qua mores
animorum deducantur ad rectam rationem: ut ex iis consequatur homo perfectam acti-
onem, quae nominatur Beatitudo ([7.2] 347).

143. Quod si sola imitatio poeseos finis est: si quicunque imitatur, is poeta est ([7.2]
347).

144. Etiam in mercatu erit institor poeta, quum Heri iussa suis verbis explicabit. Prae-
terea Epicus, ubi introducet, poeta erit. Ubi loquetur ipse, non erit. Simul Ilias & poema
erit ex personis fictis: ex Homeri persona, non erit ([7.2] 347).

145. Nam quod poetae nomine defraudat Empedoclem: minus recte fit ([7.2] 347). Cf.
Aristotle, *Poetics* 1447b17–21.

146. Poetae finem esse, docere cum delectatione ([7.2] 347).

147. Poesim vero esse politiae partem ([7.2] 347).

148. Orationis igitur proprium est significare ([7.2] 347).

149. Non ab imitatione: non enim omne poema imitatio: non, qui imitatur, omnis est
poeta. Non à fictione ac mendacio: non enim mentitur poesis, aut quae mentitur, mentitur
semper. Esset ergo poesis eadem, & non poesis. Denique imitationem esse in omni ser-
mone, quia verba sint imagines rerum. Poetae finem esse, docere cum jucunditate ([7.2]
347).

150. See also Rose Mary Ferraro, *Giudizi critici e criteri estetici nei Poetices libri
septem (1561) di Giulio Cesare Scaligero rispetto alla teoria letteraria del Rinascimento*
(Chapel Hill: University of North Carolina Press, 1971), esp. 35–42.

Chapter 5

1. Jonson, *Timber* 8:628.

2. Wittgenstein, *Philosophical Investigations* 54ᵉ.

3. In our time the *Defence* has been interpreted in this vein by Jon S. Lawry, *Sidney's
Two "Arcadias:" Pattern and Proceeding* (Ithaca: Cornell University Press, 1972), 1–13. A
new, analytical attitude is exemplified by Andrew D. Weiner, who stresses Sidney's point
that poetry should move the reader to well-doing (*Sir Philip Sidney and the Poetics of
Protestantism* [Minneapolis: University of Minnesota Press, 1978], esp. 34–50); Ronald

Levao, who reads the *Defence* as a witty exercise in learned ignorance ("Sidney's Feigned *Apology*," *PMLA* 94 [1979]: 223–33); D. H. Craig, who separates the Platonic and Aristotelian elements in order to privilege the Aristotelian ("A Hybrid Growth: Sidney's Theory of Poetry in *An Apology for Poetry*," *English Literary Renaissance* 10 [1980]: 183–201); and John C. Ulreich, Jr., who (like me) argues for the intellectual integrity of Sidney's treatise ("'The Poets Only Deliver': Sidney's Conception of *Mimesis*," *Studies in the Literary Imagination* 15.1 [1982]: 67–84).

4. Early references to Sidney's *Defence* include (1) William Temple, "Analysis tractationis de poesi contextae a nobilissimo viro Philippo Sidneio equite aurato," c. 1584 (De L'Isle and Dudley ms. 1095); see also J. P. Thorne, "A Ramistical Commentary on Sidney's *An Apologie for Poetrie*," *Modern Philology* 54 (1956–57): 158–64; and John Webster, ed. and trans., *William Temple's "Analysis" of Sir Philip Sidney's "Apology for Poetry"* (Binghamton, NY: Center for Medieval & Early Renaissance Studies, 1984); (2) Temple, "In obitum illustrissimi Philippi Sydnaei . . . carmen," *Academiae Cantabrigiensis lachrymae tumulo nobilissimi equitis, D. Philippi Sidneii*, ed. Alexander Neville (London, 1587), M1 [line 19]; (3) Gabriel Harvey, *Marginalia*, ed. G. C. Moore Smith (Stratford: Shakespeare Head, 1913), 169–70 [in 1577 Harvey acquired the book in which he has written, but the actual date of the marginalia is indeterminate]; (4) Harington 2:196, 197, 209 and passim; (5) Thomas Churchyard, *A musicall consort of heavenly harmonie . . . called Churchyards charitie* (London, 1595), 27, 43; (6) Meres fol. 276ᵛ, 279; and (7) William Vaughan, *The golden-grove* (London, 1600), fol. Y4ᵛ, Y6. G. Gregory Smith (2:408, 410) also refers several passages in Puttenham to Sidney's *Defence*. Although Spenser in his "Letter of the Authors" appended to *The Faerie Queene* does not mention Sidney's *Defence* by name, it is clear that he was familiar with the treatise because he addresses the main issues that Sidney raises. Echoes of Sidney's *Defence* are audible also in Jonson's *Timber*—e.g., 8:609–10, 635–37.

5. Although these two editions are substantially the same, there are some significant variants and the punctuation differs considerably. They were not set from the same manuscript. Generally, the Ponsonby text should be given preference, since Ponsonby served as the semiofficial printer for the Sidney family: for example, he printed both the 1590 and 1593 *Arcadias*, as well as the 1598 *Arcadia* augmented with the additional works. Furthermore, Ponsonby's text, including punctuation, closely follows the manuscript of the *Defence* owned by Robert Sidney, Philip's younger brother (De L'Isle ms. 1226), commonly known as the Penshurst manuscript. See Duncan-Jones and van Dorsten, eds., *Miscellaneous Prose of Sidney* 66–69. Already by late 1586 Ponsonby felt some allegiance to the Sidney family (or sought to secure their patronage) and acted to prevent the piratical publishing of the *Arcadia* by a competitor (see Ronald A. Rebholz, *The Life of Fulke Greville, First Lord Brooke* [Oxford: Clarendon, 1971], 75–76).

6. *The Countesse of Pembrokes Arcadia: Written by Sir Philip Sidney Knight . . . with sundry new additions* (London: William Ponsonby, 1598).

7. *The Works of the Honourable Sir Philip Sidney*, 3 vols. (London: E. Taylor, A. Bettesworth, E. Curll, W. Mears, R. Gosling, 1724–25). This edition claims on its title page to be the fourteenth, suggesting a continuity with the 1674 edition of *The Countess of Pembrokes Arcadia*, advertised as the thirteenth edition of Sidney's works.

8. *An Apology for Poetry or The Defence of Poesy*, ed. Geoffrey Shepherd (London: Thomas Nelson, 1965); *A Defence of Poetry*, ed. Jan van Dorsten (London: Oxford University Press, 1966); *Sir Philip Sidney's Defense of Poesy*, ed. Lewis Soens (Lincoln: University of Nebraska Press, 1970); and *An Apology for Poetry*, ed. Forrest G. Robinson (Indianapolis: Bobbs-Merrill, 1970). Notice must be taken also of the text printed in *Miscellaneous Prose of Sidney*, ed. Duncan-Jones and van Dorsten 73–121, which is essentially a reprint of van Dorsten's earlier text (1966).

Regrettably, most modern editors conflate the text of the 1595 Ponsonby edition and that of the 1595 Olney edition almost at whim, while changing the punctuation randomly to accord with personal readings. As a result, there is no dependable modern text of Sidney's *Defence*. The text printed by Duncan-Jones and van Dorsten in *Miscellaneous Prose of Sidney* has some claim to being the most reliable because the editors were concerned primarily with textual matters (they chose the 1595 Ponsonby edition as copy text, confirmed by and infrequently emended by the Penshurst manuscript). Even here, however, punctuation is arbitrary, spelling is modernized, capitalization is regularized, and italics are ignored. For caveats, see my "'Metaphor' and Sidney's *Defence*" 122–29. In any case, my references, except where specifically noted, are made to that text, by page and line number.

9. In addition to being frequently reprinted in its entirety, the *Defence* has been excerpted at length by later critics. G. Gregory Smith notes (1:382–83), for example, that "Charles Gildon in his *Complete Art of Poetry* (1718) incorporates long passages without acknowledgment (see Dialogue I, pp. 48–74)."

10. Like most learned men of his day, following the rhetors (cf. Quintilian 10.1.27–36), Sidney recognized several distinct disciplines that utilized the arts of language: history, philosophy, and oratory, as well as poetry (cf. Ascham, *Scholemaster* 283). In the *Defence* Sidney also considers theology and law (84.28–85.4). His differentiation of poetry from both history and philosophy is precise and becomes a prominent tactic in his strategy of defending poetry by exalting it. He never explicitly differentiates poetry from oratory, however, and on one occasion facetiously reprimands himself for confusing the two—"but," he offers by way of mild apology, "both have such an affinity in the wordish consideration, that I think this digression will make my meaning receive the fuller understanding" (119.6–8).

11. Cf. Soens xii–xxii. See also Thomas Wilson fols. 104–5ᵛ; John Rainolds, *Oratio in laudem artis poeticae* [*Circa 1572*], ed. William A. Ringler, Jr., trans. Walter Allen, Jr. (Princeton: Princeton University Press, 1940), esp. 39–41; Willes esp. 51–87. On Rainolds' *Oratio,* see James Binns, "Henry Dethick in Praise of Poetry: The First Appearance in Print of an Elizabethan Treatise," *Library* 5th ser. 30 (1975): 199–216.

12. Cf. *Timber* 8:635, which is clearly a critique of Sidney's *Defence*.

13. See Trapp esp. 13–23. Cf. also Twining 3–43.

14. See Duncan-Jones and van Dorsten, eds., *Miscellaneous Prose of Sidney* 62. See also Malcolm William Wallace, *The Life of Sir Philip Sidney* (Cambridge: Cambridge University Press, 1915), 237–38; and A. C. Hamilton, *Sidney* 107–8. For a judicious review of this argument, see Shepherd 2–3. For the most that can be said about how Sidney's *Defence* relates to Gosson, see Roger Howell 172–74. According to the Spenser-Harvey correspondence, Sidney knew *The schoole of abuse* by October 1579, and "scorned" it (*Spenser: Variorum* 9:6).

15. Richard Willes in 1573 collected the "objections which are urged by the persistent calumniators of the art of poetry" (107); see Willes 93–107.

16. See Nelson, *Fact or Fiction* 56–72; and Lawrence A. Sasek, *The Literary Temper of the English Puritans* (Baton Rouge: Louisiana State University Press, 1961), esp. 57–76, 109–26.

17. Cf. also fols. 62–64, where the evils of "lascivious, unpure and wanton bookes" are anatomized at length and by specific examples. The same sentiments are expressed by Edward Fenton, translator of Pierre Boaistuau's *Certaine secrete wonders of Nature* (London, 1569): "We see in daily experience, with howe great earnestnesse and delight the unlearned sorte runne over the fruitlesse Historie of king *Arthur* and his round table Knights, and what pleasure they take in the trifeling tales of *Gawin* and *Gargantua:* the which bisides that they passe all likelihode of truth, are utterly without either grave precept or good example" (A3–A3ᵛ).

In this climate a poet perforce had need of apology, and often called upon Horace's phrase *utile dulci,* as did Timothy Kendall. In the address to the reader that prefaces his *Flowers of epigrams* (London, 1577—and, incidentally, dedicated to Leicester), Kendall takes pains to dissociate himself "from the opinion of those that deeme Poetrie to bryng nought else, but onely a certaine naked and vaine delectation to the life of man"; and he goes on to "boldly affirme, that no where shalt thou finde profite and pleasure better linked together, than in the worthy woorkes of prudent Poets" (a4–a4ᵛ).

The sort of difficulties an author might encounter are indicated by the dedicatory epistles "to the reverende Divines" and "to al yong Gentlemen" which George Gascoigne felt constrained to place before his *Posies* (London, 1575) ¶2–¶¶4ᵛ. Gascoigne comments, for example: "It is a thing commonly seene, that (nowe adayes) fewe or no things are so well handled, but they shall be carped at by curious Readers, nor almost any thing so well ment, but may bee muche misconstrued" (¶¶2ᵛ). *The posies* are in fact a laundered version of his earlier *Hundreth sundrie flowres* (London, 1573)—in Gascoigne's words, "my Poemes gelded from all filthie phrases, corrected in all erronious places, and beautified with addition of many moral examples" (¶4). The earlier volume had run into difficulty because of certain licentious passages, especially in "The adventures passed by Master F.J."

18. The practice of legitimizing a work by allegorizing it derived ultimately from the hermeneutics of Augustine:

> I must point out the method of making sure whether a passage is literal or figurative. In general, that method is to understand as figurative anything in Holy Scripture which cannot in a literal sense be attributed either to an upright character or to a pure faith. (*De doctrina Christiana* 3.10.14)

Sidney makes an apology for this mode of interpretation (*Defence* 103.6–12). This practice of allegorization had a remarkable persistence; cf. this remark by William Webbe about Ovid:

> The worke of greatest profitte which he wrote was his Booke of *Metamorphosis,* which though it consisted of fayned Fables for the most part, and poeticall inventions, yet beeing moralized according to his meaning, and the trueth of every tale beeing discovered, it is a worke of exceeding wysedome and sounde judgment. (1:238)

Cf. also Thomas Wilson fols. 104–5.

19. *The anatomie of absurditie* (*Elizabethan Critical Essays,* ed. Smith 1:328).

20. Ascham excoriates "bookes of Chevalrie," especially the *Morte d'Arthur,* on exactly these grounds (*Scholemaster* 230–31). E.K. was another who looked askance at the "fine fablers and lowd lyers, such as were the Authors of King Arthure the great" (gloss on "April" 120). Actually, Bishop Alley and his contemporaries are echoing, although in sterner tones, the objections to chivalric tales voiced by More, Erasmus, and Vives, that generation of humanists who shaped English thought during the first half of the sixteenth century; see Robert P. Adams, "Bold Bawdry and Open Manslaughter: The English New Humanist Attack on Medieval Romance," *Huntington Library Quarterly* 23 (1959–60): 33–48. Spenser, rather boldly and surprisingly, defies this bias against the Arthurian material; in his letter to Raleigh appended to *The Faerie Queene* he states specifically, "I chose the historye of king Arthure, as most fitte for the excellency of his person, being made famous by many mens former workes" (*Spenser: Variorum* 1:167). Sidney also defends "Orlando Furioso, or honest King Arthur" (*Defence* 105.35). For Spenser's defence of chivalric romance (on the Platonic grounds that love is an ennobling experience), see *Faerie Queene* 4.proem.1–3.

21. On the status of history as a discipline in the sixteenth century, see F. J. Levy, "Sir Philip Sidney and the Idea of History," *Bibliothèque d'Humanisme et Renaissance* 26 (1964): 608–17; Kenneth Charlton, *Education in Renaissance England* (London: Rout-

ledge and Kegan Paul, 1965), 246–52; and Shepherd 36–42. On the place of reading histories in the education of a ruling elite, see *The institucion of a gentleman,* 2d ed. (London, 1568), G1–H3 [STC 14105].

22. Spenser shared Sidney's view of epic; cf. "Teares of Muses" 457–60. See also Harington 2:209.

23. C. S. Lewis formulates the problem in his own inimitable way with his unique sensibility and breadth of knowledge; see *English Literature in the Sixteenth Century Excluding Drama* (Oxford: Clarendon, 1954), 318–22.

24. In contrast, the hot-headed Nashe does; cf. *Anatomie* 1:330–31.

25. For more examples attesting to the praiseworthiness of poetry, cf. *Defence* 109.6–25, 110.11–25. Cicero's *Pro Archia poeta* (9) provides the topos for this admiration of poets by military leaders.

26. See pages 77–79. See also J. W. H. Atkins, *English Literary Criticism: The Renascence* (London: Methuen, 1947), 102–3.

27. See Ernest Hatch Wilkins, "A General Survey of Renaissance Petrarchism," *Comparative Literature* 2 (1950): 327–42, esp. 336–39; and Germaine Warkentin, "The Meeting of the Muses: Sidney and the Mid-Tudor Poets," *Sir Philip Sidney and the Interpretation of Renaissance Culture: The Poet in His Time and in Ours,* ed. Gary F. Waller and Michael D. Moore (London: Croom Helm, 1984), 17–33.

28. "We grow warm when moved by it . . ." (*Fasti* 6.5–6). This couplet from Ovid was a favorite of literary theorists: cf. Landino, ed., *Divina commedia* (1481), [*]9; Marcantonio Natta, "De poëtis liber," *Opera* (Venice, 1564), fol. 110; Estienne, *Poetae graeci* 4; Willes 98; Serres 1:528; Giovanni Antonio Viperano, *De poetica libri tres* (Antwerp, 1579), 17; and Jonson, *Timber* 8:637.

29. Frequently Sidney's vocabulary reveals a residual commitment to the Augustinian aesthetic of number, weight, and measure. For example, in his strongest support of verse, Sidney argues that the good poet "considers each word, not only (as a man may say) by his most forcible quality, but by his best measured quantity, carrying even in themselves a harmony—without, perchance, number, measure, order, proportion be in our time grown odious" (100.29–33). Cf. 77.5–6, 81.23–24, 82.1–6, 92.7–9, 119.35–120.1. See also my "Sidney and Boethian Music," *Studies in English Literature 1500–1900* 23 (1983): 37–46.

30. Sidney takes another swipe at Plato—this time, his penchant for mystical mathematics—in *Defence* 93.21–23.

31. For a judicious examination of Sidney's attitude toward "divine poetry," see Alan Sinfield, "Sidney and Du Bartas," *Comparative Literature* 27 (1975): 8–20.

32. This classification of poets is not original with Sidney. He took it over from Serres, who in turn had extracted it from Scaliger. See my "Sidney and Serranus' *Plato*" 157–58.

33. See Castor esp. 137–83.

34. See Ringler, ed., *Poems of Sidney* xxxv; and Osborn 53.

35. See Herrick, *Aristotle in England* 13–24. The only consequential reference to *mimesis* in England before Sidney is Ascham's: "The whole doctrine of Comedies and Tragedies, is a perfite *imitation,* or faire livelie painted picture of the life of everie degree of man" (*Scholemaster* 266). Ascham interprets Aristotle to mean that imitation produces a "faire livelie painted picture" of the activities of men from various ranks of society, or perhaps of both good and bad men. Oddly, however, in the next sentence he alludes to Plato, not Aristotle.

36. O. B. Hardison, Jr., makes a point of distinguishing between the Aristotelian and Platonic strains in the *Defence* and goes so far as to conjecture that Sidney composed his treatise in two stages: "The Two Voices of Sidney's *Apology for Poetry,*" *English Literary Renaissance* 2 (1972): 83–99. While I recognize distinct Platonic and Aristotelian attitudes

in the *Defence*, I do not see them as disjunctive. Rather, like Ulreich, I argue that Sidney successfully incorporates both in a systematic poetics.

37. Not all of the topics that Sidney drew from Aristotle will be dealt with in the following discussion. In order to make evident the continuing strand of Aristotelian thought which runs throughout the *Defence*, I therefore list them together here: (1) that poetry is an art of imitation (79.35–36); (2) that poetry is an art of "figuring forth to speak metaphorically" (80.1); (3) that poetry alone among the arts and sciences provides that all-embracing knowledge known as *architectonike*, conjoining both ethics and politics (82.34–83.2); (4) that poetry is more philosophical and serious than history (87.34–88.9); (5) that *praxis* rather than *gnosis* is the aim of teaching (91.13–16); (6) that poetry by imitation can render pleasurable even unpleasant things such as battles and monsters (92.24–27); (7) that comedy presents men worse than the norm, while tragedy presents noble men and results in pity and fear (95.30–96.27); (8) that poetry is a mnemonic aid (101.23–25); (9) that Aristotle wrote the "Art of Poesy" as an act of commendation for poetry (109.16–17); (10) that Aristotle specified a unity of time for the drama (113.9–12); (11) that the tragedian must carefully select and arrange the elements of his story in order to form a plot (114.1–6); (12) that delight differs from laughter, the appropriate response to comedy (116.5–9); (13) that poets should express the passions with "forcibleness or *energia*" (117.8–9); (14) that poets "were the ancient treasurers of the Grecians' divinity," as Aristotle had claimed according to Boccaccio (121.4–6).

For the placement of Sidney in the spacious tradition of Aristotelian poetics, see Hayden 100–117. On Sidney's dependence upon Aristotle for his principles of tragic design, see Donald V. Stump, "Sidney's Concept of Tragedy in the *Apology* and in the *Arcadia*," *Studies in Philology* 79 (1982): 41–61.

For the most strongly argued case against the use of Aristotle's *Poetics* as a touchstone for Sidney's *Defence*, see Lawrence C. Wolfley, "Sidney's Visual-Didactic Poetic: Some Complexities and Limitations," *Journal of Medieval and Renaissance Studies* 6 (1976): 219–22. Much is relevant in this article, but Wolfley errs in thinking that by mimesis Aristotle means the replication of actual occurrence: "For Aristotle, poetry represents recognizable *men* in action. . . . Aristotle's pervasive realism is simply lacking in Sidney" (221).

38. See Herrick, *Horatian and Aristotelian Criticism* 34–38; and Hathaway, *Age of Criticism* 65–80. This debate, of course, troubled Milton and continued into the eighteenth century without subsiding; see, for an academic view, Trapp 19–21.

39. Grammarians identified poetry by its metrics, insisting upon the mechanical distinction between prose and verse. Harington assumes a stance of professed indifference similar to Sidney's:

> Least of all do I purpose to bestow any long time to argue whether *Plato, Zenophon,* and *Erasmus* writing fictions and Dialogues in prose may justly be called Poets, or whether *Lucan* writing a story in verse be an historiographer, or whether Master *Faire* [i.e., Phaer] translating *Virgil,* Master *Golding* translating *Ovids Metamorphosis,* and my selfe in this worke that you see, be any more then versifiers. (2:196)

40. On the tradition for these genres, see Shepherd 163 (n. for 103.10f.). Sidney's list comes most immediately from Serres's preface to his translation of Plato's *Ion;* see my "Sidney and Serranus' *Plato*" 157–58. Ultimately, Sidney is responding to Aristotle's comment that "people of course attach the word 'making' to the kind of verse and speak of 'elegiac poets' ('elegiac-makers'), and of others as 'epic poets' ('epic-verse-makers'), not on the basis of their being 'poets' by virtue of their imitation, but applying the term lump-fashion by reason of their verse" (*Poetics* 1447b13–16).

41. When Sidney actually gets around to analyzing the several "parts, kinds, or species"

of poetry, he covers this list in exactly reverse order (94.33–98.28), but pays attention only to "the matter they deal with," in Aristotelian fashion, and not to "the sorts of verses they liked best to write in."

42. Abraham Fraunce echoes this passage from Sidney and goes even further in suggesting that verse is applied almost as a frivolity to make poetry pleasant:

> Poets (seeking as well to please, as to profite) have well made choyce of verse, yet the making of a verse is no part of Poetrie: otherwise, the sweete and inimitable poeme of *Heliodorus,* should be no Poeme, and every unreasonable rimer should weare a Lawrell garland.

(The third part of the Countesse of Pembrokes Yvychurch [London, 1592], fol. 3ᵛ). Harington also has Sidney in mind when he writes about "the two parts of Poetrie, namely invention or fiction and verse" (2:204). He too says that verse is "as it were the clothing or ornament" of poetry; but more indulgently, he concedes that verse "hath many good uses" (2:206).

43. The reasons for Sidney's rejection of "rhyming and versing" are quite different from those of Ascham and the earlier humanists. Actually, Ascham adheres to the requirement of versification in poetry—that is, of writing lines of determinate length comprising recognizable patterns of long and short syllables. He renounces only rhyme, which had been introduced into Italy at the fall of Rome by "the *Hunnes* and *Gothians,* and other barbarous nations" (*Scholemaster* 291). Ascham follows the neoclassical principle that vernacular poetry should not rhyme because neither Greek nor Latin poetry rhymes. Sidney, however, changes the ground for argument: metrification as well as rhyme are extraneous to poetry because its distinctive feature is the production of images.

44. That Plato was a poet because of his mythmaking was a Renaissance commonplace; see Soens 58 (n. to 6.15). Harington, as he often does, echoes Sidney (2:204).

45. Sidney regularly uses "poetical" in this Aristotelian sense of making a fictive narrative, an imitation. That which is "poetical" must be expressed by fiction; cf. *Defence* 77.17, 80.9, 81.22, 86.10, 88.28 (for this passage be sure to use Ponsonby's 1595 text, D3ᵛ), 89.8, 92.27, 93.1–6, 93.14, 99.16, 107.4, 107.36, 112.29; and *Old Arcadia,* ed. Robertson 46.11. As a further gloss on Sidney's use of "poetical" in the Aristotelian sense of imaging the actions of men, cf. his letter to his brother Robert dated 18 October 1580:

> The Historian makes himselfe a discourser for profite and an Orator, yea a Poet sometimes for ornament. An Orator in making excellent orations e *re nata* which are to be marked, but marked with the note of rhetoricall remembrances; a Poet in painting forth the effects, the motions, the whisperings of the people, which though in disputation one might say were true, yet who will marke them well shall finde them taste of a *poeticall* vaine, and in that kinde are gallantly to be marked, for though perchance they were not so, yet it is enough they might be so (last italics mine).

(Feuillerat, *Works of Sidney* 3:131). Notice also that the essence of being a poet is "*painting* forth the effects, the motions, the whisperings of the people," so that poetry is a speaking picture presenting the actions of men.

E.K. in his gloss on "Aprill" twice uses "poetical" in the sense of "fictional": cf. his gloss on "Syrinx" and on "Calliope." Spenser does not use the word "poetical"—a significant omission, in my view, indicating Spenser's innocence of Aristotelian poetics. Shakespeare seems to be joking about this definition of the term when Touchstone wishes that Audrey were "poetical": since "the truest poetry is the most feigning," if she were "poetical," she would be only feigning her honesty (*AYL* 3.3.15–27). Cf. *TN* 1.5.194–96.

46. Sidney himself vents a scorning humour against rhyming and versing when he turns his gaze on English poets. "Let but most of the verses be put in prose," he chides, "and then ask the meaning, and it will be found that one verse did but beget another." The result is "a confused mass of words, with a tingling sound of rhyme, barely accompanied by

reason" (112.30–34). The criterion for genuine poetry, once again, is a fictive element that can be expressed equally well in prose and meets the standard of reasonableness. That Sidney's early practice did not accord with this preaching is demonstrated by Frank J. Fabry, "Sidney's Poetry and Italian Song-Form," *English Literary Renaissance* 3 (1973): 232–48.

47. Cf. Aristotle, *Rhetoric* 1409b6–9.

48. Sidney's equivocal position here recalls Aristotle's double-talk about metrification in the *Rhetoric*. In a discussion of style which vacillates between what is appropriate for poetry and what for prose, Aristotle pronounces:

> The form of diction should be neither metrical nor without rhythm. If it is metrical, it lacks persuasiveness, for it appears artificial, and at the same time it distracts the reader's attention, since it sets him on the watch for the recurrence of such and such a cadence. . . . If it is without rhythm, it is unlimited, whereas it ought to be limited (but not by metre); for that which is unlimited is unpleasant and unknowable. (1480b24–32)

49. Of course, Sidney was himself an accomplished metrist; cf. Ringler, ed., *Poems of Sidney* lii–lix.

50. See R. W. Ingram, "Words and Music," *Elizabethan Poetry*, ed. John Russell Brown and Bernard Harris (London: Edward Arnold, 1960), 131–49; and Winn chap. 3.

51. See pages 154–55. For the importance of the universal in Italian literary theory, see Hathaway, *Age of Criticism* esp. 129–43, 189–202. Among the Italians, Robortello offers one of the most suggestive critiques of the Aristotelian universal (89–91).

52. For the rapprochement between the Platonic idea and the Aristotelian universal arrived at by human reasoning, cf. Tasso:

> By considering the good in various particular goodnesses, we form the idea of the good, just as Zeuxis formed the idea of the beautiful when he wished to paint Helen in Croton. And this is perhaps the difference between the ideas of natural things in the divine mind and those of artificial things which the human intellect figures to itself: with one the universal exists before, and with the other after the things themselves. (6)

Hathaway comes to the conclusion that "only to a few sixteenth-century writers did universality mean something distinct from the Platonic Idea" (*Marvels and Commonplaces* 49). Ulreich argues, rightly, that Platonic and Aristotelian conceptions of form are "ontologically contrary" rather than "logically contradictory" (as he explains, "'Form realizing matter' and 'matter expressing form' are correlative"), and that "the differences between Aristotle and Plato come to seem far less important than their fundamental affinity" (72–73).

53. In "Hymne of Beautie" Spenser describes how lovers arrive at the idealized image of the mistress by the same process, "drawing out of the object of their eyes, / A more refyned forme, which they present / Unto their mind, voide of all blemishment" (lines 213–15).

54. In the rhetorical tradition also, as a matter of practicality, the universal was preferred to the particular. Cicero explains its advantages: "The orator . . . always removes the discussion, if he can, from particular times and persons, because the discussion can be made broader about a class than about an individual, so that whatever is proved about the class must necessarily be true of the individual" (*Orator* 45).

55. Hathaway details the consternation this problem caused among the Italian critics from Robortello onwards (*Marvels and Commonplaces* 109–32). Samuel Daniel, seeking to protect his *Civile Warres* from the charge of fictitiousness, expressly states: "I versifie the troth; not Poetize" (1.6; *The Civil Wars*, ed. Laurence Michel [New Haven: Yale University Press, 1958], 72).

56. In a tightly argued essay, A. Leigh DeNeef focuses on this concern in Sidney's

poetics and demonstrates how it reveals his ontological and epistemological premises: "Rereading Sidney's *Apology," Journal of Medieval and Renaissance Studies* 10 (1980): 155–91.

57. Sidney was not the first theorist to argue that poet, like painter, must remove the incidentals in the act of universalizing his subject. Cf. Fracastoro:

> While the others [practitioners of the other arts] consider the particular, the poet considers the universal. So the others are like the painter who represents the features and other members of the body as they really are in the object; but the poet is like the painter who does not wish to represent this or that particular man as he is with many defects, but who, having contemplated the universal and supremely beautiful idea of his creator, makes things as they ought to be. (59–60)

To use Sidney's example, the poet "painteth not Lucretia whom he never saw, but painteth the outward beauty of such a virtue"—i.e., the way her inner virtue would manifest itself as beauty to the eye (*Defence* 80.35–81.2). In Shakespeare's *Merchant of Venice*, Bassanio reads Portia's portrait in the leaden casket much as Sidney advises us to read the painter's portrait of Lucrece (3.2.115–29). Cf. Spenser, *Amoretti* 17.

58. For an illuminating account of the context for this charge, see Nelson, *Fact or Fiction* 1–55. For a compelling demonstration of why William Temple demurs from Sidney's refutation of this charge, see Webster 31–33.

59. The meaning of this word "ground-plot" is problematical. It may mean no more than "plot of ground"—that is, a basis for the profitable invention: cf. John Shute, *The first and chief groundes of architecture* (London, 1563), B3. As "ground-plat," however (the spelling of the 1595 Ponsonby text), it may mean something like a diagram or blueprint: cf. Dee d3ᵛ, A4; and Wotton 66. In one passage of the old *Arcadia* (215.3–13), the rudimentary state of Cleophila's scheme to deceive both Gynecia and Basilius is called a "ground plot" and is likened to the outline-sketch a painter draws before filling in the details. Sidney does not use the term in his verse. It appears infrequently, though, in both the old and new *Arcadia:* cf. *Old Arcadia*, ed. Robertson 92.18 and 215.12; and *The Countesse of Pembrokes Arcadia* [1590], ed. Carl Dennis (Kent: Kent State University Press, 1970), fol. 99. Further references to the new *Arcadia* will be made to this edition by folio number, as here.

60. Cf. *Defence* 97.34–98.5.

61. See Marguerite Hearsey, "Sidney's *Defense of Poesy* and Amyot's *Preface* in North's *Plutarch:* A Relationship," *Studies in Philology* 30 (1933): 535–50; and Shepherd 171 (n. for 106.34f.). See also Elizabeth Story Donno, "Old Mouse-eaten Records: History in Sidney's *Apology*," *Studies in Philology* 72 (1975): 275–98.

62. On *enargeia*, see pages 96–97.

63. *Garden of eloquence* A3.

64. Cf., for example, *Defence* 89.9–26; and *Old Arcadia*, ed. Robertson 221.34–35. The etymology of these words is significant: "feign" < L. *fingere*, to make; and "counterfeit" < L. *contra* + *facere*, to make. So etymologically "feign" and "counterfeit" are synonymous, having to do with "making" an image; cf. *Astrophil and Stella* xi.23–25.

The word "counterfeit" did not, as today, necessarily imply a motive of deceit. When Bassanio opens the leaden casket and finds the portrait of Portia, for example, he rapturously proclaims, "Fair Portia's counterfeit" (*MV* 3.2.115). Falstaff, however, plays at length upon the equivocation of "counterfeit," concluding: "To counterfeit dying when a man thereby liveth is to be no counterfeit, but the true and perfect image of life indeed" (*1H4* 5.4.116–18).

65. See William Rossky, "Imagination in the English Renaissance: Psychology and Poetic," *Studies in the Renaissance* 5 (1958): 49–73, esp. 57–62.

66. See page 60. Thomas Cooper in his *Thesaurus* offers the following cogent definitions:

Fingo . . . To make, properly of earth: to fourme: to feine: to counterfeit: to imagine: to devise.

Fictus . . . Made to the likenesse of: feigned: counterfeited. (Eee5ᵛ)

Note that Cooper lists "to feine," "to counterfeit," and "to imagine" as synonyms explaining *fingere*.

67. For a cluttered discussion of this point, see Phillips Salman, "Instruction and Delight in Medieval and Renaissance Criticism," *Renaissance Quarterly* 32 (1979): 303–32.

68. Thomas Cooper provides a definition that charts the vagaries of the word's meaning: "*Imago* . . . An Image: a similitude: a representation of a thing: a likenesse: a counterfeit: a paterne: an example: the preportion: the resemblance" (Ooo1ᵛ).

69. Again, Thomas Cooper is helpful with definitions:

Imagino . . . To make images: to represent or cast the figure of ones image.

Imaginatio . . . An imagination or conceiving in thy minde. (Ooo1ᵛ)

In his usage, Sidney closely interrelates the terms "image," "imagine," and "imagination"; cf., for example, "If this imagining of matters be so fit for the imagination, then must the historian needs surpass, who bringeth you images of true matters" (*Defence* 109.19–22).

70. In this instance I am using the term "metaphor" in its expansive sense, as a figure of thought διάνοια), rather than in its more technical sense as a figure of diction (λέξις). See page 63, and pages 288–90. Agrippa offers a helpful chapter entitled "How we must find out, and examine the Vertues of things by way of similitude" (*Of occult philosophy* 34–36).

71. "Imitation" is etymologically related to "image," as the first syllable of each word indicates.

72. *Of occult philosophy* 152. This passage appears again in Mornay 3:267. Puttenham also echoes it (142–43).

73. *Of occult philosophy* 152.

74. See *Astrophil and Stella* 58.8, where the orator uses his skill to "print his owne lively forme in rudest braine." Cf. also Sidney's comments about Menenius Agrippa's fable of the belly and the rebellious members of the body, which "wrought such effect in the people, as I never read that only words brought forth but then so sudden and so good an alteration" (*Defence* 93.31–33). For the humanist's belief that the will of the rhetor eventuates in the actions of his audience, see Hanna H. Gray, "Renaissance Humanism: The Pursuit of Eloquence," *Journal of the History of Ideas* 24 (1963): 501–7.

75. See *Astrophil and Stella* 58.1–4, and Ringler's commentary (*Poems of Sidney* 477).

76. In the old *Arcadia* Sidney places the terms "imagination" and "the eyes of the mind" in synonymous juxtaposition: the "imagination" (i.e., image) of Philoclea, which Pyrocles bears continually "in the eyes of his mind," fills his fancy with beauty (ed. Robertson 28.4, 14). The collocation of the mind's eye and imagination is again demonstrated in the new *Arcadia*. When Cecropia argues with Philoclea to marry Amphialus, Philoclea only half listens, "for her thoughts had left her eares in that captivitie, and conveied themselves to behold (with such eies as imagination could lend them) the estate of her *Zelmane*" (fol. 262ᵛ).

77. Forrest G. Robinson has reconstructed the tradition of what he calls "visual epistemology" in the Renaissance and has interpreted *The defence of poesie* in this context (*The Shape of Things Known: Sidney's* "Apology" *in Its Philosophical Tradition* [Cambridge: Harvard University Press, 1972]). Where he is interested in the broad analogy between thinking and seeing, however, I am more concerned with the specific way that Sidney proposed to use the arts of language for the production of poetic images.

Richard Rorty has detailed the inhibiting effects of the theory of a mind's eye and the resulting "ocular imagery" in our cultural history (*Philosophy and the Mirror of Nature* [Princeton: Princeton University Press, 1979], esp. 38–58). Rorty associates the notion of a mind's eye with the ability to abstract from phenomena and postulate universals, and therefore, he implies, it allows an accommodation between Platonic ideas and Aristotelian universals:

> In varied forms, running the gamut between neo-Platonic notions of knowledge as a direct connection with (emanation from, reflection of) the Godhead on the one hand, and down-to-earth neo-Aristotelian hylomorphic accounts of abstraction on the other, the soul as immaterial-because-capable-of-contemplating-universals remained the Western philosopher's answer to the question "Why is man unique?" for some two thousand years [i.e., from Plato to Descartes]. (41)

Descartes's redefinition of the word ἰδέα marks the end of this era (46–51).

78. For an invaluably precise scientific account of cognition focusing upon visual perception (including its physics, physiology, and psychology), see A. Mark Smith, "Getting the Big Picture in Perspectivist Optics," *Isis* 72 (1981): 568–89. See also David C. Lindberg, *Theories of Vision from al-Kindi to Kepler* (Chicago: University of Chicago Press, 1976), esp. chap. 7. For an excellent survey of this tradition from Aristotle and Plato through Augustine and Dante to Sidney and Tasso, see Montgomery, *Reader's Eye*. For a helpful article on Dante's familiarity with and adaptation of faculty psychology, see Patrick Boyde, "Perception and the Percipient in *Convivio*, III, 9 and the *Purgatorio*," *Italian Studies* 35 (1980): 19–24. For the literature on faculty psychology, see Salman 305 (n. 4). For the placing of images derived by faculty psychology in their broad philosophical context, see Rosemond Tuve, *Elizabethan and Metaphysical Imagery: Renaissance Poetic and Twentieth-Century Critics* (Chicago: University of Chicago Press, 1947), esp. 396ff.

79. The sixth Song of *Astrophil and Stella* is a debate on which should be given preference, hearing or sight.

80. Like a photon in nuclear physics, a particle which is all energy and no mass.

81. This assumption is the basis for synesthesia. As an example, in the new *Arcadia* when Pyrocles describes his first meal with Philoclea, he reports: "So was my common sense deceived (being chiefly bent to her) that as I dranke the wine, and withall stale a looke on her, me seemed I tasted her deliciousnesse" (fol. 62ᵛ). Seeing and tasting provide interchangeable data.

82. <L. *anima,* soul.

83. For Sidney's overt use of this psychology, especially the relation of common sense to reason, see *Astrophil and Stella* vi.37–54.

84. For a suggestive study of memory as an active faculty in Renaissance culture, particularly in the provision of images, see Yates, *Art of Memory* esp. 105ff. Memory was also one of the five traditional divisions of the rhetorical exercise; see page 166, and cf. pseudo-Cicero, *Ad C. Herennium* 3.28–40, and Quintilian 11.2.1–26.

85. Because of his commitment to a visualized verbal image, Sidney often compares poetry and painting; cf. *Defence* 79.35–80.2, 80.25–81.2, 81.28–29, 81.31–32, 85.22–86.8, 87.25–29, 88.10–23, 95.17–18, 103.9–11, 103.21–23, 104.14–23.

86. Eodem namque modo auris afficitur sonis, vel oculus aspectu (Boethius, "De musica" 1.32, *Patrologia Latina,* ed. J.-P. Migne, 221 vols. (Paris, 1878–90), 63:1194. Cf. Puttenham 85.

87. Interestingly enough, landscape painting—that apparently most naturalistic of genres—began as an attempt to cross the line between the media of painting and poetry. Roger de Piles describes the two dominant styles of landscape painting in terms of two dominant genres of poetry: "The *heroick* and *the pastoral*," corresponding to the high and low styles in rhetoric as Cicero had defined them (see Gombrich, *Art and Illusion* 378–81). At the same time the topographical poem, especially the description of a country seat, came into popularity, attempting to cross the line from the other direction.

88. For the appropriate gloss on this word "poetical," see page 243.

89. For a survey of the disparate ancient tributaries that fed into this tradition, see

Coulter 26–29. For a forceful advocacy of this tradition in Elizabethan London, see Harington 2:201–4. For a provocative study of this tradition, see Michael Murrin, *The Veil of Allegory: Some Notes toward a Theory of Allegorical Rhetoric in the English Renaissance* (Chicago: University of Chicago Press, 1969).

90. As a typical example, see *Aesopi Phrygis Fabulae elegantissimis eiconibus veras animalium species ad vivum adumbrantes* (Lyons, 1570). Richard Rainolde offers "a Fable" as the first illustrative exercise in his *Foundacion of rhetorike* [1563], ed. Francis R. Johnson (New York: Scholars' Facsimiles and Reprints, 1945). He defines the term and points to its pedagogical usefulness: "A fable is a forged tale, containing in it by the colour of a lie, a matter of truthe. The moralle is called that, out of the whiche some godlie precepte, or admonicion to vertue is given, to frame and instruct our maners" (fol. 2ᵛ). Rainolde proceeds to analyze the different sorts of fable, to note "that Poetes firste invented fables, the whiche Oratours also doe use in their perswasions," to offer a brief literary history of the genre, and to provide two examples of compositions based upon a fable. The fable had been privileged in the schools at least since the time of Hermogenes (fl. 200). See also Quintilian 5.11.19–21. On the rhetorical function of the fable in *Astrophil and Stella*, see Germaine Warkentin, "Sidney and the Supple Muse: Compositional Procedures in Some Sonnets of *Astrophil and Stella*," *Studies in the Literary Imagination* 15.1 (1982): 40–41.

91. For a similar defense of beast fables in similar terms, see Thomas Wilson fols. 105ᵛ–6. A marginalium calls attention to the subject matter: "Fables how nedeful they are to teache the ignoraunte." In this same category Sidney would classify "the pretty tales of wolves and sheep" found in pastoral poetry (*Defence* 95.3–4).

For the Plutarchan origin of this quotation, see the opening of "How the Young Man Should Study Poetry." Harington explains:

> *Plutarch*, having written a whole treatise of the praise of *Homers* workes, and another of reading Poets, doth begin this latter with this comparison, that as men that are sickly and have weake stomakes or daintie tastes do many times thinke that flesh most delicate to eate that is not flesh, and those fishes that be not fish, so young men (saith he) do like best that Philosophy that is not Philosophie, or that is not delivered as Philosophie, and such are the pleasant writings of learned Poets, that are the popular Philosophers and the popular divines. (2:198–99)

The more moralizing of the English humanists had always touted fables: cf. Elyot 1:56, 2:398–401; and Ascham, *Toxophilus* 17.

92. Sidney was fond of this jest about beastliness; cf. *Defence* 74.29, 103.4–6, 104.3–4, and *Old Arcadia*, ed. Robertson 31.16–17, 307.4–6, and 408.5–7. For an instance of it in Spenser, see *Faerie Queene* 1.3.44.9.

93. *Timber* 8:618.

94. *Spenser: Variorum* 1:168.

95. W. L. Renwick has the most of theoretical consequence to say about these works; see *Edmund Spenser* (London: Edward Arnold, 1925), 59–61, 140–42. See also Thomas Hyde, "Vision, Poetry, and Authority in Spenser," *English Literary Renaissance* 13 (1983): 127–45.

96. For a similar vision, see *Amoretti* 77, where in a "dreame" the lover/poet sees "a goodly table of pure yvory: / all spred with juncats," which turns out to be his mistress's bosom. In stanza 10 of *Epithalamion*, Spenser paints a similar emblematic picture of the lady; cf. *Amoretti* 15. Petrarch was the authority for such apocalyptic visions in love poetry; cf. *Canzoniere* 323. For Shakespeare's use of the emblematic "vision," see Cleopatra's "dream" of Antony after his death (*Ant.* 5.2.76–100).

97. Puttenham demonstrates the use of "figuratively" as Sidney intended the word: "In that which the Poet speakes or reports of another mans tale or doings, as *Homer* of *Priamus*

or *Ulisses*, he is as the painter or kerver that worke by imitation and representation in a forrein subject, in that he speakes figuratively" (306–7). Cf. E.K.'s gloss to Spenser's "February" 176: ". . . figuratively, and (as they saye) κατ' ἐικασμόν"; cf. also E.K.'s gloss on "February" 215, and "April" 118.

98. A statement by Dante propounding an opposite poetics may elucidate this point. In the *Vita nuova* (25), in his apologia for ascribing to Love the ability to laugh and speak and move about as though it were an animated body, Dante concludes: "If any one should dress his poem in images and rhetorical coloring and then, being asked to strip his poem of such dress in order to reveal its true meaning, would not be able to do so—this would be a veritable cause for shame" (*Dante's "Vita Nuova,"* trans. Mark Musa [Bloomington: Indiana University Press, 1973], 56). Dante subscribes to the rhetorical model of poetry as *res* clothed in *verba,* but with the ontological *situs* of the poem remaining with the "true meaning" which has been incidentally encoded in the verbal system.

Similarly, E.K. analyzes *The Shepheardes Calender* within the coordinates of rhetorical composition. In the dedicatory epistle, he chooses to praise first the new poet's "wittinesse in devising"—that is, his *inventio;* and then "his pithinesse in uttering"—that is, his *elocutio.* And soon E.K. is commending his "seemely simplycitie of handeling his matter, and framing his words" (*Spenser: Variorum* 7:7). Not unexpectedly, E.K. in short order cites Cicero's *De oratore.* In the postscript, E.K. uses the same rhetorical terms to praise also the poems of Harvey, "which in my opinion both for invention and Elocution are very delicate, and superexcellent" (ibid. 7:11).

99. Sidney shared an increasingly common bias against the arid Ciceronianism that privileged *verba* at the expense of *res,* thereby raising style to preeminence over argument. In a letter of advice to his younger brother Robert, Sidney wrote: "So yow can speake and write Latine not barbarously I never require great study in Ciceronianisme the cheife abuse of Oxford." With an old saw in mind, which counselled "If the *res* is firmly in mind, the appropriate *verba* will naturally follow," he continues: Qui dum verba sectantur, res ipsas negligunt (Those who pay too much attention to the words do a disservice to the subject matter itself). The letter is quoted in Feuillerat 3:132. Cf. Rudenstine 131–48.

100. In a sophisticated essay à la Barthes on the rhetoricism of Sidney's style, Michael McCanles carries my proposal one step farther and argues that "the Arcadian style invites the reader to discover the complex logical interaction among the elements of a [rhetorical] figure, and, more important, to formulate for himself the logical rules that govern it" ("Reading Description in Sidney's New *Arcadia:* A Differential Analysis," *University of Toronto Quarterly* 53 [1983–84]: 37).

101. "One can learn to be an orator, but one must be born a poet."

102. I'm using Sidney's vocabulary from the following passage: ". . . these other pleasant faultfinders, who will correct the verb before they understand the noun, and confute others' knowledge before they confirm their own" (*Defence* 100.13–15).

103. Puttenham demonstrates the appropriate meaning of "stuff" as Sidney uses the word. He notes that art produces artifacts that are beyond nature's capacity, and yet the artificer must remain in constant touch with her, "nature alwaies supplying *stuffe*" (304; italics mine).

104. The slippage between the first use of the word "matter" and its second appearance in this quotation is an exact measure of the imaginative poet's achievement. In the first instance, "matter" is a given body of knowledge, a subject matter dictated in advance, which preconditions the conclusions drawn from it. In the second instance, "matter" is a mental construct, similar to the rhetorician's *res* (although devised by the poet rather than found in authorities), which by induction is abstracted from the poet's experience, his "stuff."

105. "The great Cyrus was portrayed by Xenophon not in accord with historical truth,

but as a model of just government" [Cyrus ille a Xenophonte non ad historiae fidem scriptus, sed ad effigiem justi imperii] (Cicero, *Letters to His Brother Quintus* 1.1.23). Xenophon's *Cyropaedia* was inordinately respected and praised by English humanists for the reasons that Sidney echoes: "Xenophon wrote Cyrus lyfe (as Tullie sayth) not to shewe what Cyrus did, but what all maner of princes both in pastimes and ernest matters ought to do" (Ascham, *Toxophilus* 7). Cf. ibid. 36; and Elyot 1:84.

106. For other instances of "empire" used in this verblike way, see *Old Arcadia*, ed. Robertson 246.23 and 256.19. In his commendatory verse for *The Faerie Queene*, Gabriel Harvey gives an example of "empire" used in this active sense of a verbal; he speaks of Elizabeth's ability to govern as her "Empyring spright" (line 35). In *The Faerie Queene* Spenser uses the word "rule" in a synonymous way: Gloriana provides a "mirrour" of Elizabeth's "rule" (3.proem.5.6–9).

107. Sidney uses "absolute" to describe also Thomas More's fiction in the *Utopia* (*Defence* 86.35–87.2).

108. "The Providential Plot of the *Old Arcadia*," *Studies in English Literature 1500–1900* 17 (1977): 57.

109. Perhaps with this passage from Sidney in mind, Dryden explains the mental process by which such hybrids are produced:

> But how are poetical fictions, how are hippocentaurs and chimeras, or how are angels and immaterial substances to be imaged; which, some of them, are things quite out of nature. . . . The answer is easy to the first part of it: the fiction of some beings which are not in nature (second notions, as the logicians call them) has been founded on the conjunction of two natures, which have a real separate being. So hippocentaurs were imaged, by joining the natures of a man and horse together.

("Apology for Heroic Poetry," *Essays* 1:186–87).

110. For the Aristotelian context of this statement, see Shepherd 153 (n. for 99.37ff.).

111. For the necessity of the visual percept in human knowledge, see *Defence* 85.30–86.2.

112. Cf. Augustine, *De civitate Dei* 10.2. In the *Canzoniere* (279.12–14) when Laura after her death appears to Petrarch in a vision, she consoles him by saying, "When I seemed to close my eyes, I opened them on the internal light"; cf. *Canzoniere* 72.1–6.

113. *Second part of French academie* 69.

114. For evidence of this doctrine in *Astrophil and Stella*, see 5.2, 25.8, 71.8, 88.10, 99.1–14, xi.26–30.

115. For the full implications of "poetical," see page 554 [n. 45]. "Merely" in the phrase "merely poetical" should be glossed "entirely," as van Dorsten does (*Defence*, page 189 [n. on 77.17]).

116. Sidney's view of David was common among Protestants. His interpretation of the Psalms accords with the poetics of the psalter set forth by Arthur Golding in his translation of John Calvin's commentary. In his dedicatory epistle to the earl of Oxford, Golding indicates the distinctive rhetorical features of the psalter and explains its extraordinary efficacy in leading readers to godliness:

> The thing that is peculiar to it, is the maner of the handling of the matters wherof it treateth. For whereas other partes of holy writ (whither they be historicall, morall, judiciall, ceremoniall, or propheticall) do commonly set down their treatizes in open and plaine declarations: this parte consistinge of them all, wrappeth up things in types & figures, describing them under borrowed personages, & oftentimes winding in matters by prevention, speaking of thinges too come as if they were past or present, and of things past as if they were in dooing, and every man is made a bewrayer of the secretes of his owne hart [that is, the psalms are prosopopoeiac]. . . . [Those who pray by reading the psalms] doo utterly sequester their

mindes from all earthly imaginations and fleshly conceits, and after a sort forsaking their bodies for the time, do mount uppe above the worlde by faith, and present themselves before the heavenly throne of grace, to seek the unspeakable and inestimable comfort of their soules. Such are the conteints, and suche is the maner or disposition of the ground worke of this booke.

(*The Psalmes of David and others. With M. John Calvins commentaries* [London, 1571], *4ᵛ).

117. For an alternative reading of this passage, see Rudenstine 292 (n. 3).

118. The *prosopopoeia* was a favorite rhetorical figure for Sidney, as for most authors of the Renaissance. According to Quintilian it is an impersonation, a fictitious speech in which the orator purports to express the attitudes of an assumed character in his or her own words (6.1.25; cf. 3.8.49–50, 9.2.29–31). Prosopopoeia was a familiar exercise assigned to schoolboys, and Ovid's *Heroides* were famous examples of it. Quintilian observes that "historical and poetical themes are often set for the sake of practice, such as Priam's speech to Achilles or Sulla's address to the people on his resignation of the dictatorship" (3.8.53).

When Sidney refers to the "long orations put in the mouths of great kings and captains, which it is certain they never pronounced," he is claiming that historians borrow this figure (*Defence* 75.29–31). Spenser, of course, used the term as title for "Mother Hubberds Tale," though more nearly in the sense of "personification," as Erasmus had defined the term (*Copia* 582–85). Puttenham (239) in defining *prosopopoeia* followed Erasmus.

In the rhetorical tradition *prosopopoeia* was closely associated with *mimesis;* see Sherry E3; and Peacham, *Garden of eloquence* O3–4. Cf. Quintilian 9.2.58; and Scaliger, *Poetice* [1.1] 3 and [3.48] 126.

119. Because of crucial punctuation, I quote here from *The defence of poesie* (London: William Ponsonby, 1595), C1ᵛ [STC 22535]. My concern is to keep intact the phrase "figuring forth to speake Metaphorically," and to keep it apart from the phrase "A speaking *Picture*" which immediately follows. My reasons for doing so, as well as both the textual and the interpretative evidence for such a reading, are laid out in my "'Metaphor' and Sidney's *Defence*" 120–49.

120. For Sidney's use of "representing" in this sense, see *Defence* 114.8.

121. See my "'Metaphor' and Sidney's *Defence*."

122. See page 517 (n. 19). E.K. correctly uses the term "metaphor" in this narrow sense in his gloss on "February" 171, "February" 181, "October" 14, and "December" 135.

123. See Marsh H. McCall, Jr., *Ancient Rhetorical Theories of Simile and Comparison* (Cambridge: Harvard University Press, 1969), 257.

124. Cf. also Quintilian 8.6.4–5; Erasmus, *Copia* 335; and Jonson, *Timber* 8:621.

125. See E. M. W. Tillyard, *The Elizabethan World Picture* (London: Chatto and Windus, 1943), esp. 23ff. See also my *Cosmographical Glass* 115–26.

126. George Gascoigne demonstrates the proper usage of the word "metaphorically" as Sidney means it: "For who doubteth but that Poets in their most feyned fables and imaginations, have metaphorically set forth unto us the right rewardes of vertues, and the due punishments for vices?" ("Master F. J.," *A Hundreth Sundrie Flowres*, ed. Charles T. Prouty [Columbia: University of Missouri Press, 1942], 50).

127. For Jacques Derrida's influential critique of Aristotle's definition of "metaphor," see "White Mythology: Metaphor in the Text of Philosophy," *New Literary History* 6 (1974–75): 5–74; for Michel Foucault's equally influential discussion of "similitude" in the sixteenth century, see *The Order of Things: An Archaeology of the Human Sciences* (New York: Vintage, Random House, 1973), 17–30.

128. The reassessment of platonist and neoplatonist elements in Sidney began several decades ago with the overstated case prepared by Irene Samuel, "The Influence of Plato

on Sir Philip Sidney's *Defense of Poesy*," *Modern Language Quarterly* 1 (1940): 383–91. Cf. also Cornell March Dowlin, "Sidney's Two Definitions of Poetry," *Modern Language Quarterly* 3 (1942): 573–81; F. Michael Krouse, "Plato and Sidney's *Defence of Poesie*," *Comparative Literature* 6 (1954): 138–47; John P. McIntyre, S.J., "Sidney's 'Golden World,'" *Comparative Literature* 14 (1962): 356–65; Mark Roberts, "The Pill and the Cherries: Sidney and the Neo-Classical Tradition," *Essays in Criticism* 16 (1966): 22–31; Walter R. Davis, *Idea and Act in Elizabethan Fiction* (Princeton: Princeton University Press, 1969), 29–44; Virginia Riley Hyman, "Sidney's Definition of Poetry," *Studies in English Literature 1500–1900* 10 (1970): 49–62; Morriss Henry Partee, "Sir Philip Sidney and the Renaissance Knowledge of Plato," *English Studies* 51 (1970): 411–24; Partee, "Anti-Platonism in Sidney's 'Defence,'" *English Miscellany* 22 (1971): 7–29; and Dorothy Connell, *Sir Philip Sidney: The Maker's Mind* (Oxford: Clarendon, 1977), 21 (n. 1).

129. Leonardo makes exactly this point, pages 102–3.

130. A passage from one of Cicero's most admired orations may be germane here:

> We have it on the highest and most learned authority that while other arts are matters of science and formula and technique, poetry depends solely upon an inborn faculty, is evoked by a purely mental activity, and is infused with a strange supernal inspiration. Rightly, then, did our great Ennius call poets "holy," for they seem recommended to us by the benign bestowal of God.

(*Pro Archia poeta* 18). More commonly, Sidney's statement is referred to a passage in Scaliger:

> Only poetry . . . is so much superior to the other arts, because they (as we have said) represent things just as they are, providing a veritable picture for the ears. But the poet produces both another nature and even additional events. . . . Indeed, he makes himself into another God.

> Sola poesis . . . tanto quam artes illae excellentius, quo caeterae (ut dicebamus) res ipsas, uti sunt, representant, veluti aurium pictura quadam. At poeta & naturam alteram, & fortunas plures etiam: . . . ac Deum alterum efficit. (*Poetice* [1.1] 3)

131. On this topic La Primaudaye recalled a classical authority: "*Themistocles* compared speech to a rich cloth of tapistrie, figured & set foorth with stories, bicause that both in the one and the other those things that are fashioned and represented are then seene when they are opened and displaied" (*The French academie*, trans. Thomas Bowes [London, 1586], 127).

132. Tasso makes the same point about the exhaustiveness of poetic subject matter, especially as Dante practiced the art:

> Poetic matter then seems vast beyond all others, since it embraces things lofty and lowly, serious and jocular, sad and happy, public and private, unfamiliar and familiar, new and old, national and foreign, sacred and secular, civilized and natural, human and divine, so that its boundaries seem to be not the mountains and seas that divide Italy from Spain, nor Taurus, Atlas, Bactra, Thule, nor south, north, east, or west, but heaven and earth, in fact the highest region of heaven and the deepest region of the heaviest element. Thus Dante, rising from the centre, ascends above all the fixed stars and all the heavenly spheres. (21–22)

133. For the use of "essential" with this meaning, cf. *Old Arcadia*, ed. Robertson 91.32, 134.2, 266.14, and 361.34; new *Arcadia* fol. 98ᵛ.

134. Wolfley gives references to "the major explanations of Sidney's '*Idea* or foreconceite'" (n. 10), and he offers a cogent explanation of his own (224–31). More recently

in a challenging article DeNeef proposes that "fore-conceit" is the "privileged term" in Sidney's poetics ("Rereading Sidney's *Apology*"). Using a linguistic model for the relationship between noun, infinitive, and verbal (e.g., "love," "to love," and "loving"), DeNeef argues that the fore-conceit is the "mediating term" between the Idea and the text. Taking Sidney's example of the *Cyropaedia*, he shows that "'rule' would be the Idea, 'to rule' the fore-conceit, and 'ruling' the textually bodied-forth Cyrus" (168). Cf. also his *Spenser and the Motives of Metaphor* (Durham: Duke University Press, 1982), 5–14.

135. See my *Touches of Sweet Harmony* 293–96.

136. Plutarch records a tale that exemplifies the relationship between "*idea* or fore-conceit" and "the work itself":

> It is reported, that one of *Menanders* familiar friends said unto him upon a time: *Menander*, the Bacchanale feasts are at hand, and hast not thou yet done they comoedy? who returned him this answer: Yes iwis have I, so helpe me the gods, composed it I say, I have: for the matter thereof is laid foorth, and the disposition digested already; there remaineth no more to be done, but onely to set thereto the verses that must go to it. So that you see the poets themselves reputed the things and deeds more necessary and important than words and speech. (*Morals* 984)

137. Herrick concludes, "Poetic imitation is essentially artistic feigning or fiction; it corresponds with Cicero's *inventio*" (*Horatian and Aristotelian Criticism* 34).

138. The word *conceit*, a derivative of "conception," in its original context and literal meaning implies a sexual act between a male form (usually the human soul) and a female mass of matter (usually the human body). Shakespeare's Richard II explains how soul and body interact to *conceive* a thought:

> I have been studying how I may compare
> This prison where I live unto the world;
> And for because the world is populous,
> And here is not a creature but myself,
> I cannot do it; yet I'll hammer it out.
> My brain I'll prove the female to my soul,
> My soul the father, and these two beget
> A generation of still-breeding thoughts;
> And these same thoughts people this little world.
> (5.5.1–9)

Cf. *Lr.* 1.2.57. See also Jay L. Halio, "The Metaphor of Conception and Elizabethan Theories of the Imagination," *Neophilologus* 50 (1966): 454–61; and Robert J. Bauer, "A Phenomenon of Epistemology in the Renaissance," *Journal of the History of Ideas* 31 (1970): 281–88.

139. As pure examples of Gascoigne's virtuosity in this mode, we may look at "five notable devises upon five sundry theames given to him by five sundry Gentlemen in five sundry meeters," as Gascoigne describes these poems in the table of contents of *A hundreth sundrie flowres* (A1ᵛ). In a headpiece to the poems (U2ᵛ), Gascoigne explains that he wrote them as a witty exercise to gain acceptance into a clique of five young gentlemen at Gray's Inn. The poems themselves—on such topoi as *Audaces fortuna iuvat* and *Satis sufficit*—appear U2ᵛ–X3.

140. Sidney cannily demonstrates his own ability to image forth ideas in the remarkable figures of the moral philosopher and the historian that soon appear upon the scene (83.11–84.18).

141. Van Dorsten prints "credulous" here, on the authority of the DeLisle manuscript. Both the Ponsonby and Olney texts agree that the word should be "incredulous," however, and the Norfolk manuscript concurs.

142. I see no need to insist that this interpretation of "second nature" mean the post-

lapsarian world. But see Soens 10 (n. on line 28) and 60 (n. on 9.16); and *Miscellaneous Prose of Sidney,* ed. Duncan-Jones and van Dorsten 190 (n. on 78.22–79.27).

143. Spenser's use of this phrase supplies a helpful gloss; see *Faerie Queene* 4.10.21.9ff.

144. In his informative discussion of this passage, Ulreich arrives at a similar conclusion: "In Sidney's theory, the crucial term, *making,* is an activity of poetic imagination, imitating the creative efficacy of God" (79).

145. See Frank B. Evans, "The Concept of the Fall in Sidney's *Apologie,*" *Renaissance Papers 1969* (Durham, NC: Southeastern Renaissance Conference, 1970), 9–14. Cf. also Hamilton, *Sidney* 113–16.

146. "Preface to *Lyrical Ballads* " [1802] 50.

147. *Joseph Andrews,* ed. Martin C. Battestin (Middletown: Wesleyan University Press, 1967), 189. Thomas Hobbes is a likely intermediary between Sidney and Fielding:

> They that take for Poesie whatsoever is writ in Verse . . . reckon *Empedocles,* and *Lucretius* (naturall Philosophers) for Poets, and the morall precepts of *Phocylides, Theognis,* and the Quatrains of *Pybrach,* and the History of *Lucan,* and others of that kind amongst Poems; bestowing on such Writers for honour the name of Poets, rather then of Historians or Philosophers. But the subject of a Poem is the manners of men, not naturall causes; manners presented, not dictated; and manners feigned (as the name of Poesie imports) not found in men.

(*A discourse upon Gondibert. An heroick poem written by Sir William D'Avenant. With an answer to it by Mr. Hobbes* [Paris, 1650], 122–23).

148. See Alberti, *On Painting,* ed. and trans. John R. Spencer (London: Routledge & Kegan Paul, 1956), 23–26, 70–78; and *On Painting and On Sculpture,* trans. Grayson 13–15. See also my article, "Speaking Pictures: Sidney's Rapprochement between Poetry and Painting," *Sir Philip Sidney and the Interpretation of Renaissance Culture: The Poet in His Time and in Ours,* ed. Gary F. Waller and Michael D. Moore (London: Croom Helm, 1984), 11–13.

149. That Dryden had been reading Sidney in 1664 is attested by his reference to *The defence of poesie* in the epistle dedicatory of *The Rival Ladies* (*Essays* 1:7). In 1672 Dryden alluded to Sidney as "that admirable wit" (*Essays* 1:173), and as late as 1697 he retained familiarity with the *Arcadia* (*Essays* 2:229–30).

150. "Wit" is one of Sidney's favorite words in the *Defence;* cf. 73.5, 74.26, 76.7, 78.30, 79.18, 79.25, 80.32, 82.11, 83.37, 100.4, 103.29, 104.14, 105.19, 108.1, 109.4, 110.7–8, 110.20, 111.32, 114.29, 116.32.

Chapter 6

1. Divides autem universum librum in libellos, naturae imitatione: quae partium partes facit, quibus confiat totius corporis constitutio (Scaliger, *Poetice* [3.96] 144). This comment comes in a chapter on heroic poetry.

2. See my "Sidney and Spenser at Leicester House."

3. For other instances where Sidney uses the word "poetry" in the sense of ποιητική and as a synonym for "fiction," see *Defence* 75.27, 75.34, 79.22, 81.25, 87.3, 90.4, 90.26, 92.24, 100.24. For instances where the word "poesy" is used in a similar way, see 77.21, 86.8, 88.6, 93.6, 103.14, 104.14, 109.20, 114.3

4. What is *not* poetry in *The Shepheardes Calender* is the history, what is actual fact. For example, in "June" when Hobbinol advises Colin Clout to "forsake the soyle, that so doth the bewitch" (line 18), E.K. in his gloss pointedly notes, "This is no poetical fiction, but unfeynedly spoken of the Poete selfe"; and he interprets the passage as Harvey's advice to Spenser, so that he "for his more preferment removing out of the Northparts came

into the South." Presumably, this was the occasion for Spenser's accepting employment with John Young, bishop of Rochester, as the remainder of E.K.'s gloss, with its reference to Kent, strongly suggests. In contrast, of the stanza beginning "I sawe *Calliope* wyth Muses moe" (line 57), E.K. observes, "Thys staffe is full of verie poetical invention." Again, in his gloss on the astrological positioning of the Sun in "July" ("The rampant Lyon hunts he fast, / with Dogge of noysome breath," lines 21–22), E.K. comments: "Thys is Poetically spoken, as if the Sunne did hunt a Lion with one Dogge"; and E.K. explains the meaning of this fiction at considerable length.

5. See Kathrine Koller, "Abraham Fraunce and Edmund Spenser," *ELH* 7 (1940): 108–20.

6. With valuable implications, Walter R. Davis relates *The Shepheardes Calender* to the complex but unified plotting of pastoral romance (*A Map of Arcadia: Sidney's Romance in Its Tradition, Sidney's Arcadia* (New Haven: Yale University Press, 1965), 11.

7. See my *Cosmographical Glass* 110–12.

8. See my *Touches of Sweet Harmony* 309–13.

9. This reading of the *Divina commedia* was already commonplace in the sixteenth century. Tasso reports, "Some indeed contend that the subject of Dante's poem is a contemplation because that voyage of his to Hell and Purgatory has no meaning other than the speculations of his mind" (8).

10. *On the Psalms,* trans. Dame Scholastica Hebgin and Dame Felicitas Corrigan, 2 vols. (Westminster, MD: Newman, 1960), 1:115–16.

11. Cf., albeit cautiously, Maren-Sofie Røstvig, "*The Shepheardes Calender*—A Structural Analysis," *Renaissance and Modern Studies* 13 (1969): 49–75.

12. On the ambiguity in the orthography of the title, which is impossible to maintain in modern spelling, see *Spenser: Variorum* 7:235.

13. Spenser uses the Ovidian phrase "devouring time" in *Amoretti* 58.7; cf. "Ruines of Time" 420, and "Ruines of Rome" 36.

14. Serres 3:16, quoted from Augustine, "De vera religione," *Patrologia Latina,* ed. J.-P. Migne, 221 vols. (Paris, 1878–90), 34:145 (my translation). Henry Peacham expansively echoes this passage from Augustine, connecting it with the God-given reason that sets man above the other creatures and linking it to the *ars dicendi* of orators and poets:

> God of his goodnesse hath poured forth his devine vertue into the minde of man, farre more largely, and much more aboundauntly, then in any other creature upon the face of the whole earth. Whereby he hath made man able, not onelye to governe himselfe, and to live after a most goodly order, but also to subdue the monstrous beastes to his will. By this divyne vertue, & intellective power, man doth seeke, fynde out, and comprehend the causes of thinges, he doth meditate and muse uppon the wonderfull workes of God, he searcheth out the secreates of nature, & clymeth up to the knowledge of Sapience supernaturall, he learneth the cunning reasons of numbers, the Mathematicall demonstrations, the motions of stars, the course & alteration of tymes, the musicall consent of harmonies, & diversity of tunes, he conceiveth trim devises, & is ful of many profitable and pleasant inventions, he seeth what is comely for his dignity, and to what ende he is created, which no other is able to do. And to the end that this soveraign rule of reason might spread abroade her bewtifull branches, & that wisdome might bring forth most plentifully her sweete and pleasaunt fruites, for the common use & utillity of mankind, the Lord God hath joyned to the mind of man speech, which he hath made the instrument of our understanding, & key of conceptions. (*Garden of eloquence* A2)

15. Spenser openly adheres to Augustine's advice about reading the book of nature; cf. "Hymne of Heavenly Beautie" 127–33.

16. See Lily B. Campbell, "The Christian Muse," *Huntington Library Bulletin* 8 (1935): 29–70; Frances M. Malpezzi, "Du Bartas' *L'Uranie,* The Devotional Poet's Handbook," *Allegorica* 8 (1983): 185–98; and John M. Steadman, *Milton's Biblical and Classical Imagery* (Pittsburgh: Duquesne University Press, 1984), 88–120.

17. Palingenius, *The Zodiake of Life,* trans. Barnabe Googe [1576], ed. Rosemond Tuve (New York: Scholars' Facsimiles and Reprints, 1947).

18. See my introduction to Spenser, *The Shepheardes Calender (1579)* (Delmar, NY: Scholars' Facsimiles and Reprints, 1979), v–viii.

19. For a demonstration of how Spenser's use of conflicting genres adds to the sense of totality in *The Shepheardes Calender,* see A. Leigh DeNeef, "The Dialectic of Genres in *The Shepheardes Calender,*" *Renaissance Papers 1975* (Durham, NC: Southeastern Renaissance Conference, 1976), 1–10. See also Michael D. Bristol, "Structural Patterns in Two Elizabethan Pastorals," *Studies in English Literature 1500–1900* 10 (1970): 33–48.

20. The motif of exhaustive variety is confirmed by the metrics of *The Shepheardes Calender.* No poem in English equals it for metrical variety or exactness. Spenser resorts to the same metrical scheme in only two instances, and then for carefully planned effects. First, in "February," "May," and "September" he uses rhymed couplets of a four-stressed line with an indeterminate number of unstressed syllables, the native English meter descended from the alliterative line of the Anglo-Saxons. The crude ballad stanza of "July" similarly belongs to the same family of indigenous verse based upon a four-stressed line. By repeated use of this line with four stresses, Spenser establishes a continuing linkage between "February," "May," "July," and "September," the four satirical eclogues. Second, in both "January" and "December" Spenser uses a six-line stanza rhyming a b a b c c, an artifice to indicate the likeness and therefore the continuity between "December" and "January," between the end and beginning. Otherwise, Spenser employs no less than thirteen different metrical patterns, ranging in complexity and sophistication from the rough tetrameter couplets of "February" to the highly ornate lyric stanzas in the encomium to Elisa in "April" and the dirge for Dido in "November." The metrical variety echoes and images the harmonious plenty of Creation.

21. See John W. Moore, Jr., "Colin Breaks His Pipe: A Reading of the 'January' Eclogue," *English Literary Renaissance* 5 (1975): 3–24.

22. See David R. Shore, "Colin and Rosalind: Love and Poetry in the *Shepheardes Calender,*" *Studies in Philology* 73 (1976): 176–88, esp. 182–83.

23. Perhaps the purest example of this poetic adoration occurs in *Colin Clouts Come Home Againe,* filled with praise for a lady named Cynthia representing Queen Elizabeth. Thinking on her raises the spirits of the poet and inspires him to write poetry which records her fame for posterity (see esp. lines 620–43). For the effect this use of poetry had upon Spenser's career, see Louis A. Montrose, " 'The perfect paterne of a Poete': The Poetics of Courtship in *The Shepheardes Calender,*" *Texas Studies in Literature and Language* 21 (1979): 34–67.

24. Colin breaks his pipe again on Acidale when his vision of the Graces et al. is dispelled by the approach of Calidore (*Faerie Queene* 6.10.18.1–6).

25. See Gerald H. Snare, "The Muses on Poetry: Spenser's *The Teares of the Muses,*" *Tulane Studies in English* 17 (1969): 31–52. The Muses in symphony attend upon Elisa in the April eclogue, and "so sweetely they play, / . . . That it a heaven is to heare" (lines 100–8); cf. "June" 28–29, 57–64.

26. See my *Cosmographical Glass* 179.

27. See my *Cosmographical Glass* 136–38.

28. See my *Touches of Sweet Harmony* 84–85, 151–52.

29. Cf. "Hymne in Honour of Love" 120–40, 280–93. Spenser makes further apology for what he calls "lewd layes" in "Hymne of Heavenly Love" 8–21.

30. For a valuable examination of the tradition for the literary hymn in the Renaissance and of Spenser's adaptation of it, see Philip B. Rollinson, "A Generic View of Spenser's *Four Hymns*," *Studies in Philology* 68 (1971): 292–304.

31. The sources for *Fowre Hymnes* have been much studied and debated; cf. *Spenser: Variorum* 7:662–76. The last word, at least so far, was had by Josephine Waters Bennett, "Spenser's *Fowre Hymnes*: Addenda," *Studies in Philology* 32 (1935): 131–57. For an overview, see Enid Welsford, *Spenser: "Fowre Hymnes" and "Epithalamion": A Study of Edmund Spenser's Doctrine of Love* (New York: Barnes and Noble Books, 1967), 3–63.

32. For Spenser's adherence to this principle, see "Visions of the Worlds Vanitie" 1–4.

33. See James T. Stewart, "Renaissance Psychology and the Ladder of Love in Castiglione and Spenser," *Journal of English and Germanic Philology* 56 (1957): 225–30. For the parallel ascent of the poet, see Terry Comito, "A Dialectic of Images in Spenser's *Fowre Hymnes*," *Studies in Philology* 74 (1977): 301–21.

34. Cf. *Colin Clouts Come Home Againe* 841–86.

35. Of all Spenser's characters who experience love, Britomart probably best demonstrates this crucial process of abstracting the loved one, thereby transmuting the physical object into an idea. After her viewing of Artegall in Merlin's magic mirror and after hearing Red Crosse Knight's description of "her lovers shape, and chevalrous aray," Britomart "grew pensive" as she rode along:

> A thousand thoughts she fashioned in her mind,
> And in her feigning fancie did pourtray
> Him such, as fittest she for love could find,
> Wise, warlike, personable, curteous, and kind.
> (*Faerie Queene* 3.4.5.6–9)

36. See *Spenser: Variorum* 7:558–64; and Jon A. Quitslund, "Spenser's Image of Sapience," *Studies in the Renaissance* 16 (1969): 181–213.

37. The form of *Fowre Hymnes* has been much discussed, though not in my terms. For a summary of findings, as well as a fresh look at the verbal system of the poem, see Einar Bjorvand, "Spenser's Defence of Poetry: Some Structural Aspects of the *Fowre Hymnes*," *Fair Forms: Essays in English Literature from Spenser to Jane Austen*, ed. Maren-Sofie Røstvig (Cambridge: Brewer, 1975), 13–53, 203–6.

38. Cf. "Hymne in Honour of Love" 301–2, and "Hymne in Honour of Beautie" 221–22.

39. Cf. *Faerie Queene* 3.6.12.1–2, where Spenser speaks of Venus's usual abode, "her heavenly hous, / The house of goodly formes and faire aspects, / Whence all the world derives the glorious / Features of beautie." In contrast, "when she on earth does dwel," she is localized in "her joyous Paradize," which Spenser calls the Garden of Adonis (3.6.29).

40. See my *Cosmographical Glass* 182–84, 188–91.

41. See my *Cosmographical Glass* 151–54.

42. For Guillaume Postel's version of "cosmic sexual dualism," see Marion L. Kuntz, ed. and trans., Jean Bodin's *Colloquium of the Seven about Secrets of the Divine* (Princeton: Princeton University Press, 1975), lviii–lix. The point was made in Cabbalistic terms by Johann Reuchlin: "In Ida (ἀπὸ τοῦ ἰδεῖν, from *præscience*) *Jupiter* and *Juno* sat as *one* and *two*, in the streaming Idæa of the *Tetractys*, whence flow the principles of all things, *Form* and *Matter*" (*De arte cabbalistica* [2.3], *The history of philosophy*, by Thomas Stanley, 2d ed. [London, 1687], 573).

43. See my *Touches of Sweet Harmony* 158–70.

44. Spenser uses a seven-line iambic pentameter stanza for *Daphnaida*, but the rhyme scheme is different: *a b a b c b c*.

45. Preface to *The barrons wars in the raigne of Edward the second. With Englands heroicall epistles* (London, 1603), A3. Drayton's assessment of rime royal vs. ottava rima is

confirmed by Puttenham 65. Puttenham reminds us also that "rhyme" derives from L. *rhythmus,* which in turn derives from ἀριθμός, "number" (77); see also Ing 73–74.

The consanguinity between words and numbers that Drayton and Puttenham presuppose lies in a long tradition for structuring poems according to harmonies and proportions; see Thomas Elwood Hart, "Medieval Structuralism: 'Dulcarnoun' and the Five-Book Design of Chaucer's *Troilus,*" *Chaucer Review* 16 (1981): 129–70; and Hart, "Poetry, Mathematics, and the Liberal Arts Tradition," *Syracuse Scholar* 3 (1982): 58–73. In the late sixteenth century Tasso expounded this tradition in full detail, emphasizing its grounding in music (198–202). This tradition was still viable in the third quarter of the seventeenth century; in his preface to *Annus Mirabilis,* Dryden reports: "I have chosen to write my poem in quatrains, or stanzas of four in alternate rhyme, because I have ever judged them more noble, and of greater dignity, both for the sound and number, than any other verse in use amongst us" (*Essays* 1:11).

For a recent article demonstrating how Jonson employed this tradition, see Sybil Lutz Severance, " 'To Shine in Union': Measure, Number, and Harmony in Ben Jonson's 'Poems of Devotion,' " *Studies in Philology* 80 (1983): 183–99. See also Kenneth Gross, " 'Each Heav'nly Close': Mythologies and Metrics in Spenser and the Early Poetry of Milton," *PMLA* 98 (1983): 21–36.

46. To frame a stanza as a metrical system of this sort is a vestige of an earlier poetics which considers poetic composition to be largely a musical process—that is, the stanza is defined by the ways it organizes sound. In such a poetics the stanza becomes a form which precedes the verbal system and conveys a meaning of its own independent of the verbal system (Winn 85–87). In the sixteenth century, to use Winn's vocabulary, "constructive devices . . . become highly expressive" (138)—that is, the elements of form assume a rhetorical function of moving the audience, making them aware of moral values and persuading them to act upon this awareness. The locus classicus for such theorizing lies in Plato's *Republic* 401C–E; cf. Aristotle, *Politics* 1340a–b.

47. Tasso also preferred ottava rima for the heroic poem, and he goes into considerable technical detail for this choice:

> The eight-line stanza is the best, since the number eight, according to mathematicians, is the first of the solid or cubic numbers, the ones that have fulness and weight. It is moreover perfect and fittest for action because it is composed of twos, duality being the first moved or *primum mobile.* And the fact that music is composed of odd and even numbers, of the finite and infinite, constitutes one more reason for the octave's perfection, since it is made up of a double quaternian, thus forming a solid web, or of a quadruple binary, or further of a ternary and a quinary, the first odd numbers. (201)

48. Actually, the diagram purporting to represent ottava rima is incorrect.

49. See my *Touches of Sweet Harmony* 93–95.

50. I must distinguish here between metrical analysis, which reveals the harmonious proportions in metrical forms determined by the type of foot and the length of lines and by the rhyme-scheme within a stanza, and numerological analysis, which results from counting lines in a large poetical unit. In metrical analysis the numbers rarely exceed the simple integers (1 . . . 10), although Spenser pushes his range to 12.

51. For Petrarch's exploitation of this motif, see Shapiro 10–13.

52. See *Spenser: Variorum* 8:638–43; Edwin Casady, "The Neo-Platonic Ladder in Spenser's *Amoretti,*" *Renaissance Studies in Honour of Hardin Craig,* ed. Baldwin Maxwell et al. (Stanford: Stanford University Press, 1941), 92–103; Jon A. Quitslund, "Spenser's *Amoretti* VIII and Platonic Commentaries on Petrarch," *Journal of the Warburg and Courtauld Institutes* 36 (1973): 256–76; and William C. Johnson, "Amor and Spenser's *Amoretti,*" *English Studies* 54 (1973): 217–26.

53. Cf. especially Sonnets 33 and 80, in which he speaks as author of *The Faerie Queene;* Sonnet 60, in which he gives his age as forty years; and Sonnet 74, in which he notes that his mother, his queen, and his mistress are all named Elizabeth. The autobiographical strain is undeniable.

In the final stanza of *Epithalamion,* which serves as an envoy, however, Spenser the poet and historical personage puts some distance between himself and the fictive poet/lover and speaks more directly in his own voice, as he does in the envoy to *The Shepheardes Calender.*

54. It seems now to be generally accepted that *Amoretti* and *Epithalamion* should be read as a composite work; see esp. Richard Neuse, "The Triumph over Hasty Accidents: A Note on the Symbolic Mode of the 'Epithalamion,'" *Modern Language Review* 61 (1966): 163–74; A. Kent Hieatt, "A Numerical Key for Spenser's *Amoretti* and Guyon in the House of Mammon," *Yearbook of English Studies* 3 (1973): 14–27; and Carol V. Kaske, "Spenser's *Amoretti and Epithalamion* of 1595: Structure, Genre, and Numerology," *English Literary Renaissance* 8 (1978): 271–95.

55. The wording of the opening lines strongly suggests the sun's annual journey around the earth to complete the zodiac; cf. "Mother Hubberds Tale" 305–6. But cf. also "Generall argument," *Shepheardes Calender, Spenser: Variorum* 7:13; and see Josephine Waters Bennett, "Spenser's *Amoretti* LXII and the Date of the New Year," *Renaissance Quarterly* 26 (1973): 433–36.

56. Much scholarly debate has centered on just how much time elapses in *Amoretti.* Alexander Dunlop, who confined "the *Amoretti* 'story' within a time period of a few months as against the generally accepted span of a few years" (155), sparked a controversy that remains unsettled ("The Unity of Spenser's *Amoretti,*" *Silent Poetry: Essays in Numerological Analysis,* ed. Alastair Fowler [London: Routledge and Kegan Paul, 1970], 153–69). For the most stringent review of the evidence, see G. K. Hunter, "'Unity' and Numbers in Spenser's *Amoretti,*" *Yearbook of English Studies* 5 (1975): 39–45; and Kaske 293–95. With Kaske, I stress the fact that Sonnet 60 marks the passage of a year since the poet began to love.

57. There is a tendency to misunderstand the words "short" and "moniment" in this final line. A "moniment" is usually little more than a memorial, a reminder (cf. "Ruines of Time" 5, 117, 179; "Virgils Gnat" 589; "Mother Hubberd's Tale" 1182; *Faerie Queene* 1.5.38.9, 1.7.19.8, 2.2.10.9, 2.3.25.7, 2.7.5.7, 2.10.21.9, 2.10.36.8, 2.10.46.3, 2.10.56.1, 2.10.66.8, 2.12.80.3, 3.3.2.9, 3.3.59.3, 3.4.10.7, 4.1.21.2, 4.1.24.8, 4.8.6.2, 5.5.21.4, 5.8.43.9, 5.8.45.3, 6.12.20.4). Because a "moniment" was commonly used to mark a grave, the term came to have the modern sense of "monument," a small architectural edifice for commemorative purposes (cf. "Ruines of Time" 419; *Amoretti* 51.4). In Elizabethan usage, however, the term more frequently meant a written record of some event—as, for example, John Foxe's *Actes and monuments,* or the "ancient booke, hight *Briton moniments*" that Prince Arthur reads in Eumnestes's room (*Faerie Queene* 2.9.59.6; cf. "Ruines of Time" 174; "Teares of Muses" 104; *Faerie Queene* 2.10.74.7, 3.9.50.8, 4.11.17.6). Spenser repeatedly uses "moniment" to mean specifically a poem recording memorable deeds (cf. "Ruines of Time" 682; *Amoretti* 69.10, 82.8; *Faerie Queene* ded. son. viii.12, 4.2.33.3). In the final line of *Epithalamion* the term has this meaning and indicates that the poem is a written reminder of events that Spenser wishes to commemorate.

In the phrase "short time," the word "short" means brief, limited, finite (cf. "Visions of Petrarch" 10; *Faerie Queene* 4.7.40.7, 7.8.1.9). Spenser is making a rhetorical contrast between "short" and "endlesse," thereby heightening each term; cf. "Is not *short* payne well borne, that bringes *long* ease" (*Faerie Queene* 1.9.40.6; italics mine). In the final line of *Epithalamion,* then, Spenser expresses the hope that his poem will be a lasting record of his wooing, although he won his bride in a fixed period of time and the opportunity for composing an adequate epithalamium was cut short by "hasty accidents" (line 429).

Spenser foreshadows this intention in Sonnet 69 of *Amoretti*. In the first quatrain, flush in his new-won love, the poet notes that heroes of the past erected "Trophees"—that is, commemorative plaques, "in which they would the records have enrold, / of theyr great deeds and valarous emprize." So what would be appropriate, the poet asks in the second quatrain, to commemorate his victory in love?

> What trophee then shall I most fit devize,
> in which I may record the memory
> of my loves conquest, peerelesse beauties prise,
> adorn'd with honour, love, and chastity.

The answer that he offers in the third quatrain is to write a poem:

> Even this verse vowd to eternity,
> shall be thereof immortall moniment:
> and tell her prayse to all posterity,
> that may admire such worlds rare wonderment.

That poem, of course, is the composite *Amoretti* and *Epithalamion*, an "immortall moniment." Similar sentiments are expressed in Sonnet 82.

In addition to *Epithalamion* 433, Spenser uses the phrase "endlesse moniment" in three other places: *Faerie Queene* 2.2.10.9, 2.10.46.3, and 3.3.59.3.

58. On the various antinomies resolved into concord in *Epithalamion*, see W. Speed Hill, "Order and Joy in Spenser's 'Epithalamion,'" *Southern Humanities Review* 6 (1972): 81–90.

59. Cf. *Canzoniere* 129.7–13, 178.1–8.

60. Cf., for example, Petrarch, *Canzoniere* 61. For a reconstruction of the model for the sonnet sequence, see my "Sequences, Systems, Models: Sidney and the Secularization of Sonnets," *Poems in Their Place,* ed. Neil Fraistat (Chapel Hill: University of North Carolina Press, 1986), 68–72.

61. Petrarch, *Canzoniere* 132.7; cf. 134.

62. Significantly, Sonnets 4, 5, and 6 are addressed to the reader. We are the "you" in 4.13, the "thou" in 5.1, and the understood subject of "be nought dismayd" in 6.1 and of "thinke" in 6.13. By this rhetorical strategy at an early point, we the readers are related to the narrator and enrolled as his students.

63. Cf. *Amoretti* 5, 6, 13, 21, 24, 25, 51, 59, 61, 63. For the transmutation of the "cruel fair" to the *donna angelicata* in *Amoretti,* see O. B. Hardison, Jr., "*Amoretti* and the *Dolce Stil Novo*," *English Literary Renaissance* 2 (1972): 208–16. See also Carol Thomas Neely, "The Structure of English Renaissance Sonnet Sequences," *ELH* 45 (1978): 359–89.

64. We actually arrive at this point in stanza 11 of *Epithalamion*, when we are treated to a detailed description of "that which no eyes can see, / The inward beauty of her lively spright" (lines 185–86).

65. See Ernest Hatch Wilkins, "The Invention of the Sonnet," *The Invention of the Sonnet and Other Studies in Italian Literature* (Rome: Storia e Letteratura, 1959), 11–39; Elias L. Rivers, "Certain Formal Characteristics of the Primitive Love Sonnet," *Speculum* 33 (1958): 42–55; and Christopher Kleinhenz, "Giacomo da Lentini and Dante: The Early Italian Sonnet Tradition in Perspective," *Journal of Medieval and Renaissance Studies* 8 (1978): 217–34.

66. For example, the partition of Sonnet 1 of *Amoretti* is salient, dividing it into three quatrains and a couplet, an arrangement supported by the rhyme scheme. The anaphoric repetition of "happy" in lines, 1, 5, and 9 both defines each quatrain as a separate entity and makes all three coordinate items in a single system. In the couplet, the summary phrase "leaves, lines, and rymes" gathers together the subject matter of each quatrain and completes the rhetorical organization of the sonnet, realizing and emphasizing the wholeness of the system. In contrast, however, the rhetorical organization of the next three sonnets reverts to the conventional octet-sestet arrangement. In Sonnet 2 a rhetorical division

is indicated by "But," which begins line 9; in Sonnet 3 "So" performs the same function; and "For" in Sonnet 4 does likewise. Conveniently, the rhyme scheme Spenser devised for his sonnets adapts to either rhetorical division (three quatrains and a couplet, or octet and sestet), as well as to other possibilities. For another sonnet organized like Sonnet 1, see Sonnet 56. Actually, these are examples of "correlative verse"; see Ringler, ed., *Poems of Sidney* 406.

67. Sonnet 8 rhymes *a b a b c d c d e f e f g g,* according to a scheme which originated with Surrey. This rhyme scheme for the sonnet is most frequently associated with Shakespeare, although Spenser used it as early as "Ruines of Rome," "Visions of Bellay," and "Visions of Petrarch," and even twice in his epigrams for *Theatre . . . [for] voluptuous worldlings.* For the special position of this sonnet in Spenser's canon, see L. Cummings, "Spenser's *Amoretti* VIII: New Manuscript Versions," *Studies in English Literature 1500– 1900* 4 (1964): 125–35; and Quitslund, "Spenser's *Amoretti* VIII" esp. 258–59.

68. Spenser had earlier used this metrical scheme for a sonnet in the dedication of "Virgils Gnat," in the final sonnet of "Visions of Petrarch," and consistently in "Visions of worlds vanitie."

69. In the Spenserian canon the stanzaic structure of *Epithalamion* is most nearly matched by that of *Prothalamion.* All stanzas of *Prothalamion,* however, have the same number of lines and the same rhyme scheme: *a b b a a c d c d d e e f e f f g g.* At first glance stanzas 1, 3, and 7 may seem to have an aberrant rhyme scheme; lines 6 in each instance, however, should be read as a c rhyme rather than a b rhyme.

Elsewhere in the Spenserian canon only one instance of stanzaic aberrancy occurs. The first seven lines and last five lines of *Colin Clouts Come Home Againe* have interlaced rhyme, a variation of the *a b a b* rhyme scheme of its basic metrical unit (note also a missing *b* rhyme after line 694). Although *The Shepheardes Calender* exhibits a wide variety of metrical schemes, an established metrical unit prevails in each section. The final six-line stanza of "November" attaches to "December."

70. Stanza 15 has only seventeen lines. Stanzas 1, 2, 4, 5, 6, 10, 16, 21, and 23 have eighteen lines. Stanzas 3, 7, 8, 9, 11, 12, 13, 14, 17, 18, 19, 20, and 22 have nineteen lines.

71. Two lines, 16 and 431, are tetrameters, although they fill a place in the stanza normally occupied by a trimeter, and therefore in this analysis will be considered as "short" lines.

72. Stanzas 15 and 23 are exceptions, having only two short lines, and of course the final stanza, with only one short line (a tetrameter), is also an exception.

73. The exceptions are stanza 23, which has only two short lines, and stanzas 10, 16, and 21, which have a pattern of 5 5 5 5 3 5 5 5 3 5 5 5 5 5 3 5 6. Stanza 15, the seventeen-line stanza, is anomalous, having a pattern of 5 5 5 5 5 3 5 5 5 5 5 5 5 3 5 6.

74. The only exception is the final stanza, which as envoy is aberrant in most ways.

75. See *Letters* [55], trans. Sister Wilfrid Parsons, 5 vols. (New York: Fathers of the Church, 1951–56), 1:274.

76. *Third volume of French academie* 63.

77. *Short Time's Endless Monument: The Symbolism of the Numbers in Edmund Spenser's "Epithalamion"* (New York: Columbia University Press, 1960). For the most comprehensive revision of Hieatt's analysis, see Max A. Wickert, "Structure and Ceremony in Spenser's *Epithalamion,*" *ELH* 35 (1968): 135–57; and Alastair Fowler, *Triumphal Forms: Structural Patterns in Elizabethan Poetry* (Cambridge: Cambridge University Press, 1970), 103–7, 161–73. For the most precise confirmation of Hieatt's analysis, see J. C. Eade, "The Pattern in the Astronomy of Spenser's *Epithalamion,*" *Review of English Studies* ns 23 (1972): 173–78.

78. Every critical methodology seems to have its reductive dangers. For example, in his preface to *S/Z* Richard Howard notes (by way of extolling rather than condemning) that

the reading strategy devised by Barthes reduces every text to an account of the narrative process: "His conviction of reading is that what is told is always the telling" (xi).

79. I have more to say about the "transparency" of Spenser's language pages 390–94; see also my "Words and Meter in Spenser and Scaliger," *Huntington Library Quarterly* 50 (1987): 309–22.

80. "Mother Hubberds Tale" was written during late 1579 while Elizabeth was engaged in marriage negotiations with the duc d'Anjou, as the political satire indicates. Quite possibly, however, the more general social satire to line 942 belongs to an earlier or later period of composition. It is usually assumed that the work was revised before publication in the *Complaints* volume of 1591, although there is no evidence for what exactly was changed or added at that time (*Spenser: Variorum* 8:566–68).

81. In the June eclogue Colin makes a similar disclaimer: "Of Muses *Hobbinol,* I conne no skill" (line 65). In "November," however, Colin repeatedly calls upon Melpomene and her sisters (e.g., lines 53, 111, 146–47, 151, 171), and in "December" he declares somewhat boastfully that "the wiser Muses after *Colin* ranne" (line 48; cf. also lines 37–40, 140).

Such an abstention from calling upon the Muses was something of a decorous convention when writing in purportedly simple modes such as the beast-fable and the pastoral. Sidney's persona, for example, introducing an eclogue, confides:

> I then, whose burd'ned brest but thus aspires
> Of shepheards two the seely case to show,
> > Nede not the stately Muses' helpe invoke
> > For creeping rimes.

> > > > > > (lines 5–8)

(*Poems of Sidney,* ed. Ringler 242).

82. The date of composition for *Colin Clouts Come Home Againe* can be determined only within rather broad limits. Based upon little evidence, it is generally assumed that Spenser wrote the work shortly after his return from England in 1591 and revised it, perhaps several times, before its publication in 1595. See *Spenser: Variorum* 7:450–51.

83. But see David W. Burchmore, "The Image of the Centre in *Colin Clouts Come Home Againe,*" *Review of English Studies* ns 28 (1977): 393–406, where by numerological analysis he devises a circular form for the poem with a compliment to Elizabeth Boyle at the center. The poetics of making, however, does not depend upon the arrangement of parts in a spatial configuration, but rather upon the integration of parts into a whole.

84. There is no evidence for dating the composition of this work except internal, stylistic evidence; and scholars do not agree on the interpretation of that evidence. See *Spenser: Variorum* 8:598–99. The terminus ad quem for composition is 1591, when the poem was published in the *Complaints* volume.

85. Cf. *Spenser: Variorum* 8:599–608; see also Franklin E. Court, "The Theme and Structure of Spenser's *Muiopotmos,*" *Studies in English Literature 1500–1900* 10 (1970): 1–15, esp. 1–3.

86. See Wells, "'To make a milde construction': The Significance of the Opening Stanzas of *Muiopotmos,*" *Studies in Philology* 42 (1945): 544–54.

87. See Louis S. Friedland, "Spenser as a Fabulist," *Shakespeare Association Bulletin* 12 (1937): 197–98.

88. *Aeneid* 12.950–52.

89. For a thorough analysis of the Ovidian elements in the poem, see Clark Hulse, *Metamorphic Verse: The Elizabethan Minor Epic* (Princeton: Princeton University Press, 1981), 242–62.

90. On the significance of the "dazzling surface" of the poem, see Judith Dundas, "*Muiopotmos:* A World of Art," *Yearbook of English Studies* 5 (1975): 30–38.

91. A comment by Tasso is germane here: "If the tragic and epic poets sometimes

choose the same person as subject, they regard him differently and in different aspects. In Hercules, Theseus, Agamemnon, Ajax, Pyrrhus, the epic poet considers their valour and excellence in arms; the tragic poet sees them as fallen through some error into unhappiness" (44).

92. For an excellent analysis of Sidney's *Arcadia* in terms of "playing off one genre against another" (272), see Stephen J. Greenblatt, "Sidney's *Arcadia* and the Mixed Mode," *Studies in Philology* 70 (1973): 269–78.

93. Cf. the dirge for Dido ("November" 153–59), where "*Melpomene* thou mournfulst Muse of nyne" (line 53) has been similarly invoked.

94. See Allen, *Image and Meaning* 30–31. For reservations about the too-easy identification of Clarion with the human soul, see Andrew D. Weiner, "Spenser's *Muiopotmos* and the Fates of Butterflies and Men," *Journal of English and Germanic Philology* 84 (1985): 203–20.

95. In Sonnet 72 of *Amoretti* Spenser expresses this state of mind explicitly, without the aid of fiction:

> Oft when my spirit doth spred her bolder winges,
>> in mind to mount up to the purest sky:
>> it down is weighd with thoght of earthly things
>> and clogd with burden of mortality,
> Where when that soverayne beauty it doth spy,
>> resembling heavens glory in her light:
>> drawne with sweet pleasures bayt, it back doth fly,
>> and unto heaven forgets her former flight.
> There my fraile fancy fed with full delight,
>> doth bath in blisse and mantleth most at ease:
>> ne thinks of other heaven, but how it might
>> her harts desire with most contentment please.
> Hart need not wish none other happinesse,
>> but here on earth to have such hevens blisse.

In this sonnet Spenser's soul, like Clarion, spreads its wings in flight. But also, like the journey of Clarion, the spirit's ascent is interrupted by "sweet pleasures bayt."

96. *Metamorphoses* 6.1–145.

97. Shakespeare exposes the dynamics of the oxymoron when Philostrate explains to Theseus how the "tedious brief" interlude of Pyramus and Thisbe can be "very tragical mirth" (*MND* 5.1.56–70).

98. After Josephine Waters Bennett (*The Evolution of* "The Faerie Queene" [Chicago: University of Chicago Press, 1942]), it has become increasingly common to question, and even reject, the "Letter of the Authors." To my mind, however, the Letter is a presence not so easily dismissed. While Bennett is correct that it hardly represents *The Faerie Queene* as it existed in 1580 when Spenser and Harvey were in correspondence about the poem, and while the Letter may not accord in every detail with the extant poem, it nonetheless says a great deal of immediate pertinence to *The Faerie Queene* as we have it. The authenticity of the Letter—that is, that it came from Spenser's hand—has never been challenged, and Ponsonby thought it of sufficient consequence to print it with the first edition of *The Faerie Queene* in 1590, apparently at Spenser's direction.

The early printing history of the "Letter of the Authors" is a factor in weighing its importance, and therefore should be noted. After appearing in the 1590 quarto edition of *The Faerie Queene,* the Letter was omitted from the 1596 quarto edition of the poem, which contained for the first time Books 4–6. Some have seen this as an attempt to suppress the Letter. This omission may be explained, however, by the economics of the printing house. The first three books of the poem in the 1596 edition were set from the 1590 edition, which contained only the first three books of the poem; and in the 1596 edition the last five stanzas of Book 3 in the 1590 edition were deleted and replaced by three new stanzas. Understandably, what appeared after the replaced stanzas was also omitted, including the "Letter of the Authors," four of the seven commendatory poems by diverse hands, and all of the dedicatory sonnets by Spenser.

While it is necessary to assume that the revised ending of Book 3 is directly attributable to Spenser himself, it is not appropriate to assume that the "Letter of the Authors" was actively suppressed at Spenser's request. Although it is possible to claim that Spenser ordered the omission of the Letter because his plan for the poem had altered, there is no evidence to support such a conclusion. Much more likely, the decision to omit the Letter was made by the printer. After setting type for the three new stanzas that conclude Book 3, the printer found that part of folio Oo8^r and all of folio Oo8^v were blank. In order to fill this space he chose among the additional materials that followed the poetic text in the 1590 *Faerie Queene* (i.e., "A Letter of the Authors," the commendatory poems, and the dedicatory sonnets), and in fact reprinted only the first three commendatory poems, those of greatest notoriety (i.e., the two by Raleigh and another by Harvey). As Francis R. Johnson concludes, "It seems probable that the printer selected only enough of this supplementary matter of the 1590 edition to fill out his Oo gathering and purposely omitted the rest rather than to print an additional sheet" (*A Critical Bibliography of the Works of Edmund Spenser Printed before 1700* [Baltimore: Johns Hopkins University Press, 1933], 19).

The 1609 folio edition of *The Faerie Queene* was set from the 1596 edition of the poem, and it likewise omits the "Letter of the Authors." The Letter was reinstated in the 1611 folio edition of *The Faerie Queene,* however, which includes as well the other works of Spenser. The Letter appears similarly in the 1617 folio edition of Spenser's collected works (see Francis R. Johnson 37–38), and in every major subsequent edition. To disregard this letter of explanation from poet to patron seems, therefore, beyond perversity. In consequence, I'll take my stand with those who accept the relevance of the Letter; cf. esp. A. C. Hamilton, "Spenser's *Letter to Ralegh,*" *Modern Language Notes* 73 (1958): 481–85; and Judith Dundas, "*The Faerie Queene:* The Incomplete Poem and the Whole Meaning," *Modern Philology* 71 (1973–74): 257–65.

99. There is no direct evidence that Spenser had access to either work before its publication. Given his sometime employment with the Dudley family, however, and his commerce with the stationer Ponsonby, it is not unreasonable to suppose that texts of the *Defence* and of the old *Arcadia* were available to him in manuscript, even in Ireland. That he knew the text of the new *Arcadia* before 1590 is more doubtful (since only one manuscript survives), although not impossible.

100. On this meaning of "history," see the discussion of Plutarch page 173.

101. For a digest of critics' views on "The Plan and Conduct of *The Faerie Queene,*" see *Spenser: Variorum* 1:314–62. Perhaps most noteworthy is the diversity of opinion, which stretches from 1674 to 1927 and rather accurately reflects the theoretical concerns of each era.

102. Merritt Y. Hughes refers Spenser's work to Landino's reading of Vergil and concludes: "In the allegorical interpretation of the *Aeneid* by the Neo-Platonic writers of the Renaissance we have the key to the allegory of *The Faerie Queene*" (*Virgil and Spenser* [Berkeley: University of California Press, 1929], 405).

103. For a treatment of *The Faerie Queene* as vision, see Kathleen Williams, "Vision and Rhetoric: The Poet's Voice in *The Faerie Queene,*" *ELH* 36 (1969): 131–44. See also Jerome S. Dees, "The Narrator of *The Faerie Queene:* Patterns of Response," *Texas Studies in Literature and Language* 12 (1970–71): 537–68.

104. Quoted in *Spenser: The Critical Heritage,* ed. R. M. Cummings (New York: Barnes and Noble Books, 1971), 81.

105. Dryden, for example, assumed that "the Original of every Knight, was then living in the Court of Queen *Elizabeth*" (R. M. Cummings 203).

106. According to Richard Steele in *The Spectator* (No. 540, 19 November 1712), "*Spencer's* Knights have . . . given a full and a truly Poetical System of Christian, Publick, and Low Life" (R. M. Cummings 243).

107. I have waited until this point to comment upon Spenser's own description of *The Faerie Queene* as "a continued Allegory," a phrase that he goes out of his way to place in the opening sentence of his "Letter of the Authors." While many use this phrase in an offhand way to characterize the poem, there is no consensus about what it actually means. I would suggest that the vagueness surrounding the phrase is due to an inherent ambiguity which Spenser may well have been aware of. The phrase submits to two distinct interpretations. It can mean that the poem is a Dantesque allegory of a polysemous nature, so "continued" implies contiguous layers of meaning—what we might call "vertical" allegory, leading up to the all-inclusive anagogic. Or the phrase may mean that the poem is an allegorical narrative, with "continued" implying that the allegory is maintained sequentially from one episode to another—what we might call "horizontal" allegory.

In his dedicatory sonnet to Lord Burleigh, Spenser characterizes *The Faerie Queene* as a neoplatonic allegory. First he belittles his work as "ydle rimes . . . / The labor of lost time" (lines 7–8), but then he defends it by intimating a deeper meaning hidden behind a veil:

> Yet if their deeper sence be inly wayd,
> And the dim vele, with which from comune vew
> Their fairer parts are hid, aside be layd,
> Perhaps not vaine they may appeare to you.
> (lines 9–12)

Similarly in the dedicatory verse to the earl of Oxford, Spenser claims that his poem records "th'antique glory of thine auncestry / Under a shady vele." And again in the proem to Book 2 Spenser resorts to the vocabulary of traditional allegory, explaining to Elizabeth that he "enfold[s]" his meaning "in covert vele" so that his readers will not be blinded by her glory (2.proem.5.1–5). In addition, he points continually to the Muses as his source of inspiration and calls upon their aid.

For a discussion of allegory in *The Faerie Queene* in relation to the larger tradition, see Murrin passim; and Steadman, *Lamb and Elephant* esp. 114–17. For a concise and lucid discussion of the ancient and medieval background of Spenser's allegory, see Philip Rollinson, *Classical Theories of Allegory and Christian Culture* (Pittsburgh: Duquesne University Press, 1981).

108. Actually, Spenser's letter not only sets forth a plan for twelve books to elucidate the *private* virtues of Arthur while still a prince, but it also posits the possibility that if the first twelve books are well received there will be a second twelve to elucidate his *public* virtues after becoming king. Arthur will be displayed in both "the ethic and politic consideration," which for Sidney comprised the comprehensive self-knowledge that the Greeks call ἀρχιτεκτονική (*Defence* 82.35–83.2). So the Arthur that Spenser thought of bestowing upon the world would have been a complete paradigm for the Christian life in both domestic and civic duties.

109. Edwin A. Greenlaw, I believe, was the first to make this fact a central problem in criticism; see "Spenser's Fairy Mythology," *Studies in Philology* 15 (1918): 116–17.

110. In the last stanza of the proem to Book 6 Spenser again uses the image of a water-system to explain the continual ebb and flow of visitors at Gloriana's court.

111. For an important article on how Spenser uses a fourth Grace to infold the other three Graces, analogous to how he uses Gloriana and Arthur to infold their constituent virtues, see Gerald H. Snare, "Spenser's Fourth Grace," *Journal of the Warburg and Cour-*

tauld Institutes 34 (1971): 350–55. See also Snare, "The Poetics of Vision: Patterns of Grace and Courtesy in *The Faerie Queene, VI," Renaissance Papers 1974* (Durham, NC: Southeastern Renaissance Conference, 1975), 1–8.

112. This feast is the single most significant item that Spenser took over from the Arthurian legend. As Thomas Nashe recalls from Malory, Prince Arthur "feasted all his knights of the round table together everie penticost" (*The Unfortunate Traveller, Works,* ed. R. B. McKerrow, rev. F. P. Wilson, 5 vols. [Oxford: Basil Blackwell, 1958], 2:283). For the reference in Malory, see *Le morte d'Arthur* 3.15; *Works,* ed. Eugène Vinaver, 2d ed. (Oxford: Oxford University Press, 1977).

113. For an ingenious exploitation of the word "dilate" in developing the generic aspects of romance in *The Faerie Queene,* see Patricia A. Parker, *Inescapable Romance: Studies in the Poetics of a Mode* (Princeton: Princeton University Press, 1979), 54–64.

114. At least one seventeenth-century reader concurred in this reading of *The Faerie Queene.* Peter Sterry, a Cambridge Platonist with connections to Milton, published a lengthy comment about "poetical Histories" as exemplified by "*Homer, Virgil, Tasso,* our English *Spenser*":

> The *Works* of these persons are called *Poems.* So is the Work of God in Creation, and contrivance from the beginning to the end, named ποίημα τοῦ θεοῦ, God's Poem. It is an elegant and judicious Observation of a learned and holy Divine, That the Works of Poets, in the excellencies of the imaginations and contrivances, were imitations drawn from those Original Poems, the Divine works and contrivances of the eternal Spirit. We may by the fairest lights of Reason and Religion thus judge; That excellent Poets in the heighths of their fancies and spirits, were touched and warmed with a Divine Ray, through which the supream Wisdom formed upon them, and so upon their work, some weak impression and obscure Image of it self. Thus it seemeth to be altogether *Divine,* That that work shineth in our eyes with the greatest Beauties, infuseth into our Spirits the sweetest delights, transporteth us most out of our selves unto the kindest and most ravishing touches and senses of the Divinity, which diffusing it self through the amplest Variety, and so to the remotest Distances, and most opposed Contrarieties, bindeth up all with an harmonious Order into an *exact Unity;* which conveyeth things down by a gradual descent to the lowest Depths, and deepest Darknesses; then bringeth them up again to the highest point of all most flourishing Felicities, opening the *beginning in the end,* espousing the end to the beginning.

(*A discourse of the freedom of the will* [London, 1675], 179). For a recent reading of *The Faerie Queene* that similarly presents Spenser as a Christian idealist using variety and contrarieties to adumbrate a providential scheme, see Andrew Fichter, *Poets Historical: Dynastic Epic in the Renaissance* (New Haven: Yale University Press, 1982), chap. 5.

115. See my "The Aesthetic Experience of Reading Spenser," *Contemporary Thought on Edmund Spenser,* ed. Richard C. Frushell and Bernard J. Vondersmith (Carbondale: Southern Illinois University Press, 1975), 79–98.

116. Most eloquently, perhaps, Michael O'Connell, *Mirror and Veil: The Historical Dimension of Spenser's "Faerie Queene"* (Chapel Hill: University of North Carolina Press, 1977), chap. 5–epilogue.

117. See David L. Miller, "Abandoning the Quest," *ELH* 46 (1979): 173–92; also Paul J. Alpers, "Narration in *The Faerie Queene," ELH* 44 (1977): 19–39.

118. Actually, praise for Spenser as a painter of pictures began early. Cf. the anonymous author of "The Life of Mr. Edmond Spenser" in *The Works* (London, 1679): "His Descriptions are so easie and natural, that his Pen seems to have a power of conveying *Idea's* to our mind, more just, and to the Life, than the exquisite Pencils of *Titian,* or *Raphael,* to our eyes" (A1ᵛ–A2). This notion of Spenser as a painterly poet, patterned on that of Homer

as the most painterly of poets (page 98), was intended as a neoclassical compliment. In "An Essay on Allegorical Poetry" that prefaces his edition of Spenser's works, John Hughes similarly extolls Spenser's descriptive powers. Noting that Chaucer and Spenser of the English poets have the most remarkable longevity, Hughes compares the two: "*Chaucer* excell'd in his Characters; *Spenser* in his Descriptions" (1:xxvi). Hughes confirms this assessment by claiming that Spenser "was an admirable Imager of Vertues and Vices, which was his particular Talent" (1:xxvii), and later he calls attention to "his Painter-like Genius" (1:lxvii).

The Romantics exaggerated this praise of Spenser as a painter of word pictures. For Leigh Hunt's oft-cited analysis of Spenser as the most painterly of English poets, see *Imagination and Fancy* (London, 1845), 103–35. In a section entitled "A Gallery of Pictures from Spenser," Hunt recalls Pope's anecdote about the mother of Joseph Spence, who thought of *The Faerie Queene* as a picture gallery, and quotes at length and at random various passages from the poem, which he assigns to various painters (e.g., Raphael, Titian, Rembrandt, Poussin).

119. "Upon Poetry," *Miscellanea. The second part* (London, 1690), 47.

120. See Stanley Stewart, "Sir Calidore and 'Closure,'" *Studies in English Literature 1500–1900* 24 (1984): 69–71.

121. For a similar conclusion about the non-specificity of Spenser's language based upon a rhetorical analysis of the description of tapestries in Book 3 (1.34–38 and 9.28–46), see Claud A. Thompson, "Spenser's 'Many Faire Pourtraicts, and Many a Faire Feate,'" *Studies in English Literature 1500–1900* 12 (1972): 21–32.

122. Spenser's contribution to van der Noot's *Theatre . . . [for] voluptuous worldlings* did carry illustrations in accord with the general format for the volume, and so did *The Shepheardes Calender*. It is remotely possible that the lost *Dreames* was accompanied by "Pictures," although Spenser's comments as reported in the Spenser-Harvey correspondence are difficult to interpret (*Spenser: Variorum* 9:18). But *The Faerie Queene* was not illustrated until the edition of Spenser's *Works* by John Hughes in 1715, when each of the seven books was introduced by an engraved frontispiece. Most of the other poems are similarly prefaced by an engraving, however, so the illustrations are not a response to some particular quality of *The Faerie Queene*. Rather, they reflect the taste of the eighteenth century, by which time the sisterly relationship between poetry and painting made illustrations de rigueur.

Chapter 7

1. Fulke Greville, *Life of Sir Philip Sidney* [1652], ed. Nowell Smith (Oxford: Clarendon, 1907), 15. The word "scope" means "target, aim."

2. See Ringler, ed., *Poems of Sidney* 361–62; and Duncan-Jones, ed., *Miscellaneous Prose of Sidney* 13. Scholarly opinion now seems to favor the earlier date; see Marie Axton, "The Tudor Mask and Elizabethan Court Drama," *English Drama: Forms and Development,* ed. Axton and Raymond Williams (Cambridge: Cambridge University Press, 1977), 37.

3. See Ringler, ed., *Poems of Sidney* 365; and Robertson, ed., *Old Arcadia* xv–xix.

4. *Miscellaneous Prose of Sidney* 59–63.

5. See my "Sidney and Serranus' *Plato*" 153–59.

6. *Poems of Sidney* 423. See also Germaine Warkentin, "Sidney's *Certain Sonnets:* Speculations on the Evolution of the Text," *Library* 6th ser. 2 (1980): 430–44.

7. *Poems of Sidney* 435–40. We must remember, however, that *Astrophil and Stella* is an unfinished work and that the text has survived in several states. The text in the 1598

folio of Sidney's collected works, which Ringler used as his copy text, is simply one of several. Actually, *Astrophil and Stella* is a compilation of materials that were composed and revised over a period of time. Some items in the sequence are reworkings of pieces that would otherwise appear in *Certain Sonnets*, just as Song v is a recasting of a poem that Philisides sent to Mira (cf. Ringler, ed., *Poems of Sidney* 484). There was a fluidity between the compilation printed as *Certain Sonnets* and Sidney's other works. *Certain Sonnets* 7 and 26, for example, could very well serve as songs in *Astrophil and Stella,* and later generations have regularly printed *Certain Sonnets* 31 and 32 as the final two qua-torzains of the sequence. In the new *Arcadia, Certain Sonnets* 3 appears as a love song ordered by Amphialus in his wooing of Philoclea (fols. 306–6ᵛ). Since the texts we know as *Certain Sonnets* and *Astrophil and Stella* did not come directly from Sidney's hand with his imprimatur, there is a considerable degree of uncertainty about both.

8. Ringler, ed., *Poems of Sidney* 365–66.

9. See Ringler, ed., *Poems of Sidney* 435. One can only speculate where Thomas Newman obtained copy for his unauthorized edition in 1591 (see ibid. 544; and Christopher R. Wilson, "*Astrophil and Stella:* A Tangled Editorial Web," *Library* 6th ser. 1 [1979]: 336–46). The corruptness of Newman's version, though, indicates that there was no settled manuscript tradition for *Astrophil and Stella,* a probability confirmed by the wide variation in the extant manuscripts (see Ringler, ed., *Poems of Sidney* 447–57).

10. I use the text edited by Katherine Duncan-Jones and printed in *Miscellaneous Prose of Sidney* 21–32. I make reference to page and line numbers in that volume, as here.

11. See Mary Martha Purdy, "Political Propaganda in Ballad and Masque," *If by your art: Testament to Percival Hunt,* ed. Agnes Lynch Starrett (Pittsburgh: University of Pittsburgh Press, 1948), 264–93; Ringler, ed., *Poems of Sidney* 362; Robert Kimbrough and Philip Murphy, "The Helmingham Hall Manuscript of Sidney's *The Lady of May:* A Commentary and Transcription," *Renaissance Drama* ns. 1 (1968): 103–19; Louis Adrian Montrose, "Celebration and Insinuation: Sir Philip Sidney and the Motives of Elizabethan Courtship," *Renaissance Drama* ns. 8 (1977): esp. 7–20; and Axton 37–41.

12. Cf. Rudenstine 302 (n. 37).

13. For a balanced summary of the works to which Sidney owes a discernible debt, see A. C. Hamilton, "Sidney's *Arcadia* as Prose Fiction: Its Relation to Its Sources," *English Literary Renaissance* 2 (1972): 29–60. See also Reinard Willem Zandvoort, *Sidney's Arcadia: A Comparison between the Two Versions* (Amsterdam: Swets, 1929), 189–97; Walter R. Davis, *Map of Arcadia* 7–50; Robertson, ed., *Old Arcadia* xix–xxix; and Thelma N. Greenfield, *The Eye of Judgment: Reading the New Arcadia* (Lewisburg: Bucknell University Press, 1982), 123–37. For a judicious warning against oversimplifying Sidney's debt to earlier literature, see Richard A. Lanham, *The Old "Arcadia," Sidney's Arcadia,* Yale Studies in English 158 (New Haven: Yale University Press, 1965), 384–94.

14. Ringler, for example, comments: "The eclogues, though they contribute to the design of the main action, also form an isolable unit with a structure of its own that can perfectly well stand by itself" (*Poems of Sidney* xxxviii). Cf. also Elizabeth Dipple, "The 'Fore Conceit' of Sidney's Eclogues," *Literary Monographs I,* ed. Eric Rothstein and Thomas K. Dunseath (Madison: University of Wisconsin Press, 1967), 1–47, 301–3.

15. *Eikonoklastes, The Works,* ed. Frank Allen Patterson, 18 vols. (New York: Columbia University Press, 1931–38), 5:86. Cf. Milton, *Poems and Prose,* ed. Hughes 793.

16. For provocative, if not conclusive, comments about the rhetorical function of characterization in Sidney's work, see Jane Hedley, "What Price Energeia: Personification in the Poetry of Sidney and Greville," *Studies in the Literary Imagination* 15.1 (1982): 49–66.

17. Among the "what elses," I would include the ridiculous posturing of Basilius as a *senex amans* (e.g., 95.11–31 and 176.4–7), and the envy of Philoclea's beauty felt by

Gynecia and Pamela (e.g., 39.14–17), not to mention the covetousness of Dametas, jealousy of Miso, and curiosity of Mopsa (186.19–25).

18. *Copia* 577–89.

19. Puttenham has this to say about "*Hypotiposis,* or the counterfeit representation": "The matter and occasion leadeth us many times to describe and set foorth many things, in such sort as it should appeare they were truly before our eyes though they were not present" (238). Erasmus gives the widest possible definition of hypotyposis ("This word is used for any kind of presentation to the eyes") and offers considerable advice about its construction (*Copia* 577–82). He reminds us that "descriptions of this sort consist mainly in the exposition of circumstantial details, especially those which make the incident particularly vivid, and give the narrative distinctiveness" (579). The requirement that hypotyposis set things before our eyes associates it with Aristotelian metaphor (page 288).

20. Relative to the prosopographia, Puttenham observes: "A poet or maker is woont to describe . . . the visage, speach and countenance of any person absent or dead: and this kinde of representation is called the Counterfait countenance" (238). His examples are illuminating: "As *Homer* doth in his *Iliades,* diverse personages: namely *Achilles* and *Thersites.* . . . And as our poet *Chaucer* doth in his Canterbury tales set forth the Sumner, Pardoner, Manciple, and the rest of the pilgrims, most naturally and pleasantly." Cf. Erasmus, *Copia* 582–86.

21. E.g., 30.2–13, 37.5–20, 37.21–32.

22. Connell compares Philanax's speech with the letter that Sidney wrote to the Queen upon the occasion of Anjou's proposal of marriage, suggesting that the fiction is an apologia for Sidney's own political position (104–11). Cf. also Lanham, *Arcadia* 241–44.

23. Cf. Erasmus: "Particularly appropriate to character delineation is διαλογισμός or dialogue, in which we supply each person with utterances appropriate to his age, type, country, way of life, cast of mind, and character" (*Copia* 586). See also Quintilian, who defines this figure as "imaginary conversations between men" (9.2.31); Scaliger, *Poetice* [3.48] 126; and Puttenham 235.

24. Classic examples of prosopopoeia include Cleophila's speech to the Phagonian rebels (129.24–131.7), Pamela's entreaty that Musidorus respect her virginity on their travels (196.27–197.14), Philoclea's doleful lament when Cleophila pretends to divert his attention from her to Gynecia (209.13–210.21), Pyrocles's explanation of his actions when he comes to Philoclea's bedroom (233.17–234.19), Dametas's fearful outcry when he discovers that Pamela has escaped (271.27–272.12), Gynecia's speech to Basilius after his praise of "Cleophila" as a bed partner (276.15–34), Philanax's vow for revenge over the body of Basilius (286.31–287.20), Pyrocles's apologia when Philanax arrives in Philoclea's bedroom (301.10–36), Philanax's address to the populace recommending that authority be turned over to Euarchus (353.3–354.12), and Musidorus's appeal to the Arcadians in defence of Pamela (378.6–379.7), matched by Pyrocles appeal to Euarchus on behalf of Philoclea (379.26–380.21).

25. *Old* Arcadia 249–50; cf. also Lanham's conclusion about this debate (257–58).

26. This impression is confirmed by Lanham: "The basic stylistic unit seems to be not chapter or book but scene; it is individual scenes which impress themselves graphically on the memory" (*Arcadia* 360).

27. *Old Arcadia* xx; cf. Ringler, ed., *Poems of Sidney* xxxvii. For important amplification of this point, see Robert W. Parker, "Terentian Structure and Sidney's Original *Arcadia,*" *English Literary Renaissance* 2 (1972): 61–78. See also Richard H. Perkinson, "The Epic in Five Acts," *Studies in Philology* 43 (1946): 465–75; and Clark L. Chalifour, "Sir Philip Sidney's *Old Arcadia* as Terentian Comedy," *Studies in English Literature 1500– 1900* 16 (1976): 51–63.

28. For other passages where characters think of themselves as performing in a tragedy, see 43.11, 103.29, 120.3, 281.9, 386.23, and 399.18; cf. also 193.22 and 215.31.

29. Prouty 69–70.

30. This count includes the two letters (73 lines) written by Philoclea and Pamela, and sent by them to the assembly (395.35–396.33 and 397.4–398.6). Although Philanax intercepts these letters so no other character becomes aware of them, their texts are quoted in full for the benefit of the reader, and their contents work toward revealing the individualized characters of the princesses through their own language.

31. Numerous readers have commented on the inherent drama of Book 5; e.g., Lanham: "The famous trial scene with which the Old *Arcadia* concludes is perhaps Sidney's most successful attempt to combine rhetorical declamation, abstract debate of theme, and the pleasures of *opsis*. The spectacle ought really to be acted" (*Arcadia* 233).

32. In his discussion of prosopopoeia, Quintilian notes: "We may introduce not only imaginary sayings, but imaginary writings as well" (9.2.34). After Ovid's *Heroides*, epistles from lovelorn ladies were standard items in the fictioneer's repertoire.

33. See the letter to Can Grande della Scala in Dante, *Epistolae*, ed. and trans. Paget Toynbee, 2d ed. (Oxford: Clarendon, 1966), 200–201.

34. Previously the role of the narrator has been most searchingly examined by Lanham, *Arcadia* chap. 4, "Sidney the Narrator." His comments, however, while often perceptive, are usually debilitated by not separating the narrator from Sidney. Elizabeth Dipple follows Lanham in conflating the narrator with Sidney, but she notes the "diversity of voices— condescending, comic, ironic, explosive, sententious, morally absolute" with which the narrator speaks ("'Unjust Justice' in the *Old Arcadia*," *Studies in English Literature 1500– 1900* 10 [1970]: 85).

35. Sidney was familiar with the story of Oedipus, in all likelihood as Sophocles or perhaps Seneca had dramatized it (cf. *Defence* 108.10). Alexander Neville had translated Seneca's *Oedipus* in 1563.

36. Relevant here is Foucault's discussion of "the author-function" ("Author" 148–53).

37. At this point it is appropriate to take note of the letter addressed "To my dear lady and sister the Countess of Pembroke" and printed before the 1590 (i.e., the "new") *Arcadia*. This letter, again printed before the 1593 (i.e., the "composite") *Arcadia*, has remained a standard feature of later editions. That this letter was written by Sidney has never been called into question, and I have no evidence for doing so now. However, since the only text we have for this letter is the printed version in the 1590 *Arcadia*, and since it appears with none of the nine surviving manuscripts of the old *Arcadia*, we must inquire into its relevance if not its authenticity.

In this letter Sidney reduces the *Arcadia* to an "idle work," a mere "trifle, and that triflingly handled"; and he tells his sister that it was written "in loose sheets of paper, most of it in your presence, the rest by sheets sent unto you as fast as they were done." Ringler doubts this account of the poem's composition, however, and assumes that the manuscript of the old *Arcadia* sent to the Countess of Pembroke (which Ringler designates P) was a complete version copied by a scribe from Sidney's foul papers (*Poems of Sidney* 380). In his stemma of manuscripts, Ringler places P to one side, indicating that it is not related to any of the other extant manuscripts. Robertson tacitly concurs in these conclusions. While admitting that "the matter is scarcely susceptible of proof," she continues: "But on balance Ringler thinks that, despite the suggestion in this passage of an author scribbling away, the sheets sent to the Countess of Pembroke were in fact a scribal copy (P) made from the *Old Arcadia* foul papers" (*Old Arcadia* lii). Since Sidney's account of how the *Arcadia* was composed is most unlikely, the veracity of the entire letter may be questioned.

Apparently, when Sidney sent manuscript P of the old *Arcadia* to his sister, he included this letter; and she in turn supplied this letter to those responsible for publishing the new *Arcadia* in 1590 (see Robertson, ed., *Old Arcadia* 418). Manuscript P is no longer extant, however, and the letter which accompanied it survives only by virtue of the printed version of 1590. In view of the fact that Sidney did not add this letter to his copy of the old *Arcadia* from which the other extant manuscripts were derived (see Ringler's stemma 380), I conclude that the letter was an ad hoc accessory to a single manuscript prepared with his sister in mind. It is a graceful cover letter, an intimate joke, a bit of affectionate teasing. In any case, Sidney did not consider the letter of abiding relevance to the text, since he did not add it to his foul papers, so I do not bring it to bear upon my analysis of the old *Arcadia*. And it has dubious relevance to the new *Arcadia*, since others and not Sidney juxtaposed it with that text. Unlike Spenser's letter appended to *The Faerie Queene* (see 574 [n. 98]), it gives no valid indication of the author's residual attitude toward his work.

On the irony of the phrase "idle work" in Sidney's letter to his sister, see Annabel M. Patterson, "'Under . . . Pretty Tales': Intention in Sidney's *Arcadia*," *Studies in the Literary Imagination* 15.1 (1982): 5–21; cf. also Patterson, *Censorship and Interpretation* 24–43.

38. In Book 1, cf. 27.21, 29.9, 38.3, 39.17, 40.21, 45.34, 49.25, 51.23, 54.18, 55.1, 55.14; in Book 3, cf. 172.14 and 22, 227.11, 242.30, 243.9. There are none in Book 2 or in the last two books. There may be several explanations for this uneven distribution: Sidney grew weary of this ploy, or his attitude toward the fiction changed, or he thought such facetiousness inappropriate to the serious events that occupy the concluding books of the old *Arcadia*.

39. It would be interesting to know what the Countess of Pembroke *really* thought about this aspect of her *Arcadia*. As evidence of Sidney's sensitivity to sexual politics, and therefore in argument that he was not a blind male chauvinist, we might recall Pyrocles's gallant defence of "the sex of whom I have my life" (21.9) in the debate on love with Musidorus. Pyrocles, whom Musidorus scornfully accuses of being a gentle fool with a gentle heart (20.3), calls into question the motives of his own sex in their relations with women: "It is strange to see the unmanlike cruelty of mankind who, not content with their tyrannous ambition to have brought the others' virtuous patience under them, like childish masters, think their masterhood nothing without doing injury to them who (if we will argue by reason) are framed of nature with the same parts of the mind for the exercise of virtue as we are" (21.13–18). The imputed readership of fair ladies disappears from the new *Arcadia*. Did Mary Sidney object?

40. On the problematizing function of such literary signatures, see Culler, *On Deconstruction* 192–93.

41. Cf. the plight of Sincero, most clearly delineated in prosa 7 (Sannazaro, *Arcadia*, trans. Nash 70–74). But note the contrasting experience of Carino in prosa 8.

42. See Ringler, ed., *Poems of Sidney* 410.

43. It is worthwhile to compare this with Musidorus's account of his own life in Book 2, when he conveys his identity to Pamela despite his disguise. Both episodes assume the interchangeability of fact and fiction, although they come to the interchange from opposite directions.

44. In this passage of the old *Arcadia*, where Philisides is most evidently identified as the author himself, Sidney closely follows the example of Sannazaro's most patently autobiographical performance as Sincero in the seventh prosa and eclogue of his *Arcadia* (fols. 49ᵛ–56).

45. See Ringler, ed., *Poems of Sidney* 418. John A. Galm argues, implausibly, that Philisides's courtship of Mira represents Sidney's disappointing relationship with the Queen (*Sidney's Arcadian Poems* [Salzburg: Institut für Englische Sprache und Literatur, 1973], 210–25). Dennis Moore continues Galm's argument ("Philisides and Mira: Autobiographical Allegory in the *Old Arcadia*," *Spenser Studies* 3 [1982]: 125–37).

46. I am thinking in terms of the physicist's model of a molecule, which (like mimetic fiction) is constructed by the laws of probability. The physicist presents his model of a molecule with the various particles that comprise it in fixed positions, but he warns that at any particular moment the particles in the molecule will not in fact be related in precisely

this way. In actuality, each particle oscillates around a point, and the model is no more than a diagram (a ground-plot) of those points calculated according to probability. The model is not a replication of physical nature, but a construction of what might be or should be. Moreover, no particle in the physicist's model is fixed; each is multivalent in its relationships to all the other particles.

47. As Hamilton observes (with reference to the new *Arcadia*), "Sidney acts vicariously through his characters, manifesting his virtues in them, as Harvey recognizes when he says that 'the two brave knights, Musidorus and Pyrocles [are] combined in one excellent knight, Sir Philip Sidney'" (*Sidney* 125). For corroboration of Harvey's point by evidence from the title page of the 1593 (composite) *Arcadia,* see ibid. 201 (n. 7).

48. Gynecia's progress from worthiness to despair can be readily charted: cf. 4.23–28, 37.3–5, 57.6–16, 91.9–92.23, 122.12–123.24, 222.17–23, 287.24–288.3, 366.27–368.18.

49. Cf., for example, 97.26–98.18.

50. In the new *Arcadia,* Sidney revised the oracle and inserted into it three lines which make explicit the threat of Pyrocles and Musidorus to Basilius's rule (fol. 225ᵛ). Shakespeare also in several plays explored the anxiety a father feels when a daughter reaches marriageable age—e.g., the tempest that Prospero experiences when he recognizes that Miranda is ready for a husband. Cf. also *Midsummer Night's Dream, Romeo and Juliet,* and *The Merchant of Venice,* three plays that Shakespeare wrote in the period 1594–96, just after publication of the composite *Arcadia* in 1593.

51. There is some reason, however, to question the sincerity of Basilius's devotion. Although he performs the appropriate rituals and sacrifices in worship of Apollo (cf. 134.1–6, 168.4–5, 176.4), at least on one occasion in the heat of passion he proves blasphemous, as Cleophila scornfully points out (177.4–11).

52. Michael McCanles examines Basilius as an exemplar of the Oedipean theme: "Oracular Prediction and the Fore-Conceit of Sidney's *Arcadia,*" *ELH* 50 (1983): 233–44.

53. In *De civitate Dei,* in a chapter entitled "Concerning the seventh day, whereon completeness and rest are introduced," Augustine offers comments on the number 7 which serve as an appropriate gloss on the significance of the seven lines in the oracle:

> On the seventh day, that is on the seventh repetition of the same day . . . the rest that God took is introduced, and this rest is the first thing we hear of that is hallowed. . . . The first odd integer is three, . . . four is the first even integer, and . . . the sum of these is seven. For this reason seven is often used to indicate universality. . . . In this number is God's rest, the rest that we find in him. (11.32)

In the new *Arcadia* Sidney increased the number of lines in the oracle to ten, allowing an insertion which underlines the challenge of Pyrocles and Musidorus to Basilius's authority. But, significantly, the number of lines is carefully increased to another number that represents cosmic perfection (see my *Touches of Sweet Harmony* 84).

54. For the full context of this topos as it relates to Basilius and Lear, see Alan D. Isler, "Moral Philosophy and the Family in Sidney's *Arcadia,*" *Huntington Library Quarterly* 31 (1967–68): 359–71.

55. For a cogent examination of the logic in Euarchus's speeches, see Lorna Challis, "The Use of Oratory in Sidney's *Arcadia,*" *Studies in Philology* 62 (1965): 571–72.

56. For a distinction between Spenser and Sidney in these terms, see Paul J. Alpers, *The Poetry of "The Faerie Queene"* (Princeton: Princeton University Press, 1967), 287–96.

Richard C. McCoy interprets the trial scene as a Rashamon-like construction so that it "becomes an occasion for a retrospective organization of the preceding events, and the reader is engaged in the process of judgment" (*Sir Philip Sidney: Rebellion in Arcadia* [New Brunswick: Rutgers University Press, 1979], 124). Greenfield carries over this point to a reading of the new *Arcadia* (esp. chap. 10).

57. Joan Rees reaches a similar conclusion: "Unless, as readers, we are to become as

prone to illusion and mis-judgement as the characters, we need to reenact the process of assessment and discrimination which Sidney himself has carried out in the shaping of his material" (*Exploring* "Arcadia" [Birmingham: University of Birmingham Press, 1981], 13).

58. For a concise review of this criticism, see Ann W. Astell, "Sidney's Didactic Method in The *Old Arcadia*," *Studies in English Literature 1500–1900* 24 (1984): 39–40. Astell identifies a narrative strategy for Sidney quite similar to what I propose. See also Dana, who argues that "the act of reading [the old *Arcadia*] becomes a metaphor for the difficulty of reading life itself," and that "the most convincing example Sidney offers for our emulation is not Evarchus, with his rigid literalistic interpretation of the law and Calvinistic condemnation of the individuals trapped in it, but the flexible narrator himself" (56–57).

59. See Ringler, ed., *Poems of Sidney* 458.

60. Ibid. 542.

61. For my text of Nashe's preface, I use McKerrow, ed., *Works of Nashe*, rev. Wilson 3:327–33.

62. For the fullest exposition of Stella's role, see Nona Fienberg, "The Emergence of Stella in *Astrophil and Stella*," *Studies in English Literature 1500–1900* 25 (1985): 5–19.

63. The evidence for identifying Stella as Penelope Devereux has been most thoroughly accumulated by Hoyt H. Hudson, "Penelope Devereux as Sidney's Stella," *Huntington Library Bulletin* 7 (1935): 89–129. Cf. Ringler, ed., *Poems of Sidney* 435–36. For studies dealing with the problem of autobiography in *Astrophil and Stella,* see also Jack Stillinger, "The Biographical Problem of *Astrophel and Stella*," *Journal of English and Germanic Philology* 59 (1960): 617–39; Jean Robertson, "Sir Philip Sidney and Lady Penelope Rich," *Review of English Studies* ns 15 (1964): 296–97; Ephim G. Fogel, "The Mythical Sorrows of Astrophil," *Studies in Language and Literature in Honor of Margaret Schlauch,* ed. Mieczyslaw Brahmer et al. (Warsaw: Polish Scientific Publishers, 1966), 133–52; Hamilton, *Sidney* 80–86 (esp. n. 41); and Thomas P. Roche, Jr., "Autobiographical Elements in Sidney's *Astrophil and Stella*," *Spenser Studies* 5 (1984): 209–29.

64. See Alan Sinfield, "Sidney and Astrophil," *Studies in English Literature 1500–1900* 20 (1980): 25–41. Cf. also James J. Scanlon, "Sidney's *Astrophil and Stella:* 'See what it is to Love' Sensually!" *Studies in English Literature 1500–1900* 16 (1976): 65–74.

65. *Poems of Sidney* 484.

66. This blazon turns up again in the new *Arcadia,* but there it comes from Pyrocles's mouth (disguised as Zelmane) in praise of Philoclea without reference to Philisides (fols. 150ᵛ–152ᵛ).

67. Hamilton argues that *Certain Sonnets* also fulfills this proposal (*Sidney* 75–77). It is possible that *Certain Sonnets* preserves the inchoate stage of another sequence of songs and sonnets, or perhaps merely a pool of love lyrics from which Sidney drew to ornament his other works. Rudenstine argues that "Philisides is much less sophisticated and assured than Astrophel, but it is he who begins to develop that tone of satiric bravado and strong-minded willfulness which pervades the verse of Sidney's later hero" (108); also later, "Philisides is a study for Astrophel" (114).

68. The immediate prototype for this sort of solo performance introduced by a self-effacing narrator is the third eclogue assigned to Galicio in Sannazaro's *Arcadia* fols. 28ᵛ–30. In Sannazaro's eclogue, however, the narrator does not return at the end of the song to close the event.

69. Ringler notes that the sequence between Songs iv and viii "shows clumsy joinery," and he surmises: "A possible explanation of these inconsistencies is that Sidney first began to write about Astrophil's love for Stella in a set of detached songs in the new trochaic metres he had recently been experimenting with in the *Certain Sonnets,* and that not until after he had written the songs did he think of writing the sonnets and of combining them with the songs in a single sequence" (*Poems of Sidney* xlv–xlvi). Ringler does not, however, pursue the point.

70. "The songs," Ringler admits, "present something of a problem" (*Poems of Sidney* xlv). See his discussion for what he can offer toward a solution.

71. This refrain changes in the final stanza.

72. In Song viii some readers may point to the line, "Her faire necke a foule yoke bare" (10), and say it refers to Penelope Devereux in her unhappy marriage to Lord Rich. But this line is not a historical reference. Petrarch's Laura was a married woman, so a married mistress was a commonplace of the Petrarchan code. Ovid's Corinna, incidentally, was also married, with a notably odious husband. In Song iv some may point to the line, "Jealousie it selfe doth sleepe" (10), and say it refers to Lord Rich, or at least to a husband. But "Jealousie" is only a personified abstraction, like "Danger" in the preceding line, and has no specific reference.

73. *Astrophil and Stella* begins in the past tense, as though Astrophil, in Dantesque fashion, were repeating from the book of memory. With the sestet in Sonnet 2, however, where the temporal adverb "now" occurs no less than three times (lines 9, 10, and 12), the work shifts decisively into the present. At that point Astrophil changes from storyteller to actor in a drama. The sense of immediacy is then resolutely maintained throughout the quatorzains, although some items report an event that has already happened—i.e., 16, 22, 33, 41, 53, 57, 58, 62, 87, 103. Some quatorzains based upon mythology are also placed in the past—i.e., 8, 11 (sestet), 13, 17, 20 (sestet), 55 (octet).

74. Cf. Turbervile, "The argument" (fol. 3ᵛ) and "The lover extolleth the singular beautie of his ladie" (fols. 6ᵛ–7); and Gascoigne, "Anatomy of a Lover" 4.

75. Cf. 2.14, 50.1–8, 70.10–11, 81.7, 93.3.

76. Cf. Thomas Wilson: "An Allegorie is none other thyng, but a Metaphore used throughout a whole sentence, or Oration" (fol. 93ᵛ).

77. For the continued significance of "invention" in the sequence as a whole, see Warkentin, "Sidney and Supple Muse."

78. This anguish of Astrophil may be amplified by comparison with the anguish of Musidorus in the new *Arcadia* when he composes a conciliatory set of elegiac verses addressed to Pamela after she has banished him from her presence because of an attempted kiss (fols. 245ᵛ–246).

79. On some rare occasions Astrophil reports a few lines spoken by someone else—i.e., his Muse (1), Morpheus (32), his "wit" (34), Cupid (53), young ladies of the court (54), and a poorly defined "we" comprising Astrophil and his audience (74).

80. Cogent here is Culler's discussion of apostrophe as a means of establishing poetic identity (*Pursuit of Signs* 135–46).

81. *Poems of Sidney* xliv.

82. I have dealt with this aspect of *Astrophil and Stella* in "Sequences, Systems, Models." Among several studies that consider *Astrophil and Stella* in relation to Petrarchism, the most useful to me have been Richard B. Young, *English Petrarke: A Study of Sidney's "Astrophel and Stella," Three Studies in the Renaissance: Sidney, Jonson, Milton, Yale Studies in English* 138 (New Haven: Yale University Press, 1958), 1–88; David Kalstone, "Sir Philip Sidney and 'Poore Petrarchs Long Deceased Woes,'" *Journal of English and Germanic Philology* 63 (1964): 21–32; Kalstone, *Sidney's Poetry: Contexts and Interpretations* (Cambridge: Harvard University Press, 1965), esp. 105–32; Rudenstine esp. 197–269; and Marion Campbell, "Unending Desire: Sidney's Reinvention of Petrarchan Form in *Astrophil and Stella*," *Sir Philip Sidney and the Interpretation of Renaissance Culture: The Poet in His Time and in Ours*, ed. Gary F. Waller and Michael D. Moore (London: Croom Helm, 1984), 84–94.

83. Richard A. Lanham develops (indeed, overdevelops) this point; see "*Astrophil and Stella*: Pure and Impure Persuasion," *English Literary Renaissance* 2 (1972): 100–115. Lanham's argument is seriously impaired by his refusal to distinguish between Sidney and the speaker in the poem, Astrophil.

84. For a challenging reading of *Astrophil and Stella* based upon the principle that "it is less a definable literary 'text' than a field of potential meaning," see Gary F. Waller, "Acts of Reading: The Production of Meaning in *Astrophil and Stella*," *Studies in the Literary Imagination* 15.1 (1982): 23–35.

85. Cf. 1, 3, 6, 15, 28, 40, 45, 50, 55, 58, 70, 74, 90.

86. See especially Sonnet 69, where deception is closely linked with the use of language.

87. Printed as *The Use of Poetry and the Use of Criticism* (Cambridge: Harvard University Press, 1933), 44.

88. Cf. Bertram Dobell, "New Light upon Sir Philip Sidney's 'Arcadia,'" *Quarterly Review* 211 (1909): 74–100.

89. By Albert Feuillerat as volume 4 of his *Complete Works of Sir Philip Sidney* (Cambridge: Cambridge University Press, 1912–26).

90. The old *Arcadia,* however, had its vocal proponents. For a survey of critical opinion about the relative merits of the old and the new *Arcadia* on the eve of Eliot's lecture, see Zandvoort 45–51.

91. See Ringler, ed., *Poems of Sidney* 529–33; cf. Robertson, ed., *Old Arcadia* lvi–lviii.

92. Feuillerat reprinted this text as volume 1 of his *Complete Works of Sidney.* More recently it has been reproduced in facsimile by the Kent State University Press (1970) with an introduction by Carl Dennis. My citations of the new *Arcadia* refer to this latter volume, which is paginated in folios. For a dependable résumé of the relation between the new *Arcadia* and the old, see Walter R. Davis, *Map of Arcadia* 1–4.

93. The boldest and most sophisticated conjectures about the implications of Sidney's revision are offered by Lindheim, esp. chap. 7. In no way do I wish to refute Lindheim's argument, because by and large I agree with her application of rhetoricism to Sidney's text and with her conclusion that it exemplifies "multiple unity." I do feel the need to emphasize, however, that the new *Arcadia* is an unfinished fragment that strikes out in unexpected directions, and assigning authorial intention from the evidence of what Sidney got around to reworking is at best a reconstruction of what Sidney might have intended at an early point in the protracted process of rewriting a long and artful narrative.

94. See Lawry esp. 154–66; and Farmer 1–18.

95. See fols. 51^v, 63, 64, 106, 108, 109^v, 131^v, 132^v, 145, 163, 220, 220^v, 230, 327^v, 329^v, 330^v (twice), 349^v, 352. Cf. page 418.

96. See, for example, Edwin A. Greenlaw, "Sidney's *Arcadia* as an Example of Elizabethan Allegory," *Anniversary Papers by Colleagues and Pupils of George Lyman Kittredge* (Boston: Ginn, 1913), 327–37; Lewis 335; E. M. W. Tillyard, *The English Epic and Its Background* (London: Chatto and Windus, 1954), 294–319; Kenneth Myrick, *Sir Philip Sidney as a Literary Craftsman,* 2d ed. (Lincoln: University of Nebraska Press, 1965), chap. 4; Shepherd 4; Alan D. Isler, "Heroic Poetry and Sidney's Two *Arcadias*," *PMLA* 83 (1968): 368–79; Isler, "The Allegory of the Hero and Sidney's Two *Arcadias*," *Studies in Philology* 65 (1968): 171–91; Myron Turner, "The Heroic Ideal in Sidney's Revised *Arcadia*," *Studies in English Literature 1500–1900* 10 (1970): 63–82; Hamilton, "*Arcadia* as Prose Fiction" 45–47; Josephine A. Roberts, *Architectonic Knowledge in the "New Arcadia" (1590): Sidney's Use of the Heroic Journey* (Salzburg: Institut für Englische Sprache und Literatur, 1978); Lindheim esp. chap. 6; and William Craft, "Remaking the Heroic Self in the *New Arcadia*," *Studies in English Literature 1500–1900* 25 (1985): 45–67. But Walter R. Davis makes a case "that *Arcadia* exploits the themes and techniques of pastoral romance more fully than any other work of the sixteenth century" (*Map of Arcadia* 6); and Lanham has weighty qualifications for any easy label of "epic" (*Arcadia* 395–400).

97. Cf. Ringler, ed., *Poems of Sidney* 418, 492.

98. For the distinction between "monument" and "document" as used by this historian of history, see Michel Foucault, *The Archaeology of Knowledge,* trans. A. M. Sheridan Smith (New York: Pantheon, Random House, 1972), 6–7, 138–39.

99. G. Gregory Smith 2:282.

Works Cited

Primary Texts

Unless otherwise specified, citations of Greek and Roman authors refer to texts in the Loeb Classical Library.

Aristotle. *Poetics: The Argument.* Ed. and trans. Gerald F. Else. Cambridge: Harvard University Press, 1957.

Jonson, Ben. *Ben Jonson.* Ed. C. H. Herford and Percy and Evelyn Simpson. 11 vols. Oxford: Clarendon, 1925–52.

Milton, John. *Complete Poems and Major Prose.* Ed. Merritt Y. Hughes. New York: Odyssey, 1957.

Shakespeare, William. *The Riverside Shakespeare.* Ed. G. Blakemore Evans et al. Boston: Houghton Mifflin, 1974.

Sidney, Philip. *The Poems of Sir Philip Sidney.* Ed. William A. Ringler, Jr. Oxford: Clarendon, 1962.

———. *The Countesse of Pembrokes Arcadia* [1590; the "new" *Arcadia*]. Ed. Carl Dennis. *Kent English Reprints: The Renaissance.* Kent, OH: Kent State University Press, 1970.

———. *The Countess of Pembroke's Arcadia (The Old Arcadia).* Ed. Jean Robertson. Oxford: Clarendon, 1973.

———. *Miscellaneous Prose of Sir Philip Sidney.* Ed. Katherine Duncan-Jones and Jan van Dorsten. Oxford: Clarendon, 1973.

Spenser, Edmund. *The Works: A Variorum Edition.* Ed. Edwin Greenlaw et al. 11 vols. Baltimore: Johns Hopkins University Press, 1932–57.

Secondary Materials

Abrams, M. H. *The Mirror and the Lamp: Romantic Theory and the Critical Tradition.* New York: Oxford University Press, 1953.

Adams, Robert P. "Bold Bawdry and Open Manslaughter: The English New Humanist Attack on Medieval Romance." *Huntington Library Quarterly* 23 (1959–60): 33–48.

Aesop. *Fabulae elegantissimis eiconibus veras animalium species ad vivum adumbrantes.* Lyons, 1570.

Agrippa, Heinrich Cornelius. *Of the vanitie and uncertaintie of artes and sciences*. Trans. James Sanford. London, 1569.

———. *Three books of occult philosophy*. Trans. John Freake. London, 1651.

Alberti, Leon Battista. *On Painting*. Ed. and trans. John R. Spencer. London: Routledge and Kegan Paul, 1956.

———. *On Painting and On Sculpture*. Ed. and trans. Cecil Grayson. London: Phaidon Press, 1972.

———. *Ten Books on Architecture*. Trans. James Leoni [1726]. Ed. Joseph Rykwert. London: Alec Tiranti, 1955.

Alexander of Villadei. *Doctrinale* [1199]. Ed. Dietrich Reichling. 1893. New York: Burt Franklin, 1974.

Allen, Don Cameron. *Image and Meaning: Metaphoric Traditions in Renaissance Poetry*. Rev. ed. Baltimore: Johns Hopkins University Press, 1968.

———. *Mysteriously Meant: The Rediscovery of Pagan Symbolism and Allegorical Interpretation in the Renaissance*. Baltimore: Johns Hopkins University Press, 1970.

Alley, William. Πτωχομουσεῖον: *The poore mans librarie*. London, 1565.

Alpers, Paul J. *The Poetry of "The Faerie Queene."* Princeton: Princeton University Press, 1967.

———. "Narration in *The Faerie Queene*." *ELH* 44 (1977): 19–39.

Alpers, Svetlana and Paul. "*Ut Pictura Noesis?* Criticism in Literary Studies and Art History." *New Literary History* 3 (1971–72): 437–58.

Ames, Van Meter. "What Is Music?" *Journal of Aesthetics and Art Criticism* 26 (1967–68): 241–49.

Anderson, Warren D. *Ethos and Education in Greek Music*. Cambridge: Harvard University Press, 1966.

Arbeau, Thoinot. *Orchesography* [1589]. Trans. Mary Stewart Evans. New York: Dover Publications, 1967.

Aristotle. *Poetics*. Ed. D. W. Lucas. Oxford: Clarendon, 1968.

———. *In librum Aristotelis de arte poetica explicationes*. Ed. Francesco Robortello. Florence, 1548.

———. *Treatise on Poetry*. Trans. Thomas Twining. London, 1789.

———. *Aristotle's Theory of Poetry and Fine Art*. Ed. and trans. S. H. Butcher. 4th ed. London: Macmillan, 1927.

Arnheim, Rudolf. *Art and Visual Perception: A Psychology of the Creative Eye*. Rev. ed. Berkeley: University of California Press, 1974.

Ascham, Roger. *Toxophilus. The Scholemaster. English Works*. Ed. William Aldis Wright. Cambridge: Cambridge University Press, 1904.

Astell, Ann W. "Sidney's Didactic Method in The *Old Arcadia*." *Studies in English Literature 1500–1900* 24 (1984): 39–51.

Atkins, J. W. H. *English Literary Criticism: The Renascence*. London: Methuen, 1947.

Atkinson, Dorothy F. *Edmund Spenser: A Bibliographical Supplement*. Baltimore: Johns Hopkins University Press, 1937.

Attridge, Derek. *Well-Weighed Syllables: Elizabethan Verse in Classical Metres*. London: Cambridge University Press, 1974.

Aubrey, John. *Brief Lives*. Ed. Oliver Lawson Dick. London: Martin Secker, 1949.

Augst, Bertrand. "Descartes's Compendium on Music." *Journal of the History of Ideas* 26 (1965): 119–32.

Augustine, St. *De civitate Dei*. Ed. Juan Luis Vives. Basel, 1522.

———. *Of the citie of God*. Ed. Juan Luis Vives. Trans. John Healey. London, 1610.

———. "De vera religione." *Patrologia Latina*. Ed. J.-P. Migne. 221 vols. Paris, 1878–90, 34:121–72.

———. "On Music." Trans. Robert C. Taliaferro. *Writings of St. Augustine. Fathers of the Church*. 6 vols. Washington, D.C.: Catholic University of America Press, 1947, 2:153–379.

———. *Christian Instruction* et al. Trans. John J. Gavigan, O.S.A. *Writings of St. Augustine. Fathers of the Church*. 6 vols. Washington, D.C.: Catholic University of America Press, 1947, 4:3–235.

———. *Letters*. Trans. Sister Wilfrid Parsons. *Fathers of the Church*. 5 vols. New York: Fathers of the Church, 1951–56.

———. "Faith and the Creed." Trans. Robert P. Russell. *Treatises on Marriage and Other Subjects*. Ed. Roy J. Deferrari. *Fathers of the Church*. Vol. 15. New York: Fathers of the Church, 1955, 311–45.

———. *On the Psalms*. Trans. Dame Scholastica Hebgin and Dame Felicitas Corrigan. 2 vols. Westminster, MD: Newman, 1960.

Avison, Charles. *An Essay on Musical Expression*. London, 1752.

Axton, Marie. "The Tudor Mask and Elizabethan Court Drama." *English Drama: Forms and Development*. Ed. Axton and Raymond Williams. Cambridge: Cambridge University Press, 1977, 24–47.

Babbitt, Irving. *The New Laokoon: An Essay on the Confusion of the Arts*. Boston: Houghton Mifflin, 1910.

Bacon, Francis. *Works*. Ed. James Spedding et al. 7 vols. London, 1857–59.

———. *The Advancement of Learning*. Ed. Thomas Case. London: Oxford University Press, 1974.

Baïf, Jean-Antoine de. *Étrènes de poézie fransoeze an vers mesurés* et al. Paris, 1574.

Bandini, Angelo Maria. *Specimen literaturae florentinae saeculi XV*. 2 vols. Florence, 1747.

Barbi, Michele. *Della fortuna di Dante nel secolo XVI*. Pisa, 1890.

Barkan, Leonard. *Nature's Work of Art: The Human Body as Image of the World*. New Haven: Yale University Press, 1975.

Barthes, Roland. *Le Plaisir du texte*. Paris: Seuil, 1973.

———. *S/Z*. Trans. Richard Miller. New York: Hill and Wang, Farrar, Straus and Giroux, 1974.

———. "The Death of the Author." *Image/Music/Text*. Trans. Stephen Heath. New York: Hill and Wang, Farrar, Straus and Giroux, 1977, 142–48.

Battestin, Martin C. *The Providence of Wit: Aspects of Form in Augustan Literature and the Arts*. Oxford: Clarendon, 1974.

Batteux, Charles. *Les beaux arts réduits à un même principe*. Paris, 1746.

Bauer, Robert J. "A Phenomenon of Epistemology in the Renaissance." *Journal of the History of Ideas* 31 (1970): 281–88.

Beardsley, Monroe C. *Aesthetics: Problems in the Philosophy of Criticism.* New York: Harcourt Brace Jovanovich, 1958.

———. *Aesthetics from Classical Greece to the Present.* New York: Macmillan Publishing, 1966.

———. "Verse and music." *Versification: Major Language Types.* Ed. W. K. Wimsatt, Jr. New York: Modern Language Association, 1972, 238–52.

Bebelius, Henricus. *Ars versificandi et carminum condendorum cum quantitatibus syllabarum.* Strasbourg, 1513.

Bede. "Musica theorica." *Opera.* Vol. 1. Basel, 1563. 8 vols.

Bell, Clive. *Art.* London: Chatto and Windus, 1914.

Benamou, Michel. "Wallace Stevens: Some Relations between Poetry and Painting." *Comparative Literature* 11 (1959): 47–60.

Bender, John B. *Spenser and Literary Pictorialism.* Princeton: Princeton University Press, 1972.

Bennett, Josephine Waters. "Spenser's *Fowre Hymnes:* Addenda." *Studies in Philology* 32 (1935): 131–57.

———. *The Evolution of "The Faerie Queene."* Chicago: University of Chicago Press, 1942.

———. "Spenser's *Amoretti* LXII and the Date of the New Year." *Renaissance Quarterly* 26 (1973): 433–36.

Binns, James. "Henry Dethick in Praise of Poetry: The First Appearance in Print of an Elizabethan Treatise." *Library* 5th ser. 30 (1975): 199–216.

Birch, Thomas. "The Life of Mr. Edmund Spenser." *The Faerie Queene.* Vol. 1. London, 1751. 3 vols.

Bjorvand, Einar. "Spenser's Defence of Poetry: Some Structural Aspects of the *Fowre Hymnes.*" *Fair Forms: Essays in English Literature from Spenser to Jane Austen.* Ed. Maren-Sofie Røstvig. Cambridge: Brewer, 1975, 13–53, 203–6.

Blau, Joseph Leon. *The Christian Interpretation of the Cabala in the Renaissance.* New York: Columbia University Press, 1944.

Blundeville, Thomas. *The true order and methode of wryting and reading hystories.* London, 1574.

Blunt, Anthony. *Artistic Theory in Italy 1450–1600.* Oxford: Clarendon, 1940.

Boaistuau, Pierre. *Certaine secrete wonders of Nature.* Trans. Edward Fenton. London, 1569.

Boas, George, trans. *The Hieroglyphics of Horapollo.* Bollingen Series 23. New York: Pantheon Books, 1950.

Boccaccio, Giovanni. *On Poetry.* Trans. Charles G. Osgood. Princeton: Princeton University Press, 1930.

Bodin, Jean. *Colloquium of the Seven about Secrets of the Divine.* Ed. and trans. Marion L. Kuntz. Princeton: Princeton University Press, 1975.

Boethius. "De musica." *Patrologia Latina.* Ed. J.-P. Migne. 221 vols. Paris, 1878–90, 63:1167–1300.

Bohn, Willard. "Circular Poem-Paintings by Apollinaire and Carrà." *Comparative Literature* 31 (1979): 246–71.

Bonnet, Jacques. *Histoire générale de la danse, sacrée et prophane*. Paris, 1724.

Booth, Wayne. *The Rhetoric of Fiction*. Chicago: University of Chicago Press, 1961.

Borchardt, Frank L. "Etymology in Tradition and in the Northern Renaissance." *Journal of the History of Ideas* 29 (1968): 415–29.

Boyde, Patrick. "Perception and the Percipient in *Convivio*, III,9 and the *Purgatorio*." *Italian Studies* 35 (1980): 19–24.

Brennan, Joseph X. "The *Epitome troporum ac schematum* of Joannes Susenbrotus: Text, Translation, and Commentary." Diss. University of Illinois, 1953.

Brink, J. R. "Philosophical Poetry: The Contrasting Poetics of Sidney and Scaliger." *Explorations in Renaissance Culture* 8–9 (1982–83): 45–53.

Bristol, Michael D. "Structural Patterns in Two Elizabethan Pastorals." *Studies in English Literature 1500–1900* 10 (1970): 33–48.

Brogan, T. V. F. *English Versification, 1570–1980*. Baltimore: Johns Hopkins University Press, 1981.

Bronson, Bertrand H. "Literature and Music." *Relations of Literary Study: Essays on Interdisciplinary Contributions*. Ed. James Thorpe. New York: Modern Language Association, 1967, 127–50.

Brown, Calvin S. *Music and Literature: A Comparison of the Arts*. Athens: University of Georgia Press, 1948.

———. "The Color Symphony before and after Gautier." *Comparative Literature* 5 (1953): 289–309.

———. "The Relations between Music and Literature as a Field of Study." *Comparative Literature* 22 (1970): 97–107.

Brown, Howard M. "How Opera Began: An Introduction to Jacopo Peri's *Euridice* (1600)." *The Late Italian Renaissance 1525–1630*. Ed. Eric Cochrane. New York: Torchbooks, Harper and Row Publishers, 1970, 401–43.

———. *Music in the Renaissance*. Englewood Cliffs: Prentice-Hall, 1976.

Brown, John. *A Dissertation on the Rise, Union, and Power . . . of Poetry and Music*. London, 1763.

Browne, Sir Thomas. *Religio Medici and Other Works*. Ed. L. C. Martin. Oxford: Clarendon, 1964.

Bukofzer, Manfred F. "Speculative Thinking in Mediaeval Music." *Speculum* 17 (1942): 165–80.

Burchmore, David W. "The Image of the Centre in *Colin Clouts Come Home Againe*." *Review of English Studies* ns 28 (1977): 393–406.

Burke, John G. "Hermetism as a Renaissance World View." *The Darker Vision of the Renaissance*. Ed. Robert S. Kinsman. Berkeley: University of California Press, 1974, 95–117.

Butcher, S. H., ed. and trans. *Aristotle's Theory of Poetry and Fine Art*. 4th ed. London: Macmillan, 1927.

Buxton, John. *Sir Philip Sidney and the English Renaissance.* 2d ed. New York: St. Martin's Press, 1964.

————. *Times Literary Supplement* 24 March 1972: 344.

Calvin, John, ed. *The Psalmes of David and others. With M. John Calvins commentaries.* Trans. Arthur Golding. London, 1571.

Campbell, Lily B. "The Christian Muse." *Huntington Library Bulletin* 8 (1935): 29–70.

Campbell, Marion. "Unending Desire: Sidney's Reinvention of Petrarchan Form in *Astrophil and Stella.*" *Sir Philip Sidney and the Interpretation of Renaissance Culture: The Poet in His Time and in Ours.* Ed. Gary F. Waller and Michael D. Moore. London: Croom Helm, 1984, 84–94.

Campion, Thomas. *Observations in the art of English poesie.* London, 1602.

————. *Works.* Ed. Percival Vivian. Oxford: Clarendon, 1909.

Capriano, Giovanni Pietro. *Della vera poetica libro uno.* Venice, 1555.

Carpenter, Frederic I. *A Reference Guide to Edmund Spenser.* Chicago: University of Chicago Press, 1923.

Carpenter, Nan C. *Music in the Medieval and Renaissance Universities.* Norman: University of Oklahoma Press, 1958.

Casady, Edwin. "The Neo-Platonic Ladder in Spenser's *Amoretti.*" *Renaissance Studies in Honor of Hardin Craig.* Ed. Baldwin Maxwell et al. Stanford: Stanford University Press, 1941, 92–103.

Case, John. *The praise of musicke.* Oxford, 1586.

Castelvetro, Lodovico. *Poetica d'Aristotele volgarizzata et sposta.* Basle, 1576.

Castiglione, Baldassare. *The Book of the Courtier* [1561]. Trans. Sir Thomas Hoby. Ed. Walter Raleigh. *Tudor Translations* 23. London: Nutt, 1900.

Castor, Grahame. *Pléiade Poetics: A Study in Sixteenth-Century Thought and Terminology.* Cambridge: Cambridge University Press, 1964.

Cebes. *Tablet.* Intro. by Sandra Sider. New York: Renaissance Society, 1979.

Chalifour, Clark L. "Sir Philip Sidney's *Old Arcadia* as Terentian Comedy." *Studies in English Literature 1500–1900* 16 (1976): 51–63.

Challis, Lorna. "The Use of Oratory in Sidney's *Arcadia.*" *Studies in Philology* 62 (1965): 561–76.

Chalmers, Gordon K. "'That Universal and Publick Manuscript.'" *Virginia Quarterly Review* 26 (1950): 414–30.

Charlton, H. B. *Castelvetro's Theory of Poetry.* Manchester: Manchester University Press, 1913.

Charlton, Kenneth. *Education in Renaissance England.* London: Routledge and Kegan Paul, 1965.

Chastel, André. *Marsile Ficin et l'art.* Geneva: Droz, 1954.

————. *Art et humanisme à Florence au temps de Laurent le Magnifique.* Paris: Presses Universitaires, 1959.

————. *The Myth of the Renaissance 1420–1520.* Geneva: Skira, 1969.

Chaucer, Geoffrey. *Works.* Ed. F. N. Robinson. 2d ed. Boston: Houghton Mifflin, 1957.

Chaytor, Henry J. *From Script to Print.* Cambridge: Cambridge University Press, 1945.

Church, Margaret. "The First English Pattern Poems." *PMLA* 61 (1946): 636–50.

Churchyard, Thomas. *A musicall consort of heavenly harmonie . . . called Churchyards charitie.* London, 1595.

Cibber, Theophilus. *The Lives of the Poets of Great Britain and Ireland.* 5 vols. London, 1753.

Cicero. *Three bookes of dueties.* 2d ed. Trans. Nicholas Grimald. London, 1558.

Clark, Donald L. *Rhetoric and Poetry in the Renaissance.* New York: Columbia University Press, 1922.

Clements, Robert J. *The Peregrine Muse: Studies in Comparative Renaissance Literature. University of North Carolina Studies in Romance Languages and Literatures* 31. Chapel Hill: University of North Carolina Press, 1959.

———. *Picta Poesis: Literary and Humanistic Theory in Renaissance Emblem Books.* Rome: Storia e Letteratura, 1960.

Close, A. J. "Commonplace Theories of Art and Nature in Classical Antiquity and in the Renaissance." *Journal of the History of Ideas* 30 (1969): 467–86.

Coleridge, Samuel Taylor. *Biographia Literaria.* 2 vols. London, 1817.

Colie, Rosalie L. *The Resources of Kind: Genre-Theory in the Renaissance.* Berkeley: University of California Press, 1973.

Colish, Marcia L. *The Mirror of Language: A Study in the Medieval Theory of Knowledge.* New Haven: Yale University Press, 1968.

Collingwood, R. G. "Plato's Philosophy of Art." *Mind* 34 (1925): 154–72.

———. *The Principles of Art.* Oxford: Clarendon, 1938.

———. *Essays in the Philosophy of Art.* Bloomington: Indiana University Press, 1964.

Collins, Arthur. *Letters and Memorials of State, in the Reigns of Queen Mary, Queen Elizabeth, King James, King Charles the First, Part of the Reign of King Charles the Second, and Oliver's Usurpation.* 2 vols. London, 1746.

Collinson, Patrick. *The Elizabethan Puritan Movement.* Berkeley: University of California Press, 1967.

Comito, Terry. "A Dialectic of Images in Spenser's *Fowre Hymnes.*" *Studies in Philology* 74 (1977): 301–21.

Connell, Dorothy. *Sir Philip Sidney: The Maker's Mind.* Oxford: Clarendon, 1977.

Cook, Elizabeth. "Figured Poetry." *Journal of the Warburg and Courtauld Institutes* 42 (1979): 1–15.

Cooper, Lane. *The Poetics of Aristotle: Its Meaning and Influence.* New York: Longmans, 1927.

Cooper, Thomas. *Thesaurus linguae Romanae & Britannicae.* London, 1578.

Coulter, James A. *The Literary Microcosm: Theories of Interpretation of the Later Neoplatonists.* Leiden: E. J. Brill, 1976.

Court, Franklin E. "The Theme and Structure of Spenser's *Muiopotmos.*" *Studies in English Literature 1500–1900* 10 (1970): 1–15.

Cowley, Abraham. *Poems*. Ed. A. R. Waller. Cambridge: Cambridge University Press, 1905.

Craft, William. "Remaking the Heroic Self in the *New Arcadia*." *Studies in English Literature 1500–1900* 25 (1985): 45–67.

Craig, D. H. "A Hybrid Growth: Sidney's Theory of Poetry in *An Apology for Poetry*." *English Literary Renaissance* 10 (1980): 183–201.

Craig, Martha. "The Secret Wit of Spenser's Language." *Elizabethan Poetry: Modern Essays in Criticism*. Ed Paul J. Alpers. New York: Oxford University Press, 1967, 447–72.

Crinito, Pietro. *De honesta disciplina* et al. Basel, 1532.

Crocker, Richard L. "Pythagorean Mathematics and Music." *Journal of Aesthetics and Art Criticism* 22 (1963–64): 189–98, 325–35.

Crombie, A. C. "Science and the Arts in the Renaissance: The Search for Truth and Certainty, Old and New." *History of Science* 18 (1980): 233–46.

Culler, Jonathan. *Structuralist Poetics: Structuralism, Linguistics and the Study of Literature*. Ithaca: Cornell University Press, 1975.

———. *Saussure*. Hassocks: Harvester, 1976.

———. *The Pursuit of Signs: Semiotics, Literature, Deconstruction*. Ithaca: Cornell University Press, 1981.

———. *On Deconstruction: Theory and Criticism after Structuralism*. Ithaca: Cornell University Press, 1982.

Cummings, L. "Spenser's *Amoretti* VIII: New Manuscript Versions." *Studies in English Literature 1500–1900* 4 (1964): 125–35.

Cummings, R. M., ed. *Spenser: The Critical Heritage*. New York: Barnes and Noble Books, 1971.

Curtius, Ernst R. *European Literature and the Latin Middle Ages*. Trans. Willard R. Trask. *Bollingen Series* 36. New York: Pantheon Books, 1953.

Daly, Peter M. *Literature in the Light of the Emblem*. Toronto: University of Toronto Press, 1979.

Dana, Margaret E. "The Providential Plot of the *Old Arcadia*." *Studies in English Literature 1500–1900* 17 (1977): 39–57.

Daniel, Samuel. *A defence of ryme*. London, 1603.

———. *The Civil Wars*. Ed. Laurence Michel. New Haven: Yale University Press, 1958.

———, trans. *The worthy tract of Paulus Jovius, contayning a discourse of rare inventions, both militarie and amorous called imprese*. London, 1585.

Dante. *Dante con l'espositione di Christoforo Landino, et di Alessandro Vellutello, sopra la sua Comedia dell'Inferno, del Purgatorio, & del Paradiso*. Ed. Francesco Sansovino. Venice, 1564.

———. *Vita Nuova*. Trans. Mark Musa. Bloomington: Indiana University Press, 1973.

———. *De vulgari eloquentia*. *Literary Criticism of Dante Alighieri*. Ed. and trans. Robert S. Haller. Lincoln: University of Nebraska Press, 1973.

———. *Epistolae*. Ed. and trans. Paget Toynbee. 2d ed. Oxford: Clarendon, 1966.

Davids, Roy L. *Times Literary Supplement*, 7 April 1972: 394.

Davie, Donald. *Articulate Energy: An Inquiry into the Syntax of English Poetry* [1955]. London: Routledge and Kegan Paul, 1976.

Davies, Sir John. *The Poems.* Ed. Robert Krueger. Oxford: Clarendon, 1975.

Davis, Beverly Jeanne. "Antoine de Bertrand: A View into the Aesthetics of Music in Sixteenth Century France." *Journal of Aesthetics and Art Criticism* 21 (1962–63): 189–200.

Davis, Walter R. *A Map of Arcadia: Sidney's Romance in Its Tradition. Sidney's Arcadia. Yale Studies in English* 158. New Haven: Yale University Press, 1965, 1–179.

———. *Idea and Act in Elizabethan Fiction.* Princeton: Princeton University Press, 1969.

Debus, Allen G. *Man and Nature in the Renaissance.* Cambridge: Cambridge University Press, 1978.

Dee, John. "Mathematicall praeface." *The elements of geometrie.* By Euclid. Trans. Henry Billingsley. London, 1570.

Dees, Jerome S. "The Narrator of *The Faerie Queene:* Patterns of Response." *Texas Studies in Literature and Language* 12 (1970–71): 537–68.

De Grazia, Margreta. "The Secularization of Language in the Seventeenth Century." *Journal of the History of Ideas* 41 (1980): 319–29.

Della Casa, Giovanni. *Galateo.* Trans. Robert Peterson. London, 1576.

De Man, Paul. *Allegories of Reading: Figural Language in Rousseau, Nietzsche, Rilke, and Proust.* New Haven: Yale University Press, 1979.

DeNeef, A. Leigh. "The Dialectic of Genres in *The Shepheardes Calender.*" *Renaissance Papers 1975.* Durham, NC: Southeastern Renaissance Conference, 1976, 1–10.

———. "Rereading Sidney's *Apology.*" *Journal of Medieval and Renaissance Studies* 10 (1980): 155–91.

———. *Spenser and the Motives of Metaphor.* Durham: Duke University Press, 1982.

Derrida, Jacques. "Signature Event Context" [1971]. *Margins of Philosophy.* Trans. Alan Bass. Chicago: University of Chicago Press, 1982, 307–30.

———. "White Mythology: Metaphor in the Text of Philosophy." *New Literary History* 6 (1974–75): 5–74.

———. *Positions.* Trans. Alan Bass. Chicago: University of Chicago Press, 1981.

Descartes, René. *Compendium of musick.* Trans. anon. London, 1653.

De Selincourt, Ernest, and J. C. Smith, eds. *The Poetical Works of Edmund Spenser.* London: Oxford University Press, 1912.

Dieckmann, Liselotte. *Hieroglyphics: The History of a Literary Symbol.* St. Louis: Washington University Press, 1970.

Digby, Everard. *Theoria analytica.* London, 1579.

Digby, Kenelm. *Observations on the 22. stanza in the 9th. canto of the 2d. book of Spencers Faery Queen.* London, 1644.

Dijkstra, Bram. *The Hieroglyphics of a New Speech: Cubism, Stieglitz, and the Early Poetry of William Carlos Wiliams.* Princeton: Princeton University Press, 1969.

Dipple, Elizabeth. "The 'Fore Conceit' of Sidney's Eclogues." *Literary Mono-*

graphs I. Ed. Eric Rothstein and Thomas K. Dunseath. Madison: University of Wisconsin Press, 1967, 1–47, 301–3.

———. "'Unjust Justice' in the *Old Arcadia*." *Studies in English Literature 1500–1900* 10 (1970): 83–101.

Dobell, Bertram. "New Light upon Sir Philip Sidney's 'Arcadia.'" *Quarterly Review* 211 (1909): 74–100.

Dolce, Lodovico. *Aretino*. *Dolce's "Aretino" and Venetian Art Theory of the Cinquecento*. Ed. and trans. Mark W. Roskill. *Monographs on Archaeology and the Fine Arts* 15. New York: New York University Press, 1968.

Donne, John. *The Elegies, and The Songs and Sonnets*. Ed. Helen Gardner. Oxford: Clarendon, 1965.

Donno, Elizabeth Story. "Old Mouse-eaten Records: History in Sidney's *Apology*." *Studies in Philology* 72 (1975): 275–98.

Dorsten, Jan A. van, ed. *A Defence of Poetry*. By Philip Sidney. London: Oxford University Press, 1966.

Dowlin, Cornell March. "Sidney's Two Definitions of Poetry." *Modern Language Quarterly* 3 (1942): 573–81.

Drant, Thomas, trans. *Horace His Arte of Poetrie, Pistles, and Satyrs Englished*. Ed. Peter E. Medine. Delmar, NY: Scholars' Facsimiles and Reprints, 1972.

Drayton, Michael. *The barrons wars in the raigne of Edward the second. With Englands heroicall epistles*. London, 1603.

Dryden, John. *Essays*. Ed. W. P. Ker. 2 vols. Oxford: Clarendon, 1900.

Du Bartas, Guillaume Saluste. *Devine weekes & workes*. Trans. Joshua Sylvester. London, 1605.

———. *Divine weekes and workes*. Trans. Joshua Sylvester. London, 1633.

Du Bellay, Joachim. *Deffence et illustration de la langue francoyse*. Ed. Henri Chamard. Paris: Didier, 1948.

Dubois, Claude-Gilbert. *Mythe et langage au seizième siècle*. *Collections Ducros* 8. Bordeaux: Ducros, 1970.

Duncan-Jones, Katherine. "Philip Sidney's Toys." *Proceedings of the British Academy* 66 (1980): 161–78.

Dundas, Judith. "*The Faerie Queene:* The Incomplete Poem and the Whole Meaning." *Modern Philology* 71 (1973–74): 257–65.

———. "Illusion and the Poetic Image." *Journal of Aesthetics and Art Criticism* 32 (1973–74): 197–203.

———. "*Muiopotmos:* A World of Art." *Yearbook of English Studies* 5 (1975): 30–38.

———. "Style and the Mind's Eye." *Journal of Aesthetics and Art Criticism* 37 (1978–79): 325–34.

Dunlop, Alexander. "The Unity of Spenser's *Amoretti*." *Silent Poetry: Essays in Numerological Analysis*. Ed. Alastair Fowler. London: Routledge and Kegan Paul, 1970, 153–69.

Duplessis-Mornay, Philippe. *A woorke concerning the trewnesse of the Christian religion* [1587]. Trans. Philip Sidney and Arthur Golding. *The Com-*

plete Works of Sir Philip Sidney. Ed. Albert Feuillerat. 2d ed. 4 vols. Cambridge: Cambridge University Press, 1962, 3:247–367.

Durling, Robert M. *The Figure of the Poet in Renaissance Epic.* Cambridge: Harvard University Press, 1965.

Eade, J. C. "The Pattern in the Astronomy of Spenser's *Epithalamion.*" *Review of English Studies* ns 23 (1972): 173–78.

Eco, Umberto. *L'Oeuvre ouverte.* Trans. Chantal Roux de Bézieux. Paris: Seuil, 1965.

———. *The Role of the Reader: Explorations in the Semiotics of Texts.* Bloomington: Indiana University Press, 1979.

Edgerton, Samuel Y., Jr. *The Renaissance Rediscovery of Linear Perspective.* New York: Basic Books, 1975.

Eliot, T. S. "Tradition and the Individual Talent," "The Function of Criticism." *Selected Essays 1917–1932.* New York: Harcourt Brace Jovanovich, 1932, 3–11, 12–22.

———. *The Use of Poetry and the Use of Criticism.* Cambridge: Harvard University Press, 1933.

———. "The Music of Poetry." *Selected Prose.* Ed. John Hayward. Harmondsworth: Penguin Books, 1953, 56–67.

Else, Gerald F., ed. and trans. *Aristotle's Poetics: The Argument.* Cambridge: Harvard University Press, 1957.

Elyot, Sir Thomas. *The Governour.* Ed. Henry H. S. Croft. 2 vols. London, 1883.

Erasmus. *Adagiorum chiliades quatuor, et sesquicenturia.* Lyons, 1559.

———. *De duplici copia verborum ac rerum, commentarii duo.* Antwerp, 1553.

———. *De duplici copia verborum, et rerum, commentarii duo.* London, 1569.

———. *"Copia": Foundations of the Abundant Style.* Trans. Betty I. Knott. *Collected Works of Erasmus.* Ed. Craig R. Thompson. Vol. 24. Toronto: University of Toronto Press, 1974– . 10 vols. to date.

Estienne, Henri, ed. *Poetae graeci principes heroici carminis, & alii nonnulli.* Geneva, 1566.

Evans, Frank B. "The Concept of the Fall in Sidney's *Apologie.*" *Renaissance Papers 1969.* Durham, NC: Southeastern Renaissance Conference, 1970, 9–14.

Evans, Maurice, ed. *The Countess of Pembroke's Arcadia.* By Philip Sidney. Harmondsworth: Penguin Books, 1977.

Fabry, Frank J. "Sidney's Poetry and Italian Song-Form." *English Literary Renaissance* 3 (1973): 232–48.

Farmer, Norman K., Jr. *Poets and the Visual Arts in Renaissance England.* Austin: University of Texas Press, 1984.

Fata, Frank J. "Landino on Dante." Diss. Johns Hopkins, 1966.

Fenton, Edward, trans. *Certaine secrete wonders of nature.* By Pierre Boaistuau. London, 1569.

Ferraro, Rose Mary. *Giudizi critici e criteri estetici nei Poetices libri septem (1561) di Giulio Cesare Scaligero rispetto alla teoria letteraria del Rinas-*

cimento. *University of North Carolina Studies in Comparative Literature* 52. Chapel Hill: University of North Carolina Press, 1971.

Feuillerat, Albert, ed. *The Complete Works of Sir Philip Sidney.* 4 vols. Cambridge: Cambridge University Press, 1912–26.

———, ed. *The Complete Works of Sir Philip Sidney.* 2d ed. 4 vols. Cambridge: Cambridge University Press, 1962.

Fichter, Andrew. *Poets Historical: Dynastic Epic in the Renaissance.* New Haven: Yale University Press, 1982.

Ficino, Marsilio. *Opera.* Basel, 1561.

———. *The Letters.* Ed. Paul O. Kristeller et al. 3 vols. to date. London: Shepheard-Walwyn, 1975– .

———. *Théologie Platonicienne de l'immortalité des âmes.* Ed and trans. Raymond Marcel. 3 vols. Paris: Belles Lettres, 1964–70.

———, ed. and trans. *Omnia divini Platonis opera.* Basel, 1546.

Fielding, Henry. *Joseph Andrews.* Ed. Martin C. Battestin. Middletown: Wesleyan University Press, 1967.

Fienberg, Nona. "The Emergence of Stella in *Astrophil and Stella.*" *Studies in English Literature 1500–1900* 25 (1985): 5–19.

Finney, Gretchen L. *Musical Backgrounds for English Literature: 1580–1650.* New Brunswick: Rutgers University Press, 1962.

Fish, Stanley E. *Self-Consuming Artifacts.* Berkeley: University of California Press, 1972.

———. *Is There a Text in This Class? The Authority of Interpretive Communities.* Cambridge: Harvard University Press, 1980.

Fogel, Ephim G. "The Mythical Sorrows of Astrophil." *Studies in Language and Literature in Honor of Margaret Schlauch.* Ed. Mieczyslaw Brahmer et al. Warsaw: Polish Scientific Publishers, 1966, 133–52.

Foucault, Michel. *The Archaeology of Knowledge.* Trans. A. M. Sheridan Smith. New York: Pantheon Books, Random House, 1972.

———. *The Order of Things: An Archaeology of the Human Sciences.* New York: Vintage Books, Random House, 1973.

———. "What Is an Author?" *Textual Strategies: Perspectives in Post-Structuralist Criticism.* Ed. Josué V. Harari. Ithaca: Cornell University Press, 1979, 141–60.

Fowler, Alastair. *Triumphal Forms: Structural Patterns in Elizabethan Poetry.* Cambridge: Cambridge University Press, 1970.

Fracastoro, Girolamo. *Naugerius, sive de poetica dialogus.* Ed. Murray W. Bundy. Trans. Ruth Kelso. *University of Illinois Studies in Language and Literature* 9.3. Urbana: University of Illinois Press, 1924.

Fraunce, Abraham. *The third part of the Countesse of Pembrokes Yvychurch.* London, 1592.

Freeman, Kathleen, trans. *Ancilla to "The Pre-Socratic Philosophers."* Cambridge: Harvard University Press, 1957.

Friedland, Louis S. "Spenser as a Fabulist." *Shakespeare Association Bulletin* 12 (1937): 85–108, 133–54, 197–207.

Frye, Northrop. *Anatomy of Criticism.* Princeton: Princeton University Press, 1957.

———. "Introduction: Lexis and Melos." *Sound and Poetry.* Ed. Frye. *English Institute Essays 1956.* New York: Columbia University Press, 1957, ix–xxvii.

Fuller, Thomas (?). "The Life and Death of Sir Philip Sidney." *Countess of Pembrokes Arcadia.* 10th ed. London, 1655, a2–c1.

Gadol, Joan. "The Unity of the Renaissance: Humanism, Natural Science, and Art." *From the Renaissance to the Counter-Reformation: Essays in Honor of Garrett Mattingly.* Ed. Charles H. Carter. New York: Random House, 1965, 29–55.

———. *Leon Battista Alberti: Universal Man of the Early Renaissance.* Chicago: University of Chicago Press, 1969.

Gafuri, Franchino. *Practica musicae* [1496]. Ed. and trans. Clement A. Miller. *Musicological Studies and Documents* 20. Neuhausen-Stuttgart: American Institute of Musicology, 1968.

———. *De harmonia musicorum instrumentorum opus* [1518]. Ed. and trans. Clement A. Miller. *Musicological Studies and Documents* 33. Neuhausen-Stuttgart: American Institute of Musicology, 1977.

Gager, William, ed. *Exequiae illustrissimi equitis, D. Philippi Sidnaei.* Oxford, 1587 [STC 22551].

Gale, Theophilus. *The court of the gentiles.* Oxford, 1669.

Galm, John A. *Sidney's Arcadian Poems.* Salzburg: Institut für Englische Sprache und Literatur, 1973.

Gardner, Helen. *The Business of Criticism.* Oxford: Clarendon, 1959.

Garin, Eugenio. *L'Educazione in Europa, 1400–1600: Problemi e programmi.* Rev. ed. Bari: Laterza, 1976.

———, ed. *L'Educazione umanistica in Italia: Testi scelti e illustrati.* Bari: Laterza, 1949.

Gascoigne, George. "Certayne notes of instruction concerning the making of verse or ryme in English." *Elizabethan Critical Essays.* Ed. G. Gregory Smith. 2 vols. London: Oxford University Press, 1904, 1:46–57.

———. *A hundreth sundrie flowres.* London, 1573.

———. *A Hundreth Sundrie Flowres.* Ed. Charles T. Prouty. *University of Missouri Studies* 17.2. Columbia: University of Missouri Press, 1942.

———. *The posies.* London, 1575.

Geist, Sidney. *Brancusi/The Kiss.* New York: Harper and Row, 1978.

Gent, Lucy. *Picture and Poetry 1560–1620: Relations between Literature and the Visual Arts in the English Renaissance.* Leamington Spa: Hall, 1981.

Giorgio, Francesco. *De harmonia mundi totius cantica tria.* Venice, 1525.

———. *L'Harmonie du monde.* Trans. Guy le Fèvre de la Boderie. Paris, 1579.

Giovio, Paolo. *Dialogo dell'imprese militari et amorose.* Lyons, 1574.

———. *A discourse of rare inventions, both militarie and amorous called imprese.* Trans. Samuel Daniel. London, 1585.

Glareanus, Henricus. *De ratione syllabarum brevis isagoge.* Paris, 1555.

Glowka, Arthur Wayne. "The Function of Meter According to Ancient and Medieval Theory." *Allegorica* 7 (1982): 100–109.

Golding, Arthur, trans. *The Psalmes of David and others. With M. John Calvins commentaries.* London, 1571.

Gombrich, E. H. *Art and Illusion: A Study in the Psychology of Pictorial Representation.* Bollingen Series 35. 2d ed. New York: Pantheon Books, 1961.

———. *Norm and Form: Studies in the Art of the Renaissance.* London: Phaidon Press, 1966.

———. *The Heritage of Apelles.* Ithaca: Cornell University Press, 1976.

Goodman, Nelson. *Languages of Art: An Approach to a Theory of Symbols.* Indianapolis: Bobbs-Merrill, 1968.

Gottfried, Rudolph. "The Pictorial Element in Spenser's Poetry." *ELH* 19 (1952): 203–13.

Goulart, Simon, ed. *The lives of the noble Grecians and Romaines.* By Plutarch. Trans. Thomas North. London, 1603.

Gray, Hanna H. "Renaissance Humanism: The Pursuit of Eloquence." *Journal of the History of Ideas* 24 (1963): 497–514.

Grayson, Cecil, ed. and trans. *On Painting and On Sculpture.* By Leon Battista Alberti. London: Phaidon Press, 1972.

Greenblatt, Stephen J. "Sidney's *Arcadia* and the Mixed Mode." *Studies in Philology* 70 (1973): 269–78.

Greene, Theodore Meyer. *The Arts and the Art of Criticism.* Princeton: Princeton University Press, 1940.

Greene, Thomas M. *The Light in Troy: Imitation and Discovery in Renaissance Poetry.* Elizabethan Club Series 7. New Haven: Yale University Press, 1982.

Greenfield, Thelma N. *The Eye of Judgment: Reading the New Arcadia.* Lewisburg: Bucknell University Press, 1982.

Greenlaw, Edwin A. "Spenser and the Earl of Leicester." *PMLA* 25 (1910): 535–61.

———. "Sidney's *Arcadia* as an Example of Elizabethan Allegory." *Anniversary Papers by Colleagues and Pupils of George Lyman Kittredge.* Boston: Ginn, 1913, 327–37.

———. "Spenser's Fairy Mythology." *Studies in Philology* 15 (1918): 105–22.

Greville, Fulke. *Life of Sir Philip Sidney* [1652]. Ed. Nowell Smith. Oxford: Clarendon, 1907.

Grimald, Nicholas, trans. *Marcus Tullius Ciceroes three bookes of dueties.* 2d ed. London, 1558.

Gross, Kenneth. "'Each Heav'nly Close': Mythologies and Metrics in Spenser and the Early Poetry of Milton." *PMLA* 98 (1983): 21–36.

Hagenbuechle, Helen. "Epistemology and Musical Form in Conrad Aiken's Poetry." *Studies in the Literary Imagination* 13.2 (1980): 7–25.

Hagstrum, Jean H. *The Sister Arts: The Tradition of Literary Pictorialism and English Poetry from Dryden to Gray.* Chicago: University of Chicago Press, 1958.

Halio, Jay L. "The Metaphor of Conception and Elizabethan Theories of the Imagination." *Neophilologus* 50 (1966): 454–61.

Hall, Robert W. "Plato's Theory of Art: A Reassessment." *Journal of Aesthetics and Art Criticism* 33 (1974–75): 75–82.

Hall, Vernon, Jr. "Life of Julius Caesar Scaliger." *Transactions of the American Philosophical Society* 40 (1950): 85–170.

Hamilton, A. C. "Sidney's Idea of the 'Right Poet.'" *Comparative Literature* 9 (1957): 51–59.

———. "Spenser's *Letter to Ralegh*." *Modern Language Notes* 73 (1958): 481–85.

———. *The Structure of Allegory in "The Faerie Queene."* Oxford: Clarendon, 1961.

———. "Sidney's *Arcadia* as Prose Fiction: Its Relation to Its Sources." *English Literary Renaissance* 2 (1972): 29–60.

———. *Sir Philip Sidney: A Study of His Life and Works.* Cambridge: Cambridge University Press, 1977.

Hamilton, George Heard. *Painting and Sculpture in Europe 1880–1940.* Rev. ed. Baltimore: Penguin Books, 1972.

Hanning, Barbara R. *Of Poetry and Music's Power: Humanism and the Creation of Opera. Studies in Musicology (ser. 2)* 13. Ann Arbor: University Microfilms International Research Press, 1980.

Hanslick, Eduard. *Vom Musikalisch-Schönen: Ein Beitrag zur Revision der Aesthetik der Tonkunst.* Leipzig, 1854.

Hardison, O. B., Jr. *The Enduring Monument: A Study of the Idea of Praise in Renaissance Literary Theory and Practice.* Chapel Hill: University of North Carolina Press, 1962.

———. "The Orator and the Poet: The Dilemma of Humanist Literature." *Journal of Medieval and Renaissance Studies* 1 (1971): 33–44.

———. "The Two Voices of Sidney's *Apology for Poetry*." *English Literary Renaissance* 2 (1972): 83–99.

———. "*Amoretti* and the *Dolce Stil Novo*." *English Literary Renaissance* 2 (1972): 208–16.

Harington, Sir John. "A Preface" [to his translation of *Orlando Furioso*, 1591]. *Elizabethan Critical Essays.* Ed. G. Gregory Smith. 2 vols. London: Oxford University Press, 1904, 2:194–222.

Harrison, T. P., Jr. "The Relations of Spenser and Sidney." *PMLA* 45 (1930): 712–31.

Hart, Thomas Elwood. "Medieval Structuralism: 'Dulcarnoun' and the Five-Book Design of Chaucer's *Troilus*." *Chaucer Review* 16 (1981): 129–70.

———. "Poetry, Mathematics, and the Liberal Arts Tradition." *Syracuse Scholar* 3 (1982): 58–73.

Harvey, Gabriel. *Ciceronianus.* Ed. Harold S. Wilson. Trans. Clarence A. Forbes. *University of Nebraska Studies in the Humanities* 4. Lincoln: University of Nebraska Press, 1945.

———. *Marginalia.* Ed. G. C. Moore Smith. Stratford: Shakespeare Head, 1913.

Hathaway, Baxter. *The Age of Criticism: The Late Renaissance in Italy*. Ithaca: Cornell University Press, 1962.

———. *Marvels and Commonplaces: Renaissance Literary Criticism*. New York: Random House, 1968.

Hauser, Arnold. *The Social History of Art*. 2 vols. London: Routledge and Kegan Paul, 1951.

Hayden, John O. *Polestar of the Ancients: The Aristotelian Tradition in Classical and English Literary Criticism*. Newark: University of Delaware Press, 1979.

Healey, John, trans. *Of the citie of God*. By St. Augustine. Ed. Juan Luis Vives. London, 1610.

Hearsey, Marguerite. "Sidney's *Defense of Poesy* and Amyot's *Preface* in North's *Plutarch:* A Relationship." *Studies in Philology* 30 (1933): 535–50.

Hedley, Jane. "What Price Energeia: Personification in the Poetry of Sidney and Greville." *Studies in the Literary Imagination* 15.1 (1982): 49–66.

Hegel, G. W. F. *The Philosophy of Fine Art*. Trans. F. P. B. Osmaston. 4 vols. London: Bell and Hyman, 1916–20.

Helgerson, Richard. "The New Poet Presents Himself: Spenser and the Idea of a Literary Career." *PMLA* 93 (1978): 893–911.

Hellerstein, Nina S. "Paul Claudel and Guillaume Apollinaire as Visual Poets: *Idéogrammes occidentaux* and *Calligrammes*." *Visible Language* 11 (1977): 245–70.

Heninger, S. K., Jr. *Touches of Sweet Harmony: Pythagorean Cosmology and Renaissance Poetics*. San Marino: Huntington Library, 1974.

———. "The Aesthetic Experience of Reading Spenser." *Contemporary Thought on Edmund Spenser*. Ed. Richard C. Frushell and Bernard J. Vondersmith. Carbondale: Southern Illinois University Press, 1975, 79–98.

———. *The Cosmographical Glass: Renaissance Diagrams of the Universe*. San Marino: Huntington Library, 1977.

———. "'Metaphor' and Sidney's *Defence of Poesie*." *John Donne Journal* 1 (1982): 117–49.

———. "The Semantics of Symmetry in the Arts of the Renaissance." *Hebrew University Studies in Literature and the Arts* 11 (1983): 284–303.

———. "Sidney and Boethian Music." *Studies in English Literature 1500–1900* 23 (1983): 37–46.

———. "Sidney and Serranus' *Plato*." *English Literary Renaissance* 13 (1983): 146–61.

———. "Speaking Pictures: Sidney's Rapprochement between Poetry and Painting." *Sir Philip Sidney and the Interpretation of Renaissance Culture: The Poet in His Time and in Ours*. Ed. Gary F. Waller and Michael D. Moore. London: Croom Helm, 1984, 3–16.

———. "Sequences, Systems, Models: Sidney and the Secularization of Sonnets." *Poems in Their Place*. Ed. Neil Fraistat. Chapel Hill: University of North Carolina Press, 1986, 66–94.

————. "Words and Meter in Spenser and Scaliger." *Huntington Library Quarterly* 50 (1987): 309–22.

————. "The Typographical Layout of Spenser's *Shepheardes Calender*." *The Word and the Visual Imagination*. Ed. Karl Josef Höltgen and Peter M. Daly. Erlangen: University of Erlangen Press, 1988. Forthcoming.

————. "Sidney and Spenser at Leicester House." *Spenser Studies*. Forthcoming.

————, ed. *The Shepheardes Calender (1579)*. By Edmund Spenser. Delmar, NY: Scholars' Facsimiles and Reprints, 1979.

Hermes Trismegistus. *The divine Pymander*. Trans. John Everard. London, 1650.

Herrick, Marvin T. *The Poetics of Aristotle in England*. New Haven: Yale University Press, 1930.

————. *The Fusion of Horatian and Aristotelian Literary Criticism, 1531–1555*. Urbana: University of Illinois Press, 1946.

————. "The Place of Rhetoric in Poetic Theory." *Quarterly Journal of Speech* 34 (1948): 1–22.

Hieatt, A. Kent. *Short Time's Endless Monument: The Symbolism of the Numbers in Edmund Spenser's "Epithalamion."* New York: Columbia University Press, 1960.

————. "A Numerical Key for Spenser's *Amoretti* and Guyon in the House of Mammon." *Yearbook of English Studies* 3 (1973): 14–27.

Higgins, Dick. *George Herbert's Pattern Poems: In Their Tradition*. West Glover, VT: Unpublished Editions, 1977.

Higginson, James J. *Spenser's Shepherd's Calendar in Relation to Contemporary Affairs*. New York: Columbia University Press, 1912.

Hill, Elizabeth K. "What Is an Emblem?" *Journal of Aesthetics and Art Criticism* 29 (1970–71): 261–65.

Hill, W. Speed. "Order and Joy in Spenser's 'Epithalamion.'" *Southern Humanities Review* 6 (1972): 81–90.

Hirsch, E. D., Jr. *Validity in Interpretation*. New Haven: Yale University Press, 1967.

Hobbes, Thomas. *A discourse upon Gondibert. An heroick poem written by Sir William D'Avenant. With an answer to it by Mr. Hobbes*. Paris, 1650.

Hoffman, Nancy Jo. *Spenser's Pastorals: "The Shepheardes Calender" and "Colin Clout."* Baltimore: Johns Hopkins University Press, 1977.

Holland, Philemon, trans. *The philosophie, commonlie called, the morals*. By Plutarch. London, 1603.

Hollander, John. "The Music of Poetry." *Journal of Aesthetics and Art Criticism* 15 (1956–57): 232–44.

————. *The Untuning of the Sky: Ideas of Music in English Poetry 1500–1700*. Princeton: Princeton University Press, 1961.

————. *Vision and Resonance: Two Senses of Poetic Form*. New York: Oxford University Press, 1975.

Höltgen, Karl J. "The Reformation of Images and Some Jacobean Writers on

Art." *Functions of Literature: Essays Presented to Erwin Wolff on His Sixtieth Birthday*. Tübingen: Niemeyer, 1984, 119–46.

Horace. *His Arte of Poetrie, Pistles, and Satyrs Englished*. Trans. Thomas Drant. Ed. Peter E. Medine. Delmar, NY: Scholars' Facsimiles and Reprints, 1972.

Horapollo. *De sacris Ægyptiorum notis, Ægypticè expressis libri duo*. Paris, 1574.

———. *The Hieroglyphics*. Trans. George Boas. *Bollingen Series* 23. New York: Pantheon Books, 1950.

Horn, Georg. *Historiae philosophiae libri septem*. Leiden, 1655.

Hough, Graham. *An Essay on Criticism*. London: Gerald Duckworth, 1966.

Howard, William Guild. "Ut Pictura Poesis." *PMLA* 24 (1909): 40–123.

Howell, A. C. "*Res et verba:* Words and Things." *ELH* 13 (1946): 131–42.

Howell, Roger. *Sir Philip Sidney: The Shepherd Knight*. Boston: Little, Brown, 1968.

Howell, Wilbur S. *Logic and Rhetoric in England, 1500–1700*. Princeton: Princeton University Press, 1956.

Hudson, Hoyt H. "Penelope Devereux as Sidney's Stella." *Huntington Library Bulletin* 7 (1935): 89–129.

Hughes, John, ed. *The Works of Mr. Edmund Spenser*. 6 vols. London, 1715.

Hughes, Merritt Y. *Virgil and Spenser. University of California Publications in English* 2.3. Berkeley: University of California Press, 1929.

Hulse, Clark. *Metamorphic Verse: The Elizabethan Minor Epic*. Princeton: Princeton University Press, 1981.

Hunnis, William. *A hyve full of hunnye*. London, 1578.

Hunt, Leigh. *Imagination and Fancy*. London, 1845.

Hunter, G. K. "'Unity' and Numbers in Spenser's *Amoretti*." *Yearbook of English Studies* 5 (1975): 39–45.

Hurd, Richard. "Dissertation I. On the Idea of Universal Poetry." *Works*. 8 vols. London, 1811, 2:3–26.

Hutton, James. "Some English Poems in Praise of Music." *English Miscellany* 2 (1951): 1–63.

Hyde, Thomas. "Vision, Poetry, and Authority in Spenser." *English Literary Renaissance* 13 (1983): 127–45.

Hyman, Virginia Riley. "Sidney's Definition of Poetry." *Studies in English Literature 1500–1900* 10 (1970): 49–62.

Ing, Catherine. *Elizabethan Lyrics*. London: Chatto and Windus, 1951.

Ingarden, Roman. *The Literary Work of Art*. Trans. George G. Grabowicz. Evanston: Northwestern University Press, 1973.

Ingram, R. W. "Words and Music." *Elizabethan Poetry*. Ed. John Russell Brown and Bernard Harris. *Stratford-upon-Avon Studies* 2. London: Edward Arnold, 1960, 131–49.

The institucion of a gentleman. 2d ed. London, 1568 [STC 14105].

Iser, Wolfgang. *The Implied Reader: Patterns of Communication in Prose Fiction from Bunyan to Beckett*. Baltimore: Johns Hopkins University Press, 1974.

―――. *The Act of Reading: A Theory of Aesthetic Response*. Baltimore: Johns Hopkins University Press, 1978.

Isidore of Seville. *Etymologiarum sive Originum libri XX*. Ed. W. M. Lindsay. 2 vols. Oxford: Clarendon, 1962.

Isler, Alan D. "Moral Philosophy and the Family in Sidney's *Arcadia.*" *Huntington Library Quarterly* 31 (1967–68): 359–71.

―――. "Heroic Poetry and Sidney's Two *Arcadias.*" *PMLA* 83 (1968): 368–79.

―――. "The Allegory of the Hero and Sidney's Two *Arcadias.*" *Studies in Philology* 65 (1968): 171–91.

Jacob, Hildebrand. *Of the Sister Arts: An Essay*. London, 1734.

Jakobson, Roman. "On Realism in Art." "The Dominant." *Readings in Russian Poetics: Formalist and Structuralist Views*. Ed. Ladislav Matejka and Krystyna Pomorska. Cambridge: Massachusetts Institute of Technology Press, 1971, 38–46, 82–87.

Johnson, Francis R. *A Critical Bibliography of the Works of Edmund Spenser Printed before 1700*. Baltimore: Johns Hopkins University Press, 1933.

Johnson, Paula. *Form and Transformation in Music and Poetry of the English Renaissance*. New Haven: Yale University Press, 1972.

Johnson, S. F. "Spenser's 'Shepherd's Calendar.'" *Times Literary Supplement* 7 Sept. 1951: 565.

Johnson, Wendell Stacy. "Browning's Music." *Journal of Aesthetics and Art Criticism* 22 (1963–64), 203–7.

Johnson, William C. "Amor and Spenser's *Amoretti.*" *English Studies* 54 (1973): 217–26.

Jorgens, Elise Bickford. *The Well-Tun'd Word: Musical Interpretations of English Poetry 1597–1651*. Minneapolis: University of Minnesota Press, 1982.

Joyce, James. *A Portrait of the Artist as a Young Man*. New York: Viking Penguin, 1964.

Judson, Alexander C. *A Biographical Sketch of John Young, Bishop of Rochester, with Emphasis on His Relations with Edmund Spenser. Indiana University Studies* 103. Bloomington: Indiana University Press, 1934.

―――. *The Life of Edmund Spenser*. Baltimore: Johns Hopkins University Press, 1945. Vol. 10 of *The Works of Edmund Spenser: A Variorum Edition*. Ed. Edwin Greenlaw et al. 11 vols. 1932–57.

―――. "Mother Hubberd's Ape." *Modern Language Notes* 63 (1948): 145–49.

Junius, Franciscus. *The painting of the ancients, in three books*. London, 1638.

The Kalender of Sheepehardes [c.1585]. Ed. S. K. Heninger, Jr. Delmar, NY: Scholars' Facsimiles and Reprints, 1979.

Kalstone, David. "Sir Philip Sidney and 'Poore *Petrarchs* Long Deceased Woes.'" *Journal of English and Germanic Philology* 63 (1964): 21–32.

―――. *Sidney's Poetry: Contexts and Interpretations*. Cambridge: Harvard University Press, 1965.

Karp, Theodore C. "Music." *The Seven Liberal Arts in the Middle Ages*. Ed. David L. Wagner. Bloomington: Indiana University Press, 1983, 169–95.

Kaske, Carol V. "Spenser's *Amoretti and Epithalamion* of 1595: Structure,

Genre, and Numerology." *English Literary Renaissance* 8 (1978): 271–95.

Kemp, John. "The Work of Art and the Artist's Intentions." *British Journal of Aesthetics* 4 (1964): 146–54.

Kendall, Timothy. *Flowers of epigrammes.* London, 1577.

Kennedy, George A. *Classical Rhetoric and Its Christian and Secular Tradition from Ancient to Modern Times.* Chapel Hill: University of North Carolina Press, 1980.

Kennedy, William J. *Rhetorical Norms in Renaissance Literature.* New Haven: Yale University Press, 1978.

Kenny, Anthony. *Wittgenstein.* London: Penguin Books, 1973.

Kermode, Frank. *The Sense of an Ending: Studies in the Theory of Fiction.* New York: Oxford University Press, 1967.

Kimbrough, Robert, and Philip Murphy. "The Helmingham Hall Manuscript of Sidney's *The Lady of May:* A Commentary and Transcription." *Renaissance Drama* ns 1 (1968): 103–19.

Kircher, Athanasius. *Musurgia universalis sive Ars magna consoni et dissoni in X. libros digesta.* 2 vols. Rome, 1650.

Kleinhenz, Christopher. "Giacomo da Lentini and Dante: The Early Italian Sonnet Tradition in Perspective." *Journal of Medieval and Renaissance Studies* 8 (1978): 217–34.

Koenigsberger, Dorothy. *Renaissance Man and Creative Thinking: A History of Concepts of Harmony 1400–1700.* Atlantic Highlands: Humanities Press, 1979.

Koller, Kathrine. "Abraham Fraunce and Edmund Spenser." *ELH* 7 (1940): 108–20.

Korn, A. L. "Puttenham and the Oriental Pattern-Poem." *Comparative Literature* 6 (1954): 289–303.

Kravitt, Edward F. "The Impact of Naturalism on Music and the Other Arts during the Romantic Era." *Journal of Aesthetics and Art Criticism* 30 (1971–72): 537–43.

Krieger, Murray. "*Ekphrasis* and the Still Movement of Poetry: Or, *Laokoön* Revisited." *Perspectives on Poetry.* Ed. James L. Calderwood and Harold E. Toliver. New York: Oxford University Press, 1968, 323–48.

———. *Poetic Presence and Illusion: Essays in Critical History and Theory.* Baltimore: Johns Hopkins University Press, 1979.

Kristeller, Paul Oskar. *The Philosophy of Marsilio Ficino.* Trans. Virginia Conant. New York: Columbia University Press, 1943.

———. "Music and Learning in the Early Italian Renaissance." *Journal of Renaissance and Baroque Music* 1 (1946–47): 255–74.

———. "The Modern System of the Arts." *Journal of the History of Ideas* 12 (1951): 496–527.

———. "Augustine and the Early Renaissance." *Studies in Renaissance Thought and Letters.* Rome: Storia e Letteratura, 1956, 360–72.

———. "The Platonic Academy of Florence." *Renaissance Thought II: Papers on Humanism and the Arts.* New York: Torchbooks, Harper and Row, 1965, 89–101.

Krouse, F. Michael. "Plato and Sidney's *Defence of Poesie.*" *Comparative Literature* 6 (1954): 138–47.

Kuenzli, Rudolf E. "The Intersubjective Structure of the Reading Process: A Communication-Oriented Theory of Literature." *Diacritics* 10.2 (1980): 47–56.

Kuhn, Thomas S. *The Structure of Scientific Revolutions.* Chicago: University of Chicago Press, 1962.

Kuntz, Marion L., ed. and trans. *Colloquium of the Seven about Secrets of the Divine.* By Jean Bodin. Princeton: Princeton University Press, 1975.

Kurman, George. "Ecphrasis in Epic Poetry." *Comparative Literature* 26 (1974): 1–13.

Landino, Cristoforo. *Scritti critici e teorici.* Ed. Roberto Cardino. 2 vols. Rome: Bulzoni, 1974.

———, ed. *Dante con l'espositione di Christoforo Landino, et di Alessandro Vellutello, sopra la sua Comedia dell'Inferno, del Purgatorio, & del Paradiso.* Ed. Francesco Sansovino. Venice, 1564.

———, ed. *Divina commedia.* By Dante. Florence, 1481.

Langer, Susanne. *Philosophy in a New Key: A Study in the Symbolism of Reason, Rite, and Art.* 3d ed. Cambridge: Harvard University Press, 1957.

L'Anglois, Pierre. *Discours des hieroglyphes Aegyptiens, emblemes, devises, et armoiries.* Paris, 1583.

Lanham, Richard A. *The Old "Arcadia." Sidney's Arcadia.* Yale Studies in English 158. New Haven: Yale University Press, 1965, 181–405.

———. "Sidney: The Ornament of His Age." *Southern Review: An Australian Journal of Literary Studies* 2 (1966–67): 319–40.

———. "*Astrophil and Stella:* Pure and Impure Persuasion." *English Literary Renaissance* 2 (1972): 100–15.

Lanier, Sidney. *The Science of English Verse* [1880]. Ed. Paull F. Baum. *Sidney Lanier.* Ed. Charles R. Anderson et al. 10 vols. Baltimore: Johns Hopkins University Press, 1945, 2:21–244.

La Primaudaye, Pierre de. *The French academie.* Trans. Thomas Bowes. London, 1586.

———. *The second part of the French academie.* Trans. Thomas Bowes. London, 1594.

———. *The third volume of the French academie.* Trans. R. Dolman. London, 1601.

Lawall, Sarah N. *Critics of Consciousness: The Existential Structures of Literature.* Cambridge: Harvard University Press, 1968.

Lawry, Jon S. *Sidney's Two "Arcadias": Pattern and Proceeding.* Ithaca: Cornell University Press, 1972.

LeCoat, Gerard. *The Rhetoric of the Arts, 1550–1650.* Bern: Lang, 1975.

Lee, Rensselaer W. "*Ut Pictura Poesis:* The Humanistic Theory of Painting." *Art Bulletin* 22 (1940): 197–269.

———. *Ut pictura poesis: The Humanistic Theory of Painting.* New York: W. W. Norton, 1967.

———. *Names on Trees: Ariosto into Art.* Princeton: Princeton University Press, 1977.

Lenhart, Charmenz S. *Musical Influence on American Poetry.* Athens: University of Georgia Press, 1956.

Leonardo da Vinci. *Paragone: A Comparison of the Arts.* Ed. and trans. Irma A. Richter. London: Oxford University Press, 1949.

LeRoy, Louis. *Of the interchangeable course, or variety of things in the whole world.* Trans. Robert Ashley. London, 1594.

Lessing, G. E. *Laocoön* [1766]. Trans. Ellen Frothingham. New York: Farrar, Straus and Giroux, 1961.

Levao, Ronald. "Sidney's Feigned *Apology.*" *PMLA* 94 (1979): 223–33.

Levin, Harry. "What Is Realism?" *Comparative Literature* 3 (1951): 193–99.

Levy, F. J. "Sir Philip Sidney and the Idea of History." *Bibliothèque d'Humanisme et Renaissance* 26 (1964): 608–17.

———. "Philip Sidney Reconsidered." *English Literary Renaissance* 2 (1972): 5–18.

Lewis, C. S. *English Literature in the Sixteenth Century Excluding Drama.* Oxford: Clarendon, 1954.

Lindberg, David C. *Theories of Vision from al-Kindi to Kepler.* Chicago: University of Chicago Press, 1976.

Lindheim, Nancy. *The Structures of Sidney's "Arcadia."* Toronto: University of Toronto Press, 1982.

Lipking, Lawrence. *The Ordering of the Arts in Eighteenth-Century England.* Princeton: Princeton University Press, 1970.

Lomazzo, Giovanni Paolo. *Idea del tempio della pittura.* Milan, 1590.

———. *The artes of curious paintinge, carvinge & buildinge.* Trans. Richard Haydocke. Oxford, 1598.

L'Orme, Philibert de. *Le premier tome de l'architecture.* Paris, 1568.

Lossius, Lucas. *Erotemata musicae practicae.* Nuremberg, 1563.

Lowinsky, Edward E. "The Concept of Physical and Musical Space in the Renaissance." *Papers of the American Musicological Society: Annual Meeting, 1941.* Ed. Gustave Reese. Minneapolis: American Musicological Society, 1946, 57–84.

———. "Music of the Renaissance as Viewed by Renaissance Musicians." *The Renaissance Image of Man and the World.* Ed. Bernard O'Kelly. Columbus: Ohio State University Press, 1966, 129–77.

———. "Music in the Culture of the Renaissance." *Renaissance Essays: From the "Journal of the History of Ideas."* Ed. Paul O. Kristeller and Philip P. Wiener. New York: Torchbooks, Harper and Row, 1968, 337–81.

Lucas, D. W., ed. *Poetics.* By Aristotle. Oxford: Clarendon, 1968.

MacCaffrey, Wallace T. *Queen Elizabeth and the Making of Policy, 1572–1588.* Princeton: Princeton University Press, 1981.

McCall, Marsh H., Jr. *Ancient Rhetorical Theories of Simile and Comparison.* Cambridge: Harvard University Press, 1969.

McCanles, Michael. "Oracular Prediction and the Fore-Conceit of Sidney's *Arcadia.*" *ELH* 50 (1983): 233–44.

———. "Reading Description in Sidney's New *Arcadia:* A Differential Analysis." *University of Toronto Quarterly* 53 (1983–84): 36–52.

McCoy, Richard C. *Sir Philip Sidney: Rebellion in Arcadia.* New Brunswick: Rutgers University Press, 1979.

McIntyre, John P., S.J. "Sidney's 'Golden World.'" *Comparative Literature* 14 (1962): 356–65.

McKeon, Richard. "Literary Criticism and the Concept of Imitation in Antiquity." *Modern Philology* 34 (1936–37): 1–35.

McLane, Paul E. *Spenser's Shepheardes Calender: A Study in Elizabethan Allegory.* Notre Dame: University of Notre Dame Press, 1961.

McNeir, Waldo F., and Foster Provost. *Edmund Spenser: An Annotated Bibliography 1937–1972.* 2d ed. Pittsburgh: Duquesne University Press, 1975.

Mace, Dean Tolle. "Marin Mersenne on Language and Music." *Journal of Music Theory* 14 (1970): 2–34.

———. "Ut pictura poesis: Dryden, Poussin, and the Parallel of Poetry and Painting in the Seventeenth Century." *Encounters: Essays on Literature and the Visual Arts.* Ed. John Dixon Hunt. New York: W. W. Norton, 1971, 58–81.

Macrobius. *Commentary on the Dream of Scipio.* Trans. William Harris Stahl. *Records of Civilization* 48. New York: Columbia University Press, 1952.

———. *Saturnalia.* Ed. Jakob Willis. 2 vols. Leipzig: Teubner, 1963.

Madsen, William G. *From Shadowy Types to Truth: Studies in Milton's Symbolism.* New Haven: Yale University Press, 1968.

Maier, Michael. *Atalanta fugiens.* Oppenheim, 1618.

Major, John M. "The Moralization of the Dance in Elyot's *Governour.*" *Studies in the Renaissance* 5 (1958): 27–37.

Mallarmé, Stéphane. "La Musique et les lettres" [1893]. *Studies in European Literature: Being the Taylorian Lectures 1889–1899.* Oxford: Clarendon, 1900.

Malory, Sir Thomas. *Works.* Ed. Eugène Vinaver. 2d ed. Oxford: Oxford University Press, 1977.

Malpezzi, Frances M. "Du Bartas' *L'Uranie,* The Devotional Poet's Handbook." *Allegorica* 8 (1983): 185–98.

Mancinello, Antonio. "De poetica virtute, et studio humanitatis impellente ad bonum." *Sententiae veterum poetarum, per locos communes digestae.* By Georg Major. Lyons, 1551, 263–88.

Marcus, Aaron. "An Introduction to the Visual Syntax of Concrete Poetry." *Visible Language* 8 (1974): 333–55.

Marston, John. *The metamorphosis of Pigmalion's image and certain satyres.* London, 1598.

Mason, John. *An Essay on the Power of Numbers, and the Principles of Harmony in Poetical Compositions.* London, 1749.

Mazzaro, Jerome. *Transformations in the Renaissance English Lyric.* Ithaca: Cornell University Press, 1970.

Medine, Peter E., ed. *Horace His Arte of Poetrie, Pistles, and Satyrs Englished.* Trans. Thomas Drant. Delmar, NY: Scholars' Facsimiles and Reprints, 1972.

Mei, Girolamo. *Letters on Ancient and Modern Music to Vincenzo Galilei and Giovanni Bardi.* Ed. Claude V. Palisca. Rome: American Institute of Musicology, 1960.

Mellers, Wilfrid. *Harmonious Meeting: A Study of the Relationship between English Music, Poetry and Theatre, c.1600–1900.* London: Dobson, 1965.

Mercuriale, Girolamo. *De arte gymnastica libri sex.* 2d ed. Venice, 1573.

Meres, Francis. *Palladis tamia: Wits treasury.* London, 1598.

Merriman, James D. "The Parallel of the Arts: Some Misgivings and a Faint Affirmation." *Journal of Aesthetics and Art Criticism* 31 (1972–73): 153–64, 309–21.

Mersenne, Marin. *Traité de l'harmonie universelle.* Paris, 1627.

Mexia, Pedro. *The foreste.* Trans. Thomas Fortescue. London, 1571.

Michelangelo. *Complete Poems and Selected Letters.* Ed. Robert N. Linscott. Trans. Creighton Gilbert. New York: Modern Library, 1965.

Mill, John Stuart. "What Is Poetry" [1833]. *Essays on Poetry.* Ed. F. Parvin Sharpless. Columbia: University of South Carolina Press, 1976, 3–22.

Miller, David L. "Abandoning the Quest." *ELH* 46 (1979): 173–92.

Milton, John. *The Works.* Ed. Frank Allen Patterson. 18 vols. New York: Columbia University Press, 1931–38.

Miner, Earl. "The Objective Fallacy and the Real Existence of Literature." *PTL: A Journal for Descriptive Poetics and Theory of Literature* 1 (1976): 11–31.

Minturno, Antonio Sebastiano. *De poeta.* Venice, 1559.

Montaigne, Michel de, trans. *La théologie naturelle.* By Ramòn Sabunde. *Oeuvres complètes.* Vol. 9. Paris: Conard, 1924–41. 12 vols.

Montgomery, Robert L. *Symmetry and Sense: The Poetry of Sir Philip Sidney.* Austin: University of Texas Press, 1961.

———. *The Reader's Eye: Studies in Didactic Literary Theory from Dante to Tasso.* Berkeley: University of California Press, 1979.

Montrose, Louis Adrian. "Celebration and Insinuation: Sir Philip Sidney and the Motives of Elizabethan Courtship." *Renaissance Drama* ns 8 (1977): 3–35.

———. "'The perfecte paterne of a Poete': The Poetics of Courtship in *The Shepheardes Calender.*" *Texas Studies in Literature and Language* 21 (1979): 34–67.

Moore, Dennis. "Philisides and Mira: Autobiographical Allegory in the *Old Arcadia.*" *Spenser Studies* 3 (1982): 125–37.

Moore, John W., Jr. "Colin Breaks His Pipe: A Reading of the 'January' Eclogue." *English Literary Renaissance* 5 (1975): 3–24.

Morley, Thomas. *A plaine and easie introduction to practicall musicke.* London, 1597.

Mornay: see Duplessis-Mornay, Philippe.

Mulcaster, Richard. *Positions.* London, 1581.

———. *The first part of the elementarie.* London, 1582.

Munro, Thomas. *The Arts and Their Interrelations.* New York: Liberal Arts, 1949.

Murrin, Michael. *The Veil of Allegory: Some Notes toward a Theory of Allegorical Rhetoric in the English Renaissance.* Chicago: University of Chicago Press, 1969.

Musa, Mark, trans. *Dante's "Vita Nuova."* Bloomington: Indiana University Press, 1973.

Myrick, Kenneth. *Sir Philip Sidney as a Literary Craftsman.* 2d ed. Lincoln: University of Nebraska Press, 1965.

Nashe, Thomas. *The Anatomie of Absurditie* [1589; selections]. *Elizabethan Critical Essays.* Ed. G. Gregory Smith. 2 vols. London: Oxford University Press, 1904, 1:321–37.

———. *Works.* Ed. R. B. McKerrow. Rev. F. P. Wilson. 5 vols. Oxford: Basil Blackwell, 1958.

Natta, Marcantonio. "De poëtis liber." *Opera.* Venice, 1564, fols. 110–14.

Neely, Carol Thomas. "The Structure of English Renaissance Sonnet Sequences." *ELH* 45 (1978): 359–89.

Negri, Francesco. *Grammatica.* Venice, 1480.

Nelson, Lowry, Jr. "The Fictive Reader and Literary Self-Reflexiveness." *The Disciplines of Criticism.* Ed. Peter Demetz et al. New Haven: Yale University Press, 1968, 173–91.

Nelson, William. *The Poetry of Edmund Spenser.* New York: Columbia University Press, 1963.

———. *Fact or Fiction: The Dilemma of the Renaissance Storyteller.* Cambridge: Harvard University Press, 1973.

Neuse, Richard. "The Triumph over Hasty Accidents: A Note on the Symbolic Mode of the 'Epithalamion.'" *Modern Language Review* 61 (1966): 163–74.

Nietzsche, Friedrich. *The Birth of Tragedy and The Genealogy of Morals.* Trans. Francis Golffing. New York: Anchor Press, Doubleday, 1956.

O'Connell, Michael. *Mirror and Veil: The Historical Dimension of Spenser's "Faerie Queene."* Chapel Hill: University of North Carolina Press, 1977.

Olson, Elder. "An Outline of Poetic Theory." *Critiques and Essays in Criticism 1920–1948.* Ed. Robert W. Stallman. New York: Ronald Press, 1949, 264–88.

Ong, Walter J., S.J. "System, Space, and Intellect in Renaissance Symbolism." *Bibliothèque d'Humanisme et Renaissance* 18 (1956): 222–39.

———. "From Allegory to Diagram in the Renaissance Mind: A Study in the Significance of the Allegorical Tableau." *Journal of Aesthetics and Art Criticism* 17 (1958–59): 423–40.

———. "The Province of Rhetoric and Poetic." *The Province of Rhetoric.* Ed. Joseph Schwartz and John A. Rycenga. New York: Ronald Press, 1965, 48–56.

———. "The Writer's Audience Is Always a Fiction." *PMLA* 90 (1975): 9–21.

Osborn, James M. *Young Philip Sidney 1572–1577.* Elizabethan Club Series 5. New Haven: Yale University Press, 1972.

Osborne, Harold. *Aesthetics and Art Theory: An Historical Introduction*. New York: E. P. Dutton, 1970.

Osgood, Charles G., trans. *Boccaccio on Poetry*. Princeton: Princeton University Press, 1930.

Pace, Richard. *De fructu qui ex doctrina percipitur* [1517]. Ed. and trans. Frank Manley and Richard S. Sylvester. New York: Renaissance Society, 1967.

Padelford, Frederick M., trans. *Select Translations from Scaliger's Poetics*. Yale Studies in English 26. New York: Holt, Rinehart and Winston, 1905.

Palfreyman, Thomas. *The treatise of heavenly philosophie*. London, 1578.

Palingenius. *The Zodiake of Life* [1576]. Trans. Barnabe Googe. Ed. Rosemond Tuve. New York: Scholars' Facsimiles and Reprints, 1947.

Palisca, Claude V. "Scientific Empiricism in Musical Thought." *Seventeenth Century Science and Arts*. Ed. Hedley Howell Rhys. Princeton: Princeton University Press, 1961, 91–137.

————, ed. *Girolamo Mei: Letters on Ancient and Modern Music to Vincenzo Galilei and Giovanni Bardi*. Rome: American Institute of Musicology, 1960.

Panofsky, Erwin. *Idea: A Concept in Art Theory*. Trans. Joseph J. S. Peake. Columbia: University of South Carolina Press, 1968.

————. "The Concept of Artistic Volition." *Critical Inquiry* 8 (1981–82): 17–33.

Parker, Patricia A. *Inescapable Romance: Studies in the Poetics of a Mode*. Princeton: Princeton University Press, 1979.

Parker, Robert W. "Terentian Structure and Sidney's Original *Arcadia*." *English Literary Renaissance* 2 (1972): 61–78.

Partee, Morriss Henry. "Sir Philip Sidney and the Renaissance Knowledge of Plato." *English Studies* 51 (1970): 411–24.

————. "Anti-Platonism in Sidney's 'Defence.'" *English Miscellany* 22 (1971): 7–29.

Pater, Walter. "The School of Giorgione." *Fortnightly Review* ns 22.2 (1877): 526–38.

————. *The Renaissance: Studies in Art and Poetry*, 4th ed. London, 1893.

————. *Essays from the "Guardian"*. London, 1896.

Patterson, Annabel M. "'Under . . . Pretty Tales': Intention in Sidney's *Arcadia*." *Studies in the Literary Imagination* 15.1 (1982): 5–21.

————. *Censorship and Interpretation: The Conditions of Writing and Reading in Early Modern England*. Madison: University of Wisconsin Press, 1984.

Pattison, Bruce. "Literature and Music." *The English Renaissance 1510–1688*. By Vivian de Sola Pinto. London: Cresset, 1938, 120–38.

————. *Music and Poetry of the English Renaissance*. London: Methuen, 1948.

Peacham, Henry (the Elder). *The garden of eloquence*. London, 1577.

Peacham, Henry (the Younger). *The compleat gentleman*. London, 1622.

Pears, Steuart A., ed. and trans. *The Correspondence of Sir Philip Sidney and Hubert Languet*. London, 1845.

Pepper, Stephen C. *The Basis of Criticism in the Arts*. Cambridge: Harvard University Press, 1945.

Perkinson, Richard H. "The Epic in Five Acts." *Studies in Philology* 43 (1946): 465–81.

Petrarch. *Phisicke against Fortune, as well prosperous, as adverse.* Trans. Thomas Twyne. London 1579.

———. *Lyric Poems: The "Rime sparse" and Other Lyrics.* Ed. and trans. Robert M. Durling. Cambridge: Harvard University Press, 1976.

———. *Africa.* Trans. Thomas G. Bergin and Alice S. Wilson. New Haven: Yale University Press, 1977.

Phillips, Edward. *Theatrum poetarum.* London, 1675.

Phillips, James E. "Poetry and Music in the Seventeenth Century." *Music & Literature in England in the Seventeenth and Eighteenth Centuries.* Los Angeles: Clark Library, 1953, 1–21.

Pigman, G. W., III. "Versions of Imitation in the Renaissance." *Renaissance Quarterly* 33 (1980): 1–32.

Pitcher, George. *The Philosophy of Wittgenstein.* Englewood Cliffs: Prentice-Hall, 1964.

Plato. *Omnia . . . opera.* Ed. and trans. Marsilio Ficino. Basel, 1546.

———. *Opera quae extant omnia.* Ed. Henri Estienne. Trans. Jean de Serres. 3 vols. Geneva, 1578.

Plochmann, George Kimball. "Plato, Visual Perception, and Art." *Journal of Aesthetics and Art Criticism* 35 (1976–77): 189–200.

Plotinus. *The Enneads.* Trans. Stephen MacKenna. 4th ed. London: Faber and Faber, 1969.

Plutarch. *The lives of the noble Grecians and Romaines.* Trans. Thomas North. Ed. Simon Goulart. London, 1603.

———. *The philosophie, commonlie called, the morals.* Trans. Philemon Holland. London, 1603.

———. *The amorous and tragicall tales of Plutarch whereunto is annexed the hystorie of Cariclea and Theagenes, and the sayings of the Greeke philosophers.* Trans. James Sanford. London, 1567.

Pomeroy, Elizabeth W. *The Elizabethan Miscellanies: Their Development and Conventions. University of California English Studies* 36. Berkeley: University of California Press, 1973.

Pontus de Tyard. *Solitaire premier, ou, Prose des Muses et de la fureur poétique.* Lyons, 1552.

———. *Solitaire second.* Lyons, 1552.

Pope, Alexander. *The Poems.* Ed. John Butt. New Haven: Yale University Press, 1963.

Poulet, Georges. "Phenomenology of Reading." *New Literary History* 1 (1969–70): 53–68.

Praz, Mario. *Mnemosyne: The Parallel between Literature and the Visual Arts. Bollingen Series* 35. Princeton: Princeton University Press, 1970.

Prescott, Anne Lake. *French Poets and the English Renaissance: Studies in Fame and Transformation.* New Haven: Yale University Press, 1978.

Price, Kingsley. "The Performing and the Non-Performing Arts." *Journal of Aesthetics and Art Criticism* 29 (1970–71): 53–62.

Prouty, Charles T., ed. *A Hundreth Sundrie Flowres.* By George Gascoigne. *University of Missouri Studies* 17.2. Columbia: University of Missouri Press, 1942.

Purdy, Mary Martha. "Political Propaganda in Ballad and Masque." *If by your art: Testament to Percival Hunt.* Ed. Agnes Lynch Starrett. Pittsburgh: University of Pittsburgh Press, 1948, 264–93.

Puttenham, George. *The Arte of English Poesie* [1589]. Ed. Gladys Doidge Willcock and Alice Walker. Cambridge: Cambridge University Press, 1936.

Quitslund, Jon A. "Spenser's Image of Sapience." *Studies in the Renaissance* 16 (1969): 181–213.

———. "Spenser's *Amoretti* VIII and Platonic Commentaries on Petrarch." *Journal of the Warburg and Courtauld Institutes* 36 (1973): 256–76.

Rainolde, Richard. *The foundacion of rhetorike* [1563]. Ed. Francis R. Johnson. New York: Scholars' Facsimiles and Reprints, 1945.

Rainolds, John. *Oratio in laudem artis poeticae* [*Circa 1572*]. Ed. William A. Ringler, Jr. Trans. Walter Allen, Jr. Princeton: Princeton University Press, 1940.

Raleigh, Sir Walter. *The history of the world.* London, 1614.

Ransom, John Crowe. "Poetry: A Note in Ontology." *The World's Body.* New York: Charles Scribner's Sons, 1938, 111–42.

Rasmussen, Carl J. "'How Weak Be the Passions of Woefulness': Spenser's *Ruines of Time.*" *Spenser Studies* 2 (1981): 159–81.

Read, Conyers. *Mr. Secretary Walsingham and the Policy of Queen Elizabeth.* 3 vols. Oxford: Clarendon, 1925.

Read, Herbert. *The Forms of Things Unknown.* London: Faber and Faber, 1960.

Reaney, Gilbert. "The Irrational and Late Medieval Music." *The Darker Vision of the Renaissance.* Ed. Robert S. Kinsman. Berkeley: University of California Press, 1974, 197–219.

Rebholz, Ronald A. *The Life of Fulke Greville, First Lord Brooke.* Oxford: Clarendon, 1971.

Rees, Joan. *Exploring "Arcadia."* Birmingham: University of Birmingham Press, 1981.

Reisch, Gregor. *Margarita philosophica.* Ed. Oronce Finé. Basel, 1583.

Relle, Eleanor. "Some New Marginalia and Poems of Gabriel Harvey." *Review of English Studies* ns 23 (1972): 401–16.

Renwick, W. L. *Edmund Spenser: An Essay on Renaissance Poetry.* London: Edward Arnold, 1925.

Reuchlin, Johann. *De arte cabbalistica. The history of philosophy.* By Thomas Stanley. 2d ed. London, 1687, 570–76.

Reynolds, Henry. *Mythomystes.* London, 1632.

Ringler, William A., Jr. "Master Drant's Rules." *Philological Quarterly* 29 (1950): 70–74.

———. "Spenser, Shakespeare, Honor, and Worship." *Renaissance News* 14 (1961): 159–61.

———, ed. *The Poems of Sir Philip Sidney.* Oxford: Clarendon, 1962.

Rivers, Elias L. "Certain Formal Characteristics of the Primitive Love Sonnet." *Speculum* 33 (1958): 42–55.

Roberts, Josephine A. *Architectonic Knowledge in the "New Arcadia" (1590):*

Sidney's Use of the Heroic Journey. Salzburg: Institut für Englische Sprache und Literatur, 1978.

Roberts, Mark. "The Pill and the Cherries: Sidney and the Neo-Classical Tradition." *Essays in Criticism* 16 (1966): 22–31.

Robertson, D. W., Jr. *A Preface to Chaucer: Studies in Medieval Perspectives.* Princeton: Princeton University Press, 1962.

Robertson, Jean. "Sir Philip Sidney and His Poetry." *Elizabethan Poetry,* ed. John R. Brown and Bernard Harris. *Stratford-upon-Avon Studies* 2. London: Edward Arnold, 1960, 111–29.

———. "Sir Philip Sidney and Lady Penelope Rich." *Review of English Studies* ns 15 (1964): 296–97.

———, ed. *Sir Philip Sidney: The Countess of Pembroke's Arcadia (The Old Arcadia).* Oxford: Clarendon, 1973.

Robertson, Thomas. *An Inquiry into the Fine Arts.* London, 1784.

Robinson, Forrest G. *The Shape of Things Known: Sidney's "Apology " in Its Philosophical Tradition.* Cambridge: Harvard University Press, 1972.

———, ed. *An Apology for Poetry.* By Philip Sidney. Indianapolis: Bobbs-Merrill, 1970.

Robortello, Francesco, ed. *In librum Aristotelis de arte poetica explicationes.* Florence, 1548.

Roche, Thomas P., Jr. "Autobiographical Elements in Sidney's *Astrophil and Stella.*" *Spenser Studies* 5 (1984): 209–29.

Rollinson, Philip B. "A Generic View of Spenser's *Four Hymns.*" *Studies in Philology* 68 (1971): 292–304.

———. *Classical Theories of Allegory and Christian Culture. Duquesne Studies in Language and Literature* 3. Pittsburgh: Duquesne University Press, 1981.

Ronsard, Pierre de. *Amours.* Paris, 1552.

———. "La Lyre." *Les Oeuvres . . . Texte de 1587.* Ed. Isidore Silver. 8 vols. Abbeville, Somme: Washington University Press, 1966–70, 7:53–65.

Rorty, Richard. *Philosophy and the Mirror of Nature.* Princeton: Princeton University Press, 1979.

Roscoe, William. *The Life of Lorenzo de' Medici, Called the Magnificent.* Rev. Thomas Roscoe. 9th ed. London, 1847.

Rosenberg, Eleanor. *Leicester: Patron of Letters.* New York: Columbia University Press, 1955.

Roskill, Mark W., ed. and trans. *Dolce's "Aretino" and Venetian Art Theory of the Cinquecento. Monographs on Archaeology and the Fine Arts* 15. New York: New York University Press, 1968.

Rossky, William. "Imagination in the English Renaissance: Psychology and Poetic." *Studies in the Renaissance* 5 (1958): 49–73.

Røstvig, Maren-Sofie. "*Ars Aeterna:* Renaissance Poetics and Theories of Divine Creation." *Mosaic* 3.2 (1970): 40–61.

———. "*The Shepheardes Calender*—A Structural Analysis." *Renaissance and Modern Studies* 13 (1969): 49–75.

Rousseau, Jean-Jacques. *Essay on the Origin of Languages* et al. Trans. John H. Moran and Alexander Gode. New York: Frederick Ungar, 1966.

Rudenstine, Neil L. *Sidney's Poetic Development*. Cambridge: Harvard University Press, 1967.

Ruthven, K. K. "The Poet as Etymologist." *Critical Quarterly* 11 (1969): 9–37.

Sabunde, Ramòn. *La théologie naturelle*. Trans. Michel de Montaigne. *Oeuvres complètes*. By Montaigne. Vol. 9. Paris: Conard, 1924–41. 12 vols.

Salman, Phillips. "Instruction and Delight in Medieval and Renaissance Criticism." *Renaissance Quarterly* 32 (1979): 303–32.

Samuel, Irene. "The Influence of Plato on Sir Philip Sidney's *Defense of Poesy*." *Modern Language Quarterly* 1 (1940): 383–91.

Sanford, James, trans. *The amorous and tragicall tales of Plutarch whereunto is annexed the hystorie of Cariclea and Theagenes, and the sayings of the Greeke philosophers*. London, 1567 [STC 20072].

Sannazaro, Jacopo. *Arcadia*. Ed. Francesco Sansovino. Venice, 1571.

——. *Arcadia & Piscatorial Eclogues*. Trans. Ralph Nash. Detroit: Wayne State University Press, 1966.

Sansovino, Francesco, ed. *Dante con l'espositione di Christoforo Landino, et di Alessandro Vellutello, sopra la sua Comedia dell'Inferno, del Purgatorio, & del Paradiso*. Venice, 1564.

——, ed. *Arcadia*. By Jacopo Sannazaro. Venice, 1571.

Santayana, George. *Reason in Art. The Life of Reason*. Vol. 4. New York: Charles Scribner's Sons, 1905–06. 5 vols.

Sargent, Ralph M. *At the Court of Queen Elizabeth*. London: Oxford University Press, 1935.

Sartre, Jean-Paul. *Qu'est-ce que la littérature?* Paris: Gallimard, 1948.

Sasek, Lawrence A. *The Literary Temper of the English Puritans*. Louisiana State University Studies, Humanities Series 9. Baton Rouge: Louisiana State University Press, 1961.

Saussure, Ferdinand de. *Course in General Linguistics*. Trans. Roy Harris. London: Gerald Duckworth, 1983.

Scaliger, Julius Caesar. *De causis linguae latinae libri tredecim*. Lyons, 1540.

——. *In libros duos, qui inscribuntur de plantis, Aristotele autore, libri duo*. Paris, 1556.

——. *Poetices libri septem*. Lyons, 1561.

——. *Select Translations from Scaliger's Poetics*. Trans. Frederick M. Padelford. *Yale Studies in English* 26. New York: Holt, Rinehart and Winston, 1905.

——. *Aristotelis historia de animalibus . . . cum eiusdem commentariis*. Ed. Philippus J. Maussacus. Toulouse, 1619.

Scanlon, James J. "Sidney's *Astrophil and Stella:* 'See what it is to Love' Sensually!" *Studies in English Literature 1500–1900* 16 (1976): 65–74.

Scher, Steven P. "Literature and Music." *Interrelations of Literature*. Ed. Jean-Pierre Barricelli and Joseph Gibaldi. New York: Modern Language Association, 1982, 225–50.

Scholem, Gershom G. *On the Kabbalah and Its Symbolism*. Trans. Ralph Manheim. New York: Schocken Books, 1965.

Scholes, Robert. *Structuralism in Literature*. New Haven: Yale University Press,
1974.

————. "Toward a Semiotics of Literature." *Critical Inquiry* 4 (1977–78): 105–
20.

Schopenhauer, Arthur. *The World as Will and Idea*. Trans. R. B. Haldane and
J. Kemp. 7th ed. 2 vols. London: Kegan Paul, c.1914.

Schrade, Leo. "Music in the Philosophy of Boethius." *Musical Quarterly* 33
(1947): 188–200.

Schweizer, Niklaus R. *The Ut pictura poesis Controversy in Eighteenth-Century
England and Germany*. Bern: Lang, 1972.

Seigel, Jerrold E. *Rhetoric and Philosophy in Renaissance Humanism: The
Union of Eloquence and Wisdom, Petrarch to Valla*. Princeton: Princeton
University Press, 1968.

Seneca. *The lamentable tragedie of Oedipus*. Trans. Alexander Neville. London,
1563.

Serres, Jean de, trans. *Platonis opera quae extant omnia*. Ed. Henri Estienne. 3
vols. Geneva, 1578.

Severance, Sybil Lutz. "'To Shine in Union': Measure, Number, and Harmony
in Ben Jonson's '*Poems* of Devotion.'" *Studies in Philology* 80 (1983):
183–99.

Shapiro, Marianne. *Hieroglyph of Time: The Petrarchan Sestina*. Minneapolis:
University of Minnesota Press, 1980.

Shelley, Percy Bysshe. *Critical Prose*. Ed. Bruce R. McElderry, Jr. Lincoln: University of Nebraska Press, 1967.

Shepherd, Geoffrey, ed. *An Apology for Poetry or The Defence of Poesy*. By
Philip Sidney. London: Thomas Nelson, 1965.

Sherry, Richard. *A treatise of schemes and tropes*. London, 1550.

Shore, David R. "Colin and Rosalind: Love and Poetry in the *Shepheardes Calender*." *Studies in Philology* 73 (1976): 176–88.

Shute, John. *The first and chief groundes of architecture*. London, 1563.

Sidney, Philip. *The Countesse of Pembrokes Arcadia . . . with sundry new additions*. London, 1598.

————. *The Works*. 3 vols. London, 1724–25.

————. *The Complete Works*. Ed. Albert Feuillerat. 4 vols. Cambridge: Cambridge University Press, 1912–26.

————. *The Complete Works*. Ed. Albert Feuillerat. 2d ed. 4 vols. Cambridge:
Cambridge University Press, 1962.

————. *Countess of Pembrokes Arcadia*. 10th ed. London, 1655.

————. *The Countess of Pembroke's Arcadia*. Ed. Maurice Evans. Harmondsworth: Penguin Books, 1977.

————. *An apologie for poetrie*. London: Henry Olney, 1595 [STC 22534].

————. *The defence of poesie*. London: William Ponsonby, 1595 [STC 22535].

————. *An Apology for Poetry or The Defence of Poesy*. Ed. Geoffrey Shepherd.
London: Thomas Nelson, 1965.

———. *A Defence of Poetry*. Ed. Jan van Dorsten. London: Oxford University Press, 1966.

———. *An Apology for Poetry*. Ed. Forrest G. Robinson. Indianapolis: Bobbs-Merrill, 1970.

———. *Defense of Poesy*. Ed. Lewis Soens. Lincoln: University of Nebraska Press, 1970.

Siebeck, Berta. *Das Bild Sir Philip Sidneys in der englischen Renaissance*. Weimar: Böhlaus, 1939.

Silver, Isidore. "Ronsard on the Marriage of Poetry, Music, and the Dance." *Studies in the Continental Background of Renaissance English Literature: Essays Presented to John L. Lievsay*. Ed. Dale B. J. Randall and George W. Williams. Durham: Duke University Press, 1977, 155–69.

Simson, Otto Georg von. *The Gothic Cathedral: Origins of Gothic Architecture and the Medieval Concept of Order*. 2d ed. *Bollingen Series* 48. New York: Pantheon Books, 1962.

Sinfield, Alan. "Sidney and Du Bartas." *Comparative Literature* 27 (1975): 8–20.

———. "Sidney and Astrophil." *Studies in English Literature 1500–1900* 20 (1980): 25–41.

Sloan, Thomas O. "The Crossing of Rhetoric and Poetry in the English Renaissance." *The Rhetoric of Renaissance Poetry: From Wyatt to Milton*. Ed. Sloan and Raymond B. Waddington. Berkeley: University of California Press, 1974, 212–42.

Smith, A. J. "Theory and Practice in Renaissance Poetry: Two Kinds of Imitation." *Bulletin of the John Rylands Library* 47 (1964–65): 212–43.

Smith, A. Mark. "Getting the Big Picture in Perspectivist Optics." *Isis* 72 (1981): 568–89.

Smith, Barbara Herrnstein. *Poetic Closure: A Study of How Poems End*. Chicago: University of Chicago Press, 1968.

Smith, G. Gregory, ed. *Elizabethan Critical Essays*. 2 vols. London: Oxford University Press, 1904.

Smith, Hallett. *Elizabethan Poetry: A Study in Conventions, Meaning and Expression*. Cambridge: Harvard University Press, 1952.

Snare, Gerald H. "The Muses on Poetry: Spenser's *The Teares of the Muses*." *Tulane Studies in English* 17 (1969): 31–52.

———. "Spenser's Fourth Grace." *Journal of the Warburg and Courtauld Institutes* 34 (1971): 350–55.

———. "The Poetics of Vision: Patterns of Grace and Courtesy in *The Faerie Queene*, VI." *Renaissance Papers 1974*. Durham, NC: Southeastern Renaissance Conference, 1975, 1–8.

Soens, Lewis, ed. *Sir Philip Sidney's Defense of Poesy*. Lincoln: University of Nebraska Press, 1970.

Solt, Mary Ellen, ed. *Concrete Poetry: A World View*. Bloomington: Indiana University Press, 1970.

Sonnino, Lee A. *A Handbook to Sixteenth-Century Rhetoric*. London: Routledge and Kegan Paul, 1968.

Sörbom, Göran. *Mimesis and Art: Studies in the Origin and Early Development of an Aesthetic Vocabulary.* Stockholm: Bonniers, 1966.

Sowton, Ian. "Hidden Persuaders as a Means of Literary Grace: Sixteenth-Century Poetics and Rhetoric in England." *University of Toronto Quarterly* 32 (1962–63): 55–69.

Sparrow, John. *Visible Words: A Study of Inscriptions in and as Books and Works of Art.* Cambridge: Cambridge University Press, 1969.

Spencer, John R. *"Ut Rhetorica Pictura:* A Study in Quattrocento Theory of Painting." *Journal of the Warburg and Courtauld Institutes* 20 (1957): 26–44.

———, ed. and trans. *On Painting.* By Leon Battista Alberti. London: Routledge and Kegan Paul, 1956.

Spenser, Edmund. *The Works.* London, 1679.

———. *The Works.* Ed. John Hughes. 6 vols. London, 1715.

———. *The Faerie Queene.* Ed. Thomas Birch. 3 vols. London, 1751.

———. *Faerie Queene.* Ed. John Upton. 2 vols. London, 1758.

———. *The Shepheardes Calender (1579).* Ed. S. K. Heninger, Jr. Delmar, NY: Scholars' Facsimiles and Reprints, 1979.

Spingarn, Joel E. *A History of Literary Criticism in the Renaissance.* New York, 1899.

Springer, George P. "Language and Music: Parallels and Divergencies." *For Roman Jakobson: Essays on the Occasion of His Sixtieth Birthday.* Ed. Morris Halle et al. The Hague: Mouton, 1956, 504–13.

Spurgeon, Caroline F. E. *Shakespeare's Imagery, and What It Tells Us.* Cambridge: Cambridge University Press, 1935.

Stahel, Thomas H., S.J. "Cristoforo Landino's Allegorization of the *Aeneid:* Books III and IV of the *Camaldolese Disputations.*" Diss. Johns Hopkins, 1968.

Stanley, Thomas. *The history of philosophy.* 2d ed. London, 1687.

Steadman, John M. "Timotheus in Dryden, E. K., and Gafori." *Times Literary Supplement* 16 Dec. 1960: 819.

———. *The Lamb and the Elephant: Ideal Imitation and the Context of Renaissance Allegory.* San Marino: Huntington Library, 1974.

———. *Milton's Biblical and Classical Imagery.* Pittsburgh: Duquesne University Press, 1984.

Steinberg, Theodore L. *"The English Poete* and the English Poet." *Spenser at Kalamazoo, 1979.* Cleveland: Cleveland State University, 1979, 35–53.

Stern, Virginia F. *Gabriel Harvey: His Life, Marginalia and Library.* Oxford: Clarendon, 1979.

Sterry, Peter. *A discourse of the freedom of the will.* London, 1675.

Stevens, John. *Music & Poetry in the Early Tudor Court.* London: Methuen, 1961.

Stewart, James T. "Renaissance Psychology and the Ladder of Love in Castiglione and Spenser." *Journal of English and Germanic Philology* 56 (1957): 225–30.

Stewart, Stanley. "Sir Calidore and 'Closure.'" *Studies in English Literature 1500–1900* 24 (1984): 69–86.

Stillinger, Jack. "The Biographical Problem of *Astrophel and Stella.*" *Journal of English and Germanic Philology* 59 (1960): 617–39.

Struever, Nancy S. *The Language of History in the Renaissance: Rhetoric and Historical Consciousness in Florentine Humanism.* Princeton: Princeton University Press, 1970.

Stump, Donald V. "Sidney's Concept of Tragedy in the *Apology* and in the *Arcadia.*" *Studies in Philology* 79 (1982): 41–61.

Suleiman, Susan R. "Introduction: Varieties of Audience-Oriented Criticism." *The Reader in the Text: Essays on Audience and Interpretation,* ed. Suleiman and Inge Crosman. Princeton: Princeton University Press, 1980, 3–45.

Susenbrotus, Joannes. *Epitome troporum ac schematum et grammaticorum et rhetoricorum.* London, 1621.

———. "The *Epitome troporum ac schematum* of Joannes Susenbrotus: Text, Translation, and Commentary." By Joseph X. Brennan. Diss. University of Illinois, 1953.

Sutton, Walter. "The Literary Image and the Reader: A Consideration of the Theory of Spatial Form." *Journal of Aesthetics and Art Criticism* 16 (1957–58): 112–23.

Sweeting, Elizabeth J. *Early Tudor Criticism: Linguistic & Literary.* Oxford: Basil Blackwell, 1940.

Symonds, John Addington. "The Provinces of the Several Arts." *Essays: Speculative and Suggestive.* 2 vols. London, 1890, 1:124–47.

———. *Renaissance in Italy.* 2 vols. New York: Modern Library, n.d.

Tasso, Torquato. *Discourses on the Heroic Poem.* Trans. Mariella Cavalchini and Irene Samuel. Oxford: Clarendon, 1973.

Temple, William. "Analysis tractationis de poesi contextae a nobilissimo viro Philippo Sidneio equite aurato." De L'Isle and Dudley MS 1095.

———. *"Analysis" of Sir Philip Sidney's "Apology for Poetry."* Ed. and trans. John Webster. Medieval & Renaissance Texts & Studies 32. Binghamton, NY: Center for Medieval and Early Renaissance Studies, 1984.

———. "In obitum illustrissimi Philippi Sydnaei . . . carmen." *Academiae Cantabrigiensis lachrymae tumulo nobilissimi equitis, D. Philippi Sidneii.* Ed. Alexander Neville. London, 1587 [STC 4473].

Temple, Sir William. "Upon Poetry." *Miscellanea. The second part.* London, 1690, 1–63 (Aaa1–Ddd8).

Thesiger, Sarah. "The *Orchestra* of Sir John Davies and the Image of the Dance." *Journal of the Warburg and Courtauld Institutes* 36 (1973): 277–304.

Thompson, Claud A. "Spenser's 'Many Faire Pourtraicts, and Many a Faire Feate.'" *Studies in English Literature 1500–1900* 12 (1972): 21–32.

Thorne, J. P. "A Ramistical Commentary on Sidney's *An Apologie for Poetrie.*" *Modern Philology* 54 (1956–57): 158–64.

Tillyard, E. M. W. *The Elizabethan World Picture.* London: Chatto and Windus, 1943.

———. *The English Epic and Its Background.* London: Chatto and Windus, 1954.

Todorov, Tzvetan. *Poétique de la prose.* Paris: Seuil, 1971.

Tottel, Richard, ed. *Songes and Sonettes.* London, 1557.

Trapp, Joseph. *Lectures on Poetry.* London, 1742.

Trimpi, Wesley. "The Meaning of Horace's *Ut pictura poesis.*" *Journal of the Warburg and Courtauld Institutes* 36 (1973): 1–34.

Trinkaus, Charles. *In Our Image and Likeness: Humanity and Divinity in Italian Humanist Thought.* 2 vols. London: Constable, 1970.

Trousdale, Marion. *Shakespeare and the Rhetoricians.* Chapel Hill: University of North Carolina Press, 1982.

Tung, Mason. "Spenser's 'Emblematic' Imagery: A Study of Emblematics." *Spenser Studies* 5 (1984): 185–207.

Turbervile, George. *Epitaphes, epigrams, songs and sonets.* London, 1567.

Turner, A. J. "Andrew Paschall's Tables of Plants for the Universal Language, 1678." *Bodleian Library Record* 9 (1978): 346–50.

Turner, Myron. "The Heroic Ideal in Sidney's Revised *Arcadia.*" *Studies in English Literature 1500–1900* 10 (1970): 63–82.

Tuve, Rosemond. *Elizabethan and Metaphysical Imagery: Renaissance Poetic and Twentieth-Century Critics.* Chicago: University of Chicago Press, 1947.

———, ed. *The Zodiake of Life.* By Palingenius. Trans. Barnabe Googe. New York: Scholars' Facsimiles and Reprints, 1947.

Twining, Thomas. "Dissertation I: On Poetry Considered as an Imitative Art." *Aristotle's Treatise on Poetry.* Trans. Twining. London, 1789, 3–43.

Ulivi, Ferruccio. *L'Imitazione nella poetica del Rinascimento.* Milan: Marzorati, 1959.

Ulreich, John C., Jr. "'The Poets Only Deliver': Sidney's Conception of *Mimesis.*" *Studies in the Literary Imagination* 15.1 (1982): 67–84.

Upton, John, ed. *Spenser's Faerie Queene.* 2 vols. London, 1758.

Valeriano, Giovanni Pierio. *Hieroglyphica sive De sacris Ægyptiorum literis commentarii.* Basel, 1556.

Valla, Giorgio. *De expetendis, et fugiendis rebus opus.* Venice, 1501.

Van Dorsten, see Dorsten, Jan A. van.

Vasari, Giorgio. *Lives of Seventy of the Most Eminent Painters, Sculptors and Architects.* Ed. and trans. E. H. and E. W. Blashfield and A. A. Hopkins. 4 vols. New York: Charles Scribner's Sons, 1926.

———. *On Technique.* Trans. Louisa S. Maclehose. London: Dent, 1907.

Vaughan, William. *The golden-grove.* London, 1600.

Vicaire, Paul. *Recherches sur les mots désignant la poésie et le poète dans l'oeuvre de Platon.* Paris: Presses Universitaires, 1964.

Vickers, Brian. *Classical Rhetoric in English Poetry.* London: Macmillan Press, 1970.

Vida, Marco Girolamo. *Poeticarum libri III.* Rome, 1527.

————. *De arte poetica*. Ed. and trans. Ralph G. Williams. New York: Columbia University Press, 1976.

Viperano, Giovanni Antonio. *De poetica libri tres*. Antwerp, 1579.

Vives, Juan Luis. "De tradendis disciplinis libri quinque" [1531]. *Vives: On Education*. Trans. Foster Watson. Cambridge: Cambridge University Press, 1913.

————, ed. *De civitate Dei*. By St. Augustine. Basel, 1522.

————, ed. *Of the citie of God*. By St. Augustine. Trans. John Healey. London, 1610.

Von Simson: see Simson, Otto Georg von.

Walker, D. P. "Musical Humanism in the 16th and Early 17th Centuries." *Music Review* 2 (1941): 1–13, 111–21, 220–27, 288–308, and 3 (1942): 55–71.

————. "The Aims of Baïf's Académie de Poésie et de Musique." *Journal of Renaissance and Baroque Music* 1 (1946): 91–100.

Wallace, Malcolm William. *The Life of Sir Philip Sidney*. Cambridge: Cambridge University Press, 1915.

Waller, Gary F. "Acts of Reading: The Production of Meaning in *Astrophil and Stella*." *Studies in the Literary Imagination* 15.1 (1982): 23–35.

Warkentin, Germaine. "Sidney's *Certain Sonnets:* Speculations on the Evolution of the Text." *Library* 6th ser. 2 (1980): 430–44.

————. "Sidney and the Supple Muse: Compositional Procedures in Some Sonnets of *Astrophil and Stella*." *Studies in the Literary Imagination* 15.1 (1982): 37–48.

————. "The Meeting of the Muses: Sidney and the Mid-Tudor Poets." *Sir Philip Sidney and the Interpretation of Renaissance Culture: The Poet in His Time and in Ours*. Ed. Gary F. Waller and Michael D. Moore. London: Croom Helm, 1984, 17–33.

Watson, Foster. *The English Grammar Schools to 1660: Their Curriculum and Practice*. Cambridge: Cambridge University Press, 1908.

————. *The Beginnings of the Teaching of Modern Subjects in England*. London: Pitman Books, 1909.

————, trans. *Vives on Education*. Cambridge: Cambridge University Press, 1913.

Watson, Thomas. *The Hekatompathia* [1582]. Ed. S. K. Heninger, Jr. Gainesville, FL: Scholars' Facsimiles and Reprints, 1964.

Weaver, Mike. "Concrete Poetry." *Visible Language* 1 (1967): 293–326.

Webb, Daniel. *Observations on the Correspondence between Poetry and Music*. London, 1769.

Webbe, William. *A Discourse of English Poetrie* [1586]. *Elizabethan Critical Essays*. Ed. G. Gregory Smith. 2 vols. London: Oxford University Press, 1904, 1:226–302.

Webster, John, ed. and trans. *William Temple's "Analysis" of Sir Philip Sidney's "Apology for Poetry."* Medieval & Renaissance Texts & Studies 32. Binghamton, NY: Center for Medieval and Early Renaissance Studies, 1984.

Weinberg, Bernard. *A History of Literary Criticism in the Italian Renaissance*.

2 vols. [paginated continuously]. Chicago: University of Chicago Press, 1961.

Weiner, Andrew D. *Sir Philip Sidney and the Poetics of Protestantism: A Study of Contexts*. Minneapolis: University of Minnesota Press, 1978.

———. "Spenser's *Muiopotmos* and the Fates of Butterflies and Men." *Journal of English and Germanic Philology* 84 (1985): 203–20.

Weiner, Seth. "Renaissance Prosodic Thought as a Branch of Musica Speculativa." Diss. Princeton, 1981.

Weisinger, Herbert. "Renaissance Theories of the Revival of the Fine Arts." *Italica* 20 (1943): 163–70.

Weisstein, Ulrich. *Comparative Literature and Literary Theory: Survey and Introduction*. Trans. William Riggan. Bloomington: Indiana University Press, 1968.

Welch, Roy D. "Supplementary Essay." *The Arts and the Art of Criticism*. By Theodore Meyer Greene. Princeton: Princeton University Press, 1940, 487–506.

Wellek, Albert. "The Relationship between Music and Poetry." *Journal of Aesthetics and Art Criticism* 21 (1962–63): 149–56.

Wellek, René, and Austin Warren. *Theory of Literature*. 3d ed. New York: Harvest, Harcourt Brace Jovanovich, 1956.

Wells, William. "'To make a milde construction': The Significance of the Opening Stanzas of *Muiopotmos*." *Studies in Philology* 42 (1945): 544–54.

———, ed. *Spenser Allusions: In the Sixteenth and Seventeenth Centuries*. *Studies in Philology*, Extra Series. Chapel Hill: University of North Carolina Press, 1971–72.

Welsford, Enid. *Spenser: "Fowre Hymnes" and "Epithalamion": A Study of Edmund Spenser's Doctrine of Love*. New York: Barnes and Noble Books, 1967.

Westfall, Carroll W. "Painting and the Liberal Arts: Alberti's View." *Journal of the History of Ideas* 30 (1969): 487–506.

White, Harold O. *Plagiarism and Imitation during the English Renaissance*. Cambridge: Harvard University Press, 1935.

Wickert, Max A. "Structure and Ceremony in Spenser's *Epithalamion*." *ELH* 35 (1968): 135–57.

Wilkins, Ernest Hatch. "A General Survey of Renaissance Petrarchism." *Comparative Literature* 2 (1950): 327–42.

———. "The Invention of the Sonnet." *The Invention of the Sonnet and Other Studies in Italian Literature*. Rome: Storia e Letteratura, 1959, 11–39.

Wilkins, John. *An essay towards a real character, and a philosophical language*. London, 1668.

Willes, Richard. *De re poetica* [1573]. Ed. and trans. Alastair D. S. Fowler. *Luttrell Reprints* 17. Oxford: Basil Blackwell, 1958.

Williams, Arnold. *The Common Expositor: An Account of the Commentaries on Genesis 1527–1633*. Chapel Hill: University of North Carolina Press, 1948.

Williams, Kathleen. "Vision and Rhetoric: The Poet's Voice in *The Faerie Queene*." *ELH* 36 (1969): 131–44.

Williams, Ralph G., ed. and trans. *The "De arte poetica" of Marco Girolamo Vida*. New York: Columbia University Press, 1976.

Williams, William Carlos. "Still Lifes." *Hudson Review* 16 (1963–64): 516.

Wilson, Christopher R. "*Astrophil and Stella:* A Tangled Editorial Web." *Library* 6th ser. 1 (1979): 336–46.

Wilson, Thomas. *The Arte of Rhetorique* [1553]. Ed. Robert H. Bowers. Gainesville, FL: Scholars' Facsimiles and Reprints, 1962.

Wimsatt, W. K., Jr. "In Search of Verbal Mimesis." *Day of the Leopards*. New Haven: Yale University Press, 1976, 57–73.

———, and Monroe C. Beardsley. *The Verbal Icon*. Lexington: University of Kentucky Press, 1954.

Winn, James A. *Unsuspected Eloquence: A History of the Relations between Poetry and Music*. New Haven: Yale University Press, 1981.

Wittgenstein, Ludwig. *Philosophical Investigations*. Trans. G. E. M. Anscombe. Oxford: Basil Blackwell, 1953.

———. *Lectures & Conversations on Aesthetics, Psychology and Religious Belief*. Ed. Cyril Barrett. Berkeley: University of California Press, 1966.

Wittkower, Rudolf. "Brunelleschi and 'Proportion in Perspective.'" *Journal of the Warburg and Courtauld Institutes* 16 (1953): 275–91.

———. *Architectural Principles in the Age of Humanism*. New York: Random House, 1965.

Wolfley, Lawrence C. "Sidney's Visual-Didactic Poetic: Some Complexities and Limitations." *Journal of Medieval and Renaissance Studies* 6 (1976): 217–41.

Wolterstorff, Nicholas. "Worlds of Works of Art." *Journal of Aesthetics and Art Criticism* 35 (1976–77): 121–32.

Woodward, Daniel H. "Thomas Fuller, William Dugard, and the Pseudonymous Life of Sidney (1655)." *Publications of the Bibliographical Society of America* 62 (1968): 501–10.

Woodward, William H. *Vittorino da Feltre and Other Humanist Educators*. Ed. Eugene F. Rice, Jr. *Classics in Education* 18. New York: Columbia University Press, 1963.

Wordsworth, William. "Preface to *Lyrical Ballads*" [1802]. *Literary Criticism*. Ed. Paul M. Zall. Lincoln: University of Nebraska Press, 1966.

Worringer, Wilhelm. *Abstraction and Empathy: A Contribution to the Psychology of Style* [1908]. Trans. Michael Bullock. London: Routledge and Kegan Paul, 1953.

Wotton, Sir Henry. *The elements of architecture*. London, 1624.

Yates, Frances A. *The French Academies of the Sixteenth Century*. Studies of the Warburg Institute 15. London: Warburg Institute, 1947.

———. *The Art of Memory*. London: Routledge and Kegan Paul, 1966.

Young, Richard B. *English Petrarke: A Study of Sidney's "Astrophel and Stella."* *Three Studies in the Renaissance: Sidney, Jonson, Milton*. Yale Studies in English 138. New Haven: Yale University Press, 1958, 1–88.

Zandvoort, Reinard Willem. *Sidney's Arcadia: A Comparison between the Two Versions*. Amsterdam: Swets, 1929.

Zarlino, Gioseffo. *Le istitutioni harmoniche*. Venice, 1558.

Zenck, Hermann. "Zarlino's 'Istitutioni harmoniche' als Quelle zur Musikanschauung der italienischen Renaissance." *Zeitschrift für Musikwissenschaft* 12 (1929–30): 540–78.

Zuckerkandl, Victor. *Sound and Symbol: Music and the External World*. Trans. Willard R. Trask. *Bollingen Series* 44. New York: Pantheon Books, 1956.

Zwinger, Theodor. *Theatrum vitae humanae*. Basel, 1571.

Index